Contents

KT-177-396

These are the Michelin publications to use with this guide

Regional map series
at a scale of 1: 400 000
(1 in: 6.30 miles)
Map **401** Scotland,
Map **402** The North, Midlands,
Lake District and Borders,
Map **403** Wales, West Country,
and Midlands,
Map **404** East Anglia, Midlands
and South East;

Main Road Map **986**
at a scale of 1 : 1 000 000
(1 in : 16 miles);

Motoring Atlas
of Great Britain and Ireland
at a scale of 1 : 300 000
(1 in: 4.75 miles);

Red Guide
Great Britain and Ireland
to hotels and restaurants.

Make sure it's a Michelin

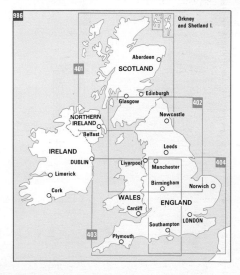

The maps and town plans in this guide are based upon the Ordnance Survey of Great Britain with the permission of the Controller of Her Majesty's Stationery Office. Crown Copyright reserved.

PRINCIPAL SIGHTS

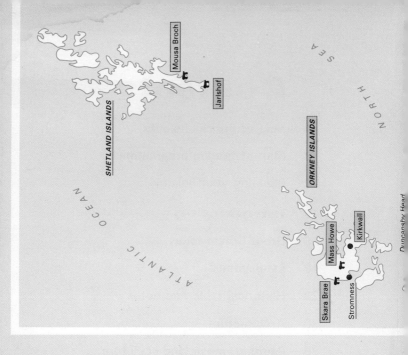

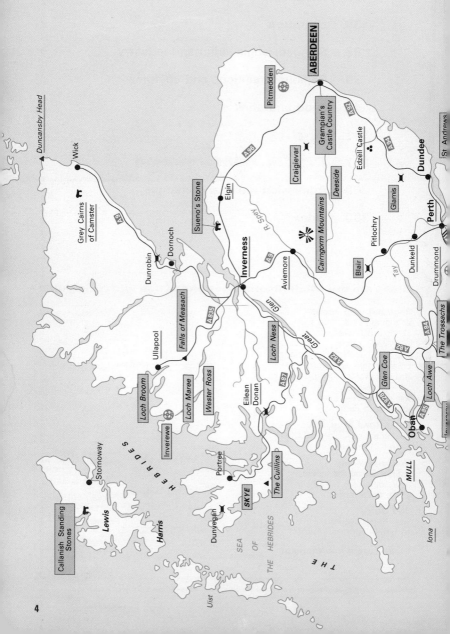

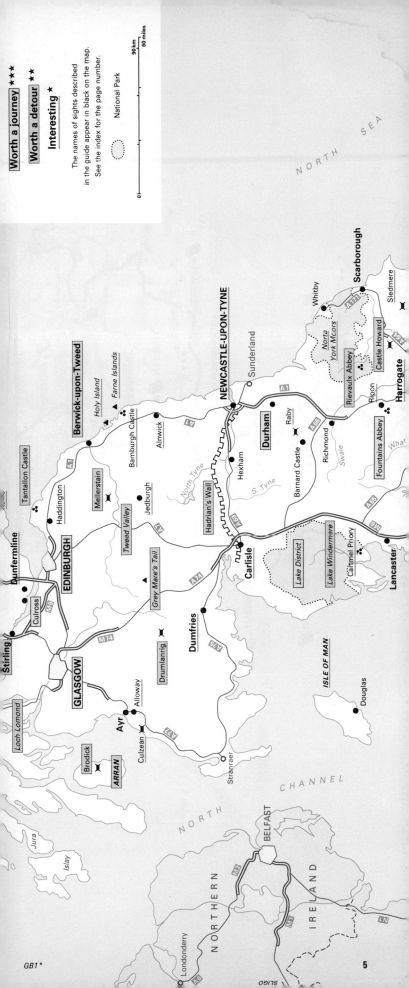

Worth a journey ★★★
Worth a detour ★★
Interesting ★

The names of sights described in the guide appear in black on the map. See the index for the page number.

National Park

90km
60 miles

NORTH SEA

Scarborough
Sledmere
Whitby
North York Moors
Castle Howard
Rievaulx Abbey
Ripon
Harrogate
Fountains Abbey
Wharfe

NEWCASTLE-UPON-TYNE
Sunderland
A1
Durham
Raby
Barnard Castle
Richmond
Swale
A66
A65
M6

Berwick-upon-Tweed
Holy Island
Farne Islands
Bamburgh Castle
Alnwick
A1
Hexham
North Tyne
Hadrian's Wall
S. Tyne
A69
Carlisle

Tantallon Castle
Haddington
A1
Mellerstain
Jedburgh
Tweed Valley
A7
Grey Mare's Tail

EDINBURGH
Dunfermline
Culross
M9
Stirling
GLASGOW
M74
A74

Loch Lomond
Brodick
ARRAN
Ayr
Alloway
Culzean
A77
Drumlanrig
Dumfries
A75
Stranraer

Lake District
Lake Windermere
Cartmel Priory
Lancaster
M6

ISLE OF MAN
Douglas

Jura
Islay

NORTH CHANNEL

BELFAST
M2
NORTHERN IRELAND
M1
Londonderry
A6
SLIGO

GB1★

5

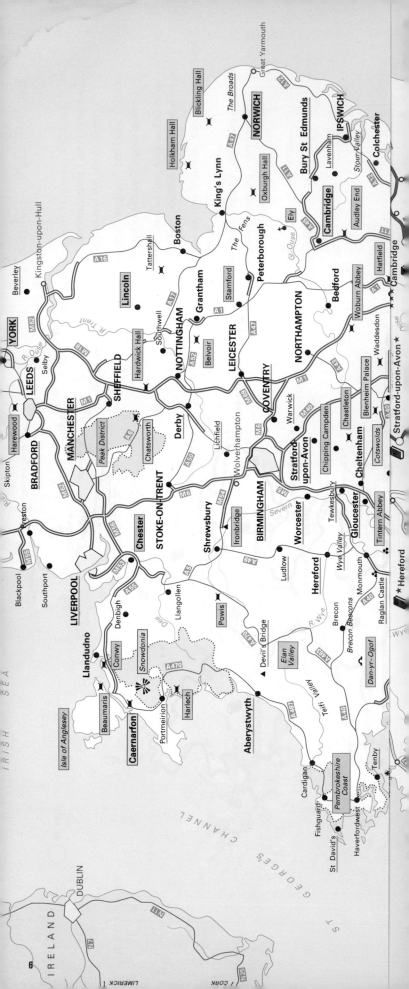

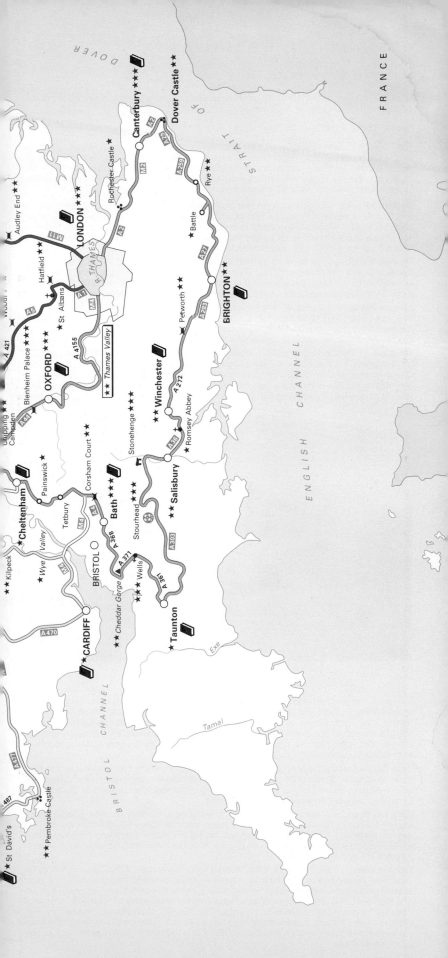

PLANNING YOUR HOLIDAY

LEISURE ACTIVITIES

In addition to the active sporting facilities available across Britain, there are a number of pleasantly recreational pastimes.

Rambling and walking

The Ramblers' Association works for the preservation of common land, ancient footpaths, trackways and rights of way, so that they may be enjoyed by walkers. Always remember to leave your itinerary and expected time of return at your base. Never underestimate the speed with which mountain weather can change, always wear adequate boots and have warm, weatherproof clothing with you.

National Parks. — There can be few better places to enjoy rambling than in any of Britain's eleven **National Parks,** the first of which were set up in 1951. In Scotland, where pressure on the wilder countryside was less, the law of trespass, too, was different and people could already walk where they would, provided they did no damage. It was decided not to extend the location of National Parks to Scotland.

The Peak District. — The deep dales and stone-walled fields of the White Peak are surrounded to east, west and north by the dramatic moors and peat bogs of the Dark Peak. In addition to walking, people come to fish and to cycle. Rock climbing on the gritstone edges has been joined as a leisure activity by gliding, hang-gliding and wind-surfing.

The Lake District. — Largest of the National Parks, it is a combination of mountain and lake, woodland and farmland. Ice shaped the troughs and corries and glacial rubble dammed the valleys, but the underlying rock dictated whether the hills were softly rounded, like Skiddaw, or wildly rugged, like Scafell and Helvellyn.

Snowdonia. — The Snowdon massif, heartland of the Park, and Cader Idris are the most popular areas — with half a million people reaching Snowdon Summit each year and only a quarter of them admit to using the railway! The Aran Mountains in the south and the rugged Rhynogydd are less crowded. Harlech Castle lies on part of the Park's twenty-plus miles of sweeping sandy coastline, backed by beautiful mountain scenery.

The Snowdon Horseshoe

Dartmoor. — Largest and wildest stretch of open country in southern Britain. Two plateaux, rising to over 2 000ft and covered with blanket bog and heather moorland, are divided by the River Dart. Ponies — descendants of those turned out in the Middle Ages — still graze much of the lower-lying heather moorland and there are hundreds of ancient sites — chambered tombs, hillforts, stone circles, medieval crosses and waymarks — in the Park.

Pembrokeshire Coast. — Second smallest of the Parks, for much of its length it is less than three miles wide. Steep cliffs display spectacularly folded and twisted rock formations, sheltered bays invite bathing and scuba-diving. Offshore islands such as Skomer and Skokholm support huge colonies of seabirds.

North York Moors. — A relatively quiet Park. The moors are clearly defined, rising sharply from Pickering in the south, Tees to the north and the Vale of York in the south. The eastern boundary is the sea, with Staithes, home of Captain Cook and Whitby famous for jet — a fossilised black amber — so popular with the Victorians. Rievaulx and Rosedale Abbeys are within the Park.

Yorkshire Dales. — Like the North York Moors Park, nearly half of the Dales is farmland. Over four centuries the monasteries' sheep walks developed into the start of a road system across the fells, the best known today being the green lane between Kilnsey and Malham Cove and Tarn, with its unique limestone pavement "grykes", sheltered habitats for lime- and shade-loving plants. The "Dales" themselves, Ribble-, Swale-, Wensley-, and Wharfe- have welcoming villages in rich valley pastures, while the limestone peaks of Ingleborough and Pen-y-Ghent are the other more rugged face of this spectacular Park.

Exmoor. — The heartland, rising to 1 500ft-460m, from Chapman Barrows to Dunkery Beacon is still the windswept haunt of falcon and hawk and cliffs, broken by deep valleys with waterfalls, make protected breeding sites for seabirds. With the Quantocks, Exmoor is the last secure habitat in the south of England for the red deer and a small breeding herd has been established to maintain the declining numbers of Exmoor ponies.

Northumberland. — Cheviot sheep graze the open moorland, mostly above 1 000ft-305m, which makes up most of this Park. A part of Hadrian's Wall runs along the southern edge of the Park. Kielder Water, just beyond the western boundary, is a much-visited recreational area.

Brecon Beacons. — High red sandstone mountains divide the ancient rocks of mid-Wales from the coalfields and industrialisation further south. Along the southern edge of the Park a limestone belt provides a dramatic change in scenery and there are hundreds of sink-holes and cave systems, the most spectacular being the Dan-yr-Ogof Caves at the head of the Tawe valley.

Norfolk and Suffolk Broads. — Established as a Park on 1 April 1989, the Broads are peat-diggings from the 9C, which flooded and became part of the river system in the 14C. Strenuous efforts by the Broads Authority in the 1980s partly halted environmental degradation, due to nutrients from effluents and fertilisers. The water is recovering its life, but care is still needed from all who use and enjoy this Park.

Steam trains

There are still many enthusiasts who indulge in their hobby of maintaining and operating steam trains. The visitor can share their fun.

The first standard-gauge steam railway to be taken over privately, in 1960, was the five miles of track near East Grinstead, in Sussex, now known as the **Bluebell Line.** Since then many lines have been preserved and steam trains with a marked Victorian and Edwardian atmosphere run frequently during the summer and less often in the winter months. The standard-gauge **North Yorkshire Moors Railway** runs through 18 miles of scenic countryside, from Pickering to Grosmont. The four miles of the **Keighley and Worth Valley** line, starting from the Brontë village of Haworth, continues to be a vital part of local community life. The **Severn Valley Railway** has more main-line engines than any other preserved line, on its sixteen miles of track between Bridgnorth and Kidderminster. The **Romney, Hythe and Dymchurch Railway** was built as a miniature line in 1927 and with 13 miles of track is the longest fully equipped 15'' gauge line in the world. The **West Somerset Railway** is the longest preserved line in Britain, with twenty miles of track from Minehead up into the Quantock Hills. The narrow-gauge **Vale of Rheidol Railway** offers a 23-mile round trip from Aberystwyth up to Devil's Bridge and the Mynach Falls and the seven miles of the **Nene Valley Railway,** near Peterborough, has locomotives from ten countries and is a regular TV and film "location".

In Scotland the **Strathspey Railway** runs the five miles from Aviemore to Boat of Garten, famed as one of the nesting spots of the osprey in the British Isles. On the **Isle of Man,** there are still 15 miles of the 3ft gauge line which used to cover the island. Trains run from Douglas to Port Erin and the line has been in almost continuous operation since 1874.

These and nearly 150 other shorter stretches of standard and miniature-gauge railway and nostalgic museums can recapture some of the aura of the Age of Steam.

Wildfowl and wetlands

The **Wildfowl and Wetlands Trust** has pioneered work in bringing larger numbers of people into contact with the natural environment. Few will remain totally indifferent to the fate of our planet and its wildlife, having had a bird, endangered in the wild, feed from their hand at one of the Trust's Centres.

Slimbridge, between Gloucester and Bristol, is probably the best known, but other Centres flourish near Arundel, outside Stockport and Sunderland, in East Anglia and outside Dumfries. A visit to any of these centres is both entertaining and informative.

Gardens

Britain has a wonderful heritage of gardens which are open to visitors. Because of the vagaries of our climate, particularly the closeness of the Gulf Stream, plant collections brought back from all over the world, particularly in the 18C and 19C, have flourished. Tucked away in Chelsea since 1673 is the **Chelsea Physic Garden,** still a centre for serious horticultural study, but also a welcome retreat from city bustle. In a churchyard alongside Lambeth Palace is the **Museum of Garden History** and a garden growing only those plants which were known to the gardener to King Charles I, John Tradescant, who is buried in the churchyard.

Gardens stretch from **Inverewe,** in Wester Ross, where, despite its northern latitude, the gardens are frost-free, thanks to the warm North Atlantic Drift, to **Tresco Abbey Gardens** in the Scilly Isles, created and maintained since 1834 by successive generations of the same family. On the Isle of Arran are the gardens of **Brodick Castle.** After a visit in 1906, Sir John Ramsden, then owner of Muncaster Castle in Cumbria, sent his hostess some rhododendrons for her garden — in all eighty tons! They, and hundreds more brought back by a 1953 expedition to Burma, flourish in the mild climate.

John Aislabie, Chancellor of the Exchequer at the time of the South Sea Bubble retired to his estate at **Studley Royal,** under something of a cloud. He designed a garden which is a work of true inspiration, anticipating **Stourhead** by forty years. It acquired the ready-made folly, so essential to Romantic landscaping, only when his son was able to purchase nearby Fountains Abbey.

Bodnant, near Llandudno, has rhododendrons, azaleas, magnolias and camellias and, in May, a wonderful tunnel of glorious yellow blossom — the laburnum walk. At **Sissinghurst,** in Kent, the garden of the Tudor house is a monument to Vita Sackville-West who, in the 1930s, created the walks, with each of the gardens opening off having its own colour scheme.

Penjerrick, in Cornwall, was begun in the 1830s and many exotic plants were grown from seed brought into nearby Falmouth by clipper captains, but rhododendrons remain one of its glories. **Lanhydrock** near Bodmin has a collection of over one hundred species of magnolia. There are many gardens to be enjoyed all over Britain.

Canals and waterways

Some 2 000 miles of what were 18C industrial and trade arteries are still conserved and managed by British Waterways, mostly today for leisure use, though working boats still operate.

The canals can be enjoyed in many ways. A floating home, in narrow-boat or cruiser, drifting along at walking pace is the fastest way of slowing down. A walk along the towpaths, a quiet day's fishing, a short trip in a diesel or horse-drawn boat or a longer cruise allow you to explore otherwise unseen aspects of our countryside and cities. There are over 120 bases from which holiday boats may be hired, usually by the week, but with 3-4 day short breaks also available.

Historical battle re-enactments

"Cavaliers and Roundheads". — Colourful re-enactments of a Civil War battle can be found during the summer in Britain. In addition, many of our battlefields are marked with museums, maps and guided tours. In the Commandery, at Worcester, is a staff who can always provide up-to-date information on all battle re-enactments and similar events which are taking place during the current year.

The National Trust for Scotland has a visitor centre and museum at **Bannockburn,** near Stirling and at **Culloden,** outside Inverness.

SOME SPORTS YOU CAN ENJOY IN BRITAIN

All will depend on the visitor's individual preference. Tennis and swimming, together with cycling and rambling, are individual activities easily arranged wherever you are on holiday. The **English Tourist Board** produces an annual guide, listing a number of contact addresses for many sports, including those mentioned below:

Angling. — Well over 3.7 million Britons are fishermen — a larger group than those who watch football matches! Britain's rivers, reservoirs and lakes offer a wide variety of coarse and game fishing. The coarse fishing season runs from 16 March to 16 June and permits can be obtained from any tackle shop, where advice will also be available on local waters. Excellent salmon and trout fishing, for which licences are required, is available in Scotland and in many rivers and lakes around England and Wales. Sea angling is popular, particularly around the southwestern and Northumbrian coastlines.

Boating and water-sports. — Ratty, in Kenneth Grahame's *Wind in the Willows,* says to his friend Mole — "there is nothing half so much worth doing as messing about in boats". In a punt on the Backs at Cambridge, a cabin cruiser on the Norfolk Broads, a narrow boat on Britain's network of canals and rivers, or sailing on lake and loch and from harbours and marinas all around the coast, Britons — and our visitors — have ample opportunity for "messing about in boats".

Bowls. — Crown green bowling is a peculiarly English, peculiarly restful summer sport, but one requiring considerable practice and skill. Local clubs can organise practice for temporary members.

Cycling and cycle touring. — Over two hundred local cycling and cycle touring groups organise tours during the summer months. These range from country lane sightseeing to more strenuous mountain climbs. Cyclists are sure to be able to find a tour geared to their age, ability and the time available.

Golf. — On the poor "links" land along the sand dunes of east coast Scotland the game of golf developed in the 15C. Undulating fairways, sandy bunkers and the brisk sea breeze conspire to ensure that no golfer ever plays two games on the same course in the same conditions. This variety has been reproduced on hundreds of courses across Great Britain, many of which are public courses, on which the visiting golfer can have a game for a modest fee. Some Golf Clubs have reciprocal arrangements allowing Members of other Clubs, inside and outside Great Britain, to avail themselves of the local facilities during their holiday.

Riding and pony trekking. — Nearly 600 approved establishments cater for riding holidays for the beginner and the enthusiast. Trekking — usually in groups and mostly at a walk — offers a marvellous way to see countryside which is inaccessible by any other transport — except your own two feet! Hacking, at a brisker overall pace, with trotting, cantering and gallops, also caters for all levels of skill.

Skiing. — Of the four ski centres in Scotland, at Lochaber, Glenshee, Lecht and Aviemore in the Cairngorms, the last is the most fully developed of the resorts. All have ski schools and forest trails have been opened up for cross-country skiing. Up to the minute snow reports are essential and the best snow conditions are probably found in March-April.

Squash. — A popular sport, squash provides maximum exercise in minimum time. There are over 9 000 courts in Leisure Centres across the country and 3 700 Clubs offer use of their courts and hire of equipment.

Tennis. —Widely available facilities make tennis one of Britain's most popular summer sports. Temporary membership of local clubs can usually be arranged and there are many public and municipal tennis courts.

Tourist signs: when motoring in Britain follow the white and brown traffic signs to help you find your way to tourist attractions.

Introduction

Beachy Head

GREAT BRITAIN TODAY

Parliament and the Constitution. — Great Britain has no written constitution. **Magna Carta** was sealed by a reluctant King John at Runnymede on 15 June 1215. (Copies in Salisbury and Lincoln Cathedrals and two in the British Library). Clause 39 guarantees every free man security from illegal interference in his person or his property. Since the reign of Henry VII 'Habeas Corpus' — 'You may have the body' as it has become known — has been used to protect individuals against arbitrary arrest, by requiring the production in Court of the person within a specified period.

The supreme legislature in Britain is Parliament, consisting of the **House of Lords** and the **House of Commons.** Medieval parliaments were mainly meetings between the king and his lords. The Commons were rarely summoned and had no place in which to meet, nor even the right of free speech until the 16C. Kings had, however, to summon Parliaments to raise money, hence frequent Parliaments were unpopular. Regular Parliaments were assured after the Glorious Revolution of 1688-89, but both Houses were dominated by the landed aristocracy until well into the 19C.

Between 1430 and 1832, the right to vote was granted to those possessing a freehold worth 40 shillings. The Reform Act of 1867 enfranchised all borough householders. 1884 brought in all county householders and in 1918 all men over 21 and women over 30 were given the vote. In 1928 this was extended to women over 21. Today all over the age of eighteen have the right to vote.

Great Britain's Members of Parliament are elected to the **House of Commons** on a 'first past the post' basis, the candidate with the largest number of votes being the winner. In 1949 Constituencies were re-organised on the principle that each should contain about 65 000 voters. Since then there have been 635 Members of the House of Commons. There is no 'proportional representation', the system which allocates to each Party seats in proportion to the number of votes cast for its candidates. This can lead to Government by the party which may not have obtained the majority of the votes, country-wide, but it does avoid the problem of having to form coalitions of several smaller parties in order to have a majority in Parliament and to govern effectively.

The **House of Lords,** the Upper House, at whose meetings, until the reign of Henry VI, the sovereign was always present, consists of the **Lords Spiritual** — the Bishops — and the **Lords Temporal** — in order of rank, Dukes, Marquesses, Earls, Viscounts and Barons. Since 1876 the Lords of Appeal — the Law Lords — have been **Life Peers,** an honour also bestowed since 1958 on other men and women of distinction. The Parliament Act of 1911 reduced the power of the House of Lords to simple delay of legislation — a time for reflection — and in 1949, this power was ended for financial legislation.

The Monarchy. — Britain is a **Constitutional Monarchy,** a form of Government in which supreme power is vested in the **Sovereign,** the King or the Queen. The origins of Monarchy lie in the seven English kingdoms of the 6C to 9C — Northumbria, East Anglia, Essex, Mercia, Wessex, Sussex and Kent. The most powerful and charismatic king was acknowledged by the others as 'bretwalda' and overlord. Alfred (871-899) began to establish effective rule, consolidated by Athelstan in 926. But it was under a Danish king, Canute, that political unification was achieved.

The Coronation ceremony, especially from the Norman conquest onwards, gave a priestly role to the anointed King. The monarchy only gradually became hereditary. Dynastic rivalry in the Wars of the Roses dominated the 15C and the Tudors gained much from their exploitation of the mystique of kingship. They manipulated anti-clericalism into a doctrine of royal supremacy and the form of address 'Your Majesty' replaced the earlier 'Your Grace'. The stubborn character of the Stuarts and the insistence of Charles I on the 'Divine Right of Kings' was in part responsible for the Civil War, his downfall and execution, leading to the only period (1649-60) during which England has not been a monarchy.

At the Restoration, considerable restraints were placed on the monarch's powers and these were increased at the Glorious Revolution of 1688-89.

During Victoria's reign the right of the monarch in relation to ministers was defined as 'the right to be consulted, to encourage and to warn', although Victoria herself clung tenaciously to her supervision of Empire and foreign affairs.

The now independent nations of the 'Empire' still have many and important links today, in the British Commonwealth of Nations. The Monarchy is the focus of goodwill, historic tradition and pageantry, in Britain and abroad.

REGIONAL ADMINISTRATION

Under the Crown, two bodies, the **Legislature** — the two Houses of Parliament — enacts and the **Judiciary** — the High Court, Criminal Court and Crown Courts — enforces the laws by which the country is governed. Directly responsible to a Minister in Parliament are the **Home Office,** the **Scottish Office** and the **Welsh Office.**

In April 1974 the administrative boundaries and counties of England and Wales were re-arranged. In seven densely populated areas **Metropolitan Counties** were formed, together with thirty nine other **Counties.** Wales was divided into eight new counties. In Scotland, in May 1975, nine **Regions** and three **Island Areas** were formed.

County Councils, with elected Chairpersons and Councillors — **Metropolitan Councils** for the large metropolitan areas — are the next link in the chain. Answerable directly to the Home Office for the maintenance of law and order is the **Metropolitan Police,** with County police forces being in part controlled by their local County Councils. Stipendiary **Magistrates** and **Justices of the Peace** — local citizens with legal training — conduct the day-to-day affairs of local courts.

The personal representative of the Sovereign in each county — and head of magistracy — is the **Lord Lieutenant,** with as his chief executive officer the **Sheriff,** or **High Sheriff. Municipal Councils,** presided over by a **Mayor,** chosen annually from the ranks of the elected **Aldermen** — a surviving Anglo-Saxon title — run the affairs of cities, towns and boroughs. Local government is carried out by **District Councils,** also elected bodies, and under them are **Parish Councils,** or in Wales, **Community Councils.**

LANGUAGE

The English language is a mighty river, fed and — for the most part, at least — enriched by streams of words from every known tongue, most of which are now quite at home in English. Rivers of Celtic, Germanic and Latin, tributaries from Anglo-Saxon, from Norman French and from centuries of our imperial connections in India make up the living language.

Old English. — Old English, a Germanic dialect spoken in 400 AD from Jutland to northern France, was established in Britain by 800 AD and, by the Renaissance, had taken on the syntax and grammar of modern English. Spoken by two million in 1600, there are probably 400 million English speakers today, those from countries where it is the second, often "official", language outnumbering by far the total population of Britain and the United States.

Anglo-Saxon. — The Anglo-Saxons pushed the Celtic speakers they encountered in Britain westward, relegating their languages to "second class" status. Then Norman French was imposed on Anglo-Saxon and by gradual process of adaptation and absorption the English language reached its zenith in the works of Shakespeare. The main Celtic languages however survived, with varying degrees of success.

Welsh. — Welsh was recognised by Edward I as an official and legal language, in his Statute of Rhuddlan in 1284. After Bosworth, Welsh nobles hopefully followed the Tudor monarchs to London, but Henry VIII decreed that "no persons shall hold office within the Realme, except they exercise the English speech".
The **bards** and **eisteddfodau** guarded a tradition of poetry and literature in the Welsh language stretching back to Taliesin, in the 7C. In 1588 Bishop Morgan published his Bible in Welsh and it was largely the willingness of the Church in Wales to preach in Welsh which saved the language from the fate suffered by Scots Gaelic and Irish. The Sunday School Movement, begun in Bala in 1789, encouraged ability to read Welsh and the University of Wales was formed in 1893. With primary school teaching in Welsh in 1939 and secondary schooling in 1956, today Channel 4 - S4C - can broadcast many hours of television in Welsh, to speakers of an everyday living language.

Gaelic. — In Scotland the **Gàidhealtachd**, the Gaelic-speaking area, is confined largely to the Western Isles. Gaelic, mother tongue of 50% of the population in the 16C, is today spoken by about 2%. The "Normanised" Kings of Scotland, particularly David I (1124-53) introduced Anglo-Norman and later contact with the English court led to English becoming the language of the aristocracy. Just after the Union of the two Kingdoms in 1603, the Statute of Iona attempted to impose the teaching of English on the sons of the chiefs and in 1616 the Westminster Parliament decreed — "that the Inglishe tongue be universallie plantit and the Scots language, one of cheif and principalle causis of the continewance of barbaritie and incivilitie amongst the inhabitantis of the Ilis and Heylandis, may be abolisheit and removeit".
Celtic Britain had always tended to be the Achilles' heel of the Protestant succession. During the Jacobite rebellions the Highlands retained their allegiance to Catholicism so that Gaelic, to the English and even to the Lowland Scots, became equated with Popery, rebellion and treason. Backing the losing side in England's quarrels with the Pope was one major reason for the suppression and decline of both Scots and Irish Gaelic. However in London, a Gaelic Society was formed in 1777, the first of many across the world which maintain and encourage Gaelic language and literature. Indeed the percentage of Gaelic speakers in Scotland is increasing slowly, many of them in Lowland areas, aware of the language as their proud heritage.

Cornish and Manx. — Cornish and Manx, two Celtic languages unsuccessful in their struggle to survive, were once widely spoken, **Cornish** being the only language of the peninsula until towards the end of the reign of Henry VIII. It is often claimed that Dolly Pentreath, born in Mousehole in 1686 and who died in December 1777, was the last speaker of Cornish, though there were doubtless other elderly speakers, none of whom would have outlived the 18C.
Manx was a similar language to the Gaelic of the Western Isles, but there has been no viable Manx-speaking community since the 1940s. Today's Manx dialect of English shows much influence from Lancashire, thanks to the fishing and tourism industries of the 19C.

Norn. — In Orkney and Shetland, **Norn,** a Viking language akin to Icelandic, survived until the 18C. The dominant tongue in Orkney until the Scottish-speaking Sinclairs became Earls of Orkney in 1379, it remained the language of Shetland until well after the pledging of the Northern Isles to James III of Scotland in 1468-9. Modern dialects of both Shetland and Orkney still contain a sizeable body of words of Norn origin: types of wind and weather, flowers and plants, animals, seasons and holidays. A high percentage of place names throughout the islands are Norn.

Immigration over the past hundred years or so has brought many other languages into everyday use by sizeable communities in Britain. Yiddish-speaking Jews came from Russia in the 19C and early 20C and their German-speaking co-religionists fled from Nazi persecution in the 1930s. The largest immigrant communities here today are from Europe, mainly Germany, Italy, Poland and Spain, with a similar number from Hong Kong, India and Pakistan. Later arrivals were from the New Commonwealth — the West Indies and from Africa. Generations born here now often speak the local dialect and with the accent they learnt at the local school; all however are tributaries, subtly altering the water chemistry of the river of English.

Admission times and charges to the sights described are listed at the end of the guide. Every sight for which there are times and charges is indicated by the symbol ⊘ in the margin in the main part of the guide.

LANDSCAPE

Britain's exceptionally diverse geological foundation has given rise to landscapes of great variety, a natural heritage enhanced by a continuous human presence over several millennia which has shaped and reshaped this given material to form the present uniquely rich pattern of fields and fells, woods and parks, villages and farmsteads. Celebrated in literature and art, this densely-textured landscape, usually domesticated but with its wilder beauties too, has become a kind of national emblem, lived in lovingly and vigorously defended against change by its inhabitants.

THE STRUCTURE OF THE COUNTRY

The complexities of rock type and structure and of relief can be reduced to a broad division into **Upland** and **Lowland** Britain. The former, generally of older, harder material, comprises much of the north and southwest of England and virtually the whole of Wales and Scotland. As well as rolling, open moorlands where the eye ranges freely over vast expanses of coarse grass, bracken or heather, there are mountain chains, modest in elevation, but exhibiting most of the features of much higher and more extensive systems elsewhere and thus attracting serious climbers as well as walkers.

To the south and east, the gentler relief of Lowland Britain is mostly composed of less resistant material of later date. Much is "scarp and vale" country where elegantly undulating chalk and limestone hills terminate in steep escarpments commanding grand panoramas over broad clay vales.

Most of the course of the Earth's history can be traced in these landscapes. From the unimaginably distant Pre-Cambrian, more than 600 million years ago, came the Torridonian sandstone and Lewisian gneiss of northwest Scotland as well as the compact, isolated uplands of Charnwood Forest and the Malvern Hills. The violent volcanic activity of Ordovician times left the shales and slates of **Snowdonia** and the **Lake District**. Extreme pressure from the southeast in the Caledonian mountain-building period produced the characteristic northeast/southwest "grain" of ridges and valleys so evident in much of Wales and Scotland. Most of the country's abundant reserves of coal had their origin in the luxuriant tropical vegetation of Carboniferous times.

Except for the extreme south, the whole country was affected by the action of the often immensely thick ice sheets of the series of Ice Ages. The characteristically sculpted forms of the high mountains testify to the great power of the glaciers as they advanced and retreated, eroding and transporting vast quantities of material, much of which was spread over the lowlands by the mighty ancestors of today's rivers. As the last of the ice melted, the sea level rose, the land bridge joining Britain to the continent of Europe was flooded, and a truncated **Thames,** hitherto a tributary of the Rhine, was given its own outlet to the sea.

Climate. — To complain about the weather is a British tradition, yet the moist and breezy oceanic climate has many compensations. Though grey days sometimes seem to prevail over sunny ones, change is frequent, and "the rain that raineth every day" is rarely unaccompanied by brighter spells. Stressful extremes of either heat or cold are rare, meaning that outdoor activity of some kind is almost always possible. Not by chance is Britain the home of outdoor sports.

Regional and local variations are pronounced. The Western mountains receive the highest amount of precipitation (an astonishing 200 inches — 5 000mm or more on some summits), yet it is in the west that the tempering effects of the **Gulf Stream** are felt and where sub-tropical plants, given shelter, can flourish. The drier, sunnier climate of the east and south is more continental in character, with colder winters and warmer summers.

Rivers and coast. — The country's irregular outline combines with its complex geology to form a long and wonderfully varied coastline. Mountains meet the sea in places to create exceptionally fine coastal scenery; there are spectacular cliffs, those of the south, in blindingly-white chalk, constituting the very symbol of English insularity. Busy resorts have appropriated many of the better stretches of sand and shingle, but quieter beaches remain, together with remote marshlands and lonely sand dunes.

The country is well-watered; the abundant rainfall, carried off the hills by a multitude of streams, feeds rivers, which, though short in length, often end in splendid estuaries bringing salt water and the feel of the sea far inland.

An ancient countryside

The taming and settling of the landscape can be traced back to the 5th millennium BC when Neolithic farmers began to clear the wildwood, the dense forests which had spread northwards in the wake of the retreating ice. The imprint of each succeeding age may be traced, not only in the obvious features of prehistoric stone circles, burial mounds and hill-forts, the planned network of Roman roads or the countless medieval churches, but also in the everyday fabric of the working countryside, where a track may first have been trodden in the Bronze Age or a hedge planted by Saxon settlers.

This many-layered landscape is now characterised by **enclosure,** a web of fields bounded in the lowlands by hedges, in the uplands by drystone walls, and, in areas reclaimed from the sea, by dykes. Small fields with irregular boundaries are likely to be ancient in origin, a regular chequerboard of hawthorn hedges the result of agricultural "Improvement" in the 18 and 19C.

In spite of conditions which are ideal for tree growth, only 8% of the land surface is wooded. About half of this consists of recent coniferous plantations, mostly in the uplands. In many parts of the lowlands, the lack of great forests is compensated for by an abundance of small woods and by the countless individual trees growing in gardens, parklands, and above all in the hedgerows.

Standing out from this orderly pattern are rough open tracts of grass and scrub, the "commons". Once the villager's source of fodder, food and game, they now provide fresh air and exercise for both town and country folk.

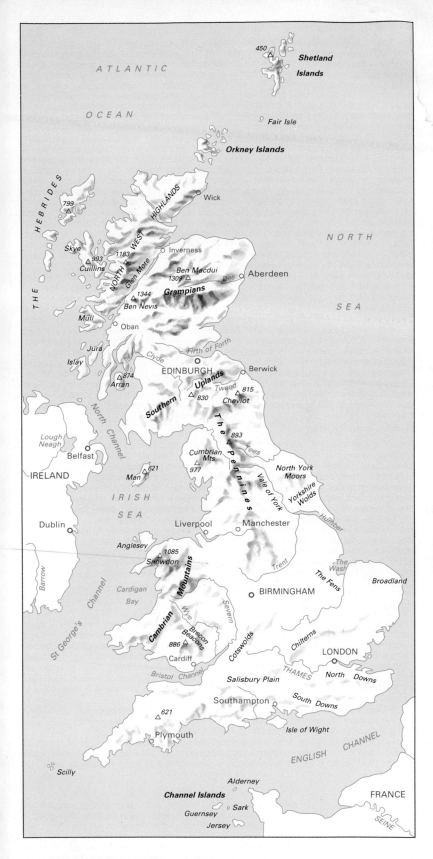

ATLANTIC

OCEAN

450 Shetland
Islands

Fair Isle

Orkney Islands

Wick

NORTH

SEA

HEBRIDES

799

NORTH WEST HIGHLANDS

Skye

993
Cuillins

1183

Glen More

Inverness

Ben Macdui
1309

Dee

Aberdeen

1344
Ben Nevis

Grampians

Mull

Oban

Jura

Islay

Clyde

Firth of Forth

EDINBURGH

Southern Uplands

Berwick

874
Arran

830

Tweed

815
Cheviot

THE

North Channel

Lough
Neagh

Belfast

IRELAND

Dublin

IRISH

SEA

621
Man

Cumbrian
Mts.
977

The Pennines

893

Tees

North York
Moors

Vale of York

Yorkshire
Wolds

Liverpool

Manchester

Humber

Anglesey

1085
Snowdon

Mountains

The
Wash

Trent

The Fens

Broadland

Barrow

St George's Channel

Cardigan
Bay

Cambrian

Wye

Severn

BIRMINGHAM

Cotswolds

Chilterns

LONDON

Dublin

886
Brecon
Beacons

Cardiff

Bristol Channel

THAMES

North Downs

Salisbury Plain

South Downs

Southampton

621

Isle of Wight

ENGLISH CHANNEL

Plymouth

Scilly

Alderney

Channel Islands

Guernsey

Sark

FRANCE

Jersey

SEINE

The Traveller's Friends for **Great Britain:**

Michelin Red Guide for hotels and restaurants
Michelin Map 986 16 miles to 1 inch
Michelin Maps 401, 402, 403 and 404 6.3 miles to 1 inch
Michelin Motoring Atlas 4.75 miles to 1 inch

Building in the landscape

From the end of the medieval period, relative civil peace meant that security was no longer of paramount importance and that the fortified castle could give way to the rural residence designed as a setting for that distinctive culture which at its best combined artistic patronage and a degree of learning with a stylish social round, field sports with progressive farm management. The results are impressive, each generation of the rich and powerful seeking to establish or consolidate its status by building or rebuilding in accord with the dictates of national or international architectural fashion.

But it is in the everyday architecture of cottage, farmhouse and barn that an intimate dialogue takes place between local materials and local skills and which expresses most strongly the individuality of particular places. The range of materials used is enormous, a reflection of the population's ingenuity as well as of the country's geological diversity. Every type of stone has been quarried and shaped, from the most intractable of Scottish Aberdeen, Peterhead and Cornish granites to the crumbling, barely suitable, chalk of the south. The limestones are often exploited to wonderful effect, as in the **Cotswolds** or the **Yorkshire Wolds.** Where stone is lacking, timber is used; structurally, as in the cruck-built cottages of Weobley and the elaborate half-timbered houses of much of the Midlands, or as cladding, in the tarred or painted "weather-boarding" of the southeast coast. In the claylands, most villages once had their own brickfield, producing distinctive tiles as well as bricks, while reedbeds might provide thatch for roofing. Less favoured areas, with no one material of particular merit, now have some of the most delightful townscapes, an amalgam of timber, tile and brick, stones and slate, even flints from the fields or pebbles from the beach (Lewes).

Building forms vary as much as materials; few contrasts could be greater than that of a solid timber-framed house of a Kentish yeoman (Weald and Downland Open Air Museum) with the humble one-roomed dwelling of a crofter in northwest Scotland (Black House).

Settlement forms too are almost infinitely varied. In the uplands, the isolated farm, sheltered perhaps by a wind-break of sycamores, is characteristic; in the well-watered west, a few cottages and farms may be loosely grouped to form a hamlet; elsewhere, true villages may predominate, street villages accompanying a road for part of its way, others clustered sociably around a green (Long Melford and Dalmeny). Many, having occupied their sites for centuries, are the very image of timeless tranquillity; others are tougher altogether, like the fishing village facing the fierce sea (Craster, Polperro and Crail), or the industrial villages of the 19C, long blank-eyed terraces stretching from pub to chapel, in the shadow of mine or factory (Pontypool and Longton).

Parks and gardens

A keen appreciation of country life and the pleasures of Nature goes back to the Middle Ages when Royal Forests covered much of the land and every person of consequence had his deer park. It was in the 18C, however, that the face of lowland Britain was transformed in pursuit of the aesthetic ideals of the country's "greatest original contribution to the arts", the **English Landscape Movement.** Ruthlessly sweeping away the grand avenues, parterres and topiary left by previous landscapers, the grandees and lesser gentry of the Georgian age, aided by professionals like **Lancelot Capability Brown** (1716-83), broke down the boundaries separating house, garden and wider countryside to make ambitious compositions fusing buildings and statuary, trees and woodland, lawns, lakes and rivers into a picturesque vision of an idealised Nature. Many of their grander creations are world-renowned (Blenheim, Stourhead), but few parts of the country remained unaffected by this national programme of landscape beautification and a continuing passion for landscaping and horticulture has left a garden heritage unequalled elsewhere.

Conservation

In this densely-populated land, urban pressures have been resisted by a system of town and country planning exercising strict control over building development. Coast and countryside are protected by an array of zonings; Green Belts; Areas of Outstanding Natural Beauty, Cotswolds, **Chiltern Hills;** Heritage Coasts and eleven National Parks. The latter comprise the finest upland scenery of England and Wales, much of it farmed and in private ownership, but controlled and managed by each of the National Park authorities to conserve the characteristic landscape beauty and make it accessible to the public.

In the countryside generally, a network of roads and lanes penetrates virtually everywhere; beyond are countless miles of paths and bridleways, among them Long Distance Footpaths leading through the best hill and coastal scenery.

Many historic houses, gardens, and landscapes now belong to the National Trusts of England and Wales and for Scotland, who successfully marry conservation with public access (visitors from abroad may find it advantageous to become members).

REGIONS

The South East. — "London's Countryside" is highly urbanised, but its varied relief and an abundance of trees, woods and parklands (in spite of the devastation wrought by the hurricane of October 1987) make an attractive habitat for its generally prosperous population.

The rim of the basin containing Greater London is formed by gracefully sculpted chalk hills; to the northwest, the Chilterns, famous for their beechwoods; to the south, the **North** and **South Downs,** running in a great arc to enfold the deep oakwoods of the **Weald** and terminating in spectacular chalk cliffs. To the east, flanked by market garden and orchard country and by many lesser creeks and inlets, is the great estuary of the **Thames.** This coastal country looks towards the Continent of Europe, with which it has many links; its outline has changed much in historical times, losses to the sea balanced by the winning of such tracts of rich pastureland as Romney Marsh.

Central Southern England. — The high and airy chalklands centred on **Salisbury Plain** were the heart of prehistoric England. Innumerable lesser earthworks and other traces form the setting for the greater monuments like Stonehenge.

Later populations have settled in the gentle river valleys and in the ports and resorts of the coast, off which lies the pretty Isle of Wight. The great stretches of salt water it shelters from the Channel are an amateur sailor's paradise. To the west, beyond the beautiful woods and heaths of the New Forest, is the geologically complex and scenically fascinating Dorset coast.

The South West. — A granite backbone unites Devon and Cornwall, showing itself in rugged high moorlands topped by wind-blasted "tors". Northwards the Exmoor National Park is formed of red sandstone, which in the Devon lowlands yields rich agricultural soils. The county's particularly luxuriant version of the English patchwork field pattern gives way in Cornwall's harsher environment to smaller fields often of ancient origin, bounded by earthen hedge-banks or stone walls.

The long coastline of the peninsula is unsurpassed; most varieties of coastal scenery are represented; spectacular rocky bastions under fierce attack from Atlantic rollers contrast with sheltered bays and beautifully wooded inlets running far inland.

East Anglia. — England's most extensive area of low relief is a region of great individuality; densely populated in medieval times, it is unequalled in its wealth of ancient villages and small towns. Its dry climate and generally good soils mean that much of its gently undulating farmland is in arable cultivation; fields are large and many trees and hedges have been removed. East of the region's capital, Norwich, is **Broadland,** extensive shallow stretches of water formed by peat extraction, rich in wildlife and thronged with pleasure craft.

Building styles express past links with the Netherlands, and it was Dutch engineers who carried out much of the work which transformed the marshes and fens around the Wash into the country's richest tract of arable land.

The Midlands. — The centre of England is firmly defined to the north and west by the mountains of the **Pennines** and Wales. To the south and east a less marked boundary is formed by a succession of broad vales watered by slowly-moving rivers overlooked by the escarpments of hill ranges. Of these, the most prominent is the belt of oolitic limestone extending from Dorset to the River Humber, at its widest in the **Cotswold Hills,** but yielding everywhere that fine stone which gives its built landscape such distinctive character.

Elsewhere, there is a less coherent pattern of modest blocks of hill country, in mixed farming except for heath and woodland tracts such as Cannock Chase and Charnwood Forest.

The regular pattern of ancient county towns sitting at the centre of their shires (Gloucester, Northampton, Lincoln) is overlaid by the later one of the Industrial Revolution. Based on the region's diverse mineral resources and given a decisive impulse at Ironbridge *(qv),* this swelled Birmingham to metropolitan size and created the chaotic urban sprawls of the Black Country and Stoke-on-Trent whose legacy of derelict land is now being transformed into parkland.

Northern England. — At a certain latitude not easy to define precisely the personality of the English landscape changes decisively. A less kindly climate, high moorlands and rugged mountains whose presence dominates the lowlands too; building stones lending themselves to a bold rather than refined treatment; the widespread impact of industry; all combine to give a distinct and strongly felt identity to "The North".

The long mountain chain of the Pennines is the region's central feature, though it is flanked by extensive lowlands; to the west, the Cheshire and Lancashire plains, the former as lush and tidy as any southern county, the latter much built over but growing horticultural crops on its reclaimed "mosses".

To the east, beyond the densely populated Yorkshire coalfield, is equally fertile country, prolonged northwards by the **Vale of York** and bounded towards the sea by chalk wolds divided by the great estuary of the **Humber.**

The **Pennines** themselves, with their three National Parks, are far from homogeneous in character. In the far north, the wild and lonely **Cheviots** of the Northumberland National Park are the well-rounded remains of ancient volcanoes. In the **Yorkshire Dales** the characteristic features of limestone country are well developed; tablelands rising to high, flat-topped eminences like **Pen-y-Gent** (2 273ft-693m), gorges, cliffs, caves and underground streams. Here and in that part of the **Peak District** where this pale carboniferous limestone occurs the rock has been used to build a harmonious landscape all of stone, much as in the far-off Cotswolds, albeit with sterner effect. Between the Peak, the mountain playground for much of industrial Lancashire and the Yorkshire Dales lie many upland miles of even more severe country, underlain by the sombre millstone grit. The abundant rainfall pours off the mountains in fast-flowing streams, feeding mills and factories of the tightly built up valley floors or, to the south and north, the unspoilt rivers of Dales and Peak. East of the Pennines, the **North York Moors** National Park forms a vast heather-covered tableland which reaches the sea in an undeveloped coastline of great beauty. To the west is the **Lake District,** with England's highest peaks (**Sca Fell** 3 206ft-978m) and an inexhaustible variety of mountain scenery ranging from the wildest of storm-blasted crags to the exquisite parkland scenery reflected in Lake Windermere.

Further north still, where the fells draw ever closer to the coast, is Northumbria, England's northernmost province, whose windy farmlands contrast with deep wooded denes and the trio of riverside conurbations flanking Tyne, Wear and Tees.

Wales. — The country is approached via the English **Marchlands,** attractive farming country interspersed with hill ranges anticipating the mountains beyond. In the south is the **Royal Forest of Dean,** pierced by the luxuriantly wooded gorge of the Wye. In the north, localised industrial landscapes give way to the narrow coastal plain of North Wales, crowded with resorts, leading via the Menai Strait to the Isle of Anglesey or to the remote Lleyn Peninsula.

Hard on the coast rise the mountains of **Snowdonia**, true highlands of a grandeur exceeded only by ranges many times their height and extent. Contrasting with their drama are the gentler, swelling forms of the sheep-grazed uplands of Mid-Wales. Southwards, a great bastion is formed by the red sandstone escarpment of the **Brecon Beacons,** beyond which lies the immense coalfield of South Wales, a high plateau deeply cut by valleys filled with mining settlements and focusing on the capital, Cardiff and the other former coal ports of the coast.

Westward, the scene is rural again, rolling country ending in the cliffs and rocks of the **Pembrokeshire Coast** National Park.

Scotland. — While many elements of the English landscape — enclosed fields, parklands — are repeated in Scotland, often in a neater, simplified form, the country's scenic personality is quite distinct; mountains and moorlands predominate; the climate is noticeably more rigorous (albeit with many compensations, mild winters in the west, sparkling air in the east); human activity is highly concentrated in the lowlands and parts of the coast, leaving much of the surface of the land free from urban intrusions and exhilaratingly open to the influences of Nature. A rich and varied landscape, it can nevertheless be broken down into three main regions.

The Southern Uplands, sparsely-inhabited borderlands, consist of gently rounded moorlands penetrated in the west by deep, narrow dales, in the east by the broader, cultivated valleys of the **Tweed** and its tributaries.

The Central Lowlands, dramatically pierced by the great firths of **Tay, Clyde** and **Forth,** this densely-populated area, rich in minerals and with a prosperous agriculture, forms the focus of Scotland's urban and industrial life. Low-lying only in contrast to the mountains to north and south, the region is enlivened by numerous hill ranges, the **Pentland Hills** and **Campsie Fells** forming a background to Edinburgh and Glasgow, the high **Ochils** seeming to bar the way northwards.

The Highlands and Islands. — Much of the area lies above 2 000ft-610m, rising above 4 000ft-1 220m, in the **Cairngorms** (**Ben Macdui** 4 296ft-1 309m) and in **Ben Nevis,** Britain's highest peak (4 406ft-1 344m). A complex geological history has left landforms as varied as the smoothly-rounded **Grampians,** the towering **Cuillins** of the Isle of Skye and the spectacular mountain and cliff-scenery of **Wester Ross.** Water is everywhere; tumbling peat-tinted burns feed fine rivers; there are salt and fresh-water lochs and in the west, the sea defines an extraordinarily indented coastline.

Cotton grass and heather clothe the mountains; tree cover becomes ever sparser northwards, though there are magnificent remains of the ancient Caledonian pine forest at Glen More.

The thinly-spread human presence favours wildlife; the coast is thronged with seabirds, including puffins; there are grey and common seals; inland the red deer is abundant, and in the wilder places live the wild cat, the eagle, and the recently re-established osprey.

Beyond the mainland lie nearly 800 islands, many uninhabited, each with its own character, like wind-swept **Islay,** almost in sight of Ireland; **Skye,** with its unsurpassed mountain and coastal scenery; **Orkney,** rich in prehistoric remains, and far-off **Shetland,** stern and treeless.

Derwentwater and Stable Hills

HISTORICAL TABLE AND NOTES

The Romans

AD 42	Roman conquest of Britain begins.
410	Alaric the Goth sacks Rome. Legions withdrawn from Britain.

Anglo-Saxons

449	First waves of Angles, Saxons and Jutes land in Britain.
597	St Augustine founds a Benedictine monastery in Canterbury.
779	Offa of Mercia regarded as the overlord of all England.
c. 840	The Danes found Dublin, and in 876 AD, York.
1016-35	Canute, first Danish king of England.
1064	Earl Harold pays homage to Duke William of Normandy.

The Normans

1066	Duke William defeats Harold at **Hastings** and is crowned as **William I.**
1086	Start of the 'Domesday Survey'.
1100-35	**Reign of Henry I** who marries Matilda, uniting Norman and Saxon royal houses.
1128	Matilda marries Geoffrey, Count of Anjou.
1135-54	**Reign of Stephen.** Treaty of Winchester accepts Henry of Anjou as heir to throne.

The Plantagenets

1154	Henry of Anjou (Plantagenet) becomes **King Henry II.**
1170	Thomas Becket murdered in Canterbury Cathedral.
1189-99	**Reign of Richard I (Cœur de Lion),** having defeated his father in battle.
1199-1216	**Reign of John.** Most of Normandy, Maine, Anjou and Brittany lost to the French.
1215	Barons force John to sign **Magna Carta.**
1216-72	**Reign of Henry III,** who marries Eleanor of Provence in 1236.
1267	Henry recognises Llywelyn as Prince of Wales.
1271-1307	**Reign of Edward I.** Start of his Welsh campaigns. Llywelyn killed 1282.
1284	Statute of Rhuddlan enacted. Prince Edward born at Caernarfon.
1296-8	William Wallace ravages northern England. Defeated at Falkirk, 1298. Executed 1305.
1307-27	**Reign of Edward II,** who marries Isabel of France.
1314	Robert I, King of Scotland, defeats Edward II at Bannockburn.
1327	Edward II murdered at Berkeley Castle.
1327-77	**Reign of Edward III.** Roger Mortimer and Isabel as Regents.
1328	Robert I recognised as King of an independent Scotland.
1330	Edward III seizes power. Executes Roger Mortimer.
1337-1453	Start of the Hundred Years War with France.
1377-99	**Reign of Richard II,** following the death of the Black Prince.
1396	Treaty of Paris. Peace between France and England.
1398	Richard II banishes Henry Bolingbroke, who returns and deposes Richard.
1399-1414	**Reign of Henry IV.** Richard dies in 1400, probably murdered.
1409	The English take Harlech. Glyndẃr disappears.
1413-22	**Reign of Henry V.**
1415	War against France. Henry wins battle of Agincourt.
1420	By the Treaty of Troyes Henry V becomes heir to the French throne.
1422-61	**Reign of Henry VI.** Dukes of Gloucester and Lancaster as Regents.
1455	Wars of the Roses begin at St Albans. Yorkists defeat Lancastrians.
1461-83	**Reign of Edward IV.**
1465	Henry VI captured and imprisoned in Tower of London.
1467-70	Warwick plots against the King. Defeated by Edward he flees to France and is reconciled with Lancastrians. Returns to England, restores Henry VI and Edward flees.
1471	Edward lands in England, defeats and kills Warwick at Barnet. After his victory at Tewkesbury, Edward murders Henry VI and Prince Edward.
1483	**Reign of Edward V.** Edward and his brother Richard imprisoned in the Tower.
1483-85	**Reign of Richard III,** defeated and killed by Henry Tudor at Bosworth.

The Tudors

1485-1509	**Reign of Henry VII,** whose marriage to Elizabeth of York ended the Wars of the Roses.
1503	Betrothal of Prince Henry to Catherine of Aragon. James IV of Scotland marries Henry VII's daughter Margaret Tudor.
1509-47	**Reign of Henry VIII.** Marriage to Catherine of Aragon, 1509.
1513	James IV of Scotland is defeated and killed at Flodden.
1515	Wolsey made Chancellor. Begins building Hampton Court Palace.
1521	Pope Leo X confers title of ''Defender of the Faith'' upon Henry VIII, for his book attacking the teachings of Martin Luther.
1533	Henry secretly marries Anne Boleyn, having obtained a divorce through Cranmer, newly appointed Archbishop of Canterbury. Princess Elizabeth born.

1535	Chancellor Sir Thomas More executed for refusing to sign the Act of Supremacy, acknowledging Henry as head of the Church, in place of the Pope.
1536-39	Suppression of the monasteries begins. Henry VIII excommunicated.
1542-67	Mary Queen of Scots born at Linlithgow.
1544-46	England at war with France. The French burn Brighton.
1547-53	**Reign of Edward VI.** First Book of Common Prayer issued in 1549.
1553-58	**Reign of Mary I.**
1554	Mary marries Philip II of Spain. Reversal of the Reformation begins.
1558-1603	**Reign of Queen Elizabeth I.** Lord Cecil becomes Secretary of State. Mary Queen of Scots marries François, Dauphin of France.
1559-60	The Protestant religion re-established. Calvinism established in Scotland.
1561	The 19-year-old Mary Queen of Scots returns from France after the death of her husband.
1565	Mary Queen of Scots marries first Darnley, then Bothwell. She remains the focus of opposition to Elizabeth's tenure of the Throne.
1567-1625	Reign of James VI, King of Scots. Moray acts as Regent.
1570	The Pope excommunicates Elizabeth.
1580	Drake circumnavigates the world.
1586	Babington Plot to assassinate Elizabeth and use Spanish help to put Mary Queen of Scots on the throne.
1587	Mary Queen of Scots executed. Drake attacks Cadiz.
1588	Spanish Armada defeated.
1592-1616	Most of Shakespeare's greatest plays produced.
1600	Incorporation of the East India Company.

The Stuarts

1603-25	**James VI of Scotland** succeeds Elizabeth as **James I of England.**
1605	Discovery of the ''Gunpowder Plot'' to assassinate the King in Parliament.
1620	The Pilgrim Fathers set sail. Start of Scottish settlement in Nova Scotia.
1624-49	**Reign of Charles I.**
1626-40	Parliament refuses to grant subsidies to the King, who dissolves it and rules without Parliament until 1640.
1640-53	The 'Long Parliament' passes the 'Triennial Act' ensuring regular Parliaments. 'Star Chamber' abolished. 'Ship Money' declared illegal.
1642	The Civil War breaks out.
1646	Charles surrenders to the Scots. The Royalists surrender at Oxford.
1647	Scots hand over Charles to the English Army. Civil War resumes a year later.
1649	Trial and execution of Charles I; abolition of the monarchy and the House of Lords. The **"Commonwealth"** established.
1651	Charles II is crowned at Scone. Flees to France after defeat at Worcester.
1652-54	War against the Dutch.
1653	Cromwell becomes Lord Protector.
1656-59	War against Spain.
1660-85	**Reign of Charles II.**
1661	The 'Clarendon Code' re-established the position of the Anglican Church.
1665-67	War against the Dutch.
1665	The Great Plague killed over 68 000 Londoners.
1666	The Great Fire of London destroyed 4/5ths of the City of London, but claimed only twenty lives. Sir Christopher Wren re-built St Paul's, and 51 other churches.
1672	'Declaration of Indulgence', relaxing penal laws against Catholics and Dissenters.
1672-74	War against the Dutch.
1673	Test Act passed, excluding non-conformists and Catholics from civil office.
1677	Princess Mary, sister to Charles II, marries William of Orange.
1679	Habeas Corpus Act strengthened existing powers protecting individuals against arbitrary imprisonment.
1685-88	**Reign of James II.**
1685	Monmouth's rebellion, followed by Judge Jeffrey's ''Bloody Assizes''.
1687	James dissolves Parliament and issues a first Declaration of Indulgence.
1688	Second Declaration of Indulgence. Trial and acquittal of the 'Seven Bishops'. William of Orange invited to England, James flees to France.
1689-1702	**Reign of William III and Mary II.**
1689	Scottish Jacobites defeated at Killiecrankie. James besieges Londonderry.
1689	War against France. 'Grand Alliance' between England, Austria, the Netherlands and German states.
1690	Irish Jacobites defeated at battle of the Boyne.
1694	**Mary II dies.** Triennial Act provided for a Parliament to meet at least once every three years and to sit for not more than three years.
1694	The Bank of England founded. The Bank of Scotland founded, 1695.
1702-14	**Reign of Queen Anne.**
1702-14	War of the Spanish Succession. French invade the Spanish Netherlands.
1704	Britain captures Gibraltar. Victory at Blenheim.
1710	Act of Union with Scotland passed.
1714	Treaties of Utrecht end War of Spanish Succession.

The Hanoverians

1714-27	**Reign of George I.**
1715	Jacobite rebellion, led by James Edward Stuart, the "Old Pretender".
1727-60	**Reign of George II.** Irish Catholics deprived of the vote in 1728.
1731	Jethro Tull's horse hoe and seed drill help revolutionise agriculture.
1733	John Kay invents the flying shuttle.
1745	"Bonnie Prince Charlie" leads second Jacobite rebellion, ended at Culloden, 1746.
1752	The Gregorian Calendar adopted.
1756	The Seven Years War starts. Pitt the Elder forms his ministry.
1757	Calcutta recaptured. Clive wins battle of Plassey.
1759	Wolfe defeats French army on the Heights of Abraham, Quebec.
1760-1820	**Reign of George III.** Conquest of Canada completed in 1760.
1763	Treaty of Paris ends the Seven Years War.
1769	Watt's steam engine and Arkwright's water frame are patented.
1773	Boston Tea Party — a protest against forced imports of cheap East India Company tea into the American colonies.
1776	American Declaration of Independence.
1781	British surrender at Yorktown. Watt patents steam engine for rotary motion.
1783	Treaty of Paris ends American War of Independence.
1787	Cartwright invents the power loom.
1793	War against Revolutionary France.
1799	Income Tax levied for the first time, to finance the war.
1805	Naval victory at Trafalgar, but Nelson is killed in the battle.
1807	Abolition of the slave trade.
1812-14	Anglo-American War ended by Treaty of Ghent.
1815	Napoleon finally defeated at Waterloo. Congress of Vienna.
1820-30	**Reign of George IV.**
1823	Peel starts to reform criminal law and prisons.
1825	Stockton and Darlington railway opened. Telford completes the Menai Bridge.
1829	Catholic Emancipation is passed. Metropolitan Police formed.
1830-37	**Reign of William IV.**
1832	First Reform Act passed.
1833	Factory Act passed. Slavery abolished.
1834	"Tolpuddle Martyrs" transported to Australia, having been found guilty of forming an agricultural 'Trade Union'.

House of Windsor

1837-1901	**Reign of Queen Victoria.**
1840	Victoria marries Prince Albert. Penny post introduced.
1842	Chartist movement campaigns for Parliamentary reforms.
1848	Cholera epidemic. Public Health Act passed.
1854	The Crimean War breaks out. Ended by Treaty of Paris - 1856.
1857	The Indian Mutiny.
1858	The Crown takes over the government of India from the East India Company.
1871	Bank holidays introduced.
1888	Local Government Act establishes county councils and county boroughs.
1900	The Labour Party is formed.
1901-10	**Reign of Edward VII.** Peace of Vereeniging ends the second Boer War in 1902.
1903	Women's suffrage movement started by Mrs Pankhurst.
1905	First motor buses run in London. Piccadilly and Bakerloo tube lines opened.
1909	Old age pensions introduced.
1910-36	**Reign of George V.**
1914	World War I breaks out. Kitchener's "Volunteer Army" formed.
1916	The Easter Rising, in Ireland.
1918	End of hostilities. Women over thirty given the vote.
1919	Treaty of Versailles signed, ending World War I.
1921	The Irish Free State is created.
1926	The General Strike.
1928	Women over 21 given the vote.
1936	**Reign of Edward VIII.** Abdication.
1936-52	**Reign of George VI.**
1939	Outbreak of World War II.
1940	Dunkirk evacuation, followed by the "Battle of Britain".
1946	National Insurance and National Health Acts introduced under Attlee government.
1947	India obtains independence and is partitioned.
	Railways and road transport are nationalised.
1949	Republic of Ireland becomes independent. The North Atlantic Treaty Organisation (NATO) is founded. Iron and steel industries nationalised.
1952	**Reign of Queen Elizabeth II begins.**
1959	Oil is discovered in the North Sea.
1967	De Gaulle vetoes, as he had done in 1963, Britain's entry into the Common Market.
1969	Prince Charles invested as Prince of Wales at Caernarfon Castle. Troubles begin in Ulster.
1973	Britain becomes member of the EC.

Great Britain is positioned at the western edge of the ancient world, and successive waves of peoples have merged their culture, language, beliefs and, above all, their energies, into the character of an island race which has explored, fought for, traded with and settled other lands right across the world.

8 000 years ago retreating glaciers caused the seas to rise and submerge the mud flats which had joined Britain to the continent of Europe. Agriculturalists arrived around 5 000 BC and gave the British landscape a basic appearance which remained largely unchanged until the 20C. Gradually the settled clans with a sound economy had the inspiration and organisational ability to build monuments to their beliefs as mighty as Stonehenge — millions of man-hours between 4 000 and 1 800 BC.

The 'Beaker Folk' arrived around 2 700 BC, bringing Aryan roots of the English language — family and tribal words such as *father, mother, sister* and *brother* and a knowledge of metal working, a benefit which was gradually absorbed as they merged into the established communities.

Skara Brae, Orkney

The Celts. — From 700 BC onwards Celtic settlers brought their language, their chariots and a love of finery, gold and ornaments. Iron swords gave them an ascendancy in battle over the native Britons, who were pushed westwards. Celtic immigrant groups, thirty or so to a boat, could scarcely supplant the established society, estimated at around a million, but by 100 BC the Celtic life style and customs were already well established in Britain. They shared little but a common dialect and it was this lack of any idea of 'nationhood' which left Celtic society an easy prey to the civilising might of Rome.

The Romans. — The offshore island of Britannia was not strategically important to Rome, but the lure of corn, gold, iron, slaves and hunting dogs was enough to make the invasion of the summer of 43 AD worthwhile. By 70 AD much of the north and Wales had been subdued. Fifty or more towns were linked by a network of roads and Rome had given Britain yet another facet of its culture, its law and had extended the use of coinage, introduced by the Celts, into a recognised system, without which trade in an 'urban' society cannot exist. Christianity was established as the official religion in Britain in 313 AD but by 411 AD the Romans had withdrawn.

The Saxons. — Germanic mercenaries manned many of the shore forts of Britain, before the final withdrawal of Roman regular troops. As pay became short they seized tracts of good farming land and with their heavier ploughs were able to till even the heavier clays.

In 597 AD Augustine, sent by Pope Gregory on a mission to convert the British to Christianity, found the King of Kent already married to a Christian princess. Differences between the Celtic and Roman churches were not, however, settled until the Synod of Whitby in 664 AD, sixty years after Augustine's death.

Christianity survived 'The Dark Ages' and with it the learning of monks, like the Venerable Bede, who in 731 AD completed his *Ecclesiastical History of the English People* at Jarrow monastery.

The Saxon kingdoms were constantly engaged in power struggles, not just with one another but with Angles and Jutes, who also came to settle. Saxons traded as far afield as Russia and Constantinople, bringing in yet further influence.

The Vikings. — From 851 AD Viking raiders wintered regularly in Britain and so became settlers themselves. One of their kinsmen, Rollo, in 911 AD, founded a kingdom which was later to play a major part in the history of Great Britain today — Normandy. The Vikings took to trading and barter as the next best thing to piracy and London became again what it had been under Roman rule, a great trading port. By 911 AD eight vassal kings paid homage to King Edgar for almost the whole island, but not all the kings were as able and strong. Norsemen attacked England during the disastrous reign of Ethelred the 'Redeless' — lacking wise counsel — who fled to Normandy, leaving his son Edmund 'Ironside' to battle against the invaders. When Edmund died the Witenagemot — parliament — preferring strength to weakness, elected the Danish invader **Canute** as King. Seven years after his death the Witan had again to choose a King and they chose Edward, son of Ethelred and his Norman wife, Emma. More abbot than king, he became **Edward the Confessor.**

Edward the Confessor gave land and positions to Normans who viewed the easy-going English with scarcely concealed contempt. **Duke William,** great-nephew of the Confessor, is said to have made Harold, son of Earl Godwin, swear an oath to help William claim the English throne on Edward's death. On 5 January 1066, only days after the consecration of his Abbey church at Westminster, the gentle Confessor died. The Witan elected Harold Godwinson as King and the stage was set for the Norman Conquest. For many, the "history" of England starts on **14 October 1066** at the **Battle of Hastings.** But it is the people, the rulers and the ruled, the thinkers, explorers, artists, soldiers and later the politicians, industrialists and reformers, who have shaped Britain today.

The Normans - 1066-1154. — With five thousand knights and followers William conquered a nation of 1.5-2 million people — descendants of Celts, Romans, Vikings and Saxons — and a strong central authority was imposed on a group of kingdoms which ranked among the richest in western Europe. This was the inheritance which allowed the Normans to consolidate their military victory so quickly.

By the time of the **Domesday Survey,** only a handful of English names feature amongst the list of 'tenants in chief', revealing a massive shift in ownership of land and only one of sixteen Bishops was an Englishman. "He destroys well who builds something better" — by 1200 almost every Anglo-Saxon cathedral and abbey — reminders for the vanquished English of their great past — had been destroyed and replaced by Norman works. But forty years after the Conquest English soldiers fought for an English-born king, **Henry I,** in his French territories. The process of conquest followed by the gradual absorption of the conquered continued.

The Plantagenets - 1154-1485. — **Henry II,** Count of Anjou, remained closely involved with his French domains. His dispute with **Thomas Becket,** whom he himself had appointed Archbishop of Canterbury, over the relative rights of Church and State, marred a reign which deserves to be remembered for Henry's restoration of order in a ravaged country. His legal reforms included the establishment of the jury and assize court system, as well as coroners courts. He twice reformed the coinage, granted many town charters and encouraged expansion of sheep farming. English wool was of high quality, heavy duties were levied on its export and it became a foundation of England's prosperity.

The despotic manner of ruling and of raising revenue adopted by his son **John** united the barons into forcing him, in 1215, to sign **Magna Carta,** guaranteeing every man freedom from illegal interference with his person or property and the basis of much subsequent English legislation.

Baronial opposition and internal strife marked the ineffectual reign of John's son, **Henry III,** but his son, **Edward I,** typical Plantagenet, fair haired, tall and energetic, was for much of his reign at war, with France, with Wales and with Scotland and upon the last two he imposed English administration and justice. The constitutional importance of Parliament increased during his reign, his 'Model Parliament' of 1295 including representatives from shire, city and borough.

But again a weak king followed a strong father. **Edward II** cared for little other than his own pleasure and his reign saw the effective loss of all that his father had won. His Queen, Isabel of France, humiliated by her husband's conduct, invaded, deposed Edward and the throne passed to his son, **Edward III,** who sought reconciliation with the barons and pursued an enlightened trade policy. He reorganised the navy, led England into the **Hundred Years War,** claiming not only Aquitaine but the throne of France and rebuilt much of Windsor Castle. Here he founded the Order of the Garter, in 1348, the year the Black Death reached England and the labour force was reduced by one-third. The 1351 Labourers' Statute, a government attempt to control wages, was one of the causes of the Peasants' Revolt in 1381. The throne passed to Richard, younger son of Edward's son, the Black Prince who had died before his father.

Richard II was much influenced by his uncle, John of Gaunt, who acted as Regent. Richard's personal bravery, demonstrated during the Peasants' Revolt (1381) could not, however, control his barons. Gaunt's son, Bolingbroke, invaded to recover his father's estates, confiscated by Richard. After Richard's abdication he became **Henry IV.** He faced rebellion by the Welsh, by the Percys, Earls of Northumberland, and threat of French invasion.

Henry V resumed the Hundred Years War and English claims to the French throne, but died leaving an infant son, who was crowned as **Henry VI,** in Westminster Abbey, in 1429 and in Notre Dame, in 1431. Yet another Regency, Henry's recurrent bouts of insanity and the counter-claims of York and Lancaster led to the outbreak of the Wars of the Roses.

York and Lancaster. — The Lancastrians, **Henry IV, V** and **VI,** claimed the throne by direct male descent from John of Gaunt, fourth son of Edward III. The Yorkists, **Edward IV, Edward V** and **Richard III,** were descended from Lionel, Edward's third son, but in the female line — The **Wars of the Roses,** thirty years of sporadic fighting and periods of armed peace, between 1455 and 1485, were ended by the marriage of Henry VII — Lancastrian and first of the Tudor dynasty — to Elizabeth of York.

The Princes in the Tower. — Edward V was imprisoned in the Tower, with his younger brother, Richard, by their uncle Richard, Duke of Gloucester, who claimed the throne by virtue of their alleged illegitimacy. Parliament accepted this and proclaimed Gloucester **Richard III.** The two princes were probably murdered.

The Tudors - 1485-1603. — **Henry VII** ruled shrewdly and his control of finances restored order after the Wars of the Roses leaving a healthy Treasury for his son. **Henry VIII** was a "Renaissance Man" — accomplished musician, linguist, scholar and soldier. An autocratic monarch of capricious temper and elastic conscience, he achieved union with Ireland and Wales and greatly strengthened the Navy. Wool, much of which had been exported raw in the previous century, was now nearly all made into cloth at home.

Henry's **Dissolution of the Monasteries** caused the greatest re-distribution of land in England since the Norman conquest.

Edward VI, son of Henry and Jane Seymour, Henry VIII's third wife, was succeeded by his half-sister **Mary,** daughter of Catherine of Aragon. Her insistence on a marriage with Philip II of Spain undermined her popularity with the English as did the burning of three hundred alleged heretics. Her war with France resulted in the loss of Calais, England's last possession in Europe.

Elizabeth I presided over a flowering of national culture and the arts. She restored a moderate Anglicanism, though potential Catholic conspiracies to supplant her were ruthlessly suppressed. The defeat of the Spanish Armada was the greatest military victory of a reign in which Elizabeth sought to avoid the needless expense of war, by her diplomacy and a network of informers controlled by her Secretaries, Cecil and Walsingham.

The Stuarts and The Commonwealth - (1603-1714).
— The economy was still largely based on agriculture and on wool. Despite an average life expectancy of only 35 years population growth — 2.5 million in the 1520s to over 5 million by 1650 — posed problems of availability of work and food. Manufacturing increased, production of iron quadrupling in the century to 1650, but small workshops producing high quality woollen cloth were still the mainstay of commerce.

James I of England and VI of Scotland seemed to ensure a **Protestant** succession. On 5 November 1605, Guy Fawkes and a **Catholic** minority attempted to assassinate James in Parliament, despite his willingness to extend a measure of toleration to all Catholics. James realised that England could not afford war and made peace with Spain. He also believed firmly in the 'divine right of Kings' and was soon in conflict with Parliament over revenues.

Charles I inherited his father's belief in absolute monarchy and attempted to rule without Parliament. His marriage to a Catholic wife did not help him in the eyes of the people. He was finally forced to recall Parliament, however, and they condemned his adviser, the Earl of Strafford, to death for treason, refused money until the King discussed their grievances and passed a Bill preventing dissolution without the consent of Parliament. The deepening constitutional crisis turned into an open breach when Charles attempted to arrest five Members in early 1642. Civil War broke out in August.

The Civil War (1642-1649). — Charles established his capital at Oxford. Scots support tilted the balance against Charles and the North was lost after Marston Moor in 1644. Formation of the New Model Army by **Cromwell** and Fairfax and its victory at Naseby in 1645 was followed by the surrender of the King who was handed over to Parliament in 1647. Attempts at compromise were fruitless. Charles wavered, playing factions in Parliament one against the other. He promised the Scots a Presbyterian England for their help and sought finance and troops from abroad. Captured after a Scottish invasion was crushed at Preston, in August 1648, the Army demanded Charles' death and he was tried and beheaded in January 1649.

Commonwealth and Protectorate (1649-1660). — The Monarchy and the House of Lords were abolished, replaced by a 40-member Council of State. Attempts by the 'Rump' Parliament to turn itself into a permanent non-elected junta caused Cromwell to dissolve it and form the Protectorate, in which he, as Lord Protector, ruled by decree. He was accepted by the majority of a war-weary population, but on his death in 1653 the realisation that no one else could successfully fill the post of Lord Protector, set in motion negotiations which led to the Restoration.

The Restoration. — **Charles II** in his Declaration of Breda, appeared to promise something for almost every political faction. The "Restoration" in May 1660, ended ten years of Puritan restriction and opened a period of sensuality, and a flourishing of theatre, painting and the arts.

The **Navigation Acts,** specifying that English goods must be carried in English ships, did much to develop commerce. Charles refused to legitimise his son, the Duke of Monmouth, who was to lead a rebellion against his uncle, **James II,** in 1685, just after Charles' death. James appeared to have everything in his favour, but his brutal repression of the Monmouth rebellion, the introduction of pro-Catholic policies, and the birth of a son James — who was to become the "Old Pretender" — all intensified fears of a Catholic succession. Disaffected politicians approached William of Orange, married to Mary, James' daughter, and he accepted the throne.

William III accepted the Declaration of Rights and following his landing in 1688 and the Glorious Revolution, was crowned with his wife Mary as his Queen, in 1689. Jacobite supporters of the exiled James II were decisively defeated in both Ireland and Scotland and much of William's reign was devoted, with the Grand Alliance he formed with Austria, the Netherlands, Spain and German states, to obstructing the territorial ambitions of Louis XIV in Europe.

In 1707, Union with Scotland was achieved, establishing Great Britain. **Queen Anne,** staunch Protestant, had supported the Glorious Revolution of 1688 which deposed her father, James II. She, too, strove to reduce the power and influence of France in Europe and to ensure a Protestant succession for Britain. Marlborough's victory at Blenheim and his successes in the Low Countries achieved much of the first aim. Anne, after eighteen pregnancies, saw the last of her surviving children die in 1701 and agreed the **Act of Settlement** providing for the throne to pass to Sophia, Electress of Hanover, grand-daughter of James I, or to her heirs.

Whigs and Tories. — Whigs' were the political party which had invited William to take the throne. They formed powerful juntas during the reigns of William and Anne and ensured the Hanoverian succession. 'Tories' accepted the Glorious Revolution, but became associated with Jacobite feelings and were out of favour until the new Tory party, under Pitt the Younger, took office in 1783. The Tories developed into the Conservative Party under Peel, in 1834. The Whigs became the Liberal Party in the 1860s.

Jacobites. — James II having been dethroned, the claim of his son, the "Old Pretender" was ignored, leading to the Jacobite rising in 1715. **Charles Edward Stuart,** "Bonnie Prince Charlie", eldest son of the Old Pretender, led a similar rising which ended at **Culloden** in 1746, the last battle fought on British soil. He died in exile in 1788 and the Stuart cause ended when his younger brother died childless in 1807.

The Hanoverians - (1714-1837). — **George I** ascended the throne of a European power, whose economic and naval strength had played a major part in weakening the influence of France in Europe. As Prince of Wales, **George II** quarrelled with his father but he retained the services of Walpole as Prime Minister. He took an active part in the war of the Austrian Succession and was the last monarch to command his forces personally in battle, at Dettingen in 1743. His grandson who succeeded him was unable to reverse the trend towards constitutional monarchy resulting from George II's virtual withdrawal from government business at the end of his reign. But **George III** did try to exercise the right of a King to govern, causing great unpopularity and he was forced to acknowledge the reality of 'party politics'. His determination to suppress the **American Revolution** dominated his foreign policy. The **Napoleonic Wars** arising from the threat that the Revolution in France posed to established powers in Europe dragged on, in Europe and on the high seas, until ended on the field of Waterloo, in 1815.

George IV was much influenced by the politician Charles James Fox, having supported the Whig cause as a symbol of opposition to his father's Tory advisers. **William IV** was sixty five when he succeeded his unpopular brother. Dissatisfaction with parliamentary representation was near to causing revolutionary radicals to join forces with the mob. Reform of the franchise, however, was not possible until the King reluctantly agreed to create fifty new Peers to ensure passage of the 1832 Reform Bill through the House of Lords. William's two daughters having died as infants, on his death in 1837 the throne passed to his niece, Victoria.

The Industrial Revolution. — The relative political stability following the Glorious Revolution had encouraged the growth of a strong banking and credit system and the overseas empire supplied both raw materials and markets for manufactured goods. Vast social changes occurred as the labour force moved from the land into overcrowded towns, often breeding unrest between worker and employer. The Napoleonic Wars both stimulated this industrialism and aggravated this unrest, but by the mid-19C it was clear that, in Britain at any rate, political revolution would not follow industrial.

The House of Windsor. — **Victoria** — in fact the last monarch of the House of Hanover — was only eighteen when she came to the throne, to become Britain's longest-reigning Sovereign and to give her name to an illustrious age. Albert was her closest adviser until his premature death in 1861. He persuaded her that the Crown should not be aligned with any political party — a principle that has endured. He was the instigator of **The Great Exhibition** (1851). Housed in the *Crystal Palace* designed by Paxton, a glasshouse 563 metres long by 124 metres broad, it contained exhibits from all nations and ran from May until October 1851. It was a proud declaration of the high point of the Industrial Revolution — the inventiveness, technical achievement and prosperity which are the hallmarks of the Victorian Age.

Edward VII, excluded from royal duties and responsibilities until 1892, greatly increased the prestige of the monarchy by his own charm and by reviving royal public ceremonial. It was **George V** who, in 1917, adopted the name **Windsor** for the dynasty. He and Queen Mary made many tours of the Empire together, visiting India in 1911, to hold a memorable Coronation Durbar. He began the tradition of the Sovereign's Christmas broadcast to the peoples of the Commonwealth and exercised the Sovereign's new restraining influence over politics.

Great Britain in the 20C. — The Great War, after ninety nine years of peace, was the beginning of many familiar modern developments in the history of Britain. Britain's sea power was challenged. The export of one third of the national industrial output was no longer sufficient to maintain a favourable balance of trade. Revenue from shipping, overseas investment and insurance could no longer make up the difference. Foreign competitors were driving British goods out of many traditional overseas markets and out of the national markets of those competitors themselves.

Liberal ideas of the 1890s gave rise to industrial unionism and to the **Labour movement** and the intense pride in "Empire" which had marked the same decade, turned to increasing self-consciousness in the 1920s and again after 1945, as the self-governing Dominions which had stood so firmly by Britain during two World Wars, changed subtly into the **British Commonwealth of Nations.**

Edward VIII achieved popularity by his charm and by his concern for the unemployed during the Depression. On Edward's abdication his younger brother became **George VI.** Both he and his Queen — Elizabeth Bowes-Lyon, whom he had married in 1923 — became beloved and respected symbols of British determination and resistance during World War II. After the evacuation from Dunkirk in 1940 and the frustration of Hitler's invasion plans, during the **Battle of Britain,** from July to October that year, Great Britain stood alone and many towns and cities experienced massive aerial bombardment — "the Blitz". Actively supported by the United States, which came into the conflict after Pearl Harbour in December 1941, British and Commonwealth forces fought world-wide and Britain became the springboard for the invasion of Europe and final victory.

After 1945 the **Welfare State** was born, with the National Health Service and improved pension and unemployment benefits and nationalisation of key industries. Starting with India in 1947, virtually all Britain's overseas dependencies achieved independence within the ten years to 1957.

Queen Elizabeth II, who succeeded to the throne in 1952, together with her husband, Prince Philip, Duke of Edinburgh, have done much to strengthen the role of monarchy both at home and abroad.

Since 1945 Britain has adjusted to the realities of the modern world. Despite reduced economic strengths, Britain retains her traditional role in international affairs while forging new economic links within the EC.

Great Britain and Ireland are now covered by an Atlas at a scale of 1 inch to 4.75 miles. Three easy to use versions: paperback, spiralbound, hardback.

ARCHITECTURE

Pre-Romanesque. — Few buildings survive from this period, c650AD to the Norman Conquest. Much Saxon work, in timber, was destroyed in Viking raids **All Saints, Brixworth** (c680) in Northamptonshire makes use of Roman brick, and the apse was surrounded by an external ring-crypt, a feature first found in St Peter's Rome, (c590). Nearby **All Saints**, at Earl's Barton has a late Saxon tower and Saxon crypts remain at **Hexham, Repton** and **Ripon**.

Romanesque or **Norman.** — These bold, massive buildings continued to be erected until after the death of Henry II in 1189 and nowhere else in Europe is there such a richness or variation of Norman work, nor such an abundance of surviving examples. In English cathedrals, the naves tend to be much longer than on the Continent, for example **Ely** (13 bays) and **Norwich** (14), whilst the eastern end was usually shorter. **Durham Cathedral,** begun in 1093, where the whole interior is one Romanesque scheme, is a fine example of Norman work in Britain, though externally only the lower parts of the tower and nave and the choir show true Romanesque work. Its stone vaulting, completed 1133, survives in original form. **Southwell Minster** has a west front c1130, with later Perpendicular windows. The eastern end of **Norwich** cathedral is tri-apsidal. Its spire and clerestory are later Gothic, but the remainder is Norman. **Rochester, Gloucester, Peterborough, Hereford, St Albans,** and the abbey churches of **Tewkesbury** and **Waltham,** also **Lincoln** and **Exeter,** are all part of England's heritage of Norman work.

South Door, Kilpeck

Every county boasts many parish churches with Norman nave or tower, west doorway, or south porch or chancel arch. **Iffley Church,** Oxfordshire, west front (c1170), **St Mary and St David, Kilpeck,** Herefordshire (c1140), with Scandinavian influence in the carving and **St Nicholas, Barfreston,** Kent, are just some of the hundreds well worth visiting. Most secular buildings are fortifications, such as the **White Tower** at the Tower of London, the Keep of William's first work (1080) with four storeys, over 90ft - 27m high, massive walls over 20ft - 6m thick at base, openings small and well protected. **Rochester Castle,** c1130, though ruined, gives an impression of living conditions, with passages, garderobes and bedchambers in the 12ft - 3.5m thickness of the walls. **Chepstow Castle** (1067) is one of the earliest stone secular buildings in Britain.

Gothic. — Evolved in northern France, the Abbey of St Denis outside Paris being the earliest example, Gothic designs allowed larger and higher buildings, flooded with light. Heavy columns were replaced by slender clustered column shafts, towers became taller and more slender. Four phases kept Gothic architecture in use in England much longer than elsewhere in Europe, each phase retaining its distinctive English style.

Transitional. — Began in England around 1145 and lasted until the accession of Richard I, in 1189. Transitional buildings have both pointed and round arches, especially in windows and vaults. **Ripon Cathedral** (1181) is an example, but the most outstanding must be the choir of **Canterbury Cathedral.**

Early English. — Lasted from around 1190 until the death of Edward I in 1307. Distinctive features are the ribbed vaults, narrow pointed arches and lancet windows. **Salisbury Cathedral** *(photograph p 32),* built, apart from tower and spire, between 1220 and 1258, is the only English cathedral to have been built virtually in one operation, hence in a single style. See also **Wells,** the façades of **Peterborough** and **Ripon,** much of **Lichfield,** and the Abbeys of **Tintern** and **Fountains,** and **Bolton Priory.**

Decorated. — This third phase of English Gothic, beginning around 1280, lasted roughly until the death of Edward III in 1377. **Ely Cathedral,** with its octagon and lantern (1323-30) was one of the early experiments in new spatial form and lighting. Other examples include the west façades of **Exeter** and **York.**

Perpendicular. — The last — and longest — phase of Gothic architecture in Britain and uniquely English in style. There is an emphasis on vertical lines, but the principal features are panelled decoration all over the building, an increase in window area, and the consequent development — very much later than in France — of the flying buttress. Fan-vault roofing, a peculiarly English design, can best be seen in **King's College Chapel,** Cambridge (1446-1515), **Eton College Chapel** (1441) and **St George's Chapel,** Windsor (1475-1509).

Longleat House

Contemporary with the fan-vault, and equally English, was the development of the **timber roof**. Tie and collar designs from the 13 and 14C developed into more complex 15 and 16C **hammerbeam** roofs over churches and guildhalls, of which **Westminster Hall** (Hugh Herland, *c*1395) is an example. Others are the Great Hall at **Hampton Court** (1535) and **Rufford Old Hall,** near Ormskirk, Lancashire (1505).

Tudor Gothic. — Starting from the accession of Henry VII in 1485, the secular variety is best seen in the brick-built **Hampton Court Palace,** whilst **Bath Abbey** is a high point of the ecclesiastical style. England also has a wealth of medieval timber-framed houses, built in areas where stone was scarce. **Rufford Old Hall,** and the **Guildhall** at Lavenham, in Suffolk, are examples, as is the **Feathers Hotel,** in Ludlow.
From 1550 to 1620 building was largely domestic, for a thriving middle class and a wealthy aristocracy. **Longleat House** (1550-80), in Wiltshire, **Montacute House** (1588-1601), in Somerset, and Bess of Hardwick's **Hardwick Hall** (1591-7), in Derbyshire are outstanding examples. The courtyard layout of medieval days was abandoned for the E or H shaped plan, a central rectangular block with projecting wings. The **Long Gallery** — used for exercise on winter days — became a feature of all the great houses of this period — Montacute 170ft-52m, Hardwick 166ft-51m. Half-timbered houses were built in areas where stone was scarce — **Little Moreton Hall** (1559), in Cheshire, and **Speke Hall,** begun in 1490 and still being added to in 1612, near Liverpool. The staircase began to assume an importance in the design of Elizabethan houses and by Jacobean times, had become, in many houses, the focus of the whole interior — Hatfield, Knole, Audley End and Ham. Garden design, too, took on an aesthetic importance.

Renaissance. — Architects in England who had never seen an ancient Classical building, based their work on "Pattern Books" published by Renaissance designers. **Inigo Jones** (1573-1652) brought the Renaissance to England and his two most outstanding public buildings are the **Banqueting Hall** (1619-22), in Whitehall, and the **Queen's House** (1616-35), in Greenwich. He rebuilt part of **Wilton House** (1647-53), in Wiltshire, and the "Double Cube" room shows his adherence to classical proportions.

Classicism. — Though introduced by Inigo Jones, it was in the reign of Charles I, from 1625, that classicism really began to make its mark on the English scene. Vanbrugh and Adam were outstanding, but **Sir Christopher Wren** (1632-1723) dominated the English scene for years, even after his death. After the Great Fire of London, he was responsible for 53 churches, the new **St Paul's Cathedral,** as well as the **Royal Naval College** at Greenwich and a new wing for **Hampton Court Palace,** which harmonises well with the Tudor brickwork. The **Sheldonian Theatre** (1669) at Oxford, and the **Library** of **Trinity College,** Cambridge (1676-84) are two of his best-known works outside London.
Sir John Vanbrugh (1664-1726), soldier and playwright, turned architect in 1699. One of the chief exponents of the **baroque** in England, his masterpieces, produced in collaboration with **Nicholas Hawksmoor** (1661-1736), are **Castle Howard, Blenheim Palace** and **Seaton Delaval.** Hawksmoor, under a commission of 1711, designed six London churches. **St Mary Woolnoth,** in the City, survives to show his style.
Baroque architecture brought fantasy and movement to the classical order, but found little favour in England and was replaced in the 1720s with **Palladianism.** This, too, was a foreign 'implant', but one with a symmetry which was eagerly adapted by architects such as **Campbell (Houghton Hall)** and **Kent (Holkham Hall).** Palladian houses were set carefully in landscaped parks — many by Capability Brown — a far cry from the formality of French and Italian gardens of the period.
Robert Adam (1728-92), son of a Scottish architect, returned from the Grand Tour, having absorbed the principles of ancient buildings and learnt much neo-classical theory. He and his brothers set up in practice in London, in 1758, introducing a lighter, more decorative style than the Palladian work then in vogue. Most of Adam's buildings are domestic and he also had great flair as an interior designer.

19 and 20C Architecture. — The 19C was predominantly an age of stylistic revivals. The Industrial Revolution and the movement of people into towns, sparked off a drive to house them and to build the factories and mills in which they worked. Iron and glass played a part in the mass-production of buildings, though individual craftsmanship was still evident in mouldings, decoration and furniture. By 1900, though, much of this craftsmanship had vanished.

John Nash (1752-1835), builder of many terraces round Regent's Park, also designed London's Regent Street, and the **Royal Pavilion** at Brighton. **Sir John Soane** (1753-1837), probably the last of the original designers, is represented by his house at Lincoln's Inn Fields, now the **Sir John Soane Museum.**

From 1840 the trend was towards the Gothic revival which reached its height between 1855 and 1885. **Sir Charles Barry** (1795-1860) rebuilt the **Palace of Westminster** after the 1834 fire. Alfred Waterhouse (1830-1905) designed the Natural History Museum and built Manchester Town Hall.

The 19C was also the Railway Age with **Isambard K Brunel** (1806-59), Chief Engineer to the Great Western Railway in 1833, who designed the Clifton Suspension Bridge, which through lack of funds was not built until after his death. **Thomas Telford** (1757-1834) built roads, bridges and canals across the length and breadth of Britain. His London-Holyhead road crosses the Menai Strait on the bridge he built, opened in 1826.

In the 20C the British paid scant attention to Art Nouveau in architecture, though there was passing interest in interior decoration, fabrics and stained glass in the new style. Reinforced concrete was the main structural development as iron and steel had been in the 19C.

Between the Wars, the outstanding figure was probably **Sir Edwin Lutyens** (1869-1944), who adapted classicism to the needs of the day, in civic and housing design as well as ecclesiastical. His was the genius behind New Delhi, and he also designed the **Cenotaph,** in Whitehall, and **Hampstead Garden Suburb. Sir Giles Gilbert Scott** (1880-1960), grandson of Sir George, the 19C architect, built the last great cathedral in Gothic style, the red sandstone **Anglican Cathedral** of Liverpool. He also set the pattern for power stations with his 1929 design for **Battersea Power Station.**

''Urban planning'' was not a 20C idea. Haussmann re-designed much of Paris in the 1860s and the Italian Renaissance painter Martini has left us his picture, painted in 1475, of *The Ideal City.* In Britain, **Welwyn Garden City,** built near St Albans in 1920, was the first of the New Towns, an extension of the idea of the Garden Suburb, designed by Lutyens and built at Hampstead in 1907. The planned layout of streets, cul-de-sacs and closes, romantically named and lined with semi-detached and detached houses, was copied all over the country after the 1939-45 war, in an attempt to check the ''urban sprawl'' in London, Lancashire, the Clyde Valley and South Wales. The 1946 New Towns Act provided for 28 such New Towns; **Harlow New Town** was built by Gibberd in 1947, **Cumbernauld,** near Glasgow, in the 1950s and **Milton Keynes** arose in rural Buckinghamshire in the 1970s. But as costs escalated and concern grew over the decay of city centres the building of complete new towns was halted. Pedestrian zones and the banishing of traffic have gone some way towards saving both the fabric and spirit of those town and city centres.

Outstanding among examples of 20C architecture is Sir Basil Spence's **Coventry Cathedral** (1956-62), remarkable in itself and in the way it blends with the older buildings around it. The imaginative circular design of **The Metropolitan Cathedral of Christ the King** (1926-27) in Liverpool was the work of Sir Frederick Gibberd. In the secular sphere, education — established and new universities — and the arts provided good opportunities for pioneering work. Custom-built galleries were designed by Norman Foster for the Sainsbury Collection (1970s) at Norwich and Burrell's donation in Glasgow.

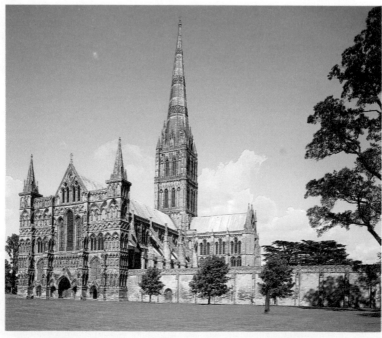

Salisbury Cathedral

GLOSSARY OF ARCHITECTURAL TERMS

The glossary may help you to understand descriptions of buildings in this Guide, and also in other guides to individual cathedrals, churches, abbeys and castles.

Abacus: top member of a capital, usually a square or curved-sided slab of stone or marble.

Abutment: solid masonry acting as a support against the lateral pressure of an arch.

Aisle: lateral divisions running parallel with the nave in medieval and other buildings, usually churches.

Ambulatory: passage giving access between the choir and apse of a church.

Apse: rounded or polygonal end — often the eastern end of the choir — of a church or chapel *(see chevet)*.

Arcade: a series of arches, open or closed with masonry, supported on piers or columns. May be attached to or detached from, the wall.

Arch: a structure — usually curved — supporting itself and capable of carrying a load over an opening, thus supporting the weight of the building above.

Architrave: the beam, or lowest portion of the entablature *(qv)*, extending from column to column. Also used of the moulded frame around the head and sides of a window or door opening.

Archivolt: concentric mouldings on the face of an arch resting on the impost.

Ashlar: hewn masonry or squared stones laid in regular courses, as distinguished from rubble work.

Atlantes: sculptured human male figures serving as supports *(see caryatids)*.

Bailey: space enclosed by the outer walls of a medieval castle.

Baldachin: canopy supported by pillars set over an altar, throne or tomb.

Ball-flower: globular 3-lobed flower ornament carved along a hollow moulding. Characteristic of English Decorated Gothic architecture.

Baptistery: building, separate from the church, containing the font.

Barbican: outwork of a medieval castle, often with a tower, defending a gate or bridge.

Barrel vaulting: continuous arched vault of semicircular section.

Basilica: an aisled hall, in Roman times, for the administration of justice. Used of a Christian church of similar form, with aisles and clerestory *(qv)*.

Batter: slight inward tilt of a wall from its base upwards.

Battlements: parapet of medieval fortifications, with a walkway for archers or crossbowmen, protected by merlons *(qv)*, with embrasures *(qv)* between them.

Billet: design used in Norman times consisting of short cylindrical or squared pieces carved at intervals along a moulding.

Broach spire: octagonal spire rising from a square tower without a parapet, having pyramidal broaches at the angles.

Buttress: vertical mass of masonry built against a wall, so strengthening it and resisting the outward pressure of a vaulted roof *(see flying buttress)*.

Capital: crowning feature of a column or pillar.

Caryatids: sculptured human female figures serving as supports *(see atlantes)*.

Chancel: part of the church set aside for clergy and choir, to the east of the nave. Several steps and a screen often separate the chancel from the nave.

Chantry chapel: chapel endowed for religious services for the soul of the founder.

Chapter house: place of assembly for the governing body of a monastery or cathedral. In medieval England, often multi-sided, with vaulting supported on a central pillar.

Charnel-house: room used for the storage of bones found whilst digging new graves.

Chevet: French term for the circular or polygonal eastern end of a church *(see apse)*, when surrounded by an ambulatory from which radiate chapels.

Chevron: Norman decoration of zig-zag moulding used around windows and doorways.

Choir: western part of the chancel, used by the choir, immediately east of the screen separating nave and chancel.

Clerestory: upper storey of the nave *(qv)* of a church, generally pierced by a row of windows.

Corbel: stone bracket, often richly carved, projecting from a wall to support roof beams, the ribs of a vault, a statue or an oriel window.

Corinthian: most slender of the three Greek orders of architecture with capitals decorated with acanthus leaves. Extensively used during the Renaissance.

Cornice: crowning projection, the upper part of the entablature in classical architecture. Also used for the projecting decoration around the ceiling of a room.

Crossing: central area of a cruciform church, where the transepts cross the nave and choir. A tower is often set above this space.

Crypt: underground chamber beneath a church, used as places of burial or charnel-houses. They often also housed the bones or relics of a saint or martyr.

Cupola: hemispherical roof.

Curtain wall: in medieval castles, the length of wall, with towers at intervals, enclosing the bailey or courtyard. In modern architecture, a non-structural wall.

Dog-tooth: ornamentation used in the Early English period, consisting of a row of tooth-like projections, each carved into four leaves.

Donjon: French term for the keep of a castle.

Doric: first and simplest of the three orders of Greek architecture.

Drum: vertical walling supporting a dome in which windows can be placed to introduce light into the part of the building below the dome.

Embrasure: the space between two merlons *(qv)*, on a battlement, through which archers could fire, whilst protected by the merlons.

Entablature: in classical architecture, the entire portion above the columns, comprising architrave, frieze *(qv)* and cornice *(qv)*.

Fan vaulting: system of vaulting peculiar to English Perpendicular architecture, all ribs having the same curve, resembling the frame-work of a fan.

Fillet: narrow flat band, used chiefly to separate mouldings from one another.

Finial: top or finishing portion of a pinnacle, gable, bench end or other feature.

Fluting: narrow concave channelling cut vertically on a shaft or column.

Flying buttress: external arch springing over the roof of an aisle and supporting the clerestory wall, counteracting the thrust of the nave vault.

Folly: a purely decorative structure, raised to romanticise the landscape, usually 18C.

Fresco: wall-painting executed whilst the plaster is still wet.

Frieze: central division of the entablature — any long, horizontal decorative design at high level.

Gable: triangular end section of a wall of a building, enclosed by the line of the roof.

Gallery: long passage, sometimes hung with pictures, and serving as communication between rooms.

Greek Cross: used of church plan, where all four limbs are of equal length.

Hammerbeam roof: late Gothic form of roof construction with no tie-beam. Wooden arches rest on corbels and short beams bracketed to the walls and eaves.

Harling: wall plastered with roughcast. Often painted or with colour incorporated.

Ionic: second order of Greek architecture with capitals decorated with large volutes or scrolls at the corners.

Jamb: upright side of a window or door opening.

Keep: inner tower and strongest part of a medieval fortress *(see donjon)*.

Keystone: central, wedge-shaped stone which locks an arch together *(see voussoir)*.

Lancet: Early English (13C) sharp-pointed arch.

Lantern: glazed construction, for ventilation and light, often surmounting a dome.

Latin Cross: cross with one limb longer than the other three. (Used of church plan, as distinct from Greek Cross.)

Lierne: short intermediate rib in Gothic vaulting.

Loggia: open-sided gallery or arcade.

Machicolation: in medieval military architecture, a row of openings below a projecting parapet through which missiles could be rained down on the enemy.

Merlon: upstanding portion between two embrasures on a battlement.

Misericord: tip-up seat in choir stalls, with a small projection on the underside, to support a person having to stand through a long service. Often fancifully and grotesquely carved.

Mullions: vertical ribs dividing a window into a number of lights.

Narthex: western portico at the entrance to early Christian churches.

Nave: central main body of a church, west of the choir, into which lay persons were admitted, chancel and choir being reserved for the priests.

Newel: central shaft around which a spiral staircase climbs. Also post at a junction of a flight of stairs and a landing.

Ogee: arch used in late Gothic period, combining convex and concave curve, ending in a point.

Oriel: window projecting from a wall on corbels.

Pediment: triangular termination above the entablature, in classical architecture. Sometimes 'broken' in Renaissance designs.

Pier: supporting mass of masonry, as opposed to a pillar, supporting an arch or a bridge. Applied also to portion of wall between doors and windows.

Pilaster: rectangular pillar, projecting about one-sixth of its breadth from the wall.

Piscina: basin, with drain, in a small niche near the altar, for the washing of sacramental vessels.

Plinth: projecting square block at the base of a column.

Putto / Putti: term applied to the cherubs and babies sculptured in baroque architecture.

Quoin: dressed corner-stone at the angle of a building.

Reredos: decorative screen or panel above and behind an altar.

Retro-choir: area behind the High Altar.

Rococo: debased form of decoration at the end of the baroque era, characterised by abstract assemblages of scrolls and shells.

Rose window: circular window with mullions converging like the spokes of a wheel.

Screen: partition, often richly carved, separating nave from choir and chancel.

Sedilia: seat for priests, cut into the south wall of chancel.

Skewputt: gable's corner stone.

Spandrel: triangular space between the curves of arches and the frame in which they are set.

Squinch: arch placed diagonally across the internal corner angles of a square tower, converting the square into an octagonal form.

Stucco: fine plaster much used in Renaissance and later periods for decorations in relief on ceilings and walls.

Tierceron: secondary rib in Gothic vaulting.

Transept: arms of a cruciform church set at right angles to nave and choir.

Transom: horizontal cross-bar or division of a window *(see mullions)*.

Tympanum: space between the flat lintel and the arch of a doorway.

Undercroft: vaulted chamber partly or wholly below ground, in a medieval building. In a church this would be the crypt; in a house, it would be used for storage.

Volute: spiral scroll used at the ends of Ionic, Corinthian and composite capitals.

Voussoir: wedge-shaped stones of an arch, their sides tapering towards the imaginary centre of the circle of the arch.

PAINTING, MUSIC and SCULPTURE

PAINTING

The Celtic peoples loved rhythm and curvilinear scroll patterns, which they used in jewellery and later in manuscripts. The Romans brought their wall paintings and mosaics and both later inspired the medieval church murals — allegories to impress and instruct — some of Britain's earliest paintings. Surviving painting from the Saxon and medieval periods consists largely of exquisite work on illuminated manuscripts, such as the **Lindisfarne Gospels** *(photograph p 54)*, though the drawings of **Matthew Paris** are notable departures from this stylised work. One of the earliest English paintings is the **Wilton Diptych** *(c*1400), now in the National Gallery.

British artists never enjoyed that scale of patronage given to European artists by absolute monarchs and the Papacy. Much early portraiture, other than the **Holbein** pictures of Henry VIII and his court, tend to be flat and stiff, but the art of the miniature flourished at the court of Elizabeth, where **Nicholas Hilliard** and **Isaac Oliver** created their masterpieces, capturing both the likeness and something of the spirit of the sitters.

The Dutchman **Sir Anthony van Dyck**, knighted by Charles I, enjoyed his patronage and was the first to record the atmosphere of the Stuart Court, in full size paintings, before the Civil War. Canaletto, a Venetian, enjoyed some aristocratic support in the 1740s, as did **Sir Peter Lely** and **Godfrey Kneller**, both of German origin, but who worked in England for long enough to be considered founders of the English portrait painting school. **William Hogarth**, English-born and bred, famous for his vivid commentaries on the life of his day, started the idea of public exhibitions of painting, leading ultimately to the founding in 1768 of the **Royal Academy**, with **Sir Joshua Reynolds** as its first President. Together with his contemporary, **Thomas Gainsborough**, Reynolds raised the status of English painting and especially portraiture, though it was still much influenced by Dutch and Italian example.

Richard Wilson, founder Member of the Royal Academy, was much inspired by the French masters, Claude and Poussin and founded the English school of **landscape painting**, a fashion which developed in England and spread to include marine scenes as well as country houses and estates. The visionary, **William Blake**, heralded the dawn of English Romanticism. Portraiture by **Sir Thomas Lawrence** — notably his "Congress of Vienna" series at Windsor — and the works of **Sir Henry Raeburn** in Scotland added Romanticism to the traditions of Reynolds. **John Crome** founded the Norwich School in 1803, a regional treatment of landscape painting which was uniquely English. It was continued after his death by **John Cotman**. **John Constable** and **Joseph Turner** carried this tradition and its studies of the effects of ever-changing light into the 19C. From 1840 to 1850 **Dante Gabriel Rossetti's** group, the **Pre-Raphaelites** and **Sir Edward Burne-Jones**, made a short-lived return to primitive values and religious and moral subjects. Their designs inspired *Art Nouveau*, best expressed in England by the work of **William Morris** and **Aubrey Beardsley**.

Born in Paris, but of English parents, was **Alfred Sisely**, an Impressionist whose sense of colour and tone owed much to the founder of the movement, Claude Monet. The **Camden Town Group**, around **Walter Sickert**, returned to the realism of the Post-Impressionists, whose work **Roger Fry** had exhibited in 1911 and the next twenty years saw many short-lived and loose "movements", such as the **Bloomsbury Group**. **Augustus John** chose an almost Impressionist style for his fashionable portraits, while his sister, **Gwendolen**, adopted the quiet tones she learnt from Whistler, in Paris.

Between the Wars, **Graham Sutherland** and the paintings of **Sir Stanley Spencer**, depicted Biblical scenes in the everyday setting of places such as his birthplace at Cookham. **Robert Mason** has carried on in Spencer's social style, his current series of paintings of developments in the City of London recalling Spencer's official Clydeside ship building series during the Second World War, while the work of **David Hockney** is usually known by a term he himself dislikes — **"pop art"**.

MUSIC

Much, as with painting and sculpture, early and medieval English music was largely inspired by religion. The **Chapel Royal** — an institution, not a building — has fostered English music since 1135. By the Elizabethan age **madrigals**, in the Italian manner, with amorous or satirical themes, had become firmly established as part of English entertainment. Folk music dating back much further accompanied the country dance, which survives today as the **Morris Dance**. Composers such as **William Byrd** and **Thomas Morley**, who wrote settings for several of Shakespeare's plays, spread music into the theatre. **Ben Jonson** and **Henry Lawes** among others were leading exponents of the **masque**, which became popular in the 17C, combining music, dance and pageantry. **Orlando Gibbons**, organist of the Chapel Royal under James I, wrote madrigals, anthems and much church music. **Henry Purcell**, in the 1680s, wrote music for State occasions which far transcended the doggerel verses.

Music, like painting and architecture, followed first a classical, then a baroque and rococo course, before, in the 18C, **chamber music** came into fashion, as did the first English **operas** and **oratorio**, perhaps the greatest exponent of the latter being **Georg Friederich Handel**. The composer **Thomas Arne** set to music the words of James Thomson, *Rule Britannia,* in a masque for the Prince of Wales in 1740. Romantic song cycles became fashionable in the 19C.

Two remarkable Englishmen met in 1875, **Sir William Gilbert** and **Sir Arthur Sullivan** and with Richard D'Oyly Carte, created the "Gilbert and Sullivan" operas. **Musical comedy**, an English development of the European operetta, began in the 1890s, with shows like *The Gaiety Girl* and another typically British institution, the **music hall** also became popular — variety entertainment with the audience being able to eat and drink while watching the performance. Two names, **Ivor Novello** and **Noël Coward**, will always be associated with British musical comedy between the Wars. Still popular since their inception in 1895 are the **Promenade Concerts**, a season of which is held at the Albert Hall every summer.

Andrew Lloyd-Webber has maintained the tradition of British musicals, and conductors and composers such as Peter Maxwell Davies, Neville Mariner and Simon Rattle ensure the continuation of healthy British music. Eisteddfods in Wales and Mods in Scotland carry on a tradition of the Celtic bards. Festivals, such as the **Three Choirs** at Hereford, Worcester and Gloucester Cathedrals and — in completely different spheres — opera productions at **Glyndebourne** and the **English National Opera** contribute to this aim.

SCULPTURE

The idea of erecting statues, in stone and bronze, introduced largely by the Romans, fell into disuse in Britain in the Dark Ages. Gradually, however, pagan influences and Celtic scroll-work were put to Christian service, in standing crosses and in church decoration. Massive carving in Norman churches gave way to glorious tracery, windows, ribs and vaults in our Early English and Perpendicular churches and cathedrals, complemented by carved wooden misericords, bench ends, altar screens and font covers. Impressive statuary such as that on the west front of Wells Cathedral has survived Reformation and Puritan depredations, to give an idea of the skills of unknown craftsmen but, until the flowering of British art between 1720 and 1840, statuary did tend to be confined to tombs and memorials. The fashion for portrait busts, however, was brought back by those who made the "Grand Tour" and first classical, then baroque, memorials abound in our cathedrals and parish churches. In the Victorian age statues were erected to the memory of industrialists and benefactors, municipal worthies and military heroes in every town and city in the land. Wars, too, have resulted in sculpted memorials, some of very fine quality, others less so. This century, British sculpture has been enlivened by the sometimes controversial work of **Jacob Epstein,** and of **Henry Moore,** whose technique of "natural carving" allowed the grain and shape of the material to dictate final form. Other sculptors, such as **Barbara Hepworth, Reg Butler** and **Kenneth Armitage,** maintain the tradition today.

LITERATURE

The Medieval Age — **Geoffrey Chaucer** (*c*1340-1400), the first great English poet, was influential in the evolution of 'standard' English from cruder medieval dialects. The language of the *Canterbury Tales* is consequently as recognisable to us today as are Chaucer's vividly-etched characters. **William Langland** (*c*1330-1400) in the *Vision of Piers Plowman,* and **Sir Thomas Malory** (d1471) in *Le Morte D'Arthur,* also brought a new depth and expressiveness to literature.

The English Renaissance and the Elizabethan Age — The sonnet was introduced and blank verse became the regular measure of English dramatic and epic poetry. The supreme achievement of this dynamic, expansive period was in the

William Shakespeare by Coblitz

theatre. Ambitious dramatic forms developed by the fiery **Christopher Marlowe** (1564-94) were perfected by the protean genius of **William Shakespeare** (1564-1616), the greatest dramatist and poet of this or any age. His monumental 37 plays appealed to all classes, from 'the groundlings' to the nobility. **Ben Jonson** (1572-1637) created the English comedy of humours.

The Seventeenth Century — **John Donne** (1572-1631), courtier, soldier and latterly Dean of St Paul's, was the most important of the Metaphysical poets whose "witty conceits" were concerned with the interaction between soul and body, sensuality and spirit. **John Milton** (1608-74), after Shakespeare arguably England's greatest poet, was also a powerful pamphleteer for the Puritan cause. He overcame blindness and political disappointment to write his epic masterpiece *Paradise Lost* in 1667. Puritan control was responsible for closing the theatres for nearly twenty years until the Restoration of Charles II in 1660. Restoration drama primarily reflected the licentiousness of the Court by the use of broad satire, farce, wit and bawdy comedy.
In prose, the language of the Bible — particularly the Authorised Version of 1611 — exerted a strong influence, most notably in the work of **John Bunyan** (1628-88) whose *Pilgrim's Progress* was more widely read than any book in English except the Bible itself. Enormously popular too, but in a very different vein, was *The Compleat Angler* by **Izaak Walton** (1593-1683), which not only gave instruction on fishing but also offered a personal contemplation of nature. The diaries of **John Evelyn** (1620-1706) and **Samuel Pepys** (1633-1703) detailed the minutiae of everyday life at the time.

The Eighteenth Century — The early development of the novel is probably best exemplified in the work of **Daniel Defoe** (1660-1731). While his *Journal of the Plague Year* is a lively but primarily factual piece of journalism, *Robinson Crusoe,* though it utilises similar reporting techniques, is entirely fiction. Defoe's style was imitated and developed by **Samuel Richardson** (1689-1761), **Henry Fielding** (1707-1754), in *The Rake's Progress* and **Laurence Sterne** (1713-1768), in *Tristam Shandy.*

Though the rise of the novel (together with the newspaper) and the expansion of a newly literate middle class were signposts for future developments, the Age of Reason was as notable for other literary achievements. **Alexander Pope** (1688-1744), the finest satirical poet of the time, was matched in both poetry and prose by **Jonathan Swift** (1667-1745), famous for the incisive political and social satire of *Gulliver's Travels*. The age was overshadowed, however, by the influence of **Samuel Johnson** (1709-1784), now best remembered as the subject of Boswell's famous biography and the author of the first *English Dictionary* in 1755.

The Nineteenth Century — The French Revolution was a primary inspiration for the Romantic movement, which stressed intensity of emotion rather than elegance and art, freedom of expression rather than stylistic rules. The rebellious spirit of the movement was epitomised in the life of **Lord Byron** (1788-1824) though perhaps a better representative of Romantic poetry is **William Wordsworth** (1770-1850) whose best poems reflect his belief that intense joy could arise from deep harmony with nature. **Percy Bysshe Shelley** (1792-1822) wrote more directly of the power of joy as a reforming influence, while the intense, lyrical verse of **John Keats** (1795-1821) stressed the power of beauty. Though lyricism, nature and the exotic continued to attract Victorian poets such as **Robert Browning** (1812-89), faith in joy and the senses waned and the verse of **Alfred, Lord Tennyson** (1809-1902) is noble but sombre.

The novel, meanwhile, had continued to develop in range and appeal. The carefully structured domestic comedies of **Jane Austen** (1775-1817) are at once amusing and deeply serious, though the historical novels of her contemporary, **Walter Scott** (1771-1832), proved to be more popular. Popular too were Scott's Victorian successors, **William Makepeace Thackeray** (1811-63), **Anthony Trollope** (1815-82) and, above all, **Charles Dickens** (1812-70), whose sentimental but funny and sometimes despairing vision of city life in the Industrial Revolution struck a deep chord with the reading public. Mary Ann Evans (1819-80), under the pseudonym **George Eliot**, wrote realistic works about the problems of the provincial middle class. Her novels are notable as much for the development and interplay of character as for plot and action. The **Brontë** sisters, **Charlotte** (1816-55) and **Emily** (1818-48), took inspiration from their upbringing on the wild moors of Yorkshire to write their respective masterpieces, *Jane Eyre* (1846) and *Wuthering Heights* (1847). Most important of the later writers of the century is **Thomas Hardy** (1840-1928), whose novels express a passionate feeling for man's tragic involvement in nature and estrangement from it.

Influenced by the new drama in Europe, **George Bernard Shaw** (1856-1950) brought a new purpose and seriousness to the English theatre which had, for nearly two centuries, failed to find a meaningful direction. The witty comedies of **Oscar Wilde** (1854-1900) were less profound but equally well crafted. They reflected the aims of the Decadent movement which stressed flagrantly amoral beauty — a direct reaction against the undue moral earnestness of the Victorian Age.

The Twentieth Century — The early modern masters of the novel — **Henry James** (1843-1916), **Joseph Conrad** (1857-1924), and **E M Forster** (1879-1970) — were still working in a recognisably Victorian tradition. However, the need for new forms of self-expression able to encompass a growing awareness of the unconscious gave rise to a strong individualistic movement. The Dubliner **James Joyce** (1882-1941) used the stream-of-consciousness technique in the highly experimental *Ulysses* (1922) and *Finnegan's Wake* (1939). This insistent excavation of personal experience is also to be found in the very different novels of **Virginia Woolf** (1882-1941) and **D H Lawrence** (1885-1930) who challenged the taboos of class and sex in novels such as *Lady Chatterley's Lover*. Concurrent with the serious 'literary' novel, there developed a growing market for lighter fiction — entertainments — to serve the needs of an increasingly literate public; from the adventure novels of **Robert Louis Stevenson** (1850-94) and the *Sherlock Holmes* stories of **Arthur Conan Doyle** (1859-1930), to the spy thrillers of **John Le Carré** and **Len Deighton** in our own time.

The novel has, in all its forms, become the dominant vehicle of literary expression in the modern age. Poetry, comparatively speaking, is less widely read than in previous times. Here too though, fundamental changes have been wrought. The Romantic decadence of the early 20C was swept aside by the modernist poets **Ezra Pound** (1885-1972) and **TS Eliot** (1888-1965) whose *Waste Land* (1922) is a dense and highly literary meditation on the situation of modern man. Less dramatically modern but equally influential was the slightly earlier poetry of **Thomas Hardy** and **WB Yeats** (1865-1939). The poets of the First World War, particularly **Wilfred Owen** (1893-1918) and **Siegfried Sassoon** (1886-1967), voiced their horror of mass warfare in realistic, pungent images which also looked forward not back. **WH Auden** (1907-73) led a prominent group of intellectual left-wing poets in the twenties, though it was the exuberant imagery and lyrical rhetoric of **Dylan Thomas** (1914-53) that caught the public's imagination. Only **John Betjeman** (1906-84), with his sympathetic eulogies to the mundane and everyday, has achieved comparable popularity in recent times.

Throughout the century there have been a number of important and stylish writers — less iconoclastic than their more innovative peers — who have continued to work with more traditional subjects and themes. The novelists **Aldous Huxley** (1894-1963), **Evelyn Waugh** (1903-66), and **Graham Greene** (1904-91) achieved considerable critical as well as commercial success, while **Somerset Maugham** (1874-1965) and **JB Priestley** (1894-1984) triumphed equally as playwrights and novelists.

The theatre of the first half of the century was dominated by well-crafted 'traditional' plays and the sophisticated comedies of **Noël Coward** (1899-1973). In the 50s however, new voices started to be heard. The Theatre of the Absurd, which saw man as a helpless creature in a meaningless universe, was explored by the Irish writer **Samuel Beckett** (1906-89) and, later in the decade, disillusionment with contemporary Britain was vented by **John Osborne** (b1929) in his play *Look Back In Anger*. The pithy "comedies of menace" by **Harold Pinter** (b1930) and the socialist plays of writers such as **Arnold Wesker** (b1932) were also highly influential and subsequently led to the development of a diverse and challenging contemporary theatre which reflected the fragmentation and problems of modern society.

SCIENCE, ENGINEERING and INDUSTRY

Between 1760 and 1850 the **Industrial Revolution** turned Britain into the first industrial nation of the world. Power-driven machines replaced human muscle and factory production replaced medieval craft work carried out in the home. New methods supplied expanding markets — new machines were invented to satisfy growing demand.

Power. — In 1712 **Thomas Newcomen** designed the first practical piston and steam engine, and his idea was later much improved by **James Watt.** Such engines were needed to pump water and to raise men and ore from mines and soon replaced water wheels as the power source for the cotton factories which sprang up in Lancashire. Then **Richard Trevithick** (1771-1833), Cornish tin miner, designed a boiler with fire box inside which he showed to **George Stephenson** (1781-1848) and his son, **Robert** (1803-59) and this became the basis of the early "locomotives".

Without abundant coal, however, sufficient iron could never have been produced for all the new machines. By 1880, 154 million tons of coal were being transported across Britain. Cast iron had been produced by Shropshire ironmaster **Abraham Darby,** in Coalbrookdale *(qv)* in 1709 and was used for the cylinders of early steam engines and for bridges and aqueducts. Wrought iron with greater tensile strength was developed in the 1790s, allowing more accurate and stronger machine parts, railway lines and bridging materials. In 1856 **Sir Henry Bessemer** devised a system in which compressed air is blown through the molten metal, burning off impurities and producing a stronger steel.

Transport. — "Turnpike trusts" had laid the foundation of a coherent road network between 1751 and 1772, and by the 1830s there were 20 000 miles of roads. But these were often impassable and cheap transport for bulk goods was by canal. There were 4 000 miles of canals, pioneered by **James Brindley** (1716-72). **Thomas Telford** (1757-1834) built roads and bridges along which stage-coaches and broad-wheeled wagons could transport people and goods. These held onto their trade until the railways took the long distance passenger traffic and the canals the heavy goods.

Stephenson engineered the Stockton and Darlington Railway in 1825, the world's first passenger-carrying public steam railway. By 1835, with twin tracks and a time-table, the railway had become the vital element of the Industrial Revolution — swift, efficient and cheap transport for raw materials and finished goods all over the country. The success of Stephenson's *Rocket* proved the feasibility of locomotives. **Isambard Kingdom Brunel** (1806-59), Chief Engineer to the Great Western Railway, designed the Clifton Suspension Bridge and also the first successful trans-Atlantic steamship, the *Great Western* in 1837. His father Sir Marc Isambard Brunel (1769-1849) was responsible for the first tunnel under the Thames, between 1825 and 1843.

William Henry Morris — Lord Nuffield — the most influential of British car manufacturers, began with bicycles and made his first car in 1913. He is probably best remembered, along with his philanthropic foundations in medicine, for his 1959 "Mini". **John Boyd Dunlop** started with bicycles too. In 1888 this Scottish veterinary surgeon invented the first pneumatic tyre. It was **John Loudon McAdam,** an Ayrshire engineer, who devised the "Tarmacadam" surfacing for roads.

More recently **Christopher Cockerell** patented a design for the first hovercraft in 1955.

Aviation. — The names of **Charles Rolls** and **Henry Royce** will always be associated with the grand cars they pioneered although their contribution to aviation is arguably even greater. A Rolls Royce engine powered Sir Frank Whittle's Gloster E28/29, the first jet aircraft, and the De Havilland Comet, the world's first commercial passenger-carrying jet airliner which made its maiden flight in 1949. British aerospace designers worked with their French counterparts in the development of Concorde, the world's first supersonic airliner.

Science. — In 1660 Sir Francis Bacon (1561-1626) had founded the Royal Society, granted its Charter by Charles II in 1662, "to promote discussion, particularly in the physical sciences". Robert Boyle and Sir Christopher Wren were founder members and Sir Isaac Newton was its President from 1703 to 1727. **Michael Faraday** was appointed assistant to Sir Humphrey Davy, inventor of the miners' Safety Lamp, in 1812. It was Faraday's work with electromagnetism which led to the development of the electric dynamo and motor. An early form of computer, the "difference engine" was invented by **Charles Babbage** in 1833 and can be seen in the library of King's College, Cambridge.

Edmond Halley, friend of Newton, became Astronomer Royal in 1720. He is best remembered for the comet named after him, and for correctly predicting its 76-year cycle and return in 1758. When Halley's Comet returned in 1985, it was a British Aerospace probe — Giotto — which intercepted it and relayed much information about its composition and nature.

Set up by Sir Bernard Lovell in 1955, the radio telescope at Jodrell Bank is still one of the largest in the world and contributes to our widening knowledge of our Universe. It was Antony Hewish, a British astronomer at Cambridge, however, who in 1968 first discovered pulsars, cosmic sources of light or radio energy.

Medicine. — It was **William Harvey,** physician to James I and Charles I, who discovered the circulation of the blood. More recent British achievements in medicine have been those of Dr Jacob Bell who, with Dr Simpson from Edinburgh, introduced chloroform anaesthesia, which met with public approval after Queen Victoria had used it during the birth of Prince Leopold in 1853. **Sir Alexander Fleming** discovered the effects of penicillin in killing bacteria, in 1928, though large-scale production did not start until 1943. The "double-helix" structure of DNA (deoxyribonucleic acid) — the major component of chromosomes which carry genetic information and control inheritance of characteristics — was proposed by Francis Crick working at the Cavendish Laboratory in Cambridge, with his American colleague, James Watson, in 1953. Yet another British medical discovery was cyclosporin, discovered by Dr Tony Allison, in Cambridge, to minimise rejection by the body of donated organs, thus increasing the chances of successful heart, lung and kidney transplants.

REGIONAL TRADITIONS and CUSTOMS

Folk customs carry us back to our earliest recorded beginnings and beyond. Many declined and disappeared with the shifting populations, the building over of land long dedicated to festivals and because of new farming methods which have done away with shearing and harvest ceremonies.

Ceremony of the Keys. — Every night, at 9.53pm the Chief Warder of the Tower of London makes the rounds with an escort of Guardsmen and locks all the gates. The party is ceremonially challenged on return to the Bloody Tower archway and when identified, the Chief Warder doffs his cap and says 'God Save Queen Elizabeth' to which all reply 'Amen'. On the stroke of 10pm Last Post is sounded and the Keys are left in the care of the Governor for the night.

Cheese rolling. — Parish of Brockworth, Gloucestershire. A Whit Monday / Spring Bank Holiday festival. A cheese is rolled down a steep slope, with the youth of the village allowed to chase it after a count of three. Cheese used to be paraded around the church in Randwick, Gloucestershire, on May Day.

Furry dance - Helston . — The sole remaining example of a communal spring festival dance in Britain, this dance has taken place in Helston, Cornwall, for centuries, on 8 May, feast day of St Michael the Archangel, patron saint of the church. The young folk of the town dance in the morning, but the main dance of the day, with the Mayor in chain of office, starts at midday. The song which is sung shows very clearly the origin of the event — 'For Summer is a-come-O and Winter is a-gone-O'. The dancers go in and out of all the houses, shops and gardens of the town, in one door and out of the other, to bring luck and summer. Despite the thousands of tourists who come to see the dance, it has remained of unchanging character, never being used to raise funds for charity or being anything but the communal spring festival — a rite that any pre-Christian ancestor of today's inhabitants of the town would have had no difficulty in recognising.

Maypole. — A fertility symbol, the Maypole, too, belongs to the beginning of summer. Many parishes, before the Civil War, had permanent maypoles, witness to another pagan festival tacitly accepted and tamed by the Christian church. The Puritans, however, would have none of them and few survived. At Barwick-in-Elmet, Yorkshire, there is still a permanent Maypole, some eighty feet tall, whilst that of Welford-on-Avon is about seventy feet. The church of St Andrew Undershaft in Leadenhall Street in the City of London, is so named for the maypole which stood before its south door until torn down by apprentices, rioting against foreign traders, in 1517. The Maypole was banned throughout England in 1644, but returned triumphant at the Restoration, marking both May Day and Oak Apple Day, 29 May, anniversary of Charles II's triumphal entry into London.

Oyster Feast - Colchester. — King Richard I gave the oyster fishery rights in the Colne estuary to the town of Colchester, in 1186. To open the dredging season, the Mayor and Council set out in a boat, read a proclamation asserting the rights, toast the Sovereign with gin and gingerbread and ceremonially dredge up the first oysters. The Oyster Feast is held on or about 20 October each year.

Well dressing. — Even in the damp climate of northern Europe a well or a spring, providing water, the basic necessity of all life, has long been venerated as home of a mysterious power to whom sacrifice and propitiation were due. Christianity forbade the worship of water spirits as such, but many wells were simply 'purged' and re-dedicated to the Blessed Virgin or one of the saints. In Derbyshire the custom of decking wells or springs with flowers still continues, under the auspices of the church. Large pictures are formed on boards covered with clay, the design being picked out in

Well dressing at Youlgreave

flowers, pebbles, shells or any natural object. Tin, glass or manufactured materials are not used. At Tissington it is said, variously, that well dressing in its present form, started after a prolonged drought in 1615, when alone amongst the wells of the district only those of Tissington continued to give water. Another tale has it that it was in thanksgiving for deliverance from the Black Death of 1348-9. St Anne's Well, near Buxton, is dressed on the Thursday nearest Midsummer Day. The well is named for a statue — possibly a Roman votive offering to a water spirit — found in the spring in the Middle Ages and piously enshrined in a chapel which was swept away by one of Thomas Cromwell's agents in 1538, together with 'all the crutches, shifts, shirts and was offered' by grateful pilgrims. Buxton later became a spa, where the cures were medical, rather than of any religious significance.

FOOD and DRINK

Great Britain provides a cosmopolitan choice of food but also has a rich tradition of regional dishes, all using local fish, game, fruit and dairy products to best advantage.

SOME REGIONAL SPECIALITIES

London and the South East. — **Steak and kidney pie** is chief among the many varieties of pie found. The Kentish marshes nurture fine **lamb** while **Dover sole** and other fresh fish are available along the coast. Sussex produces a range of **hotpots** and **pies**, mostly lamb and mutton based and excellent **smoked mackerel**. Whitstable, in Kent, is famous for its **oysters**. An "Arnold Bennett omelette", made with haddock and cheese, is a London dish, as are **Chelsea Buns**, dough buns folded round dried fruit and enjoyed since Georgian days. **Maids of Honour** are small puff pastry tarts with ground almond.

The West Country. — Cornwall is known for its **clotted cream**, served on scones with strawberry jam. It is delicious on the **apple pies**, richly flavoured with cinnamon and cloves, for which the region is renowned. **Devon junket** is made with rum or brandy — a reminder of smugglers' tastes from the past. **Dorset jugged steak**, cooked with sausage meat and port, could be followed by **Widecombe gingerbreads**, or by a **Taunton cider cake**, made with raisins and a large apple, the cider reduced to concentrate the apple flavour. **Fresh and potted mackerel** are a coastal delicacy, as are **pilchards**. **Cheddar cheese** is named after the caves in which it is ripened.

Thames and Chilterns. — **Brown Windsor soup** made with beef, mutton, butter carrots and onions is delicious. **Aylesbury duck** and green peas, Hertfordshire **pork puffs**, and **harvest rabbit** with forcemeat balls, could be followed by **Bucks cherry bumpers**, cherries in shortcrust pastry, or some **Banbury apple pie**. Breakfasts should always finish with chunky **Oxford marmalade** on toast.

Heart of England. — The Vale of Evesham is England's fruit growing area — **plums** and **greengages** are a speciality, with **apples** and pears. Herefordshire raises fine **beef** and local **cider**, a refreshing but deceptive potent drink, is skilfully combined in local dishes, including a **pigeon casserole**, with cider and orange. Gloucestershire produces excellent **cheeses**. Worcestershire **asparagus**, in season, rivals any in flavour and **Worcestershire sauce**, a blend of anchovies, garlic, treacle and spices, has been enjoyed worldwide since 1839.

East Midlands. — Lincolnshire grows fine **potatoes** and these feature in many dishes, particularly with delicate pink, green and white slices of **stuffed chine of pork**, a piece of back of fat pig, stuffed with green herbs. Three regional cheeses enjoyed country-wide are **Stilton**, **Red Leicester** and **Derby sage**. **Bakewell tarts** are made of puff pastry with an almond and jam filling. Ashbourne produces a **gingerbread** as does Grantham, and **pikelets**, a cross between a crumpet and a pancake, are a regional speciality. **Melton Mowbray pies**, succulent lean pork in jelly, with a little anchovy flavouring in a pastry case, vie with **Sherwood Venison pie**, eaten hot or cold with redcurrant jelly. **Veal collops with orange** are said to have been a favourite dish of Oliver Cromwell.

East Anglia. — Norfolk is famed for its **dumplings**. Another delicacy is **mussels in cider and mustard** and during the summer **samphire**, "poor man's asparagus", grows wild along the salt marshes and is eaten with melted butter. In Suffolk they serve a **spicy shrimp pie**, cooked with wine, mace and cloves in a puff pastry case. **Black caps** are large baked apples, the cores scooped out and filled with brown sugar, citrus peel and raisins. **Cromer crabs** are full of flavour and the Colchester **oysters**, introduced by the Romans, are the equal of the best from France.

Yorkshire, Humberside and the Northeast. — **Roast beef and Yorkshire pudding** — a succulent batter pudding on which the juices of the roasting meat have been allowed to drop — rivals **York ham** and **parkin** — a dark oatmeal cake made with cinnamon, ginger, nutmeg and treacle — as Yorkshire's greatest contribution to British gastronomy. **Wensleydale cheese** goes well after any of the many **game pies** or **potted grouse** for which the area is renowned. Humberside offers many fish dishes. Newcastle has **potted salmon** and along the Northumberland coast, **baked herrings**, cooked with mint, sage and pepper, are a delicacy, hot or cold.

Cumbria, the Northwest and the Isle of Man. — Fish of all sorts from the Irish Sea, **cockles**, **scallops**, the smaller flavourful "Queenies" from the Isle of Man, **potted shrimps in butter**, from Morecambe Bay, and **Manx kippers**, are the glory of this region. **Char**, a fish from the deepwater lakes of the Lake District, are eaten fresh-caught or potted, **Goosnargh cakes** are the local gingerbread. Cheshire produces two fine **cheeses**, one white and one a **blue vein**. **Cumberland sauce** is not to be missed as an accompaniment to ham or game pies.

Scotland. — **Scottish beef and lamb** are deservedly renowned, as is Scottish **venison**, **grouse** (in season) and **salmon**. **Partan Bree** is a tasty **crab** soup and there are **Arbroath smokies** and **kippers** to rival **kedgeree**, made with salmon, haddock or other fish, with rice, hard-boiled eggs and butter. **Haggis** served with swedes — "haggis and neeps" — is a tasty meal accompanied by a wee dram of whisky. **Mutton pies** are made with hot water pastry and **oatmeal bannocks** are spread with local honey. Dundee makes an **orange marmalade** as rich, dark and chunky as that from Oxford. **Aberdeen buttery rowies** are flaky pastry rolls.

Wales. — In Britain lamb is traditionally eaten with mint sauce, mutton with red currant jelly. **Welsh honey lamb** is delicious, cooked in cider, with thyme and garlic, basted with honey. Caerphilly produces a light, crumbly **cheese**. **Leeks**, the national emblem of Wales, appear in many dishes, including **cawl cenin**, a tasty leek soup. **Baked crab and cockle pie** is a speciality of the Gower peninsula and the local sea trout — **sewin** — is stuffed with herbs before being cooked. **Welsh cakes**, griddle scones with currants, and **crempog**, small soft pancakes, are best eaten hot with butter. **Bara brith** is a rich moist cake bread, full of raisins, currants, sultanas and citrus peel.

Sights

Eilean Donan Castle

Michelin Map 401 N 12 or Atlas G Britain p 69

The ''Granite City'' lies between the Rivers Don and Dee. It has a rich agricultural hinterland, while the North Sea has brought it fisheries and more recently, the oil industry.

Twin Burghs. — The present city developed from two separate fishing villages on the Dee and the Don. An episcopal city by the 12C, Old Aberdeen had an ever increasing secular community outside the precincts. In the late 15C, Bishop Elphinstone founded a University. The second distinct burgh grew up around the King's castle and became an active trading centre, based on the coastal and Baltic trades.

The Granite City. — Following the lead of Edinburgh and Perth, Aberdeen implemented its own expansion plan with the laying out in 1801 of Union and King Streets. It was Archibald Simpson (1790-1847), an Aberdonian himself, who gave much of the character to the city by his masterly use of local granite. The streets were lined with impressive public and private buildings, but all with a simplicity and dignity befitting the nature of granite as a building material.

Maritime Connections. — The recorded history of the harbour dates back to 1136 and the prosperity of Aberdeen has always been closely linked with the sea. There has always been a strong tradition of shipbuilding in Aberdeen; firstly vessels for whaling, then the Clipper ships, which gave Britain supremacy in the China tea trade. From wooden vessels through composite-built to iron ships in the 1870s, when sail yielded to steam, shipbuilding has remained an important activity.

Whaling was carried on from the 1750s, but it was the herring boom of the 1870s that made Aberdeen a major fishing port. Since 1900 and the switch to white fishing it remains Scotland's premier fishing port.

More recently Aberdeen has become the ''off-shore Capital of Europe'' for the North Sea oil industry and exploration and supply base activities continue to play an important role.

ABERDEEN

Alford Pl.	X 2	
Belmont Rd	V 3	
Causewayend	V 9	
College Bounds	V 10	
Craigie Loanings	X 13	
Leslie Rd	V 18	
Maberley St.	VX 20	
Menzies Rd	X 24	
Mount St.	VX 25	
North Esplanade West	X 27	
Powis Pl	X 28	
Powis Terrace	V 30	
Riverside Drive	X 31	
Rosehill Drive	V 32	
Rosemount Viaduct	X 34	
South College St.	X 37	
South Esplanade West	X 38	
Springbank Terrace	X 39	
Victoria Bridge	X 41	
Victoria Street	X 42	
Waverley Pl.	X 44	
Wellington Pl.	X 45	
Wellington Rd	X 46	
Whinhill Rd	X 48	

ABERDEEN
CENTRE

George St. .... Y
St Nicholas St. .... YZ 35

Schopping Centre ...... Y
Union St. .... YZ

Carnegies Brae .... Y 6
Castle St. .... Y 7
Exchequer Row .... Y 14

Flourmill Lane .... Y 15
Hadden St. .... Z 17
Marywell St. .... Z 21
Meal Market St. .... Y 23
Rosemount Viaduct .... Y 34
Windmill Brae .... Z 49

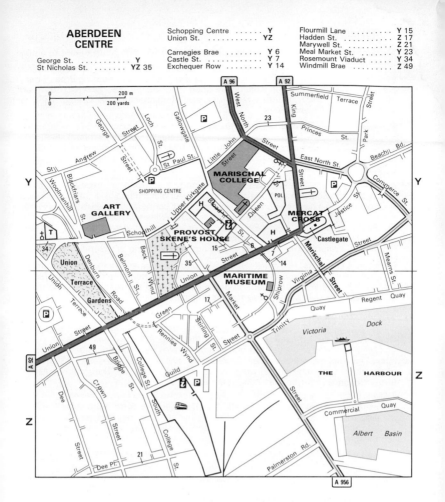

★★OLD ABERDEEN (V)

Old Aberdeen became a burgh in 1489 and retained this status until 1891. The quarter from King's College Chapel to St Machar's Cathedral is part of a conservation area where the character of the old burgh is well retained.

★ **King's College Chapel.** — Of Bishop Elphinstone's University, the beautiful chapel in its campus setting is the only original building left. It is famous for its Renaissance **crown spire**★★★, restored in the 17C following storm damage. The arms on the west front buttresses include those of James IV and of his Queen, Margaret Tudor, sister of England's Henry VIII.
Pass the **Old Town House (V A)**, an attractive 18C Georgian house, and then the **Chanonry**, a walled precinct for the dependent residences of the bishop, canons and chaplains.

★★ **St Machar's Cathedral.** — The twin spires have long been one of the landmarks of Old Aberdeen. The cathedral dates from the 14 and 15C and was built "overlooking the crook of the Don" in compliance with instructions from St Columba. Impressive though the exterior is, it is the 16C **heraldic ceiling**★★★ which should not be missed. The brightly coloured coats of arms present a vision of the European scene around 1520 the year of the Field of Cloth of Gold, and strongly assert the place of Scotland in a united Europe and a united Church.

★ **Brig o'Balgownie.** — *Approach via Don Street* (V)
This early 14C bridge with a defensive kink at the south end, is one of Aberdeen's most important medieval buildings.

CITY CENTRE

★ **Maritime Museum** (Z). — *Provost Ross's House, Shiprow.*
The museum, in two 16C houses bordering Shiprow, a medieval thoroughfare winding up from the harbour, traces the development of the harbour, the various fishing booms, shipbuilding and the recent North Sea oil industry and the effect all these have had on Aberdeen.

Castlegate (Y). — The medieval market place, on the way up to the site of the castle ("gata" from the Viking word for street and not a gateway in today's English sense). Here, too, is the Mannie fountain (1706), a reminder of Aberdeen's first piped water supply, and the elaborate platform **Mercat Cross**★★ (Y) dating from 1686. The decoration of this arcaded structure includes a series of royal portrait medallions and the royal unicorn. The cross marked the focal point of the burgh and was the place for public punishment and proclamations.

Marischal Street (YZ). — A street laid out in 1767-8 with houses built to a uniform design of three storeys and an attic.

★ **Marischal College** (Y). — The intricate granite street front overlooking Broad Street was a 20C addition to the college founded in 1593 by George Keith, 5th Earl Marischal. King's (qv), older by a century, and Marischal amalgamated in 1860 to form Aberdeen University.

★ **Provost Skene's House** (Y). — With title deeds going back to 1545, this house ⊘acquired its present form when owned by **Sir George Skene** (1619-1707). Restored in the 1950s it contains tastefully furnished period rooms. Most outstanding, however, is the chapel with its 17C **painted ceiling** of New Testament scenes within a geometrical framework.

★★ **Art Gallery** (Y). — The permanent collection has a strong emphasis on contem-
⊘porary art. The Scottish section has important works including William McTaggart's *A Ground Swell* in his own personal "impressionist" style, and Lavery's *Tennis Party*. Also well represented are two local artists, 19C William Dyce, a precursor of the Pre-Raphaelites (*Titian's First Essay in Colour, A Scene in Arran*) and the 17C portraitist George Jamesone. The **Macdonald Collection★★** of British artists' portraits, ninety-two in number, is a highly revealing survey of the art world in the 19C.

Parks and Gardens. — Aberdeen's parks and gardens are justly worthy of mention, for the city has won the Britain in Bloom competition nine times. **Union Terrace Gardens** (YZ), the Winter Gardens in **Duthie Park** (X) and the rose garden and maze at **Hazlehead** (X) have some amazing floral displays.

EXCURSIONS

★★ **Deeside.** — *About 64 miles - 103km by the A93. Allow at least a day.*
The splendid valley of the salmon-rich Dee penetrates deep into the Grampian Moun-
⊘tains. There are many fine castles, **Drum, Crathes** (qv), and, some 8 miles - 13km north of the river, the architectural masterpiece of **Craigievar** (qv). The green at **Aboyne** forms the setting for colourful **Highland Games** in August.

⊘**Balmoral Castle** has been the summer residence of the Royal Family since Queen Victoria's reign. **Braemar** too has its castle, but the village is better known for the **Braemar Highland Gathering** held annually in September and normally attended by royalty. At the road's end is the famous beauty spot of **Linn o'Dee**, where salmon may be seen leaping.

★★ **Pitmedden Garden.** — *14 miles north of Aberdeen by the A92* (V).

⊘**Sir Alexander Seton** (c 1639-1719), possibly influenced by designs of Le Nôtre or the gardens of Sir William Bruce at Holyrood, laid out the original formal gardens. The garden is seen at its best in July and August, when some 30-40 000 annuals are in bloom. Within this walled garden a belvedere provides the best viewing point. The Museum of Farming Life adjoins the Great Garden.

★★ **Grampian's Castle Country.** — *Description p 128.*

★ **ABERYSTWYTH** Dyfed   Pop 8 636
Michelin Map 🔢 H 26 or Atlas G Britain p 24

From the top of Penglais Hill, standing in front of the National Library of Wales, one has a magnificent **view★** across this seaside town. The **University College of Wales** was founded here, in 1872, in an hotel building which still stands on the sea front.

⊘**National Library of Wales.** — The library houses a priceless collection of early manuscripts and treasures of Welsh and Celtic literature, and there is usually an exhibition of selected treasures in the Gregynog Gallery.

Castle. — Built by Edmund of Lancaster, brother to Edward I, between 1277 and 1289, it was here, in 1406, that Owain Glyndwr proposed the establishment of an independent Welsh church and the founding of two universities. Little remains, on the commanding site, of the diamond-shaped castle.

⊘**Vale of Rheidol Light Railway.** — The last steam train service still operated by British Rail takes visitors up from Aberystwyth Station, to the Devil's Bridge Falls *(see below)*. The journey of 12 miles - 19km takes an hour as the train climbs slowly up to 639ft - 195m. The rail link was put in, in 1902, to service the lead mines up the Vale of Rheidol, and the engines and rolling stock, with their 1ft 11 1/2 in gauge are all originals.

EXCURSIONS

★★ **Elan Valley.** — *34 miles - 55km by the A44 to Rhayader; circuit of lakes 25 miles - 40km.* Reservoirs were built in the Elan Valley, 1892-1904, to supply water to Birmingham, 73 miles - 116km away. The Claerwen dam, built to increase
⊘the supply, was opened by Queen Elizabeth in 1952. The **Elan Valley Visitor Centre** in the village has displays and a twenty minute audio-visual presentation explaining the need for, the history of and the building of the whole scheme, in the words of James Mansergh, the engineer responsible. The resultant lakes have become very attractive, justifying the title given to the whole 70 square mile - 180km² region, of "The Welsh Lake District". Submerged under the waters are the remains of Nant-gwyllt, the house where the poet Shelley and his young bride spent some time in 1811-12.

Near the junction of the Elan and Claerwen valleys the road crosses the Caban Coch reservoir on a viaduct over the Garreg Odu dam; it is here that the water is drawn off for the Midlands. The four dams are best seen in flood conditions when huge waterfalls cascade over them.

★**Devil's Bridge (Pontarfynach).** — *12 miles - 19km from Aberystwyth, on the A4120. If intending to get to the Falls by rail, plan your journey to leave at least an hour for your visit.* The rivers Rheidol and Mynach join here and form a spectacular 300ft - 90m waterfall, Mynach Falls. The original bridge was probably built by the monks of Strata Florida in the 12C, though legend says it was the Devil who built it to allow a local woman to take her cattle across the torrent. There are now three bridges, one atop the other, the second one being built in 1753 and an iron one on top of this, in 1901, to level off the roadway and allow motor cars to cross, on an easier gradient.

★**Strata Florida.** — *16 miles - 26km - southeast of Aberystwyth on the B4340 to Pontrhydfendigaid- "Bridge of the Blessed Ford" - then on minor road.* Little other than the Norman arch of the west door and the lines of the walls remains of this Cistercian abbey founded in 1164. Cistercian ideals of simplicity and poverty, rather than the Benedictine Rule, appealed to the Welsh temperament. Strata Florida, completed by 1201, became a centre of Welsh culture and influence. It was here that Llywelyn the Great assembled all the Welsh princes to swear allegiance to his son Dafydd. Many of those early princes are buried here, in the angle between the presbytery and the south transept. The abbey suffered at the hands of Edward I and Henry IV, and at the Dissolution the monks took with them their most precious possession, an olive-wood cup, believed to be the Holy Grail.

Llanbadarn Fawr. — *Outskirts of Aberystwyth, on the A44.* Early 13C church, restored in the 19C, on the site of a 6C centre of Christianity. In the south transept, two Celtic crosses, probably 9-11C, have been preserved in a chapel which is in the modern image.

★ **ALNWICK** Northumberland   Pop 6 972

Michelin Map 402 O 17 or Atlas G Britain p 51

The attractive grey stone town grew up around the great medieval castle whose stern walls still seem to bar the route from Scotland.

★★**Castle.** — Among the many fortifications of this much contested border country Alnwick's castle is the most formidable. Begun in Norman times, it was acquired in 1309 by the **Percys**, the region's greatest family, and has remained in their hands ever since. Though much remodelled in the 19C, its basic features are all intact and in an exquisite setting by the River Aln, it epitomises the romantic ideal of a mighty medieval fortress.
The approach from the town is defended by an impressive early 14C **gatehouse** and **barbican** whose battlements, here as elsewhere around the castle, are guarded by 18C stone warriors. Beyond, the extensive walls enclose the broad lawns of the outer and middle baileys. These are separated by the imposing **keep**, largely rebuilt by the 4th Duke in the mid-19C. The baronial gothic of its courtyard conceals a sequence of sumptuously-furnished rooms decorated in a lavish Renaissance style by a team of Italian designers and master craftsmen. Among the many good paintings (Titians, Tintorettos, a Turner...) there is a Van Dyck portrait of the 10th Earl. From the north-facing terrace there are fine views over the castle's extensive parklands. These were landscaped in the mid 18C by Lancelot Capability Brown and are enlivened by a number of follies such as the sham castle on Ratheugh Crags, 2 1/2 miles - 4km to the northeast.
To the northwest, Hulne Park contains the ruins of Hulne Priory as well as the 18C Brislee Tower which offers wide prospects over the country.

★**Town.** — Though its streets were laid out in the Middle Ages, Alnwick's present sober and harmonious appearance dates from the 18C when much dignified rebuilding in stone took place. It is still compact, with countryside everywhere close at hand and, as the market centre for a wide area, has a busy life of its own. Even so, there are many reminders of the Percys' dominating presence; their emblem, a poker-tailed lion, stands on the bridge over the Aln to the north and atop the tall **Tenantry Column** to the south; and the only surviving fragment of the town walls, the 15C **Hotspur Gate**, is named after Harry Hotspur, celebrated in Shakespeare's *Henry IV*.

EXCURSIONS

★**Dunstanburgh Castle.** — *8 miles - 13km including 2 1/2 miles - 4km on foot. Leave Alnwick on the B1340 to the northeast. After 3 miles - 5km turn right.*
Craster. — A tough little fishing village built in dark stone and noted for its kippers.
A grassy footpath leads northwards along the low-lying but rocky coast.

★**Dunstanburgh Castle.** — The skeletal ruin on its lonely crag of volcanic rock is one of the most stirring sights of the Northumbrian coast.
Seen from the south the long wall and its lesser towers are dominated by the substantial remains of two massive gatehouse towers. Beyond is an immense grassy space, the outer bailey, protected on the west by a wall and tower topping the steep slope and on the north and east by the sea itself, whose breakers crash against cliffs alive with seabirds. There are long views up and down this wonderfully unspoiled coastline of rocky headlands and sweeping sandy bays backed by dunes.

Warkworth. — *7 1/2 miles - 12km.* Pop 1 280. *Leave Alnwick on the A1068 to the east.*
Within the easily defended site formed by a loop in the River Coquet is a remarkable sequence of castle ruin, dependent township, church and fortified bridge.

★ **Warkworth Castle.** — Perched high above the river, the castle dates from the 12C and ⊘ since 1332 has belonged to the Percys. Its general layout can be appreciated from the upper floor of the fine 13C **gatehouse.** The outer walls, punctuated by towers, enclose a compact area divided into an inner and an outer ward by the foundations of the castle church. The tower entrance to the **Great Hall** on the west is decorated with an odd, dog-faced version of the Percy lion. The most prominent feature is the exceptionally beautiful restored **keep,** designed for comfort and convenience as much as for defence.
From the castle the single street of the little planned town runs steeply downhill to the Norman **church of St Lawrence** and to the river crossing with its rare medieval **bridge tower.**

⊘ **Warkworth Hermitage.** — *1/2 mile - 1km upstream. Reached by hired boat or by footpath and then ferry.*
In its peaceful riverside setting this extraordinary late medieval retreat, partly hewn into the sandstone cliff, accommodated its hermit in some style, with a chapel and living quarters on two levels.

Rothbury. — *11 1/2 miles - 18km. Leave Alnwick on the B6341 to the southwest.*
The road climbs up over the fells. After 4 1/2 miles - 7km there are good views northwestwards towards the rounded hills building up to the summit of The Cheviot (2676ft-816m).

★ **Cragside House.** — The stupendous success of his engineering and armament works ⊘ at Newcastle enabled **Lord Armstrong** (1810-1900), perhaps the greatest of Victorian inventor / industrialists, to build this extraordinary country house in which Old English and Germanic styles are romantically combined. The many rooms of its wellpreserved **interior**★ give a fascinating insight into the comforts and pretensions of late-Victorian domestic life.

Rothbury. — Pop 1 694. The pleasant little stone town on the River Coquet is overlooked to the south by the crags of the Simonside Hills and is a good centre for ⊘ exploring the **Northumberland National Park.** This vast tract of wild and sparsely populated upland extends from the Cheviot in the north to Hadrian's Wall in the south.

⊘ **Chillingham Wild Cattle.** — *8 miles - 13km northwest by the B6346, right fork onto minor road to Chillingham, a further four miles.*
A herd of wild white cattle, last of the species which once roamed free through the forest stretching from the North Sea to the Clyde, still remains at Chillingham. Pure bred, uncrossed with domestic cattle, they have been in the Park for the past 700 years. Their genetic survival is attributed to the fact that only the "King" bull sires the calves, thus breeding from strength.

★★ Isle of ANGLESEY (Ynys Môn) Gwynedd

Michelin Map **403** G,H 23 and 24 or Atlas G Britain p 32

Môn - Mam Cymru: Anglesey. - Mother of Wales - the island, separated from the rest of Wales by the **Menai Strait**, has a landscape of low undulating hills, unlike anywhere else in the Principality. Anglesey and the Strait offer walkers and yachtsmen marvellous opportunities to follow their pastimes.

Llanfairpwllgwyngyllgogerychwyrndrobwllllantysiliogogogoch. — *The church of St Mary in a hollow of white hazel, near to a rapid whirlpool by the red cave near St Tysilio's church.* The village name, Llanfair P.G. for short, was almost certainly strung together in the 19C to amuse - and baffle - English tourists. Rising 112ft - 34m on its hill above the village is the column and statue erected in memory of William Henry Paget, 1st Marquess of Anglesey (1768-1854), one of the Duke of Wellington's most trusted commanders.

Menai Bridge. — Thomas Telford (1757-1834) built the suspension bridge to carry his road to Holyhead. The Admiralty insisted upon a clearance of 100ft-30m between water and roadway, and the bridge, with its span of 579ft-176m between towers, was the longest iron bridge in the world, when it was opened in 1826.

Britannia Tubular Bridge. — Designed by Robert Stephenson it carried the railway across the Strait, in 1850. The railway ran in two separate tubes; these were badly damaged by fire in 1970 and separate decks, between the original towers, now carry both road and rail.

★★ **Plas Newydd.** — Home of the Marquess of Anglesey, this magnificently sited late ⊘ 18C mansion in 169 acres-68ha of parkland and garden looking over the Strait to the mountains of Snowdonia, was given to the National Trust in 1976. During alterations to the house in 1936, the artist **Rex Whistler** was commissioned to decorate the long dining room. His whimsical masterpiece of *trompe l'œil* includes frequent references to the Paget family and contains a small portrait of himself, as a gardener sweeping up leaves.

★★ **Beaumaris Castle.** — Begun in 1295, Beaumaris was the last, and largest, of the ⊘ castles built by Edward I in Wales. Though never finished, it is the finest example in Britain of a concentric castle. A moat surrounds it and there was a defended dock, capable of taking ships of up to 40 tons. The gatehouses were planned to have lavish accommodation; the **Great Hall**, impressive enough as it stands, would have risen to twice its present height, dominating the inner ward.

St Nicholas Church. — 14C church, built to serve the new town which grew up around the castle. In the porch is the stone coffin of Princess Joan, daughter of King John and wife of Llywelyn the Great, who died in 1237.

⊙ **Court House and Gaol.** — The quaint Court House dates from 1614 and contrasts with Beaumaris Gaol, in use from 1829-75 and a grim reminder of the Victorian penal system, with stone floors, shackles and treadmill.

★★ Isle of ARRAN Strathclyde   Pop 4 726

Michelin Map 401 E 17 or Atlas G Britain p 53
Access: see the current Michelin Red Guide Great Britain and Ireland

Arran is the largest of the islands in the Firth of Clyde, some 20 miles-32km long by 10 miles-16km wide. Cut in two by the Highland Boundary Fault, Arran presents ''Scotland in miniature''. A mountainous northern part (**Goat Fell** 2 866ft - 874m) has deep valleys and moorlands, whilst the southern half consists of more typically lowland scenery.
Sheltered bays and sandy beaches, together with ample facilities for yachting, swimming, golf, sea angling and fishing, make tourism the principal industry on Arran today.

TOUR OF THE ISLAND

56 miles - 90km - about 1/2 day, not includIng visiting time Make sure the petrol tank is full before setting out. There are few petrol pumps.

Mainly a coastal route, the road affords views of the diversity of scenery; but as well as the coast road, try the 10 mile - 16km String Road across the waist of the island, between Blackwaterfoot and Brodick.

★★ **Brodick Castle.** — Historic stronghold of the Hamiltons, Earls of Arran, the 13C
⊙ castle was extended by Cromwell's troops in 1652 and again in the baronial style by Gillespie Graham in 1844. The Hamilton and Beckford treasures comprise a fine collection of silver, porcelain, family portraits as well as paintings by Watteau, Turner and Herring.
There is a formal walled garden from 1710 and, thanks to the mild climate, a 65 acre - 26ha rhododendron garden, one of the finest in Britain.

Machrie Moor Stone Circles. — *1 1/2 miles - 3km inland off the road north of Blackwaterfoot.*
Moorland backed by mountains makes an impressive setting for these remnants of Bronze Age stone circles, built about the same time as the later parts of Stonehenge. Arran was on the main migration route for Neolithic agriculturalists up the western seaboard of Scotland.
As the road swings round Arran's southern tip the 1 000ft - 300m high granite island of **Ailsa Craig** can be seen to the south. The road from Lamlash Bay, sheltered by Holy Island, to Brodick gives a spectacular view of Brodick Castle dominated by Goat Fell.

★★ AVEBURY Wiltshire

Michelin Map 403 O 29 or Atlas G Britain p 17

Though less famous than Stonehenge, the 28 acre - 11ha earthwork and stones at Avebury form one of the most impressive prehistoric monuments in Europe, the more fascinating as the present day village lies inside the circle of stones within the earth ''ramparts''. **St James Church★**, in which Anglo-Saxon work is found alongside Norman, Perpendicular and 19C, certainly merits a visit.

The Stones. — It is difficult to take in all the stones from one vantage point; but by standing on the circular earthen banks, particularly at the south entrance, one can see part of the **Circle of sarsen stones**, the two inner rings and the **Avenue** which leads 1 1/2 miles - 2 1/2km southeast to the burial site known as the Sanctuary.
The circle of bank and ditch is broken at four opposite points, now used by modern roads entering the village. The Avenue consisted of approximately 100 pairs of thirty to forty ton stones of two distinct shapes alternating in each file - broad and square or tall and slender - which may represent male and female symbols. Not all the stones have survived from c1800 BC to the present; in the 18C a number of stones from the circle were broken up as building material for the village. Thanks to the plans drawn up by the 18C antiquary William Stukeley it is possible to picture the site before this vandalism, and concrete obelisks now stand in the position of vanished
⊙ stones. A visit to the **Alexander Keiller Museum** gives a valuable insight into this and neighbouring sites.

NEIGHBOURING PREHISTORIC SITES

★ **Silbury Hill.** — *1 mile south of Avebury, north of the A4.* This 130ft - 40m high man-made mound of chalk, 550ft - 168m in diameter at the base and 100ft - 30m across its flat top, is surrounded by a ditch, the whole covering 5 1/4 acres - 2ha. It was built in four stages starting c2500 BC, but despite excavations in the 18C and 20C its purpose remains a mystery.

★ **West Kennet Long Barrow.** — *3/4 mile - 1km southeast of Silbury Hill, footpath from the A4.* This is England's finest example of a burial barrow, dating from 3500-3000 BC. The entrance to the 340ft - 104m long by 75ft - 23m wide earthen mound is at the east end between giant sarsens. The passage, the two lateral chambers and the terminal chamber are roofed with massive capstones supported on upright sarsens and drystone walling. Some 50 skeletons from the late Mesolithic period were discovered in the vaults.

Windmill Hill. — *4 miles - 6km northwest return, on foot.* This causewayed camp gives its name to the earliest Neolithic culture in Britain. It comprises three concentric ditches and embankments in which herds were assembled in the autumn.

AYR Strathclyde	Pop 48 493

Michelin Map 401 G 17 or Atlas G Britain p 48
Town plan in the current Michelin Red Guide Great Britain and Ireland

Once the busiest port on Scotland's west coast, in the 17C even larger than Glasgow, Ayr is now a thriving resort, the hub of **Burns Country.** The sandy beaches are splendid; the country's premier racecourse is here and there is good golfing nearby.

Auld Brig. — 13C bridge, said to have been financed by two sisters who lost their fiancés, drowned whilst trying to ford the river in spate. It stood, whilst a later bridge was carried away in a storm in 1870.

★ **Alloway.** — *3 miles - 5km to the south by the B7024.*
Alloway is famed as the birthplace of the poet Robert Burns (1759-96), whose birthday on 25 January is celebrated by Scots (and others) throughout the world.
⊙ The **Burns Cottage and Museum**★ evoke his humble origins and house an extensive and well-displayed collection of manuscripts and relics.
⊙ Nearer the **Burns Monument** and the **Brig o'Doon**, a visitor centre, the **Land o'Burns**, recalls the bard's life and times as well as introducing the visitor to southwest Scotland.

EXCURSION

★ **Culzean Castle.** — *12 miles - 19km southwest of Ayr by the A719.*
The coast road takes you through Dunure, an attractive fishing village and on to the **Electric Brae,** where a curious optical illusion caused by the lie of the surrounding countryside, makes the road appear to be descending, when it is, in fact, going uphill.

   Continue for a further 4 miles - 6km.

★ **Culzean Castle** (pronounced Cullane) in its dramatic clifftop **setting**★★★, was the work
⊙ of **Robert Adam** (1728-92), designer also of Hopetoun House and of Charlotte Square in Edinburgh. Though a classicist, Adam added arrow slits and battlements to this his most spectacular castle, to complete the mock-medieval touch. There is an "Eisenhower Exhibition" in the castle.

BARNARD CASTLE Durham	Pop 6 075

Michelin Map 402 O 20 or Atlas G Britain p 45

⊙ The ruined **castle** stands high up on the steep left bank of the River Tees, overlooking the town that has grown up beneath it. It was built early in the 11C, on land given by William II to the Baliols, who founded Balliol College, Oxford in 1263, and Sweetheart Abbey in Scotland. Of the original four wards, only the town, middle and the inner ward survive, the **Baliol Tower,** *c*1250, straddling the curtain wall of the inner ward, being the best preserved part.

★ **Bowes Museum.** — *In Barnard Castle itself, not in Bowes village. Follow road*
⊙ *signs.* A French-designed château, set in 20 acres of landscaped gardens is an unexpected surprise in this area. It was built, from 1869 onwards, to house the extraordinary array of ceramics, pictures, tapestries, furniture and other objets d'art amassed by John Bowes and his French wife. Their treasures include novelties like an automated silver swan but there are also paintings of the first rank; a magnificent **St Peter** by El Greco, two Goyas and works by Primaticcio, Boucher, Boudin and Courbet.

EXCURSION

★ **Raby Castle.** — *6 miles - 10km northeast of Barnard Castle, by the A688.* Built
⊙ in the 14C by the Nevill family, Raby Castle was forfeit to the Crown after the "Rising of the North" against Queen Elizabeth in 1569. In 1626 it was sold to Sir Henry Vane, Treasurer to Charles I, and his descendants, now the Lords Barnard, live there still. Though it appears to be a moated 14C castle, the interiors date mainly from the 18C and 19C. The house contains a good collection of paintings and furniture, and some excellent Meissen porcelain. The graceful statue of a manacled **Greek Slave** is by Hiram Powers, an American sculptor who caused a sensation when he exhibited it at the Great Exhibition of 1851.
There is a fine **Walled Garden**, where a 200-year old fig and ancient yews blend with more recent features.

★ BARNSTAPLE Devon   Pop 24 490

Michelin Map 403 H 30 or Atlas G Britain p 6

Barnstaple received its first charter as a burgh in 930, one of the earliest recorded in Britain. Ever since it has been the regional centre for trade, agriculture and industry. The 19C cast iron, glass-roofed **Pannier Market**, which adjoins the unique **Butchers' Row**, is still used for its traditional function on each Tuesday, Friday and Saturday throughout the year.

★ **Long Bridge.** — The 520ft - 158m long stone bridge was first constructed c1273, consisting of 16 arches, the three on the town side being replaced probably in 1539. Downriver is **Queen Anne's Walk**, built as a merchants' exchange in 1609 and comprising a single lavishly adorned colonnade above which stands a statue of Queen Anne.

⊙ **Parish Church.** — This 13C church, extensively restored by Gilbert Scott in 1866-82, is notable for its lead-covered broach spire of the second half of the 17C. Inside are a large number of 17C **memorial monuments** (south aisle).

Horwood and Paiges Almshouses and **Alice Paige School.** — The school and almshouses, with wooden mullioned windows, were built in the 17C in the quiet cobbled Church Lane (small oblong courtyard, through the arch).

EXCURSIONS

★★ **Clovelly.** — Pop 419. 20 miles - 32km west on the A39 and B3237. One of the show villages of England, it remains surprisingly unspoilt considering the numbers of visitors. The steep cobbled High Street lined with small, whitewashed 19C houses, leads down to **Quay Pool**, the minute harbour, where the **view** extends from Lundy to Baggy Point.

Bideford. — Pop 12 296. 9 miles - 15km on the A39. The town is known chiefly for its beautiful **stone bridge**★★ (c1460), replacing a late 13C oak bridge. Most of the present stonework dates from the various repairs, especially the widening of 1865.

*The **Michelin Sectional Map Series** is revised regularly.*
These maps make the perfect travelling companion.

★★★ BATH Avon   Pop 84 283

Michelin Map 403 M 29 or Atlas G Britain p 17

Bath combines the grace and elegance of the 18C with a long and varied past.

Legend and history. — Britain's only hot springs surfaced c100 000 years ago. In 500 BC, legend tells, **Prince Bladud**, a swineherd since being smitten by leprosy, saw his swine healed of their skin ailments after wallowing in the mud; he plunged in himself and was cured. He returned to court, was crowned, fathered King Lear and settled in Bath. True or not, Bath was known for its warm springs before the arrival of the **Romans** in the 1C AD. They made Bath England's first spa resort, building baths, a temple and possibly a gymnasium or theatre. When the Romans left in the 5C the city declined; in the 6C the Saxons took Bath and built a town within the Roman walls and an abbey near the site of the Roman temple. In the 9C Alfred is said to have fortified Bath; in 973 **Edgar**, first King of all England, was re-crowned in the Saxon abbey.

Feuding Norman barons so reduced the city that **John de Villula** of Tours, Bishop of Somerset and physician, bought it for £500. He began the creation of a vast Benedictine cathedral priory, built a palace, guesthouse, new baths, and a school, and encouraged the treatment of the sick. His cathedral was never completed, the present abbey standing on the site of the nave. Bath became a prosperous wool town, but at the Dissolution the monks lost their power and sold off parts of the abbey. In 1574 Queen Elizabeth I had a fund set up to restore the abbey and St John's Hospital and render "an unsavoury town... a most sweet town".

In 1668 Pepys praised the town but had reservations about the hygiene of the baths. However, crowds of less fastidious people followed royalty to Bath and by the early 18C it was a fashionable, though dull and unorganised city.

Beau Nash. — "The Beau" (1673-1762) followed fashion to Bath in 1704. Quickly appointed Master of Ceremonies he made a programme for the high-flyers, from morning bathing to evening assemblies; he had the streets lit and made safe, swords forbidden in town and sedan chair tariffs controlled. He opened the first Pump Room for taking the waters and meeting in civilised society. He organised concerts, balls, gambling and laid down rules. Bath prospered - as did Nash - and became the most fashionable city in England.

Ralph Allen and John Wood. — As Nash refashioned Bath Society, Allen and Wood transformed its architecture and urban plan. Allen (1694-1764), a Cornish postmaster, came to Bath in 1710 and made his fortune by creating an efficient postal service for the region. He then bought quarries at Claverton and on Combe Down in order to build a new city with the honey-coloured stone. Wood (1700-54), a Yorkshireman, had settled in Bath by 1728. He and his son, John Wood (1728-81), were classicists, inspired by Bath's Roman past; they built in the Palladian style with stone from Combe Down, now known as Bath stone.

SIGHTS

The city is best seen on foot; watch out everywhere for street vistas.

★★ Roman Baths (BX B). — The baths are fed by a spring which pours out approximately 280 000 gallons - about 1 250 000 litres of water per day at a temperature
of 116 °F - 46.5 °C.

The Roman complex consisted of the Great Bath, a large warm swimming pool,
now open to the sky, and two baths of decreasing heat; later a *frigidarium* was built
on the west side with openings at the north, overlooking the sacred spring, and two
more heated chambers *(tepidarium* and *caldarium)*. The east end was subsequently enlarged, the baths were elaborated and the *frigidarium* transformed into a cold
plunge circular bath. North of the reservoir was an altar and to its west, a temple.
When the Romans left, the drains clogged; so much mud overflowed that today Stall
Street lies above the temple site, the Pump Room above the altar and its court.
In the Middle Ages the King's Bath was constructed over the Roman reservoir.
In 1727 workmen building a sewer along Stall Street found the gilded bronze head
of **Minerva**, the goddess of the spring. Since then excavations have revealed the temple
and baths complex and a wide variety of artefacts now in the museum.

★ Bath Abbey (BX). — The sanctuary was begun in 1499 by Bishop King. From the
pillars of the Norman church arose the pure late Perpendicular abbey. Inside nave,
chancel, narrow transepts soar to **fan vaulting** by Robert and William Vertue (designers of the fan vaulting in the Henry VII Chapel, Westminster Abbey). Outside
five-light windows stand between flying buttresses, crocketed pinnacles and a
castellated pierced parapet. The **west end** has a Perpendicular window, 17C door
and, in the stone, tall ladders with angels ascending and descending.

★ Pump Room (BX A). — Though the present Pump Room was built in 1790-95
after Nash's death, he still presides in the form of a **statue**. There are fluted pilasters
with gilded capitals beneath a coved ceiling, apsed ends, a rounded bay with the
former drinking fountain and a view of the King's Bath, Chippendale style chairs,
a glass chandelier - the perfect meeting place for Catherine and Mr Tilney in Jane
Austen's *Northanger Abbey.*

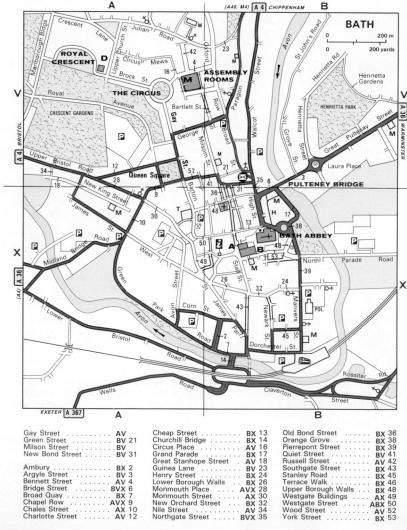

EIGHTEENTH CENTURY ELEGANCE

★★★ **The Royal Crescent (AV).** — The great arc of thirty terrace houses in which the horizontal lines are counterbalanced by 114 giant Ionic columns rising from the first floor to the pierced parapet, was the great achievement of John Wood II, in 1767-74.

⊘ **No 1 Royal Crescent★★ (D)** has been authentically restored, providing a perfect setting for Chippendale, Sheraton and Hepplewhite furniture and for porcelain and 18C glassware. **Brock Street**, which links the Crescent to the Circus, was also built by John Wood II in 1767.

The Circus, Bath

★★★ **The Circus (AV).** — Although one of the elder Wood's earliest concepts, the Circus was built as late as 1754. It is a tight circle of identical houses, pierced by three equidistant access roads. The houses of pale Bath stone, decorated with coupled columns, rise three floors to a frieze and acorn-topped balustrade. It is a design of classical proportions and control.

Gay Street (AV), linking the Circus to **Queen Square (AV)**, was the work of the two Woods, father and son, from 1734 to 60, while Queen Square was the elder Wood's first example of urban planning.

★ **Assembly Rooms (AV).** —
⊘ These elegant rooms were built in 1769-71 for the evening assemblies - at which people met to dance, play cards, drink tea and to gossip. The long ballroom is as high as it is wide, its decoration concentrated above in columns, entablature and a deep Naples yellow ceiling with five magnificent crystal chandeliers. The **Octagon** was intended as a small card room. The **Tea Room** has a rich interior with a splendid two-tiered screen of columns at its west end.

⊘ The **Museum of Costume★★★** presents a colourful and elegant display of the rich range of styles, textures and patterns used in every sort of garment from the Stuart period to the present day.

★ **Pulteney Bridge (BV).** — The bridge, built in 1769-74 to Robert Adam's design, has small shops on both sides, domed end pavilions and a central Venetian window.

EXCURSIONS

★★ **Bradford-on-Avon.** — Pop 8 000. *8 miles - 13km on the A4, then the A363 to the southeast.*
The houses rising tier upon tier up the hillside from the River Avon give the town its charm and character. The larger houses built in the local creamy-yellow ochre limestone reflect the affluence of the 17-18C clothiers when the town prospered as a wool centre. The nine-arched **bridge★**, built in 1610 with a small square, domed chapel topped by a weather-vane, is the best starting point for the walk to the top of this attractive town.
The Saxon **St Laurence Church★★** may date from the 7-8C when, as William of Malmesbury records, St Aldhelm built a church here. Having served as a school, cottage and charnel house, the church was re-discovered in 1856. The minute building of stone is impressive for its dimensions, being exceedingly high in proportion to its width; the arch separating nave from chancel is no more than 3 1/2ft - 105cm wide. The west wall was rebuilt in 1875.
⊘ The vast early 14C **tithe barn** has gabled doorways and a superbly constructed wooden roof.

★★ **Corsham Court.** — *11 miles - 18km to the northeast by the A4.*
⊘ Built in 1582 this Elizabethan mansion was bought by Paul Methuen in the mid-18C. Corsham was altered and enlarged on several occasions to house the extensive Methuen collection of **paintings** (16 and 17C Italian and 17C Flemish), **statuary, bronzes** and **furniture**. The excellent collection in the **Picture Gallery** includes Caravaggio's *Tobias and the Angel,* Veronese's *Annunciation,* and *Wolf Hunt* by Rubens. The **Cabinet Room** contains **Fra Filippo Lippi's** *Annunciation* (1463), Chippendale side tables and pier glasses by the brothers **Adam**, while the highlight of the **Octagon Room**, designed by Nash, is **Michelangelo's** *Sleeping Cupid* (1696). Note also fine family portraits by Reynolds in the **Dining Room**.

★ **Lacock.** — *14 miles - 22km east by the A4 then the A350 to the south.*
The calm, attractive stone and brick-built village has always been under special patronage: first of the abbey, then the Talbots and now the National Trust. The village comprises four streets which form a hollow square and are lined by cottage-shops, houses and inns of every height and size, as various in date as in design.

⊘ **St Cyriac's★** is a Perpendicular "wool church" from the time of Lacock's prosperity in the 14-17C as a wool and cloth centre. Distinctive features include the large pin-nacled porch, the 15C lierne vaulting and 16C tombchest in the Talbot Chapel.

⊘ The **Fox-Talbot Museum★** near the abbey gate specialises in 19C photography, with the accent on the achievements of **William Henry Fox-Talbot** (1800-77), scientist, philosopher and photographer. With his pioneering work in the early 1840s he laid down the foundations of the negative-positive process of photography.

⊘ To the east is **Lacock Abbey★** founded in the 13C and converted into a house by William Sharington, following the Dissolution. The cloisters, sacristy and chapter house survived. Lacock Abbey passed to the Talbot family and in the 19C the oriel window was the subject of the first photographic negative, taken in August 1835 by William Henry Fox-Talbot *(see above).*

★ **Dyrham Park.** — *9 miles - 15km north on the A46.* The 17C mansion was built
⊘ for William Blathwayt (1649-1717), Secretary of State to William III. His first ar-chitect took back the existing Tudor house to the Great Hall and built instead a for-mal regular entrance front of local stone. In 1700 the second phase began with "the ingenious **Mr Talman**" as architect; his 130ft - 40m long **east front**, with two storeys and an attic, the same balustrades and urns as on the other side, is light-ened by touches of baroque ornament. The house contains various 17C and 18C furnishings, objects and works of art, mainly from England and the Low Countries. The **garden** and **park** were designed by Talman and George London, but were later replanned by **Humphry Repton** (1752-1818).

⊘ **Claverton.** — Pop 109. *2 miles - 3km east on the A36.* The **American Museum★★** is housed in Claverton Manor, a neo-classical country house. The nucleus of its col-lection is a series of furnished rooms dating from the late 17C to the middle of the 19C presenting 200 years of American life and styles. Besides special galleries, there are also various exhibits in the spacious grounds, including a colonial herb garden and an arboretum.

★ **BATTLE** East Sussex   Pop 4 662

Michelin Map **404** V 31 or Atlas G Britain p 12

The momentous victory, on 14 October 1066, of the Normans over King Harold's English army is marked on its hill-top site by the remains of the great commemora-tive abbey built by William the Conqueror and also in the name of the little town which grew up to serve it.

★ABBEY AND THE SITE OF THE BATTLE OF HASTINGS
⊘ *time: 1 1/2 hours*

Over the humble buildings of the town's market place rises the imposing but graceful mass of the 14C gatehouse, battlemented and richly decorated. Most of the great Benedictine abbey beyond was systematically dismantled at the Dissolution, though its outlines may be traced among the remaining fragments. The abbey church's high altar, erected at William's command over the spot where Harold fell, is identi-fied by a plaque. Stepping down the steep slope are the impressive remains of the **monks' dormitory,** its high gable with three rows of lancet windows staring blankly south towards the battlefield. The most complete survival is the west range of the cloister, now a private school.

★ **Battlefield.** — From the **terrace walk** there is a commanding view of the tranquil scene over which this most decisive of English battles was fought. It was on this ridge that Harold deployed his men after their exhausting forced march from York. On the far side of the swampy valley were ranged their Norman adversaries with their French and Breton allies, fresh from their nearby beachhead at Hastings. The day-long battle was fierce and bloody; a pathway with topographical models at inter-vals follows its course up and down the fateful slopes.

★★ **BEAULIEU** Hampshire   Pop 1 027

Michelin Map **404** P 31 or Atlas G Britain p 9

This pretty village at the head of the Beaulieu River is famous for the National Motor Museum, one of the most comprehensive collections of motor vehicles, set in the grounds of the Cistercian monastery founded in 1204 by King John.

Abbey. — After the Dissolution the abbey fell into ruin, its stone being in demand for Henry VIII's coastal forts. Only the footings remain of what was once the larg-est Cistercian abbey in England. The cloister has partly survived, notably the lay brothers' quarters (now housing an exhibition of monastic life) and the 13C refec-tory, converted into the parish church; note, behind a screen of Purbeck marble columns, the staircase leading to what was the lector's pulpit.

Palace House, the home of the 1st Lord Montagu; it is a strange mixture of medieval monastic architecture, Victorian home comforts and mementoes of the Montagu family; however the most notable memento is the motor museum started by the second Lord Montagu.

1913 Rolls-Royce Alpine Eagle

★★ **National Motor Museum.** — The collection of more than 250 vehicles including
many veteran and vintage cars in excellent condition and working order, presents
the story of motoring from 1895 to the present day. The "Classic Car" Hall of
Fame celebrates the great motoring pioneers; its outer walls are adorned with
replicas of the tiled panels from Michelin House, former offices of Michelin in
Fulham Road, London.
The **Veteran Cars** (pre-1919) include an 1899 Daimler (12hp), 1906 Renault (20-30hp),
one of the first closed cars; the beautiful Silver Ghost (40-50hp) which earned Rolls-
Royce the title "best car in the world" and the Ford Model T, the first mass-produced
car — £135 in 1914. The **Vintage and 1930s** section displays the benefits which mass
production brought to the American and European motor industries, epitomised by
the Austin Seven and 1924 Morris Cowley. The market for exclusive cars is represented by a 1925 Rolls-Royce Phantom I and a 1924 Delaye boat-tailed tourer.
The **Racing** and **Record-Breaking Car** section is notable for the 1961 Bluebird in which
Donald Campbell attained 404mph - 649km/h in 1964. The **post-1945** section displays achievements of the modern motor industry. The **Commercial Vehicles** include
a variety of delivery vans and a 1950 London bus. The **Motorcycle Gallery** features
eighty machines and traces the history of motorcycling. **"Wheels"**, located on the
ground floor, is a ride in automated "pods" through 100 years of motoring.

ENVIRONS

★ **Buckler's Hard.** — *2 miles - 3km southeast. 1 1/2 hours.* This charming hamlet,
one very wide street of 18C cottages running down to the Beaulieu River, was founded in the early 18C by John, 2nd Duke of Montagu; his hopes of using the port
for trading with the West Indies came to nothing and in the 1740s the village became a shipbuilding centre for the Royal Dockyard in Portsmouth. As iron replaced
wood in shipbuilding the industry declined, but in the 20C the hard became popular among yachtsmen, notably **Sir Francis Chichester** (1901-72) who began and ended
his single-handed round-the-world voyage from the little harbour.
The **Maritime Museum★** evokes many aspects of life and work in Buckler's Hard in
the 18C, with reconstructed interiors of two cottages and the New Inn, furnished
as they might have been in the 1790s. **Boat trips** can be taken from the wharf at
the end of the street.

★★ BERKELEY Castle Gloucestershire

Michelin Map 403 M 28 or Atlas G Britain p 17

Its rugged walls of pink and grey stone a reminder of 800 and more years of history, this archetypal medieval stronghold commanded the narrow strip of lowland
between the Cotswolds and Severn.
William Berkeley was the first Governor of Virginia from 1641 to 1677. Part of the
library of the famous metaphysician Bishop Berkeley passed on his death in 1753
to Yale University and then to the California university which bears his name.

TOUR *time: 1 hour*

The inner courtyard is dominated by the great drum of the **keep** of 1153; its outer
wall still displays the breach made by Cromwellian cannon in the siege of 1645.
From near the entrance gate there is a prospect of water meadows which could
be flooded to strengthen the castle's defences. Beyond, a curious castellated building
houses horses and hounds of the famous Berkeley Hunt.

Interior. — A confusion of twisting passages and stairways, vaulted cellars, ancient kitchens and deep dungeons reminds the visitor that this is a fortress, adapted only slowly over centuries to reconcile comfort and convenience with the demands
of defence. Through a grille in the King's Gallery can be seen the chamber, simply
and evocatively furnished, where the deposed **Edward II** was kept prisoner and then
foully murdered. Other rooms are richly furnished with reminders of the castle's
continuous occupation since the 12C by the Berkeley family.
Outstanding are the **Great Hall,** with its 32ft - 10m high timber roof and printed screen
and the **Morning Room,** once a chapel, the decoration of its ceiling incorporating lines
from the 14C Norman French translation of the Bible, which was worked on here
by the castle chaplain, John Trevisa.

EXCURSION

★ **Wildfowl and Wetlands Trust, Slimbridge.** — *7 miles - 11km. Leave Berkeley on the B4066, turning northwards on the A38 and then left after 3 miles - 5km down a minor road.* Bordering the extensive wetlands of the tidal Severn, this water-bird sanctuary, created over a period of 40 years by the late Sir Peter Scott, has acquired an international reputation for research and conservation and as a place where the public can observe at fascinatingly close quarters a great variety of native and exotic wildfowl, pink flamingoes and countless migrant birds.

★★ BERWICK-UPON-TWEED Northumberland   Pop 12 772

Michelin Map 402 O 16 or Atlas G Britain p 57 - Local map p 237

Berwick has been alternately held by English and Scots, since the 12C. The **Walls★** were replaced from 1558 onwards with ramparts and bastions in the style just being introduced in Verona, Antwerp and other European cities. Not much remains of the castle where, on 17 November 1292, Edward I heard the petitions of thirteen contenders for the throne of Scotland and gave his decision in favour of John Baliol. Some of its stones were used, in 1651, to build Holy Trinity Church, one of the few to have been built during the Commonwealth. Then, in 1720, it was 'quarried' for **Berwick Barracks,** which now houses the **Kings Own Scottish Borderers Museum** and finally, in the 19C, the railway station was built over what remained of the castle site. The Clock Block of the Barracks also contains the **Burrell at Berwick Collection,** displaying excellently crafted pieces (Imari ware, brassware, medieval religious art, Chinese bronzes and glassware) collected by the 'magpie millionaire', Sir William Burrell. The elegant 15-arch **Old Bridge,** built in 1611, is the fifth known to have been built between Berwick and Tweedmouth.

EXCURSIONS

★★ **Lower Tweed Valley.** — *Description p 236.*

★ **Holy Island and Bamburgh Castle.** — *8 miles - 13km south on the A1, left onto minor road, then 5 miles - 8km including causeway — can only be crossed at low tide — to Holy Island.*

The Lindisfarne Gospels (detail)

Saint Cuthbert (635-87AD), hermit monk from Holy Island, who became Bishop of Lindisfarne in 685 AD, is buried in Durham Cathedral. Here were written and magnificently illuminated in Celtic tradition the **Lindisfarne Gospels** *(photograph opposite)*, now preserved in the British Museum. The **Priory ruins★** visible today are those of a Benedictine house, founded, from Durham, in 1093.

★ **Lindisfarne Castle.** — 16C castle, restored in 1902 by **Edwin Lutyens,** as a holiday home for the founder of *Country Life* magazine, Edward Hudson. Austere but beautifully designed interior, in the inimitable 'Lutyens' style.

Return to the A1, south 12 miles - 19km then left onto the B1342 to Bamburgh.

★ **Bamburgh Castle.** — The **Norman keep** still dominates this castle, which was restored in the Victorian era. Bought by Lord Armstrong in 1894, it houses a fine collection of arms and armour from the Tower of London and much Sèvres, Crown Derby, Worcester and Chelsea porcelain. There are exquisite small collections of silver vinaigrettes, Fabergé carvings and jade and in what was probably the Norman guard room, now the Court Room, a number of family portraits, including one of the present Lady Armstrong by Annigoni.

★ **Farne Islands.** — *15 miles - 24km - south on the A1, turn left onto B1342/1340 to Seahouses. Boats leave the harbour here for trips of about 3 hours, around the bird sanctuary islands with landings, when permitted.* The islands, 15 to 28 of them depending upon the tide, provide nesting sites for eighteen species of seabirds, and are home to the largest British colony of the grey seal. On Inner Farne, where landing is permitted dependent on the breeding dates, is a small chapel, dedicated to St Cuthbert, who lived on the islands from 676-685AD. The islands were home to **Grace Darling**, who, on 7 September 1838, with her lighthouse-keeper father rowed to the rescue of nine persons from the paddle-steamer *Forfarshire,* aground on Harcar's Rock.

★ **BEVERLEY** Humberside   Pop 19 368

Michelin Map 402 S 22 or Atlas G Britain p 41

Georgian façades hide the ancient timber buildings of a town which in 1377, with 5 000 inhabitants, was half the size of York and twice as big as Hull. Behind its 1832 façade, the **Guildhall** built in 1762 has a fine courtroom, with a glorious stucco ceiling by Cortese.

★★ **Beverley Minster.** — John of Beverley, Bishop of Hexham and York, sought seclusion in his old age and died here in 721. He was buried in the church he had founded thirty years before. Today's Minster was begun about 1220, an earlier church having been burnt down on 20 September 1188. The Minster is 332ft - 101m in length, of almost "Cathedral" proportions.

Building began at the east end, and the Early English style with shafted lancet windows is carried back to the transepts. The nave is Decorated, early 1300s, with the clerestory transitional between Decorated and Perpendicular. The **west front** is wholly Perpendicular, being completed by 1420.

The great east window, a Perpendicular nine-lighted window containing all the fragments of medieval glass the Minster once possessed, was bequeathed in 1416.

The **Percy Tomb** and its canopy, with angels, symbolic beasts, and leaf carvings, is the most splendid of funerary monuments from the Decorated period. Built 1340-9 the tomb probably commemorates Lady Idonea, who died in 1365. Sixty eight **misericords** in the choir stalls, work of the Ripon school of woodcarvers early in the 16C, are some of the finest in Britain.

★ **St Mary's Church.** — Founded *c*1120, St Mary's soon became adopted by the trade Guilds, and transepts and nave aisles were quickly added. The tiny (36 × 18ft - 11 × 5.5m) Chapel of St Michael with its ingenious "telescopic" spiral staircase, is contemporary with the Percy Tomb in the Minster. The Perpendicular west front with slim shafts and fine mouldings is comparable with King's College Chapel in Cambridge *(qv).* By 1524 the addition of the **tower** completed what is one of the finest parish churches.

Kings of England Ceiling

BEVERLEY

An extensive collection of carvings of medieval musical instruments is shared between the Minster and St Mary's at Beverley. All told there are 140 represented. Three of the musicians on the brightly painted **Minstrels' Pillar** in the nave, donated by the Guild of Musicians in 1524, have, unfortunately, lost their instruments, but there are many others, on pew ends, choir stalls, ceiling bosses and in the south porch. The **chancel ceiling**, painted in 1445, with its pictorial record of 40 English kings, is unique. The keen observer will see a portrait of George VI, which, in 1939, replaced one of the legendary kings in the original design. Twenty three misericords with extraordinary carvings of animals and men adorn the choir stalls. A 'Pilgrim Rabbit' carved about 1325, on a doorway to the sacristy, may have influenced Sir John Tenniel when he drew the 'White Rabbit' in his illustrations of *Alice in Wonderland.*

EXCURSIONS

⋆**Burton Constable.** — *16 miles - 27km - east, by the A1035, south onto the A165, then minor road to left towards Sproatley.*

Built by Sir Henry Constable, about 1600. The **east front**, brick with mullion windows and two projecting wings, still gives the first and strongest impression. The **Entrance Hall**, the Great Hall of the Elizabethan house, is by Thomas Lightoller (1760), as is the portal with Tuscan columns and window above, by which the visitor enters.

In the **Muniment Room,** the remodelling of the house in Georgian times can be followed from documents of the period. A **Long Gallery**, of noble proportions and decoration, was designed by William Constable in the mid-18C and contains many family portraits. The marble **fireplace**, the work of a Beverley master-mason, is inlaid with flowers and birds by **Domenico Bartoli**.

In the Chapel, Ballroom and Dining Rooms, the delicate plasterwork is by Guiseppe Cortese, the Italian master who created the courtroom ceiling in Beverley. In these rooms and in the **Chinese Room**, many fine pieces of Chippendale furniture are displayed.

⋆**Burton Agnes Hall.** — *18 miles - 29km - north by the A164, to Great Driffield, then A166 towards Bridlington.*

An outstanding example of late Elizabethan architecture, a mellow red brick house, started in 1598, finished 1610 and little altered since.

In the **Great Hall** are a screen and alabaster chimneypiece, crowded with fantastic and allegorical carvings, unmatched in Britain. A **Dance of Death** carving, gruesome but magnificently detailed, is above the fireplace in the **Drawing Room**. The **Staircase** allowed generous scope for the Elizabethan woodcarvers to display their talents. The **Long Gallery**, with its restored plasterwork tunnel-vault ceiling, is now displayed in its 1610 condition and houses many of the Impressionist and Post-Impressionist paintings collected by the family.

Kingston upon Hull. — Pop 322 144. Town plan in the current Michelin Red Guide Great Britain and Ireland. *9 miles - 15km south of Beverley on the A1174 and A1079.*

Medieval and 17C Hull was contained between the river and the old docks. Queen's Dock, built 1775-8 is now Queen's Gardens. A statue to one of Hull's celebrated citizens, **William Wilberforce** (1758-1833), stands nearby. His Bill to abolish the slave trade became law in 1807 and he lived to see the abolition of slavery in British territories, in 1833. His birthplace in High Street, is now a **museum. Holy Trinity Church** is the largest of all parish churches in Britain 285ft - 87m long, with a tower 150ft - 46m high. The transepts, *c*1330, are remarkable for being built partly in brick, as is the lower stage of the **tower**, for Hull had a municipal brickyard as early as 1303.

Trinity House. — A religious Guild founded 1369 became a Mariners' Guild by royal charter in 1541 and took on the control of navigation and shipping in the 17C and 18C. The stuccoed, pedimented building in Trinity House Lane dates from 1753-4.

Humber Bridge. — Started in 1972, it was opened by HM the Queen on July 17 1981 and, until completion in 1988 of the Akashi Kaikyo bridge in Japan with its main span of 5 425ft - 1 780m, this was the world's longest single span suspension bridge. At 4 626ft - 1 410m it beats the Verrazano Narrows Bridge in New York by 366ft - 111m.

GREEN TOURIST GUIDES

Scenery,
Buildings,
Scenic routes,
Geography,
History, Art,
Touring programmes,
Plans of towns and building.

Guides for your holidays

Michelin Maps 403 or 404 O 26 or Atlas G Britain p 27

The second city of the Kingdom and one of the centres of the Industrial Revolution, Birmingham still produces a high proportion of Britain's manufactured exports. Industrialisation began in the mid-16C, the city ''swarming with inhabitants and echoing with the noise of anvils'' (William Camden). By the mid-17C, in keeping with its radical tradition, it was supplying the Parliamentarians with swords and guns, which provoked Prince Rupert to sack the city. Its 18C growth, marked by the miles of canals radiating from the centre (Birmingham has more miles of canal than Venice) attracted **James Watt** (1736-1819), inventor of the double-action steam engine, **William Murdock** (1754-1839), inventor of coal-gas lighting, and **Matthew Boulton** (1728-1809), whose Soho factory was the first to be lit by gas.

Reaction to the grim conditions caused by the city's phenomenal growth in the 19C came in two ways: a radical approach to civic improvement, pioneered by Joseph Chamberlain (1869-1940), many times mayor and father of Neville Chamberlain, mayor in his time, but ill-fated as Prime Minister; it came also in the private philanthropy of the cocoa manufacturer, George Cadbury (1839-1922), responsible for one of the world's first garden suburbs, Bournville.

The face of the modern city owes much to the ambitious development projects following the Second World War. Expressways, underpasses and high-rise buildings have not created the most attractive of townscapes, but the indoor shopping centres are convenient and there are new landmarks like the Rotunda towering over the **Bull Ring** (KZ), the huge Central Library and the uncompromisingly contemporary

International Convention Centre. The position of the city and its West Midland hinterland at the hub of industrial Britain is emphasised by its centrality in the national motorway network; a particularly elaborate interchange is known with perverse pride as **Spaghetti Junction.** Especially well served by transport links of all kinds, including Birmingham's international airport, are the vast modern halls of the National Exhibition Centre.

After a century of city status Britain's second city is acquiring a new image as a European business centre with a flourishing cultural life: a new symphony hall in the International Convention Centre will be home to the CBSO, the refurbished Hippodrome Theatre is the new headquarters for the Birmingham Royal Ballet, formerly Sadler's Wells, and the National Exhibition Centre hosts a myriad sporting and entertainment events.

MUSEUMS AND GALLERIES

★★ **Birmingham Museum and Art Gallery** (JZ M²). — The pride of a city whose coat
⊘ of arms is flanked by a masculine Industry and a feminine Art, Birmingham's gallery is famed for its outstanding collection of **Pre-Raphaelite paintings.**

The visitor is greeted at the top of the entrance stairs by a charming fresco, a street scene of 1914 by the local artist Joseph Southall, then by the superb *Sultanganj Buddha,* the right hand offering peace, the left a blessing. The spacious round room, the original gallery, is crowded with 18C and 19C paintings, among them Leader's *February Fill Dyke.* The elaborate ironwork of the two-tiered Industrial Gallery is a late-Victorian marvel, a fascinating setting for the well-displayed ceramics and stained glass. Beyond it, is the surprise of the *Edwardian Tea Room,* presided over by Jacob Epstein's *Lucifer.*

Much gallery space is devoted to the extensive holdings of European paintings, among them outstanding works like the *Madonna and Child* by Bellini, a Claude *Landscape near Rome* and a *Roman Beggar Woman* by Degas. English paintings include works by Wright, Hogarth, Gainsborough, Constable and David Roberts, and by the Birmingham landscape painter, David Cox, but at the heart of the collection are the Pre-Raphaelites; all the masters of the Brotherhood are represented, mostly by key works like *The Last of England* by Ford Madox Brown, *The Blind Girl* by Millais, **Beata Beatrix** by Rossetti and *Two Gentlemen of Verona (photograph below)* by Hunt. A series of panels showing Cupid and Psyche is by Burne-Jones, a native of Birmingham. Another famous 19C work is Augustus Leopold Egg's *The Travelling Companions,* sitting timelessly in their Italian railway carriage, while a selection of 20C paintings includes Sickert's *Miner* and Paul Nash's *Landscape of the Moon's First Quarter.*

Further rooms are given over to local history, archaeology and natural history; there is a spectacular fossilised skull of a triceratops, 6 feet - 2m long. The Pinto Gallery contains an extraordinary array of wooden objects from medieval times onwards.

Two Gentlemen of Verona by William Holman Hunt

★★ **Barber Institute of Fine Arts** (HX U). — *University of Birmingham. 2 1/2 miles*
⊘ *- 4km south of the city centre. From the Bristol Road turn right up Edgbaston Park Road to the University south car park. By train: from New Street station to University station.*

The Institute is part of the sprawling campus of England's archetypal ''red-brick'' university, a civic foundation which achieved full university status in 1900. Brick of a most uncompromising redness was used in the crescent of ponderous edifices around Chancellor's Court and in the extraordinary Sienese campanile, the 328ft - 100m high Chamberlain Tower.

The gallery itself is in a severe stone and brick building begun in 1935. Within is a small but lovingly chosen and representative collection, built up with the bequest of Lady M C H Barber (d 1933). Displayed together with furniture and other objets d'art it has the pleasingly intimate atmosphere of a private collection. Sir Henry

BIRMINGHAM CENTRE

did not appreciate modern art and stipulated that all works had to be pre-1900; though policy has since changed there is a still a predominance of Old Masters. Among the Italian works there are several Venetians, a *Portrait of a Boy* by Bellini, a *Crucifixion* by Cima, and a *Regatta* by Guardi. Flemish paintings include Brueghel the Younger's *Two Peasants Binding Faggots,* and the wonderfully fresh, ''pure'' *Landscape near Malines* by Rubens.

The French School is well represented, with works by Poussin, Watteau, Delacroix, Ingres, Corot and Courbet. There is a bright portrait of the Countess Golovine by Elisabeth Vigée-Lebrun and an outstanding group of Impressionists and Post-Impressionists, including Bonnard, Degas, Gauguin, Manet, Monet, Renoir, Vuillard and Van Gogh.

Among the English painters is the *Harvest Wagon* by Gainsborough, a *View near Harwich* by John Bernay Crome, Turner's *Sun Rising through Vapour* and Whistler's sensitive study of two girls *Symphony in White.*

★ **Museum of Science and Industry** (JY M³). — Flanked by a restored run of canal locks, the museum records Birmingham's industrial progress. Of the various sections note in particular the Locomotive Hall with the imposing form of the steam engine *City of Birmingham* (no 46235) in its gold and green livery, the James Watt Building with probably the oldest working steam engine, the Smethwick Engine of 1779. On the first and third Wednesdays of each month the beam engine is put through its paces. The life and work of **James Watt** (1736-1819) is retraced until his meeting with Boulton. Amidst the various exhibits of the transport section are a double-decker cable tram which ran on part of the Birmingham network until 1911, John Cobb's record-breaking Railton Mobil Special Car (394.196mph in the United States in 1947) and World War II fighter aircraft including R J Mitchell's Spitfire MK LFIX. Additional exhibits include other examples of Birmingham's engineering prowess: machine tools, textile and other industrial machinery as well as recreated workshops.

ADDITIONAL SIGHTS

★★Aston Hall (HV M[1]). — *2 miles - 3km north of the city centre.*
Built 1618-35 by John Thorpe for Sir Thomas Holte, besieged by the Parliamentarians in 1643 (shot marks punctuate its staircase balustrade of sea monsters), used as the setting for Washington Irving's novel *Bracebridge Hall* (1822), leased 1819-48 to James Watt's son, Aston Hall remains more than ever a ''noble fabric which for beauty and state much exceedeth anything in these parts''.

Interior. — Typically Jacobean (''uniformed without, though severely partitioned within'': Francis Bacon) and characterised by splendidly barbaric ceilings and fireplaces. Its most gorgeous rooms are the long gallery, with its strapwork ceiling, arcaded oak panelling and de la Planche tapestries of the *Acts of the Apostles;* and the great dining room, with more extravagant strapwork, a frieze of the Nine Worthies (Alexander, Hector, Caesar, Joshua, David, Judas Maccabeus, Arthur, Charlemagne and Godfrey of Bouillon) and paintings by Romney and Gainsborough.

Cathedral of St Philip (KY Z). — Thomas Archer's first major commission and built 1711-25 in a very English classical baroque, its exterior is saved from severity by its exuberant west tower (concave sided with dome and lantern) and its west door (a baroque joke incorporating as many styles as possible).
Of the interior, Archer's nave, arcades and galleries make a moving contrast to Burne-Jones' gigantic **stained glass portrayals★** of the Nativity, Crucifixion, Ascension and Last Judgement.

Canal Walkway to Gas Street Basin. — A canal walkway *(3/4 mile - 1.2km)* leads from the Museum of Science and Industry past the canals, locks, bridges and buildings, all products of the city's 19C industrial expansion.

> *Go slightly beyond the junction of the Worcester Canal to take the footbridge and follow the canal to the left.*

Overlooking the canal junction on the right is the site of the new National Indoor Sports Arena. Further round you pass the modern form of the **International Convention Centre** (HV A) providing comprehensive facilities including 11 major halls around a central mall and a custom-built Symphony Hall for Simon Rattle's City of Birmingham Symphony Orchestra.
The **Gas Street Basin** (JZ), a restored canal basin, is overlooked by the new 23-storey Hyatt Regency Hotel, and surrounded by both new and restored 18 and 19C buildings including Matthew Boulton's factory — The Brasshouse (Broad Street) — refurbished to accommodate a restaurant and pub. The gaily painted narrow boats moored alongside the canal are typical of the craft which once plied the Midlands' canal network.

EXCURSIONS

★★Ironbridge Gorge Museum. — *Description p 139.*

Black Country Museum. — *Dudley 10 miles - 15km northwest of Birmingham by the A4123 or 3 miles - 4km from junction 2 on the M5.*
The sprawling landscape of the South Staffordshire coalfield may have given rise to the name Black Country, which now designates the boroughs of Wolverhampton, Walsall, Dudley and Sandwell. Now a fast growing revitalised industrial region it has a rich heritage to attract visitors. The museum occupies 26 acres - 11ha with buildings rescued from the Black Country. The coal mining industry is represented by a reconstructed pit head and an impressive underground display of the conditions in a 'Thick Coal' mine in the 1850s. Nearby is a working replica of the world's first steam engine of 1712. An electric tramway carries visitors to the core of the displays, an industrial village between two canal arms. The main exhibits are houses, a grocery, hardware shop, baker's, chemist's, sweet shop, glasscutter's, chainmaker's, nail shop, rolling mill, anchor forge, boatdock, Methodist chapel and pub. Boat trips are organised into the spectacular limestone caverns beneath the adjacent Castle Hill.

BLACKPOOL Lancashire   Pop 146 297

Michelin Map 402 K 22 or Atlas G Britain p 38
Town plan in the current Michelin Red Guide Great Britain and Ireland

Thousands upon thousands of holidaymakers have been coming here each year since 1846 when the railway first made seaside holidays a possibility. About a third of these visitors now come in September and October, when the famous **Blackpool Illuminations** are switched on. Seemingly endless beaches, three piers, and entertainments galore ensure fun for everybody. A tramway system, unique now in mainland Britain, plies 7 miles - 11km of Promenade and continues north to the sister port of Fleetwood. **Blackpool Tower★**, 518ft - 158m high, was inspired by the Eiffel Tower; opened in 1894, with its ballroom and circus, it has been the resort's trade mark ever since.

EXCURSION

Lytham St Anne's. — Pop 39 599. With its white **Windmill**, survivor of the many which used to work along this foreshore, Lytham St Anne's offers a more tranquil and leisurely atmosphere of beaches and sand dunes. There are four superb championship golf courses, including The Royal, and many good walks and beauty spots.

Michelin Map 404 P 28 or Atlas G Britain p 18

This greatest building of the English baroque, residence of the Dukes of Marlborough, is matched in splendour by the sublime landscape of its vast park.

"Royall and National Monument". — The Royal Manor of Woodstock, once the hunting ground of Saxon kings, was given by Queen Anne to **John Churchill, Duke of Marlborough** (1650-1722), to mark his victory of 1704 over the armies of Louis XIV at Blenheim in Bavaria. Seemingly limitless funds were made available for a "Royall and National Monument" to be erected in celebration of this decisive check to France's pan-European ambitions. Leading architects and craftsmen were employed, foremost among them **Sir John Vanbrugh**, one of England's most original architects, whose inventiveness and sense of drama found full expression here. Alas, court intrigues led to Marlborough's fall from the Queen's favour; the flow of money was cut off and building stopped. When it resumed it was at the Duke's own expense. His disputatious Duchess, Sarah, her sense of value for money now sharpened, quarrelled constantly over supposed extravagance, provoking Vanbrugh's resignation. The grandiose project, truly a monument rather than a home, was completed but only after the first Duke's death in 1722. A century and a half later, on 30 November 1874, his direct descendant, **Winston Churchill**, was born here. This most illustrious of Englishmen is now buried in the nearby village churchyard at Bladon.

🕐 **PALACE** *time: 3/4 hour*

The palace's huge scale and fortress-like character is relieved by dynamic, almost theatrical composition and exuberant detail. Thus its **silhouette** has a romantic, even medieval air, with an array of **turrets**, pinnacles and disguised chimney-pots, and the Great Court, some 450ft - 137m long is like a stage set, a succession of colonnades, towers and arcades, leading the eye inexorably to the main façade with its imposing portico. Symbols of military prowess and patriotism abound, from heaped up trophies to centurions standing proudly on the parapet; over the courtyard gateway the unfortunate cockerel of France is mauled by the haughty English lion.

Interior. — A series of splendidly-decorated rooms continues the monumental theme. The **Great Hall's** ceiling, 67ft - 20m high, is painted with an allegory of Marlborough's victory. Sir Winston Churchill's life is celebrated in a suite of rooms, including the one in which he was born. State apartments are furnished with original pieces, many of the highest quality. There are portraits by Reynolds, Romney, Van Dyck and one, by Sargent, of the ninth Duke with his family and American-born wife Consuelo. The vast **Saloon** has a great painted colonnade, apparently open to the sky, thronged with figures representing the four continents. The main axis of the park runs through this room, terminating in the church spire at Bladon. The **Long Library**, with a magnificent stucco ceiling, runs for 180ft - 55m, the entire length of the west front. In the Chapel is the overwhelming marble **tomb** of the first Duke.

★★★**THE GROUNDS**

The ancient hunting park, with its venerable trees and 9 mile - 15km long deer-proof wall, was worked upon in the early 18C by the royal gardeners. The **Italian Garden** to the east of the palace and the spectacular **Water Garden** to the west are modern, as is the symbolic maze of trophies, cannon and trumpets in the walled garden, but they capture something of the spirit of the formal avenues and geometrical parterres which were mostly swept away by **Lancelot Capability Brown**, the greatest of English landscape architects. The redesigned park is his masterpiece, offering from the Woodstock Gate what has been described as "the finest view in England". Sweeping grassy slopes, noble groves of trees and the curving outline of the great lake, crossed by Vanbrugh's **Grand Bridge**, combine to "improve upon Dame Nature" and provide a more than worthy setting for the palace.

A huge **Doric column**, 134ft - 41m high, topped by a statue of the first Duke with Victory in his grasp, forms one focal point of the recently replanted axis which on the north side of the palace runs to the Ditchley Gate, two miles - 3km distant. By the lake is the site of old **Woodstock Manor**, long demolished, and **Fair Rosamund's Well**, a reminder of this favourite of Henry II. Downstream, Brown's water engineering terminates in his **Grand Cascade**, over which the little River Glyme foams to rejoin its former bed.

WOODSTOCK Pop 3 057

In complete contrast to the immense scale of the palace and park are the trim streets of this little stone town with its coaching inns and classical town hall. The medieval royal palace *(see above)* was the birthplace in 1330 of Edward the Black Prince who was known as Edward of Woodstock.

EXCURSION

Burford. — *16 miles - 26km. Leave Woodstock southeastwards on the A44, turning right at a roundabout onto the A4095 in the direction of Witney.*

Bladon. — The village churchyard is the modest burial place of Sir Winston Churchill.

Continue on the A4095 to Witney, then follow the B4047 and the A40.

Burford. — Pop 1 371. One of the focal points of the wool trade, later an important coaching town, Burford's growth stopped when the turnpike road, now the A40, bypassed it in 1812. With its wealth of beautifully preserved buildings, nearly all of Cotswold limestone, it now welcomes the modern traveller to this beautiful region of which it is so typical.

The single main street descends steeply, then more gently, to cross the pretty River Windrush. About half-way down is the 16C Tolsey, once the courthouse, now the local museum. Slightly apart from the town is the large **Church of St John the Baptist★**, its tall spire rising gracefully above the watermeadows. Norman in origin, the church exhibits a rich variety of work from many periods; the pinnacled 3-storeyed 15C porch is outstanding. Among the memorials is the exuberant wall-monument to Edward Harman (d 1569), decorated with Red Indians and rows of kneeling children.

BOSTON Lincolnshire   Pop 33 908
Michelin Map **404** T 25 or Atlas G Britain p 37

The second largest port in England in the 13C, a centre of Puritanism and prison of the Pilgrim Fathers, Boston's elegant Georgian houses and warehouses line the banks of the River Witham, a fitting setting for the mother-town of a great city.

★St Botolph's Church. — *Market Place.*
⊘ The largest parish church when it was built in the 14C, its 272ft - 83m high tower, the **Boston Stump**, is visible from 20 miles - 32km away. It possesses a unity of which few churches can boast: the body Decorated and the stump and octagonal lantern Perpendicular. Note the 14C **misericords**: a bear playing an organ, a virgin and a unicorn and a hunter chased by his wife. The southwest chapel is dedicated to John Cotton (1584-1652), vicar of St Botolph's before sailing to Boston, Massachusetts.

⊘ **Boston Guildhall Museum.** — This fine brick building dating back to 1450 has a spectacular five-light window above the doorway. It was once the hall of St Mary's Guild, later the town hall, and is now the Borough Museum. The cells and courtroom were where William Brewster and other Pilgrim Fathers were imprisoned and tried, following their unsuccessful attempt to flee the country for Holland in 1607. The Banqueting Hall and Maritime Room still have their original roofs, while the Court Room and Council Chamber have changed very little since the 18C.

⊘ **Fydell House.** — *South Street.*
Built for William Fydell about 1720 with elegant Georgian interiors, it has been called by Pevsner ''the grandest house in town''.

EXCURSIONS

★Tattershall Castle. — *15 miles - 24km northwest on the A1121 and the B1192,*
⊘ *follow signs.*
Built by Ralph, Lord Cromwell (veteran of Agincourt and Lord Treasurer), Tattershall is closer to a French Château than a 15C castle, heralding the Renaissance castle-as-status-symbol (Oxburgh Hall *qv*). Well fortified, nevertheless, with double moat and 16ft - 5m thick walls, it is built of brick and stands out 100ft - 30m above the Lincolnshire flatlands. Its 4 floors contain exceptional mid-15C chimneypieces and the battlements provide panoramic **views**. By the early 20C the castle was in ruins, its site about to be sold off to speculators. It was saved by Lord Curzon, Viceroy of India, an intervention that led to the Ancient Monuments Act of 1913.

Spalding. — *16 miles - 26km south on the A16.*
On the northern edge of **The Fens** *(qv)* and set beside the River Welland, Spalding is as Georgian as Boston and blazes with a million flowers each spring during its
⊘ **Bulb Festival**. **Ayscoughfee Hall** *(Churchgate),* built in 1430 but much altered in the 18 and 19C, was the home of Maurice Johnson, founder of the **Spalding Gentlemen's Society** (1710), the second oldest antiquarian society in England, its members including Newton, Pope, Addison and Gray. It is now a local history museum. With 25 acres - 10ha of changing displays of 250 000 bedding plants, the gardens at
⊘ **Springfields** *(Camelgate off Holbeach Road),* are the centre of the British bulb industry and are famous for their tulips and roses.

BOURNEMOUTH Dorset   Pop 142 829
Michelin Map **403** O 31 or Atlas G Britain p 9

Bournemouth has been a popular summer and winter resort since the late 19C. Its amenities include **two piers,** the pavilion, now a theatre, and the always colourful **public gardens.**

⊘ **Russell-Cotes Art Gallery and Museum.** *Russell-Cotes Road.*
Each room, furnished in Victorian style, contains a varied collection from English fine china to oriental armour. Among the numerous paintings are William Frith's *Ramsgate Sands* and *Venus* by Rossetti.

⊘ **Shelley Rooms.** — *Shelley Park, Beechwood Avenue, Boscombe.* An important collection including the poet's letters, revolutionary leaflets and portraits.

EXCURSIONS

★Poole. — Pop 119 316. *4 miles - 6km west.* Poole with its fine sandy beach situated on one of the largest harbours in the world is both a popular yachting haven and a major roll-on-roll-off port. Near the quay is the famous **Poole Pottery** and also
⊘ the **Old Quarter,** with its 18C town houses. Of interest is **Waterfront Museum,** telling the history of the port and town, **Scaplen's Court,** a preserved domestic building dating from the late medieval period, and the fine 18C Guildhall building.

★★ **Compton Acres.** — *3 miles - 5km east of Poole by the B3369.*

⊘ This series of nine separate and distinct **gardens** (Italian, rock, water, Japanese...), spreads over 15 acres - 6ha in a rift in the sandstone cliffs, is famous for having flowers in bloom throughout the year. The **English Garden** lies open to sunsets and a westerly **view★★★** of Poole harbour, Brownsea Island and the Purbeck Hills.

★ **Corfe Castle.** — *18 miles - 29km southwest by the A35 and the A351.*

⊘ Corfe Castle has dominated the landscape since the 11C, first as a towering strong-hold and since 1646 as a dramatic ruin. From the high mound on which it stands, the **views★★** are spectacular. In 987 the 17 year-old King Edward, son of Edgar, visiting his half-brother at the castle, was murdered by his stepmother, Queen Aelfryth; in 1001 he was canonised as **St Edward, King and Martyr.** It was the home of Sir John Bankes, Chief Justice to King Charles I. His wife resolutely defended it from 1643-45 and when it fell, owing to the treachery of one of the garrison, it was looted and blown up by the Parliamentarians.

★ **BRADFORD** West Yorkshire   Pop 293 336

Michelin Map 402 O 22 or Atlas G Britain p 39
Town plan in the current Michelin Red Guide Great Britain and Ireland (see under Leeds)

Bradford, like Leeds its neighbour, prospered on the wool trade. In 1500 it was a bustling market town "which already standeth much by clothing". The Bradford canal opened in 1774, to improve communications and trade. By 1850 there were 120 mills and Bradford had become the world's worsted capital. Among its famous sons are the author **JB Priestley** (1894-1984), composer **Frederick Delius** (1862-1934) and the contemporary painter **David Hockney** (b1937). It is essentially a Victorian city, but one which, rather than being planned, just grew.

⊘ **National Museum of Photography, Film and Television.** — *Prince's View.*
Part of the Science Museum, opened in 1983, this museum houses Britain's largest cinema projector and a curved screen 52ft - 16m high and 64ft - 20m wide, designed to show the Canadian IMAX projection system. The displays trace the history and practice of photography, the cinema and television.

⊘ **Wool Exchange.** — *Market Street.* Built 1867 in Italian style, it was the centre of the world's wool trade. Brokers still meet here once a week. The statues at the entrance are those of St Blaize, patron saint of wool combers, and of Edward III, who did much to encourage the wool industry.

Cathedral. — *Church Bank.* The battlemented exterior does not give the impression of a building which, in parts, dates back to the 1440s; the west tower with battlements and pinnacles dates from 1493. The church was raised to cathedral status in 1919 and the chancel has some fine stained glass, *c*1862, by William Morris, Rossetti and Burne-Jones.

BRECON BEACONS Dyfed, Gwent, Mid Glamorgan, Powys

Michelin Map 403 I, J, K 28 or Atlas G Britain pp 15 and 16

These red standstone mountains culminate in a spectacular north-facing escarpment overlooking the lesser uplands of mid-Wales. South from this great barrier (highest point Pen y Fan, 2 907ft - 886m) extend high rolling moorlands cut by lush valleys, the broadest of them formed by the River Usk. Downstream from Brecon, centrally placed for exploring the **Brecon Beacons National Park,** the river is accompanied by the most delightful of waterways, the 32 mile - 52km Monmouthshire and Brecon Canal.

Places to visit in and around the National Park

Brecon (Aberhonddu). — Pop 7 166. The Normans constructed a castle here, whose ruins overlook the meeting of the rivers Honddu and Usk, and a priory too, whose church is now the Cathedral. The stone-built former county town has kept its intri-
⊘ cate medieval street pattern and numerous dignified 18C houses. The **Brecknock Museum** has good local displays and there is also the museum of the South Wales Borderers (24th Foot).

⊘ **Brecon Beacons Mountain Centre.** — *5 miles - 8km southwest of Brecon by the A470 and minor road.*
The first of its kind in Britain, beautifully sited on the edge of moorland, the centre continues to welcome visitors wanting to know more about the Park.

★★ **Dan-yr-Ogof Caves.** — *19 miles - 30km southwest of Brecon on the A40 and*
⊘ *A4067.*
The underground complex includes the largest as well as the longest single chamber cave open to visitors in Britain. There are archaeological displays, a "Dinosaur Park" and an interpretive exhibition.

Hay-on-Wye. — Pop 1 578. *16 miles - 30km northeast of Brecon on the A470, A438 and B4350.*
The quiet market town at the northern end of the Black Mountains has become internationally known for its numerous second-hand bookshops.

Michelin Map 404 T 31 or Atlas G Britain p 11
Town plan in the current Michelin Red Guide Great Britain and Ireland

With its south-facing beach punctuated by piers and backed by a wide promenade, its elegant Georgian, Regency and Victorian architecture, the labyrinthine lanes of the old fishing town contrasting with lavishly planted open spaces and parkways, Brighton is where the English seaside was invented and brought to a pitch of perfection.

Modern Brighton began in the mid-18C with the promotion by Dr Richard Russell of the healthy effect of drinking and bathing in seawater. The new modishness of the once decayed fishing town of Brighthelmstone was confirmed by the allure it exercised throughout his lifetime on the Prince of Wales, following his first visit in 1783. From the 1840s the London, Brighton and South Coast Railway brought ever-increasing numbers of holidaymakers of all classes to what had truly become "London- by -the - Sea". Today's mature town has remained young, stage-managing its raffish appeal to attract successive generations of visitors from home and abroad, while acquiring the ingredients of a miniature metropolis: specialist shops, uncountable restaurants, entertainments of all kinds, and even, on its outskirts, the modern University of Sussex.

Royal Pavilion, Brighton

★★★ROYAL PAVILION *time: 1 hour*

⊘ This fantastic oriental confection in stucco and stone reflects the brilliant personality of George Augustus Frederick, Prince of Wales (1762-1811), later Regent (1811-1820), finally King George IV. A year after his clandestine marriage in 1785 to the young and attractive commoner and Catholic, Mrs Fitzherbert, "Prinny" rented Brighton House, and this "superior farmhouse" he successively enlarged and transformed until, between 1815 and 1824, in genial collaboration with the architect John Nash and with inspired interior designers, he created a uniquely flamboyant setting for the extravagant festivities of his seaside court, a pleasure palace which is the representative monument of the Regency Age.

The Pavilion is approached via two exotic gateways. Its extraordinary silhouette, all bulbous domes, pinnacles, turrets and spikes pricking the skyline, is a free interpretation of "Hindoo" architecture. Within, throughout a series of gorgeously furnished and decorated interiors, Chinoiserie prevails, taken to astonishing lengths in the **Music Room,** lit by lotus-shaped gasoliers, where painted serpents and dragons writhe beneath the gilded scales of a great dome. Equally sumptuous is the great **Banqueting Room,** from whose 45ft - 14m high dome hangs a one-ton crystal lighting device, at its apex a huge winged dragon in silver outlined against enormous *trompe l'œil* plantain leaves.

All this exuberance is set in restored gardens, bounded on the northwest by the former royal stables, a massive building in subdued Oriental style housing municipal library and museum and the Dome concert hall.

★★SEAFRONT

The meeting of Victorian Brighton and the sea is marked by a broad **promenade,** carried on massive brick vaults and with generous ramps and stairs leading to a roadway at beach level. A wealth of light-hearted detail, from splendid decorative ironwork to jaunty little kiosks and shelters, sets the holiday mood, and is extended into the sea on the **West Pier** of 1866, now sadly derelict, and the later **Palace Pier,** a raucous place of fun and refreshment. The pioneering electric **Volks Railway** of 1883 runs eastwards along the foot of the rising chalk cliff to the somewhat remote modern **Marina,** claimed with its 2 000 moorings to be the largest in Europe.

Within the continuous wall of seafront building is a succession of architectural set-pieces, designed to enhance the status of early visitors and offer at the very least a glimpse of the waves. Of these, the most distinguished, just in the adjoining borough of Hove, is **Brunswick Square** of 1825-7, with stucco, bow windows, classical details and elegant ironwork; the earliest, Royal Crescent of 1798-1807, in black mathematical tiles, and the grandest, far to the east, the vast expanse of **Lewes Crescent/Sussex Square**, core of Thomas Reid Kemp's ambitiously planned Kemp Town, developed from 1823 onwards. Victorian building, exemplified in the many-storeyed and richly-decorated Grand and Metropole hotels, stresses panache as much as elegance.

ADDITIONAL SIGHTS

★ **The Lanes.** — This maze of animated alleyways in the old town, lined with countless boutiques and antique shops, focuses on **Brighton Square**, an intimate modern piazza.

★ **St Bartholomew's.** — Of Brighton's many Victorian churches this large edifice of 1872-4 is outstanding. The sublime simplicity of patterned brick walls carrying the nave to the awesome height of 135ft - 41m contrasts with rich furnishings (Lady Altar, main altarpiece, giant candlesticks), masterworks of the Arts and Crafts Movement.

Art Gallery and Museum. — In addition to its local history collection, Dutch and English paintings, porcelain and pottery, and its fashion and ethnographical gallery, the intimate interior of this section of the Royal Pavilion's fomer stables also houses a well-presented display of **20C decorative arts**★, ranging from Art Nouveau to post-war Scandinavian design.

EXCURSION

Devil's Dyke. — *5 miles - 8km. Leave Brighton by the Dyke Road to the north-west.*
The sweeping expanses of the South Downs, their steep north-facing scarp followed by the Long Distance Footpath of the **South Downs Way**, offer relief from the congestion of the coast. Magnificent northward **views**★ over the woods and villages of the Sussex Weald can be enjoyed from the prehistoric earthworks overlooking the **Devil's Dyke**, a deep coombe cutting into the hills.

★★ BRISTOL Avon | Pop 413 861

Michelin Map **403** M 29 or Atlas G Britain p 16

Bristol is a trading city. In the 10C it was a settlement at the western limit of Saxon influence, trading with Ireland. Its port flourished and by the Middle Ages Bristol was England's second city. By the 17C its trade had expanded to the Canaries, South and North America, Africa and the West Indies. In the 18-19C new industries developed locally: iron, brass, copper, porcelain, glass, chocolate and tobacco. The Industrial Revolution drew interests north, but as a communications centre, and with high technology and aircraft industries, Bristol regained its importance.

Architecturally, Bristol prospered from Domesday to the 18C, or from the Norman, through Gothic — particularly the Perpendicular — to the Jacobean and Palladian periods. Its medieval churches were mostly spared 19C restoration, while the city benefited from the genius of the visionary engineer **Isambard Kingdom Brunel** (1806-59), designer of the Clifton Suspension Bridge and the steamship *Great Britain* and architect of the impeccably planned, broad-gauge Great Western Railway, which reached its terminus here, **Station Building (BZ)**, in 1841. In 1940-42 the city was heavily bombed and today's centre is mostly the result of post-war rebuilding.

PRINCIPAL SIGHTS

★★ **The Floating Harbour Area (AZ).** — To overcome the problems caused in the port by the exceptional tidal range, an elaborate system of locks was constructed in 1804-9 to maintain a constant water level along the city's extensive quaysides. Modern docks on the estuary of the Severn now enable virtually all commercial shipping to avoid the difficult passage through the Avon Gorge, and the Floating Harbour is enjoying a new life as a splendid leisure and recreation area.

St Augustine's Reach penetrates into the heart of the city. On the west are the shops and the media centre of the **Watershed** and exhibition halls ; on the east a mixture of new office buildings and converted warehouses, including the Arnolfini Arts Centre. On the quayside to the south are two fascinating museums; the **Industrial Museum**★★ **(AZ M²)** which celebrates the city's long and famous history of manufacturing, from pinmaking to Concorde, and the new **Maritime Heritage Centre (AX G)**, telling the story of Bristol shipbuilding since the 18C.

Beyond lies the **SS Great Britain**★ **(AX B)**. Launched in 1843, this first iron-built, propeller-driven Atlantic liner lies in her original dry dock. Her vast carcase, 322ft - 98m long and 51ft - 16m across, is being painstakingly restored. The innovations of Brunel's design and the saga of the great vessel's history are described in the museum.

★★ **St Mary Redcliffe (BZ).** — Queen Elizabeth I called St Mary's "the fairest, goodliest and most famous parish church in England". The church, built in pale Dundry stone and begun in 1280, represents the Perpendicular style at its most perfect. Elaborately carved pinnacles mark the west end, the same foliage being continued among transepts, porches and the angles of the tower. Finialled buttresses between

BRISTOL

the wide pointed windows of the nave and chancel fly up to support the immense clerestory windows. The hexagonal **north porch,** a late 13C jewel set off-centre in its two tiers of decorated gables and with figures of the saints, has an exquisite door carved with three rows of stars, antechamber to the c1180 inner porch containing the shrine of Our Lady. From the massive, richly decorated tower a 19C spire rises 292ft - 89m above the city.

Interior. — Slender shafted pillars sweep up to break into **lierne vaulting,** in which every one of the 1 200 and more intersections is masked by a different boss, all, except those below the tower, gilded in 1740 and well worth studying with binoculars. By the pillars of the **American** or **St John the Baptist Chapel** is a painted wooden statue of Queen Elizabeth I, probably made after her visit in 1574. On the nave side hangs the armour of **Admiral Sir William Penn** (d 1670), whose son founded Pennsylvania. In the south aisle note the Perpendicular octagonal **font** with panelling; the richly coloured arms of Charles II over the porch and the stellate tomb recesses. The **south transept** is almost a chapel to William Canynges (1400-74), mayor and MP for Bristol, a pious businessman who paid for the completion of the church. In one tomb he lies beside his wife, in the other he wears the vestments of the holy order he joined in 1474 after his wife's death. In the Lady Chapel note the elegant 18C brass **candelabra.** In the chancel are brasses to John Jay (d 1480), merchant, and to John Brook (d 1512), servant-at-law to Henry VIII. Note also the fierce eagle **lectern** at the crossing.

★ **Bristol Cathedral (AZ).** — The cathedral is a 14-15C Perpendicular Gothic church with a crenellated and pinnacled crossing tower, tall pointed windows framed by finialled buttresses and pinnacled parapets. The nave and twin west towers were added in 1868-88. It was an Augustinian abbey and already 400 years old when dissolved by Henry VIII in 1539; three years later it was reconstituted as the Cathedral Church.

Interior. — From the crossing, look through the screen and carved, canopied choir stalls (lively 15C **misericords)** at the high altar before the 19C reconstructed reredos, then up at the highly original vault. The sight is unique in English cathedrals, a feat of early 14C construction. The east end is a **hall church** with chancel and aisles rising to an equal 50ft - 15m. Over the choir the ribbed vaulting sweeps up directly from the pillars to form cusp lined kites at the crest.

The **Elder Lady Chapel** (off the north transept) of 1210-20 with vaulting of 1270, is notable for its sobriety, its foliated capitals on slender Purbeck columns and its small carved figures — St Michael and the dragon, a fox and goose, a lizard and monkeys. The **East Lady Chapel,** a 100ft - 30m extension added when the Norman chancel was rebuilt in 1298-1330, is memorable for its riot of medieval colour highlighting stone carved into cusped arches, gabled niches, fleurons, heads and crests. The minute **sacristy** (off the south chancel aisle) is covered by a vault of flying ribs and arches beneath a flat stone roof; the ribs are bossed and the corbels foliated. In the south transept is the **Harrowing of Hell,** a remarkable 1 000 year old Saxon sculpture. The late Norman rib-vaulted **chapter house** and columned vestibule were built 1150-70. The walls have elaborate interlacing, the cross-ribs bold zig-zags.

Lord Mayor's Chapel (AY Z). — St Mark's Chapel, part of the medieval hospital of the Gaunts, was purchased at the Dissolution for £1 000 by the City Corporation. To the right of the narrow north-south nave is the impressive Perpendicular chapel containing 15-17C **tombs.** As well as early Renaissance French glass, note the mayor's hatchments and a fine gilded sword rest, wrought, like the iron gates, by William Edney in 1702.

★★ **Georgian House (AX A).** — No 7 Great George Street was built c1790 for the successful merchant and sugar planter John Pinney. The architect William Paty produced for him a typical late 18C design in Bath stone with a pedimented door and rooms with Adam style decoration, while Pinney himself attended to every detail.

ADDITIONAL SIGHTS

Red Lodge (AY). — The exterior of this c1590 house is much altered, but its glory is the 16C woodwork and stone fireplaces inside, notably in the Great Oak Room.

Corn Street (AY). — The four **brass nails,** on which corn merchants struck deals and paid in cash (hence the expression "cash on the nail"), testify to the importance of this street in Bristol trade. Behind them stands the giant pilastered and pedimented Corn Exchange, built by John Wood the Elder in the mid-18C. To the left of the sober 19C Greek Doric Council House is the richly exuberant Venetian Cinquecento façade of Lloyds Bank, which dates from 1854. Note also the 18C Coffee House.

St Nicholas Church Museum (ABY M³). — A fine Georgian church, gutted in 1941, houses a vast Hogarth triptych, rare plate and vestments. The 14C crypt is a brass-rubbing centre.

King Street (AZ). — This cobbled street contains 18 and 19C warehouses at the harbour end, 17C almshouses and pubs and the **Theatre Royal★★ (T),** which opened in 1766 but was granted a royal licence by George III in 1778 and is the oldest playhouse in the country still in use.

Quakers Friars (BY D). — These 13C buildings were occupied by Dominican, or Black Friars, until the Dissolution and by the Society of Friends from the 17C to the mid-20C. Inside, the Baker's Hall has a splendidly ordered roof of 14C oak beams.

⊘ **John Wesley's New Room** (BY E). — This chapel, built in 1739, with its banistered gallery and statues of John Wesley on horseback and Charles Wesley preaching, is the oldest building specifically built for Methodist worship.

⊘ **Temple Meads: Brunel's Station Building** (BZ). — No visit to Bristol would be complete without paying suitable homage to Brunel at the station he built for the Great Western Railway in 1841 and which now serves as an exhibition centre.

★★ CLIFTON

The elegant suburb of Clifton began to take shape on the heights above the Avon Gorge in the early 1790s, with a mad rush of building abruptly halted by a wave of bankruptcies. When building picked up again in about 1810 a more assured Grecian style was applied, giving birth to distinguished crescents, squares and terraces generously interspersed with greenery. Streets such as The Mall, Caledonia Place, Princess Victoria Street and Royal York Crescent make up the delightful **Clifton Village★** (AX) with terraced houses, small shops and GE Street's 1868 **All Saints Church** (AX) with John Piper windows.

★★ **Clifton Suspension Bridge** (AX). — The bridge, designed by Brunel 1829-31, is arguably the most beautiful of early English suspension bridges. Unfortunately funds ran out and Brunel never saw his 702ft - 214m long bridge completed; he died five years too soon, in 1859. Close to the suspension bridge on the cliff stands the 1729 Observatory Tower at the top of which is an 18C ''camera obscura'', affording views for miles around.

★★ **Cathedral of SS Peter and Paul** (AX F). — Consecrated in 1973, the Roman Cathol-
⊘ ic cathedral is an impressive hexagonal edifice in white concrete, pink granite, black fibreglass, lead and glass. Note the windows and the Stations of the Cross carved in stone.

★★ **Bristol Zoological Gardens** (AX). — Opened in 1836, the zoo still attracts visi-
⊘ tors eager to see the reptiles, apes, elephants, pink flamingoes, rare okapi and Sumatran tigers.

EXCURSION

★ **Clevedon Court.** — *11 miles - 16km west on the A370* (AX), *B3128 and B3130.*
⊘ This well preserved early 14C house with *c*1575 alterations, displays evidence of every period in its interior furnishings. The 14C Great Hall has Tudor windows and fireplaces; the remarkable Hanging Chapel, with its unusual reticulated window tracery, contains 17C prayer desks and 15 and 16C Biblical carvings. The contents of the 14C State Bedroom reflect ten generations of family taste, while the Justice Room displays local Nailsea glass made between 1788 and 1873.

★ BURY ST EDMUNDS Suffolk   Pop 30 563

Michelin Map ▨404 W 27 or Atlas G Britain p 22 .

''The nicest town in the world'' according to William Cobbett, Bury St Edmunds boasts the ruins of one of the richest abbeys in Christendom, a cathedral built by John Wastell (architect of King's College Chapel, Cambridge) and an 11C grid-shaped town centre, the earliest example of town planning since the Romans.

★★ ABBEY AND CATHEDRAL *time: 1 hour*

⊘ **St Edmundsbury Abbey.** — Founded in 633 and later renamed in honour of the Saxon king and martyr Edmund (d 870), rebuilt by Benedictine monks in the 11C, only two of its monumental crossing towers still stand upright (one bearing a plaque to Archbishop Langton and the 20 barons who forced on King John the **Magna Carta**). Remnants of nave, chancel and transepts, together with the **Great Gate**, give some idea of its vastness (505ft - 154m long with 12 bays).
The **Norman Tower's** richly decorated gateway frames Elizabeth Frink's bronze of St Edmund and the cathedral precinct houses built into the abbey's west end.

⊘ **Cathedral of St James.** — Bury's parish church from 1530 until it was granted cathedral status in 1914. A perfect late Perpendicular composition of nine bays leads the eye to Stephen Dykes Bower's 1960s chancel and transepts. Note the 16C Flemish stained glass window of Susanna.

⊘ **St Mary's Church.** — The 1430 church is famous for its spectacular **nave roof** (alternating arched braces and hammerbeams held up by angels, the spandrels carved with dragons, unicorns, fish and birds), for the wagon roof of the chancel with its many carved bosses and for the grave of Mary Tudor (1496-1533), sister of Henry VIII.

EXCURSIONS

★ **Ickworth House.** — *A143 southwest for 3 miles - 5km.*
⊘ A rotunda dominated by ribboned friezes based on Flaxman's Homer, with two wings curving inward and set in one of the first semi-formal Italianate gardens in England, Ickworth was built between 1795 and 1829 by the fabulously rich Frederick Hervey, 4th Earl of Bristol, Bishop of Derry, Irish nationalist and eccentric traveller after whom the Hotel Bristols throughout Europe are named.

Interior. — The four scagliola columns in the **Hall's** entrance frame Flaxman's *Fury of Athamas*. In the **Library** is Hogarth's *Holland House Group* and Gravelot's conversation piece of Augustus Hervey, his command *Princesa* and members of the family. In the **Dining Room** are works by Lawrence, Reynolds and Gainsborough and in the **Smoking Room,** Titian's *Portrait of a Man* and Velazquez's *Infante Balthaser Carlos.* In the West Corridor is an extensive collection of Georgian silver. The beautifully painted neo-classical walls of the Pompeian Room are by J D Crace, who painted the library at Longleat *(qv)* and the National Gallery *(qv)* staircase.

National Horse Racing Museum, Newmarket. — *12 miles - 19km west on the A45.* Devoted to the only Sport of Kings that embraces all English social classes, the museum tells the story of racing from 2 000 BC. Exhibits include fine paintings by Stubbs and Herring, bronzes, the skeleton of Eclipse, video clips of Persimmon, Arkle and Red Rum.

★ **Lavenham.** — Pop 1 658. *11 miles - 18 km southeast by the A134 and A1141.* A medieval wool town crowded with timber-framed houses, its showpieces are the late 15C **Church of SS Peter and Paul★** , one of the great ''wool'' churches (with a noble tower and porch and enchanting misericords) and the *c*1520 **Guildhall** facing the Market Place, the interior a museum depicting the East Anglian wool trade.

★★★ CAERNARFON Gwynedd   Pop 9 271

Michelin Map 403 H 24 or Atlas G Britain p 32

Caernarfon, bristling with towers and turrets, stands guard over the Menai Strait and its wall encircled town. The town's site has been appreciated from earliest times: the Romans built their fort of Segontium nearby, the Normans chose the castle's present site for their stronghold, to be followed by the stone castle of the Welsh princes and finally Edward's indomitable structure, designed as a seat of power. Today the town is a centre for visitors to Snowdonia and for yachtsmen.

CASTLES OF EDWARD I IN WALES

Welsh Wars of Independence. — In the 13C two great Welsh princes, Llywelyn the Great (1173-1240) and his grandson, Llywelyn ap Gruffydd (d1282) strove to create a united principality and secure firm control. Their achievement was recognised by Henry III in the Treaty of Montgomery, 1267. It was his son, the determined Edward I who demolished the new found unity with his campaigns of 1277-8 and 1282-3. Following the death in battle of Llywelyn ap Gruffydd in December 1282, Edward set out on his programme of military re-settlement.

Edward's castle building. — In the twenty years following 1276, seventeen castles were built or re-fortified by Edward and his Marcher lords (Denbigh, Ruthin, Hawarden and Holt), to consolidate English power in North Wales.
The major castles were the work of the greatest military architect of the day, **Master James of St George,** brought by Edward from Savoy. Most were built to be supplied from the sea, for travel by land in Snowdonia was impossible for Edward's forces. Round towers, less vulnerable to undermining, replaced square; concentric defences, the inner overlooking outer, made their appearance; planned walled towns, after the manner of the ''bastides'' of southern France, housed the settlers who would help hold the territories.

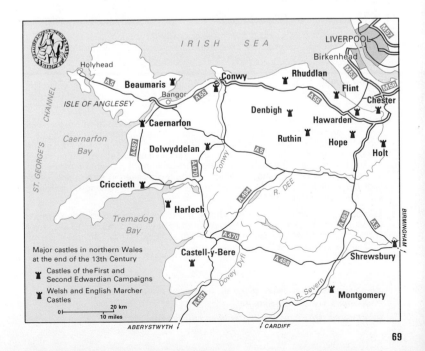

Major castles in northern Wales at the end of the 13th Century

✠ Castles of the First and Second Edwardian Campaigns

✠ Welsh and English Marcher Castles

The four best-preserved castles — **Conwy** *(qv)*, **Caernarfon** *(see below)*, **Harlech** *(qv)* and **Beaumaris** *(qv)* are among the most remarkable group of medieval monuments to be seen in Europe. Documents detailing the conscription of labour from all across England, the costs of timber, stone, transport, a wall, a turret, even a latrine, are still to be read, bringing alive the people who built and lived in these massive stone fortifications. The garrisons were small — only some thirty men-at-arms, plus a few cavalry and crossbowmen would hold a castle for the king. A journey starting at Chester, visiting the castles of **Flint, Rhuddlan, Conwy, Beaumaris, Caernarfon,** to **Harlech** and on to **Aberystwyth,** will throw much light on the turbulent period in which they were built and on the people who built them.

★★★ **Caernarfon Castle.** — *Time: 1 hour excluding the regimental museum.*
Building work started in 1283 under Master James of St George (*c*1235-1308), who built for his royal patron a castle with walls decorated with bands of coloured stone and polygonal towers like those of Constantinople. Grandiose in design, it was to serve as the seat of English government in the principality.
We owe the appearance of the castle today to the vision of the Constable in the 1840s, **Sir Llewelyn Turner** (1823-1903), who cleared, restored, re-roofed and renewed, in the teeth of local opposition.
Massive curtain walls link the towers to form a figure of eight with the lower bailey to the right and upper to the left. The great twin-towered gatehouse, **King's Gate,** was defended by five doors and six portcullises.
The **Eagle Tower,** crowned by triple turrets, each, as in Constantinople and *The Mabinogion,* crested with an eagle, had accommodation on a grand scale. Currently it houses the exhibition: *"A Prospect of Caernarfon",* recreating the **Investiture of Charles, Prince of Wales,** in July 1969. It was here that the first English Prince of Wales was born in April 1284, Edward of Caernarfon, later Edward II. The **Queen's Tower** houses the Regimental Museum of the Royal Welch Fusiliers. The Great Hall once stood between this and the Chamberlain Tower.
In **Castle Square,** opposite the balcony from which Charles, Prince of Wales, greeted his subjects, is the statue of **David Lloyd George** (1863-1945), Liberal MP for Caernarfon for 55 years and Prime Minister 1916-22.

Caernarfon Castle

ADDITIONAL SIGHTS

Town walls. — The 800yd - 734m circuit of walls and towers encircling the medieval town was built as a single operation at the same time as the castle. The walls are punctuated at regular intervals by eight towers and two twin-towered gates.

Segontium Roman Fort. — *Southeast outskirts of Caernarfon on the A487*
The Roman auxiliary fort of Segontium, overlooking Caernarfon town, is one of the most famous in Britain. The remains of Roman buildings in a large area of the fort are on view to the public. An exhibition in the site **museum** tells of the conquest and occupation of Wales by the Roman army, the military organisation of the day, the garrisons of Segontium and the history of the fort as seen in its remains; secondly, it displays selected finds excavated on the site which throw light upon daily life in this remote Roman outpost.

Llanbeblig Church. — Situated outside the town, near to Segontium, this is the parish church of Caernarfon. Peblig, reputed to have been the son of Magnus Maximus, is said to have returned to introduce Christianity. Mainly 14C, there is a striking 16C alabaster tomb in the Vaynol chapel.

Admission charges, when given at the end of the guide, are for adults.
Reductions are often available
for children, OAPs, students, families and groups.

Michelin Map **401** I,J,K 11 and 12 or Atlas G Britain pp 67 and 68

This granitic range between the Spey Valley and Braemar has some of Britain's wildest and most dramatic mountain scenery. Lying mainly above 3 000ft - about 900m, with Ben Macdui (4 296ft-1 309m) as its highest point, the region is named for Cairn Gorm (4 084ft-1 245m). Glacial erosion has worn the summits down to form flat plateaux and at the same time glaciers have gouged out the trough of Loch Avon and the Dee valley.

Climbing and hill walking. — The fact that no motorable roads cross these mountain fastnesses make them all the more attractive to the dedicated walker and mountaineer. The severe climate of the windswept summits allows only an Arctic-Alpine flora to flourish, and they are the home of the ptarmigan, snow bunting and dotterel. The **Cairngorm National Nature Reserve** was founded in 1954 to protect the scientific as well as the scenic value of these 64 000 acres - 26 000ha.

It is this very remoteness and the fickleness of the weather which makes the Cairngorms a treacherous place to all but the well-equipped and experienced, be they true mountaineers or just walkers.

★★★ **Panorama from Cairn Gorm.** — The chairlift used by skiers in the winter provides
⊘ the less than energetic summer visitor with an easy way of appreciating something of the magic and beauty of this mountainous region. The already good view from the car park unfolds still further at the second stage. From the terminal near the Ptarmigan Restaurant at 3 600ft - about 1 100m, there is an extensive view★★★ westwards down the Spey Valley where it widens into a basin, with Loch Morlich below and the ski centre of Aviemore beyond. A further climb of 500ft - 150m, this time on foot, to the summit of Cairn Gorm, will give an all round panorama which amply repays the minimal effort required.

★ **Aviemore.** — Pop 1 510. The building in the 1960s of the Aviemore Centre, a complex of shops, hotels and entertainment facilities with an ''après-ski'' flavour, transformed the village into Britain's first winter sports resort. There are ice-rinks
⊘ for skating and curling, a dry ski slope and a swimming pool. The **Strathspey Railway** operates a steam service on the five miles of track between Aviemore and Boat of Garten.

SPEYSIDE from Kingussie to Spey Bay
50 miles - 80km — allow a day

The itinerary follows Speyside taking in the main attractions and several distilleries along the way.

⊘ **Highland Folk Museum.** — Kingussie. Exhibits relate to the everyday life of the Highlanders, clothes - in particular tartans and the kilt - musical instruments, farm implements and relics of old crafts. There is a **black house** typical of the Western Isles, and a **clack mill**. Kingussie is also a pony-trekking centre, set in the wooded countryside of Strathspey.

Continue on the A86 and then the A9.

★ **Highland Wildlife Park.** — Opened in 1972 to show the wildlife that has existed in Bri-
⊘ tain from the Ice Ages to the present day.

Continue north and just before Aviemore take the B970 to the right.

Loch Garten. — The RSPB observation point has a hide from which visitors may watch many species of birds, including the rare osprey; this species has returned to nest after an absence of 40 years.

The B970 and the A95 lead to Grantown-on-Spey.

Grantown-on-Spey. — Pop 1 800. Planned as a residential resort in 1776, Grantown's 18C elegance has persisted to the present day. It is a major centre for anglers seeking the Spey salmon and is considerably involved with the winter sports industry.

Return to the A95 to follow Strathspey northwards; at Bridge of Avon turn right onto the B9008.

⊘ **Glenlivet.** — Fine malt whisky has been distilled here since 1824 and the methods used in today's modern distillery have not changed much since the days of clandestine distilling by the crofters.

From here there are two possible routes to Dufftown. Either take the B9009 down Glen Rinnes, or return to the A95 and turn right along Strathspey, then right again onto the A941 at Craigellachie. Either way it is possible to visit some of the distilleries on the Malt Whisky Trail. At Craigellachie, take the A941 to Dufftown.

Dufftown. — Pop 1 613. Capital of the malt whisky industry, the trim town of Dufftown is also interesting for Mortlach Church, one of the earliest places of Christian wor-
⊘ ship, and a ruined courtyard castle, Balvenie Castle. **Glenfiddich Distillery** provides an excellent introduction to the art of whisky distilling.

The A941 takes you back to Craigellachie and then on to Rothes where you take the B9015 right to Mosstodloch. Turn right onto the A96.

⊘ At the roadside is **Baxters**, a family firm producing quality foods. After an introductory film guided tours of the premises are available.

Once over the River Spey turn left to take the B9104 leading to the Spey estuary and Spey Bay.

⊘ **Tugnet Ice House.** — Interesting exhibition on the salmon fisheries of the Spey. This is the northern end of the Speyside Way, which winds northwards from the Cairngorms *(see Michelin map* **401***).*

Michelin Map 404 U 27 or Atlas G Britain p 29

England's second oldest university, Cambridge established its academic reputation in the early 13C when scholars from Paris and Oxford fled there. **Peterhouse** was founded in 1284 and seven more colleges had been built by 1352, all with their characteristic four-sided monastic court.

The burgeoning academic community was recognised by a Papal Bull in 1318. As with Peterhouse, other colleges were founded to provide lodgings. Today the thirty-one colleges are totally independent self-governing bodies while the University undertakes all public teaching and confers the degrees.

King's College Chapel, Cambridge

ST JOHN'S TO QUEENS' *time: allow a day*

Walk down St John's Street, Trinity Street, King's Parade, Trumpington Street.

★★★ **St John's College** (Y). — A walk through St John's (founded 1511) is a walk through architectural history. **First**, **Second** and **Third Courts** are predominantly Tudor, Ruskin calling the Second the most perfect in Cambridge. Behind Third Court is the 18C Kitchen Bridge, with its **view** of Hutchinson's exquisite **Bridge of Sighs**. That in turn prepares you for his neo-Gothic **New Court**, so obsessively symmetrical that he once reprimanded a student for leaning out of the window. Beyond is Powell and Moya's 20C **Cripps Building** and the 13C **School of Pythagoras**.

★★ **Trinity College** (Y). — Founded 1546 by Henry VIII, the largest Cambridge college, its oldest buildings surround the **Great Court**; the 1432 **King Edward's Tower**, the 1533 **gatehouse** and the deliberately conservative **chapel**, built by Queen Mary and aspiring to a Perpendicular world where the Renaissance never happened. In the 1612 cloistered **Neville's Court** stands Robert Grumbold's Tribune and **Wren's Library**, the statues of Divinity, Law, Physic and Mathematics by Gabriel Cibber, looking down from the balustrade. The masonry is by Grumbold, who learnt his trade from Wren, the wood carvings by Grinling Gibbons and the Byron statue by Thorwaldsen.

CAMBRIDGE

⊘**Gonville and Caius College** (Y A). — Founded 1348 by Edmund Gonville and in 1557 by John Caius (pronounced "keys"), Renaissance scholar and physician to Edward VI and Queen Mary. Its charm is its gates, conceived by Caius to symbolise the scholar's progress. He enters the college through the **Gate of Humility** (now relocated in the Master's Garden) into the **Tree Court**; progresses through the **Gate of Virtue** into **Caius Court**, before finally passing through the **Gate of Honour** to receive his degree at what is today the Senate House.

⊘**Trinity Hall** (Y B). — *To the rear of Gonville and Caius, down Senate House Passage.* Founded 1350, behind the 18C ashlar of **Principal Court** are three 1350 ranges (best viewed from North Court) and beyond the delightful Elizabethan **Library** is the garden Henry James called "the prettiest corner of the world".

★**Clare College** (Y). — *Adjacent to Trinity Hall.* Founded 1326 as University Hall ⊘ and again in 1338 as Clare Hall. The 17C ranges are the work of **Robert Grumbold** and his father **Thomas** and are among the most serene in Cambridge. **Clare Bridge** was built by Thomas Grumbold, before the 17C ranges. Note the missing segment of one of the stone balls on the bridge's parapet. He had vowed never to complete the bridge unless he was paid. He never was.

⊘**Old Schools, Squire Law Library, Senate House.** — These are the oldest of the university's central buildings. **Old Schools** was the School of Law and Divinity before assuming its Palladian frontage; **Squire Law Library** (Y D) is the 19C classicism by CR Cockerell and **Senate House** (Y E) is an 18C blend of Roman Wren and new Palladianism by James Gibbs.

Great St Mary (Y). — The rebuilding of the university church began in 1478 in late Perpendicular style and did not finish until 1608 when **Robert Grumbold's** grandfather, also Robert, built the **tower** that affords such a fine **view**.

★★ **King's College** (YZ). — Founded 1441 and set back behind **William Wilkins'** Gothic revival **screen** and **gatehouse,** King's is dominated by Gibb's classical **Fellows Building** and the soaring late Perpendicular buttresses of King's College Chapel.

★★★ **King's College Chapel.** — Built between 1446 and 1515 mainly by three Kings (Henry VI, Henry VII and Henry VIII), King's College Chapel is the final and most glorious flowering of Perpendicular. Turner painted its exterior, Wordsworth wrote three sonnets about it, and Wren, marvelling at the largest single span vaulted roof in existence, offered to make one himself, if only someone would tell him where to lay the first stone.

Exterior. — Its dimensions (289ft - 88m long, 94ft - 88m high, 40ft - 12m across) suggest a cathedral choir rather than a college chapel, the eighteen side chapels and door emphasising the height of the twenty-two buttresses taking the weight of the roof.

Interior. — The 12-bay nave rises upwards on buttresses so slender they become mere frames to the twenty-five 16C stained-glass windows illustrating episodes from the Old Testament. The nearly two thousand tons of vaults *(photograph p 72)*, Wordsworth's "branching roofs", appear weightless above. Note the splendid early Renaissance **screen** and **stalls** by foreign craftsmen and **Rubens'** *Adoration of the Magi.*

⊘ **Corpus Christi College** (Z F). — *Enter Old Court via Bene't Street, return via New Court.* Founded in 1352 **Old Court** still retains its 1352-77 monastery style ranges of stone rubble with clunch dressings. The Saxon **St Bene't's Church** adjoining Old Court is the oldest in Cambridge. **New Court** is by William Wilkins. It was his favourite neo-Gothic building and he is buried in the chapel.

⊘ **St Catharine's College** (Z G). — Founded 1473. The three Restoration ranges were built by Robert Grumbold, the **chapel** clearly influenced by his apprenticeship under Wren.

★ **Queens' College** (Z). — *Behind St Catharine's, entry via Silver Street and Queens' Lane.*
Founded 1446 and again in 1465 in memory of two queens, Margaret of Anjou and Elizabeth Woodville, **Old Court** is another unchanged example of a medieval college court, while **Cloister Court,** with its half-timbered **President's Lodge** and **Gallery** were the first cloistered courts in Cambridge. In **Erasmus' Tower** to the south of Cloister Court Erasmus complained about the "windy" beer.

St Botolph's Church (Z). — Enchanting Perpendicular with nave built 1300-50 and tower added *c*1400. Inside is a memorial to **Robert Grumbold,** master-builder of Cambridge.

MUSEUMS

★★ **Fitzwilliam Museum** (Z). — *Trumpington Street.*
Neo-classical and monumental, on the edge of Victorian baroque, the University's renowned museum was designed by George Basevi and opened to the public in 1843.
Among the profuse and well-arranged collections of Oriental, Near Eastern, Classical and medieval antiquities are many superb objects; Assyrian reliefs, the massive granite tomb lid of Rameses III, Greek vases in abundance, a Roman marble sarcophagus, a Chinese buffalo in jade and fine examples of medieval carving, metal and enamel work. The porcelain and pottery is outstanding.
But it is the paintings which command the greatest attention. There are a number of Old Masters of exceptional quality; Italian works include pictures by Simone Martini and Domenico Veneziano, Titian, Veronese and Palma Vecchio. Among the numerous Dutch and Flemish paintings are landscapes and portraits by Cuyp, Van Ruisdael and Hobbema.
The English School is strongly represented. A highly stylised portrait of 1603 of the 3rd Countess of Southampton contrasts with a flamboyant portrait by Van Dyck of the 4th Countess, *La belle et vertueuse Huguenote.* These show the extraordinary developments in court portraiture within one generation. There is a good selection of 18C works by Gainsborough, Reynolds, Stubbs and Hogarth, including the last-named's wry evocation of courtship, *Before* and *After.* Paintings by Constable range from tiny delicate studies of atmospheric effects to one of his finest landscapes of Hampstead Heath. From the later 19C are the melodramatic *On the Brink* by Arthur Elmore and Alma Tadema's *94° in the Shade.*
The moderns include an impressive range of works by Sickert and Augustus John, Wilson Steer's skinny girls paddling at Walberswick and a quizzical self-portrait by Stanley Spencer. These works are more than balanced by the exceptional French collection; among the array of works by Bonnard, Vuillard, Pissarro, Matisse and other major artists are the exhilarating *Coup de Vent* and *Place Clichy* by Renoir and several Monet landscapes.

★ **Kettle's Yard** (Y M[1]). — In complete contrast to the academic atmosphere of the Fitzwilliam is Kettle's Yard, "a living place where works of art can be enjoyed inherent in the domestic setting...", according to its creator Jim Ede. The works, littered about the house amid books you can read, furniture you can sit on, are by Ben Nicholson, Henry Moore, Barbara Hepworth, Eric Gill, Gaudier-Brzeska and Joan Miro, most of whom were friends of Ede.

ADDITIONAL SIGHTS

⊘ **Magdalene College** (Y). — Founded 1542 by Lord Audley of Audley End *(qv)* on the site of a Benedictine college. The **First Court** is essentially 15C except for the 16C **gatehouse** and hall. Beyond in the late 16C and early 17C **Second Court** is the **Pepys Building** which contains Samuel Pepys' own library left by him to the college in 1703 and which includes the cipher manuscript of his Diary.

⊘ **Jesus College** (Y). — Founded 1496, Jesus was a former Benedictine Nunnery, growing up around **Cloister Court** and the 12C Priory Chapel: **First Court** with its robust early Tudor **gatehouse** was added in the 16C, **Second Court** and **Chapel Court** in the 19C, **North Court** in the 20C.

⊘ **Emmanuel College** (Z). — Founded 1584 by Sir Walter Mildmay. "I have set an acorn, which when it becomes an oak, God alone knows what will be the fruit thereof" he told Queen Elizabeth. The only surviving buildings of the Dominican, or Black Friars, priory are the **Hall** and **Old library** (with Tudor façades) forming the south and east ranges of **New Court**. The **Chapel** was built by Wren (1668-74) in a classical style touching on baroque and has a memorial to John Harvard, founder of Harvard College in the 17C.

⊘ **Pembroke College Chapel** (Z). — Wren's first completed building and the first classical building in Cambridge, the commission was a gift from his uncle, Matthew Wren, Bishop of Ely. The ceiling is by Henry Doogood who worked on the ceilings of thirty Wren churches.

Round Church (Y). — Holy Sepulchre Church is one of only five circular Norman Churches in the country.

★★ **The Backs** (YZ). — The **Backs** (of the colleges) along the River Cam are as fine as the fronts; best viewed from a punt which can be hired by Silver Street Bridge, these are a wonderful combination of buildings and lawns in a riverside setting.

OXBRIDGE: halls and colleges

Prior to the existence of universities, teaching was confined to ecclesiastical schools. The scholars usually lodged with the townspeople or lived in hostels known as Halls and by the early 15C all undergraduates had to belong to a hall. The foundation of Colleges came later and these were exclusively reserved for graduates. As with other medieval corporate bodies the members, in this case graduates, enjoyed separate living quarters but a common hall and chapel. William Wykeham's New College, founded in 1379 was the first to accommodate both undergraduates and graduates.

The charm of many of today's colleges derives from the self-contained collegiate plan of inter-communicating courts, a direct heritage of their medieval origins.

The Colleges are working academic institutions and are closed to the public during the examination period (between early April and late June but varies from college to college). Notices to this effect are usually displayed at the porter's lodge. For guided tours apply to the tourist information centres in Oxford and Cambridge.

EXCURSION

★★ **Audley End.** — *13 miles - 21km south on Trumpington Road, the A1309, the A1301*
⊘ *and then the B1383.*
A Benedictine monastery here was granted to Sir Thomas Audley. The house he built was replaced in 1605-14 by another when the estate came into the possession of Thomas Howard, Earl of Suffolk and Lord High Treasurer. It was one of the greatest Jacobean houses in England and cost £200 000. "Too large for a king, but might do for a Lord Treasurer" said James I who unintentionally helped to finance it and later imprisoned the Earl for embezzlement. Briefly owned by Charles II it was partially demolished in 1721 when the interior was redesigned by **Robert Adam** and the grounds by **Capability Brown**. The present house, vast enough, is but a shadow of its former glory.

Interior. — The heart of the house is the **Great Hall,** its two screens, the splendid Jacobean oak screen and Vanbrugh's *c*1721 stone screen confronting each other. In total contrast are the Adamesque **Great Drawing Room** (to make such a small room "great", Adam designed the furniture deliberately small, giving the room the impression of a doll's house) and the **Little Drawing Room** (domestic classicism with lovingly detailed ceiling and wall panels by Biagio Rebecca and unforgettably funny cherubs painted on the inner door panels by Cipriani). Upstairs the outstanding features of the **State Rooms** are the ceilings and the 200-year-old four-poster bed covered in embroidered hangings in the **State Bedroom,** built for a visit by George III which never took place.

The ecclesiastical capital of England, rich in medieval atmosphere, is dominated by its renowned cathedral. Long open to influences from the Continent, the city lies on Watling Street, the great Roman thoroughfare linking London with the port of Dover. It also forms the terminus of the **Pilgrims' Way**, a trackway of prehistoric origin used by some of the worshippers at the shrine of St Thomas, England's best-known martyr. Today it is the thriving centre of the eastern part of Kent, seat of a new university and exerts as strong a pull on the modern tourist as once on the medieval pilgrim.

HISTORICAL NOTES

Although certain Neolithic and Bronze Age finds indicate the earliest of settlements, Canterbury's history really begins with Emperor Claudius' invasion of AD 43 and the foundation of the walled town of Durovernum. After the Roman withdrawal early in the 5C, the city was settled by Jutish invaders and renamed Cantwaraby-rig - ''stronghold of the Men of Kent''. In AD 597 it received **St Augustine**, sent by Rome to convert the pagan population to Christianity. The impact of his mission was such that the city became the centre of the English Church and Augustine himself was consecrated as first archbishop.

The original cathedral was destroyed in a fire in 1067 and replaced by a large-scale building by the first Norman Archbishop, Lanfranc. In 1170 a later Archbishop, Becket, was bloodily assassinated in the cathedral's north transept by four of Henry II's knights who had taken all too literally their ruler's desire to be rid of ''this turbulent priest''. Thomas was canonised two years later and his shrine immediately attracted countless pilgrims, many of whose stories are recounted in **Chaucer's** *Canterbury Tales*.

The cathedral's monastery was the largest in the country and by the 13C Grey and Black Friars were established as well. This thriving monastic life came to an end at the Dissolution; the cathedral's treasures were appropriated by Henry VIII, the saint's shrine destroyed, the pilgrimages ended.

The post-Reformation period saw the arrival of French Huguenot refugees at the invitation of Elizabeth I. Skilled craftsmen, they contributed to Canterbury's prosperity. The city continued to flourish, in spite of the depredations of Puritans in the Civil War. Greater damage was suffered in the ''Baedeker'' raids of 1942, when Luftwaffe bombs reduced part of the historic centre to rubble; providentially, the cathedral remained untouched and the rebuilding of the devastated area is now complete.

★★★CANTERBURY CATHEDRAL (B) *time: 1 hour*

Lanfranc's work in rebuilding the cathedral, destroyed in the conflagration of 1067, proceeded rapidly and was virtually complete after seven years. An equally vigorous Archbishop, **Anselm**, nevertheless replaced his predecessor's choir by a vastly more ambitious structure, exceeding the nave in length. Dedicated in 1130, it too was gutted by fire in 1174, four years after Becket's murder, though crypt and nave were spared. Now that the cathedral had become the most important centre of pilgrimage in Northern Europe, the opportunity was seized to rebuild in a manner worthy of the martyr; an early Gothic style was employed, of great subsequent influence in both the choir and its extension eastwards to Trinity Chapel and Corona.

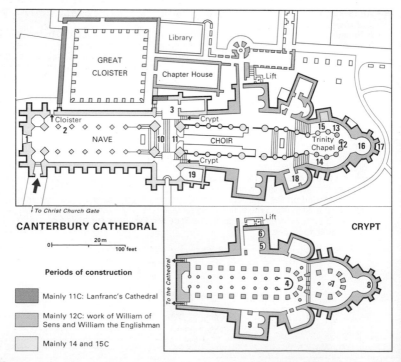

CANTERBURY CATHEDRAL

CRYPT

Periods of construction

Mainly 11C: Lanfranc's Cathedral

Mainly 12C: work of William of Sens and William the Englishman

Mainly 14 and 15C

The nave and cloisters were rebuilt in Perpendicular style in the 14C, while the 15C saw the completion of the transepts and reconstruction of the towers. **Bell Harry Tower**, crowning the entire building, was completed at the end of the 15C. Since then, apart from the damage inflicted by Puritans to glass, sculpture and furnishings, the great edifice has undergone little notable change. The northwest tower was demolished in 1832 and replaced by a copy of the southwest tower.

Built between 1504 and 1521 **Christ Church Gate★ (A)** is the main entrance to the cathedral precincts. The imposing structure, decorated with coats of arms believed to commemorate the son of Henry VII, Prince Arthur, was restored in the 1930s.

Enter through the southwest porch and turn right into the nave.

Constructed between 1391 and 1404, the nave is the work of the royal architect, Henry Yevele. The slender shafts of columns rising uninterruptedly into the high vault, the lofty aisles and the abundant light create a majestic calm. The great west window (**1**) contains 12C glass, including a fine representation of Adam delving. Towards the north door stands the 17C classical marble **font** (**2**) decorated with figures of the Four Evangelists and the Twelve Apostles.

Leave the main building to visit the Great Cloister.

The **Great Cloister** walks were rebuilt in Perpendicular style around 1400. More than 800 coats of arms adorn the elaborate vaulting. Off the eastern walk is the **Chapter House** with its high, intricately ribbed oak roof and Perpendicular windows with glass depicting characters in the cathedral's history.

Return to the main building then turn left into the northwest transept.

Here is the site of **Becket's martyrdom** (**3**), strikingly commemorated by the restored ''Altar of the Sword's Point'' and a modern cruciform sculpture. Pope John-Paul II and Archbishop Runcie prayed together on this spot on 29 May 1982.

Descend a short flight of steps into the Crypt.

The mysterious vaults of the 12C crypt with its nave, aisles and transepts contain rich items from the cathedral treasury, the exquisitely delicate screens of the **Chapel of Our Lady Undercroft** (**4**) and a series of vigorously carved capitals, superb examples of the Romanesque sculptor's imagination and skill. The transept houses the altars of St Nicholas (**5**) and St Mary Magdalene (**6**), whereas at the eastern end of the crypt is the post-1174 extension with massive columns and pointed vaults heralding the new Gothic style. It was here that the body of St Thomas Becket was entombed (**7**) until 1220. Beyond is the admirable Jesus Chapel (**8**). The southern side was the Black Prince's Chantry (**9**), subsequently the Huguenots' church, and is still used for services in French today.

Leave the crypt on the south side and turn right into the crossing.

Far above is the beautiful lace-like **fan vaulting** underneath the central Bell Harry Tower (**10**); the bosses are decorated with the coats of arms of those responsible for the tower's construction.

Go into the choir through the iron gates.

The **screen** (**11**) with its figures of six kings is mid-15C. From here the full length of the early Gothic construction replacing Anselm's choir is visible, leading up to **Trinity Chapel**, the High Altar and the 13C marble **St Augustine's Chair** (**12**) which has served throughout the ages to enthrone the Archbishop, Primate of All England.

The new work was entrusted to a French architect, **William of Sens.** Crippled by a fall from the scaffolding he was replaced by another William, ''the Englishman'', who completed the choir and engineered the building of the eastern crypt and Trinity Chapel.

The long vistas back to the nave at its much lower level from either of the irregularly aligned choir aisles reveal the evolution of Gothic style over three centuries; the cool Perpendicular of the nave contrasts with the work of the two Williams, with its lavish use of polished Purbeck marble, particularly for shafts and columns, dark against the pale limestone.

There is much wonderful **medieval glass**; that in the Trinity Chapel depicts the miracles (**13**) wrought by

Black Prince's effigy

St Thomas. His shrine, placed here in 1220, has gone, though the fine Roman mosaic pavement in front of it remains. Among the remarkable tombs is that of the **Black Prince** (**14**). Above the famous effigy hang replicas of his helm, crest, shield, gauntlets and sword, the originals normally being displayed nearby. To the north is the sumptuous alabaster **tomb of Henry IV** (**15**) buried in 1413 with Queen Joan of Navarre. He is the only English king to be buried in the cathedral.

Beyond the Trinity Chapel the building culminates in the **Corona (16)**, a circular chapel so called because it is said to have once housed the top of St Thomas' skull. The early 13C **Redemption window (17)** behind the altar is of particular interest; it portrays scenes of the Crucifixion, Entombment, Resurrection and Ascension of Christ. Off the southwest corner of the Trinity Chapel is the mostly Norman **Chapel of St Anselm (18)**; high up in its apse is that rarity in England, a fine 12C wall painting, its subject St Paul.

Return to the south transept, where the main exit is located.

Off the transept is the **Chapel of St Michael (19)**, filled with a wealth of Renaissance and baroque memorials.

ADDITIONAL SIGHTS

Approach the city centre from the northwest along London Road.

⊙ **St Dunstan's Church** (A). — Founded towards the end of the 11C by Lanfranc, the church was used by Henry II in 1174 when he changed into penitential garments for his involvement in the murder of St Thomas Becket. When Sir Thomas More, Lord Chancellor of England, was beheaded in 1535 his daughter Margaret, wife of William Roper, recovered her father's head, which now rests in the Roper family vault within the church.

Walk down St Dunstan's Street to the town centre.

★ **West Gate** (A). — This is the last of the gatehouses which once formed part of ⊙ the city walls and later served as a prison. A museum with an interesting arms collection has now been installed over the gate proper.

From the battlements there is a fine panoramic view of the city centre, dominated by the cathedral.

Continue along St Peter's Street towards the centre.

★ **Canterbury Weavers** (A B). — This group of picturesque Tudor houses overlooking the River Stour takes its name from the refugee Huguenot weavers who settled in the area.

★ **Hospital of St Thomas the Martyr, Eastbridge** (A D). — Founded 1180 by Ed- ⊙ ward Fitzoldbold, a wealthy citizen of Canterbury, the original buildings served as accommodation for pilgrims to the shrine of St Thomas. After constant use during the 14C and 15C the hospital shared the fate of the monasteries at the Dissolution. By the late 16C, Archbishop John Whitgift had secured the future of the property by an Act of Parliament ordering that the hospital provide ten homes for poor people as well as a boys' school. Today the buildings still offer accommodation for the elderly.

The entrance hall was built towards the end of the 11C. Immediately on the left is the 14C chantry chapel, still in use today for regular worship. Facing the entrance doorway is the 12C undercroft, originally a pilgrims' dormitory. Upstairs is the late 12C refectory. The north wall boasts a painting of Christ among the Four Evangelists, discovered in 1879. The chapel, directly above the entrance hall, dates from the 12C and is remarkable for its fine timber roof.

Turn right into Stour Street and pass through a right-hand gate.

⊙ **Franciscan Gardens and Greyfriars Monastery** (A). — A charming 13C home built over the River Stour, the building originally housed the Franciscan Grey Friars. The upstairs room is now a chapel open to all.

Continue along Stour Street.

★ **Poor Priests Hospital** (A M¹). — Founded in the 13C as an almshouse. The ⊙ present buildings, according to the 17C Canterbury antiquary, Thomas Wyke, date from 1373. They house a museum relating to the history of Canterbury and its immediate surroundings. On the ground floor are Roman, Anglo-Saxon and Viking remains, while on the first floor are exhibits of the Norman period, including a remarkable model of the rebuilding of the Cathedral choir after the fire of 1174.

Continue to the end of Stour Street.

Norman Castle (A). — Only the keep remains of the 11C Norman castle.

Turn southeast towards Pin Hill.

City Walls, Dane John Fortification and Garden (A). — A walk runs along the top of the well-preserved **medieval walls (AB)**, stoutly built on Roman foundations. The Dane John mound, probably part of an earlier defensive system although popular legend connects the name with the French "donjon", offers a charming view of the **memorial (A E)** to **Christopher Marlowe**, Canterbury's famous playwright.

Continue along Broad Street and turn right into Church Street then Longport.

★★ **St Augustine's Abbey** (B). — The abbey was founded in AD 597 by St Augustine. ⊙ Considerable ruins remain of the great abbey church of the Norman period which replaced earlier Saxon buildings. Also to be discovered are the vestiges of Saxon burial places and, to the east, the church of St Pancras, adapted by Christians from an earlier pagan temple. The abbey was dissolved in 1538 and the church demolished.

The ruins are approached from the south side (Longport). Reaching the centre through a maze of ground-level remains, the visitor may descend into the crypt of the Saxon abbot Wulfric and its chapel, before proceeding east to St Pancras church. Built in the 7C, the remains of its walls are entirely of Roman brick.

Continue along Longport towards the east.

★ **St Martin's Church** (B). — Built on St Martin's Hill and claimed to be the oldest parish church in England, St Martin's has an imposing Perpendicular tower. Note the Roman brick used in the construction of its walls. Of simple design, the church has a Norman font, a "Leper Window" 2ft - 60cm from the ground at the back of the nave and a Norman piscina opposite the pulpit.

Return towards the town centre by Longport and Monastery Street.

St Augustine's College (B). — The missionary college founded here in the 19C occupied both medieval buildings and others designed by the Victorian architect William Butterfield. Of particular interest is the early 14C **Great Gateway**. The buildings are now used by the King's School *(see below)*.

Continue across Broad Street and along Burgate.

★ **Mercery Lane** (AB 21). — A well-known Canterbury thoroughfare, this bustling little street has kept its medieval charm and offers an impressive view of Christ Church Gate and the western towers of the cathedral.

Turn northwest along Sun Street and then right into Palace Street.

★ **The King's School** (B). — An ancient foundation remodelled by Henry VIII in 1541, the school occupies buildings of the former cathedral monastery grouped in the main around the pleasant grassy space of Green Court. The immense length of the cathedral is best appreciated from this point. In the northwest corner are the Norman Court Gate and the splendid Norman **staircase** (12C).

Return along King Street and The Friars as far as St Peter's Street. Turn right and right again after St Peter's Church into St Peter's Lane.

Blackfriars Monastery (A). — All that remains of a 13C Dominican Friary, dissolved during the Reformation, are the Guest Hall, seen from St Peter's Lane, and the Refectory, now used as The King's School Arts Centre.

EXCURSION

East Kent. — *Round tour of 63 miles - 100km. Allow at least a day.*
With its chalk cliffs offering a prospect over the Straits of Dover to the coastline of the Continent, England's "Bulwark Shore" (Caroline Hillier) bears many traces of its vulnerability to attack and invasion as well as to more peaceful influences from abroad.
It was here that the Romans first set foot in Britain in 55 BC, later fortifying the "Saxon Shore". English history has been said to have begun with the landing of Hengist and Horsa at Ebbsfleet in AD 449, English Christianity with the arrival of St Augustine at the same spot in AD 597. In the Middle Ages, the maritime federa-

tion known as the **Cinque Ports** was established by Edward the Confessor, grouping Sandwich, Dover, Hythe, Romney and Hastings together to supply the ships and men for the protection of the realm. Succeeding ages contributed new defences, from Henry VIII's castles and the elaborate precautions taken to repel Napoleon, such as the Royal Military Canal, built to facilitate troop movements, to the pill-boxes, airfields and gun emplacements of the year of Dunkirk and the Battle of Britain, the latter fought largely in Kentish skies.

In part on the Roman highways radiating from Canterbury and passing through the quiet rural interior of East Kent, the tour visits ports of the coast, some dreaming still of medieval glories, some striving to meet the coming challenge of the Channel Tunnel.

Leave Canterbury on Watling Street, the A257, to the east.

Wingham. — Pop 1 429. The village's wide well-treed street is lined with attractive old buildings, some timber-framed.

Continue on the A257 and after 5 miles - 8km turn left on minor road and follow signs to Richborough Castle.

⊙**Richborough Castle.** — This is where Emperor Claudius' invading forces probably landed in AD 43. Roman Rutupiae remained one of the province's most important ports and was latterly the headquarters of the Count of the Saxon Shore, responsible for repelling the ever-growing pressure from Germanic sea-borne raiders. The massive walls still impress, though the prospect from them is no longer of the sea, now 2 miles - 3km distant, but of the monotonous levels of the River Stour.

Return to the A257 and continue into Sandwich.

★**Sandwich.** — Pop 4 184. One of the original Cinque Ports, this fascinating medieval borough is still largely contained within its earthen ramparts and seems to have changed little since the River Stour began to silt up in the 15C. Its pretty houses of all periods cluster around its three churches, St Clement's, with a sturdy, arcaded Norman tower, St Peter's, with a bulbous cupola reflecting Flemish influence, and St Mary's. By the quayside is the quaint Barbican guarding the river crossing and the medieval Fisher Gate.

Go south on the A258 towards Deal.

Deal. — Pop 26 548. A modern pier protrudes eastwards from Deal's shingle beach towards the notorious wreck-littered Goodwin Sands. Landward is a long line of mostly Georgian houses, backed by narrow streets of fishermen's cottages. The Tudor-rose shaped castle was built in Henry VIII's reign and its twin at Walmer, just a mile - 2km south, is the official residence of the Warden of the Cinque Ports.

Continue on the A258 towards Dover. At a roundabout after 5 miles - 8km there is a choice of route into Dover; by the A2 which descends to the port or the A258 which leads directly to Dover Castle.

Dover. — *Description p 109.*

Take the A20 westwards towards Folkestone. After 4 miles - 6km turn left onto the clifftop road.

The Warren. — The 480ft - 146m high cliffs drop away to a chaos of tumbled chalk and scrub, held in now by extensive sea defences protecting the main London-Folkestone-Dover railway.

Continue on the A20.

Folkestone. — Pop 42 949. As well as being a cross-Channel ferry port second only to Dover in importance, Folkestone has an attractive fishing harbour. On the clifftop to the west is a splendid grassy promenade, **The Leas**★, laid out in the mid-19C at the start of the town's heyday as one of the most fashionable of resorts. The magnificent seaward **panorama**★ extends to the coast of France on clear days. Immediately to the northwest of the town is the **Eurotunnel Exhibition Centre** enabling the vast scale of the Channel Tunnel terminal works to be appreciated.

Take the coast road, the A259, to the west.

Hythe. — Pop 13 118. The High Street of this Cinque Port is now half a mile, nearly 1km, from the modern seafront promenade, Hythe Haven having silted up centuries ago. Picturesque alleyways rise steeply to **St Leonard's Church**, perched imposingly halfway up the slope of the former cliff. The beautiful 13C chancel is unusually ambitious for a parish church, a reflection of the town's ancient prosperity. In a vault is a macabre ossuary of 500 skulls and countless thighbones. Over the roofs of the town are fine views of the Channel and of the coastline of Romney Marsh *(qv)* curving away to the remote spit of Dungeness. The Royal Military Canal passes through the town, its banks the setting for a biennial water carnival, the Venetian Fête. Hythe is also the terminus of the famous miniature Romney, Hythe and Dymchurch Railway *(see under Rye).*

Go west on the A261, then the B2067.

⊙**Port Lympne Zoo Park.** — Built for Sir Philip Sassoon in 1912, the red brick house and its formal gardens command extensive views over Romney Marsh to the sea. Inside there is a fascinating *trompe l'œil* Tent Room, painted by Rex Whistler and an Asian animals mural by Spencer Roberts. Outside in enclosures and on the open slopes below, the rhinos, tigers, lions, elephants and other animals of John Aspinall's Zoo Park.

Return northwards to Canterbury on the Roman Stane Street, the B2068.

*Make life easier by using **Michelin Maps** with your **Michelin Guide**.*

★ **CARDIFF** (CAERDYDD) South Glamorgan   Pop 262 313

Michelin Map 403 K 29 or Atlas G Britain p 16

Cardiff, capital city of Wales, arose around the Roman fort guarding the crossing of the Taff, on the road between Caerleon and Carmarthen. It was the world's principal coal port at the start of the 20C and much of its appearance today can be directly attributed to this era. Rugby football, the national sport of Wales, has its headquarters in the National Stadium (Cardiff Arms Park).

★**Cardiff Castle** (Z). — After Hastings, William gave Robert FitzHamon a free hand in the southern borderlands, and he built a timber motte and bailey castle within the ruins of the Roman fort. The twelve-sided stone keep is 12C.

But it was the third **Marquess of Bute** (1847-1900), reputedly the richest man in Britain at the time, who in 1868, commissioned the architect William Burges (1827-81); his romantic imagination was given free rein in an extraordinary series of exotic **interiors★**, Arab, Gothic and Greek, to create the unique monument to the Victorian age we see today. Also in the grounds are the **Welch Regiment Museum** (M¹) and the Queen's Dragoon Guards Museum.

★**National Museum of Wales** (Y M²). — The impressive headquarters of the National Museum is situated in **Cathays Park**, the city's spacious early 20C Civic Centre. The museum has excellent displays of archaeology, silver and 18C porcelain and the natural sciences; its **picture collection★** is particularly rich.

The Old Masters on display include works by Claude and Poussin, but it is the 19C and early 20C French paintings that command attention, with canvases by many of the important Impressionists and Post-Impressionists including several superb pictures by Monet and Cézanne and a poignant study *Rain at Auvers,* painted by Van Gogh just before his death.

Another, natural, emphasis is on **Welsh painting**. The great 18C landscape artist **Richard Wilson** is represented by numerous works, including his *Caernarvon Castle,* and his pupil Thomas Jones by several sparkling Italian views. There are works by the flamboyant **Augustus John** (1878-1961) and his sister Gwen.

Rodin bronzes are among the treasures of the sculpture displays.

CARDIFF

Duke Street	Z 26
High Street	Z
Queen Street	Z
St. David's Centre	Z
St. Mary Street	Z
Working Street	Z 67
Castle Street	Z 9
Cathays Terrace	Y 10
Central Square	Z 12
Church Street	Z 14
City Hall Road	Y 15
College Road	Y 20
Corbett Road	Y 21
Customhouse Street	Z 23
David Street	Z 25
Dumfries Place	Y 28
Greyfriars Road	Y 29
Guilford Street	Z 30
Hayes (The)	Z 32
King Edward VII Avenue	Y 36
Mary Ann Street	Z 39
Moira Terrace	Z 42
Museum Avenue	Y 43
Nantes (Boulevard de)	Y 44
Newport Road	Y 46
Penarth Road	Z 49
St. Andrews Place	Y 6
St. John Street	Z 58
Station Terrace	Z 61
Stuttgart Street	Y 62

81

★ **Llandaff Cathedral.** — *By the A4119* (**Z**). Tradition has it that St Teilo founded
⊘a community here in about 560 AD, naming his *'Llan'* after the Taff river nearby.
The cathedral was built between 1120 and 1280 but fell into decay after the Reformation. The 13C tower and roof collapsed in a storm in 1723 and it was not until
the 18C that John Wood was chosen to restore the cathedral. Almost the whole
of his work was destroyed by a land-mine which fell to the south of the cathedral
on 2 January 1941. The choir is now divided from the nave by a concrete arch
embellished with some of the 19C figures from the choir stalls and by a huge alumini-
um *Christ in Majesty* by Epstein. In the Memorial Chapel of the Welch Regiment
is a triptych - *The Seed of David* - by Rossetti.

⊘**Welsh Industrial and Maritime Museum.** — *To the south by Bute Street* (**Z**). Sited in Butetown, one of the foremost dockland development schemes, the museum
comprises four galleries devoted to power, transport, shipping and railways, the
last housed in the old terminus building of the Taff Vale Railway.

EXCURSIONS

★★ **Welsh Folk Museum, St Fagans.** — *On the western outskirts of Cardiff in the*
⊘*village of St Fagans.* One of the finest collections of vernacular buildings in Britain
stands in the parkland of St Fagans Castle, an Elizabethan mansion. These re-erected
buildings, from all over Wales include cottages, farmhouses, a chapel, bakehouse,
school, corn mill, woollen mill, tannery, a village store and unusual edifices like a
toll house and a cockpit. A unique collection of coracles, a working farmstead and
an award-winning terrace of miners' cottages add to the variety of the exhibits,
while a number of traditional craftsmen demonstrate their skills in their craft workshops. Modern galleries present the traditional domestic, social and cultural life of
the country and there are displays on costume and on agriculture.

St Fagans Castle itself was built *c*1580 on the site of an earlier castle. It has been
restored to its 19C appearance and furnished appropriately. Its fine formal gardens
include a mulberry grove and there are fishponds, stocked as in the 17C with carp,
bream and tench.

★ **Castell Coch.** — *5 miles - 8km north by the A470* (**Y**); *signposted from Tongwynlais.*
⊘A pseudo-medieval stronghold, created, as was Cardiff Castle, by the wealth of
the Marquess of Bute and the imagination of William Burges, who in 1875 started
to build a fantasy 13C castle, with turrets inspired by Chillon and Carcassonne and
complete with drawbridge, portcullis and 'murder holes'. French, Gothic and Moorish
influences combine in the interior decorations.

★★ **Caerphilly Castle** (**Caerffili**). — *7 miles - 11km north by the A470* (**Y**) *then the A469.*
⊘This massive stronghold sits threateningly behind its extensive water defences,
reducing to apparent insignificance the busy town gathered round the outer limits
of its vast site.
Begun in 1268 by the powerful baron Gilbert de Clare, the castle was the first in
Britain to be built from new on a regular concentric plan; the design of its walls,
towers and gateways embodied many innovative features too and it served as a
model for the castles of Edward I shortly to be built in North Wales, *(p 69).* One
of its owners was **Hugh Despenser**, favourite of Edward II, who himself made a brief
sojourn here in 1326 in flight from his Queen, Isabella, and her lover Mortimer.
The castle's later decay was accelerated in the Civil War by deliberate destruction,
of which the half-ruined ''leaning tower'' in the southeast corner of the main ward
is a poignant reminder. The present state of the impressive complex is largely due
to the general restoration carried out in the 19C and 20C by the 3rd and 4th Marquesses of Bute *(p 81).*
The visitor's approach to the castle is via the great gatehouse; this is set in the
immensely long **East Barbican**, a fortified dam separating the outer moat from the
inner moat and its flanking lakes to north and south. Behind these defences is the
castle's core, an outer ward with semicircular bastions and an inner ward with
drum towers, mighty gatehouses and **Great Hall**, the last rebuilt *c*1317 by Despenser.
Protecting the western gatehouse, the original entrance, is an extensive western
outwork and beyond this, the 17C redoubt on the site of a Roman fort.

⊘**Caerleon.** — *12 miles - 19km east by the M4* (**Y**) *to Junction 25, then follow signs.*
Isca to the Romans, Caerleon, or 'City of the Legions' in Welsh, was home to the
5-6 000 men of the Legio II Augusta, from 75 AD until 300 AD. They built the enormous **Fortress Baths★**, magnificently preserved and presented. The newly opened
⊘**Roman Legionary Museum** nearby displays other finds from this important site in an exemplary way. The **amphitheatre★** (car park) just outside the fortress walls was built
about AD 90. The **barrack buildings**, in pairs, with verandahs onto a central street,
eight men to a room and the centurion at the end of the block, are the only remaining Roman Legionary barracks to be seen in Europe.

Pontypool and Blaenavon. — *20 miles - 30km on the M4* (**Y**) *to Junction 26 then*
north onto the A4042 and A472. Immediately to the north of Cardiff and the other
ports of South Wales lie **The Valleys**, one of Britain's greatest coalfields. Its remaining metalworks, pitheads and attendant railways, overlooked by teeming rows of
terraced houses, occupy the floors of deep parallel valleys, separated from each
other by high green hills. From this place of coexistence between wild nature and
heavy industry came Aneurin Bevan, eloquent politician and founder of the National Health Service. His statue, pointing northwards to the coalfield, stands in Cardiff;
another memorial to him is on the breezy heights above Ebbw Vale, whose MP he
was from 1929 until his death in 1960.
The whole area is rich in the relics of an industrial age. This tour introduces the
visitor to some of the industrial archaeology of Gwent's eastern valleys.

Pontypool. — Pop 36 579. In the 18C this industrial town saw the first successful production of tinplate. In the fine stable buildings of Hanbury Park, an ironmaster's ⊘ mansion, is the **Valley Inheritance Centre**, with exhibits evoking local industrial history.

⊘ **Big Pit, Blaenavon.** — *10 miles - 16km north on the A4043.*
Here on the eastern edge of the coalfield, large-scale extraction of coal and iron began in the 18C. **Big Pit Colliery** stopped work in 1980; its pithead installations now welcome visitors with displays on mining history and there are guided tours, led by former miners, of the **underground workings.**

CARDIGAN (ABERTEIFI), Dyfed   Pop 3 815
Michelin Map 403 G 27 or Atlas G Britain p 24 - Local map p 198

The remains of the Norman castle still guard the southern approaches to Cardigan, but today the town has a mainly Victorian character. The fine six-arched **town bridge**, originally Norman, was rebuilt in 1640, after being damaged in the Civil War. There is a fine view from the cliffs at nearby Gwbert.

EXCURSION

Teifi Valley. — *17 miles - 27km. Leave Cardigan to south by the A478 then turn left towards Cilgerran.* This most delightful of rivers is known for its salmon fishing.

⊘ **Cilgerran Castle.** — Subject of paintings by Turner, one of which is in the Leicestershire Museum and Art Gallery, the romantic ruins perch on a promontory high above the deep wooded gorge of the Teifi. This was probably the castle from which, in 1109, Owain, Prince of Powys, abducted the beautiful Nest, wife of Gerald of Windsor. Her sons, FitzRoys, FitzOwens and FitzGeralds, all founded powerful Anglo-Irish families. **Drum towers**, four storeys high, defended the landward approach and still dominate the scene.

Follow signs to Llechryd and turn east on A484.

Cenarth Falls. — Downstream from the pretty falls the river is the setting for an annual coracle race. Pairs of coracles - small boats made from interwoven ash ribs covered with tarred canvas - are still used to trawl for salmon and sea-trout here and on the River Twyi.

Continue on A484; turn right on minor road 3 miles after Newcastle Emlyn.

⊘ **Museum of the Welsh Woollen Industry.** — A branch of the National Museum of Wales, housed in impressive mill buildings at Dre-fach Felindre, tells the story of an important rural industry in Wales from its very early domestic origins to the factory system of this century.

★ CARLISLE Cumbria   Pop 72 206
Michelin Map 402 L 19 or Atlas G Britain p 44 - Local map p 132
Town plan in the current Michelin Red Guide Great Britain and Ireland

The **Market Cross**, in the city centre, stands on the site of the Forum of Roman Luguvalium. Four hundred years of Roman presence were followed, for Carlisle, by five hundred years of decline and decay, and four hundred years of border warfare and strife between England and Scotland. These years of turmoil did not encourage the inhabitants to build grandly, or for posterity ! The **Guildhall** is a timber-framed house of 1407, built by Richard de Redness, and another surviving house, **Tullie** ⊘ **House**, dates from 1689, and still has its original oak staircase. It now houses a part of the City Museum.
On 17 November 1745, **Prince Charles Edward**, on the way south to Derby, entered Carlisle and proclaimed his father King James III, from the Market Cross. The Young Pretender stayed in Highmoor House, as did his adversary, the **Duke of Cumberland**, who re-took the city on 30 December of that year, before chasing the Jacobite army back into Scotland.

★ **Cathedral.** — Henry I gave the responsibility for a Border priory, probably founded by Walter the Priest in about 1100, to the Augustinians in 1122, creating a See of Carlisle in 1133. All that remains of the Norman building is the truncated **nave** and the south transept. Hugh of Beaulieu became bishop in 1219 and new work was begun in 1225. The new choir was twelve feet broader than the nave. The extension had to be to the north, for the monastic buildings were all on the south side, hence the "offset" between nave and choir. The two most important works from this period are the **east window**, a fine example of Decorated tracery, containing much original 14C glass in the upper section and the choir, with its set of **sculptured capitals**, a unique series of fourteen, twelve of which represent the occupations and pursuits of the months of the year. In the choir, too, is a magnificent **painted ceiling★**, completed in 1360, featuring golden suns and stars on a blue ground, not unlike the later nave ceiling of St Mary's, Beverley. The 16C **Brougham Triptych** in the north transept is a masterpiece of Flemish craftsmanship.

⊘ **Castle.** — Established by William II in 1092, the castle served to block the passage of Scots raiders. The Norman **keep** was altered in Tudor times to accommodate cannon in place of archers. Opposite the entrance to the keep is the shell of the medieval hall, which now houses the museum of the **King's Own Royal Border Regiment**. All that remains of the tower, in which Mary Queen of Scots was held, is the staircase to the east of the museum building. A feature of the outer ward is the Tudor **half-moon battery**, built in the 1540s for the deployment of cannon.

⊘**Church of St Cuthbert with St Mary.** — A galleried church of 1779, it has an unusual pulpit, installed in 1905, to enable the preacher to speak to the galleries. This was so massive that it completely hid the chancel from the congregation; so it was placed on rails, and is moved into position before the sermon.

★**Tithe Barn.** — Built for convenience near the road leading from the rich corn lands ⊘to the west, the tithe barn, c1502, measures 115ft-34m by 27ft-8m and is of red sandstone with massive oak tie-beams. Restored 1968-71, it now serves as the church hall.

EXCURSIONS

★★**Hadrian's Wall.** — *Description p 131.*

⊘**Lanercost Priory.** — *11 miles - 18km northeast by the B6264 to Brampton, then minor road.*
Built between 1200 and 1220, much of the stone being brought from Hadrian's Wall nearby. At the Dissolution, in 1536, the lead was stripped from the roof, apart from the north aisle which was left as the parish church. The **west front** is a fine example of Early English work, with a figure of St Mary Magdalene, the Priory's patron saint, in a lancet in the gable end. The nave and north aisle are today roofed over and still serve as the parish church. The choir, transepts and sanctuary, all open to the sky, contain tombs of the Dacre family, including that of Sir Thomas Dacre of Kirkoswald, Lord of the Marches.

★★ CASTLE HOWARD North Yorkshire

Michelin Map 402 R 21 or Atlas G Britain p 40

Castle Howard, **Sir John Vanbrugh's** great piece of architectural theatre, was the first building he had ever designed. Soldier, turned dramatist on his return to England in 1692, Vanbrugh attracted the attention of the Whig nobility of his day - perhaps thanks to his popular, if bawdy, plays, and came to the notice of **Charles Howard**, 3rd Earl of Carlisle, through the select circle of the Kit Kat Club. Vanbrugh was not, however, alone in the task, for the realisation of his ideas and much of the detail was the work of **Nicholas Hawksmoor**, already an established architect. When Vanbrugh, enthusiastic amateur, was chosen to build a home fitted to the position of the Earl, Jonathan Swift commented: "Van's genius, without thought or lecture, is hugely turned to Architecture." But 'Genius' was assuredly there.
The striking entrance topped by a painted and gilded dome, reaching more than 80ft-24m into the air, is familiar to many as the castle served as principal location for the television series *Brideshead Revisited*.

⊘**TOUR** *time: 1 hour*

The **statuary** in the **Grand Entrance** and elsewhere is from but two of the three shiploads collected by the 4th Earl in Italy, the third vessel having been lost at sea. A remarkable piece is the **altar** from the Temple of Delphi, its top slotted to receive the tripod which held the sacred flame. On the **China Landing**, among portrait busts, are displayed services of Meissen, Crown Derby and Chelsea, together with a Dutch **tulip vase**, from c1704.
The heart of the house is the **Great Hall**. Rising through two storeys into the painted dome, it is the most light-hearted but impressive concept of English architecture. Samuel Carpenter, a Yorkshire mason, carved the columns and capitals. A Huguenot refugee, Nadauld, carved the cupola and both worked on the flowing pinewood swags in the **Music Room** and **Tapestry Room**. In the **Long Gallery** and its **Octagon** are pictures by Lely, Kneller and Van Dyck, but probably the finest are the two **Holbeins**. His portrait of **Henry VIII**, a disillusioned and stricken monarch, was painted in 1542, just after the execution of Catherine Howard, and the 1538 portrait of Thomas Howard, 3rd Duke of Norfolk, Catherine's uncle, who escaped the block himself only because the King died on the day appointed for the execution. The **Chapel** has magnificent stained-glass windows by the 19C artist Edward Burne-Jones.
In the **Stable Court**, is the largest private collection of period costume in Britain, from the 17C onwards. The displays change annually.
The scale of the **Park★★★** is superhuman. It is one of the most grandiose projects of the great age of landscaping, a series of compositions focused on some of the most ambitious and beautiful garden structures ever built, notably the **Temple of the Four Winds**, Vanbrugh's last work and, most extraordinary of all, crowning a distant rise, Hawksmoor's colossal colonnaded **Mausoleum.**

★★ CHANNEL Islands   Pop 120 272

Michelin Map 403 P, Q 33 or Atlas G Britain p 5
Access: see the current Michelin Red Guide Great Britain and Ireland

The Islands, west of the Cherbourg peninsula of the Normandy coast, are composed of fertile granite plateaux sloping to open sand dunes. The southerly latitude and the Gulf Stream ensure a mild climate which explains the role agriculture plays in the islands' economy. Tourism is an important source of revenue and the islands' tax status has attracted banks and finance houses as well as a number of "tax exiles". The islands are rich in prehistoric tombs and monuments indicating human habitation from 7 500-2 500 BC. Few traces remain of the brief Roman occupation. The islands were annexed by the Normans in 933 and later attached to the English crown by William I. Some customs and traditions and the Norman-French dialect sometimes heard on these English-speaking islands date back to this period. In 1204 the French took Normandy and tried repeatedly to capture the islands; a papal Bull of Neutrality was issued in 1483 and remained in force technically until 1689 although it became a dead letter once the islands became Protestant in the 1540s. In the Civil War Jersey was Royalist while Guernsey supported Cromwell. Threats of invasion by Napoleon account for many defence towers built along the coasts. The islands were occupied by the Germans from 1940-45.

★★ JERSEY Pop 72 970

The largest and southernmost of the group is thick with flowers in spring and summer. The sandy bays which characterise the coastline occur even among the steep pink granite cliffs of the sparsely populated north coast.

St Helier. — The capital is named after the 6C hermit saint who brought Christianity to the island. On an islet *(access by causeway at low tide)* stands **Elizabeth Castle**, begun in the mid-16C on the site of a 12C abbey. In the Civil War it was adapted to resist attacks by the Parliamentarians and in World War II the occupying German forces made their own additions. West of the Royal Jersey Militia Museum the Upper Ward encloses the Mount (keep) affording **views★** across St Aubin's Bay. Today a breakwater leads south to the 12C hermitage chapel on the rock on which St Helier lived. The centre of the town is the charming **Royal Square** with a 1751 statue of George II dressed as a Roman emperor. The pink granite **parish church**, dating back to the 11C was restored in the 19C. Other features are the **Jersey Museum**, containing maritime exhibits and the story of Jersey and **Fort Regent**, built 1806-14 to protect Jersey from invasion by Napoleon, now used as a leisure centre.

La Hougue Bie. — In Grouville, La Hougue Bie is notable for the cruciform **Neolithic tomb★** dating from 3000 BC, a 33ft - 10m passage roofed with granite slabs leading to a 10ft × 30ft - 3m × 9m funeral chamber and three side chambers. On top of the mound stand the 12C **Chapel of Our Lady of the Dawn** and the 1520 **Jerusalem Chapel** containing early 16C frescoes of archangels.

Gorey. — This charming old port at the north of the Royal Bay of Grouville is dominated by **Mont Orgueil Castle★** which dates back to the 13C. Set on a rocky promontory, its position and defensive strength account for the name (Mount Pride). A spiral network of steps and passages between separate defence systems leads up to excellent **views★★** at the top. Other sights include the **Jersey Pottery workshops★** set in a magnificent garden and the 49ft - 15m **Faldouet Dolmen**, dating from 2500 BC, with a 20ft - 6m wide funeral chamber.

St Matthew's Church, Millbrook. — Built in 1840, it is remarkable for **René Lalique's** rich **glasswork★** interior executed in 1934 as a memorial to Lord Trent. Another notable church is the **Fishermen's Chapel** at St Brelade, decorated with 14C and 15C **frescoes★**. The manor houses at St Ouen, Trinity and **Samarès**, much altered through generations of use, remain characteristic features of the Jersey scene, with dovecotes in their grounds. Special mention must be made of the **Jersey Zoo★** which Gerald Durrell founded to preserve rare species.

★GUERNSEY Pop 53 637

The second largest of the islands has many greenhouses except along the wild, dramatic **southern cliffs** and the sandy beaches and rocky promontories of the west and north coasts, excellent for bathing, surfing and exploring rock pools.

★★St Peter Port.

St Peter Port. — The capital, attractively situated on a hillside on the east coast, overlooks a sheltered harbour. The medieval town was rebuilt after the Civil War in which Guernsey had supported Cromwell. A late 18C building boom produced a delightful Regency town built in local granite. **Castle Cornet★**, dating back to c1206, reinforced under Elizabeth I, remained loyal to the king in the Civil War, being the last of the royal strongholds to surrender, after eight years of siege. In 1672 the gunpowder store was struck by lightning and the castle was seriously damaged and had to be rebuilt. It now houses the Royal Guernsey Militia Museum and the Guernsey Maritime History Museum. St Peter Port **Church★** dates back as far as 1048 when it also served as a fort. It now contains several memorials to famous Guernseymen. One well-known inhabitant of Guernsey was the French poet Victor Hugo, in political exile from 1851-70; in 1856 he bought **Hauteville House★** and decorated it himself - in a highly individual way !
The finest house is **Sausmarez Manor**, an elegant, mostly Queen Anne house, not to be confused with **Saumarez Park★** the venue for the annual **Battle of the Flowers**. The **Guernsey Folk Museum** is housed in the outbuildings.

St Sampson. — Guernsey's second port. The oldest church on the island was built where the Welsh monk St Sampson came ashore in the 6C; the oldest part of the present church is the early Norman saddle-back tower. The ruined medieval **Château des Marais** crowns a low knoll, first used in the Bronze Age. Excavations in 1975-77 produced 13C coins found in a chapel dedicated to Our Lady of the Marshes.

Prehistoric remains. — The most notable are the burial chambers **Déhus Dolmen** *(north)*, le **Trepied Dolmen** *(west)* and **La Gran'mère du Chimquiere★**, a Stone Age figure at the gate to St Martin's churchyard. A similar female figure stands outside the 12C church of **Ste Marie du Câtel** which also contains 13C frescoes of the Last Supper and the three living and the three dead.

Alderney, Herm and **Sark★★**, the other islands making up the Bailiwick of Guernsey, are well worth a visit. Sark has stayed remarkably remote from modern society, even to the extent of being totally free of cars.

Michelin Map 402 P 24 or Atlas G Britain p 35

The original Chatsworth was begun in 1551 by Sir William Cavendish and **Bess of Hardwick**, that indomitable Elizabethan who went through four husbands, multiplying her wealth with each marriage. It was at Chatsworth that she first exercised her passion for building. She built one Renaissance palace, decided that her third husband, the Earl of Shrewsbury, was a ''knave, fool and beast'' and that he had had an affair with his prisoner, Mary Queen of Scots, returned to her Hardwick home fifteen miles away and built another. Transformed between 1686 and 1707 by the first Duke of Devonshire, it became a baroque palace. Greatly extended by the 6th Duke between 1820 and 1827, Chatsworth was in 1854 called by Charles de Saint-Amant ''le second Versailles''.

Painted Hall. — Unashamedly baroque, as only **Laguerre** can do it, the ceilings and walls are a soaring profusion of colours depicting the triumphs of Caesar.

Great Stairs. — The bronze Mercury is after Giambologna, the three sculptured figures by Caius Gabriel Cibber (1630-1700) and the ceiling by Verrio. Beneath the stairs (and holding them up) is the **grotto**, with superb stone carvings by Samuel Watson.

Mary Queen of Scots Rooms. — Rebuilt and clad in Regency **chinoiserie** by Sir Jeffry Wyatville since Mary's involuntary stay: the two coronation chairs in the lobby were used by William IV and Queen Adelaide in 1830. The long landscape by Gaspard Poussin in the **Green Satin Dressing Room** is ''not only among the most beautiful works of the master, but among the finest landscapes in the world'' (Gustave Waagen), and a rare portrait of the architect, William Kent (1685-1748), hangs in the **Green Satin Bedroom**.

State Drawing Room, Chatsworth

State Rooms. — The grandest rooms in the house, characterised by unrestrained ceilings by Laguerre and Verrio and Louis XIV furniture; the gilt side tables in the **Dining Room** are by Kent; the **Drawing Room tapestries**, based on Raphael, are from Mortlake (c1635); the violin on the inner door of the **Music Room** is a *trompe l'œil* by Jan van der Vaart (c1653-1727). Notice **Breughel the Elder's** *Casting out of the Swine* and **Hans Schauffen's** *Wheel of Fortune* (1533), in the **China Closet**.

West Stairs. — The wrought-iron panels on the landings are by Jean Tijou, the ceiling depicting *The Fall of Phaeton* is an early work by Sir James Thornhill, (1675-1734) and the painting of *Samson and Delilah* by Tintoretto (1518-94). Three more paintings on the stairs, one being of the house in Bess of Hardwick's time, show the changes in Chatsworth up to the mid-18C. In the corridor are two 3 800 year old Egyptian memorial tablets.

Chapel. — Unchanged since 1694 with ceiling choreography by Laguerre and a *Doubting Thomas* by Verrio over the altar; the limewood carving and cedar panels are by Samuel Watson and the gloriously baroque altarpiece by Cibber. Outside in the passage hangs Paolo Veronese's *Adoration of the Magi.*

The Library. — 90ft - 28m long, containing 17 000 books and stretching almost the entire length of the east range; the books are almost lost in the splendid gilded stucco ceiling by Edward Goudge (Wren's best pupil) framing Verrio's paintings.

Sculpture Gallery. — Built by the 6th Duke to house an incomparable collection of sculptures, among the finest of which are **Antonio Canova's** *Hebe,* his *Endymion* and *Napoleon's Mother* and **Bertel Thorwaldsen's** bas reliefs *Day* and *Night.* Hanging amid these glories is **Rembrandt's** *King Uzziah.*

★★★ **Park and garden.** — The genius of Capability Brown made this one of the grandest of 18C parks. The garden's most majestic feature is the **Cascade**, designed in 1696 by Grillet, a pupil of Le Nôtre, each step a different height, to vary the sound of the falling water that disappears into pipes, to reappear out of the **Sea Horse Fountain** on the south lawn. The garden as we see it today, however, is mostly the creation of **Joseph Paxton** (1803-65), working for the 6th Duke. To the north of the Cascade is his "Conservative Wall" - a pun on "conservatory" - as well as the 1698 Greenhouse and Rose Garden, while to the south are the 1842 rockeries and the 1692 Willow Tree Fountain, later restored, which so intrigued Celia Fiennes. She wrote of it, in 1696, "by turning a sluce it raines from each leafe and from the branches like a shower, it being made of brass and pipes to each leafe, but in appearance is exactly like any willow". A maze now covers the ground plan of Paxton's Great Conservatory, which was demolished in 1920. He built it eleven years before designing the Crystal Palace for the Great Exhibition of 1851.

EXCURSIONS

★★ **Hardwick Hall.** — *15 miles - 24km east on the A619 and the A617, turn right ⊙ 2 miles - 3km after the M1.*
Of the modest manor house where **Bess of Hardwick** was born, little remains. Directly after building Chatsworth and abandoning her husband the Earl of Shrewsbury she rebuilt it. Not satisfied with that she built another Hall, 100 yards away, at the age of 70. "Hardwick Hall, more glass than wall", designed by **Robert Smythson.** Of the two family homes in such close proximity her descendants preferred Chatsworth. Bess's Old Hall fell into ruins and her New Hall was left unlived in, frozen in time and one of the purest examples of 16C design and decor in the country.

Interior. — Famous for its stupendous late Elizabethan fireplaces, friezes, **tapestries** and **embroideries** on its walls; an embroidery in the Paved Room is by Mary Queen of Scots. Note also the *Fancie of a Fowler.* The three embroideries in the Drawing Room, *Diana and Actaeon,* the *Fall of Phaeton* and *Europa and the Bull* are by Bess herself. Both the Hall and the Long Gallery contain portraits of her.

★★ **Haddon Hall.** — *3 miles - 5km south and west on the B6012 and the A6.*
⊙ Overlooking the River Wye since the 12C, rambling, unaggressive and very English, Haddon Hall was successively enlarged until the early 17C. Saved from Victorian romanticism, it was lovingly restored by the 9th Duke of Rutland in the early 20C.

Interior. — The interior, like the exterior, is in a multitude of styles; the Hall (1370) is medieval, the Dining Room and Great Chamber are Tudor and the Long Gallery (note Rex Whistler's painting of Haddon) is Elizabethan. As splendid as the rooms are the Mortlake **tapestries** of Aesop's Fables *(Feeling, Hearing, Seeing, Tasting and Smelling).* The glory of the miniscule chapel is its **murals**; St Nicholas calming the sea (north wall), St Christopher carrying Jesus (south wall) and the Holy Family (in the chancel).
The terraced **gardens** date from the 17C, perhaps even earlier. Lavishly planted with roses they tumble prettily to the river with its venerable stone packhorse bridge.

★ **Bolsover Castle.** — *16 miles - 26km east on the A619 and the A632.*
⊙ A fairy-tale castle perched on a hill above the coal mines and pitheads, Bolsover was built by the Earl of Shrewsbury, husband to Bess of Hardwick; a Gothic folly by Bess's builder Robert Smythson, his son John and grandson Huntingdon adding the **Terrace Range** and **Riding School.** Completed in 1633, it provided the magical setting for Ben Jonson's masque, *Love's Welcome to Bolsover,* performed the next year before Charles I at a cost of £15 000. The interior is rich in carved Jacobean fireplaces, panelling, strapwork and ceiling paintings, particularly the **Elysium** and **Heaven Rooms**, a foretaste of baroque.

★ **CHELTENHAM** Gloucestershire   Pop 87 188
Michelin Map **403** N 28 or Atlas G Britain p 17
Town plan in the current Michelin Red Guide Great Britain and Ireland

The benefits of the waters of this most elegant of English spas were discovered early in the 18C, but it was at its most fashionable in the Regency period, becoming a pleasure town of classical architecture, its squares, terraces and crescents in a delightful setting of trees and gardens which are still its pride. Long favoured for residence, retirement and recreation, it has an animated cultural life, with internationally important musical and literary festivals. It is an excellent centre for exploring the varied landscapes around the Severn Vale, the Wye Valley and the Forest of Dean, the Malvern Hills and the Cotswolds themselves, whose escarpment rears up just outside the town.

CHELTENHAM

★ Town Centre. — Of pre-spa Cheltenham there remains the secluded Church of St Mary and the line of the much rebuilt High Street. At right angles to this old thoroughfare is the **Promenade**; its lower part, the most spacious of shopping streets, is lined on one side by the **Municipal Offices**, an imposing terrace of 1823; its upper part, twice as broad, rises gently to the stately stuccoed façade of the **Queen's Hotel** of 1838. To the east are the **Imperial Gardens**, a multicoloured floral cocktail in summer; to the west, behind a double avenue of parkland trees, are some of the refined **Regency houses** with classical details and exquisite balcony ironwork which characterise the town. Further south is **Montpellier Walk**, whose mid-19C shop-fronts are divided up by Grecian caryatids and which terminates in the colonnade and dome of **Montpellier Spa** (now Lloyds Bank).

⊘ **Museum and Art Gallery.** — Among the paintings, porcelain and pottery and many exhibits of local interest is a good **collection of applied art** illustrating the importance of the Cotswolds in the Arts and Crafts Movement.

Pittville. — Joseph Pitt's distinguished district of classical terraces and villas focuses on the romantic landscape of **Pittville Park**, whose picturesque lake, great ⊘ trees and sweeping lawns are the setting for the **Pittville Pump Room★** of 1825-30. This outstanding Grecian building with its Ionic colonnade and domed interior houses a small **gallery of fashion** where costumed figures are displayed in historic settings.

⊘ Near the entrance to the park, in Clarence Road, is the **Gustav Holst Birthplace Museum**, a Regency house where the composer of *The Planets* was born in 1874.

EXCURSIONS

★ Sudeley Castle. — *7 miles - 11km. Leave northeastwards on the B4632.* The road climbs over the shoulder of Cleeve Hill, one of the Cotswolds' highest points.

Winchcombe. — Pop 4 754. In the long winding High Street of this once important Saxon town is the fine Perpendicular **Church of St Peter**, its exterior enlivened by grotesque carvings.

★ Sudeley Castle. — Sudeley is surrounded by the dramatic scenery of the Cotswolds ⊘ escarpment. Once a medieval stronghold, later the home of **Katherine Parr**, widow of Henry VIII, it was besieged and demolished in the Civil War. In the 19C the house was restored, although some parts were left in a ruined state.
The interior's fascinatingly varied collection of furniture and relics includes a small number of outstanding **paintings★** by Constable, Turner, Van Dyck and Rubens, as well as the late 16C Sheldon Tapestry. The nostalgic Victorian landscape scene embraces the pretty Church of St Mary where Katherine Parr is buried, the romantic ruins of the Tithe Barn and Banqueting Hall, to form a harmonious whole with the formal gardens and great parkland trees. The formal Queen's Garden is flanked by the famous double yew hedges.

★★ CHESTER Cheshire   Pop 80 154
Michelin Map 403 L 24 or Atlas G Britain p 34

The Roman legionary fortress and fleet base of Deva, covering sixty acres - about 24ha, on a sandstone ridge in a loop of the River Dee, was one of the largest in Britain and home to the XX Valeria Victrix Legion for 200 years. Watergate and East Gate follow the Via Principalis, where Watling Street entered the fort, and Bridge Street marks the Via Praetoria, along lines laid out by a Roman surveyor 1 900 years ago. St Peter's Church (at the junction of Watergate and Northgate Streets) stands on the site of the legionary headquarters. Chester was re-fortified at the start of the 10C by Aethelflaeda, daughter of Alfred the Great; she extended the Roman walls down to the river making the present two-mile circuit.
Hugh Lupus, the alleged nephew of William the Conqueror, became Norman Earl of Chester in 1070. The Earldom reverted to the Crown in 1237 and since 1301, when Henry III conferred it upon his son, later Edward I, it has remained one of the titles of the eldest son of the monarch.
Sea-going vessels had used the port since Roman times, Chester's greatest prosperity being from the 12C to 14C. Until the end of the 16C, Chester regarded Liverpool as a 'creek of the Port of Chester'. Silting of the Dee estuary from the 15C forced ships to anchor some twelve miles downstream. Where once Roman galleys tied up, punters now win - or lose - on the horse of their choice, for the **Roodee** - a name derived from Anglo-Saxon, meaning 'Island of the Cross', is now a racecourse. Horse racing has been held here since 1540, when the City Fathers banned the games of football which traditionally took place, because of increasing spectator violence and hooliganism.

★ City Walls. — No other city in Britain has been able to preserve a continuous circuit as has Chester. Parts of the Roman walls are to be seen between **King Charles' Tower (A)** - so called because from here King Charles I is said to have watched the defeat of his troops in September 1645 - and the Northgate. Stand on the **Eastgate (B)** by the Clock Tower and look westward to the spire of Holy Trinity Church (now the Guildhall). This view marks the width of the Roman fortress.
By the cathedral is the **Kaleyards Gate (D)** which allowed the monks of the Middle Ages to reach their vegetable garden. A petition to King Edward I was necessary before the abbot was permitted to breach the wall, and then only with a gate too low for a man on horseback to pass through. The cathedral authorities are still responsible, after 700 years, for the securing of this gate at nine o'clock, sharp, every night.

★ **Cathedral.** — From the outer courtyard of the abbey, now Abbey Square, the 14C abbey gateway leads to the cloister and the cathedral. Today's magnificent red sandstone building, built between 1250 and 1540, carefully restored since 1868, replaced the Norman abbey church. Many of the original abbey buildings, however, are still grouped around the 12C cloister.

On leaving the cathedral by the south transept, visit the Cheshire Regiment Memorial Garden to the east, and the nearby **campanile**, clad in Bethesda slate, opened in 1975 to accommodate the ring of twelve bells. On the outside of the transept are satirical corbels of the two political opponents Gladstone and Disraeli, carved during the Victorian restorations.

Entering by the steps down into the cloister, the visitor comes to the **refectory** with its magnificently re-created hammerbeam roof. The dean and chapter still meet in the 13C **chapter house**, and the clergy and choir assemble before services in the vestibule. The **camber beam** roof of the north transept, dating from 1518-24 carries a splendid display of Tudor heraldry; here is the monument to John Pearson, Bishop of Chester 1673-86, author of the *Exposition of the Creed* and here too is the 11C round arch and arcade, the oldest part of the cathedral. It pre-dates by some forty years the arches intended to support a tower over the baptistery in the northwest corner of the nave. The choir has stalls and misericords dating from 1390, comparable with those at Lincoln and Beverley, with richly carved Victorian tabernacle work over the stalls blending perfectly with the rest of the carvings. The **Lady Chapel** was carefully restored to its 1250 appearance and the 14C **shrine of St Werburgh**, daughter of the King of Mercia, who died about 700AD, has now been placed at the back of the chapel behind the High Altar.

⊙ **Town Hall** (H). — This fine Gothic style building, in red and grey sandstone, with its 160ft - 49m tower, replaced in 1869 the earlier Town Hall which had been destroyed by fire. Council Chamber and Assembly Rooms are open to the public.

⊙ **Grosvenor Museum** (M). — Whilst reflecting the local history of the City, with proud emphasis on the Roman period, it possesses an interesting collection of coins, minted in Chester in Saxon and Norman times and during the Civil War.

★★ **The Rows.** — These shopping arcades, unique in Britain, first appear in the city records for 1331. Since they extend no further than the original Roman fort walls, they probably originated when 14C merchants began putting their shops hard up to the packed rubble from Roman buildings that had lined the streets a thousand years earlier. Other shopkeepers put their stalls on the top of the stone rubble; steps and a walkway would have been built, then upper floors to provide accommodation for the merchant and his family. Whether or not this is the correct theory of their beginnings, The Rows make for convenient wet-weather shopping and freedom from traffic hazards. Beneath the crooked front of a house dating from 1664, now a bookshop, lies a 13C crypt; beneath a neighbouring shop is a Roman hypocaust system — just two of the many discoveries to be made around the city.

St John's Church. — Begun in 1075, the unfinished building was left unroofed for a hundred years. Norman drum columns lean deliberately outwards, an unnerving technique seen, apart from here, only at Orvieto and at Reims. Above the arches, three arcades show clearly the change from Norman to Transitional to Early English work in the clerestory.

EXCURSION

★ **Chester Zoo**. — *3 miles - 5km north, by the A5116.* A splendid Zoo, with the animals ⊙ displayed in spacious enclosures, with moats and flower borders, rather than cages separating them from the public.

★ CHICHESTER West Sussex   Pop 26 050

Michelin Map 403 R 31 or Atlas G Britain p 10
Town plan in the current Michelin Red Guide Great Britain and Ireland

On the flatlands between the South Downs and the sea, Chichester and its spire present one of the most English of English views. Many English towns grew up around their cathedral, but Chichester was already a thousand years old before the cathedral was thought about; its North, South, East and West Streets running off the 1501 ornamental **Market Cross** still conform to their Roman plan.
Chichester enjoyed a golden age in the 18C and its domestic architecture is almost wholly of this period; the resulting harmonious Georgian townscape is best seen in **The Pallants**. The 20C is represented, beyond the walls, by Powell and Moya's hexagonal Chichester Festival Theatre of 1962.

★ **Cathedral**. — Begun in 1091, finished in 1184, the nave is Norman; porches, ⊙ retrochoir and clerestories are early English; tower, side chapels and Lady Chapel are Decorative; and the cloisters, the unique bell tower and splendid spire (rebuilt 1861), are Perpendicular.

Interior. — Romanesque in style and spirit, though every architectural movement of the Middle Ages has left its mark. In spite of its Norman austerity, the **nave** (best viewed looking west) appears small, almost intimate. The splendid **screen** is Perpendicular. In the **south transept**, lit by a Decorated window, are early 16C paintings of the cathedral; in the **north transept** is the grave of the composer Gustav Holst (1874-1934); east of it, a stained-glass window by the French painter Marc Chagall (1887-1985).
The Lady Chapel ceiling paintings are notable, too, but the cathedral's greatest treasures are the 12C stone panels in the south choir aisle; they depict scenes from the Raising of Lazarus and are among the finest examples of Norman sculpture in England.

★ **St Mary's Hospital**. — *St Martin's Square.*
⊙ A medieval hospital (1290) with an aisled infirmary hall prolonged by a chapel. The hall provided accommodation for elderly people "of good character... from within five miles of Chichester". The compartmented hall retains its 17C brick chimneys rising up through the medieval roof. The chapel has interesting misericords.

★ **Pallant House**. — *9 North Pallant.*
⊙ Built in 1712 for the wine merchant, Henry Peckham, the tastefully furnished
period rooms of this Queen Anne town house are the setting for collections of Bow porcelain and paintings (Henry Moore, Graham Sutherland, John Piper and Paul Nash).

EXCURSIONS

★★ **Petworth House**. — *14* ⊙ *miles - 22km northeast by the A27 and the A285.*
This grand 17C mansion (1688) is the nearest there is to a Louis XIV château in England. The restrained west front is the perfect complement to the Capability Brown grounds with their view of the South Downs. The rooms contain exquisite carvings by Grinling Gibbons and John Selden, antique statuary and a considerable collection of paintings, including many by Turner, who was a frequent guest. The most spectacular feature is the **Grand Staircase** with its painted walls and ceiling by Laguerre. The **Turner Room**

Limewood carving by Grinling Gibbons (c1691) (detail)

contains the largest collection of his works outside the Tate Gallery *(qv)*. The Marble Hall is mostly Reynolds, the Square Dining Room, Van Dyck and the Beauty Room, Kneller. Lely's *Children of Charles I* is in the Oak Hall, Bosch's *Adoration of the Magi* in the Dining Room and **Grinling Gibbons'** carvings are in the **Carved Room**.

★ **Arundel Castle.** — *11 miles - 18km east on the A27.*
Home of the Duke of Norfolk, foremost Catholic layman in England, the original Norman **gatehouse and keep** (1138) survive after 750 years of assaults and sieges, unlike the lower bailey which was largely rebuilt by the Victorian 15th Duke, 1875-1900. The ashlared **keep** *(119 steps)* looks out over Arundel Cathedral (by Joseph Hansom, designer of the Hansom Cab), the meeting place of two revivals, the Catholic and the Gothic.

The finest Victorian rooms are the **Chapel** and **Barons' Hall** (paintings by Mytens, Kneller, Van Loo and Van Dyck); hanging in the **Drawing Room** are portraits by Mytens, Van Dyck, Gainsborough and Reynolds, while the **Library** (*c*1800) is 122ft - 70m of Gothic revival, displaying a Fabergé silver icon and a portrait of Richard III.

Fitzalan Chapel. — On the boundary of the castle grounds and forming the east end of the parish church, the Decorated private **Fitzalan Chapel** is crowded with tombs and monuments to the Howards. Originally the church and the chapel were one. The church became Protestant but with the establishment of the Howards' ownership of the east end, the chapel remained Catholic; thus the two denominations worship under one roof.

★ **Weald and Downland Open Air Museum.** — *6 miles - 10km north on the A286.*
Follow signs.
Over thirty historic buildings have been re-erected on the beautiful Downland slopes of this attractively located museum, launched in 1967 to rescue vernacular rural buildings in southeast England. They include a cottage, shop, medieval farmhouse, Tudor market hall, working watermill, toll cottage and a school.

Goodwood House. — *5 miles - 8km northeast, take the A27 and A285, follow signs.*
A Jacobean mansion, the home of George Lennox, Duke of Richmond, the illegitimate son of Charles II and Louise de Kerouaille, the house was extended in the 18C, first by Chambers, then by Wyatt, who planned an octagon but completed only three sides before the third Duke ran out of money. His best work is in the interiors, designed to house the Duke's 18C French furniture; particularly the **Tapestry Drawing Room** (with Gobelins tapestries depicting scenes from *Don Quixote*) where the colour scheme of pink, green and gold - a potential disaster - is superbly handled. In the **Round Reception Room** is Lely's portrait of *Frances Teresa Stewart* (the model for Britannia on coins); in the **Yellow Room** are works by Reynolds and Romney and in the **Long Hall** equestrian paintings (suitable for a house whose name is synonymous with horse racing) by Stubbs and Wootton. In the Entrance Hall there are four Canalettos.

Fishbourne Roman Palace. — *1 mile - 2km west on the A259.*
The most luxurious Roman palace yet excavated in England, built *c* 75AD, it may have been the home of Cogidubnus, a British collaborator with Imperial Rome. **Mosaics★** were laid over mosaics, as Roman fashions changed, until the 3C when the palace burnt down. Stumbled over by a workman digging a pipeline in 1960, the north wing shows off both the glorious mosaics and the luxury in which the Roman élite basked.

Bignor Roman Villa. — *13 miles - 21km northeast on the A27 and A29, follow signs.*
More modest than Fishbourne, a farm rather than a palace, but with exceptional **mosaics★**, in particular the **Ganymede Mosaic**, in the piscina, **Head of Venus** and chillingly austere **Winter** in the north range and a **Medusa Head** in the bathhouse.

Medusa Head Mosaic

When visiting London use the **Michelin Green Guide ''London''**

— *Detailed descriptions of places of interest*
— *Useful local information*
— *A section on the historic square-mile of the City of London with a detailed fold-out plan*
— *The lesser known London boroughs - their people, places and sights*
— *Plans of selected areas and important buildings.*

Michelin Map **403** O 27 or Atlas G Britain p 27

Its long curving High Street, lined with buildings of all periods in the mellowest of limestone, makes Chipping Campden the embodiment of Cotswold townscape at its most refined. Its welcome is warm, yet discreet, with little of the commercialisation to which some less favoured places have succumbed. Quietly prospering ever since the great days of the medieval wool trade, in the early 20C it attracted artists and craftspeople to whose care and skill is due something of its present perfect state of preservation.

Many of the **High Street's** houses are substantial, but more than individual distinction it is the overall harmony of the street scene which impresses. The centre of the town is marked by the arched and gabled **Market Hall** of 1627. Further north, distinguished by its two-storeyed bay window, is the **house of William Grevel**, "the flower of the wool merchants of all England", who died in 1401 and is commemorated by a fine brass in the parish church. In Church Street stand the Almshouses built in 1617 by Sir Baptist Hicks, whose own mansion opposite was destroyed in the Civil War. Two pavilions survive, together with pepperpot lodges and the gateway, near the entrance to the churchyard of **St James' Church**. Almost entirely remodelled in the 15C in the Perpendicular style and conveying a great sense of unity and repose, this is one of the noblest Cotswold "wool" churches.

EXCURSIONS

★★ **Hidcote Manor Garden.** — *3 1/2 miles - 5km north on minor roads.*
In creating one of the greatest English gardens of the 20C, the horticulturalist Lawrence Johnstone contrived an enchanting variety of effects in the small space of 10 acres - about 4ha. Calm expanses of lawns, vistas down avenues or into the countryside beyond, contrast with places of luxuriant but carefully controlled wildness. A labyrinth of "garden rooms" encloses an intricate arrangement of herbs, a composition of plants entirely in white, a mysterious pool... the whole is stitched together into a unified design by trim hedges of yew, beech and holly.

★★ **Chastleton House.** — *11 miles - 18km. Leave Chipping Campden on a minor road southeastwards, passing through the pretty village of Broad Campden. At Blockley, once a centre of silk manufacture, take the B4479 southwards, turning left after one mile onto the A44.*

Moreton-in-Marsh. — Pop 2 545. The Fosse Way broadens out to form the main street of this dignified little town.

2 miles further eastwards on the A44 turn right into a lane signposted to Chastleton.

★★ **Chastleton House.** — Hidden down narrow lanes is this perfect example of a Jacobean country house, built in the early 17C by a rich wool merchant and hardly altered since.

The gabled **front**, in grey and gold Cotswold stone, is grandly symmetrical and is flanked by two massive towers containing the staircases. Within, the décor, particularly panelling and plasterwork, has the rough vitality of the period and is complemented by original furniture. From the **Great Hall**, one of the last of its kind to be built, via the richly decorated **Great Chamber**, to the tunnel vaulted Long Gallery running the whole length of the top floor, the rooms open to the public evoke with unforced authenticity the atmosphere of domestic life in the 17C. Off one of the bedrooms is a secret chamber where Chastleton's owner may have hidden from Cromwell's troops after the battle of Worcester in 1651.

On one side of the forecourt are the 17C stables; on the other the modest little **Church of St Mary.** To the east of the house is a great rarity, a small formal **garden** dating from about 1700.

Michelin Map **403** O 28 or Atlas G Britain p 17

Founded as a fort early in the Roman conquest, by the second century AD Corinium had become a walled city second only to London in size, the centre of a flourishing countryside of great villa estates and the crossroads of the long-distance routeways of Ermine and Akeman Streets and the Fosse Way.

The confusion and destruction of the Dark Ages was followed by a long period of wool-based wealth, whose monument is the fine parish church. The "Capital of the Cotswolds" is still the market town for a prosperous rural region and has kept a traditional townscape, little marred by incongruous intrusions.

★ **Church of St John the Baptist.** — This most important example of a Cotswold "wool church" is of great interest and beauty. The lofty tower of 1400-20, supported by powerful spur buttresses, rises grandly above the town, a focal point of views from far around. The unusual three-storeyed porch giving onto the market place once served as the town hall.

The nave is exceptionally high and spacious; its immensely tall piers carry angels bearing the coats of arms of those pious townsfolk responsible for the ambitious rebuilding of 1516-30. Throughout the interior there is a wealth of detail: an unusual pre-Reformation pulpit; the **Boleyn Cup**, a gilt cup made for Anne Boleyn; memorial brasses grouped in the Chapel of the Holy Trinity; and, in the Lady Chapel, the charming effigies of Humfry Bridges (d 1598), his wife and their numerous children, their solemn demeanour contrasting with the insouciant air of the semi-reclining figure opposite of Sir Thomas Master (d 1680).

Town Centre. — The old town is compact, hemmed in by the green spaces of two ancient estates: the Abbey, completely demolished at the Dissolution, whose gardens lead down to the pretty River Churn and **Cirencester Park**, one of the most grandiose of formal landscapes, its **Broad Avenue** striding nearly five miles across country. The great house jealously preserves its privacy by turning to the town a shoulder of high wall and even higher yew hedge.

★ **Corinium Museum,** — This modern and well-ordered museum explains Cotswold
⊙ history from geological to recent times. The Roman heritage is emphasised with many local finds, including a series of superb **mosaic pavements**★ .

EXCURSIONS

★ **Westonbirt Arboretum.** — *14 miles - 23km southwestwards by the A433.*

Tetbury. — Pop 4 467. The focal point of this gracious little town with its elegant houses and inns in silver-grey stone is the quaint Market House of 1655. The architecture of the spacious Church of St Mary is a refined 18C interpretation of medieval motifs.

Continue on the A433 towards Bath. Shortly afterwards on the right is High-grove, a residence of the Prince of Wales.

★ **Westonbirt Arboretum.** — Since 1829 when Robert Halford planted the first trees here,
⊙ this most important plant collection has grown steadily to comprise some 14 000 trees and shrubs from all over the world. The Forestry Commission pursues serious research here, but tourists are well provided for with a modern visitor centre and many miles of signposted walks. Some trees are the largest of their species in Britain. The many varieties of maple guarantee a spectacular autumn display.

Fairford. — Pop 2 408. *8 1/2 miles- 14km eastwards by the A417.*
This old coaching village is famous for the **Church of St Mary**★ , harmoniously rebuilt in the late 15C. Sculptures, some humorously grotesque, enrich the exterior. Inside, the screens, stalls and misericords of the choir are of exceptional quality. But the church's glory is its wonderful set of **stained glass windows**★★ (c1500), tracing in colour the Bible story from Adam and Eve to Last Judgement. The twelve apostles face the twelve prophets and in the clerestory the twelve martyrs afront the twelve wicked enemies of the faith.

⊙ **Chedworth Roman Villa.** — *9 1/2 miles - 15km northwards on a minor road, the White Way. After 7 miles - 11km follow National Trust signposts.*
This large and rich villa stood at the head of a small valley beside its own spring. It was undoubtedly one of the grandest buildings of the Roman Cotswolds. The remains, including good mosaic floors, have been carefully excavated and are well presented. The museum presents items found on the site.

COLCHESTER Essex — Pop 87 476

Michelin Map 404 W 28 or Atlas G Britain p 23

Originally Camulodunum, the ancient British capital of King Cunobelin (Shakespeare's Cymbeline), Colchester became a Roman colonia under Claudius in 50 AD and soon established the reputation for **oysters** which it still has. After the Conquest the town became the site of the largest Norman keep and one of the richest priories in Europe. The oyster remained the principal source of wealth until the late Middle Ages when **wool** took over. Colchester continues to prosper today, the epitome of the economically thriving south and east of England.

Roman Walls. — *Balkerne Hill, Roman Road, Priory Street and Eld Lane.*
Encircling the town centre the 9ft - 3m thick walls are built of stone in concrete between brick bonding courses; best **viewed** from Balkerne Hill where **Balkerne Gate**, with arches and flanking towers, extends 30ft - 9m in front of the wall.

★ **Castle and Museum.** — Built with 12ft - 4m thick walls on the vaults of the
⊙ Roman Temple of Claudius, its massive dimensions (151ft - 46m by 110ft - 34m) make it half again the size of the White Tower at the Tower of London *(qv)*. Gutted and re-roofed, it is now a **museum** housing one of the largest collections of Roman antiquities gathered from one site in Britain.

⊙ **St Botolph's Priory.** — *Priory Street.*
Only the skeleton remains of the 12C priory, yet it gives a hint of its grandeur. Built, like the castle, of Roman brick, only the piers, west front (with the earliest circular windows in Britain) and 120ft - 37m nave survive.

EXCURSIONS

★ **Stour Valley.** — ''I associate my careless boyhood to all that lies on the banks of the Stour'', wrote **John Constable** (1776-1837). ''They made me a painter and I am grateful''. The lower Stour is **Constable Country**, the upper Stour **Gainsborough Country**, the frontier being Sudbury, where Gainsborough was born and where Constable went to school.

Take the A12 north for 8 miles - 13km, turn right onto the B1070 and follow signs.

★ **Flatford Mill.** — Home of Constable (his father was a miller), both the 1773 **Mill, Willy**
⊙ **Lott's Cottage** and the river valley are the subjects of his best-loved landscapes, including *The Haywain, Boatbuilding* and *Flatford Mill.*

The Haywain by Constable

2 miles - 3km west of Flatford, or by riverbank path.

Dedham. — Pop 1 905. A quintessentially English village, the subject of many Constable landscapes, ''there is nothing to hurt the eye in Dedham'' (Pevsner).

Cross under the A12 and take the B1068 and B1087 for 6 miles - 10km.

St James' Church, Nayland. — Built in the 15C. Inside is Constable's painting **The Last Supper.**

Take the B1087 to Bures, then the B1508.

Sudbury. — Pop 17 723. A silk-weaving centre and market town, Sudbury is blessed with three monumental Perpendicular churches, **St Gregory's**, **St Peter's** and **All Saints**, and lines of Georgian houses peppered with older half-timbered cottages.

★ **Gainsborough's House.** — *46 Gainsborough Street.* The birthplace of **Thomas Gainsborough**
⊘ (1727-88) is a late medieval building behind an elegant 18C façade. The holding includes Gainsborough memorabilia, two portraits of **Abel Moysey**, the recently discovered *Portrait of a Young Boy* and *The Gypsies*.

Continue 3 miles - 5km north on the A134.

Long Melford. — Pop 2 739. Long it is, with a 2 mile - 3km long main street, lined with 16, 17 and 18C timbered and pink plastered houses. At its end is a green and spacious triangle, marked by the 1573 **Trinity Hospital**, the late 15C **Church of the Holy Trinity**, one of the great ''wool churches'' of East Anglia. Note the 14C alabaster relief of the Adoration of the Magi and the 15C stained glass.

⊘ Nearby is **Melford Hall★**, Early Elizabethan, around three sides of a courtyard. Only the **Main Hall** retains its Elizabethan features. The Drawing Room is splendidly rococo and the 1813 Greek Revival staircase is by Thomas Hopper. In the West Bedroom, where **Beatrix Potter** *(qv)* frequently slept, is the original Jemima Puddle-Duck and on the walls are **watercolours** by the famous children's authoress.

★ **CONWY** Gwynedd   Pop 3 649

Michelin Map 403 I 24 or Atlas G Britain p 33

Viewed from across the river, Conwy Castle, massive and bristling with towers, the walled town, the river and bestriding bridges, make a breathtaking sight against the mountain background. An ideal site, controlling the estuary, Llywelyn the Great had already chosen it for his burial place and to this end had endowed a Cistercian abbey. With the building of Edward I's mighty fortress and garrison town, the monks were moved upstream to Maenan. All of Edward I's castles in Wales - with the exception of Harlech - were built in association with a ''bastide'', a town laid out on a rectangular grid. The town developed with the castle but remained contained by its circuit of walls.

Conwy Castle

★★**Conwy Castle.** — This masterpiece of medieval architecture, like Edward's other
⊘ Welsh castles was supplied from the sea. Building started in 1283 and was under
the direction of Master James of St George. Towards the end of June, building was
sufficiently advanced for the king and queen to stay here and by 1287 work was
almost completed.
Eight massive drum towers with pinnacled battlements protect the two wards of
the castle, set on its rocky ridge. The inner ward with the royal apartments was
approached by water and the large outer ward from the town. In the outer ward
the Great Hall lines the right hand side. Beyond the well the Middle Gate gives access to the inner ward, heart of the castle with on the right the King's Hall and
King's Tower. The now vanished Water Gate was to the east of the Chapel Tower.

Town. — Built at the same time as the castle the 13C **town walls★★**, 35ft - 11m
high and 6ft - 2m thick, girdle the town on three sides. The circuit is defended by
twenty-two towers and three gateways and provides a good wall walk between
Upper Church Gate and Berry Street. The founder of Conwy, Llywelyn the Great,
dominates all from his column in Lancester Square. Further down the High Street
⊘ at the corner of Crown Lane is **Plas Mawr★★** a mansion built in 1577 by Robert
Wynne, a truly "Elizabethan adventurer". Its rooms today still evoke a picture of the
more gracious moments of the age in which it was built. At the junction with Berry
⊘ and Castle Streets is **Aberconwy**, a medieval town house of c1300. Its ground floor,
some two feet below today's street level, houses an interesting "History of Conwy"
exhibition. On the quayside nearby is what is claimed to be the 'Smallest House
in Great Britain'.

Bridges. — In 1826 Thomas Telford built the first of the three bridges which seem
to lead straight into the castle, the most recent of which is to be replaced in its
turn, this time by a tunnel. Thomas Telford's 1826 suspension bridge is now for
pedestrians, the railway crosses Stephenson's medievalised 1848 bridge and road
traffic uses the 1958 road bridge.

EXCURSIONS

★★**Bodnant Garden.** — *8 miles - 13km south of Conwy by the A470.*
⊘ Mostly laid out in the late 19C and early 20C, the 99 acres - 40ha of garden offer
the visitor formal terraces around the house and "The Dell", an area of shrubbery
and woodland walks. Noted for rhododendrons, camellias and magnolias, it is
justly famed for the "Laburnum Arch", a curved tunnel of golden racemes, when
seen on a sunny day in late May and early June.

Sychnant Pass. — *Leave Conwy to the west by the minor road to the left.*
A mile west of the town the road suddenly comes to the head of the **Sychnant Pass**,
'Dry Ravine' in Welsh, with a stunning **view★★** down the deep slopes, held together,
it seems, by a minimum of vegetation.

★★★ CORNWALL Coast

Michelin Map 403 D to H 32 and 33 or Atlas G Britain pp 2 and 3

Remoteness and wildness are the charms of the Cornwall peninsula with its long
rugged coastline. The **Cornwall Coast Path** winds a sinuous course (268 miles - 430km)
above the sheer cliffs and indented coves and is the ideal way to discover the scenic
splendours of the peninsula. The path is clearly waymarked and there is a wide choice
of inland paths as short cuts.

SOUTH COAST

From Plymouth to St Just-in-Penwith
205 miles - 330km - allow 2 days - local map pp 96-97

The southern coastline of Cornwall has two contrasting features: weather-beaten
headlands jutting defiantly into the sea; and the tidal estuaries of the Tamar, Fowey,
Fal and Helford, with their sheltered creeks where even sub-tropical vegetation can
grow - which explains the abundance of gardens in this region. This fragmentation
of the land slows down the tempo of life (particularly suitable for holidays !), for
where there is no ferry or bridge a long detour must be made to move from one
remote village to another. The adventurous traveller who departs from this itinerary will find many hidden treasures - even if it means coming to a dead end at times !

★★**Plymouth.** — *Description p 203.*

★**Antony House.** — Sir William Carew built this classical grey stone house in 1721.
⊘ It contains a varied collection of 18C furniture and distinguished portraits, including three by Reynolds in the panelled salon and Edward Bower's memorable portrait of King Charles I at his trial.

St Germans. — Pop 2 136. In the centre of this old village are Sir William Moyle's
attractive **almshouses**, built in 1583. The **church★** is one of the finest examples of Norman architecture in Cornwall. Dissimilar towers frame a majestic west front. Note
the splendid **west portal** richly encircled by seven decorated orders carved in the
local blue-grey Elvan stone. The east window designed by Burne-Jones has glass
by William Morris.

★**Polperro.** — Pop 1 199. This attractive fishing town is particularly worth visiting
outside the tourist season.

★★Fowey. — Pop 2 092. This small town on the hillside above an excellent natural harbour in the mouth of the River Fowey was once one of England's busiest ports. There are walks out towards **Gribbin Head**, which affords **views★★** for miles around. It is well worth taking a boat trip round the harbour and coast where the cliffs rise dark and sheer from the water, or upriver along wooded hillsides. Try also to find the time to walk around the town, along Fore Street to visit the Elizabethan house called **Noah's Ark** and the 14C **St Fimbarrus Church** with its richly decorated tower, two-storeyed south porch, fine old wagon roof and Norman font.

★★Mevagissey. — Pop 1 896. Old quayside boathouses, a maze of twisting back streets and steps, nets of all shapes, sizes and colours lure crowds of tourists to this picturesque old fishing village. All the more reason for concentrating on its particular feature - the **double harbour** with its 1770s pier.

★Veryan. — Pop 880. Five small white round houses with Gothic windows and conical thatched roofs surmounted by a cross give this village its unique charm.

★★St Just-in-Roseland. — The church here, built on a 6C Celtic site in the 13C and restored in the 19C, is remarkable for its enchanting steep churchyard garden. The church stands so close to the creek and little harbour that at high tide it is reflected in the water.

★St Mawes. — In 1539-43 Henry VIII erected this cloverleaf shaped castle and Pendennis Castle on the opposite bank of the Fal (known as the Carrick Roads), to safeguard the mile-wide entrance to the estuary. The castle, situated in pleasant gardens, affords excellent **views★** right out to Manacle Point *(see below)* 10 miles to the south.

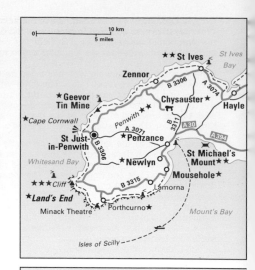

★★Trelissick Garden. — There are three gardens at Trelissick: the woodland Valley Garden, the East Lawn Garden and the Flower Garden. From the drive and the porticoed house of 1825 are splendid views of Falmouth and the open sea. In early summer the rhododendrons are in full bloom and in mid-August the gardens play host to performances of Shakespeare.

2 miles - 3km along the B3289 stands the 18C Quaker meeting-house at Come-to-Good.

Truro. — Pop 17 852. *Local map in the Michelin Green Tourist Guide The West Country.* A one-time river port and mining centre, Truro was considered by the 18-19C, with its theatre and assembly rooms, county library (1792) and its cathedral (since 1850) to be the county "metropolis". It is the most notable Georgian town west of Bath, with 18C houses in, for example, Boscawen and Lemon Streets.

Requests made throughout centuries for Cornwall once more to become an independent see were finally accepted and in 1880 the cathedral foundation stone was laid. Completed by 1910 **Truro Cathedral** is a mixture of Normandy Gothic with upswept vaulting, vistas through tall arcades and, outside, three steeple towers which give the building its characteristic outline.

★Falmouth. — Pop 17 810. *Local map in the Michelin Green Tourist Guide The West Country.* A low crest, crowned at its seaward point by **Pendennis Castle★**, divides the town in two: the hotel-residential area facing south and the old town, looking north up the Fal estuary. The waterfront extends for over half a mile, from **Greenbank Quay** to **Prince of Wales Pier**. Between these points the river is overlooked by 18C houses and warehouses standing on the 17C harbour wall. The quays which enclose the inner basin date back to c1670.

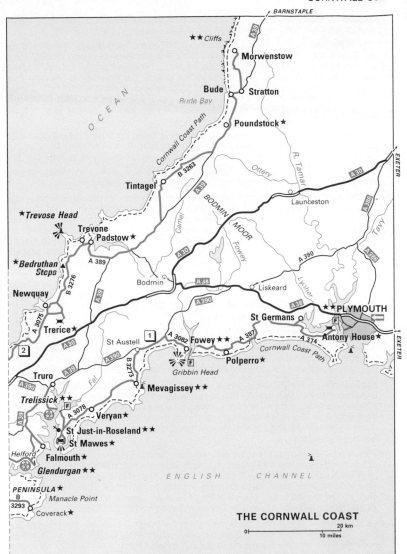

THE CORNWALL COAST

0   20 km

0   10 miles

Carlyon Bay, Cornwall

★★ **Glendurgan Garden.** — This richly-planted garden, dropping down to Durgan hamlet ⊘on the Helford River, is notable for its maze.

★ **Lizard Peninsula.** — *Local map in the Michelin Green Tourist Guide The West Country.* There is no coastal road running round this southernmost part of England so ⊘it is advisable to be selective in your exploration, choosing from the following : **Gweek Seal Sanctuary★** ; the south side of the **Helford estuary**; the **Manacles** off Manacle Point (an underwater reef responsible for many a shipwreck); the famous old fishing smuggling village of **Coverack★** ; the **Lizard** and its famous 1751 **lighthouse** (altered in 1903) on the southernmost tip of England ; and the very popular **Kynance Cove★★★** and **Mullion Cove★★★**.

Helston. — Pop 10 809. Helston is the market town for the Lizard Peninsula, but on 8 May, or the previous Saturday if the 8th falls on a Sunday or Monday, the town is closed to traffic and becomes the home of the famous **Flora Day Furry Dance★★**. Five processional dances are performed at 7, 8.30 and 10 am, at noon and at 5 pm, the most spectacular being at 10 am and at noon.

★★ **St Michael's Mount.** — *Causeway road from Marazion.* Mediterranean tin traders ⊘are said to have settled on what they called the island of Ictis, in 4BC. Cornish legend tells how, in 495 AD, fishermen saw the Archangel Michael on the granite rock rising out of the sea. The island became a place of pilgrimage and a Celtic monastery is said to have stood on the rock from the 8 to 11C. In c1150 Abbot Bernard of Mont-St-Michel in Normandy built a Benedictine monastery which as alien property was appropriated by the Crown in 1425 and finally dissolved in 1539.
The rock frequently served as a strongpoint from the Middle Ages to 1647, when its last military commander, Colonel John St Aubyn, bought the castle as a family residence. It is now a hybrid of 14-19C styles, with a Tudor **doorway** bearing the St Aubyn arms, a 14C **entrance hall**, a restored 14C **church** with 15C windows, and an 18C Rococo-Gothic **drawing room**.

★ **Penzance.** — *Description p 200.*

★ **Newlyn.** — Pop 2 090. Newlyn is the major fishing village in the southwest. The beautiful light and the charm of the cottages clustered round the harbour and on the hillside attracted a group of painters, the **Newlyn School,** in the 1880s.

★ **Mousehole.** — Mousehole is a very attractive and much-visited village. Its harbour is almost enclosed by a quay of Lamorna granite and a breakwater dating from 1393. Close to the low granite fishermen's cottages by the water's edge is the half-timbered Keigwin Arms, the only house left standing after a Spanish raid in 1595. One mile south of Mousehole is Spaniards' Point where the raiders landed to pillage the country for miles around.

★★ **Penwith.** — Penwith is the most westerly headland in England. It has a bleak beauty of its own deriving from its granite foundation, the wind, the blue of the ocean and its small granite churches and Celtic wayside crosses. This sparsely-populated region almost speaks for itself. Take any opportunity to leave the B3315 to admire the views from the cliffs and the sheltered coves of **Lamorna** and **Porthcurno★** and the **Minack Theatre** with its ocean back-drop, created in 1929.

★ **Land's End.** — The journey ends fittingly at the magical westernmost point of England, where the Atlantic surges perpetually, relentlessly buffeting the cliffs. For a peaceful view of this, perhaps the finest **cliff scenery★★★** in the West Country, come early and walk the coastal path, or come at sunset and stay to see the display put on by the many lighthouses.

St Just-in-Penwith. — *See below.*

NORTH COAST

From St Just-in-Penwith to Morwenstow
103 miles - 165km - allow 2 days - local map pp 96-97

The northern coast of Cornwall is the longest stretch of land in the southwest peninsula exposed to the wild Atlantic Ocean. At the same time it benefits from the warm Gulf Stream and this combination of warm water and sandy beaches with rolling waves explains north Cornwall's popularity with holidaymakers, particularly surfers.

St Just-in-Penwith. — Pop 2 680. The buildings lining the triangular square reflect the prosperity enjoyed by this tin-mining town in the 19C. The **church★** has a 15C pinnacled tower, walls of dressed granite, an elaborate 16C porch, wall paintings and a 5C tomb in the north aisle. 1 mile - 1 1/2km to the west (partly on foot), the hillock of **Cape Cornwall★** rises 230ft - 70m, affording **views★★** of Brisons Rocks, Land's End and the Longships lighthouse.

★ **Geevor Tin Mine.** — *Near Pendeen Lighthouse.* The tour of one of Cornwall's three ⊘ **working mines** and its **museum** demonstrates the process by which tin, copper, iron and arsenic are separated from the bedrock.

★ **Chysauster.** — The best-preserved **prehistoric Cornish village,** probably inhabited from ⊘ 100 BC to 250 AD, consists of eight circular stone houses, now open to the sky but originally roofed with turf or thatch, in two lines of four just below the crest of the hill.

⊘ **Zennor.** — Pop 213. The outdoor **Wayside Museum** shows the evolution of implements from stone to iron. On a 6C site stands the 12C granite **church★** of St Senner, enlarged in the 15C. Inside are an ornate late 13C font of Hayle limestone and on a bench end the 16C carving of the pretty Mermaid of Zennor.

★★**St Ives.** — Pop 9 439. *Town plan in the current Michelin Red Guide Great Britain and Ireland.* This attractive fishing harbour, with winding alleys and hillside terraces, is a much-visited summer resort and a favourite with artists since the late 19C. The church of **St Ia**, its 85ft - 26m **tower** of Zennor granite clearly visible from the harbour, was built in one phase in the 15C. Notable features are the **wagon roof, bench ends,** the 15C **font** and, in the **Lady Chapel**, the tender *Madonna and Child* (1953) by **Barbara Hepworth**, who came here in 1953 with **Ben Nicholson** and stayed until her death in 1975. Her studio is now the **Barbara Hepworth Museum**★★ containing an excellent collection of her abstract sculptures. **Smeaton Pier** and its octagonal domed lookout were constructed in 1767-70 by the builder of the original Eddystone Lighthouse, which now stands on Plymouth Hoe.

Hayle. — Pop 6 179. This estuary town, formerly important for copper, tin and iron smelting, is now popular for its miles of sandy beaches.

★★**St Agnes Beacon.** — The 628ft - 191m beacon affords a **panorama**★★ of the wild north Cornwall landscape, extending from Trevose Head in the northeast to St Michael's Mount to the southwest.

★**Trerice.** — This excellent Elizabethan manor house was built in 1572-73; the east front is highly decorated with scrolled gables, the **great hall** has a beautiful stone mullioned window containing 16C glass and the interior is notable for the quality of its 16C **plasterwork**, fireplaces and fine furniture.

Newquay. — Pop 16 050. *Town plan in the current Michelin Red Guide Great Britain and Ireland.* This popular resort, with sandy beaches at the foot of cliffs in a sheltered north-facing bay, takes its name from the new quay, built in 1439. By the 18-19C Newquay was a pilchard port, exporting salted fish to Italy and Spain, and from this period dates the **Huar's House** on the headland, from which the huar summoned the fishermen when he saw shoals of fish enter the bay.

★**Bedruthan Steps.** — Look over the cliff edge at the 1 1/2 mile arc of sand spectacularly scattered with giant rocks, worn to the same angle by waves and wind — the stepping stones, legend says, of the giant Bedruthan!

★**Trevose Head.** — From the 1847 lighthouse on the 243ft - 74m head, one can see that of Hartland Point, 40 miles - 64km northeast and that of Pendeen on West Penwith. By day the **views**★★ are of bay after sandy cove after rocky island...

Trevone. — For the more energetic the Cornwall Coast Path *(5 miles - 8km on foot)* is a spectacular approach from this village to Padstow, passing the natural rock arches of Porthmeissen Bridge and around the 242ft - 74m Stepper Point.

★**Padstow.** — Pop 2 256. *Local map in the Michelin Green Tourist Guide The West Country.* In the 6C St Petroc, landing from Wales, founded a Celtic minster at the mouth of the Camel estuary. It was destroyed by the Vikings, along with the town, in 981. The town recovered, developing into an important port until the 19C when ships became too large to pass the sand bar, known as Doom Bar, at the estuary mouth. The **harbour** is enclosed on three sides by quays lined with attractive old houses, while a network of narrow streets behind the quay ends at **St Petroc's Church** and **Prideaux Place,** a Tudor house with 18C battlements, still in the Prideaux family. The church, with its embattled west tower, dating from the 13C, contains an octagonal 15C font of Catacleuse stone and a bench end depicting the fox preaching to the geese; in the churchyard stands a Celtic cross-shaft.

Tintagel. — *Description p 235.*

★**Poundstock.** — Pop 665. In a secluded wooded dell stand a 13-15C **church**★ with square unbuttressed tower and square 13C granite font, and the sturdily built 14C Guildhall, two-storeyed, buttressed and with a slate roof.

Bude. — Pop 2 679. *Local map in the Michelin Green Tourist Guide The West Country.*
This harbour town in the cliffs which stand tall against the incoming Atlantic is a very popular holiday resort with golden sandy beaches and breakers ideal for surfing.

Stratton. — Pop 1 288. The narrow streets of this old market town climb to the **church**★ begun in 1348, the granite south arcade being added in the mid-15C, the chancel and 90ft - 27m tower in the 16C. The font is Norman, the pulpit Jacobean.

Morwenstow. — Pop 619. Cornwall's northernmost parish, situated on spectacular 450ft - 133m **cliffs**★★, possesses a fine **church**★ with a Norman **south door** and a north **arcade**, the last two bays of which are Early English. Beneath the original wagon roof are an egg-shaped Saxon font with cable moulding and mid-16C bench ends.

FOLLOW THE COUNTRY CODE

Guard against all risk of fire.
Fasten all gates.
Keep dogs under proper control.
Keep to the paths across farmland.
Avoid damaging fences, hedges and walls.
Leave no litter.
Safeguard water supplies.
Protect wildlife, wild plants and trees.
Go carefully on country roads.
Respect the life of the countryside.

Rising gently from the Upper Thames valley in the southeast to a dramatic escarpment overlooking the Severn Vale in the west, the Cotswolds offer the essence of rural England in concentrated form. Airy open uplands, sheltered in places by stately belts of beech trees, alternate with deep valleys enfolding exquisite villages and small towns.

The region has long been favoured for settlement. The commanding heights in the west are crowned more often than not by the hill-forts of prehistoric man, whose burial places abound, too, from the chambered tombs of the Neolithic to the round barrows of the Bronze Age. Great estates were farmed from the Roman villas lying just off the ruler-straight Ermin Street and the Foss Way. In the Middle Ages it was the wool from countless sheep grazing on the fine pasture of the wolds which gave rise to a trade of European importance and to a class of prosperous merchants, whose monuments are the great "wool" churches which they built from the underlying **oolitic limestone.** Quarried everywhere and ranging in colour from silver or cream to deepest gold, this loveliest of building stone is inseparable from any definition of "Cotswold character". Yielding the sophisticated masonry of manor house, the "tiles" of cottage roof, rough dressed wall of barn and even the drystone boundaries of fields, it creates a rare harmony of building and landscape.

Far removed from coalfields and big cities, the area escaped the effects of industrialisation; its rural pattern is intact, an idyllic setting for quiet exploration of the past.

From Cirencester to Chipping Campden

40 miles - 64km - allow 1 day

Starting in the centre of the Cotswolds, the tour runs northwards through some of the region's most delightful small towns and villages towards the spectacular prospect from the escarpment high above Broadway.

★ **Cirencester.** — *Description p 92.*

> *Leave Cirencester eastwards on the A429 and then the B4425.*

★ **Bibury.** — Pop 603. The friendly River Coln, stone bridges, weavers' cottages and the gables of Bibury Court against a wooded background combine to justify
⊘ William Morris' epithet of "the most beautiful village in England". The restored **Arlington Mill** is an interesting folk museum.

> *Continue on the B4425, turning left after 1 1/2 miles - 2km onto a minor road and follow signs to Northleach.*

★ **Northleach Church of SS Peter and Paul.** — This fine example of a "wool" church dominates the market place of this little stone town. The graceful two-storeyed south porch is adorned with medieval carvings. Inside, a remarkable set of **wool merchants' brasses**★ recalls former prosperity.

⊘ The region's rural past is evoked in the **Cotswold Countryside Collection,** a well-arranged modern museum intriguingly accommodated in the "House of Correction", a jail and courthouse from 1791 until 1974. The displays recreate a way of life now long gone from the Cotswold hills and farms.

> *Continue northwards on the A429, the Roman Foss Way.*

★ **Bourton-on-the-Water.** — Pop 2 538. A focal point of Cotswold tourism, with a model village, "Birdland" and a motor museum, Bourton owes its special charm to the clear waters of the Windrush which run through well-tended lawns alongside the main street and under elegant stone bridges.

Arlington Row, Bibury

Cross the A429 and follow signs west to the Slaughters.

The villages of **Lower** and **Upper Slaughter** are both picturesquely sited by the River Eye.

Leave Upper Slaughter to the northwest, turning left almost immediately onto the B4068 towards Ford. Cross the B4077 and turn left after 3 miles - 5km to Snowshill.

★ **Snowshill Manor.** — Snugly sited below the escarpment's brim, Snowshill Manor, a good example of a Cotswold manor of about 1500, is crammed with a wondrous array of objects acquired in a lifetime of collecting by the eccentric Charles Wade, who also laid out the enchanting **terraced garden★**.

Continue northwest to Broadway.

★ **Broadway.** — Pop 1 931. Favoured by its position at the junction of two main roads, this "show village of England" devotes itself wholeheartedly to the needs of its many visitors with a variety of antique and craft shops, cafés and restaurants, hotels and guest houses. The long, partly tree-lined "broad way" rises gently from the village green at the western end to the foot of the escarpment, flanked by mellow stone buildings which range from the stately Lygon Arms to picturesque thatched cottages.

Take the A44 east and shortly after reaching the summit of the long climb, turn right to Broadway Tower Country Park.

In the Country Park is **Broadway Tower,** a battlemented folly of 1800, marking one of the highest points (1 024ft - 312m) in the Cotswolds. The vast westward **panorama★★** is one of the most magnificent in England. The eye soars freely over the fertile Vale of Evesham to the jagged line of the Malvern Hills and beyond, in clear weather, to the far distant landmarks of the Welsh border country; the Forest of Dean and the Black Mountains in the southwest, Clee Hill and the Wrekin to the northwest.

Cross the A44 and follow signs to Chipping Campden.

★★ **Chipping Campden.** — *Description p 92.*

★ COVENTRY West Midlands

Pop 318 718

Michelin Map 404 P 26 or Atlas G Britain p 27

Coventry's history stretches back to Saxon times; Leofric, Earl of Mercia, founded a Benedictine Priory in 1043 and his wife Godiva saved the town from the wrath of the Earl by riding naked through the streets. The priory became a cathedral and the ride became a legend. The city grew rich in the Middle Ages through the cloth and wool trade and a new church, St Michael's, was built *c*1200. 20C light industries brought a new kind of wealth and the church became a cathedral in 1918, the population growing from 70 000 in 1900 to 250 000 in 1930.

Most of the city was burnt on 14 November 1940 in the biggest bombing raid of its time. The new city built in its place, planned by Sir Donald Gibson and Arthur Ling and epitomised by **Sir Basil Spence's** new cathedral, is both a visual and functional success, thanks to its human scale and respect for what little of medieval Coventry remains, the timber-framed properties of the **Spon Street** (Y) scheme.

St Michael defeating the Devil by Jacob Epstein

TWO CATHEDRALS *visit 1 hour*

★ **Old St Michael's** (Y B). — *South of the new cathedral.*
Late 13C with large-scale Decorated and Perpendicular additions, all but the walls, crypt and 294ft - 90m tower and spire (one of the architectural glories of England, exceeded only by Norwich and Salisbury in height) were gutted in 1940. At the east end the altar is marked by a simple cross of charred timber, a replica of one erected by an anonymous fireman out of two roof beams in the aftermath of the firestorm.

★★★ **New St Michael's** (Y). — Regarded by traditionalists as too modern and modernists as too traditional, Coventry Cathedral is one of the few post-war buildings to meet with the approval of the ordinary person. Its success lies in its synthesis of traditional dimensions and structural possibilities and in its use of light.

Exterior. — Facing north so that it appears to be a part of the old St Michael's, its nave walls are simple, showing off Epstein's *St Michael defeating the Devil*, at the entrance steps. The majestic porch was designed to link the two cathedrals and dramatically expresses the meaning of death and resurrection. In the ruins, the Altar of Reconciliation is the focus of the Friday liturgy, while the 100ft - 91m tower and spire with newly-restored bells dominates the city which is well-known as the city of the three spires. The flèche on the new cathedral (sometimes described as a TV aerial) has been both criticised and praised.

Interior. — The overwhelming impression is of height, light and colour - height from Spence's soaring slender nave pillars which support the canopied roof; light from the great west screen - a wall of glass engraved with patriarchs, prophets, saints and angels by John Hutton; a symphony of colour from Piper's Baptistery window - symbolically showing the light of truth breaking through the conflicts and confusions of the world. The font is the most ancient of all, a great rough boulder from the hillside of Bethlehem. The orientation of the ten great windows southwards to form angled recesses enables the sun to pour light through the beautiful colours to light the nave. Dominating the whole cathedral is the huge tapestry designed by Graham Sutherland, *Christ in Glory* (the nearby Herbert Art Gallery has Sutherland's studies for this work). At the foot of the tapestry is the Lady Chapel with its exquisite statue of the Blessed Virgin Mary. Adjacent, the Chapel of Christ in Gethsemane depicting the Angel with the shining chalice, and beyond is the Chapel of Christ the Servant with its unique hanging cross and Crown of Thorns. The Chapel of Unity, under the control of the Joint Council, has many interesting features. The floor is the work of the Swedish artist Einar Forseth, its centre piece the Dove on a nest of flame, the symbol of the Holy Spirit, surrounded by representations of the five continents as well as traditional Christian symbols. The tall windows are the work of Margaret Traherne and are a beautiful sequence of colour, which casts exciting lighting patterns on the floor when the sun shines.

ADDITIONAL SIGHTS

⊙ **Guildhall of St Mary** (Z D). — Founded in 1342, it was the prison of Mary Queen of Scots in 1569. Its treasures are two tapestries (one Flemish *c*1500), showing Henry VII kneeling, the other showing Queen Elizabeth and her courtiers. The **Hall** with a splendid timber roof, is lit by stained glass windows portraying the Kings and Queens of England.

⊙ **Whitefriars** (Z E). — A Carmelite monastery from 1342 until the Reformation and after that a workhouse, the beautifully vaulted eastern **cloisters** and the **monks' dormitory** survive.

Ford's Hospital (Z). — *Exterior only.*
Much restored after war damage the 1509 half-timbered almshouses form a tranquil courtyard, a picture, with its flowers and creepers, in the heart of the late 20C city.

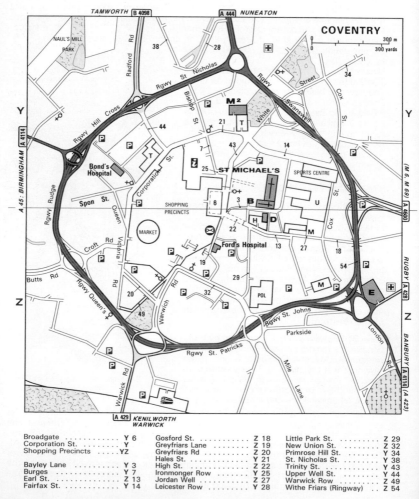

Bond's Hospital (Y). — *Exterior only.*
Another enchanting half-timbered almshouse, forming a courtyard with **Bablake Old School** and looking out on the 14C **St John's Church.** The oldest part is the **east range** (*c*1500), founded by Thomas Bond, "for as long as the world shall endure".

★ **Museum of British Road Transport** (Y M²). — Appropriately for the city that was
⊙ the birthplace of the British car industry - with Daimler in 1896 - and subsequently home to over 100 different manufacturers of motor vehicles (Daimler, Standard, Rover, Riley, Humbor, Lea & Francis, Singer, Hillman, Triumph...) and motor cycles (Swift, Rudge Whitworth, Raleigh, Norton...) this display illustrates the industry, its growth and decline in the present century. The earliest models are attractively presented in an authentic turn of the century street scene. In the line-up look for the 1908 Riley with its carbide lighting system as an optional extra, the well loved bull-nosed Morris (1922), the no 1 state car a 1947 Daimler and the latest Jaguar XJ6 2.9, an epitome of comfort and elegance. The display ends with Thrust 2, holder of the world speed record at 633.468mph - 1 019.47km/h.

★★★ CULROSS Fife   Pop 460

Michelin Map **401** J 15 or Atlas G Britain p 56

An attractively restored small Scottish burgh, on the north shore of the Firth of Forth. Legend has it that St Mungo, patron saint of Glasgow, was born here. A Cistercian house was founded here in the 13C, but it was trade with the Low Countries, salt panning and coal mining that brought the status of Royal Burgh, accorded by James VI in 1588.
It is, however, as a place where the visitor can see in all its richness of detail Scottish domestic architecture of the 16 and 17C that Culross (pronounced Cuross), is best known today.

★★★ **Village.** — When wandering round note the inscribed lintels, decorative finials, skewputts, crow stepped gables, forestairs, harling and rubble stonework with door and window trims.
⊙ The **Town House** (NTS Visitor Centre) is a stone and slate building, built 1625 in Flemish style, and contrasts with the white harling and red pantiles of the surrounding buildings.
The **Back Causeway**, behind, has a central line of paving stones slightly raised above the rest - for the exclusive use of local notables, in order to keep their feet out of the filth and damp of the narrow alleyway.
⊙ The **Study★**, a delightful example of 17C burgh architecture dating from 1610, has a restored 17C **painted ceiling** in the main room and original panelling dating from 1633. Directly opposite is the oldest house in Culross, with a replica of the 1588 mercat cross in front of its gable end.

★★ **Palace.** — Built between 1597 and 1611 by George Bruce, a merchant and coal
⊙ owner who, like Danzig Willie (Craigievar Castle) and Provost Skene (Aberdeen), used his wealth to build himself a fine and comfortable house. The rooms are small and pine-panelled for warmth, and there are 21 fireplaces, in which coal, rather than logs, was burnt. Dutch tiles, carried as ballast in his ships, were used for flooring and roofing, and the whole house gives us an insight into the domestic surroundings of the prosperous merchants of the period.

★★ DARTMOOR Devon

Michelin Map **403** H, I 32 or Atlas G Britain p 4

Dartmoor, 365 square miles in extent, is the largest of the five granite masses which form the core of southwest England. The centre is open moorland, approximately 1 000ft - 300m high, while the **tors**, mainly to the north and west, rise to as much as 2 000ft - 600m, though the two highest **High Willhays** (2 038ft - 621m) and **Yes Tor** (2 030ft - 619m) are in the military training area and thus often inaccessible. To the east and southeast are wooded valleys, cascading streams and small villages. About 109 sq miles - 282 sq km of the land are owned by the Duchy of Cornwall (since 1503 the estate of the monarch's eldest son), the rest by farmers, Devon County Council, the Forestry Commission, the Water Authority and the Ministry of Defence. Ponies, sheep and cattle graze freely on the moor, buzzards, kestrels and ravens may be sighted and beside the streams, woodpeckers, wagtails and dippers...

Landmarks, towns and villages on the Moor

See local map in the Michelin Green Guide The West Country

Ashburton. — Pop 3 610. This former stannary, or coinage, town stands on a tributary of the River Dart at the beginning of the old road (B3357) across the moor to Tavistock. The church with its tall Perpendicular granite tower was built in the 15C when the town was a wool centre. Slate-hung houses indicate its importance as a slate mining centre from the 16-18C.

Brent Tor. — The 1 130ft - 344m hill of volcanic stone is crowned by **St Michael's,** a small 13C stone church with a low stalwart tower affording excellent **views★★** for miles around.

Buckfastleigh. — Pop 2 894. This market town on the southeast edge of the moor,
⊙ with its 13C church, is best known as the terminus of the **Buckfast Steam Railway**, a former GWR line, one of the most picturesque in England.

Buckland in the Moor. — Pop 93. Thatched stone cottages set in a wooded dell and the late medieval moorstone church form a particularly characteristic Devon village.

★ **Castle Drogo.** — On discovering his descent from a 12C Norman nobleman Dru or Drogo, the successful grocer Julius Drewe commissioned **Edwin Lutyens** (1869-1944) to create an extravagant castle to the glory of his name. The castle was built 1911-30 of granite partly from Drewe's own quarry; the exterior shows Norman and Tudor influences while the interior is very much Lutyens at his best.

Chagford. — Pop 1 400. The medieval market town, one of four Devon towns chartered as stannary towns in the Middle Ages, stands high above the Teign valley, with good views of high tors and of Castle Drogo. The **market square** is surrounded by small granite or whitewashed houses, a 13-16C inn built as the manor house and the quaint market house known as the Pepperpot, all overlooked by the tall 15C pinnacled **church tower**.

Dartmeet. — The West and East Dart Rivers converge from the uplands to flow on through a gorge-like valley between wooded hillsides lively with bird and animal life.

Fingle Bridge. — The three-arched 16C granite bridge spans the most picturesque reach of Fingle Gorge. On the 700ft - 213m hilltop to the north stand the ruins of an Iron Age hillfort, Prestonbury Castle.

Lydford. — Pop 1 880. The village descends from the main road towards the River Lyd and the gorge, the buildings increasing in age to the 16C oak-timbered cottages and the inn. The castle testifies to Lydford's military importance as a Saxon outpost from the 7C to the 13C; the two-storey **keep**, now in ruins, was built in 1195 to hold prisoners. **St Petroc's Church** founded in the 6C was rebuilt and enlarged on Norman foundations in the 13C, the south aisle and tower in the 15C, and further changes were made in the 19C.

★★ **Lydford Gorge.** — *2 hours for the joint Upper and Lower Path walk.*
The wooded gorge is about 1 1/2 miles - 2km long with rock walls in places about 60ft - 18m high. There are three marked paths from the main entrance; the **Upper Path** following the northeast - southwest course of the gorge giving excellent views of the river below and glimpses of Dartmoor. The **Lower Path** skirts the northwest bank at the water's edge. The **Third Path** leads from the Pixie Glen to the Bell Cavern via the thundering whirlpool known as the **Devil's Cauldron.** At the south end is the 100ft - 30m **White Lady Waterfall.**

Moretonhampstead. — Pop 1 420. Known locally as Moreton this old market town was a coaching stage on the Exeter-Bodmin road. The 14-15C granite **church** has a commanding west tower but the most remarkable building is the row of thatched, colonnaded granite **almshouses**, dating from 1637.

Postbridge. — Pop 121. The **clapper bridge** made of large granite slabs, is believed to date from the 13C when tin-mining and farming were being developed on the moor. The three openings are spanned by slabs weighing up to 8 tons, each about 15ft - 5m long.

Princetown. — Pop 842. The town, the highest in England at 1 400ft - 425m, is dominated by one of the best-known prisons in England — the least welcoming place in Devon. Originally built in 1806-08 to hold Napoleonic prisoners of war, it already held 5 000 men in 1809 and 9 000 by 1813. After a period as a factory it was re-opened as a convict prison in the 1840s, when the practice of deportation had ceased.

Rough Tor. — The 1 791ft - 346m tor stands at the centre of the moor north of Two Bridges.

Scorhill Circle. — *4 miles - 6km west of Chagford on the Teigncombe road to Batworthy, then 1 mile - 2km over Teign footbridge.* A rare Bronze Age stone circle on the moor.

Shovel Down. — *1 mile - 2km south of Batworthy on foot.* An interesting Bronze Age group of a monolith and five stone alignments is to be seen at Shovel Down.

Two Bridges. — The Two Bridges, one a medieval **clapper bridge**, cross the West Dart at the junction of two ancient tracks across the moor (now the B3357/B3212).

Widecombe in the Moor. — Pop 603. A cluster of mostly granite-built cottages, grouped around the church, stands in the shallow valley surrounded by granite ridges which rise to 1 500ft - 460m. The Perpendicular **Church of St Pancras**, a vast building 104ft - 32m long with an imposing pinnacled tall tower is sometimes known as the **Cathedral of the Moor.** The plain barrel roof is decorated with a series of well carved **bosses.** The traditional ballad, about Tom Pearse's grey mare and Old Uncle Tom Cobleigh and all riding to the fair, has made Widecombe itself a popular legend.

Wistman's Wood. — *3 miles - 5km on foot, return, north of Two Bridges.* On the steep and rocky slopes of the West Dart River grow stunted mossy oaks, survivors and descendants of the primeval woodland which once clothed these uplands. Nearby are large groups of Bronze Age remains.

When visiting the West Country
*use the **Michelin Green Guide "England: The West Country".***

— Detailed descriptions of places of interest
— Touring programmes by county
— Maps and street plans
— The history of the region
— Photographs and drawings of monuments, beauty spots, houses...

★★ DARTMOUTH Devon

Michelin Map **403** J 32 or Atlas G Britain p 4

A deepwater haven in a beautiful setting, almost invisible from the sea, the town grew wealthy on trade. In the 17C, however, when trading concentrated on Bristol and London, Dartmouth became purely a naval port, as the presence of the Britannia Royal Naval College, built at the turn of the century, now testifies. The Quay was constructed in 1548 when it served as the centre of the town's activities. Along its length stand merchants' houses, built in the 17C.

St Saviour's Church. — *Anzac Street.* The tall square pinnacled tower has been a landmark for those sailing upriver since it was constructed in 1372. Note especially the south door with its two ironwork lions and rooted Tree of Life and the medieval altar with legs carved like ships' figureheads.

High Street. — The Shambles, or main street of the medieval town, is still lined with houses of the medieval period. Most notable are the early 17C four-storey **Tudor House** and, on the corner, **The Cherub**, a late 14C half-timbered merchant's house, now an inn.

⊙ **Dartmouth Castle.** — *1 mile - 1 1/2km by Newcomen Road, South Town and Castle Road.* The fort was begun in 1481 by the merchants of Dartmouth to protect their homes and deepwater anchorage and altered and added to in the 16C and 18C. It commands excellent **views★★★** out to sea and across and up the estuary.

EXCURSIONS

★ **Totnes.** — Pop 6 133. *12 miles - 19km north on the B3207 then the A38.*
The ancient town of Totnes still guards the lower Dart valley at its tidal and navigable limit. The narrow main street climbs uphill beyond the East Gate, a reminder that
⊙ Totnes was once a walled town. The half-timbered **Elizabethan Museum** *(No 70 Fore*
⊙ *Street)*, the **Guildhall**, a former cloth merchants' hall and numerous other attractive buildings testify to Totnes' prosperity as a wool and cloth centre in the 16C. **St Mary's★** with its red sandstone tower has a beautiful Beer stone rood screen dating from 1459. High on its mound sits the **castle**, encircled by 14C ramparts built to strengthen the motte and bailey earthworks raised in the early 12C. The castle walls command excellent **views★★★** of the Dart River valley, upstream to Dartmoor *(qv)* and downstream towards Dartmouth.
⊙ **Ferry boats** ply the 10 mile - 16km stretch of the Dart between Totnes and Dartmouth; a good way to discover its lushly green and intricate shoreline.

Torquay. — Pop 54 430. *10 miles - 16km. Ferry across the Dart estuary, then the A379 and A3022.*
A mild climate, exotic vegetation, sea views and wide sandy beaches all help to explain why Torquay is a bustling South Devon summer resort.
⊙ Excavations in the group of limestone caves, known as **Kents Cavern★** *(Wellswood, Ilsham Road, right off Babbacombe Road, the B3199)* have shown that they were inhabited by prehistoric animals and by men for long periods from the Palaeolithic era, 100 000 years ago, until Roman times. The tour *(1/2 mile - 800m)* leads through contrasting chambers with petrified ''waterfalls'', beautiful white, red-brown and green crystals and many **stalactites** and **stalagmites.**
⊙ **Torre Abbey** *(Torbay Road)*, in luxuriant gardens, comprises an 18C house, the so-called Spanish Barn and the ruins of the medieval abbey. The house, now a museum, contains collections of **English pewter**, 18-19C glass and a rare set of proof copies of **William Blake's** illustrations for the *Book of Job.*

DENBIGH (DINBYCH) Clwyd

Michelin Map **403** J 24 or Atlas G Britain p 33

The market town of Denbigh is clustered on a hillside overlooking the Vale of Clwyd
⊙ to the east. Interesting side streets lead up to the ruins of the **castle★** built by Henry de Lacy in 1282, on the orders of Edward I after he defeated Llywelyn. The three interlinked 14C towers of the gatehouse, similar in plan to Caernarfon, probably show the influence of the King's master mason, James of St George. The town walls, still almost complete, date from the same period, with the Burgess Gate being the main entrance to the town.
Robert Dudley was created Earl of Leicester and Baron Denbigh in 1564. In 1579 work began on **Leicester's Church**, the first purpose-built Protestant church in Britain, but it was unfinished at his death in 1588. The walls still stand to roof height.

Henry Morton Stanley (1841-1904), african explorer in his own right, but best known for his remark 'Doctor Livingstone, I presume', was born in Denbigh and brought up in the workhouse at St Asaph *(see below).*

EXCURSION

St Asaph (Llanelwy). — Pop 3 156. *5 miles - 8km north by the A525.*
St Kentigern founded the cathedral and a monastic community on the site in 560 AD.
⊙ The present **cathedral★**, mainly 13C (in the second smallest cathedral city in the country, after St David's), houses the memorial of Bishop William Morgan, translator of the Bible into Welsh in 1588 — ''Religion, if not taught in the mother tongue, will lie hidden and unknown'' — and the Bible used at the Investiture of the Prince of Wales in 1969.

Michelin Map 402 P 25 or Atlas G Britain p 35
Town plan in the current Michelin Red Guide Great Britain and Ireland

Originally Roman (Derventio was on the opposite bank of the Derwent) and now the home of Rolls Royce, Derby was one of the five Daneburghs, with Leicester, Lincoln, Nottingham and Stamford *(qv)* and the furthest point south to which Bonnie Prince Charlie's army penetrated before its retreat to Culloden (1746). Ten years later William Duesbury founded the Derby porcelain industry, excelling in table-ware and unglazed figures in light neo-classical mode.

⊘ **Cathedral.** — *Queen Street.*
A sublime blending of three eras; early 16C (the high tower), early 18C (James Gibbs' nave) and late 20C (retrochoir). Inside, the impression of classical simplicity is coun-tered by the magnificent Bakewell wrought iron **screen and gates**, and the pediment-ed baldachin over the high altar. South of the chancel rests Bess of Hardwick *(qv)*, outshining her neighbours in death as in life.

★ **Museum and Art Gallery.** — *The Strand.*
⊘ Derby Museum and Art Gallery is home to two superb collections. The China Gallery contains the largest **collection of Derby Porcelain★**, some 3 000 pieces covering the

different periods of manufacture. Of par-ticular interest are works typical of the early period by André Planché; unglazed biscuit figures and groups by Pierre Ste-phan dating from the Chelsea Derby peri-od (1770-84); painted scenes from the Crown Derby period (1784-1811) by John Brewer, especially naturalistic flow-ers and landscapes, George Robertson shipping scenes, Zachariah Boreman's Derbyshire landscapes, as well as more elaborate items from the Robert Bloor period (1811-48). In addition there is a good selection from the Crown Derby Company production since its foundation in 1876 to the present day.

The Wright Gallery holds many of the finest paintings and drawings of **Joseph Wright of Derby** (1734-97); his early studies in artificial light *(Blacksmith's Shop, A Philosopher lecturing on the Orrery)*, his portraits *(The Rev d'Ewes Coke group)* and the romantic masterpieces in natur-al light *(Landscape with Rainbow, Indian Widow)* of his later life.

★ **Royal Crown Derby Museum.** — *Os-*
⊘ *maston Road.*
The new works, founded in 1847, house a collection of Derby porcelain, dating from 1756 to the present day. George III accorded royal patronage in 1773 and the

Derby Candlestick (1756-60)

Royal Crown Derby title was granted by Queen Victoria in 1890. In the **Raven Room** a priceless mint collection of Royal Crown Derby is displayed as it would have been in a Victorian house.

EXCURSIONS

★★ **Kedleston Hall.** — *4 miles - 6km northwest on Kedleston Road.*
⊘ Sir Nathaniel Curzon began to pull down his Restoration house in 1758, employing Matthew Brettingham to replace it with a Palladian mansion connected by curving arcades to four detached wings. James Paine built the north front and in 1760 Robert Adam, fresh from his Italian Grand Tour, was called in to add the south front and to design the interior, one of his earliest great works. The disastrous effects which such a triple change of architects might have had was avoided since all three worked in the neo-classical context, creating one of the grandest 18C houses in England. The Curzons have lived at Kedleston for over 500 years and one, Lord Curzon, was Viceroy of India 1898-1905.
Paine's north front is Palladian. In contrast, Adam's south front bursts out of clas-sical constrictions with the movement of its stairs and dome.
Interior. — The rooms centre on the **Marble Hall**, lit from above so as not to detract from the Greek and Roman splendours of gods and goddesses in the alcoves. The arabesque stucco ceiling is by Joseph Rose, Adam's own plasterer. The **State Draw-ing Room** shows Adam at his most colourful; (note the Cuyp *Landscape* and the Veronese *Achilles*). As grand as the Marble Hall but as warm as the State Drawing Room is the **Saloon** or **Rotunda**, reaching to the 62ft - 19m coffered **dome**, as surpris-ing as Biagio Rebecca's neo-classical *Scenes from British History*. The final Adam surprise is the **Ante Room** and **Dressing Room**, graced by a neo-classical screen with a segmental arch above the entablature, in a room covered by 17 and 18C Masters including Van Dyck, Lely, Kneller and Jansen.

★★ **Sudbury Hall.** — *15 miles - 24km west on the A516 and A50.*
⊘ Built between 1660 and 1702 the **Jacobean exterior** is deliberately conservative, the **interior** a radical combination of late Renaissance classicism and budding baroque. The old formal gardens were swept away in the 18C to make way for a naturalis-tically landscaped park.

The Hall is packed with 18C paintings, beautified by the work of Grinling Gibbons, Edward Pierce and James Pettifer (all craftsmen who had worked with Wren on many of his London churches) and capped by Louis Laguerre's ceiling paintings. In the **Entrance** and **Great Hall** is Griffier's bird's-eye view of Sudbury and portraits by Reynolds and Lawrence; the **Staircase** was built by Pierce and the exquisite plaster-work above it is by Pettifer; two Griffiers and a Hoppner hang beneath Pettifer's ceiling of winged cherubs in the **Drawing Room**, while the finest ceiling of all is in the **Long Gallery**.

★★ **Dovedale.** — *Description p 197.*

DEVIZES Wiltshire   Pop 12 430

Michelin Map **403** O 29 or Atlas G Britain p 17

Devizes developed around the early Norman castle, which was rebuilt by Bishop Roger of Sarum in the 12C, became Crown property, but being ''utterly ruinated and decayed'' by 1596, was finally demolished by Cromwell's forces in 1645. The town itself flourished as a sheep market which accounts for the size of the half-moon-shaped **Market Place★**, with its handsome 1814 cross and 1879 fountain. It is overlooked by 18C houses and a number of old inns, notably the 18C **Black Swan** and early 18C **Bear Hotel**, known for the portrait sketches of customers drawn in the 18C by the landlord's son **Thomas Lawrence** (1769-1830). Note **Parnella House** (no 23), built in *c*1740 by a doctor who decorated the front with a statue of Aesculapius, the Classical god of medicine (modern copy).

★★ **St John's.** — This major Norman church has a mighty oblong **crossing tower** with, on the inside, round arches towards the nave and chancel and an early example of pointed arches towards the transepts. The chancel has low rib vaulting and walls patterned with intersecting arches. Note the broad mouldings sharp with zig-zag decoration and in the chapels, Norman corbels with grimacing human faces and monster masks.

★ **Devizes Museum.** — *41 Long Street.* In addition to geology and natural history ⊘ collections and an art gallery, the museum has a famous **archaeological department** where models of nearby Stonehenge and Avebury are displayed among a collection of local finds.

Town Buildings. — The arcaded and balustraded **Corn Exchange**, crowned with the gilded figure of Ceres, dates from 1857. Facing down onto the Market Place stands the **Old Town Hall**, a fine stone building of 1750-52, built with an open ground floor to serve as a market, beneath Ionic columned and pedimented upper halls and offices. The elegant 1806 **Town Hall**, at the end of St John's Street, has a rusticated ground floor with arched windows and above the bow to the front, tall Ionic columns.

St John's Alley. — Obliquely opposite the Town Hall is the best display of timber-framing in the town - a range of Elizabethan houses with oversailing upper floors.

EXCURSIONS

★ **Bowood House.** — *10 miles - 16km northwest by the A342, then the A4 to the* ⊘ *right.*
Begun in 1725, the house was sold, still uncompleted, in 1754 to the Lansdowne family, later Earls of Shelburne. It underwent change upon change by a succession of famous architects and in 1955 the ''big house'' was demolished except for the Orangery (R Adam) and its attendant pavilions, which provide an admirable set-ting for the Lansdowne collections of paintings, statuary, ceramics and silver.
The grounds, laid out mostly by **Capability Brown**, are as beautiful as ever and include such features as Adam's noble mausoleum, an 18C Doric temple and a grotto interweaving with the spectacular cascade at the foot of the lake.

Potterne. — Pop 1 590. *2 miles - 3km south by the A360.*
The pride of this village is the fine 15C half-timbered **Porch House★★**. In spite of later additions, **St Mary's Church** is a good example of Early English architecture.

★ DORCHESTER Dorset   Pop 13 734

Michelin Map **403** M 31 or Atlas G Britain p 8

Thomas Hardy (1840-1928), born near Dorchester, attended school in this county town and was articled to a local architect from 1856-61. At various stages in his life he returned to live in or near his home town, which features frequently in his novels under the name of Casterbridge.
The Romans built the settlement of Durnovaria in the 1C AD on the London-Exeter highway, but Dorchester is now notable for its 17C houses, many of them refaced or rebuilt in the 19C, producing façades of infinite variety.

Dorchester Streeets. — The 17C **King's Arms**, boasting an expansive early 19C front with broad porch on Tuscan columns, is to be found on High East Street, one of Dorchester's main thoroughfares. South Street starts with an impressive row of 18C red brick fronts. No 10, now a bank, is a distinguished late 18C three-storey house faced with lustred brick headers and redbrick dressings. In High West Street stands the much restored **St Peter's Church** with white stone doorway, white stone tower, battlements and pinnacles. No 6, where the notorious Judge Jeffreys stayed when trying over 500 of Monmouth's men in the **Bloody Assizes** *(qv)*, is the town's only half-timbered building, early 17C with overhangs at two levels.

Located at the top of the street, Eric Kennington's 1931 **Thomas Hardy Memorial** is a portrait of the author as an old man, hat on knee, seated on a flowery tree-stump.

★ **Dorset County Museum.** — *High West Street.* A splendid **Victorian gallery,** with painted cast iron columns and arches supporting a glass roof, houses **Thomas Hardy** memorabilia: furniture and paintings and papers from **Max Gate**, the house Hardy built for himself in 1885, as well as a reconstruction of his study as it was at his death. Note also the **Maiden Castle Gallery** *(see below)* and the collection of local fossils.

EXCURSIONS

★★ **Maiden Castle.** — *2 miles - 3km south on the A354.* Britain's finest **earthwork ramparts** were begun in *c*350 BC on the site of a Neolithic settlement dating back to *c*3000 BC. There were four main building phases before this massive 47 acre - 19ha complex was fully equipped with its defence system in *c*60 BC. However the hillfort was stormed by the future Roman Emperor Vespasian in 43 AD, when his infantry cut through rampart after rampart, reached the inner bay and burnt the huts.

★★ **Chesil Beach.** — *10 miles - 16km southwest via Martinstown, the Admiral Hardy Monument and Portesham.* The village of Abbotsbury is situated at the end of the lagoon formed by Chesil Beach, a remarkable 15 mile - 24km shingle bank. It takes its name from the 11C Benedictine abbey, dissolved in 1541 and now a ruin. The unique **swannery★** was founded by the monks *c*1390 and now accommodates more than 400 birds and their cygnets. The lushness of the **sub-tropical gardens★** contrasts with the ruggedness of the wind-blown 14C **St Catherine's Chapel★** on its 250ft - 76m downland crest.

★ **Cerne Abbas.** — *8 miles - 13km north of Dorchester on the A352.* The 180ft - 55m high figure of a giant, displaying his manliness in more ways than one, has been connected with local fertility rituals. With his club, he resembles Roman representations of Hercules and may, therefore, date from the Roman occupation. The **village★** is notable for the beautiful range of timber-fronted 16C houses in Abbey Street, and **St Mary's Church**, a mixture of Early English and Perpendicular, with a spectacular **tower** built in Ham Hill stone.

★ **Bere Regis Church.** — *11 miles - 18km east by the A35.* The fine Perpendicular church of **St John the Baptist** is the only building to have survived the last of a series of fires in 1788. Its **roof★★** is a pure joy: a structure of oak tie beams and braces, posts outlined by cresting, filled with tracery, decorated in rich colours, with bosses masking the meeting points and the not-in-fact hammers disguised by almost lifesize, clearly recognisable carved figures of the apostles. Note the capitals in the late 12C arcade with carved figures in agony with toothache and sore throat...

Milton Abbas. — Pop 433. *12 miles - 19km northeast by the A354 and by-road.* The **Abbey Church** was rebuilt after a fire in 1309 in the Early English and Decorated styles, but work was stopped by the Black Death in 1348. The 136ft - 41m long church consists of choir, crossing and transepts only. The **house** with its impressive **staterooms** was built by Sir William Chambers for Lord Milton in the centre of a park designed by Capability Brown. He had the village rebuilt out of sight of the abbey; twin lines of identical thatched cottages marked in the centre by the 1786 church and the **Tregonwell Almshouses**, a rebuilding of the original 16C houses.

DORNOCH Highland   Pop 1 006

Michelin Map **401** H 10 or Atlas G Britain p 67

A Royal Burgh, Dornoch is built around its medieval cathedral. With its golf courses and miles of sandy beaches, it is a popular family resort and is also an excellent centre for touring the north of Scotland.

Cathedral. — The site had been occupied by a Celtic community since the 6C, but it was in the early 13C that Gilbert de Moravia (1222-45), the Bishop of Caithness, made Dornoch his episcopal seat and started to build a cathedral. Today's building has been greatly altered, though much of the original stonework remains.

EXCURSION

Dunrobin Castle. — *12 miles - 19km to the north by the A9.*
The Mound causeway, built by Thomas Telford, carries the road across the head of **Loch Fleet** which, like the Cromarty Firth and others along this coast, is a feeding and roosting ground for migrant wildfowl in winter.
In Golspie, visit St Andrew's Church to admire the finely carved Sutherland loft (1739).

Dunrobin Castle. — The ancestral seat of the earls and dukes of Sutherland, Dunrobin Castle stands on a natural terrace overlooking the sea. Later additions now surround the original tower of 1400. **Charles Barry,** architect of the Houses of Parliament, remodelled the interior in the 1850s. After a fire, **Robert Lorimer**, designer of the Thistle Chapel in St Giles' Cathedral in Edinburgh, made good and redecorated the interior. The principal rooms provided the setting for family portraits by masters of the art (Jamesone, Ramsay, Reynolds, Hoppner, Lawrence and Wright). The castle has attractive formal gardens which can be admired from the terrace.

DOVER Kent

Michelin Map 404 X, Y 30 or Atlas G Britain p 13
Town plan in the current Michelin Red Guide Great Britain and Ireland

Flanked by the famous white cliffs, Dover has been the gateway to England since Roman times, receiving sailing ships, steam ships and hovercraft, though much will be diverted to the Channel Tunnel emerging at nearby Folkestone *(qv)* in the 1990s. The town was badly damaged during World War II and of her two Norman churches, **St Mary's** survived, St James' stands in ruins. Of the other buildings the 14C **Maison Dieu**, the 17C **Maison Dieu House**, both in Biggin Street, and Philip Hardwick's late Regency **Waterloo Crescent**, have survived; giving Dover islands of elegance rare amongst working ports.

★★ **Castle.** — *Castle Hill Road.* The high land to the east, commanding town and port, has been fortified since the Iron Age. The Romans built a lighthouse (Pharos) which still stands within the castle walls, and the Saxons a church (St-Mary-in-Castro). The defences were strengthened by William the Conqueror, then by Henry II, who in the 1180s added the splendid **keep**, set within a curtain wall. The spectacular **Constable's Tower** dates from the early 13C. Underneath the castle is a warren of tunnels and secret chambers built for defensive purposes.

Western Heights. — Evidence that the threat of Napoleonic invasion was taken very seriously abounds on England's southeast coast; seventy-three stout **"Martello Towers"**, small circular brick forts, were built between Folkestone and Eastbourne; a military waterway, the **Royal Military Canal**, was dug between Hythe and Rye. Here on the chalk downland rising from the harbour towards Shakespeare Cliff are some two square miles - 5km of elaborate defences, among them the **Drop Redoubt** of 1808 and the unique triple staircase of the **Grand Shaft**, completed a year later, 140ft - 42m in height.

★ DUMFRIES Dumfries and Galloway

Michelin Map 401 J 18 or Atlas G Britain p 49
Town plan in the current Michelin Red Guide Great Britain and Ireland

''Queen of the South'', Dumfries has long been the chief town in Scotland's southwest, probably best known for its connection with **Robert Burns** (1759-96) who lived and farmed in and around the town. Another Robert, **Robert the Bruce**, started his long campaign to free Scotland from Edward I in Dumfries, by killing John Comyn, one of the Competitors for the crown, and having himself crowned at Scone in 1306. Eight years later, his victory at Bannockburn was crucial in obtaining that Independence.

Robert Burns Centre. — *Mill Road.* An excellent introduction to Burns and the last few years of his life spent in Dumfries. The presentation includes an audio-visual display, an exhibition as well as a diorama and a scale model of the town in his day.

Burns' House. — *Burns Street.* Here Burns spent the last three years of his life. He had given up his farm at Ellisland, outside Dumfries, and accepted a full-time post with the Excise. The house, now a museum, has examples of the poet's abundant correspondence.

Burns Mausoleum. — Behind the red sandstone church of St Michael's is the mausoleum where Burns, his wife Jean Armour and several of their children are buried.

Dervorgilla Bridge. — Dervorgilla, wife of John Balliol, and founder of Sweetheart Abbey *(qv)*, built a wooden bridge across the Nith, in the 1270s. It was replaced by the present narrow six-arch bridge in the 15C.

EXCURSIONS

★★ **Drumlanrig Castle.** — *18 miles - 29km northwest of Dumfries by the A76.*
The castle was a Douglas stronghold from the 14C until the 18C. In the 17C William, 1st Duke of Queensberry, built a mansion worthy of his station; he was so appalled by the cost, however, that he spent only one night there, before returning to the family seat at Sanquhar. James, 2nd Duke, was the High Commissioner who presented the Treaty of Union to Queen Anne in 1707. The property now belongs to the Montagu-Douglas-Scott family.
The castle stands impressively with four square towers quartering — in true native tradition — the courtyard structure. Innovation comes with the main façade and its terraces, horseshoe staircase, dramatic turreted skyline and rich sculptural detail such as the entrance breast with ducal crown aloft.

Interior. — There is a varied and superb collection of paintings, including a Holbein, a Leonardo and Rembrandt's *Old Woman Reading* (1655) and fine furniture and clocks are to be seen throughout the castle. In the oak-panelled Dining Room, carved panels attributed to Grinling Gibbons alternate with 17C silver sconces and family portraits. The Douglas crest of the ''winged heart'' appears on plasterwork, on wall hangings and wood carvings and even on picture frames, to remind the visitor that Drumlanrig is a Douglas seat.

★ **Sweetheart Abbey.** — *8 miles - 13km southwest, by the New Abbey Road, the A710.*
Founded 1273, by Dervorgilla, Sweetheart was the last Cistercian foundation in Scotland. Its name derives from the fact that the foundress was laid to rest in the presbytery together with a casket containing the embalmed heart of her husband. The beauty and charm of the ruins derive from the contrast between the warm red sandstone and the clipped green of the surrounding lawns.

On the way back to Dumfries turn left just out of New Abbey.

Shambellie House contains a delightfully presented **costume collection★**, donated to the Royal Scottish Museum in 1977, by Charles Stewart. Both historical and modern costume are displayed in the charming setting of a small country house.

★ Caerlaverock Castle. — *9 miles - 15km southeast, by the B725.*
The attractive ruins of this castle have a formidable outward appearance, but the inner courtyard has great refinement and is an early example of Scottish Renaissance style. Finished in 1300, the castle was besieged by Edward I the same year. It became the principal seat of the Maxwells, until it was abandoned following an attack in the Covenanting Wars, after which it fell into disrepair.

★ Ruthwell Cross. — *16 miles - 26km by the B725 from Dumfries, but fork left at Bankend, rather than right for Caerlaverock.*
An outstanding example of early Christian art stands in the church - the 7C Ruthwell Cross, telling in sculpture the Life and Passion of Christ. The tracery, animals and birds, together with runic inscriptions are a credit to the artistry and skill of the sculptor. The cross was demolished in 1642 on orders from the General Assembly; the pieces were re-assembled in the 19C, by the Rev Dr Henry Duncan and installed in the church in 1887. Duncan's other claim to fame was the founding, in Ruthwell, in 1810, of the first Savings Bank, forerunner of today's widespread movement.

DUNDEE Tayside   Pop 172 294

Michelin Map 401 K, L 14 or Atlas G Britain p 62
Town plan in the current Michelin Red Guide Great Britain and Ireland

Dundee enjoys a nigh-perfect situation on the northern shore of the Tay with the Sidlaw Hills as a backdrop. Prosperity accrued from the three ''j's'' — jute, jam (Mrs Keiller first made her renowned Dundee marmalade in 1797) and journalism in the Victorian era. Traditional industries have given way to modern, high-technology industries. As Scotland's fourth city, it is a busy seaport, educational centre and capital of the Tayside Region.
It was home to the inventor of the adhesive postage stamp, James Chalmers (1823-53) and the cradle of the Thomson publishing empire. Dundee took over as Britain's chief whaling port in the 1860s, from Peterhead, which had itself superseded Hull some twenty years earlier. Whale oil was used in another of Dundee's industries, jute milling, to soften the fibres before processing. As the tobacco trade enriched Glasgow, so the whaling and jute industries were the prosperity of Dundee.

Tay Railway Bridge. — The Tay estuary was the site of the world's first train ferry (1850). In 1878 its replacement, a bridge just short of two miles - 3km long was completed. Disaster struck on a stormy winter night in December 1879, when the structure gave way and a train plunged into the icy water with the loss of 75 lives. The bridge's designer, Thomas Bouch, died shortly afterwards, broken by the tragedy and it was not until ten years later that both the Forth and the Tay estuaries were successfully bridged.

★ The Frigate Unicorn. — *Victoria Dock.*
The Unicorn was launched in 1824 as a 46-gun frigate for the Royal Navy. She is now the oldest British-built ship still afloat. Visitors can explore the main gun decks, with their 18 pounders — each manned by a crew of nine men, who lived and slept alongside their guns — and the Captain's and officers' quarters and discover the flavour of life in the Royal Navy in the golden age of sail.

★ RRS Discovery. — *Victoria Dock.*
Custom-built in Dundee in 1901 for scientific exploration and a landmark on the Thames in London for 45 years, *Discovery* is now back in her home port. Captain Scott commanded the vessel on the 1901-04 Antarctic Expedition.

EXCURSION

Broughty Ferry. — *To the east by the A930.*
Leaving Dundee along the coast, the road passes some of the substantial houses built by the 19C jute ''barons''. Broughty Ferry was the ferry terminus in the 1850s and has become Dundee's own seaside resort today. The Museum has an interesting section on whaling. Just to the north is **Claypotts Castle,** a perfect example of a 16C Z-plan tower house, with rounded towers at the opposite corners of the rectangular centrepiece.

When visiting Scotland,
*use the **Michelin Green Guide ''Scotland''.***

— *Detailed descriptions of places of interest*
— *Touring programmes*
— *Maps and street plans*
— *The history of the country*
— *Photographs and drawings of monuments, beauty spots, houses...*

★ DUNFERMLINE Fife

Michelin Map 401 J 15 or Atlas G Britain p 56

One-time capital of Scotland, Dunfermline figures frequently in Scottish history, largely in association with its great abbey and royal palace. It has long been a thriving industrial centre, with coal mining and linen weaving, and new industries maintain this tradition today.

Royal residence. — **Malcolm Canmore** (*c*1031-93) sheltered the heir to the English throne, **Edgar Atheling** and his family, fleeing from William the Conqueror after Hastings (1066). Edgar's sister **Margaret** married the Scots king in 1070. She was a devout Catholic and was largely responsible for introducing the ideas which gradually supplanted the rituals of the Celtic church. The Benedictine abbey was founded by **David I**, son of Queen Margaret. It grew in importance with the revenues from coal, salt panning, land and ferry dues and the town prospered with it until, following the untimely deaths of Alexander III and Margaret of Norway, Edward I of England was called in as mediator in the struggle for succession. On his departure in 1304 the monastic buildings were a smouldering ruin.

Robert the Bruce (1274-1329) helped with the reconstruction and is buried in the abbey - although his heart is in Melrose Abbey, in the Borders.

The guest house was refurbished for James V's French wife, but it was James VI who gave the palace to his Queen, Anne of Denmark, and it was here that Charles I was born, together with his sister, the Winter Queen. There were fleeting royal visits, after the Union of the Crowns in 1603, by James as well as by Charles I and his son, later Charles II in 1633, but the palace was never again a royal residence for long.

SIGHTS

★ **Dunfermline Abbey.** — The interior is one of Scotland's finest **Norman naves**, its simple, massive forms and round-headed arches recalling both Durham and St Magnus, Kirkwall. The east end was rebuilt in 1818-21 and serves as the parish church. Outside are the few remains of the once great monastic ensemble (visitor centre). All that is left of the Royal Palace is a single wall, best seen from the attractive Pittencrieff Park.

Dunfermline District Museum. — The making of **damask** on hand looms as a cottage industry lasted until the late 19C, when power looms took over. Displays illustrate the techniques and the intricate product.

Andrew Carnegie Birthplace. — *Moodie Street.* The self-made steel baron and great philanthropist (1835-1919) was born in this house before emigrating to America with his family in 1848.

EXCURSION

Loch Leven Castle. — *12 miles - 19km north by the M90. Ferry service from Kinross.* Mary Queen of Scots was imprisoned on this island stronghold from June 1567 until her escape the following May. The Douglas fortress comprises a 14C tower, its entrance at second-floor level, and a later curtain wall.

★★ DUNSTER Somerset   Pop 793

Michelin Map 403 J 30 or Atlas G Britain p 7

The beautiful old town of Dunster on the northeast edge of Exmoor *(qv)* enjoyed a flourishing coastal and continental trade with Bordeaux, Spain, Italy and Wales, until the sea retreated in the 15-16C, whereupon it became a wool market and weaving centre.

★★ **Castle.** — The red sandstone castle dominates the town from the tor on which a fortification has stood since Saxon times. The present castle was begun by the Norman baron William de Mohun, but by 1374 the de Mohun line was dying out and the castle was sold to Lady Elizabeth Luttrell, in whose family it remained until 1971. The castle defences were put to the test in the Civil War and finally avoided being destroyed when the owner paid a heavy fine and swore allegiance to Cromwell. In the late 17C Colonel Francis Luttrell spent extravagantly on the house, but all the work ceased when he died in 1690. When George Fownes Luttrell inherited the property in 1867 he commissioned the architect **Anthony Salvin** to transform the castle to its present appearance of a fortified Jacobean mansion.

★ **Dunster Water Mill.** — The mill on the River Avill, rebuilt and improved since Domesday, ground corn until the late 19C, came back into use during the 1939-45 war and was rebuilt and restored to working order by the previous tenants in 1979-80.

Town. — The long, wide **High Street**, lined with 17-19C houses and shops, is characterised by the octagonal Yarn Market, whose most recent rebuilding dates from the 17C. The **Luttrell Arms**, dating back to *c*1500, has in the Great Hall a hammerbeam roof, a twelve-light window and a huge fireplace with a 17C overmantel. **Church Street** is marked by buildings related to the priory founded in 1090 and dissolved in 1539. The Nunnery and Priest's House both date from the 14C, the latter heavily restored in the 19C. Beyond the gate in the end wall of the Priory Garden stands a 20ft - 6m high early medieval **dovecote**★.

★ **St George's Church.** — The church was originally built by the Normans in the 12C then rebuilt by the monks in the 14C. Its 110ft - 34m **tower**, dating from 1443, houses a carillon which plays daily at 9am and at 1, 5 and 9pm. Inside are **wagon roofs**, a splendid 54ft - 16m carved **screen**, a 16C Perpendicular font and the Luttrell tombs.

Michelin Map 401 P 19 or Atlas G Britain p 46
Town plan in the current Michelin Red Guide Great Britain and Ireland

The quiet streets of the little medieval city with its castle are the perfect foil for
the great sandstone mass of the Norman cathedral rising above the deep wooded
gorge of the River Wear in a sublime fusion of architecture and landscape.

HISTORICAL NOTES

Christianity flourished early in the Saxon Kingdom of Northumbria but conditions
were rarely stable in this border country with its coastline exposed to raiders from
the east. In 875 the monks of Lindisfarne fled south from Danish attacks, carrying
with them the body of **St Cuthbert** (d 687), but it was not until more than 100 years
later that his much venerated remains found their final resting place on easily defended bluffs carved out by the Wear. From the 1070s the site's natural advantages
were strengthened by the Normans, who built their castle to command the peninsula's narrow neck. In 1093 the cathedral's foundation stone was laid. Uniquely
in England, Durham's bishop was not only spiritual leader but lay lord, the powerful Prince Palatine of a long-troubled province.

The city has remained compact, physically unaffected by the once intense industrial activity all around it. Its scholarly character was confirmed with the foundation in 1832 of the University, after Oxford and Cambridge England's oldest. But
it is also the county town, an important administrative and shopping centre and,
on the second Saturday in July, is thronged with the thousands attending one of
Britain's great popular festivals of modern times, the famous **Miners' Gala.**

★★★CATHEDRAL *time: 1 hour*

> *Parking is difficult near the Cathedral and Castle and cars should be left in one
> of the car parks on the edge of the city centre.*

Durham's beauty lies in its unity: its fabric was mostly completed in the short
period between 1095 and 1133 and though added to since, it remains a supremely
harmonious achievement of Norman architecture on the grandest possible scale.

Exterior. — The calm and level space of **Palace Green**, bounded to the north by the
castle wall and to the east and west by a mixture of university buildings, is dominated by the imposing north elevation of the Cathedral running its entire width. The
solemn rhythm of nave and chancel is set off by the two west towers, richly decorated, by the high central tower, mostly 15C and, to the east, by the great Early
English Chapel of the Nine Altars.

Entry to the Cathedral is normally by the many-arched portal (northwest), with its
celebrated lion's head **Sanctuary Knocker★**, *(photograph p 257)*, a 12C masterpiece
of expressive stylisation.

Interior. — In the nave★★★ the first impression is one of overwhelming power.
Huge deeply-grooved columns alternate with massive many-shafted piers to form
an arcade supporting a gallery, clerestory and beautiful vault, whose pointed ribs
are an important technical and aesthetic innovation, heralding the lightness and
grace of Gothic architecture. The great weight of masonry, its arches enriched with
various zig-zag patterning, is however so well proportioned that the final effect is
one of repose, of great forces held in equilibrium.

From the crossing there is a stupendous view up into the vault under the central
tower, while in the south transept is an extraordinary brightly painted 16C clock.
In the choir there are fine **stalls** and the splendidly vain **throne** and **tomb** of the 14C
Bishop Hatfield. Beyond the 14C **Neville Screen** with its delicate stonework is the
shrine of St Cuthbert and finally, its floor sunk to gain as much height as possible,
the 13C **Chapel of the Nine Altars★★★**. This Early English addition to the cathedral,
paralleled elsewhere only at Fountains Abbey *(qv)*, has its extravagantly tall lancet windows separated by columns of clustered shafts and reveals a new preoccu-
pation with lightness and verticality. The carved stonework of its bosses and capitals
is exceptionally rich.

At the extreme western end of the building, perched on the very edge of the ravine, is the **Galilee Chapel.** Twelve slender columns, their arches profusely decorated
with zig-zag carvings, subdivide the interior, which contains the tomb of the **Venerable Bede** (d 735), England's first historian.

Monastic buildings. — Around the much rebuilt cloisters are grouped the buildings of the former abbey. They include the monks' dormitory and the **Cathedral
Treasury★**, with its collection of Anglo-Saxon embroideries, precious objects and
manuscripts and, above all, the evocative relics associated with St Cuthbert; his
tiny portable altar, his pectoral cross, fragments of his oak coffin... To the south
is the tranquil precinct of **The College**, its mellow, mostly 18C buildings resting on
medieval foundations.

From the top of the cathedral's central tower *(a long climb of 325 steps: access
from south transept)* spectacular **views★** reinforce the full drama of Durham's site.

ADDITIONAL SIGHTS

★ Castle. — Its Norman architecture much modified by successive Prince Bishops,
the castle now forms part of Durham University, its keep having been converted
into student residences as early as 1840.

From the courtyard, protected by the much rebuilt gatehouse and overlooked by
the **keep** on its great earth mound, the visitor is taken via the 15C **kitchen** into the
imposing **Great Hall**, then to galleries built around the original castle wall, whose fine
arched doorway is still intact. The upper floors are reached by the broad steps of
the spectacular **Black Staircase** of 1662. There are two chapels, one of the 16C with

humorous misericords including a bagpipe-playing pig and a nagging wife in a wheel-barrow. The **Norman chapel★**, deep below, dates from the castle's earliest days and evokes a more primitive world, with its close-set columns hewn from a strangely patterned sandstone and capitals crudely ornamented with weird figures and savage faces.

City and riverside. — Most traffic has been removed from the centre and some streets have been attractively repaved. From the **Market Place**, sited at the very neck of the peninsula and mostly 19C in character, streets descend steeply to the slop-ing **Elvet Bridge** on the east and to **Framwellgate Bridge** on the west. From here there is a fine **view★★** upstream of the Cathedral with the stern walls of the Castle in the foreground.

North Bailey and **South Bailey**, with their many pleasant 18C houses, follow the line of the town wall. Near the church of St Mary-le-Bow, now housing the Durham Heritage Centre, a lane leads downhill to Kingsgate footbridge of 1963, elegantly spanning the gorge to link the city with the uncompromisingly modern building of the University Students' Union, **Dunelm House**. South Bailey ends at the Watergate, from which a track leads down to **Prebends' Bridge.** From here, from the path on the far bank and from the riverside itself are those **views★★★** which have long capti-vated writers and artists; a perfect composition is created by the elements of water, massed trees and humble mill buildings enhancing the grandeur of the noble architecture above.

ENVIRONS

★★**Oriental Museum** (Durham University). — *Leave the city on the A1050 to the A167 towards Darlington.*
In a leafy setting among other buildings of the University of which it forms part is this modern museum, a treasure house of oriental art and artefacts. Its changing displays range from Ancient Egypt via India and South East Asia to Japan, but of outstanding interest are ceramics, a range of jade and other hardstone pieces and an extraordinary room-like bed, all from China.

EASTBOURNE East Sussex   Pop 86 715

Michelin Map 404 U 31 or Atlas G Britain p 12
Town plan in the current Red Guide Great Britain and Ireland

Sheltered by the South Downs and enjoying an exceptionally sunny climate, East-bourne owes its transformation, from an unassuming farming village a mile inland into England's most gentlemanly resort, to William Cavendish, the Duke of Devon-shire (1808-91). Careful development of his extensive estates from the 1850s onward created a decorous seaside town of dignified hotels and picturesque villas in tree-lined roads. Now recognised as a model of Victorian town planning, Eastbourne continues to attract visitors appreciative, like Claude Debussy, who wrote part of *La Mer* while here, of a place "where the sea displays herself with strictly British correctness".

★**Seafront.** — Eastbourne's long southeast-facing promenade, backed by trim lawns and carefully tended flower beds, is free from commercialism and forms a fitting setting for traditional seaside pleasures.
The holiday mood is set by the spick and span **pier** of 1870 and continued by the remarkable bandstand of 1935, an integral part of the lower promenade. This cen-tral part of the seafront is defined by defence works of Napoleon's time; eastwards the great **Redoubt**, home to the museums of the Royal Sussex Regiment and the Queen's Royal Irish Hussars; to the west, on rising ground and giving good views, the **Wish Tower**, one of 74 "Martello Towers" protecting the Kent and Sussex coast from French invasion. Beyond, the clifftop rises via King Edward's Parade to the foot of the Downs and many bracing walks, while the lower promenade leads to gardens with fine views across the bay to Hastings.

Eastbourne Heritage Centre. — *A short distance from the seafront and near the Congress Theatre.* The displays in this quaint little tower give a good explanation of the town's development since 1800. Nearby is the entertainment complex ad-joining Devonshire Park, the Victorian theatre of that name, the historic Winter Garden and the modern Congress Theatre.

EXCURSION

★★★**Beachy Head.** — *4 miles - 6km. Leave on the B2103, turning left at the top of the rise outside the town.*
Few prospects are more exhilarating on a sunny day than that of the blue sea washing against the toy-like lighthouse at the foot of the dazzling white 500ft - 150m cliffs *(photograph 15).* West of this wonderful viewpoint extends a "Heritage Coast" of sweeping downland ending in lesser, but still spectacular, chalk headlands, the **Seven Sisters**, mostly accessible only on foot.

The grid references U 30
*given in the line under each heading are common to both
the Motoring Atlas (1:300 000 or 1/in: 4.75 miles) and
the Regional Map Series (1:400 000 or 1/in: 6.30 miles).*

Michelin Map 401 K 16 or Atlas G Britain p 56

Edinburgh, capital of Scotland, is set on a series of volcanic hills, each giving a different vantage point from which to view this beautiful city. Perhaps the best known is Arthur's Seat (823ft - 251m), overlooking Holyrood Park. Edinburgh boasts a past rich in history; the Old Town, huddled for years on the ridge running down from the Castle Rock, contrasts with the New, with its elegant Georgian streets and squares.

It is best to visit Edinburgh, especially the Old Town, on foot. But before doing so, take one of the conducted coach tours around the City lasting about an hour - to obtain an overall impression and choose what you may wish to explore further.

★★★ **Edinburgh International Festival.** — This prestigious festival *(3 weeks in August; see p 262)* has provided a quality programme of performances in all the art forms since its inception in 1947. The **Military Tattoo** presents a spectacle rich in colour, tradition, music and excitement, under the floodlights of the Castle Esplanade. Also a part of festival time, **The Fringe** spills out onto the streets and squares of Edinburgh, with over 20 different nations presenting 1 000 or more productions, often avantgarde, sometimes just plain eccentric. Also part of the festival are the **Jazz** and **Film Festivals**.

Secure stronghold to capital. — The Castle Rock had been a secure refuge for generations when in the late 11C it was associated as a residence with Malcolm Canmore and his Queen Margaret. Their son, David I, favoured the site by founding the Abbey of the Holy Rood. During the reign of the early Stuarts Edinburgh gradually assumed the roles of royal residence, seat of government and capital of Scotland. With the Union of the Crowns (1603) and subsequent departure of James VI of Scotland and I of England for London, Edinburgh lost much of its pageantry, cultural activity and in 1707 with the Union of the Parliaments its parliament. It was in the late 18C during the Enlightenment, a period of intellectual ferment, that plans were mooted for a civic project of boldness and imagination: the creation of the Georgian New Town.

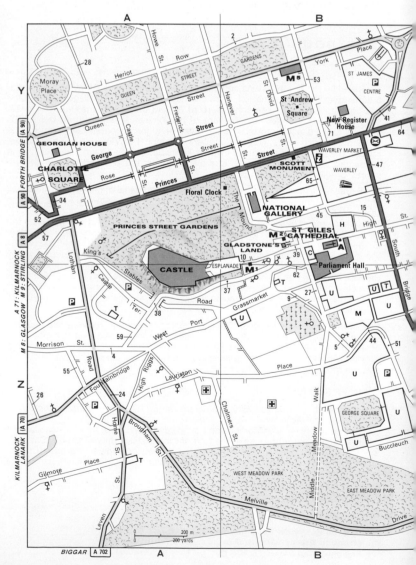

★★THE ROYAL MILE FROM CASTLE TO PALACE

Allow a day, including Castle and Palace visits

The principal thoroughfare of Old Edinburgh runs from the Castle down the ridge to the Abbey and Palace of Holyroodhouse. For two centuries the city's Flodden Wall (16C) restricted the spread of Edinburgh, confining expansion to the ten- and twelve-storey "tenements", with narrow wynds and closes, so typical of the Old Town.

Defoe, in the 18C, called it "perhaps the longest, largest and finest street, not in Britain only, but in the world". The few original buildings which remain can still today give the impression of what medieval and 17C Edinburgh must have looked like.

★★ **Castle** (AYZ). — The impressive silhouette of the castle and its **rock**★★ is prob-
ⓧ ably the best known feature of views of Edinburgh. Though a royal residence since the 11C most of the buildings today are basically those resulting from its use as a military garrison over recent centuries.

The esplanade, an 18C parade ground, is the setting for the Festival's most popular event, the Military Tattoo. The fortifications afford splendid views across Princes Street to the New Town. The one o'clock salute is fired from one of the batteries. The main points of interest include the **Honours of Scotland**★★★ (the Scottish Crown Jewels) on display in the Crown Room, Mons Meg, one of the oldest cannon in
ⓧ the world and the **Royal Scots Regimental Museum** (the senior regiment in the British Army, raised in 1633). The small 12C St Margaret's Chapel is dedicated to Malcolm's Queen Margaret. Around Crown Square are: the Scottish National War Memorial (north side); the Scottish United Services Museum (west side); the 16C Great Hall with its hammerbeam roof and 15C Palace containing the royal apartments.

ⓧ **Scotch Whisky Heritage Centre** (BY M¹). — The ground floor exhibition and a film recount the whisky making process, its various products and the workings of a distillery.

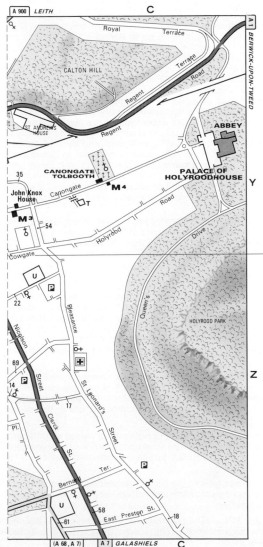

We suggest:

*For a sucessful tour,
that you prepare it in advance.
Michelin maps and guides
will give you much useful
information on route planning,
places of interest,
accommodation, prices, etc.*

★ **Gladstone's Land** (BY). — This narrow six-storey tenement is typical of the type
⊘ of building erected within the Flodden Wall in 17C Edinburgh. Thomas Gledstanes, a merchant, bought the building in 1617. The National Trust for Scotland has restored the premises and on the first floor above the shop is a good example of a town house of the period.

⊘ Down the close of the same name is **Lady Stair's House** (BY M²) with an exhibition on three of Scotland's greatest literary figures, Robert Burns (1759-96), Sir Walter Scott (1771-1832) and Robert Louis Stevenson (1850-94).

★★ **St Giles' Cathedral** (BY). — The High Kirk of Edinburgh is probably the third church
⊘ to occupy this site. Alterations and restorations have, however, drastically changed its character since its rebuilding in the 14C. The only original exterior feature is the crown **spire**★★★ dating from 1495. Inside, it is the monuments and details that provide much of the interest. Of note is the Thistle Chapel, designed by **Robert Lorimer** in 1911 in Flamboyant Gothic style for the Most Noble Order of the Thistle, founded in 1687. There are monuments to John Knox and to Covenanter-turned Royalist, the Marquess of Montrose.

⊘ Nearby is **Parliament Hall** (BYZ), the 17C hall decreed by Charles I, now behind a Georgian façade, in which the Scottish Parliament met from 1693 to 1707. In Parliament Square is the **Mercat Cross** (BY A), the one-time hub of Edinburgh life, meeting place of traders and merchants and scene of royal proclamations, demonstrations and executions.

⊘ The **John Knox House** (CY) was built in about 1490. It is associated with both John Knox, the religious reformer and with James Mossman, the goldsmith to Mary Queen of Scots. The exhibition incorporates details on both men and recreates the atmosphere of 16C Edinburgh.

⊘ Just opposite the John Knox house, on the south side of the Royal Mile, is the **Museum of Childhood** (CY M³). Anything and everything to do with childhood is the theme of this unusual collection. Children discover while parents reminisce.

⊘ Further down on the left is the attractive 16C **Canongate Tolbooth**★ (CY) with its tur-
⊘ reted steeple and opposite three 16C mansions known as **Huntly House** (CY M⁴) housing the local history museum. The independent burgh of Canongate was where the nobility and officers of the Royal Household resided in proximity to the palace.

★★ **Abbey and Palace of Holyroodhouse** (CY). — At the east end of the Royal Mile,
⊘ amid the green slopes of Holyrood Park, leading up to Arthur's Seat, stands the Palace of Holyrood, official residence of the monarch in Scotland. The abbey was founded by David I, in 1128. James IV started to transform the guesthouse accommodation of the abbey into a royal palace but it was Charles II, though he never set foot in the palace, who had his architect Sir William Bruce draw up designs; and, influenced perhaps by the work of Inigo Jones in Whitehall, it was Bruce who created the magnificent example of Palladian style we see today.

The inner court elevations are outstanding Renaissance work of the Stuart period and among Scotland's earliest examples. The decoration of the **State Apartments** is lavish, the craftsmanship outstanding. Particularly noteworthy are the **plasterwork ceilings**★★★, the fruit of ten years: labour by "gentlemen modellers" who had worked for the Lauderdales, patrons of Sir William, at Ham House in London and also for Charles II at Windsor. The **Historic Apartments** in the 16C round tower, with close associations with Mary Queen of Scots, contain tapestries from the Mortlake workshop founded by her son; the painted ceilings are magnificent. It was in the small room adjoining the bedchamber that Mary's Italian secretary, Rizzio, was murdered in 1566.

⊘ **Abbey.** — The roofless nave is all that is left of this once great abbey, dating from the late 12C and early 13C. Here are buried the remains of David II, James II, James V and also of Lord Darnley, father of James VI of Scotland, who united the Crowns in 1603.

★★**NEW TOWN 1767-1830** (ABCY)

When the decision had been taken to extend the Royalty of Edinburgh, it was a then unknown architect, James Craig, whose design won the competition and who organised the development. The North Bridge was thrown across the valley and the New Town was laid out on a gridiron pattern, with vistas and focal points. It was not until 1782 that regulations were introduced to control uniformity of façades and storeys. The wealthy soon took up residence in these splendid squares and elegant streets.

★★★ **Charlotte Square** (AY). — It was Robert Adam who was commissioned in 1791 to design what is New Town's most elegant square. No 5 is occupied by the Na-
⊘ tional Trust for Scotland, who have also refurbished No 7, the **Georgian House**★ (AY); its lower floors now give a delightful impression of domestic life in the period 1790-1810.

George Street (ABY). — The principal Street of Craig's plan is closed at either end by Charlotte and St Andrew Squares. From the street intersections there are good views away to the Forth or down to Princes Street Gardens with the castle as backdrop.

St Andrew Square (BY). — It has none of the unified elegance of its counterpart, Charlotte Square, but its houses of great charm and individuality are today occupied by banks and insurance companies.

Queen Street Museums (BY M⁵). — The two museums are housed in a building
⊘ provided by a donation from the proprietor of *The Scotsman* in 1882. The **National Portrait Gallery**★ "illustrates Scottish history by likeness of the chief actors in it".

There are masterpieces of portraiture of royalty, statesmen, politicians and literary
figures. The **Royal Museum of Scotland: Antiquities**★★ was founded in 1780, to show
the whole history of Scottish life and culture. Items are on show from Skara Brae,
the Neolithic settlement from 4 500 years ago, and from Jarlshof, continuously
occupied from the Bronze Age to the 17C. Pictish sculptured stones, Doune pistols
and Roman silverware vie for attention with a collection of 16-19C Scottish silver.

New Register House (BY). — Fronted by fine wrought-iron gates are the offices of the
Registrar General for Scotland and the Court of the Lord Lyon King of Arms. Lord
Lyon regulates all heraldic matters in Scotland, and officiates at state and public
ceremonial of all sorts.

Princes Street and Gardens (ABY). — Originally the southern boundary of the
New Town development, **Princes Street** has grown from a totally residential street,
looking out onto gardens in the newly filled-in Nor'Loch, into Edinburgh's prime
shopping street. The railway came in 1845-6, followed by commercial development. The south side of the street was protected from building by Act of Parliament and the gardens opened to the public in 1876.

Following Sir Walter Scott's death in 1832, a public appeal was launched and the
foundation stone of the **Scott Monument**★ (BY) was laid in 1840. The 200ft - 61m
tall Gothic spire, as well as sheltering a Carrara marble statue of Scott, is surrounded
by statuettes of 64 characters from his novels and by the busts of 16 Scottish poets.
For the agile *(287 narrow stairs to the top)* a viewing platform affords a magnificent **view**★ over central Edinburgh.
Dividing Princes Street Gardens into East and West are two imposing classical buildings, the National Gallery and the Royal Scottish Academy.

★★★ **National Gallery of Scotland** (BY). — The building designed by William Playfair
and built 1850-7 with its tastefully refurbished and furnished galleries makes an
ideal home for this small but selective collection. The paintings are hung in chrono-
logical order and include works by Raphael, Titian, Tintoretto and Velazquez, by
Rubens and Frans Hals. Both the British 18C portraitists (Gainsborough, Reynolds,
Romney and Raeburn) and French Impressionists are well represented. The basement galleries are devoted to Scottish painting.

In West Princes Street Gardens, nearby, is the **Floral Clock** (BY) composed of 20 000
annuals.

EXCURSIONS

★ **Dalmeny.** — Pop 319. *6 miles - 10km west by the A90.*
The village is famous for its parish **church**★ , an exceptionally fine example of Norman ecclesiastical architecture, with an intricately carved south **doorway**★★ . To the
east of the village is **Dalmeny House**★ , home of the earls of Rosebery. Archibald the
4th Earl commissioned William Wilkins to build the Gothic revival house which was
completed in 1817. Archibald the 5th Earl married Hannah de Rothschild and it was
he who succeeded Gladstone as Prime Minister in 1894. Of particular interest is
the Rothschild collection of 18C French furniture, porcelain and tapestries and the
memorabilia of the Napoleon Room collected by the Prime Minister 5th Earl.

★★ **Forth Bridges.** — *Best viewed from the esplanade at South Queensferry, 9 miles -
15km via the A90.*
The first ferry across this, the narrowest part of the Forth, was instituted by Queen
Margaret in the 1070s, and was operated by the monks of Dunfermline, for pilgrims travelling to the abbey. By the 17C it was the busiest ferry crossing in Scotland. The **Forth Rail Bridge** was begun in 1883 - an intrepid endeavour so soon after
the Tay Bridge disaster of 1879 - and was opened in 1890. The **Road Bridge**, a slim-
line elegant suspension bridge, with its amazing ''curve'', was built 1958-64. It
carries two 24ft - 7m wide carriageways, cycle tracks and pathways.

★★ **Hopetoun House.** — *11 miles - 18km to the west by the A90 then the A904.*
Set in beautiful landscaped grounds, Hopetoun House is a mansion of contrasts.
The original house, built 1699-1707, displays the mature classicism of **Sir William
Bruce**, its main staircase richly embellished with carving leading the eye upward to
the painted cupola - a unique survival of decorative art of the baroque period. The
later flamboyant extensions and frontage, 1721-67, are the work of **William Adam**,
completed by his son John. The grandeur of the State Apartments is complemented by the original furnishings, magnificent plaster ceilings and a notable art collection. An interesting exhibition covering the architects and craftsmen at Hopetoun
includes advice from Robert Adam, while on the Grand Tour with the Hope family.

The Binns. — *15 miles - 24km west of Edinburgh by the A8 and the M9.*
The home of the Dalyell family has interesting plasterwork ceilings in the Drawing
Room and the King's Room. The history of the house is dominated by the colourful
personality of **General Tam** (1615-85) a staunch Royalist who refused to cut his hair
or beard until the monarchy was restored and founder of the Royal Scots Greys.

★★ **Linlithgow Palace.** — *19 miles - 31km west of Edinburgh by the A8 and the M9.*
The history of the town is that of its royal palace around which it grew from the
12C. Following the rebuilding of the palace in 1424 it enjoyed over a century of
grandeur as the centre of Scotland's court until the Union of the Crowns (1603).
The roofless and forbidding four-square ruin still shelters several delicate features,
notably the 1530s **fountain**★ in the courtyard and a superbly carved **fireplace** at the
dais end of the Great Hall.
Alongside the palace stands the 15-16C late Gothic St Michael's Church★ with its controversial spire (1964).

★ **Cairnpapple.** — *24 miles - 39km west of Edinburgh by the A8 and the M9 to Lin-*
⊘ *lithgow then the A707 to Torphichen. Cairnpapple is a mile beyond.*
The site is unique in that five distinct phases in prehistoric evolution are represented. The earliest consists of cremation burials of the late Neolithic (*c*3000-2500 BC).
A henge with a bank and ditch and a stone circle were built *c*2500-2000 BC.
Within and slightly overlying this are two successive burial cairns, the first dating
to *c*1600 BC (now reconstructed with a concrete dome) and the second, larger,
cairn to *c*1300 BC. The final phase is represented by four Iron Age burials.

★★ **Rosslyn Chapel.** — *7 miles - 11km south of Edinburgh near the village of*
⊘ *Roslin.*
A bewildering example of craftsmanship, on the edge of the Esk Valley, Rosslyn
Chapel was built at the orders of Sir William St Clair, third and last Prince of Orkney
(1396-1484). Work lasted from 1446 until 1486, just after Sir William's death. By
then, only the choir of the planned collegiate church had been completed; this was
damaged in 1592, and used as a stable for the horses of General Monck's men
in 1650. Amongst the incredible riches of decoration, perhaps the best known single item is the **Apprentice Pillar★★★**. Legend has it that whilst the master mason was
abroad, his apprentice carved the pillar. The enraged master mason, on his return,
is said to have killed his too-gifted apprentice.

★ **ELGIN** Grampian   Pop 18 702

Michelin Map **401** K 11 or Atlas G Britain p 68

Elgin stands on the banks of the Lossie. The original plan has been well preserved,
with the main street linking the two mainstays of a medieval burgh, cathedral and
castle.

★ **Cathedral.** — The ruins stand as a monument to that period of intensive church
⊘ building, the 13C. The diocese dates back to 1120, but the ruins here are those
of a cathedral built in 1270, replacing one destroyed by fire. In 1390 the **Wolf of
Badenoch**, second son of King Robert II, destroyed both cathedral and town. Both
were repaired, and the 13C **chapter house★★** was reconstructed in the 15C, but the
cathedral suffered further deterioration since after the Reformation it was no longer
used as a place of worship. After the collapse of the tower in 1711, the ruins became a quarry for building materials. Conservation was begun in the early 19C.

EXCURSIONS

★★ **Sueno's Stone.** — *12 miles - 19km to the west by the A96 to Forres then the B9011.*
This superbly carved Pictish stone is probably a funerary monument commemorating a battle. A 20ft - 6m high sandstone slab, dating from the 9C, it has no parallel
in Britain. Three sides are decorative - one carved with a wheel cross. The fourth
side, the most spectacular, is narrative, and shows horsemen, warriors and head-
less corpses.

ELY Cambridgeshire   Pop 9 006

Michelin Map **404** U 26 or Atlas G Britain p 29

A mound of clay astride the River Ouse, Ely (Eel Island, according to Bede) rises
70ft - 21m above the Fen flatlands; a place of worship since St Etheldreda (7C),
it was sacked by the Danes in 870 and was the site of Hereward the Wake's last
stand against the Normans.

★★CATHEDRAL

⊘ The superb Norman nave and transepts little prepare you for the surprises beyond:
the wonderful Decorated east end and Lady Chapel, and that 14C masterpiece the
Octagon. The cathedral was begun in 1083; then in 1250, the east end of the original
Norman building was reconstructed, using Purbeck marble. In 1321 work started
on the Lady Chapel under the monastery surveyor Alan de Walsingham. Next year
the great Norman crossing tower fell down. Alan did not know ''where to turn or
what to do''. What he did was a triumph of medieval engineering. He cut off the
four Norman corners of the crossing and built on the eight points an octagonal space
three times the size of the Norman tower.

Exterior. — The cathedral is best viewed from the northwest to appreciate its length
(537ft - 164m), castellated west tower (215ft - 66m), Early English Galilee Porch,
the Decorated **Octagon** (170ft - 52m) and the wooden lantern above it.

Interior. — The relentless rhythm of the long and slender Norman nave (the triforium almost as tall as the arcades, the clerestory almost as tall as the triforium),
broken only by the ornate Norman work of the **Prior's Doorway**, leads the eye to the
Octagon above the crossing, its pillars embellished with the life of St Etheldreda.
Beyond George Gilbert Scott's **screen** is the beautifully vaulted Early English choir,
with its splendid 14C **choir stalls**, Perpendicular **Bishop Alcock's Chantry** and **Bishop West's
Chapel, tomb** to Bishop Redman, and the site of the shrine to St Etheldreda. The north
transept provides access to both the exquisite **Lady Chapel** (the largest single span
of vaulting in its time, above a rhythm of niches, canopies, windows and bosses)
and a **Stained-Glass Museum** in the triforium; while the **Monk's Door** by the **south transept**
provides access to the ruined cloisters and precincts (note the 1396 **Ely Porta**).

EXCURSIONS

The Fens. — Mostly below sea-level and stretching from Cambridge *(qv)* to Boston *(qv)*, the swamps and marshes were comprehensively drained by Dutch engineer Cornelius Vermuyden in the 17C and are now a very fertile agricultural region.

★ **Wicken Fen.** — *4 miles - 7km south on the A10 to Stretham then 5 miles - 8km east on the A1123.* This wilderness of swamp and scrub, Britain's oldest nature reserve, harbours the characteristic plant and animal species of the primeval fenland in a landscape little changed since Hereward's times.

★★ EXETER Devon   Pop 88 235

Michelin Map 403 J 31 or Atlas G Britain p 4

In the 1C AD the Romans captured the settlements of the Dumnonii tribe on the western bank of the River Exe, making it their most westerly strongpoint. The Saxon town which succeeded it was largely devastated by Danish invaders from 876 to 1003, but was rebuilt enough for the bishop's see to be transferred from Crediton to Exeter in 1050. In the Middle Ages trade prospered thanks to the city's position at the head of the navigable waters of the River Exe and it became one of the chief markets of country woollens. With the advent of steam power and machinery, however, Exeter's share of the woollen trade declined and the city settled down to the calm life of a county town. Today, despite heavy bombing in 1942, a visit to Exeter is rewarding for the charm of its crescents and terraces and in particular for its cathedral, standing out in elephant grey against the red sandstone of the city churches and the city wall, and the red brick of Georgian houses.

★★ **Cathedral** (Z). — The **Norman transept towers** are the earliest part of the cathedral, since the majority of the building was remodelled and improved in the 13C by Bishop Bronescombe and finally completed a century later by Bishop Grandisson. Set in its Close, an island of calm amid the city's traffic, and surrounded by buildings from many periods, the west front of the cathedral rises through tier upon tier of carved angels, bishops and monarchs, through Decorated tracery to castellated parapets. The towers, twin but not identical (the northern one being earlier), mount

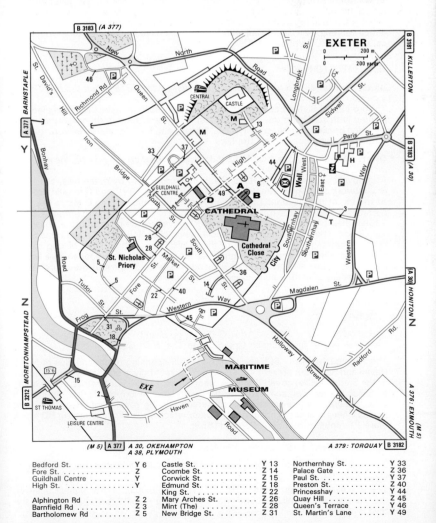

solidly through tiers of blind arcading and intersecting arches to castellations and the angle turrets with pepperpot roofs, substituted in the 15C for the traditional Norman pyramids. At the west end the upper gable window is half-hidden by the main window which in turn is masked at the base by the pierced parapet edging the **image screen.**

Interior. — The most striking feature is the **nave vaulting**, extending 300ft - 91m from west to east in an uninterrupted line of meeting ribs, with huge gilded and coloured bosses studding the intersections. Also impressive are the 14C **corbels** between the pointed arches of the arcade, supported on piers of sixteen clustered columns with plain ring capitals. Note the 14C **minstrels' gallery** *(north side)* with 14 angels playing instruments.

Behind the high altar stands the **Exeter Pillar**, the prototype of all the others in the cathedral. Through the two barely pointed arches behind the high altar can be seen the clustered pillars of the ambulatory and beyond them the Lady Chapel which is alive with bosses and corbels. The 19C canopied choir stalls incorporate the oldest complete set of **misericords** in the country, carved in 1260-80. The exquisite **bishop's throne** was carved in oak in 1312. Above the high altar the late 14C **east window** contains much original glass. In the north transept note the 15C clock with the sun and moon revolving around the earth.

Cathedral Close (Z). — The Close is diamond-shaped with the cathedral at its centre, almost abutted to the east by the gabled red sandstone bishop's palace. Marking the limits are the old **city wall (YZ)**, **St Martin's Church (Y A)**, **Mol's Coffee Shop (Y B)** - the four-storey timber-framed house dated 1596 - the cathedral choir school and a curving line of tall 17-19C shops and houses ending in a white, four-storey Georgian house now a hotel.

★★**Maritime Museum** (Z). — In warehouses by the old tidal river port Canal Basin, ⊘alongside, is a fascinating collection of more than 150 ships and boats of all shapes and sizes and from every corner of the globe.

⊘**Guildhall (Y D)**. — The more striking parts of this ancient municipal building are the decorated Tudor portico added in 1593 and the **Chamber** which has a timber roof of 1468-70 and ornate Elizabethan **panelling.**

⊘**St Nicholas Priory** (Z). — The sandstone building was the former guest wing of a small Benedictine priory founded in 1087 which later became an Elizabethan merchant's home. In the Norman undercroft crypt massive round columns support low ribbed vaulting. The Guest Hall and Prior's Room have handsome timber roofs and contain 16-17C furniture.

EXCURSIONS

★**Bicton Gardens.** — *8 miles - 13km southeast by the B3182 then the B3179 and ⊘a minor road.*
The grounds of Bicton house, now an agricultural college, have been designed and planted with specimen trees over the last 200 years. Among other features are a secluded **Hermitage Garden**, an early 19C **Orangery** and the Woodland Railway running through the grounds and by the lake.

★**Ottery St Mary.** — Pop 4 034. *12 miles - 19km east on the B3183, the A30 and B3174.*
Attractively situated on the River Otter and surrounded by green hills, the town is a network of winding streets and small squares with 17C and Georgian houses. At the top of the hill stands the twin-towered parish church of **St Mary's★★**, consecrated in 1260 on the manor which belonged to Rouen Cathedral from 1061 to 1336, when Bishop Grandisson of Exeter converted the church into a collegiate foundation. The Bishop had the chancel, nave, aisle and Lady Chapel remodelled in the Decorated style and many of the furnishings of the church belong to this period, including the **clock** in the south transept and the gilded wooden **eagle lectern,** one of the oldest and grandest in England. A special feature of the church is its varied **vaulting,** superb coloured **bosses** and corbels.

★★ EXMOOR

Michelin Map 403 I, J 30 or Atlas G Britain pp 6 and 7
See local map in the Michelin Green Guide The West Country

The 265 square miles - 665 square km of moor spanning the boundaries of North Devon and Somerset present varied scenery, beautifully in scale; the upland ridges of the Brendon Hills, covered in blue moor-grass, bracken or heather, ripple away as far as the eye can see, while to the north lies the Exmoor Forest, until 1818 a Royal Forest where game was preserved for the royal hunt. Red deer, wild ponies, sheep and cattle still roam the moor which is vividly described in RD Blackmore's famous novel *Lorna Doone* (1869).

Landmarks, towns and villages on the Moor

Although Exmoor is one of the smallest of the National Parks its many varied sights invite exploration.

★★★**View from Dunkery Beacon.** — At 1 705ft - 519m the Beacon is the highest point on the Moor, visible for miles around and commanding **views★★★** of the moor and sixteen counties.

★ **Lynton and Lynmouth.** — Pop 2 075. These complementary towns in a hollow at the top and at the foot of 500ft - 152m North Devon cliffs rejoice in glorious **views**★ across the Bristol Channel to the distant Welsh coast. Lynton is predominantly Victorian-Edwardian while Lynmouth remains a traditional fishing village with small stone cottages and houses. The **Valley of the Rocks**★ *(1 mile - 2km west)* is a group of rocks rising from the wide grass-covered valley to crests of bare sandstone and shale spectacularly carved by the wind.

Oare. — Pop 85. This tiny village in a green valley only a couple of miles from the sea owes its fame entirely to *Lorna Doone (see opposite)*. The Doone family is said to have lived here and it was in the restored 14-15C church that Lorna was married to John Ridd. A path leads to **Doone Valley**★ *(6 miles - 9km)* which came to fame with the publication of Blackmore's novel, based on tales of a group of outlaws and cut-throats who settled in Badgworthy Valley in the 1620s.

★ **Porlock.** — Pop 1 368. An attractive, though much visited, village - rendered infamous by "the man from Porlock" who interrupted Coleridge as he was writing *Kubla Khan*. The 13C **St Dubricius Church**★ with its truncated shingle-covered spire, is a reminder of Dubricius, a legendary figure who died aged 120 and is said to have been a friend of King Arthur. Inside is a remarkable canopied tomb with alabaster effigies.

★★ **Tarr Steps.** — The finest **clapper bridge**★★ in the country, dating back to the Middle Ages or earlier, crosses the River Barle at this point.

★ **Watersmeet.** — A beauty spot where the Rivers East Lyn and Hoaroak meet in a deep wooded valley, the river bed strewn with boulders around which the water swirls endlessly.

★ **Winsford.** — Pop 340. With its seven bridges within yards of each other, Winsford's oldest is the **packhorse bridge** over the River Exe.

★ **FALKLAND** Fife   Pop 896

Michelin Map 401 K 15 or Atlas G Britain p 56

Falkland town and palace, tucked away as they have long been from the depredations of war, retain the charm of an ancient royal burgh.

★ **Palace of Falkland.** — The earls of Fife stronghold passed to the Crown in 1425
⊘ and the hunting seat of Falkland became one of the Stewarts' favourite royal palaces. James IV, a typical prince of the Renaissance, entertained a splendid court at Falkland, but it was his son James V who, while preparing the palace for his French bride, gave it its unusual feature the Renaissance ornament of the courtyard façade of the south range, was a radical departure from the Gothic of the time. It makes a sharp contrast with the gatehouse and street front built by James IV in Gothic.

Interior. — The tour includes the private apartments of the keeper in the gatehouse. Attractively refurbished the apartments are hung with portraits of the occupants, and contain fine examples of period furniture. The east range housed the royal apartments, the king's suite on the first floor and that of the queen above. The first floor level affords a good view of the south range front.

★ **Gardens.** — At the far end of the attractive and varied gardens is a **real tennis court** built prior to Henry VIII's one at Hampton Court.

★ **Town.** — Take the time to stroll round the town and discover something of the lives of the court officials, the servants and the tradesmen who have left their houses, their carved lintels and marriage stones. A restoration programme has preserved much of the original character of the town.

★★★ **FOUNTAINS Abbey** North Yorkshire

Michelin Map 402 P 21 or Atlas G Britain p 39

This most complete of Cistercian ruins, set in the wooded valley of the little River Skell, is wonderfully evocative of monastic life in the Middle Ages.
In 1132 a small band of Benedictines, in revolt against slack discipline at their abbey in York, were granted land in this "place remote from all the world". Accepted by St Benedict into his austere order, the monks set about transforming the northern wilderness into the flourishing and productive countryside characteristic of Cistercian endeavour. Within a century, Fountains was the centre of an enormous enterprise, managing fish-farms and ironworkings, as well as forests and vast tracts of agricultural land, the profits from which paid for an ambitious building programme. The great complex fell into decay following the Dissolution, but in 1768 it was bought by the Aislabie family who had long desired it as the ultimate in picturesque ruins to complete their lavish landscaping of the adjacent **Studley Royal** estate.

> *The single estate comprising both Fountains Abbey and the gardens of Studley Royal may be entered from the west, for the abbey, or from the north. The entrances are about 1 mile - 1.5km apart, or further if the visitor approaches from the north and first sees the abbey as Aislabie intended, from a viewpoint on a high level walk.*

⊘ The splendid five-storey Jacobean mansion, **Fountains Hall**, with its striking main **façade**★ was built in 1611 with materials taken from the abbey. Beyond, a small gatehouse **museum** contains a large-scale model of the abbey.

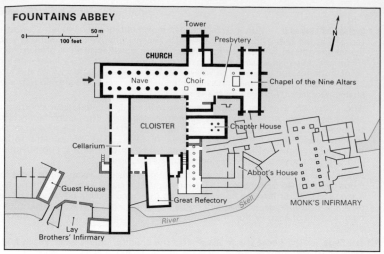

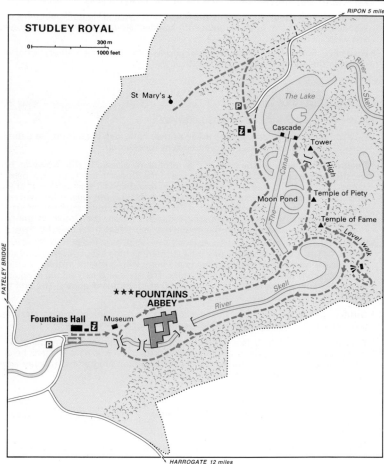

★★★ FOUNTAINS ABBEY *time: 1 hour*

⏱ The grassy levels of the valley floor sweep up to the western front of the roofless abbey church. An immensely long range of monastic buildings, with the lay brothers' dormitory above the cellarium, stretches away to the right. The church's tall tower of about 1500 rises above the stately Norman nave, while in the east is the spectacular 13C **Chapel of the Nine Altars**, an unusual feature later repeated at Durham Cathedral, with soaring arches and a huge Perpendicular window.

To the south the **monastic quarters** extend for hundreds of feet along the river, bridging it in places. Their scale and diversity suggest the varied activities of the great community of monks and lay brothers. The foundations and lower walls of the monk's infirmary and abbot's house to the east are impressive, but the most complete and beautiful remains are those of the buildings grouped around the **cloister** according to the standard Cistercian plan: to the east the **chapter house**, entered through three fine Norman arches; to the south the **great refectory**, its single doorway a masterpiece of elaborate moulding; and to the west the **cellarium**, with its astounding 300ft - 90m vaulted interior.

Outside the precinct there are the **guest house** and the **lay brothers' infirmary**.

★★ STUDLEY ROYAL

A vast personal fortune enabled John Aislabie, a disgraced former Chancellor of the Exchequer, to spend his retirement years (1720-42) transforming the sinuous valley of the Skell into a spectacular landscape in which woodland, water and buildings were manipulated to celebrate Nature and evoke a romanticised past.

Hundreds of workmen remodelled the valley floor to create a series of formal water features; **Moon Pons** is overlooked by a classical **Temple of Piety**, while the canalised river, emerging from a dark grotto, is led over a weir and finally discharges into a lake over a **grand cascade** flanked by symmetrical pavilions.

A high-level walk through the woods is approached via a dark, twisting tunnel. The path leads past a **Gothic Tower** and an elegant little **Temple of Fame**, to "Anne Boleyn's Seat", where the most notable of contrived garden **views★** opens out, that of the abbey itself, finally acquired in 1768 by William Aislabie after his father's death.

High up in the expansive deer-grazed parkland beyond the formal garden is **St Mary's Church**, a masterpiece of High Victorian Gothic, by William Burges. From it a long avenue extends eastwards, aligned on the twin towers of Ripon Cathedral.

★★ GLAMIS Castle Tayside

Michelin Map 401 K, L 14 or Atlas G Britain p 62

Set in the rich agricultural Vale of Strathmore, Glamis is the epitome of a Scottish castle; the massive sandstone pile bristles with towers, turrets, conical roofs and chimneys; it has a ghost (Lady Glamis, burnt as a witch), literary associations (Macbeth was Thane of Glamis) and has been the home of the Lyon family (forebears of the present Queen Mother) since 1372.

Exterior. — The 14C L-shaped core of the castle has been added to and altered, apparently at random through the centuries, giving the present building its impressive appearance.

Interior. — Family and other portraits, Jacobean armour and furniture, and interiors of many periods, form the charm of the guided tour. The chapel has a series of paintings of the Apostles and scenes from the Bible by Jacob de Wet (1695-1754), a Dutch artist who also worked at Blair and Holyrood House. In the splendid **Drawing Room** is a **plasterwork ceiling** (1621), and a magnificent fireplace. Here, as in Holyroodhouse, are tapestries from the workshop founded at Mortlake by James VI and I, after his accession to the English throne.

Statues of James and his son, Charles I, flank the driveway. To the side is a beautiful **Italian Garden**.

A attractive row of cottages in the nearby village of Glamis houses the **Angus Folk Museum★** with a fascinating collection of domestic and agricultural items depicting rural life in days gone by.

EXCURSIONS

Pictish Stones. — The area around Glamis is rich in carved stones of the Picts. Their enigmatic carving, from the 7C onwards, with Christian symbols incorporated in later centuries, vividly illustrate their life and art. The Pictish Kingdom and its distinctive art lasted for some 500 years, but faded away after Kenneth MacAlpine unified the thrones of Picts and Scots in 843 AD.

★ Aberlemno Stones. — *6 miles - 10km northeast of Forfar, on the B9134.* Four sculptured stones, with animal and abstract symbols, hunting and battle scenes and a cross with flanking angels, stand at the roadside and in the churchyard.

★★ Meigle Museum. — *7 miles - 11km west of Glamis.* Here are displayed, in the former village school behind the church, an outstanding collection of **early Christian monuments** in the Pictish tradition, all found locally. The carving is full of vitality and shows a high degree of skill.

★ Arbroath. — Pop 23 934. This fishing port on the Angus coast is famous for its abbey - though there are those who remember it also for its "smokies" - flavourful smoked haddock. The **Abbey★** was founded by William the Lion, in 1178, in memory of his childhood friend, Thomas Becket, murdered in Canterbury eight years previously. William died before the abbey was finished and is buried before the High Altar. The **Declaration of Arbroath** was drawn up and signed here on 6 April 1320, asserting Scotland's independence. Even as they are now, these "fragments of magnificence", as Dr Johnson called them, give some idea of its former splendour.

★ Edzell Castle. — *25 miles - 40km northeast, by the A94 and B966 to Edzell village.* Seat of the Lindsay family, the castle possesses a formal walled garden, **The Pleasance★★★** which is without equal in Scotland - or some say, elsewhere in Britain. Sir David Lindsay (*c*1550-1610) created this garden in 1604, a product of the Renaissance ideas he had absorbed on his wide travels. The blaze of summer colour against the rich red of the walls may divert the attention from the heraldic and symbolic **sculptures** on the walls, but these, too, reward closer inspection.

Scotland's most populous city, Glasgow is an important industrial centre and port, and is enjoying a growing reputation as a cultural centre.

HISTORICAL NOTES

It was to this part of the embattled Kingdom of Strathclyde that **St Mungo** came in the mid-6C: setting up his wooden church on the banks of the Molendinar Burn, and becoming the first bishop, then patron saint of the city. In the 17C Glasgow - always a radical city - became the centre of the Protestant cause. By the 18C the city was rich from trade in textiles, sugar and tobacco, her wealth increasing in the 19C through banking, shipbuilding and heavy industry. The arts prospered amid the wealth: neither the **Glasgow Boys** (hard-headed realists W Y MacGregor, James Guthrie, George Henry and John Lavery, painting in an age of romanticism), nor the pioneer modern movement led by Charles Mackintosh, could have so flourished in any other city, the realist and radical traditions continuing in the Glasgow painters of the 1980s (Steven Campbell, Ken Currie, Peter Howson and Adrian Wiesnewski). Today Glasgow is the home of the Scottish Opera, Scottish Ballet and several notable art collections.

★★★BURRELL COLLECTION Pollok Park

⊘ *3 miles - 5km to the southwest by the M77* (**AZ**)

The collection of one man, the shipowner **Sir William Burrell** (1861-1958) who gifted it to his native city in 1944, it is now on display in a custom-built gallery surrounded by a parkland, "as simple as possible" as Burrell wished. The collection is spaciously laid out in six sections. The Ancient Civilisations section includes items from Egypt, Mesopotamia, Italy and Greece, notably the 2C AD Warwick Vase and the porphyry Head of Zeus or Poseidon 4C AD. The section Oriental Art incorporates ceramics, bronzes and jades from the 3rd millennium BC to the 19C, and features the enamelled Ming figure of a lohan, or disciple of Buddha, which is dated to 1484. Burrell's particular interest was in Medieval and Post-Medieval European Art and two delightful specimens are the 15C Tournai tapestry *Peasants Hunting Rabbits with Ferrets* and the fragment of 12C stained glass depicting the Prophet Jeremiah. Of the early works to be found in Paintings, Drawings and Bronzes Bellini's *Virgin and Child* is notable. There is an important group of 19C French works with the pastel *Jockeys in the Rain* by Degas among them. The Hutton Castle Rooms, once part of Burrell's own home, are complete with medieval and antique furnishings.

★**Pollok House.** — The highlight of this 18C man-
⊘ sion is the representative collection of **Spanish paintings**★★ acquired by Sir William Stirling Maxwell (1818-78). The paintings, including portraits by El Greco, etchings by Goya as well as works by Tristan, Alonso Cano and Murillo, are displayed in tastefully furnished rooms.

MEDIEVAL GLASGOW

★★★**Cathedral** (**CY**). — The Gothic cathedral, fourth
⊘ church on the site of St Mungo's original building, and best viewed from the heights of the nearby Necropolis, is mostly 13 and 14C with 15C additions (chapter house, Blacader Aisle, central tower and stone spire). The nave is late Gothic; its elevation of richly moulded and pointed arches, more numerous at each level, rises to the timber roof. Beyond the 15C stone screen - unique in Scotland - is the choir, mid-13C in finest early pointed style, the triple lancets of the clerestory echoed in the lines of the east window. Beyond the ambulatory, through one of the four chapels leading off from it, is the upper chapter room (rebuilt in the 15C) where the medieval university held its classes. The lower church is another Gothic delight, where light and shade play effectively amidst the piers enshrining the tomb of St Mungo, Glasgow's patron saint, whose legend is illustrated on the St Kentigern Tapestry (1979). Before leaving the cathedral visit the 15C Blacader Aisle, an extension by Glasgow's first archbishop with its decorative ribbed vaulting.

Cathedral Square (**CY**). — The pre-Reformation heart of the ecclesiastical city; of the original buildings only the Cathedral and Provand's Lordship (1471) survive. The 20C Royal Infirmary replaces an earlier Adam brothers' one (1792), built near the site of the medieval Bishop's Castle.

GLASGOW

Glasgow Cross (CZ). — The heart of Glasgow until Victorian times; the **Tolbooth Steeple★** is the last reminder of its faded elegance.

Bridgegate (CZ 9). — Once a fashionable thoroughfare to Glasgow's first stone bridge (1345); all that is left of its better days is the 164ft - 50m steeple of Glasgow's Merchants Hall (1659), which served as a look-out for homecoming ships.

Glasgow Green (CZ). — A place used for grazing, jousting, parades, public hangings and above all free speech; the most historic piece of common land in the city.
⊘ The **People's Palace** is a social history museum with exotic winter gardens.

The Barras (CZ). — A weekend market, providing some of the most attractive and colourful street scenes in the city.

GLASGOW UNIVERSITY AREA

Founded in 1451 and centred around George Gilbert Scott's neo-Gothic Gilmorehill Building (completed by his son John Oldrid), the University with 10 000 students is home to two fine collections.

⊘ **Hunterian Museum** (M¹). — First floor, main building, East Quadrangle. The collection of William Hunter (1718-83), anatomist and pioneer obstetrician, is now divided between the museum and art gallery. The geological, anatomical, archaeological and ethnographical collections are complemented by a fine coin and medal collection.

★★ **Hunterian Art Gallery** (M²). — The University's art collection has an important
⊘ holding of works by **James McNeill Whistler** (1843-1903) with such favourites as *Rose et Argent: La Jolie Mutine*, *Red and Black: The Fan* and *Blue and Silver: Screen with Old Battersea Bridge*.
The **Mackintosh Wing** is a reconstruction of the home of Charles Rennie Mackintosh (1869-1928), the Glasgow architect and designer.

★★ **Art Gallery and Museum Kelvingrove** (M³). — Opened in 1902, financed by the
⊘ 1888 Glasgow International Exhibition, to house the various donations by local captains of industry. The European art section is displayed in the first-floor galleries. The Dutch and Flemish holding includes works by Jordaens, Rubens, Bruegel the Elder, Rembrandt *(A Man in Armour)* as well as Ruisdael landscapes. French

Trongate	CZ	Castle St.	CY 17	Morrison St.	BZ 38
Union St.	CYZ	Commerce St.	BZ 18	Oxford St.	BZ 40
		Ferry Rd	AY 19	Pitt St.	BY 42
Albert Bridge	CZ 2	Finnieston St.	BYZ 21	Port Dundas St.	CY 43
Arcadia St.	CZ 3	George V Bridge	BZ 22	Queen St.	CZ 45
Bain St.	CZ 4	Glasgow Bridge	BZ 25	Scott St.	BY 47
Binnie Pl.	CZ 6	Glasford St.	CZ 26	South Portland St.	CZ 49
Bridge St.	BZ 7	Kilbirnie St.	BZ 31	Stirling Rd	CY 50
Bridgegate	CZ 9	Killermont St.	CY 32	Stockwell St.	CZ 52
Buccleuch St.	BY 10	Kingston St.	BZ 33	Victoria Bridge	CZ 55
Caledonia Rd	CZ 14	Laurieston Rd	CZ 35	West Graham St.	BY 54
Cambridge St.	BY 15	Morris Pl.	CZ 36	West Nile St.	CY 56

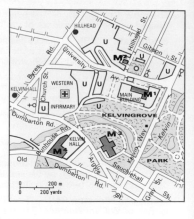

19C and early 20C movements are represented by Millet *(Going to Work),* Fantin-Latour, Courbet; and Monet, Pissarro, Renoir and Sisley for the Impressionists. Van Gogh's 1887 portrait depicts the Glasgow art dealer, Alexander Reid, with whom he shared a flat in Paris. In the British section note the portraits of Ramsey, Raeburn, Reynolds and Romney and the work of the Pre-Raphaelites. Remark the luminous quality of William McTaggart's outdoor works, precursors of the late 19C Glasgow Boys, a school contemporary with the Barbizon and Hague Schools. Henry's *A Galloway Landscape* is typical, while the combined compositions of Henry and Hornel show a strong Japanese influence. The highly distinctive works of the Scottish Colourists (Peploe, Hunter, Cadell and Fergusson) are enjoying a growing reputation.

★★ **Museum of Transport** (M⁴). — The museum in its new home has comprehensive displays of trams and trolley buses from 1872-1967, vintage cars with the emphasis on Scottish built-cars (Argyll, Albion and Arrol-Johnston), fire vehicles and bicycles. In the Kelvin Street exhibit there is a reminder of the subway prior to modernisation. The Clyde Room of Model Ships displays the varied and impressive output of Scottish shipyards, in particular those of Clydeside.

ADDITIONAL SIGHTS

George Square (CY). — Though started in 1782 George Square is magnificently Victorian. Note especially the 1869 **Merchant's House** (CY A) and, opposite, the **City Chambers★** (CY C) where the grandeur and opulence of the loggia, council and banqueting halls are reminders that Glasgow was the second city of the Empire in Victorian times.

Hutchesons' Hall (CZ B). — The original hospital was endowed in 1639 by the Hutcheson brothers, whose statues adorn the frontage of the 1802-5 hall. It is now a National Trust for Scotland visitor centre.

Royal Exchange (CZ F). —Glasgow's most splendid late 17C mansion, home of the tobacco millionaire William Cunninghame, it was turned into the Royal Exchange in the early 18C and extended. Now a public library, the great hall with its magnificent coffered ceiling can still be admired.

★ **Glasgow School of Art** (BY E). — Designed by Charles Rennie Mackintosh when he was only 28, this unique working educational institution remains his masterpiece. It was built in 1897-9 and 1907-9 and holds his acclaimed library with its three-storey-high windows and suspended ceiling, and the furniture gallery with items from Miss Cranston's Tea Rooms.

Tenement House (BY D). — A piece of social history. The flat, consisting of two rooms, kitchen and bathroom complete with original fittings, portrays turn of the century tenement life, at once private and centred on the back court and its community.

EXCURSIONS

★ **Hill House, Helensburgh.** — *21 miles - 34km northwest by the A82 and the A814.* The road follows the north shore of the Clyde Estuary. On entering the town of Dumbarton the bonded warehouses and distillery on the left are guarded by geese, Roman style. Perched on the basaltic Dumbarton Rock (240ft - 73m) once the capital of the Kingdom of Strathclyde, **Dumbarton Castle** provides panoramic views of the Clyde from its 18C fortifications.

★ **Hill House.** — *Upper Colquhoun Street, Helensburgh.* On a hillside overlooking the Clyde and designed by Mackintosh, Hill House (1902-4) is a first-rate example of pioneer modern architecture and interior design.

★ **Bothwell Castle.** — *9 miles - 15km southeast.*
The vast red sandstone fortress, now in ruins, dominates the Clyde Valley as it has since it was built in the late 13C. The massive circular keep is 13C while the great hall, chapel and southeast tower are 15C.

In nearby Blantyre an 18C mill tenement, Shuttle Row, houses the **David Livingstone Museum★** presenting the life and work of the missionary cum explorer (1813-73). The displays evoke his pioneering journeys through the ''dark continent'' and his encounter with Stanley *(qv).*

★★ GLASTONBURY Abbey Somerset

Michelin Map 403 L 30 or Atlas G Britain p 8

Although a ruin for centuries the name immediately conjures up the great abbey, one of the richest in the land and famous as a centre of learning.

Legend and history. — Glastonbury Tor and the Polden Hills were once islands in the marshes which were connected to the open sea by tidal channels; by the Iron Age (450 BC) the hilltops were occupied by forts enclosing hut settlements. According to the Grail legends an abbey was founded by Joseph of Arimathea, who caught the blood of the crucified Christ in the cup of the Last Supper; when he planted his staff in the ground it sprouted and became the famous **Glastonbury Thorn**,

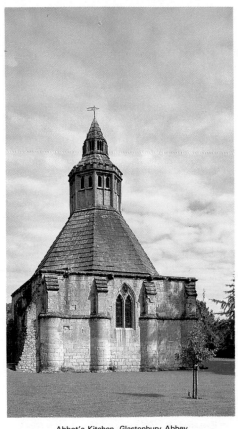

Abbot's Kitchen, Glastonbury Abbey

a tree which flowers at Christmas and in May. Another legend claims that **King Arthur** and his queen Guinevere were buried here, their bodies "discovered" in the abbey cemetery in 1191. The historian William of Malmesbury *(qv)*, in his ecclesiastical history of Glastonbury begun in 1120, gives us the first solid date: 688, when Ine, King of the West Saxons, having driven the Celts from Somerset, built, with **Aldhelm's** guidance, an additional church to that already on the site. Although **Dunstan**, Abbot of Glastonbury from 943 to 959, enlarged and rebuilt the abbey, the abbot appointed after the Norman Conquest considered the church inadequate for the richest abbey in the land and began to rebuild it. After a fire entirely destroyed the buildings in 1184, rebuilding began with the Lady Chapel, completed within two years, and continued over the next two centuries. Having acquired vast manorial holdings, it was annihilated at the Dissolution in 1539.

Ruins. — Extending far across the lawns, they stand tall amidst majestic trees. The Lady Chapel in Doulting stone, has a corner turret, decorated walls, and rounded doorways, with that to the north enriched by carved figures of the Annunciation, the Magi and Herod. East on the impressive Gothic transept piers remain the chancel walls and beyond them the site of the Edgar Chapel, a mausoleum for the Saxon Kings. The 14C **Abbot's Kitchen**, the sole building to survive intact, is square with an eight-sided roof rising to superimposed lanterns, which served to draw the smoke from the corner fires in the kitchen up the flues in the roof. North of the abbey stands the **Glastonbury Thorn Tree**.

★**Glastonbury Tor.** — 521ft - 159m high, it is a landmark for miles around. The tower at its summit is the last remnant of a Church to St Michael, built in the 14C. The view★★★ includes the Quantocks, Bristol Channel and the Mendips.

★★ GLEN COE Highland and Strathclyde

Michelin Map 401 E, F 13 or Atlas G Britain p 60

It was in this stark and grandiose setting that over forty of the pro-Stuart **MacDonald clan** were treacherously massacred in 1692 by the pro-Whig **Campbells** after giving an oath of allegiance to the British Crown in return for a pardon.
Approach the 11 mile - 18km long glen on the A82 from the south, via the desolation of Rannoch Moor, the **Meall a Bhuiridh** (Hill of the Roaring Stags) 3 636ft - 1 108m, the **Buachaille Etive Mor** (Big Herdsman of Etive) 3 345ft - 1 022m, and the glacial valley, Glen Etive, between them. The flat-topped rock, the Study, lying to the right, pinpoints the head of Glen Coe. Once in the glen, beyond the waterfall you are dwarfed by mighty rock faces; the **Three Sisters**, outliers of the **Bidean nam Bian** (Peak of the Bens), rising to 3 766ft - 1 141m, stretch out to the left, and the serrated ridge of **Anoach Eagach** to the right; Loch Achtriochtan spreads out on the valley floor.
The **Glen Coe Centre** provides information on local walks and climbs.
On the shores of Loch Leven, the village of **Glencoe** (Pop 315) has a small **folk museum.**

★ GLOUCESTER Pop 106 526

Michelin Map **403** N 28 or Atlas G Britain p 17
Town plan in the current Michelin Red Guide Great Britain and Ireland

At the lowest crossing point of the River Severn, Roman Glevum commanded the approaches to Wales. The medieval city's four "Gates" which still meet at the central Cross, reflect the plan of the legionary fort. Now a busy centre of administration, manufacturing and commerce, Gloucester's successive efforts at modernisation mean that much of its past, endearingly described in Beatrix Potter's children's classic *The Tailor of Gloucester,* can only be imagined. But the city is still dominated by its glorious cathedral and many traces of a history lasting nearly 2 000 years.

★★ CATHEDRAL *time: 1 hour*

Today's structure is essentially the creation of the Norman Benedictine abbot, Serlo, and of his successors in the 14C, who pioneered the Perpendicular style and adorned the transepts and choir under royal patronage and from the gifts of the pilgrims drawn to the tomb of Edward II, murdered in 1327 at nearby Berkeley Castle. The building was extended in the 15C by the addition of the Lady Chapel.

In the nave, massive Norman columns, reddened at the base by a fire in 1122, give an impression of enormous strength. Further east, Perpendicular elegance prevails: in the exquisite tracery of the 92ft - 28m - high **vault** of the choir; in the magical **east window**, the largest of its kind in medieval glass, commemorating the Battle of Crecy; and in the wonderfully light **Lady Chapel** of about 1500. Edward's effigy, north of the choir, is protected by a 14C stonework canopy of rare delicacy.

In the **cloisters**, the 14C **fan vaulting**, the earliest of its kind, is of exceptional richness, while the lavatorium evokes the rigours of monastic life. William the Conqueror is said to have ordered the Domesday Survey from the adjoining chapter house.

The 225ft - 69m **tower** of the mid-15C, with its unmistakable crown of parapet and pinnacles, rises gracefully above **College Green**, a pleasant combination of mainly 18C houses, replacements of earlier monastic buildings. **St Mary's Gate** is an impressive medieval survival.

ADDITIONAL SIGHTS

★ **The Docks.** — This fine 19C inland port is being actively conserved, with new uses being found for its sturdy warehouses, such as the **National Waterways Museum** which explores the long history of river and canal navigation in Britain. The exhibits inside are complemented by historic vessels moored at the quay-side.

The centre of the city, the Cross, is marked by **St Michael's Tower** (Tourist Information Centre). **Bishop Hooper's Lodging**★ in Westgate Street, housing the **Folk Museum** and the **New Inn** in Northgate Street are excellent examples of late medieval timber buildings.

Via Sacra. — This distinctively-paved pedestrian route roughly follows the line of the Roman walls and links Cathedral with modern shopping centre and with other points of interest, notably **Blackfriars**, a medieval Dominican friary.

EXCURSION

★ **Painswick.** — *7 miles - 11km. Leave Gloucester by the A417. Turn left at roundabout at the summit of the hill and follow signs to Crickley Hill Country Park.*

Crickley Hill Country Park. — From the dramatic promontory of the Cotswold escarpment, site of successive Neolithic and Iron Age settlements (explanatory information available, annual excavations), there are extensive **views**★ over the Severn Vale, Forest of Dean and, in the far distance, the Black Mountains of Wales.

> *Return to the A417, continue to Birdlip and follow signs to Painswick. The road passes through magnificent hanging beechwoods.*

★ **Painswick.** — Pop 1 757. The intimate streets of this hilltop village, with its many old buildings of golden Cotswold stone, should be explored before visiting the parish churchyard with its elaborate baroque tombstones and 99 clipped yew trees.

> *Return to Gloucester on the B4073.*

★★ GRAMPIAN'S Castle Country Grampian

Michelin Map **401** L, M and N 12 and 13 or Atlas G Britain p 69

Aberdeen's hinterland is rich in castles, from Norman to the golden age of castle building (16-17C), the Scottish baronial style. The masterpieces of the latter are representative of a flourishing native tradition revelling in both an imaginative and an inventive approach.

★ **Haddo House.** — *26 miles - 42km north of Aberdeen by the A92 to Ellon, then onto the B9005.*
On the estate acquired by the Gordons in 1469, William 2nd Earl of Aberdeen (1679-1745) commissioned William Adam to design the present house. George Hamilton Gordon (1784-1860), Prime Minister during the Crimean War, still found time to repair the house, by then derelict, and to landscape the parkland. The interior was transformed when his youngest son refurbished it in the Adam Revival style. Elegant rooms are a perfect setting for family portraits and mementoes.

★**Fyvie Castle.** — *26 miles - 42km north of Aberdeen by the A947.*
⊙ Alexander Seton, Lord Chancellor (*c*1639-1719), creator of Pitmedden Garden *(qv)*, remodelled Fyvie incorporating the Preston and Meldrum towers, thus giving us the spectacular 150ft - 46m long front, an impressive example of 17C baronial architecture, and the wheel stair, dating from 1603. In the late 19C Fyvie was purchased by Lord Leith and refurbished in an opulent Edwardian manner. He also collected, in the manner of other American millionaires, in particular portraits by the Scottish master of the art Henry Raeburn.

★★**Crathes Castle.** — *15 miles - 24km southwest of Aberdeen by the A93.*
⊙ The wonderfully crowded and detailed skyline of this 16C tower house is a striking example of the inventive native tradition. The interiors include some fine early vernacular furniture as well as some outstanding examples of painted ceilings (Room of the Nine Nobles and the Muses Room). This lively form of decoration, peculiar to the east coast, may well have been copied from Scandinavian contacts. By the mid-17C decorative painting was eclipsed by ornate plasterwork ceilings. The whole is enhanced by the delightful gardens, the lifetime achievement of the late Sir James and Lady Burnett. The visitor is lured through a series of distinct and separate gardens, each a delight in the wealth and colour of the planting.

★★★**Craigievar Castle.** — *26 miles - 42km west of Aberdeen by the A944, turn left*
⊙ *just before Westhill onto the B9119 then onto the A980.*
Danzig Willie, William Forbes (d 1627), an Aberdeen merchant who made his fortune in the Baltic trade, financed this crowning glory of 17C Scottish castle building. Ingenuity and skill are everywhere apparent as this traditional Scottish tower house rises gracefully but starkly to the wallhead cluster where conical roofed turrets, crow stepped gables, dormers, chimney stacks and balustrade jostle for position. Every elevation of this six-storey tower house is different and every one is worthy of close attention. Inside little has changed since the great hall, its plasterwork ceiling covered with medallion portraits and pendants was finished in 1625, and the interior reflects the lifestyle of a 16-17C Scottish laird.

★**Castle Fraser.** — *15 miles - 24km west of Aberdeen by the A944, then onto the*
⊙ *B993 at Dunecht.*
Built between 1575 and 1636, Castle Fraser is one of the grander Castles of Mar, a traditional tower house with highly individual decoration. The local style with its harmonious combination of traditional features - turrets, conical roofs, crowstepped gables, chimney stacks, decorative dormers and gargoyles - was Scotland's unique contribution to Renaissance architecture. The central block of this Z-plan castle is distinguished by a magnificent heraldic achievement. The refurbished interiors bring to life the homely lifestyle of a 17C laird.

★**Kildrummy Castle.** — *38 miles - 61km west of Aberdeen by the A944, turning*
⊙ *left at Mossat.*
The extensive ruins of this 13C courtyard castle, the "noblest of northern castles", incorporates two different concepts of defensive design. The late 13-14C gatehouse, which may have been built for King Edward I of England, displays striking similarities with the gatehouse at Harlech Castle in Wales, while the circular tower, known as the Snow Tower, displays parallels with the great castle of Coucy in France, which was built by the father of Alexander II's queen. Although these important elements are no more than foundations, substantial fragments of the castle still survive and the overall layout is clearly visible.

★★**Dunnottar Castle.** — *18 miles - 29km south of Aberdeen by the A92.*
⊙ Legend has it that St Ninian founded a Christian settlement here in the 5C. Sir William Keith founded the present castle on the site in the 14C and was excommunicated for building on consecrated ground. Set on an almost inaccessible promontory with sheer cliffs on three sides, it was the last castle remaining in Royalist hands during the Commonwealth. Here the Honours of Scotland were held during an eight-month siege by Cromwell's troops in 1651-2, being finally smuggled out and hidden in nearby Old Kinneff church, where they remained until the Restoration.

GRANTHAM Lincolnshire   Pop 30 700

Michelin Map **402** S 25 or Atlas G Britain p 36

An important staging point on the road north from London, Grantham thrived in the Middle Ages and continues to prosper. St Wulfram's is one of England's most beautiful parish churches.
Sir Isaac Newton (1643-1727) was born here, as was Britain's first woman Prime Minister.

★**St Wulfram's Church.** — With one of the tallest spires in Britain (272ft - 83m), so beautiful that Ruskin swooned, St Wulfram's is largely Early English, with a *c*1340 Lady Chapel and rare **chained library** of over 300 books in the south porch.
Facing the churchyard is the *c*1500 Grammar School where Isaac Newton was educated.

Angel and Royal Inn. — *High Street.* One of the great medieval inns of England established by the Knights Templar, and with a stone front, the Angel has played host to monarchs from King John to Richard III, who signed the death warrant for the Duke of Buckingham here.

EXCURSIONS

★★**Belvoir Castle.** — *6 miles - 10km west on the A607 to Denton, follow signs.*
Built by John Webb (pupil of Inigo Jones) in 1654-68, Belvoir (pronounced "Beever") was romanticised by James Wyatt into an early 19C "castle on a hill".

Interior. — Part Gothick fantasy, part baroque fantasy, the Ballroom contains Thomas Becket's illuminated breviary, and the Elizabeth Saloon a ceiling of Jupiter, Juno, Mercury and Venus. In the picture gallery are miniatures (Hilliard and Oliver) and paintings, including *Grace before Meat* (Jan Steen), the *Earl of Southampton,* Shakespeare's patron (Cornelius Janssen), *Proverbs* (David Teniers II), *Seven Sacrements* (Poussin) and the *Woodcutter's Return* (Gainsborough). In the Regent's Gallery, 131ft - 40m long and hung with vast Gobelins tapestries recording the *Adventures of Don Quixote,* is Canova's sculpture of the *Three Graces.*

★**Belton House.** — *3 miles - 5km northeast on the A607, follow signs.*
A late 17C mansion crowned by balustrade and cupola with late 18C neo-classical alterations by James Wyatt, Belton is the fulfilment of the golden age of English domestic architecture from Wren to Adam.

Interior. — The classical simplicity of the Marble Hall provides the setting for the paintings by Reynolds, Hoppner and Romney; the exquisite woodcarvings in the Salon are possibly the work of Grinling Gibbons; the Red Drawing Room is graced by Fra Bartolomeo's *Madonna and Child*; the Tyrconnel Room boasts a rare Greek Revival painted floor; the two glorious 1681 "oriental" tapestries in the Chapel Ante Room are by John Vanderbanc (partly copied from Mogul miniatures); the Chapel's ceiling is by Edward Goudge and the wood carvings by Edmund Carpenter.

★ GREAT GLEN Highland

Michelin Map 401 E and F 13, F and G 12, G and H 11 or Atlas G Britain pp 60 and 67

The geological fault of the Great Glen, running southwest to northeast, cuts across the Highlands, linking the Atlantic Ocean with the North Sea through a series of narrows lochs joined together by 22 miles - 35km of Thomas Telford's **Caledonian Canal** (1803-22). The lochs and canals are now used principally for pleasure craft; some operators offer "Monster Hunting" trips on Loch Ness.

FORT WILLIAM TO INVERNESS

65 miles - 105 km - allow an afternoon for the drive excluding Inverness and Fort William

★**Fort William.** — Pop 10 805. Fort William lies on the shore of Loch Linnhe in the shadow of Britain's highest mountain, **Ben Nevis** (4 406ft - 1 344m). The town makes an ideal touring centre from which to discover the beauty of the surrounding countryside.

Take the A82 northwards.

Beyond the World War II Commando Memorial lies the 10 mile - 16km long Loch Lochy, flanked by forests on both sides. Once beyond the loch take the time to turn off at Laggan and watch the pleasure boats negotiate the **Laggan Locks**, built to overcome the 13ft - 4m difference between the two lochs.
Shortly after Laggan the road crosses to the west side of the glen before skirting the shallow waters of Loch Oich.

Fort Augustus. — Pop 575. Sitting astride the Caledonian Canal at the southern end of Loch Ness, this busy little town becomes a bottleneck in summer as traffic negotiates the swing bridge. On the site of General Wade's 18C fort stands Fort Augustus Abbey, known for its Catholic school.

★★**Loch Ness.** — The dark waters of this 754ft - 230m deep loch are renowned the world over as the home of the elusive **Nessie.** First espied in the 8C by a local monk Nessie has continued to captivate, intrigue, and despite modern technology, preserve her true identity. A roadside monument commemorates the death of the racing driver John Cobb in 1952, while attempting to break the water speed record.

Urquhart Castle. — *Fairly steep path and stairs down to its lochside site.* The ruins are strategically set on a promontory jutting out into the loch and the stronghold was one of a chain controlling this natural route. The landward gatehouse leads to a double bailey courtyard. The viewing platform in the tower house affords good **views** of the castle's layout and of the loch in its mountain setting.

Drumnadrochit. — Pop 542. The village's **Official Loch Ness Monster Exhibition★** provides an interesting and informative introduction to the Nessie enigma.

The final stretch of lochside road provides some good views of the loch before reaching the capital of the Highlands.

★**Inverness.** — *Description p 137.*

Passing places
are provided to allow vehicles to pass one another,
but also to permit overtaking.
Do not park in passing places. Do not hold up a following vehicle.

Michelin Map **401** L 16 or Atlas G Britain p 56

This handsome market town grew up in the 12C around a royal palace; by the 16C it was the fourth largest town in Scotland, and in the 18C entered a golden age based on agricultural wealth.

⊘ Start with the 14-15C **St Mary's Collegiate Church** in its peaceful riverside setting. Its impressive dimensions remind us that it was built as one of the great burgh churches. Inside note the Burne-Jones window in the south transept and the four recumbent effigies of the Maitland family in the 17C **Lauderdale Aisle**.

Follow The Sands past the 16C **Nungate Bridge** with its pointed cutwaters up to the **High Street★** and its continuous line of frontages, often gable ended. This type of colourful and varied streetscape was typical of Scottish burgh architecture in the past. Beyond, in Lodge Street, a pend leads to the childhood home of Jane Welsh, the wife of Thomas Carlyle *(qv)*. At the junction of High and Market Streets is William Adam's dignified 18C town house.

EXCURSIONS

★★**Tantallon Castle.** — *13 miles - 21km by the A1 then the A198 in the direction*
⊘ *of North Berwick.*

The formidable ruin of this Douglas stronghold clings to its clifftop site defying both waves and winds, as so aptly described by Scott in his narrative poem *Marmion*. Ditches and earthen ramparts defend the landward side of this gaunt red sandstone ruin, now attractively weathered.

★**Lennoxlove.** — *1 mile - 0.5km south of Haddington.*
⊘ This historic home has been the seat of Maitlands and latterly the Dukes of Hamilton and houses some of the family collections from the now demolished Hamilton Palace. There are numerous historic associations with such personalities as Mary Queen of Scots, Frances Teresa Stewart or La Belle Stewart, the Duke of Lauderdale sometimes referred to as the ''King of Scotland'' as well as that other personality, ''Il Magnifico'', the 10th Duke of Hamilton. The many portraits bring these and other figures to life for us.

★**Gifford.** — Pop 663. *4 miles - 6km south on the B6369.*
This late 17C early 18C estate village is one of the several attractive villages (East Saltoun, Pencaitland, Garvald and Stenton) nestling in the rolling countryside of the northern foothills of the Lammermuir Hills. The T-shaped church (1710) has an emblazoned laird's loft and in the churchyard a monument to John Witherspoon, the only clergyman signatory of the American Declaration of Independence.

★★ **HADRIAN'S WALL** Cumbria, Northumberland

Michelin Map **402** L 19 M, N and O 18 or Atlas G Britain pp 50 and 51

In AD 122, Emperor Hadrian, touring the western provinces of the Empire, visited Britain. He ordered the building of a defensive wall, across the northernmost boundary of the Empire, 73 miles - 117km, from Wallsend on the Tyne, to Bowness on the Solway Firth; parts of this wall can still be seen today. Museums, camps and settlements give a picture of military and civilian life on Rome's ''North West Frontier''.

The Wall. — The wall was built by legionaries, citizens of Rome, and garrisoned by as many as 24 000 auxiliaries from conquered territories. With its ditch to the north, a military road and ''vallum'', defining the military zone, to the south, the wall was built in stone and turf, with forts, milecastles and turrets at regular intervals along its length. It follows the best strategic and geographical line, and at places such as Cawfields and at Walltown Crags, commands splendid **views**. Milecastles along Hadrian's Wall have been numbered, from east to west, starting at Wallsend (0), and finishing at Bowness (80). The Roman mile was about 1 620yds - 1 481m, somewhat shorter than today's mile of 1 760yds - 1 609m. Many of the guidebooks specific to the wall refer to this system.

MAIN SITES AND LANDMARKS ALONG THE WALL

Follow the B6318 which is hilly. The main sites all have car parks (police warning: beware of car thieves, leave no valuables) and are indicated by light brown signposts. They are listed in their geographical order going from east to west. Refer to the local map overleaf for exact locations.

★**Museum of Antiquities.** — Newcastle upon Tyne. The exhibits (scale models and artifacts) provide a good introduction to the wall and its different elements *(p 184)*.

Corbridge. — Pop 2 757. The attractive town of Corbridge had its origins in the settlement of civilians and camp followers which grew up alongside the Roman station of Corstopitum. In Saxon times it was relocated here. Corbridge has an interesting Vicar's Pele, a 14C fortified dwelling within the churchyard, three storeys high, built of Roman worked stones.

★**Corstopitum.** — West of Corbridge. This site was occupied for longer than any
⊘ other on the wall. The township sprang up around the fort and supply-base which lay north of the bridge carrying Dere Street and it also marked the junction with the east-west Stanegate. The wall runs along the rise to the north. The **museum** of the Corbridge Roman Station presents the layout of the site with its **granaries**, foun-

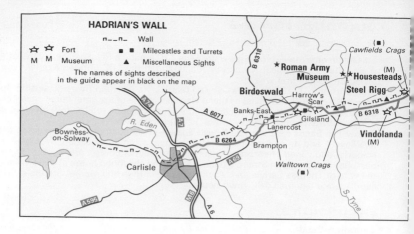

tain, headquarters building and temples. From the elevated viewpoint there is a good overall view of the visible remains which represent only a small central part of the supply-base and settlement.

Beyond the Planetrees roadside fragment of the Wall and once down in the valley take the A6079 to the left. Almost immediately on the left is **Brunton Turret**.

★Chesters. — Near Chollerford. The fort lies just west of the point where the wall crossed the River Tyne, and remains of the bridge can still be discerned on the far bank. The four gateways, headquarters building and barrack blocks of this fort can still be traced from their foundations. Down by the river are the fascinating remains of a **bath house★**. The **museum** contains a selection of sculptured stones collected among and around the wall in the 19C.

Temple of Mithras. — Carrawburgh. *5 minute walk from the car park.* An unexpected find in such a desolate stretch of moorland, this compact mithraeum is the only one visible of the three discovered in the vicinity of the Wall. Inside the lobby is a statue of the mother goddess, beyond, earth benches for worshippers flanked a narrow nave with three altars at the end. The originals can be seen in a reconstruction of the temple in the Museum of Antiquities in Newcastle *(qv)*. The temple was destroyed early in the 4C, probably by the Christians, who saw, in the Mithraic ritual of taking bread and water, a caricature of their own sacrament.

★★Housesteads. — Covering 5 acres - 2ha the fort is perched high on the ridge and is the most complete example on the Wall. Still clearly visible are the foundations of the large courtyard house of the commandant, the granaries, barracks, headquarters building, the four main gateways, the **hospital** and 24-seater **latrine block** as well as part of the civilian settlement, clustering round the south gate.

The Wall is visible to east and west as it undulates over the whinsill ridge.

View along Hadrian's Wall

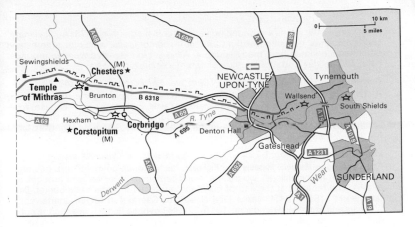

Steel Rigg. — The car park high up on the sill gives a good **view★** of and access to Wall sections winding east to Peel Crags and west to Winshields Crags. The section of the Wall from Steel Rigg to Housesteads is popular with walkers.

Vindolanda. — Chesterholm. The fort and civilian settlement on the Stanegate to the south of the Wall date from the period before the building of the wall. Full-scale replicas have been built of a stretch of the Wall with a stone turret, as well as of the turf wall, which was the earliest barrier, with a timber milecastle. As well as objects of metal, bone and stone, there is an interesting collection of writing tablets, leather goods, textiles and wooden objects in the **museum★**. These records, stores accounts and letters add significantly to information about the Roman life-style.

The road to the right in the direction of Whiteside leads to a quarry car park. A short climb gives access to the precariously-perched **Cawfields Milecastle** 42. These fort-lets could accommodate from 8 to 32 soldiers.

★Roman Army Museum. — At Carvoran. With an audio-visual presentation and examples of Roman armour, dress and weapons, it is the largest and most modern of the Wall museums and presents a lively picture of the Wall and its garrison. The adjoining unexcavated fort of Carvoran was on the pre-Hadrianic frontier. To the east the quarry viewing point provides a good view of one of the finest sections of the Wall, **Walltown Crags**.

When the B6318 comes to a dead end take the A69.

Birdoswald. — Of this fort, fine sections of gateways and granaries have been excavated. To the west is the **Banks East** section of the Wall.

★★ HARLECH Castle Gwynedd

Michelin Map 403 H 25 or Atlas G Britain p 32

Started during Edward I's second campaign in Wales, Harlech Castle, command-ing a prospect of sea and mountains from its 200ft-60m crag, was built from 1283 to 1289. Its position with the fortified "Way from the Sea" protected by walls and "artillery platforms", ensured its defences. **James of St George**, master mason of most of Edward's castles in Wales, was rewarded by being appointed Constable of Harlech, from July 1290, at a salary of 100 marks a year — over £120 000 at 1988 values. The song *Men of Harlech* commemorates the holding of the castle for the Lancas-trians, for eight years, during the Wars of the Roses, when it gave shelter to Henry VI's Queen, Margaret of Anjou. The garrison was permitted to march out in triumph in 1468, rather than being put to the sword or hanged — a more usual treatment for losers in those times.

⊘ TOUR *time: 1/2 hour*

Before entering, pause to look at the massive east front with its **Gatehouse**, and solid drum towers — the daunting sight which confronted would-be attackers. Enter by the modern wooden stairs, at the spot where a second, inner drawbridge pivoted to come down on bridge towers behind you, of which only the foundations now remain. Inside the castle, the strength and importance of the gatehouse becomes apparent. Traceried windows, facing the Inner Ward, gave ample light to self-contained suites with fireplaces and a chapel. Here, in contrast to the purely "mili-tary" character of towers and curtain wall, is one of the finest examples of the 'for-tified domestic' architecture of the time.

EXCURSIONS

★Portmeirion. — *18 miles - 29km north by the A496, turning left and crossing the river in Maentwrog onto the A487. A toll-road across the estuary marshes cuts 10 miles from this trip.*
The village was designed in 1925 by Sir Clough Williams-Ellis (1883-1978), an architect intent on proving that a beautiful site could be developed without being defiled, as he himself explains in the audio-visual presentation of the project.

He developed the site as a self-funding venture until his death in 1978. An 'Italianate' style dominates, combined with a Celtic profusion of ideas, buildings, statues and other items donated from many sources. All is set in extensive wooded grounds; hotel and holiday cottages provide accommodation for visitors.

Criccieth. — Pop 1 535. *6 miles - 10km west of Portmeirion by the A497.*

A charming Victorian seaside holiday spot, base for exploring the **Lleyn Peninsula,** with its sandy beaches and wild scenery. The **Castle,** with its great gatehouse, towers above the town. A Welsh castle dating from the 1230s, it was here that Llywelyn the Last lived with his wife, daughter of his old ally Simon de Montfort, until his death at Builth in 1282.

Llanystumdwy. — Pop 1 794. *2 miles - 3 km west of Criccieth on the A497.*

The **Lloyd George Memorial Museum** and **Highgate,** his Victorian boyhood cottage home, are situated in this village, where the world-famous statesman was brought up, to which he returned at the end of his life and where he chose to be buried. **David Lloyd George** (1863-1945) was a Liberal MP for Caernarfon for an uninterrupted 55 years and Prime Minister during 1916-22. His boyhood home is open to the public and the museum illustrates his life through varied displays (memorabilia, cartoons, costumes). The grave is a short walk away on the bank of the River Dwyfor.

★ HARROGATE North Yorkshire   Pop 63 637

Michelin Map 402 P 22 or Atlas G Britain p 40
Town plan in the current Michelin Red Guide Great Britain and Ireland

The **Royal Pump Room,** built in 1842, and the **Royal Baths Assembly Rooms,** built in 1897, were the hub of this spa town in its heyday at the end of the 19C, when some 60 000 people a year came to 'take the waters'. There are 36 springs within an area of an acre, less than half a hectare, mostly sulphurous, but no two with water of identical chemical composition. An interesting aspect of the town today is the **Stray,** 200 acres - 80ha of grassland surrounding the town centre. For a town that scarcely existed on a map of 1821, Harrogate today, with its fine shops, hotels and new **International Exhibition and Conference Centre,** is an admirable touring base.

EXCURSIONS

★★**Harewood House.** — *8 miles - 13km south, by the A61.*

Edwin Lascelles started to construct Harewood House in 1759. The building is an essay in Palladian architecture by John Carr of York; most of its interiors are neo-classical, lighter in spirit, one of the greatest achievements of **Robert Adam,** recently returned from Italy. Lascelles chose **Thomas Chippendale** (1718-79), born at nearby Otley, to make the furniture, and Capability Brown to develop the grounds.

Entrance Hall. — The only room to retain John Carr's original form. The fine plasterwork ceiling, as are all the ceilings in the house, is the work of a York craftsman Joseph Rose. Old Master paintings are hung throughout, mostly English and Italian, but note the superb El Greco *A Man, a Woman and a Monkey* in the Green Drawing Room; there is much rare Chinese porcelain, as well as Sèvres pieces collected at the beginning of the 19C. **The Gallery★** is perhaps the pinnacle of Adam's work at Harewood. The wooden curtain swags were "carved and painted under the direction of Mr Chippendale, in so masterly a manner as to deceive any beholder". In the **Music Room,** the ceiling and the Axminster carpet were designed by Adam, to give an illusion of "roundness" in a square room.
In the grounds is the **Bird Garden.** The **Tropical House** has been refurbished to simulate one of the earth's rapidly-disappearing natural wonders, the Rain Forest. River Bank and Waterfall display plants, birds and butterflies, all in authentic environments.

Knaresborough. — Pop 12 910. *2 miles - 3km east of Harrogate by the A59.*

A small market town on the River Nidd, overlooked by the ruins of its castle **keep,** started about 1130. Hugh de Morville, the Constable, fled to the castle with his three companions, after murdering Thomas Becket in Canterbury Cathedral in December 1170. From here they went on a pilgrimage for pardon to Jerusalem, three dying there and the fourth on his way home. **Mother Shipton's Cave** and the **Dropping Well** lie alongside the river. Mother Shipton, born *c*1488, was reputed to have lived and prophesied in this cave. The **Dropping Well,** unique in Britain, is a cascade of water falling into a pool. Objects hung in the water become covered with a stalactite deposit, seemingly "turned to stone".

Harlow Carr Botanical Gardens. — *2 miles - 3km by the B6162.*
The Northern Horticultural Society's Trial Gardens cover some sixty acres - 24ha.

*Admission times and charges
to the sights described are listed at the end of the guide.*

*Every sight for which there are times and charges is indicated by the symbol ⊙
in the margin
in the main part of the guide.*

★★ HATFIELD House Hertfordshire

Michelin Map 404 T 28 or Atlas G Britain p 19

One of the finest and largest Jacobean houses in England, Hatfield House was built by Robert Lyminge, architect of Blickling Hall *(qv)* for Robert Cecil, chief minister to Elizabeth I and James I (VI of Scotland). The earlier palace built by Cardinal Morton had been Elizabeth's childhood home and there under an oak tree she heard of her succession. ''It is the Lord's doing and it is marvellous in our eyes.'' Hatfield has remained the home of the Cecil family who, after two chief ministers, produced a three-times Prime Minister, Lord Salisbury (1830-1903).

Exterior. — Having exchanged Theobalds for Hatfield with his monarch, Cecil pulled down three ranges of the earlier palace, leaving the Hall (''one of the foremost monuments to medieval brickwork in the country'': Pevsner). With the bricks Lyminge built a palace to the traditional E-plan, adding decorative detail with the use of stone quoins and openwork balustrades. The south front has a striking façade of Caen stone.

Interior. — The house has several characteristic features of the period, notably the hall, staircase and long gallery. In the **Marble Hall** the magnificently carved screen, minstrels' gallery and panels are Jacobean, the gigantic 17C allegorical tapestry from Brussels and the ceiling and gallery panels by Taldini. The **Ermine Portrait** of Elizabeth I is attributed to Nicholas Hilliard while the one of her cousin *Mary Queen of Scots* is said to be by Rowland Lockey. The **grand oak staircase** is Jacobean carving at its best. Note the relief of the horticulturist John Tradescant *(qv)*, gardener to Charles I, on one of the newels at the top of the stairs, and the *Rainbow Portrait* of Elizabeth I.

Extended the length of the range in the 19C, the **long gallery** has the crystal Posset Set (believed to be a betrothal gift to Queen Mary and King Philip of Spain) by Cellini at one end, Queen Elizabeth's silk stockings, hat and gloves at the other. In the library amid the 10 000 volumes and the mosaic portrait of the builder, Robert Cecil, are displayed a letter from Mary Queen of Scots and her execution warrant, signed by Lord Burghley, Cecil's father. In the chapel the biblical stained glass with its wonderful clarity is Flemish.

An Elizabethan **knot garden** and a traditional **herb garden** are recent additions.

★ HEREFORD Hereford and Worcester   Pop 48 277

Michelin Map 403 L 27 or Atlas G Britain p 26
Town plan in the current Michelin Red Guide Great Britain and Ireland

Seat of a bishop in 676 AD, Hereford was a flourishing city and became capital of Saxon Mercia, with its own mint. William FitzOsborn, builder of Chepstow castle, established a new market where the roads converged north of the town in 1070. Today Hereford is the flourishing centre for a rich agricultural region. Outstanding amongst the wealth of half-timbered buildings preserved in the city is the **Old House★**, dating from 1621, a fine example of Jacobean domestic architecture.

★★ Cathedral. — The red sandstone building is mainly of the 12C. The massive tower was added in the 14C, largely funded by offerings from pilgrims to the shrine of St Thomas Cantilupe, Bishop from 1275-82. His shrine, minus effigy, stands in the north transept. The chantry to John Stanbury, Bishop from 1453-74, is a fine example of Perpendicular architecture. Among the treasures is the **Mappa Mundi★**. This is a map of the world, with Jerusalem at its centre, made by Richard of Haldingham in Lincolnshire. Here too is one of the finest **chained libraries** in the country, with 1 400 books and over 200 manuscripts, dating from the 8C to the 15C. The ''Cider Bible'', so called because ''strong drink'' of the Authorised version has been translated as ''cidir'', is but one of these. There is a small 13C Limoges enamel reliquary, which used to contain a relic of St Thomas Becket, whose murder is depicted on the side. Hereford is unique in possessing yet another chained library in All Saints Church. Every third year the Cathedral is the setting for the **Three Choirs Festival**, which it has shared with Gloucester and Worcester since the 18C.

Bulmer Railway Centre. — The Hereford-based cider company, HP Bulmer, restored the GWR steam locomotive *King George V*, in 1968, and the Centre now houses other steam locomotives and rolling stock. It is a working depot for steam operation on the main line between Newport and Chester.

Cider Museum. — *Pomona Place, Whitecross Road.* Housed in a former cider factory the museum tells the story of cider making through the ages.

EXCURSIONS

Kilpeck. — *8 miles - 13km southwest on the A465, then right for 1 mile - 1 1/2km on a minor road.*
The manor was held from the king, at the time of Domesday, for ''fifteen sesters of honey and ten shillings annually''. The **Church of SS Mary and David★★**, built in 1135, replaced a Saxon church which had been on the site since 650 AD. Nowhere else in Britain has such rich Norman carving and decoration survived. The South Door *(photograph p 30)* with its portal and columns is particularly fine. Of the 70 grotesques around the corbel only two have any religious significance. The gargoyle heads on the west wall are pure Viking in inspiration and might have been lifted straight from the prows of their longships. Beyond the graveyard are the lonely remains of the ruined castle.

Abbey Dore. — Pop 261. *9 miles - 15 km southwest on the A465, turn left onto unmarked road, 3 miles - 5 km.*
An abbey was founded here in 1147, and the present building was begun in 1180. This, thanks to the restoration put in hand in 1632, by Lord Scudamore, is now the village's church. John Abel, the architect commissioned to do the job, used 204 tons of timber to re-roof the nave and presbytery, and it was he who carved the magnificent screen from Hereford oak. Since the re-consecration on Scudamore's birthday, Palm Sunday 1634, Abbey Dore has been one of the few Cistercian churches in England regularly used for worship.

★ HEVER Castle Kent

Michelin Map 404 U 30 or Atlas G Britain p 12

The idyllic setting in deep Kent countryside of this enchanting fortified manor house and its association with the romantic, then tragic story of Anne Boleyn and King Henry VIII, make it an irresistible attraction. Its allure was felt too by William Waldorf Astor, the anglophile American multi-millionaire who acquired it in 1903. His lavish restoration of the neglected castle and ambitious landscaping of its grounds added a further layer to an already rich history.
Externally, the castle is much as it appeared in the late Middle Ages; it sits securely, protected by its moat and the drawbridge and portcullis of its massive rectangular gatehouse.

Hever Castle

⊘ **Interior.** — The decor of the rooms around the intimate courtyard is more opulent than in the Boleyns' time; in particular, much of the **woodwork** is a triumphant recreation of the finest Renaissance craftsmanship. There are portraits of Anne, and one, by Holbein, of Henry; in her little room is the Book of Hours the young queen took to her execution on 19 May 1536. Tableaux representing scenes from the life and times of Anne Boleyn have been set up in the 100ft - 30m long gallery.

Gardens. — Astor's enthusiasm for garden styles of many periods resulted in an assemblage of diverse landscapes, whose main focus is the 38 acre - 15ha artificial lake, approached via an elaborate loggia and an Italian garden; the frame for his important **collection of antique statuary and sculpture** from Italy. There is topiary, a maze, and leading through fine parkland trees, Anne Boleyn's Walk.

HEXHAM Northumberland   Pop 8 914

Michelin Map 402 N 19 or Atlas G Britain p 51 — Local map p 133

The importance of this attractive market town on the River Tyne goes back to Saxon times; in 664AD the supremacy of the Roman ritual had been established at the Synod of Whitby, under the leadership of the Northumbrian Wilfrid. A decade later he was granted land by Queen Etheldreda on which he founded a great monastery dedicated to St Andrew. Of this apparently splendid edifice only the crypt survives, most of today's abbey dating from 1180-1250.

★ **Hexham Abbey.** — Above the evocative **Saxon Crypt**★★, built with stones taken
⊘ from the Roman settlement of Corstopitum (Corbridge), is a fine Early English
choir with imposing transepts. From the south transept a stone staircase, the Night
Stair, leads to what was the canons' dormitory. The **Leschman Chantry**★, dating from
1491, has amusing stone carvings on the base, and delicate woodwork above.

EXCURSIONS

ᴧ ᴧ **Hadrian's Wall.** — *Description p 131.*

★★ INVERARAY Castle Strathclyde

Michelin Map **401** E 15 or Atlas G Britain p 54

The whitewashed township on the shores of Loch Fyne lies only a short distance
from the present-day castle. The original 15C seat of Clan Campbell with its attendant settlement was replaced in the 18C and a new planned village was rebuilt at
a distance. The rebuilder, the 3rd Duke of Argyll, commissioned Roger Morris as
architect and William Adam as clerk of works. The castle's exterior remains a good
example of Gothic revival in spite of 19C alterations.

⊘ **Interior.** — The 5th Duke refurbished the interiors in the neo-classical style after
the fashion of Carlton House in London. In particular, the dining room is a masterpiece of delicately detailed plasterwork and painting. The Tapestry Drawing Room
reveals an Adam-designed compartmentalised ceiling, decorative panels and over
doors by Girard. The armoury hall with its decorative display of pole-arms, Lochaber
axes and broadswords is where the duke's personal piper plays a medley of Campbell tunes to awaken the household. In the Saloon Pompeo Batoni's *8th Duke of
Hamilton* faces Gainsborough's *Conway*. Among the portraits in the northwest hall
and staircase note the rebuilding *3rd Duke* (Allan Ramsay), the redecorating *5th
Duke* (Gainsborough) and his Duchess *Elizabeth Gunning.*

EXCURSIONS

West shore of Loch Fyne to Crinan. — *33 miles - 53km by the A83.*
The great sea loch of **Loch Fyne**★★ stretches from the heart of the Argyll mountains
down the arm of Loch Gilp where it turns due south to reach the open sea. In the
19C this was the scene of a successful herring fishery.

★ **Auchindrain.** — The open-air folk museum evokes life in the communal-tenancy farms.
⊘ Once the commonest kind of Scottish farming, they survived longest in the Highlands. Farming methods, domestic interiors, barns and byres are among the many
aspects of life presented here.

> *Continue along the A83 to Lochgilphead then follow the A816 to Cairnbaan.
> The B841 leads westwards to Crinan.*

The rocky eminence, **Dunadd Fort** *(access is from the A816)*, rising abruptly out of
the flat lands to the right, was a Dark Age fortification and capital of the Scots Kingdom of Dalriada from 498 to 843 AD.

★ **Crinan.** — A delightful hamlet at the western end of the Crinan Canal, linking the
Sound of Jura with Loch Fyne.

★ INVERNESS Highland   Pop 38 204

Michelin Map **401** H 11 or Atlas G Britain p 67
Town plan in the current Michelin Red Guide Great Britain and Ireland

Inverness, standing at the northern end of the Great Glen *(qv)*, astride the River
Ness flowing from Loch Ness, is the traditional capital of the Scottish Highlands.
It was strategically important from the days of the Picts; St Columba visited King
Brude in the vicinity, and King Duncan (murdered by Macbeth in the 11C) had his
castle here. Its strategic value was its downfall, and fought over by Scottish
monarchs, Highland clans, Jacobites and English, it now has few significant buildings from before the 19C.

Inverness Castle. — 19C, the most recent of a series of castles, it now serves
as a courthouse and administrative building; with a good **view** of the town and the
River Ness from the statue of Flora MacDonald on the esplanade.

★ **Museum and Art Gallery.** — *Castle Wynd.* On the first floor an imaginative and
⊘ well-presented exhibition "Inverness, Hub of the Highlands" interprets the region's
rich heritage. Exhibits on the Great Glen, the Picts, General Wade's roads and Telford's Caledonian Canal are of special interest. The Highlanders' way of life is presented on the upper floor.

⊘ **St Andrew's Cathedral.** — *Ardross Street.* A richly decorated neo-Gothic church
of 1866-9; its nave piers are of polished Peterhead granite, the reredos and pulpit
of carved stone. Both choir screen and rood cross are by Robert Lorimer.

Kessock Bridge. — Opened in 1982, suspended across the Beauly Firth and
carrying the A9 north to the Black Isle, it is 345ft - 1 052m long and 95ft - 29m
above high water.

EXCURSIONS

★ **Cawdor Castle.** — *13 miles - 21km northeast of Inverness by the A96 then the B9090 to the right.*
Built in the late 14C by the Thanes of Cawdor (this was the title Shakespeare's witches promised Macbeth), the central tower was the 14C keep. The castle was added to in the 17C. During a visit to this historic home note the lovely tapestries and amidst the many portraits one of the 18th thane, resplendently attired in an assortment of tartans refuting the idea of one clan one sett.

Return to the A96 and continue straight over to Fort George on the coast.

★ **Fort George.** — Set on a peninsula jutting out into the Moray Firth, this impressive artillery fortress was built (1745-46), on the orders of George II, to prevent once and for all Hanoverian law and order from being disrupted by the Highland clans. The fort, its elaborate defences as well as several exhibitions bring to life the lot of the troops in the 17 and 18C.

Culloden. — *6 miles - 10km east of Inverness by the A9 then the B9006 to the east. National Trust for Scotland Visitor Centre.*
Here on 16 April 1746 the Jacobite army under Bonnie Prince Charlie was slaughtered by Government troops under "Butcher Cumberland", George II's younger son, finally ending the hopes of a Stuart restoration to the British throne. On the Battlefield site are the Memorial Cairn and the Clan Graves. Footpaths demarcate the front lines. The visitor centre has an audio-visual programme and exhibition area explaining the battle. The restored Old Leanach Cottage can also be viewed.

Continue on the B9006 as far as the Cumberland stone then turn right.

★ **Clava Cairns.** — Of the three Neolithic cairns, girdled by stone circles and a small ring of boulders in a unified design, the middle one was always open to the sky while the other two had roofed entrance passages leading to burial chambers.

★ **Isle of IONA** Strathclyde   Pop 268

Michelin Map **401** A 14 and 15 or Atlas G Britain p 59 — Access: see the current Michelin Red Guide Great Britain and Ireland. No cars permitted.

The remote and windswept Isle of Iona, where **St Columba** established his monastic settlement 1 400 years ago, is one of the most venerated places in Scotland. His community grew (the intricately carved crosses and grave slabs a testament to its artistic accomplishments) until brought to an end by the Norse raids of the 8 and 9C. A monastery was re-established in the early 13C, this time Benedictine, disappearing at the Reformation. In 1938 a third religious brotherhood - now an ecumenical community - came to the isle and a major restoration programme was completed in 1966.

Visit. — Take the road from the old Benedictine **Nunnery** (restored late 19C). Go through the gate past the intricately carved 15C **Maclean's Cross★** and the early Christian burial ground, **Reilig Odhrain** (where Scotland's kings from Kenneth MacAlpine to Malcom III were buried) to the 12C **St Oran's Chapel**, oldest building on the island, with a fine Norman west door. Walk down the **Street of the Dead**, where three **High Crosses** catch the eye (an 8C Cross of St Martin, a 9-10C truncated shaft of St Matthew and a replica of an 8C St John's Cross). On the other side of the Street of the Dead is St Columba's cell, Tor Abb.
The **abbey** stands on the site of its Columban predecessor; the original 13C church was enlarged in the 15C with a tower at the crossing and a south aisle to the choir. Fragments of the 13C Benedictine church include the north transept and arcade of the choir's north wall. The elaborate trefoil-headed doorway below was inserted when the north aisle was converted into a sacristy (15C).
Beyond the abbey is the **Infirmary Museum★**, with an outstanding collection of early Christian and medieval stonework.

IPSWICH Suffolk   Pop 129 660

Michelin Map **404** X 27 or Atlas G Britain p 23
Town plan in the current Michelin Red Guide Great Britain and Ireland

A rich port and trading centre in the Middle Ages, reviving in the 19C, this bustling country town at the head of the Orwell estuary is now mostly Victorian and modern in character, though the street layout and several flint and stone churches recall its early origins.

Christchurch Mansion. — *Christchurch Park.* In its pleasant parkland setting, this much-restored Tudor building is notable for the King Arthur tapestry and charmingly naive early 17C allegorical painted Hawstead panels (eg *The World Turned Upside Down*). Of greater importance is the fine **collection*** of paintings by **Gainsborough** *(Portrait of William Wellerston, Crossing the Ford, The Cottage Door* and *View Near the Coast)* and by **Constable** *(Mill Stream, Willy Lott's House,* and two Stour Valley *(qv)* landscapes of his father's kitchen and flower gardens). There are also works by members of the **Camden Town** group and *Knucklebones* by Wilson Steer, painted at Walberswick on the Norfolk coast.

Near the entrance to Christchurch Park is the fine St Margaret's Church, elaborate stone and flint outside, with a good hammerbeam roof inside.

⊙ **Ancient House.** — *Buttermarket.* A wedding cake of a house overflowing with Restoration plasterwork, pargeting and stucco reliefs of nymphs, pelicans and the then-known continents: Asia (an Oriental dome), America (a tobacco pipe), Africa (an African with a sunshade astride a crocodile) and Europe (a Gothic Church). The interior is even more ancient, with a 15C hammerbeam roof, *c*1603 oak panelling, a 17C fireplace and plastered ceiling.

EXCURSIONS

★ **Stour Valley.** — *Description p 93.*

Snape Maltings. — *20 miles - 32km northeast by the A12 and the A1094 to the right.*
The early 19C malthouses standing serenely on the River Alde are now a musical arts complex, home of the late Benjamin Britten's **Aldeburgh Festival**.

★★ IRONBRIDGE GORGE Museum Shropshire

Michelin Map 403 M 26 or Atlas G Britain p 26 — 12 miles - 19km east of Shrewsbury

This important industrial museum consists of a number of sites along the densely-wooded, mineral-rich Severn Gorge, "birthplace of the Industrial Revolution". In the autumn of 1708 **Abraham Darby** (1678-1717), Bristol ironmaster, came to Coalbrookdale; he was the first to use coke in 1709 as a fuel for smelting iron, replacing traditional charcoal. His experiments revolutionised the industry, making possible the use of iron in transport (wheels, rails), in engineering (steam engines, locomotives and ships), and in construction (buildings and bridges, including the area's emblem, the famous Iron Bridge).

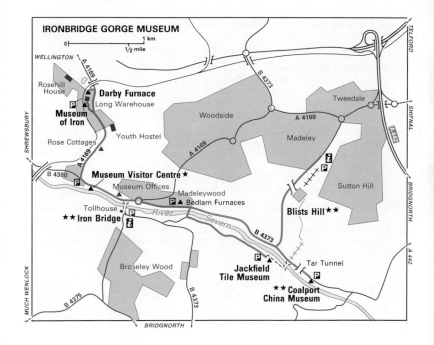

⊙ **Sightseeing.** — This museum site can be approached from either the northwest or the northeast. The map above gives the location of the various sights described and indicates the main parking areas. As the various attractions are quite far apart organise your visit around sites with car parks.

Museum of Iron. — The museum illustrates the history of ironmaking and the story of the Coalbrookdale Company. It is housed in the great warehouse, built in 1838, which has cast iron windows, sills and lintels. By the time of the Great Exhibition in 1851, the Coalbrookdale Company employed 4 000 men and boys and produced 2 000 tons of cast iron a week, for railway stations, bridges, fireplaces and a multitude of other uses.

Beyond the car park is a full-scale working model of the railway locomotive built by the Coalbrookdale Company for Richard Trevithick in 1802, a quarter of a century before Stephenson's *Rocket*.

Darby Furnace. — This is where in 1709 Abraham Darby pioneered his techniques using coke rather than charcoal as fuel, and smelting continued until *c*1818. Beyond, the Upper Furnace Pool, along with five other pools, provided power for five ironworks.

Further to the north the fine houses of the ironmasters stand close by the cottages of their workers (Carpenters Row). On the opposite or west side of the valley are two of the Darby family homes. Rosehill House built in 1734 to supersede neighbouring Dale House (restoration in progress) is furnished as it might have been in Victorian times with items from other family homes. An exhibition presents the various members of the Darby family. Further uphill is the Quaker burial ground.

★ **Museum of the River and Visitor Centre.** — An 1840s wharf and warehouse have been restored and now house an exhibition and audio-visual introduction to Ironbridge Gorge.

★★ **The Iron Bridge.** — A bridge across the Severn Gorge at Coalbrookdale was needed to replace the hazardous ferry crossing, the only other bridges being at Buildwas and Bridgnorth. A design by Shrewsbury architect, Thomas Pritchard, was chosen and the Act of Parliament obtained in February 1776. Work began under **Abraham Darby III** in November 1777 and the Iron Bridge was opened on New Year's Day 1781. The bridge's single graceful span was a triumph of the

Iron Bridge (c1845)

application of new technology to the solution of a difficult problem. The ironwork weighs over 378 tonnes - the builders, unfamiliar with the new technology, undoubtedly erred on the side of caution. In the old **Tollhouse** is an information centre with a display illustrating the history of the bridge.

On the north bank are the **Bedlam Furnaces** (1757), among the first custom-built for coke smelting.

Take the bridge over the Severn (10 ton limit).

Jackfield Tile Museum. — *On the south bank of the river.*
Only partly restored, the former tilery contains a small museum of the colourful wall and floor tiles once manufactured here in immense quantities in the 19C. The visitor is able to view tile manufacturing and decoration.

Return to the north bank then turn right (B4373).

★★ **Coalport China Museum.** — Coalport china was made here from 1792 until the works moved to Stoke-on-Trent in 1926. The old works have been restored as a museum of china, showing techniques of manufacture and particularly the products of Coalport.

Near here is the **Tar Tunnel**, cut in 1786 to aid drainage from the Blists Hill Mine. It was found to ooze bitumen through the mortar of the brick lining.

★★ **Blists Hill Open Air Museum.** — On this 50 acre - 20ha site the visitor steps back into a working community of the 1890s, with bank, pub, butcher's shop, mine and candle factory, as well as the inclined plane which carried boats from Blists Hill to the Severn and Coalport. Many of the buildings have been brought from elsewhere and rebuilt on site.

★ **JEDBURGH** Borders   Pop 4 053

Michelin Map **401** M 17 or Atlas G Britain p 50

The royal burgh of Jedburgh, spanning the Jed Water with a mid-12C triple-arched bridge was once a much fought-over border town. Today it is a peaceful market town on one of the main routes into Scotland.

★★ **Jedburgh Abbey.** — Founded by David I in 1138 for the Augustinian order, it was ⊘ one of the many Border abbeys founded by this king to spread monasticism in 12C Scotland. The mellow stone church took 75 years to build but was often plundered and attacked before the final destructive raid in 1545. The ruined abbey church is a majestic example of 12C architecture and has a powerful west front, while the rhythm and design of the nave display the assurance of an art well-mastered. Although only the foundations of the cloister buildings survive, their layout can be clearly distinguished following the usual pattern.

★ **Mary Queen of Scots House** (Visitor Centre). — This is the attractive 16C tower ⊘ house where Mary Queen of Scots stayed when she made her 20 mile - 32km ride to Hermitage Castle. Engraved glass panels, paintings and documents relate the life of this hapless queen.

⊘ **Jedburgh Castle and Jail.** — The Howard Penal Reform prison, built in 1823 on the site of the original castle, was considered one of the most modern jails of its day. It centred around the governor's block which overlooked the three centrally-heated cell blocks and was linked to them by first-floor gangways. There are exhibits interpreting Jedburgh's local and industrial history.

EXCURSIONS

★★Bowhill. — *19 miles - 31km via the A68 to St Boswells then the A699 and A7*
⊘ *to Selkirk. The A708 leads to Bowhill.*
The Border home of the Duke of Buccleuch and Queensberry, Bowhill has an important collection of paintings including Reynolds' *Winter* and *The Pink Boy*, a Canaletto of *Montagu House* in London, Wilkie's *King George IV in Highland Dress* as well as an impressive collection of miniatures (Cooper, the Hilliards and the Olivers).
There are many personal belongings of the Duke and Duchess of Monmouth.

★Hermitage Castle. — *26 miles - 42km on the B6358 and A693 to Hawick, then*
⊘ *south on the B6399.*
In its isolated moorland setting this massive ruin evokes the Borders' troubled past. A stronghold of the Wardens of the March, it was here that Mary Queen of Scots came on her dash to the injured Earl of Bothwell. Although deceptively uniform from the outside, Hermitage is in fact the result of a complex sequence of building phases, the earliest dating from the mid-14C, absorbed by later additions.

KING'S LYNN Norfolk   Pop 37 323

Michelin Map ▨ V 25 or Atlas G Britain p 30

As old as the Conquest, the original town grew up around Saturday Market, its 12C extension northwards around Tuesday Market. Surrounded by walls (best remnants at Southgate), Bishop's Lynn (as it was then called) was one of the busiest ports of the Middle Ages. Its fine townscape is based on its ancient street pattern and its exceptionally rich inheritance of buildings from the medieval period onward.

From Saturday Market to Tuesday Market. — In **Saturday Market** is the chequered flint Guildhall of 1421 and the 13C **Church of St Margaret's** with its splendid west front and two of the best **brasses** in the country (Adam de Walsoken d 1349 and Robert Braunche d 1364). Queen Street, mainly Georgian in character, leads north past the gables of Thorseby College of 1500 towards the splendid 17C Custom House, Dutch in flavour and most dignified. Down King's Staithe Lane to the quayside on the River Ouse are warehouses of the 16 and 17C and in King's Staithe Square stands Bank House, one of Lynn's grandest buildings, with a statue of Charles I in a niche. Further north, **King Street** is a delightful succession of houses of varied dates and materials; just before the spacious Tuesday Market is St George's Guildhall, where by tradition Shakespeare acted, now the home of the July King's Lynn Festival.

EXCURSIONS

★★Houghton Hall. — *13 miles - 21km east on the A1076 and the A148, then a minor*
⊘ *road to the left.*
Transitional between baroque and Palladian, inspired by Colen Campbell, Houghton Hall was built (1722-35) for Sir Robert Walpole, Britain's first Prime Minister; its main rooms by **William Kent** are dedicated to "taste, expense, state and parade". Its joys are its ceilings and Kent furniture, the Sèvres porcelain in the Marble Parlour, the thrones by Pugin and 17C Mortlake tapestries of the Royal Stuarts in the Tapestry Dressing Room and Oudry's *White Duck* in the White Drawing Room.

★★Oxburgh Hall. — *18 miles - 29km southeast on the A10, the A134 then on a minor*
⊘ *road following the signs.*
Constructed in 1482, this was one of the first fortified manor houses to be built as status symbols. Its **gatehouse** ("one of the noblest specimens of domestic architecture in the 15C": Pugin) and flanking ranges are 15C, the hall range 19C. Inside are elaborate **embroideries** depicting mammals, fish and plants by Mary Queen of Scots and Bess of Hardwick *(qv)* in the Marian Needlework Room; letters from Henry VIII, Queen Mary and Queen Elizabeth I, and woodcarvings by Grinling Gibbons in the King's Room (note the priesthole under the floor in the adjoining octagonal chamber); and the Sheldon tapestry map of the Heart of England (1647) in the Queen's Room; the floors are linked by staircases, their walls clad in 17C Cordova leather.

★★Holkham Hall. — *31 miles - 50km north, then east on the A149.*
⊘ Seat of the Earls of Leicester and Coke of Norfolk (1754-1842), the inventor of modern agriculture, Holkham Hall is palatial Palladian designed by William Kent. Most monumental of the interiors is the Marble Hall *(photograph overleaf)*, faced with polished pink alabaster, carrying a gallery of pink Ionic columns, and dramatically setting off the surrounding neo-classical sculpture (more of which can be seen in the Statue Gallery). Almost as grand are the Drawing Room (with works by Claude, Poussin) and the Saloon (works by Rubens, Van Dyck). In the South Sitting Room hang Titian's *Unknown Lady,* Guido Reni's *Joseph taking leave of Potiphar's Wife*, a Gainsborough and Battoni's *Coke of Norfolk*; the Landscape Room is devoted to Poussin and Claude.

★Sandringham House. — *8 miles - 13km northeast on the A1076 then the A149.*
⊘ "Dear old Sandringham, the place I love better than anywhere else in the world", wrote George V of the Royal Family's neo-Jacobean country home since 1862. In the largest room in the house, the Saloon, are family portraits by Von Angeli and Winterhalter, and 17C tapestries of *Emperor Constantine* by Brier of Brussels. The corridor is hung with intricately-wrought Oriental arms and armour. In the main Drawing Room - "a very long and handsome drawing room with painted ceiling and panels and two fireplaces" (Queen Victoria) - is Russian silver and Chinese jade. And in the Ballroom, bedecked with armour, is a photo exhibition on the owners.

Castle Rising. — *4 miles - 6km northeast by the A149.*
Surrounded by 12 acres - 5ha of earthworks, with walls 8ft - 2m thick, Castle Rising (1138) was built by William d'Albini, Earl of Sussex, for his wife, widowed queen of Henry I. In 1331 it became home to another dowager queen, the disgraced Isabella, lover of Roger Mortimer and murderer of her husband Edward II.
The Norman gatehouse leads to the intricately - and almost uniquely - decorated keep forebuilding with stairs leading to the portal (converted into a fireplace in the 16C). Apart from the figured corbels for the hall roofbeams only the gallery and chapel (with Early English doorway and Norman arcading) have survived.

Castle Acre. — *18 miles - 29km to the east on the A47, then the A1065.*
Here are those two great supports of the medieval nobility: a castle for security in this world, a priory to help ensure it in the next. The **castle** built by William de Warenne, one of William the Conqueror's most trusted supporters, on 15 acres - 6ha of earthworks, is unusual in originally being a fortified stone manor house. The keep was not built until the *c*1140 civil wars. Of the **priory** founded for Cluniac monks only the west wall, prior's lodgings and late 12C porch still stand, though remnants still mark the ''bare ruin'd choirs'', chapter house, dormitories, kitchens and latrines south of the church.

★ **Four Fenland Churches.** — The Fens' *(qv)* glories are its churches and sunsets both well set against the flat and featureless landscape.

Leave King's Lynn to the west by the A17 and after 5 miles - 8km turn right.

Terrington St Clement. — St Clement's Church, big and Perpendicular, boasts a splendid west window and northwest tower. The interior has exquisite Georgian panelling at the west end and a 17C **font cover** with paintings of New Testament scenes inside.

2 miles - 3km southwest across the A17, passing through Walpole St Andrew.

Walpole St Peter. — St Peter's Church built in the 14C transition between Decorated (west window and tower) and Perpendicular (nave windows and chancel stalls) is known as the Cathedral of the Fens. Among its charms are its raised altar (to provide space for a groined right of way underneath), 17C woodwork and embossed south porch. Huge plain glass windows illuminate a magnificent interior.

3 miles - 5km along the Wisbech Road.

West Walton. — St Mary's Church is mid-13C Early English at its most profuse and extravagant: beautifully ornate arcading and doorways, and wall paintings in the clerestory.

1 1/2 miles - 2km continuing towards Wisbech.

Walsoken. — All Saints' Church, ''the grandest Norman parish church in Norfolk'' (Pevsner), built in 1146, with zig-zag mouldings on arcade arch and chancel arch, a hammerbeam and cambered tie-beam roof, an eight-sided **font** portraying the Seven Sacraments and Crucifixion, and a 16C wall painting of the Judgement of Solomon.

Marble Hall, Holkham Hall

Michelin Map 402 K, L 20 or Atlas G Britain p 44

880 square miles - 2 280 square km of lakes and mountains, England's largest and most visited National Park. ''I do not know of any tract of country in which, in so narrow a compass, may be found an equal variety in the influences of light and shadow upon the sublime and beautiful'' (Wordsworth).

The mountains rise abruptly from glaciated valleys, most of them occupied by one of the beautiful stretches of water which give the area its name and which radiate out from a high central core of volcanic rocks. Here are cliffs, crags and precipices, and many famous peaks, among them the stony wastes of **Scafell Pike** (3 206ft - 977m), highest point in England. Elsewhere, it is slate which has formed much of the landscape: to the north, in the gently rounded but majestic heights of the Skiddaw group; to the south, in the more broken country reaching its highest point in the commanding presence of **The Old Man**, looming over Coniston Water. The drama of the fells is set off by the gentler, pastoral character of much of the lowland, particularly in the park-like surroundings of Lake Windermere. The remote valleys of the west are lush too; though near the head of Wasdale is the sternest of the lakes, Wast Water, where awesome screes plunge hundreds of feet to the shore.

Rainfall is high among these western mountains; the many tarns and the tumbling becks are wellfed. While peaks are often capped in cloud and slopes shrouded in mist, the air is soft, and the changing light plays continuously with the rich and subtle colour-mix of rock and vegetation: coarse grasses, heathers and bracken clothing the mountainsides, bright-berried rowans and white-stemmed birches sheltering in mossy clefts, dark pines standing elegantly by the lakeside and bright green pastures interspersed with the luxuriant foliage of oak and sycamore.

The rocks occur again in the man-made structures of the countryside; in ancient bridges, in the drystone walls which climb high into the fells; in the rough-hewn stone of sturdy barns, cottages and whitewashed farmhouses with massive roofs of slate. Busy as they are with the traffic and tourists, even the little towns are mostly of stone and slate and thus form part of the mountain scene too.

Lakeland can be appreciated in many ways: idling by the shore, aboard a launch, or exploring the narrow - and often congested - lanes by car. But above all it is the realm of the walker for whom ''there is no such thing as bad weather, only unsuitable clothing''. Climbers and hill walkers may be tempted by the many possibilities in Lakeland. Never venture onto the mountains without being properly shod, clothed and equipped. Do not set out if daylight is failing or weather conditions worsening. Take the necessary maps and make sure you are tackling the route most suited to your experience.

1 LAKELAND POETS TOUR

30 miles - 48km - local map p 144

This itinerary takes in the busier central area of the Lake District and evokes the poets (Wordsworth, Coleridge and Southey) who were variously inspired by the Lakeland landscapes. The busy centres of Ambleside and Windermere on the lake shore, both make good touring centres from which to discover the Lake District.

Windermere. — Pop 6 835. A railhead town built mostly of slate, created in the 19C Lakeland tourist boom and lapped by the waters of Lake Windermere.

★★ **Lake Windermere.** — The longest lake in England, Windermere is over 10 miles - 16km long and attractively framed by wooded slopes and rising fells. The liveliest lake, it is popular for both sailing and water skiing and **boat trips** allow visitors to admire at close quarters the unspoilt west bank and its many islets including Belle Isle.

Bowness-on-Windermere. — Pop 1 264. The pretty village is known for its promenade skirting the bay. This is the starting point for trips on the lake with stops at Waterhead in the north and Lake Side in the south. A **ferry** (car and pedestrian) plies the waters of the lake to the far side, or the motorist may choose to drive round the southern end of Windermere via Newby Bridge.

Hill Top. — In Near Sawrey on the west side of Windermere. Home of Peter Rabbit, Benjamin Bunny, Jemima Puddle-Duck and retreat of Beatrix Potter (who, incidentally, saw herself primarily as a sheep farmer and was embarrassed at the acclaim conferred on her for her children's books), unchanged since her death in 1943, and attracting thousands of searchers of lost childhoods each year. Inside the 17C house are her watercolours, dolls' house and mementoes.

★ **Hawkshead.** — Pop 660. The narrow slate-walled lanes and paths of this traditional Lakeland village are bordered by flower-decked cottages. Wordsworth attended the local grammar school from 1779 to 1787.

Coming over the rise you see the lake and the surrounding area dominated by the form of **The Old Man** rising to a height of 2 631ft - 801m.

★ **Coniston Water.** — Lying parallel to and to the west of Windermere, Coniston Water is a smaller version of its august neighbour. It was on this stretch of water that Donald Campbell died in 1967 trying to beat the world water speed record.

★ **Brantwood.** — On the east side of Coniston Water, this was the home of John Ruskin *(see over)*, one of the greatest figures of the Victorian age. On the walls are exquisite watercolours by himself and by Pre-Raphaelite contemporaries whom he championed. His study turret provides a splendid **view**★ of Coniston in its attractive lakeside setting with the form of The Old Man to the left, perfectly mirrored in the tranquil waters of the lake.

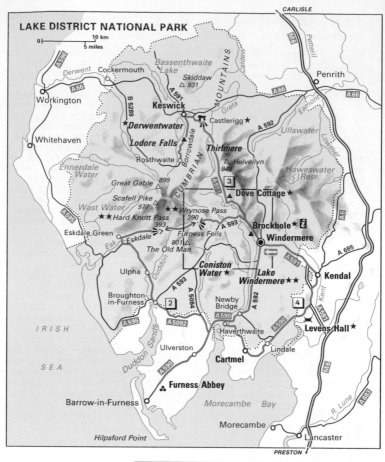

LAKE DISTRICT NATIONAL PARK

Other National Parks described in the Guide:

Brecon Beacons
Dartmoor
Exmoor
Norfolk and Suffolk
Broads
Northumberland
North York Moors
Peak District
Pembrokeshire Coast
Snowdonia
Yorkshire Dales

Coniston. — Pop 1 713. The little slate-grey town is known for its associations with the author, artist and social reformer **John Ruskin** (1819-1900) who came to live at nearby Brantwood in 1872. He is buried in the local churchyard. Nearby a small **Ruskin Museum** with drawings, manuscripts and other mementoes illustrates his many talents.

Leave Coniston by the A593 and continue to Skelwith Bridge before turning left towards Grasmere in its attractive lakeside setting.

Grasmere. — The village would be beautiful even if **Wordsworth** had never existed. It was here that the family lived in two different dwellings between 1799 and 1850 Dove Cottage and Rydal Mount. The churchyard of 13C St Oswald's is where Wordsworth, various members of the family and Coleridge's son David Hartley are buried.

    ''Not raised in nice proportion was the pile.
    But large and massy; for duration built.
    With pillars crowded, and the roof upheld.
    By naked rafters intricately crossed''. (Wordsworth).

★ **Dove Cottage.** — In Town End just off the A591. An early 17C converted inn (The Dove and Olive Bough) and home of William and his sister Dorothy from 1799 to 1808, Dove Cottage became a magnet for the early 19C literary romantics: Coleridge, Southey and De Quincey. In the kitchen where Dorothy cooked the inhabitants' two meals per day (both porridge) are three chairs embroidered by the poet's daughter, Dora Wordsworth, Sara Coleridge and Edith Southey, while the room off it was first Dorothy's, then William's. Upstairs is the sitting room, looking out over the waters of Grasmere (in Wordsworth's time the cottage stood on its own), the main bedroom (first William's, then Dorothy's), the Newspaper Room, wallpapered in newspaper to keep it warm, and the pantry-cum-spare room. The cottage was for a short period home to De Quincey. Behind is a **museum** containing manuscripts, memorabilia and Lakeland paintings.

⊘ **Rydal Mount.** — In the hamlet of Rydal overlooking Rydal Water. A c1574 cottage extended in the 18C into a farmhouse, Rydal Mount was the home of William Wordsworth (1770-1850) from 1813, through his decline from revolutionary poet to reactionary Poet Laureate, to his death in 1850. Here he wrote his most financially successful book, *Guide to the Lakes*. Inside, his library now forms part of the drawing room, and the study ceiling is still painted with the Renaissance design he copied from a visit to Italy.

Ambleside. — Pop 2 689. North of Windermere this village makes a good touring resort.

★ **Brockhole National Park Centre.** — *Description below.*

② ESKDALE VIA WRYNOSE PASS
50 miles - 80km - local map opposite

Starting at Windermere, this itinerary leads to the less-frequented, wilder and at times desolate expanses of Ulpha Fell and Furness Fell. The road up to these highlands dominated by the Cumbrian Mountains negotiates two difficult passes. Extreme caution is required on this road which is narrow with severe bends and very steep gradients, sometimes over 1:3 - 30%. All along the route there are possibilities for walks but be properly shod and clad with warm and waterproof clothing as conditions change rapidly on the hills.

Leave Windermere to the north by the A591.

★ **Brockhole National Park Centre.** — A comprehensive and imaginatively-run in-
⊘ formation centre with displays on the ecology and history of Lakeland, a Beatrix Potter exhibition and lakeside walk.

Before Ambleside turn left to take the A593; after Skelwith Bridge, turn right.

Initially the road is dyke-enclosed, then starts the climb up this v-shaped valley with its bare slopes, hill sheep country. Having negotiated **Wrynose Pass★★** (1 280ft - 390m) stop to admire the **view** back down to Little Langdale. The road runs parallel to the River Duddon all along Wrynose Bottom between the two passes. Stop to appreciate the wild splendour of the scenery and the gently rounded forms of the summits which rarely exceed 3 280ft - 1 000m, but are scarred by steep scree slopes. These are the grazing grounds for hill sheep.

Continue westwards; the road climbs steeply again to cross the second pass.

Hard Knott Pass★★ is at an altitude of 1 289ft - 393m. Again take the time to enjoy the view westwards of the more pastoral valley of **Eskdale**. Even the Romans had an outpost in this remote spot, as part of their northern frontier to contain the northern native tribes.

Here the motorist has the choice of returning by the same route or of making a long detour by Ulpha, Broughton-in-Furness, and Newby Bridge at the southern end of Windermere.

③ KESWICK AND NORTHERN LAKELAND
29 miles - 47km - local map opposite

★ **Brockhole National Park Centre.** — *Description above.*

Ambleside. — *Description above.*

Rydal Mount. — *Description above.*

★ **Dove Cottage.** — *Description opposite.*

The road following the Rothay rises to Dunmail Raise before descending to Thirlmere which is overshadowed by "the dark brow of mighty" **Helvellyn** (3 114ft - 949m) to the east. Wordsworth used to walk this route to visit Coleridge and Southey installed with their families at Greta Hall in Keswick.

Thirlmere. — Graced by mountains and forests it looks almost too good to be true. It isn't. The forest is a plantation, the lake a reservoir, raised 50ft - 15m by a dam. Again the road negotiates two rises before descending to Keswick. On the outskirts lookout for the signpost leading right to a stone circle. **Castlerigg Stone Circle★** set on a grassy eminence and older than Stonehenge guards the secret of its purpose. The site affords far-flung **views** away towards Thirlmere and Helvellyn and westwards to Derwentwater and Keswick below.

Keswick. — Pop 4 777. This lakeland town, medieval in origin, was home to the extended families of Coleridge and Southey when they shared Greta Hall (private). With the mining of graphite at Borrowdale as early as the mid-16C Keswick claims
⊘ the world's first pencil factory (1832) and today has a small but interesting **Pencil Museum** recounting the process of high-quality pencil making. The local museum has both Wordsworth and Southey manuscripts, a 500-year-old cat and the famous musical stones.

★ **Derwentwater.** — Three miles - 5km long, one mile - 1/2km wide and flanked by clerestories of crags. Southey called it the most beautiful of English lakes (photograph p 22).

Lodore Falls. — The most literary cascade of the lakes, according to Southey ''it comes thundering and floundering, and thumping and plumping and bumping and jumping and whizzing and hissing and dripping and skipping and grumbling and rumbling and tumbling and falling and brawling and sprawling'' (but only after heavy rain).

Beyond the attractive valley of **Borrowdale**, where graphite was first mined in the mid-16C, leads to the tiny hamlet of Rosthwaite set in a mountain-rimmed clearing in characteristic Lakeland scenery. Away to the south are two of the region's most prominent summits, **Great Gable** (2 949ft - 899 m) and **Scafell Pike** (3 205ft - 977m).

④ KENDAL AND THE SOUTH

40 miles - 64km - local map p 144

Leave Windermere by the A591.

Kendal. — Pop 23 710. The ''Auld Grey Town'', built out of the local limestone, is the thriving centre for a wide area. It was the birthplace of Henry VIII's sixth wife, Catherine Parr, but long before her day was already famous for its wool trade. It has the excellent **Museum of Lakeland Life** and there is a fine view of the town in its setting of foothills from the castle ruins.

Continue south on the A591 then the A590.

★ **Levens Hall and Garden.** — An Elizabethan manor has been added to a 13C pele tower to give us the graceful residence we see today. The Great Hall with its panelling of local oak and ornate ceiling, is an introduction to equally outstanding carving and **plasterwork**, Elizabethan and later, throughout the rest of the rooms. The dining room, covered in Cordova leather in 1692, has a magnificent set of Charles II walnut dining chairs. The **Topiary Gardens** are unique in that the 1690 design has been preserved intact. They are the only surviving examples of the work of Monsieur Beaumont, who also worked for James II at Hampton Court.

Go west on the A590 and after Lindale follow signs on minor roads to Cartmel.

Cartmel. — Pop 306. With its 17C and 18C houses and Priory Gatehouse, the village's market square has an urbane air. **Cartmel Priory★** is Lakeland's grandest medieval building, having survived the Dissolution to become the parish church. It is mostly 12C; its curious tower is in fact two, one set diagonally upon the other. Inside there is a fine Perpendicular east window, and above the choir's droll misericords is a beautifully carved screen of 1620.

Take the local road to Haverthwaite then turn left onto the A590.

Furness Abbey. — Stephen, Count of Boulogne, later King of England, gave a site near Preston to the Order of Savigny, for a convent, in 1123. The group moved to a more secluded site in Furness in 1127 and became part of the Cistercian Order. The red sandstone ruins of the abbey sit in a secluded vale. The transepts and choir walls stand almost to their original height, as does the western tower. In the south wall of the Presbytery are four seats (sedilia) and basin (piscina), with relatively little damage to their canopied heads. The mid-13C vestibule and chapter house have the graceful simplicity associated with Cistercian building of the period.

LANCASTER Lancashire   Pop 43 902

Michelin Map **402** L 21 or Atlas G Britain p 38

Lancaster Castle and the Priory Church of St Mary share the same hill on which the Romans had established their fort guarding the crossing of the River Lune. The town prospered in the 18C from trade with the West Indies and contains many fine buildings from this period, including the Georgian **Customs House** (see below).

★ **Castle.** — The massive **John of Gaunt Gatehouse** dominates the approach up the hill; it was built c1407-13, by Henry IV, John of Gaunt's son. Much of the rest of medieval castle, like the **Great Keep** and **Hadrian's Tower**, was incorporated into the structure of the substantial late-18C additions to the prison; the walls were rebuilt at this time, though they follow the original 14C alignment. The Gothick **Shire Hall** has a notable ceiling of carved stone, and a display of heraldic shields of monarchs and sheriffs. Nearby, on the site of the Great Hall, seat of the Assizes since 1176, are the **Crown Court** and the **Drop Room**, from which prisoners were led out to execution. All three are splendid examples of the style of the period 1796-8.

Priory Church. — A priory dedicated to St Mary was founded nearby in 1094, but the present building is predominantly Perpendicular in style. The south porch doorway dates from c1180, but the glory of the church is the late-medieval **chancel stalls** with elaborate carvings of foliage.

Maritime Museum. — *St George's Quay.* The Customs House was designed by a member of the Gillow family in 1764, and is now home to the Maritime Museum where various aspects of local maritime history are well illustrated. Note the packet boat for canal travel, the diligence for 'crossing the sands' and the exhibit on the growth of the nearby seaside towns such as Morecambe and Heysham (see opposite).

EXCURSIONS

Morecambe and Heysham. — Pop 41 432. *5 miles - 8km west by the A589.* Traditional seaside holiday resorts on the broad sweep of Morecambe Bay with views of the Lakeland hills. Heysham is now a port for Ireland and the Isle of Man, as well as the site of a nuclear power station. On the headland overlooking the port are six graves, cut into the living rock, probably by Irish monks in the 8C and nearby are the ruins of **St Patrick's Chapel.** In **St Peter's Church** just below the headland is a strange 'Hogback tombstone' intermingling Christian and Norse figures.

Blackpool and Lytham St Anne's. — *Description p 60.*

★ **LEEDS** West Yorkshire   Pop 445242

Michelin Map 402 P 22 or Atlas G Britain p 40
Town plan in the current Michelin Red Guide Great Britain and Ireland

Though medieval in origin, Leeds is above all a great Victorian city, its population multiplying tenfold between 1800 and 1900. Ranking third in size among England's provincial cities, it has now replaced heavy industry with light engineering, and clothing manufacture with retail trade. A network of pedestrian precincts and shopping arcades leading off Briggate and Headrow makes for easy exploration of the Victorian heart of the city. Headingley, just outside the city, is the home of Yorkshire cricket.

Town Hall and Victoria Square. — This was the winning design in a competition in 1853. Corinthian columns all around the building, the 225ft - 69m - high baroque tower and the splendour of the interior made it a symbol of civic pride when opened by Queen Victoria in 1858. On fine days, chess enthusiasts can be seen playing 'Giant Chess' on the boards marked out in Victoria Square.

★ **City Art Gallery.** — The gallery's strength lies in its collection of **19C/20C British art**, particularly in its holdings of paintings of the early to mid-20C, virtually all major artists of the period being represented. A selection from its rich collection of British watercolours is normally also on display.
Dominating a limited number of Pre-Raphaelite paintings is the striking *The Shadow of Death* by Holman Hunt. There are several of the large narrative paintings so popular in the 19C, among them Lady Butler's *Scotland for Ever!* and some characteristically atmospheric scenes by the local painter Atkinson Grimshaw.
Most of the early 20C painting is arranged around the grand stairway and on the upper floor. At the top of the stairs is a stunning Vorticist portrait, *Praxitella* by Wyndham Lewis. The more muted work of the Camden Town School includes a Charles Ginner landscape of 1914, *The Leeds Canal* and there is a range of the highly individual work of Stanley Spencer. Native surrealism is well represented, with canvases by Paul Nash, John Armstrong, Tristram Hillier and Edward Wadsworth; the later strain of neo-Romanticism is present too, in the work of John Minton, Graham Sutherland and John Piper. Post-war trends, international as well as British, are illustrated as well in, for example, the disturbing *Painting* of 1950 by Francis Bacon.
The dominance of British art is relieved by the presence of some French paintings: a Courbet, several Impressionists and a brilliant Derain of 1905, *Barges on the Thames.*
The greatest British sculptor of the 20C, **Henry Moore** (1898-1986) was a Yorkshireman; as well as having work by some of his contemporaries, the **Henry Moore Centre for the Study of Sculpture** shows the range of the master's achievement, from exquisite small-scale studies to the *Reclining Figure* of 1929 and the powerful, post-war *Meat Porters.*

St John's Church. — *New Briggate* — The oldest church in central Leeds. A sensitive restoration in 1868 left the interior virtually unchanged since the church was built in 1632-4. Sumptuous screen and pulpit.

Grand Theatre. — *New Briggate* — Gothic, 1877-8, and modelled on La Scala, Milan, this is the home of ''Opera North''.

★ **Kirkstall Abbey.** — *2 miles - 3km from city centre by the A65.* Little imagination is needed to place roofs on these buildings, which still stand almost to roof height. An austerely traditional Cistercian Abbey, started in 1152 by monks from Fountains, the exterior is dominated by the crossing tower, raised in height between 1509 and 1528.

EXCURSIONS

★ **Temple Newsam.** — *Near Whitkirk, 5 miles - 8km east by the A63.* The birthplace of Lord Darnley, husband of Mary Queen of Scots, this is a brick Jacobean-style house forming three sides of a court. Begun in the late 15C it was substantially rebuilt in the first part of the 17C. An inscription from this period, praising God, honouring the King and calling for prosperity for those within the house, runs all round the balustrade.
Inside, the collection of English, European and oriental **decorative arts**★ is outstanding. The displays are enhanced by the appropriateness and attractiveness of their setting and by the presence of many of the city's Old Master paintings. The park, once landscaped by Capability Brown, has a variety of gardens.

★**Nostell Priory.** — *18 miles - 29km by the A61 then the A638.*
⊘ Palladian mansion near the site of a 12C priory dedicated to St Oswald. The house, started in 1733 by James Paine then still only nineteen years old, is in *piano nobile* design, all the chief rooms being on the one floor approached by an external flight of steps.

Robert Adam was commissioned in 1765 to complete the State Rooms and they are amongst his finest interiors. **Thomas Chippendale**, once an apprentice on the estate, designed furniture especially for the house.

The **Library Table** and the green and gold **chinoiserie** furniture of the State Bedroom are some of his finest pieces. The **Dolls' House**, complete with original furniture and fittings, is probably also by him.

LEICESTER Leicestershire — Pop 324 394

Michelin Map 404 Q 26 or Atlas G Britain p 28

Known as Ratae Coritanorum in Roman times, Leicester was the capital of Lear's kingdom, the seat of the 8C East Mercian bishops and one of the five Danelaw towns (with Derby, Lincoln, Nottingham and Stamford *qv*). William I built a castle there, its tenants including Simon de Montfort (Earl of Leicester) and John of Gaunt. Other industries have been added to the hosiery manufacture on which the city's medieval wealth was based.

LEICESTER

Belgrave Gate	CZ
Belvoir Street	CZ
Gallowtree Gate	CZ 20
Gramby Street	CZ 22
High Street	BC
Humberstone Gate	CZ
Bishop Street	CZ 4
Burleys Way	AY 7
Castle Street	CZ 9
Castle View	BZ 10
Causeway lane	BZ 12
Fleet Street	CZ 15
Fosse Road North	AY 16
Frog Island	AY 19
Glenfield Road	AY 21
Guildhall Lane	BZ 26
Horsefair Street	CZ 29
King Richards Road	AY 33
Lee Street	CZ 34
London Road	AY 35
Market Place	CZ 36
Millstone Lane	CZ 37
New Bond Street	CZ 41
Oxford Street	BZ 42
Peacock Lane	BZ 43
St. Augustine Road	BZ 45
St. Margaret's Way	AY 46
St. Martin's	CZ 47
St. Matthews Way	AY 49
St. Nicholas Circle	BZ 50

Southgate Street	BZ 52		Western Boulevard	BZ 58
Welford Place	CZ 55		Wood Gate	AY 59
Welford Road	CZ 56		Woodville Road	AY 60

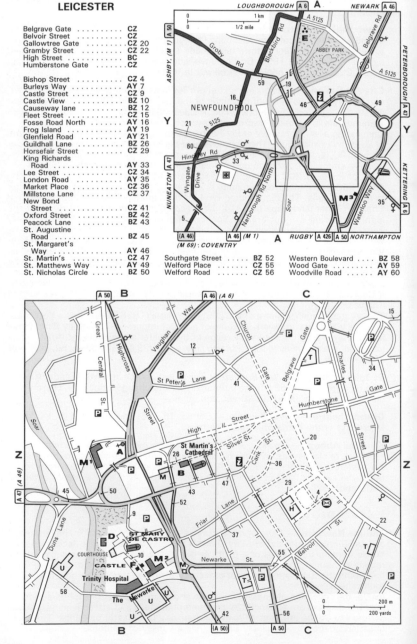

⊘**Jewry Wall and Archaeology Museum** (BZ M¹). — On the site of the excavated Roman baths the museum contains excellent Roman relics, including two fine mosaics, the Blackfriars Mosaic and the Peacock Pavement.

St Nicholas Church (BZ A). — The oldest church in Leicester, begun in late Saxon times incorporates re-used Roman bricks. The present length of the church dates from then (see the small nave windows and chancel wall). The tower is 11 and 12C, restored 1905; the attractive south chancel chapel c1220.

★**Guildhall** (BZ B). — The oldest part built in the 14C, the remainder in the 16C and ⊘forming a courtyard, the Guildhall was the site of the last stand of the Leicester Parliamentarians in the Civil War. Note the robust timber roof and uprights in the Hall, the c1500 glass depicting the Four Seasons in the Mayor's parlour and upstairs one of the earliest public libraries in England.

St Martin's Cathedral (BZ). — A cathedral since 1927, the first St Martin's was Norman. The church that replaced it is Early English, with a Perpendicular clerestory and east end and a very "correct" Victorian interpretation of an Early English exterior (including the tower and spire). Note the Robert Herrick family memorials in the north choir aisle dating back to 1589, the Richard III memorial stone in the chancel and the rare 15C oak-vaulted roof of the north porch.

★**St Mary de Castro Church** (BZ). — The shadowy and attractive interior, a "pat-⊘tern book of architectural styles" (Pevsner), goes back to 1107. The best Norman work is the sedilia. The south aisle and tower are 13C, the chancel roof 14C.

Castle (BZ). — The c1150 **Great Hall** (D) still stands, hidden behind the 1695 Courthouse façade. The **Turret Gateway** (F) (1423), gutted during pro-Reform Act riots in 1832, still acts as the division between the castle precinct and the Newarke.

The Newarke (BZ). — Built by Henry Earl of Lancaster and his son the first Duke ⊘of Lancaster around the **Trinity Hospital**, a 1331 almshouse. In the chapel is the grave said to be of Mary Bohun (d 1394), mother of Henry V.

⊘**Newarke Houses Museum** (BZ M²). — Housed in the c1512 **Wyggeston Chantry House** and the c1600 **Skeffington House**, displaying furniture, toys, clocks and musical instruments.

★**Museum and Art Gallery** (AY M³). — *New Walk.*
⊘An excellent collection of English painters, including Gainsborough, Wright of Derby, Lawrence, Hogarth, Rossetti, Stanley Spencer, Laura Knight and LS Lowry. There is also the country's largest collection of works by the German Expressionists.

Leicester Abbey (AY E). — *Abbey Park, St Margaret's Way.*
Founded in 1132, it became the second richest Augustinian Abbey in England. It was here that the dying Cardinal Wolsey came in 1530 - "an old man, broken with the storms of state". Demolished during the Reformation, its stones were used to build the now ruined Cavendish House next door, headquarters of Charles I before the Battle of Naseby (1645).

★ **LEWES** East Sussex   Pop 14 499
Michelin Map 404 T, U 31 or Atlas G Britain p 11

The downland spur on which the long High Street of this most attractive of county towns is built drops abruptly to the gap cut through the surrounding hills by the River Ouse. The site's strategic value was appreciated by William de Warenne who built his castle here soon after the Conquest. With his wife Gundrada, once thought to be the daughter of William the Conqueror, he also established a great priory, of which very little remains. In 1264, Simon de Montfort's rebellion against Henry III led to the defeat of the royal forces at the **Battle of Lewes**, fought on nearby Mount Harry. Apart from its many architectural delights, the town is famous for its robust celebrations of **5 November**, when torchlight processions, tar-barrel rolling, fireworks and giant bonfires commemorate not only Guy Fawkes and the Gunpowder Plot but also the burning here in the mid-16C of 17 Protestant martyrs.
Beyond the chalk massif of Caburn, looming over the town to the east, is **Glyndebourne**, the country house internationally famous for its annual opera festival.

⊘**Castle.** — Entry to the castle remains is via **Barbican House**, a fine 16C timber-framed building with a late-Georgian façade. It contains good displays on Sussex archaeology. A perfect flint-built 14C **barbican** guards the castle precinct, in which, unusually, there are two mounds, on one of which, high above the rooftops, is perched the **keep**. From one of its towers there are fine **views**★ of the town and the gracefully-sculpted outlines of the chalk hills all around.
⊘The **Lewes Living History Model** is housed nearby; the town's history is brought to life by an audio-visual show accompanying a detailed scale model.

★**Town.** — In the well-preserved **High Street**★ there is a delightful variety of traditional building materials: flint, stone, brick, timber, stucco, hung tiles, and the local speciality, "mathematical tiles", which in the 18C were used on older timber buildings to simulate a fashionable brick façade. Cobbled **Keere Street**★ is very pretty, dropping steeply downhill to a fragment of the old town walls back to **Southover Grange**, built of stone taken from the priory. In Southover High Street is the timber-framed ⊘**Anne of Cleves' House**, a museum of local history; it has a particularly interesting gallery devoted to the iron industry which once flourished among the deep oak forests of the Sussex Weald.

EXCURSIONS

★**Sheffield Park Garden.** — *9 1/2 miles - 15km north on the A275.*

⊘ This large 18C and 19C landscaped park with its four lakes linked by cascades was enriched early in this century with thousands of trees and shrubs from all over the world.

As a plant collection it is outstanding and the effects obtained by waterside planting are dramatic; the varied shapes of conifers contrast with each other and with the exotic outline of the Gothicised mansion *(not open to the public)*, half-hidden in drifts of shrubs; azaleas and rhododendrons give magnificent colour effects in spring and the autumn leaf show has few equals.

⊘ **Bluebell Railway.** — Five miles of former London Brighton and South Coast Railway track now carry the steam trains of Britain's first full-scale preserved railway between Sheffield Park and Horsted Keynes. Everything — trim stations, uniformed staff, carriages and locomotives in authentic livery — evokes the atmosphere of yesterday's country railway.

LEWIS and HARRIS Islands Area

Michelin Map ▨▨▨ Z, A 8, 9 and 10 or Atlas G Britain p 71
Access: see the current Michelin Red Guide Great Britain and Ireland

The island is part of the chain of islands known as the Western Isles which extends some 130 miles - more than 200km from Barra Head in the south to the Butt of Lewis in the north. Buffeted by Atlantic waves, they are treeless and windswept, but rejoice in glistening lochans, superb sandy beaches, and crystal-clear waters. Lewis and Harris, one island, is almost cut in two by West and East Loch Tarbert. Lewis consists largely of rolling moorlands, while Harris is altogether more mountainous. Gaelic is still spoken, peat dug, and Harris Tweed woven (the orb trademark is a guarantee of quality).

Stornoway. — Pop 5 152. Lewis. Capital and only sizeable town, the slopes fronting the land-locked harbour, overlooked by the 19C castle (now a college), Stornoway is the base for any excursion inland where hotels and petrol stations are scarce. Eye peninsula to the northeast has some fine sandy beaches.

EXCURSIONS FROM STORNOWAY

★★**Callanish Standing Stones.** — Lewis. *16 miles - 26km west of Stornoway, well signposted off the A858.*
Over 4 000 years old and contemporary with Stonehenge *(qv)*, the stones, of Lewisian gneiss, form a circle plus alignments with the points of the compass and it is generally assumed that they were used for astronomical observations. A central burial chamber is a later Neolithic addition (2 500-2 000 BC).

★**Carloway Broch.** — Lewis. *5 miles - 8km beyond Callanish Standing Stones, signposted off the A858.*
Although not a complete example of a broch (small fortified farms going back to 500 BC), enough remains of the galleried walls and entrance chamber for the builders' skill to be admired.

⊘ **Arnol Black House.** — Lewis. *6 miles - 10km beyond Carloway, signposted off the main A858.*
Typical of the island dwellings (living area, sleeping area, kitchen and stable-cum-barn all under one thatched roof), called black houses because of their open hearth. Arnol Black House has been preserved as a reminder of island life as it was until half a century ago.

St Clement's Church. — Harris. *60 miles - 97km to the southeast of Stornoway by the A859.*
In the town of Rodel near the southern tip of Harris is a church with the outstanding **tomb**★ of its 16C builder, Alexander MacLeod (d 1546), decorated with carvings, including the Twelve Apostles, the Virgin and Child and the galley emblem of the Lord of the Isles.

★ LICHFIELD Staffordshire   Pop 25 408

Michelin Map ▨▨▨ O 25 or Atlas G Britain p 27

''A place of conversation and good company'', according to Daniel Defoe, predominantly Georgian Lichfield is graced by one of the most beautiful and picturesquely-sited cathedrals in England. ''Every man has a lurking wish to appear considerable in his native place'', **Samuel Johnson** (1709-84) once wrote; and he stands
⊘ in the Market Place opposite his **birthplace** looking eminently considerable.

★★ CATHEDRAL

⊘ On a Christian site since at least the 7C, the present building replaced a Norman cathedral of the 11C. Begun in 1195 it is a fine synthesis of the Early English and Decorated styles, with some Perpendicular work. The Close was three times besieged in the Civil War, the cathedral much bombarded and its central spire collapsed in 1646. Restoration took place during the 1660s, the interior of the building was changed substantially by Wyatt in the 18C, but Sir George Gilbert Scott carried out thoroughgoing and sensitive work from 1857 to 1901, restoring the cathedral to its medieval grandeur.

Exterior. — Built of mellow red sandstone and, uniquely in England, with three spires, its most moving characteristic is its richly-textured west front, alive with sandstone saints. These date from the 13C but most from the work of Scott in the 1880s.

Interior. — One of the smallest, narrowest and most beautiful of England's cathedrals, the wooden roof **bosses** of the nave, decorated **capitals** and perfectly proportioned nave lead the eye past the Transitional crossing and western choir to the Lady Chapel and the fine 16C Flemish glass at the east end. Look out for monuments to Anna Seward *(The Swan of Lichfield)*, 18C authoress, and the diplomat and orientalist Lady Mary Wortley Montagu at the west end, to Johnson and Garrick in the south transept and Erasmus Darwin in the south choir aisle. The tenderly carved *Sleeping Children* by Sir Francis Chantrey is also in the south choir aisle.

Cathedral Close. — Beautifully sited by the water of the Minster Pool, amongst Georgian, early Victorian and neo-Georgian buildings; the best are the 1704 **Deanery** and the 1687 **Bishop's Palace** (now the school) by Wren's pupil Edward Pierce, on the north side.

★★ LINCOLN Lincolnshire   Pop 79 980

Michelin Map **402** S 24 or Atlas G Britain p 36

High on a limestone plateau beside the River Witham, the triple towers of the cathedral are visible for miles around. Lincoln was originally Lindon, latinised by the Romans into Lindum and anglicised by the Anglo-Saxons into Lincoln.

Lindum Colonia. — A settlement since the Bronze Age, occupied by the Ninth Legion in *c* 60 AD, it was turned into a colonia in *c* 96 AD and confined to the plateau top, 42 acres - 17ha surrounded by a wooden palisade. In the 3C Lincoln, now one of the four provincial capitals of Roman Britain, doubled in size. The city spread down the southern slopes to the river and was encased in a 4 1/2ft - 1.5m thick stone wall, with six gates, best viewed from the Bishop's Palace or East Bight.

Medieval Lincoln. — Lincoln survived the Roman decline, emerging as the capital of the Anglo-Saxon kingdom of Lindsey and converted to Christianity in *c*630. It became one of the five Danish burgh towns (with Derby, Leicester, Nottingham and Stamford *(qv)*, gained in importance after the Conquest with the building of the castle and cathedral, and became one of the most prosperous cities in medieval England, shipping its wool direct to Flanders from Brayford Pool on the River Witham.

★★★ CATHEDRAL AND PRECINCTS (Y) *time: 2 hours*

The first cathedral, built by Remigius, was early Norman, the result of a short and decisive programme between 1072 and 1092. Alexander, Lincoln's third bishop, builder of Newark Castle *(qv)*, re-roofed the cathedral following a fire in 1141. Hugh of Avalon, a French monk, built the present Early English cathedral on the orders of Henry II, following the earthquake of 1185 which virtually destroyed the original Norman building.

Exterior. — Visible for miles, few cathedrals have achieved such even proportions: the chancel is as long as the nave, the west towers almost as high as the crossing tower. The **west front** is its most famous view, the central sections early Norman, surrounded by a cliff-face of Early English blind arcading. The south side is graced by the intricate carving of the **Galilee Porch** and **Judgement Porch** and the north side provides a splendid and varied view of the buttressed Decorated **east end**, the north transept, Wren's Library and the flying-buttressed chapter house.

Interior. — Wide and harmonious, Lincoln limestone and Purbeck marble combine to create columns of contrasted texture which support the triforium, aisles and arcading, showing Early English architecture as its best.

Nave. — Seven bays long (with an exceptional font of Tournai marble in the second south bay), the nave is rich in Victorian stained glass. The crossing is flooded with light from the windows of the **Dean's Eye** (13C glass) in the north transept and the **Bishop's Eye** (14C glass) in the south.

St Hugh's Choir. — East of the magnificent 14C stone screen is the Choir, still with its 14C oak **misericords**. Its surprise is its vault, the so-called "crazy vault of Lincoln", the first rib-vault of purely decorative intentions in Europe, curiously asymmetrical yet "easier to criticise than improve" (Pevsner).

Angel Choir. — Undiluted Decorated, rich, light and spacious, the soaring **East Window** depicts Biblical scenes in geometric pattern. High on the northeast pillar, the **Lincoln Imp**, the grotesque that has become the city's emblem, looks down on the shrine of St Hugh.

Cloister and Chapter House. — North of St Hugh's Choir is the 13C cloister, vaulted in wood (note the bosses: a man pulling a face, a man sticking his tongue out). Forming the north range is Christopher Wren's **Library**, above a classical arcade. East of the cloister is the **Chapter House** (early 13C) - the vaulting springing from a central shaft and externally supported by flying buttresses - where Edwards I and II held some of the early English Parliaments.

Precincts. — Amidst the mostly Georgian and Victorian houses are two gems: the **Bishop's Palace (Y)** and the **Vicar's Court.** Grand and intimidating, built on the plateau's slopes, the palace, though only ruins, gives an idea of the richness of Lincoln's medieval prelates. The East Hall is Norman, the West Hall, built by St Hugh, Early

English. According to a description before its destruction in the Civil War, ''the great hall is very fair, lightsome and strong... one large middle alley and 2 out alleys on either side with 8 grey marble pillars bearing up the arches and free-stone windows very full of stories in painting glass of the Kings of this land''.

Vicar's Court (Y A). — Mid-14C, the four ranges and barn behind are a rare survival of medieval domestic architecture and one of the prettiest examples in England.

ADDITIONAL SIGHTS

Castle Hill (Y 3). — Surrounded by 16-19C houses; to the east the 14C **Exchequer gate** (B) leads to the cathedral; at the other end the East Gate leads to the castle.

★**Castle** (Y). — Of the original Norman keep and wooden stockade built by William the Conqueror nothing remains. It covered 13 acres - 5ha and involved the demolition of 166 houses. The keep's mound is now crowned by the late 12C **Lucy Tower**. The **East Gate** was added in the 12C, **Cobb Hall** in the 13C. A Norman tower was enlarged in the 14C and heightened in the 19C when it became known as the Observatory Tower. Although besieged in the wars of 1135-54 and 1216-17, the castle gradually lost its military significance, but became more important as a centre for the administration of justice.

The **Prison Building**, built between 1787 and 1791, was enlarged in 1845-6; the **Prison Chapel**, with its devilishly-designed self-locking cubicles which prevented the prisoners from seeing each other, seems an eminently suitable monument for an age more concerned with bringing prisons into the house of God, than God into prisons.

Aaron the Jew's House (Y D). — Built about the same time as the Jew's House; Aaron, who never actually lived there, was one of the most successful bankers in England.

★ **Jew's House** (Y E). — Built c1170, with beautifully designed Norman windows and doorway, the adjoining **Jews' Court** was once used as a synagogue.

★★ **Usher Gallery** (YZ M¹). — Financed from a legacy by James Ward Usher (who made a fortune at the turn of the century selling replicas of the Lincoln Imp), to house his collections of 16-19C **miniatures**, 17 and 18C French and English **clocks**, Chinese, Sèvres, Meissen and English **porcelain**; it also has well-chosen selections of 17C Italian and Dutch **paintings** and an excellent collection of topographical views of Lincolnshire. The collections include works of **Peter de Wint** (1784-1849), *Gleam of Sunshine after Rain, Newark Castle* and *Lincoln Cathedral.*

Greyfriars (Z M²). — Earliest surviving chapel of the Franciscan Order in England, the 13C building with its robust barrel roof and vaulted undercroft now holds collections of Roman, Saxon and medieval antiquities.

Stonebow (Z F). — Site of the southernmost Roman gate, Stonebow is a replacement of an earlier 14C gate. The east range is late 14C, the west early 16C. The gate and guildhall above it were built between the two. The niches in the flanking towers contain statues of the Virgin Mary and the Archangel Gabriel.

★★ **High Bridge** (Z). — Medieval (though much restored), with the River Witham flowing through its Norman vaults (the Glory Hole), its timber-framed houses are a unique reminder of what Old London Bridge *(qv)* must have looked like. The projection on the other side of the bridge once carried the Chapel of Thomas Becket.
Upstream is **Brayford Pool** (Z), Lincoln's medieval port, while downstream are two historic inns, the 14C "Green Dragon" and the 15C "Witch and Wardrobe".

EXCURSIONS

★ **Doddington Hall.** — *5 miles - 8km southwest by the A15* (Z) *and the A1434.*
Late Elizabethan, built by Robert Smythson, who had worked on Longleat *(qv),* Hardwick Hall, *(qv)* and Wollaton Hall *(qv),* it is E-shaped and outward-looking, abandoning the traditional internal courtyard, a sign of a self-confident age.

Interior. — With the exception of the Parlour, all was refurbished in 1764 by Thomas Lumby, a local builder. The **Parlour** itself is in Queen Anne style, its walls graced with paintings, including Sir Thomas Lawrence's *Mrs Sarah Gunman,* Sir Peter Lely's *Cymon and Iphegenia* and Ghaerardt's portrait of *Meg of Meldon,* a local witch. The **White Hall** and the **Stairs** are Lumby's masterpieces. The **Long Gallery** has displays of paintings and porcelain.

★ **Gainsborough Old Hall.** — *18 miles - 29km west on the A57* (Z) *and north on the A156.*
One of the best-preserved late medieval manor houses in England, the timber-framed hall with two flanking ranges was built by Sir Thomas Burgh between 1460 and 1480. Richard III visited it in 1483. Originally all timber-framed except for the brick kitchen, brick tower and stone bay window, Elizabethan features were added to the two ranges. The Hall itself has a sturdy single-arched braced roof; the **kitchen** gives an unforgettable memory of medieval life below stairs. The east wing contains great chambers, while the west wing, in contrast, is a unique example of 15C lodgings. The tower is furnished as a late 15C bedchamber.

★ **LIVERPOOL** Merseyside   Pop 535 809

Michelin Map 402 L 23 or Atlas G Britain p 34

On 28 August 1207 King John granted a Charter for settlers to establish a port on the Mersey. Gradual silting up of the Dee estuary, on which, since Roman times, had stood the port of Chester, turned this new village into England's second port - Liverpool. Centred around seven streets, which can still be followed today - Castle and Old Hall, Water and Dale, Chapel and Tithebarn, up to Hatton Garden - and the "Pool", an inlet following today's Canning and Paradise Streets and Whitechapel, Liverpool started to expand when trade with the West Indies - sugar, rum, cotton and, until 1807, slaves, - brought such prosperity that by 1800 there were more than 80 000 "Liverpudlians". In the 19C Liverpool, home to the Cunard and White Star liners, was Britain's gateway to the empire and the world. The Mersey Docks and Harbour Company handled the cargo traffic, employing some 20 000 men in the immediate post-war period. Today, with container ships and mechanical handling just over 2 500 men now work in the docks.
Though its days of mercantile splendour are long over, Liverpool remains an eminently handsome city, with a wealth of glorious architecture and fine civic buildings, reflecting some of the energy, taste and philanthropy of the Victorian age. Today it is intent on its own revival, leisure developments leading the way, like the country's first Garden Festival in 1984, the Albert Dock and the Tate Gallery.

Pier Head (CY). — To absorb the spirit of Liverpool and the Mersey, stand with your back to the river, looking up Water Street. The ferries behind you have been part of the scene here since the monks of Birkenhead Priory began rowing travellers across in about 1150. The green-domed **Port of Liverpool Building**, built 1907, with its neighbours the **Cunard Building** (1913) and the **Royal Liver Building** (1908), with its "Liver Birds" on the cupolas are, perhaps before even the cathedrals, the best known symbols of Liverpool.

★ **Albert Dock** (CZ). — A series of massive brick warehouses encloses a 7 acre - 3ha basin. Completed in 1846, finally closed in 1972, the complex has now been revitalised with shops, cafés and apartments, a maritime museum and the northern extension of the Tate Gallery.

LIVERPOOL

Green Tourist Guides

*Scenery
Buildings,
Scenic routes,
Geography,
History, Art,
Touring programmes,
Plans of towns and buildings.*

Guides for your holidays.

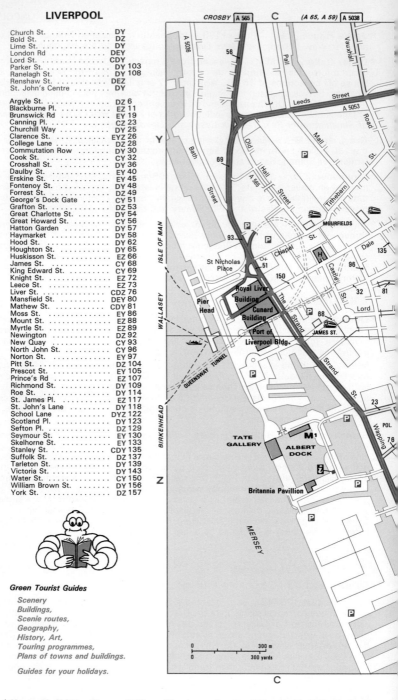

★ **Merseyside Maritime Museum (M¹).** — The many facets of Liverpool's intimate involvement with the sea are recounted on five floors (start on the fourth floor and work down). Liverpool's seafaring past is presented through displays on the history of shipbuilding, the evolution of the port, navigation and the growth of maritime insurance, ship models and paintings. The most poignant is that devoted to the nine million emigrants to the New World who passed through Liverpool between 1830 and 1930.

It also includes a maritime park with historic vessels and boat displays, the piermaster's house and the pilotage buildings.

★ **Tate Gallery Liverpool.** — The Tate family originated in Liverpool and the choice of the city to house part of the national collection of 20C art was a happy one. The architect James Stirling, who also designed the Clore Gallery at the Tate in London, has created unobstructed display areas by retaining the cast-iron supports and perimeter wall. The transformed warehouse will eventually offer as much space as the parent gallery for semi-permanent exhibitions from the primary collections of 20C art and for temporary exhibitions.

The Beatles Story. — *Britannia Pavilion.* Relive or discover the decade of the Beatles, the 1960s, known for the phenomena of rock'n'roll, teenagers, the Merseybeat and Beatlemania. The group (John, Paul, George and Ringo), their manager the late Brian Epstein, the places (the basement cellar club The Cavern, Strawberry Fields,

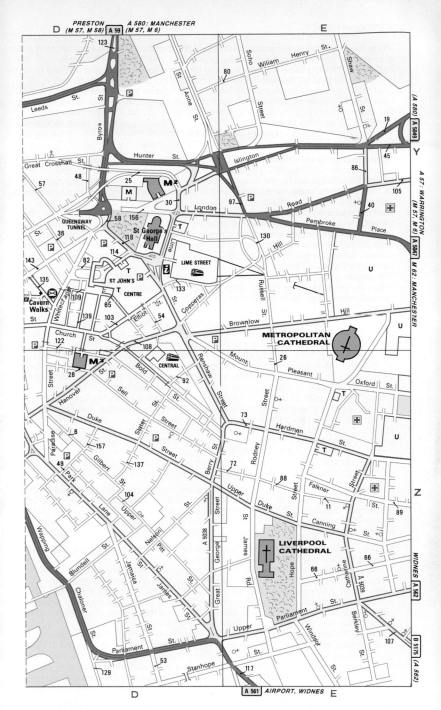

PRESTON (M 57, M 58) A 59 A 580: MANCHESTER (M 57, M 6)

Penny Lane, Hamburg) and the hits *(Strawberry Fields, Magical Mystery Tour, Sergeant Pepper's Lonely Hearts Club Band, The Yellow Submarine)* are presented in a lively and entertaining manner in this walk-through presentation.

★★ **Liverpool Cathedral** (EZ). − *The cathedral is not traditionally oriented east-west, but the cardinal points are here used as though the high altar were at the east end.* On its ridge overlooking the Mersey, this monumental edifice in red sandstone is the largest Anglican church in the world. Work on it began in 1904 and it has taken most of the century to build, a triumphant reinterpretation of the Gothic tradition by its architect **Sir Giles Gilbert Scott** (1880-1960). On entering the Nave, one's first impression is that of the poet Sir John Betjeman - *vastness, strength and height no words can describe.* Turn at the **nave bridge** and look back at Carl Edwards' west window. Its Old Testament theme of the Benedict - *O all ye works of the Lord, bless ye the Lord,* balances the New Testament Te Deum window at the east end. Scott's unusual design includes double western and eastern transepts and a 15 000sq ft - *c*1 400m² **central space** under the tower, giving an uninterrupted view of altar and pulpit. The 331ft - 100m high tower extends the full width of the building and houses the heaviest ringing peal of bells in the world (31 tonnes). Set in the floor immediately below is the memorial to the architect, who once said of his design: ''Don't look at my arches, look at my spaces''. A Roman Catholic, he is buried just outside the west door.

In the western of the two south transepts is the **Baptistery**, with its marble font and a baldachin and font cover containing some of the finest wood carving in the cathedral. Through the **choir**, with its Liver Birds on the steps leading into the stalls, one comes to the **Lady Chapel★**. It served as the cathedral from its completion in 1910 until consecration of the main building in 1924. It has a notable reredos and a 15C Madonna by Giovanni della Robbia. In the south choir aisle is a memorial to **Bishop Chavasse**, who inspired the building of the cathedral. The foundation stone had been laid in 1904 by King Edward VII; in 1978, at the service of dedication, his great-granddaughter Queen Elizabeth II unveiled a commemorative stone, fulfilling the hopes of three generations in the completed cathedral.

★★ **Metropolitan Cathedral of Christ the King** (EYZ). — Its stands on Brownlow Hill, occupied from 1771 to 1928 by the Poor Law Institute, haven for Liverpool's destitute; the site seemed to the Diocesan authorities an apt one for the new cathedral. In 1930 **Sir Edwin Lutyens** was chosen as the architect and the foundation stone was laid on Whit Monday, 1933.

Building stopped in 1941; the crypt was completed after the war but inflation had raised the cost of the cathedral as planned to over £27 million. Architects were invited to submit plans which would make use of the existing crypt, cost no more than £1 million - and be completed in five years. Sir Frederick Gibberd's design was chosen, building began in October 1962 and the completed cathedral was consecrated on the Feast of Pentecost, 14 May 1967.

The **exterior** is unmistakable, an extraordinary buttressed circular structure in concrete, culminating in the 290ft - 88m high lantern with its crown of pinnacles. The main entrance, with its bronzed fibreglass doors carrying the emblems of the Evangelists, is set into the wedge-shaped belltower.

Interior . — From the inner porch the High Altar is immediately visible, at the centre of the 194ft - 60m diameter circular nave. The **tower**, its stained glass in the colours of the spectrum with three bursts of white light representing the Trinity, rises above the **High Altar**, architectural as well as liturgical focal point. The baldachin is suspended from above; the candlesticks are short; the Crucifix is purposely narrow - all to ensure an uninterrupted view of the celebrant at the altar for every member of a full 2 300-strong congregation. To the right, as you enter, is the circular **Baptistery**. The font, with its dull silver cover, is a simple design in white marble, matching the High Altar. Largest of the chapels around the circumference, the **Lady Chapel** is almost feminine in its gentleness and elegance.

Below, in the crypt, Lutyens' massive brick vaults now form four main areas, including a parochial hall, a venue for regular concerts and a museum recounting the story of the building of the cathedral. This last area also has the **Chapel of Relics**, burial place of the Archbishops, which has as its door a fretted six-tonne marble disc, which rolls back as did the stone sealing the tomb of Christ.

St George's Hall area. — The city's landward focal point, partly bounded by neo-classical civic buildings of considerable grandeur, is dominated by the awesome presence of **St George's Hall** (DY), ''one of the finest neo-Grecian buildings in the world'' (Pevsner). Completed in 1854 it contains the circular Concert Room with caryatid gallery and the vast tunnel-vaulted Great Hall of more than Roman opulence.

★★ **Walker Art Gallery** (DY M²). — The gallery's collection of paintings, British and European, is among the best in the country.

Numerous painters of the Italian school are represented, from the 14C to the Renaissance and after, among them an exquisite Simone Martini *Christ Discovered in the Temple* and a Salvator Rosa *Landscape with Hermit.* There is a fine precisely-constructed Poussin, *Landscape with the Ashes of Phocion,* while the extensive holdings of Northern European art include works by Rembrandt, Eisheimer and the invitingly drowsy *Nymph of the Fountain* by Cranach.

The range of British work is particularly complete, extending from Elizabethan and later portraits to key works by Stubbs *(Horse frightened by a Lion),* Wright of Derby *(Easter Sunday at Rome)* and Richard Wilson *(Snowdon from Llan Nantlle);* there are typically uncanny works by Fuseli, and many **Pre-Raphaelites**, including Millais' *Lorenzo and Isabella* and Ford Madox Brown's *Coat of Many Colours* and narrative paintings like WR Yeames' *When did you last see your Father ?* The gaslit murk of Victorian Liverpool is evoked by Atkinson Grimshaw's *The Custom House,* a world away from the rustics and fisherfolk of Stanhope Forbes and George Clausen.

A small number of French Impressionists, Degas, Seurat and Monet, are juxtaposed with their British contemporaries like Sickert, whose *Bathers at Dieppe* are observed as through a camera's telephoto lens.

The good selection of modern British artists includes Gilman, Ginner and Bevan of the **Camden Town School**, Stanley Spencer and Lucian Freud, with a townscape, *Villas at Cookham* and *Interior near Paddington* respectively, both paintings of disturbing intensity. Paul Nash's surreal *Landscape of the Moon's Last Phase* contrasts with the cheerful townscape of Dame Laura Knight's *Spring in St John's Wood* or with the meticulously-detailed rural scenes of James McIntosh Patrick and Stanley Badmin.

Bluecoat Chambers (DZ M³). — *School Lane.* A Queen Anne building set round a cobbled court, founded 1717 as a charity school, now houses the Merseyside Arts Trust and series of exhibitions.

Cavern Walks (DY). — *Mathew Street.* This modern precinct marks the site of the Cavern Club, starting point of the careers of **The Beatles** *(p 154),* Liverpool's best known 20C sons. In Stanley Street, just around the corner, is the statue of Eleanor Rigby, by Tommy Steele, a contemporary of The Beatles. As in the song, she sits on a bench, with shopping bag and headscarf, sharing her few crumbs with the sparrows. A plaque behind her dedicates the statue ''To all the lonely people''.

EXCURSIONS

★ **Speke Hall.** — *Near the Airport, 8 miles - 13km southeast by the A561* (EZ).
⊘This "black and white" Elizabethan manor house was built between 1490 and 1612 by successive generations of the Norris family. The **Great Hall** is the oldest part of the building; its panelling, including the Great Wainscot of 1564, is particularly fine. The many smaller rooms reflect the Victorian preference for privacy and comfort. In the courtyard are two ancient yews, possibly pre-dating the house.

The Wirral. — *By the Queensway Tunnel* (DY), *then south on the A41.* The Wirral peninsula is a tongue of land bounded by the Rivers Mersey and Dee.

Birkenhead. — Pop 99 075. On the west bank of the Mersey, Birkenhead with its sweeping Victorian terraces and imposing stone houses, grew rapidly in the 19C following the starting of a regular ferry service in the 1820s and the opening of the docks in 1847.

4 miles - 6km south on the A41.

Port Sunlight. — The model village was established in the late 19C by William Hesketh Lever for the workers of his soap factory, giving them a style of life very different from that of the crowded slums of the period. Lord Leverhulme's company became Unilever, one of the largest manufacturers of consumer goods. The
⊘**Lady Lever Art Gallery** also founded by Lord Leverhulme and opened in 1922, contains period furniture, British paintings including Pre-Raphaelite works, and a Wedgwood collection.

A further 4 miles - 6km south on the A41, then onto the M53 as far as Junction 9.

⊘**Ellesmere Port.** — Pop 65 829. The **Boat Museum**, located where the Shropshire Union Canal meets the Manchester Ship Canal, has over fifty historic canal boats. Visitors can make canal trips and, in the workshops, see restoration work being carried out.

⊘**Ness Gardens.** — *14 miles - 23km by Queensway Tunnel* (DY) *south on the M53 to Junction 4, then the B5136 to Neston.* Nelson's Lady Hamilton was born at Ness. The University of Liverpool Botanic Gardens has an extensive collection, particularly of rhododendrons, azaleas, alpines and heathers.

⊘**Pilkington Glass Museum, St Helens.** — *12 miles - 18km east along the A5047* (EY) *then right onto the A57.* Opened 1964, the museum traces the evolution of glass-making and the many applications of glass. Exhibits range from an Egyptian amphora of *c*1350 BC to the working lighthouse optic.

⊘**Knowsley Safari Park.** — *8 miles - 13km east by the A5047* (EY), *the only entrance is on east-bound carriageway of the A58 (Prescot by-pass).*
The Earl of Derby established a menagerie here in the 19C. It was here that **Edward Lear** made many of his animal drawings and the tales he told to Lord Derby's grandchildren became his *Book of Nonsense*. Today twenty-one species of animal from all over the world make this one of the most interesting of private collections.

⊘**Wigan.** — *19 miles - 31km northeast by the A59* (DY) *and the M58.*
George Formby Senior joked about the pier at this inland town on the Leeds-Liverpool Canal. In 1936 when **George Orwell** was preparing *The Road to Wigan Pier* he had set his heart on seeing the celebrated Pier but he had to admit "Alas ! Wigan Pier has been demolished, and even the spot where it used to stand is no longer certain". The canal warehouses here were built in 1770, and had indeed sadly decayed until they were restored and turned into a Heritage Centre, showing life as it was at the turn of the century.

LLANDUDNO Gwynedd   Pop 13 202

Michelin Map 403 I 24 or Atlas G Britain p 33
Town plan in current Michelin Red Guide Great Britain and Ireland

Safe sandy beaches make Llandudno a popular family summer holiday resort. It is also a good centre from which to explore nearby Snowdonia. Owen Williams, a Liverpool surveyor, developed the town in the 1850s and planned the promenade and wide streets. **Great Ormes Head** (679ft - 207m), reached by the Tramway which dates from 1902, by road or cabin lift, offers superb views of the coast and mountains of Snowdonia. The energetic can even walk up ! It was whilst walking on the beach here with Alice Liddell over a century ago, that **Lewis Carroll** was inspired to write *Alice in Wonderland.* The **'White Rabbit'** memorial on the West Shore commemorates this.

EXCURSION

★★ **Rhuddlan Castle.** — *16 miles - 26km east on the A470, A55 and the A547.*

Colwyn Bay (Bae Colwyn). — Pop 27 002. A more restrained version of the Victorian seaside resort than Llandudno, with a long promenade giving onto the sandy beach.

Go east on the A55.

Shortly before Abergele the vast pile of **Gwrych Castle** becomes visible, a romantic folly built in 1815. Commanding the coastline from its hillside site, it evokes all the atmosphere of the Middle Ages.

Go east on the A547.

★★ **Rhuddlan Castle.** — Diggers from the Fens and elsewhere laboured for three years during
⊘ the war of 1277 to divert the River Clwyd, so that a castle which could be supplied from the sea could be built. A town grew up which, in the war of 1282, replaced

Chester as the main base of operations against the Welsh in Snowdonia. In 1284 the''Statute of Wales'' was issued here, as the plaque on the so-called ''Parliament House'' in the High Street records, ''securing to the Principality of Wales its judicial rights and independence''. A few beam holes, foundations and roof creases are all that remind us today of the splendour of the black and white timber-framed buildings around the Inner Ward, which rang then with laughter and music, and no trace at all remains of the little garden made for the Queen. It is likely that Edward presented his Welsh-born son, the future Edward II, to the assembled princes of Wales at Rhuddlan, rather than at Caernarfon, as tradition has it. The castle was partly demolished after the Civil War. Entry to the remains is by the **west gatehouse**, best surviving feature. First and second floors provided comfortable apartments with fireplaces. Similar suites must have existed in the east gatehouse. The concentric plan of the castle within its wide dry moat, with lower walls to the outer ward and a defended river wall and dock, can still be traced on the ground.

LLANGOLLEN Clwyd   Pop 2 546

Michelin Map ▨ K 25 or Atlas G Britain p 33

Home of the **International Eisteddfod**, held annually in July since 1947, Llangollen is dominated by the ruins of the 12C Welsh fortress of Dinas Bran on its dramatic hilltop site. (A visit is only for the energetic; the pathway up becomes very steep.)

★ **Plas Newydd.** — *A ten-minute walk from the town centre.* From 1780, when they arrived from Ireland and set up house together, it was the home of **The Ladies of Llangollen.** Lady Eleanor Butler and Miss Sarah Ponsonby caused considerable comment at the time, but entertained a constant stream of distinguished visitors at their home. They began the transformation of a humble cottage into the eccentric ''black and white'' building we see today. They are buried in the nearby St Collen's Church, under a roof believed to have been taken from Valle Crucis Abbey at the Dissolution.

EXCURSIONS

Detail of porch door Plas Newydd

⊘ **Valle Crucis Abbey.** — *2 miles - 3km north on A542.* Beautifully-sited ruins of an important Cistercian abbey, founded 1201, whose name is taken from the **Pillar of Eliseg,** a 9C cross commemorating the ancient Kings of Powys. The abbey was well known for its patronage of the bards and Iolo Goch, a 14C poet from Dyffryn, is buried here. The Early English west front still stands and the vaulted and ribbed 14C **chapter house** is intact.

Wrexham (Wrecsam). — Pop 39 929. *13 miles - 21km northeast by the A539, then the A483.* The largest town in North Wales, its long-standing prosperity stems from its position between profitable coal seams and rich agricultural land. In the

⊘ churchyard of the fine Perpendicular Gothic **St Giles Church★** is buried **Elihu Yale** (1649-1721). His gifts to Newhaven College in America caused it to be named **Yale University** in his honour. His family had come from near Wrexham, returning to Britain when Elihu was two years old. He spent much of his life in the East India Company and his epitaph starts: ''Born in America, in Europe bred, in Africa travelled, and in Asia wed, where long he liv'd and thriv'd: in London dead...''. The **Royal Welch Fusiliers** have their Memorial Chapel, Roll of Honour and Colours in St Giles.

★ **Erddig.** — *2 miles - 3km south of Wrexham (see above), off the A525.* Late 17C
⊘ house rescued in 1973 from dereliction due to mining subsidence. It contains much furniture of outstanding quality, supplied for it in the 1720's, as well as magnificent porcelain, tapestries and paintings. There is also a unique collection of portraits, photographs and poetic descriptions of staff. The restored joiner's shop, sawpit, laundry, bakehouse, kitchen and servants' hall all furnish an insight into the running of that complex organism, the country estate. The **State Bedroom** with 18C Chinese wallpaper contains the magnificently restored bed from 1720. The early 18C formal garden survived, at least in outline and has now been restored.

★ **Chirk Castle.** — *7 miles - 11km east by the A5.* Chirk Castle, or Castell y Waun,
⊘ was built, to a design similar to that of Beaumaris, started the same year, 1295. It is unique in having been in continuous occupation from then until the present day and here we see the adaptation of a great fortress to the changing needs of later times. The **State Rooms** in the north wing are the great glory of Chirk today.

Pont Cysyllte. — *4 miles - 6 1/2km east on the A5 and minor road at Froncysyllte.* Built 1794-1805 by Telford and one of his most achievements, the 1 007ft - 307m long aqueduct carries the Llangollen branch canal 127ft - 39m above the River Dee.

One of the great financial centres of the world is also important in the world of entertainment and fashion. Though there is nothing unique about such a combination of roles, the peculiarity of London is that they function side by side - in two separate cities ! Even before the Middle Ages the **City of London** was the scene of busy trading, while the Palace and Abbey which Edward the Confessor (1042-66) had built 2 miles west of the city were the beginnings of the City of Westminster. The differences between the two are still very evident: the City of London - the **City** - is very much a place of business and finance, the City of Westminster - the **West End** is characterised by elegant shops, theatres, clubs, parks, the Houses of Parliament and Buckingham Palace.

HISTORICAL SKETCH

Though the name London is of Celtic origin the city only began to take shape when the Romans made it the hub of their road system and built the first London Bridge. There was little resistance to the Romans in the southeast, a notable exception being Queen Boadicea's attack on London in 61 AD, after which the Romans encircled the city with defensive walls. Remains of these walls, reinforced in the Middle Ages, can be seen on the street called London Wall and its continuation southeast to the Tower.

By building the royal palace at Westminster, Edward the Confessor set a precedent which was followed by the kings after the Norman Conquest. Indeed London only officially became the capital of England in the mid-12C, for until then Winchester (qv) was administratively more important. The City and its busy port gained considerable freedom and independence thanks to the monarchs' preferring to reside outside its confines; in fact the Crown was often dependent on City merchants to finance expeditions and military campaigns. The City did not encroach on Westminster and, with few notable exceptions, citizens held no office under the Crown or Parliament. In time, however, a number of merchants and bankers chose to build their houses in the less crowded West End or in villages such as Islington, Chelsea and Holborn.

The problems of overcrowding, particularly in the City, became all too apparent when London was ravaged by the **Great Plague** in 1665 and then the **Great Fire** in 1666, which left only one fifth of the City standing - but did at least put an end to the plague ! Within six days of the end of the fire, 33-year-old **Christopher Wren** submitted a plan for rebuilding the City. It was not accepted, however, and only St Paul's Cathedral was built entirely to his designs, though the City is graced by several Wren churches.

As the metropolis expanded individual parishes proved ill-equipped to control housing, transport and sanitation. The appalling conditions of the 18C are strikingly illustrated in **William Hogarth's** works and in the 19C **Charles Dickens'** journalism and novels provide vivid descriptions of poverty, as does Henry Mayhew's *Survey of the London Poor, 1850*. In 1855 the Government at last established a central body, the Metropolitan Board of Works, with special responsibility for main sewerage and to act as co-ordinator of the parish vestries, which had hitherto been in charge of local drainage, paving, lighting and the maintenance of streets.

In 1888 the County of London was created with an area equivalent to the present 12 inner London boroughs. In 1965 the Greater London Council superseded the London County Council to control an area of 610 square miles - 1 580km² and a population of 6 700 000. On 1 April 1986 the GLC was abolished and its functions have devolved largely to the borough councils and newly-created statutory bodies.

The City was heavily bombed in World War II, which explains the profusion of modern architecture, one of the most imaginative examples being the **Barbican**, a residential neighbourhood incorporating schools, shops, open spaces and an arts centre which plays just as active a part in London cultural life as does the **South Bank Arts Centre**. Without doubt, the most ambitious project is the regeneration of great tracts of disused dockland east of the City. The London Docklands Development scheme, begun in 1981, is already changing the face of London, with exciting prospects for the future.

LONDON TODAY

The historical sketch above ends with the future. Today's visitor is likely to have the impression that the centre of London is busy, noisy but hardly lived-in. This applies particularly to the City and other business quarters to which thousands of commuters travel distances of up to 100 miles - 160km and beyond - every day. However, a walk around any of the "villages" could quickly dispel this impression. Although the villages have become completely absorbed in the metropolis, many of them have retained their own particular character of which their inhabitants are proud. The visitor who takes the time to explore such boroughs as **Southwark**, **Hackney**, **Islington**, **Camden** or elegant **Kensington** and **Chelsea** will have a more realistic impression of life in London.

London has a long been a cosmopolitan city, but since Britain joined the European Community in 1972 it has been slowly becoming even more international, with an increasing number of foreign food stores and restaurants as more and more Londoners discover the pleasures of eating out.

With the creation of the London Docklands Development Corporation in 1981 and the computerisation of the Stock Exchange in 1986, London, which has so proudly cherished its ancient traditions, has also become one of the fastest-developing cities of Europe.

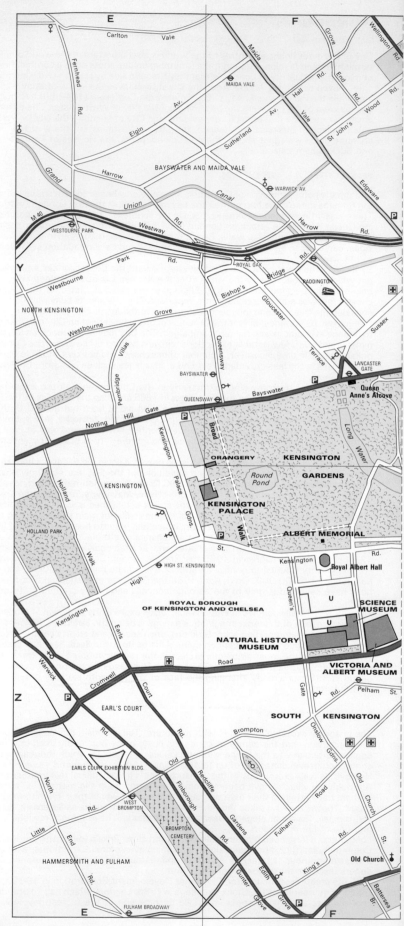

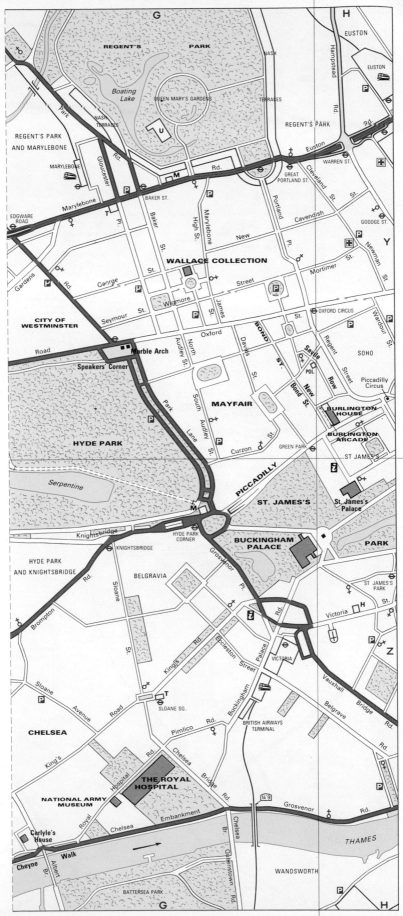

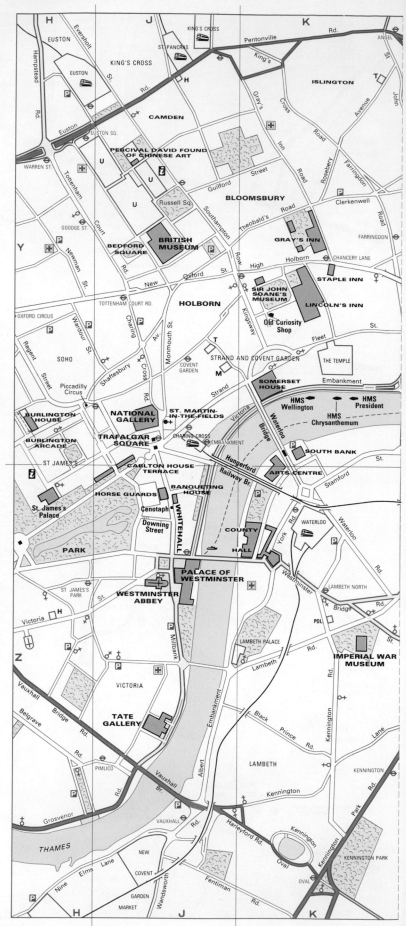

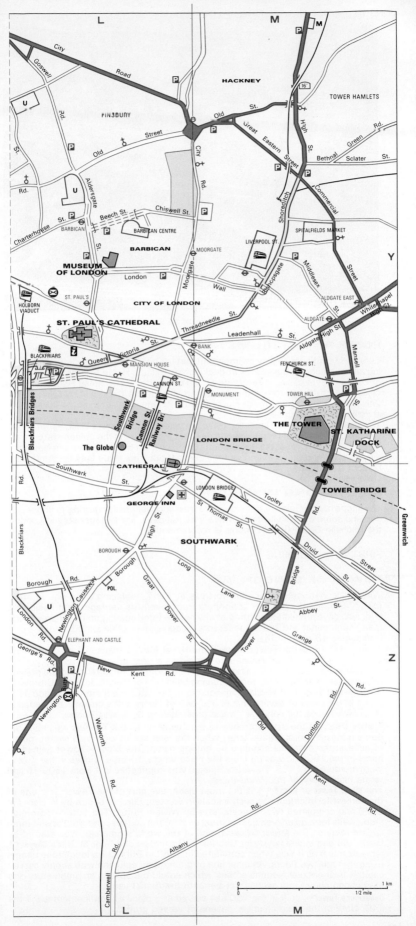

Aeriel view of the City

POMP AND CIRCUMSTANCE

Ceremony continues to play an important part in London life. The ceremonial mounting and changing of the guards at Buckingham Palace, Horse Guards or the Tower of London never cease to fascinate crowds of visitors. The Royal Household provides colourful pageantry when the Queen attends the **Trooping of the Colour** on the 2nd or 3rd Saturday in June at Horse Guards Parade, and again at the **State Opening of Parliament** in November.

The second Saturday in November sees the colourful **Lord Mayor's Show,** as the newly elected Lord Mayor of London proceeds through the City in the golden state coach, before taking his oath at the Royal Courts of Justice. On the first Sunday in November a large number of veteran and vintage cars set out from Hyde Park on the famous London to Brighton Rally.

SIGHTSEEING IN LONDON

The scope of this Guide permits no more than suggestions for getting to know London and some of its "villages" in five very full days. For a longer stay in London, the Michelin Green Guide London is recommended.

FIRST DAY MORNING

★★★TOWER OF LONDON (MY)

William I constructed a wooden fortress in 1067, replacing it by one in stone (c1077-97) in order to deter Londoners from revolt; its vantage point beside the river also gave immediate sighting of any hostile force coming up the Thames. Norman, Plantagenet and Tudor successors recognised its value and extended it until it occupied 18 acres - 7ha.

From 1300-1810 the Tower housed the Royal Mint; because of its defences it became the Royal Jewel House and served as a grim prison.

In the **Jewel House** are kept the **Crown Jewels★★★** from the Restoration to the present day, almost all of the earlier regalia having been sold or melted down by Cromwell.

The **Chapel of St Peter ad Vincula,** consecrated in the 12C, rebuilt in the 13 and 16C, is the burial place of several dukes and two of Henry VIII's queens, beheaded in the Tower. Note the carvings on the organ casing by **Grinling Gibbons.**

Traitors' Gate was the main entrance to the Tower when the Thames was still London's principal thoroughfare; later, when the river served only as a secret means of access, the entrance acquired its chilling name. The Bloody Tower gained its name in the 16C and was perhaps the place where the little Princes in the Tower were murdered in 1483. Sir Walter Raleigh was imprisoned in it from 1603-15 and wrote his *History of the World* there.

The **White Tower** or **Keep★★★** is the most distinctive part of the Tower; it is one of the earliest fortifications on such a scale in western Europe, begun by William I in 1078 and completed twenty years later by William Rufus. The 100ft - 31m high stone walls form an uneven quadrilateral with, at the corners, one circular and three square towers. The **Armour Collection,** one of the world's greatest, was started by Henry VIII and increased under Charles II. On the second floor **St John's Chapel★★** remains much as it was when completed in 1080, a 55ft - 17m long stone chapel rising through two floors. An inner line of great round columns with simply carved capitals bear circular Norman arches which enfold the apse in an ambulatory and are echoed above in a second tier beneath the tunnel vault.

Beauchamp Tower★, built in the 13C has served as a place of confinement since the 14C. Note in the main chamber dozens of carved graffiti.

TOWER BRIDGE and ST KATHARINE DOCK

★★**Tower Bridge** (MYZ). — The familiar Gothic towers, high-level walkways *(lift or 200 steps)* and the original engine rooms were opened in 1982 as a museum demonstrating the functioning of the hydraulic mechanism which raised the 1 100 ton bascules, from 1886-94, when Sir John Wolfe-Barry and Horace Jones built the bridge, until 1976.

★**St Katharine Dock** (MY). — In 1828, on the site of the 12C Hospital of St Katharine by the Tower, **Thomas Telford** developed a series of basins and warehouses; the dock was the nearest to the City and prospered for over a hundred years. After wartime bombing the dock was abandoned until 1968, when moorings were organised for private yachts. Telford's Italianate building was restored as Ivory House with apartments above a shopping arcade.

FIRST DAY AFTERNOON

★★★**ST PAUL'S CATHEDRAL** (LY)

The present cathedral, the fourth or fifth on a site dating back to 604 AD, is considered to be the masterpiece of **Sir Christopher Wren** (1632-1723), though it is worth visiting some of his other churches in the City (eg St Stephen Walbrook, St Margaret Lothbury) to gain a fuller impression of the flexibility and ingenuity of Wren's art. After the Great Fire Old St Paul's was a sad ruin; Wren submitted plans for a new cathedral to the authorities before going ahead as Surveyor General to the King's Works. The foundation stone was laid on 21 June 1675. 33 years later Wren saw his son set the final stone in place - the topmost in the lantern. When Wren died 15 years later he was buried within the walls; beneath the dome his own epitaph reads in Latin: "Reader, if you seek his monument, look around you".

Exterior. — The most striking feature is the **dome**, even today a dominant feature of the City skyline. Unlike the dome of St Peter's, which fascinated and influenced Wren, it is not a true hemisphere. The drum below it is in two tiers, the lower encircled by columns and crowned by a balustrade, the upper recessed behind the balustrade so as to afford a circular viewing gallery, the **Stone Gallery**. On top of the dome, the lantern is restrained English baroque with columns on all four sides and a small cupola serving as a plinth to the 6 1/2ft - 2m diameter golden ball.
The **west end** presents, at the top of the two wide flights of steps, a two-tier portico of Corinthian and composite columns below a decorated pediment surmounted by the figure of Saint Paul. On either side rise Wren's most baroque spires as a foil to the dome. A notable feature is the rich carving all around the exterior by Gibbons and others.

Interior. — The immediate impression is one of space, of almost luminescent stone and, in the distance, gold and mosaic. In the **nave** the entire space between two piers in the north aisle is occupied by the Wellington monument and in the south aisle hangs Holman Hunt's *The Light of the World*. From the **Whispering Gallery** in the dome *(259 steps)* there are impressive views of the concourse below, the choir, arches and clerestory, and close views of the interior of the dome, painted by Thornhill. Note the curious acoustic effect, giving the gallery its name. The **views**★★★ from the **Golden Gallery** at the top of the dome are better than from the Stone Gallery *(543 steps)*. The **transepts** are shallow, that to the north serving as baptistery with a font carved in 1727 by Francis Bird, that to the south including Flaxman's fine statue of **Nelson**. In the **choir** the dark oak stalls are the exquisite work of **Grinling Gibbons**. The iron railing, the gates to the choir aisles and the great gilded screens enclosing the sanctuary are the work of Jean Tijou. The graceful sculpture of the Virgin and Child in the north aisle is by Henry Moore (1984). In the south aisle is a rare pre-Fire relic, a statue of **John Donne**, the great poet and Dean of St Paul's 1621-31. The **Crypt** contains tombs of many illustrious individuals and memorials to the dead of many wars and to others, too numerous to list.

SECOND DAY MORNING

★★**TRAFALGAR SQUARE** (JY)

The square was laid out by Nash in 1820 as part of a north-south communication between Bloomsbury and Westminster. Begun in 1829, the square was completed in the 1840s, when Charles Barry levelled it and built the north terrace for the National Gallery. In 1842 **Nelson's Column** was erected; the monument is 185ft - 56m tall, with the pedestal, fluted granite column, bronze capital and a 17ft - 4 1/2m statue of the great admiral who lost his life winning the Battle of Trafalgar. The church of **St Martin-in-the-Fields**★ *(northeast)* was built by James Gibbs in 1722-26, with a Corinthian portico and elegant spire. Note the equestrian statue of **Charles I** cast by Le Sueur in 1633 *(south)* and *(west)* **Canada House**, a classical building of Bath stone (1824-27) by Robert Smirke.

★★★**NATIONAL GALLERY** (JY)

After more than a century of discussion the collection was founded by Parliamentary purchase in 1824, its nucleus being 38 pictures collected by City merchant and banker **John Julius Angerstein** (1735-1823). Only in 1838 was the new gallery completed, its pedimented portico of Corinthian columns forming a climax to Trafalgar Square. The 1973-75 extension is the fifth to William Wilkins' original building and affords additional space for the permanent and special exhibitions.

There are now more than 2 000 paintings in the collection; they represent the jewels in the public domain from Early to High Renaissance Italian painting, early Netherlandish, German, Flemish, Dutch, French and Spanish pictures and masterpieces of the English 18C. (The fuller representation of British art, particularly the more modern and 20C work of all schools is in the Tate Gallery.)

To give an impression of the richness of the collection let the following names, just some of the bright stars in a brilliant constellation, speak for themselves: Duccio, Giotto, Uccello, Fra Angelico, Piero della Francesca, Botticelli, Leonardo da Vinci, Michelangelo, Raphael, Titian, Tintoretto, Veronese, Bellini, Caravaggio, Canaletto and Guardi among the Italians. From the Low Countries Frans Hals, Jan Steen, Vermeer, Rembrandt, de Hooch, Avercamp, Cuyp, Van Dyck and Rubens. Earlier German and Netherlandish work is represented by Dürer, Cranach, Holbein, van der Weyden, Bosch and Memlinc. Hogarth, Reynolds, Gainsborough, Constable, Turner and Lawrence figure among British artists of the 17-18C. Spanish artists are represented by Velazquez, El Greco and Goya, and the French and other European painting after 1800 by artists such as Manet, Degas, Cezanne, Monet, Renoir, Seurat, Klimt and Friedrich.

★★ WHITEHALL (JZ)

Government offices and buildings line Whitehall which leads from Trafalgar Square to the Houses of Parliament. On the right, halfway down, stands **Horse Guards★**, a mid-18C building by William Kent and John Vardy around three sides of a shallow forecourt, pierced by a central arch, with clock tower above. The unadorned building is completed by the statue-like presence of the Household Cavalry sentries. Directly opposite stands part of Whitehall Palace, the two-storey **Banqueting House★★** which **Inigo Jones** began for James I in 1619 (though the north entrance and staircase were added in 1809 and the exterior refaced in 1829). Inside, the hall is a double cube 110 × 55 × 55ft - 33.5 × 16.75 × 16.75m, with a delicate balcony on gilded corbels; above, richly decorated beams divide the ceiling into compartments filled with magnificent paintings (1634-5) by Rubens.

Just before the **Cenotaph**, Luytens' austerely impressive war memorial in the middle of the street, is **Downing Street**, with a row of modest Georgian Houses, of which No 10, rebuilt for Sir Robert Walpole in 1732, has been the Prime Minister's residence ever since.

SECOND DAY AFTERNOON

★★★ PALACE OF WESTMINSTER (JZ)

England's medieval kings enlarged and embellished Edward the Confessor's Palace, but most of the surviving buildings occupied by Parliament were destroyed in a disastrous fire in 1834. The oldest remaining part is **Westminster Hall★★** which William Rufus added to his father's palace between 1097 and 1099. This scene of royal banquets and jousts in the Middle Ages was altered and re-roofed by command of Richard II between 1394 and 1399. For this the upper parts were rebuilt and what is perhaps the finest timber roof of all time was built, a superb **hammerbeam★★★** designed by the king's master carpenter, Hugh Herland, carved with flying angels. After the 1834 fire which, fortunately, did not damage Westminster Hall, **Charles Barry** and **Augustus Pugin** won a competition for a new design for the Palace, or Houses, of Parliament as it became known. These committed Gothicists gave London a masterpiece of Victorian Gothic architecture. It was completed in 1860, with over 1 000 rooms, 100 staircases and 2 miles - 3km of corridors spread over 8 acres - 3ha.

The Clock Tower - **Big Ben★** - the most famous feature of this distinctive building, was completed by 1859. The name Big Ben applied originally to the great bell in the 316ft - 96m tower; its diameter is 9ft - 2.75m, its height 7ft - 2.1m and it weighs 13 1/2 tons. The light above the clock remains lit while the House of Commons is sitting.

The **House of Commons★** seats 437 of the 650 elected Members of Parliament; at the end of this simply, decorated chamber is the canopied Speaker's Chair. Red stripes on both sides of the green carpet mark the limit to which a Member may advance to address the House - the distance between the stripes is reputedly that of two drawn swords.

The **House of Lords★★** is a symphony of design and workmanship in encrusted gold and scarlet. The throne and steps, beneath a Gothic canopy mounted on a wide screen, all in gold, occupies one end of the chamber. The ceiling is divided by ribs and gold patterning above the red buttoned leather benches and the Woolsack, seat of the Lord Chancellor since the reign of Edward III, adopted as a symbol of the importance to England of the wool trade.

★★★ WESTMINSTER ABBEY (JZ)

The abbey in which the Conqueror was crowned as **William I** on Christmas Day 1066 had been built by **Edward the Confessor** in the Norman style; only after the rebuilding by the Plantagenet Henry III in 1220 did it acquire its Gothic appearance. Inspired by the style of Amiens and Reims, Henry III began with the Lady Chapel, to provide a noble shrine for the Confessor, who had been canonised in 1163. Continuing west the existing building was demolished as new replaced the old; progress halted after the construction of the first bay of the nave and it was another two centuries before the nave was finished. When Henry VII constructed his **chapel** at the east end (1503-19), Perpendicular Gothic was still the ecclesiastical style and he produced the jewel of the age. The west towers by Wren and Nicholas Hawksmoor (1722-45) and repairs by George Gilbert Scott kept to the Gothic spirit. The Dissolution in 1540 meant the confiscation of the abbey's treasure, forfeiture of its property, the disbanding of the 600-year-old Benedictine community of 50 monks, but not the destruction of the buildings. In 1560 Queen Elizabeth I granted a charter establishing the Collegiate Church of St Peter with a royally appointed Dean and chapter of 12 canons and the College of St Peter, generally known as Westminster School.

Interior. — The vaulting is glorious, the carving on screens and arches delicate, often beautiful, sometimes humorous; the ancient tombs in **Henry VII's, St Edward's** and the ambulatory chapels are dignified and sometimes revealing in expression (some being derived from death masks). The transepts and aisles abound with sculpted monuments, particularly the south transept with the famous **Poets' Corner★**.

The **Sanctuary** beyond the **Choir** is where the **Coronation ceremony** is performed. To the right hangs a 16C tapestry behind a large 15C altarpiece of rare beauty. Beyond is an ancient 13C sedilia painted with full length royal figures (Henry III, Edward I). The **Henry VII Chapel★★★** with its superb fan-vaulted roof is the most glorious of the abbey's many treasures. The banners of the Knights Grand Cross of the **Order of the Bath** hang still and brilliant above the stalls patterned with the heraldic plates of former occupants and those of their esquires, with inventive 16-18C misericords. The **Chapel of Edward the Confessor★★** is rich in history, with the Confessor's shrine ringed with the tombs of five kings and three queens. In the centre is the **Coronation Chair and Screen**, the carved stone screen completed in 1441 and below the oaken seat the **Stone of Scone**.

The **Chapter House★★** (1248-53) is an octagonal chamber 60ft - 18m in diameter with vaulting springing from a slim central pier of attached Purbeck marble columns. Its walls are partially decorated with medieval paintings.

★★BUCKINGHAM PALACE (GZ)

The walk from Westminster to Buckingham Palace includes **St James's Park★★** (GHJZ), the oldest royal park in London, dating back to 1532 when Henry VIII had **St James's Palace (HZ)** built in place of an old hospital for lepers. The park was landscaped in the 19C by Nash who was also responsible for the majestic **Carlton House Terrace★** (JYZ) at its north corner.

In 1703 the newly-created Duke of Buckingham built for himself a brick town house on land which Queen Anne had granted him at the west end of St James's Park. In 1762 the mansion was purchased by **George III** and presented to his bride, Charlotte. Few alterations were made to it until 1825 when George IV summoned John Nash who produced a palace clad in Bath stone around the core of the old brick mansion. When the King died in 1830, Nash was not permitted to complete his extravagant work and the task was taken over by Edward Blore, who completed it in 1837 after the death of William IV. Ten years after Queen Victoria's accession the wings were linked to the east front, enclosing the forecourt and including what has become the focal point on public occasions, the balcony. Nash's Marble Arch, rendered superfluous as a grand entrance, was removed to its present position at the northeast corner of Hyde Park.

Changing of the Guard★★ takes place at 11.30am in the forecourt. When the Sovereign is in residence, the Royal Standard flies over the Palace.

The **Queen's Gallery★★**, on the site of a former domestic chapel, presents exhibitions of the portraits, paintings, drawings and furniture in the superb Royal Collection.

THIRD DAY MORNING

SOUTH KENSINGTON: Museums and Colleges (FZ)

In 1851 Prince Albert opened the **Great Exhibition** in Hyde Park, after two years of planning and despite Parliamentary opposition. In Joseph Paxton's 19 acre - 7 1/2ha glasshouse or **Crystal Palace**, 13 937 exhibitors demonstrated man's inventiveness and 19C British achievement in particular. The Exhibition attracted 6 039 195 excited visitors and made a net profit of just under £200 000, which Prince Albert proposed should be spent in creating a great educational centre in South Kensington by buying land on which the famous museums and colleges were established. On the 86 acre - 34ha area now stand the Royal College of Art, the Royal College of Organists with its ornate façade, the Royal Geographical Society, the Royal College of Music, the Royal School of Mines, the Imperial College of Science and Technology and the Science and Natural History Museums, as well as the remarkable Victoria and Albert Museum.

★★★Victoria and Albert Museum. — This fabulously rich and varied collection was started, in part, with the purchase of contemporary works manufactured for the Exhibition. It includes the national collection of furniture, British sculpture, textiles, ceramics, silver and watercolours, as well as world-famous displays of fashionable dress, jewellery, Italian Renaissance sculpture and art from India and the Far East. Since 1909 the Museum has been housed in Aston Webb's idiosyncratic building of brick, terracotta and stone, fittingly adorned with a figure of Prince Albert.

★★★Science Museum. — This factory-laboratory of Man's continuing invention extends over 7 acres - nearly 3ha. There are innumerable working models, handles to pull, buttons to push as well as a hands-on experience area, the Launch Pad. The Wellcome Galleries on the History of Medicine were opened in the early 1980s.

★★Natural History Museum. — Alfred Waterhouse's vast symmetrical palace, inspired by medieval Rhineland architecture, was opened in 1881 to house the British Museum's ever-growing natural history collection, which today illustrates all forms of life, from the smallest bacteria to the largest creatures, fossils and dinosaurs, minerals and rocks as well as an exhibition of Man's place in evolution.

★ **Albert Memorial.** — At the summit of four wide flights of steps George Gilbert Scott's neo-Gothic spire is ornamented with mosaics, pinnacles and a cross. At the centre, surrounded by allegorical statues and a frieze of 169 named figures of poets, artists, architects and composers, sits a 14ft - 4.25m bronze statue of the Prince Consort who did so much to further the arts and learning, until his premature death in 1861. The memorial was unveiled in 1876, the figure of Albert gazing across at the enormous, round **Royal Albert Hall** (1867-71), still an active venue for meetings, conferences and concerts, notably the eight-week summer season of **Promenade Concerts.**

THIRD DAY AFTERNOON

★★KENSINGTON PALACE, GARDENS AND HYDE PARK (FGYZ)

⊙ Since its purchase in 1689 by William III this early 17C Jacobean house has passed through three phases: under the House of Orange it was the monarch's private residence, with **Wren** as principal architect; under the early Hanoverians it became a royal palace, with Colen Campbell and William Kent in charge of decorative schemes; since 1760 it has been a residence for members of the royal family.

The **State Apartments** are approached by the **Queen's Staircase** designed by Wren. The **Queen's Gallery** has carving by Grinling Gibbons and portraits by Kneller and Lely; in the Queen's Drawing Room hangs a painting by Kneller of the first Royal Gardener, Henry Wise, who was in charge of Kensington Gardens. The **Privy** and lofty **Presence Chamber, Cupola** and **Drawing Rooms,** added for George I in 1718-20, were decorated by William Kent during 1722-7. The staircase, built by Wren in 1689, was altered in 1692-3 and again when Kent coverd the walls and ceiling with *trompe l'œil* paintings including a dome and gallery of contemporary courtiers. The gallery was built to house William's finest pictures. Kent's ceiling depicts scenes from the story of Ulysses.

The Court Dress Collection is displayed in period room settings on the ground floor and shows the dresses and uniforms which have been worn at the select court occasions spanning 12 reigns from 1750.

Hyde Park Bandstand

The **Gardens★**, originally 26 acres - 10ha and extended finally to 275 acres - 110ha, were at their prime under the Queens Mary, Anne and Caroline (George II's consort) and the royal gardeners, Henry Wise and his successor in 1728, Charles Bridgeman. In the 18C the **Round Pond** was dug, facing the State Apartments, as the focal point for avenues radiating northeast, east and southeast to the **Serpentine** and **Long Water,** which terminates at its northernmost point in the 19C Italian Gardens and Queen Anne's Alcove. Other features of the period are the **Broad Walk** and the early 18C **Orangery★**, Hawksmoor's splendidly baroque centrepiece (1705). Beyond the Serpentine is the less formal **Hyde Park★★** (GYZ), which, together with Kensington Gardens, Pitt the Elder called "the lungs of London"; two centuries later the park plays the same essential role for tourists and office-workers in their lunch-hour, all enjoying the fresh air and feeding the ducks.

Speakers' Corner (GY) is a relatively modern feature of the park; not until 1872 did the government recognise the need for a place of public assembly and free discussion. To its north stands **Marble Arch** (GY), the triumphal arch of Italian marble which was designed by John Nash in 1827 as a grand entrance to Buckingham Palace, in commemoration of the battles of Trafalgar and Waterloo.

FOURTH DAY MORNING

★★★TATE GALLERY (JZ)

⊙ The gallery developed because within 50 years of the founding of the National Gallery in 1824 the nation had acquired a large number of pictures - notably through the Turner bequest of 282 oils and 19 000 watercolours (1856), the Chantrey bequest for the purchase of works by living artists as well as early masters and through two major collections. These pictures were variously exhibited in the National Gallery, the Victoria and Albert and Marlborough House until, in 1891, Henry Tate, sugar broker and collector of modern art, offered his collection to the nation and £80 000 for a building, if the government would provide a site.

The site of the former Millbank prison was offered and in 1897 the Tate opened as the Gallery of Modern British Art. Tate and the Duveens funded extensions, Sir Hugh Lane bequeathed 39 paintings, including some superb Impressionists, in 1923 Samuel Courtauld funded the purchase of modern French paintings and in 1955 the Tate became legally independent of the National Gallery.

A major extension, opened in 1979, enables about one twelfth of the British and Modern Art collections of some 14 000 paintings, sculptures and prints acquired since the Gallery's foundation, to be displayed at one time. 1987 saw the opening of the **Clore Gallery**, devoted wholly to the display of works by Turner. Frequent special exhibitions are another feature which ensures that the gallery always remains very much alive.

⊘ BOAT TRIP from WESTMINSTER (JZ) to GREENWICH *time: 45 minutes*

A trip downriver to Greenwich gives a different view of the heart of London, showing the city's new interest in the river as a way of life or as a thoroughfare between Westminster and the Docklands. Opposite Westminster pier **County Hall★** (KZ), opened in 1922, is still one of London's most distinctive buildings. Beyond Hungerford railway bridge (JKYZ) the **Royal Festival Hall★** built for the 1951 Festival of Britain marks the beginning of the **South Bank Arts Centre★★** (KY); it is followed by the smaller concert halls, the **Queen Elizabeth Hall** and **Purcell Room** (1967), almost hiding the 1968 **Hayward Gallery** from view. Beyond it, after Waterloo Bridge (KY), stands Denys Lasdun's **National Theatre★**, incorporating three theatres seating audiences of 1 100, 890 and 400. On the other side of the river can be seen the impressive riverfront of Chambers' **Somerset House★** (KY), dating from 1777-90. After passing the three vessels HMS *Wellington*, *Chrysanthemum* and *President*, then under Blackfriars road and rail bridges and Southwark and Cannon Street rail bridges (LY), **Southwark Cathedral★★** (LYZ) is seen on the right. It stands just before **London Bridge★** (LY), on the site of the oldest crossing of the Thames. The present bridge is the newest (1973) in London — its latest predecessor (1831) having been sold for £1 000 000 is now in Arizona. Passing **Tower Bridge★★** *(qv)* and the **Tower of London★★★** *(qv)* one can see everywhere the work which is revitalising the disused Surrey Docks *(south side)* and on the Isle of Dogs. Every trip will bear witness to new progress in these exciting projects.

FOURTH DAY AFTERNOON

★★★GREENWICH (DX)

Greenwich has been in the royal domain since King Alfred's time. Henry V's brother, Humphrey, Duke of Gloucester, first enclosed the park and transformed the manor into a castle which he named Bella Court. The Tudors preferred Greenwich to their other residences and Henry VIII, who was born there, magnified the castle into a vast palace with a royal armoury; he also founded naval dockyards up and downstream at Deptford and Woolwich. Rich as the Tudor palace was, James I commissioned **Inigo Jones** in 1615 to build a house for his queen, Anne of Denmark. Jones created a Palladian villa but work ceased on Anne's death, to be resumed when Charles I gave the house to his queen, Henrietta Maria, whose name and the date 1635 appear on the north front.

The Queen's House was the only part of the palace relatively unscathed during the Commonwealth. Charles II disliked the derelict palace and commissioned a King's House from John Webb, a student of Inigo Jones. This house - the King Charles Block - and the Observatory were the only parts of Charles II's palace to be completed.

William and Mary, preferring Hampton Court as a royal residence, granted a charter for the foundation of a Royal Hospital for Seamen at Greenwich, with **Wren** as surveyor. In 1873 these buildings were transformed into the Royal Naval College, while the Queen's House, extended by two wings in 1807, became the National Maritime Museum in 1937.

★★ **Royal Naval College** (DX A). — At Queen Mary's insistence, Wren retained the ⊘ Queen's House, giving it a 150ft - 46m wide river vista (after demolition of the Tudor palace). To the King Charles Block he added three symmetrical blocks, the King William, Queen Mary and Queen Anne. The vista was focused by twin advanced cupolas above the refectory and chapel and the course of the Thames was modified and embanked.

The **Painted Hall★** in the domed refectory building is the work of **Sir James Thornhill**, exuberant baroque representations of William and Mary, Anne, George I and his descendants, in an allegorical celebration of British maritime power, painted 1708-27. The **Chapel★** by Wren was redecorated after a fire in 1779 by "**Athenian**" **Stuart** and **William Newton** as a rococo interior in Wedgwood pastels. In contrast to such delicate patterns, at the apse is *St Paul after the Shipwreck at Malta* by **Benjamin West**, who designed the stone medallions for the pulpit which is made from the top of a three-decker.

★★ **National Maritime Museum** (DX M¹). — The elegant white **Queen's House★★** was ⊘ the first Palladian villa to be built in England. Inigo Jones matched the beauty of the horseshoe-shaped staircase leading to the terrace, a first-floor loggia on the park side, with an equally attractive interior. The galleries in the **West Wing** trace Britain's marine history, from **Captain Cook's** exploration of the Pacific to **Nelson's** battles, in paintings, maps, ships' logs and models. Other galleries cover shipbuilding in wood, iron and steel, navigation and maritime archaeology and conservation.

★ **The Park and Old Royal Observatory** (DX). — The Park, the oldest enclosed royal domain, extends for 180 acres - 72ha, rising to a point 155ft - 47m above the river, crowned by the Old Royal Observatory and the General Wolfe Monument. In 1675 Charles II directed Wren to ''build a small observatory within our park at Greenwich, upon the highest ground at or near the place where the castle stood'' for the ''finding out of the longitude of places for perfect navigation and astronomy''. Until the inauguration of the annual *Nautical Almanack* in 1767 map makers fixed the zero meridian where they chose; thereafter they began to base their calculations on Greenwich and by 1884 75% of the world's charts were based on the Greenwich Meridian.

Inside Wren's brick **Flamsteed House** is the lofty Octagon Room, beautifully proportioned, equipped with what John Evelyn called ''the choicest instrument''. The **Meridian Building** was added in the mid-18C to house the growing **collection**★★ of telescopes. Note Airey's Transit Circle, through which the meridian passes and outside, the brass meridian of 0°, the clocks showing world times and the 24-hour clock.

★★ **Cutty Sark** (DX D). — Emphasising Greenwich's maritime importance, this splendid clipper, launched in 1869 for the China tea trade, stands in a dry dock by the river. Famous in her heyday as the fastest clipper afloat, her best day's run, with all 32 000 sq ft - 3 000 m² of canvas fully spread, was 323 miles - 584km. Beside her, the 53ft - 16m **Gipsy Moth IV,** in which Sir Francis Chichester made his solo circumnavigation of the world in 1966-67, looks incredibly small. The best way to return to London is to take the foot tunnel *(lift or 100 steps)* to the other side of the river, from which the **view**★★ of Greenwich Palace is excellent, and then the Docklands Light Railway which affords views of the developing dockland areas.

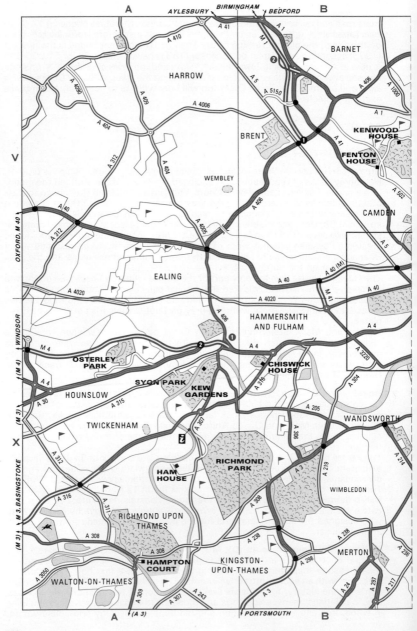

FIFTH DAY MORNING

★★★HAMPTON COURT (AX)

⊙ This grand Tudor palace was begun (1514-29) by **Cardinal Wolsey**, son of an Ipswich butcher, who rose to a position of power second only to that of Henry VIII. Its size and sumptuousness, indicative of Wolsey's wealth (together with Wolsey's failure to obtain, from the Pope, Henry's divorce from Catherine of Aragon) angered the king, who dispossessed his most ambitious subject in 1529 on his fall from favour; he died in disgrace the following year.

Henry VIII then set about enlarging the palace; he built wings on the imposing **west front**, the splendid **Great Hall** with its hammerbeam roof and lavishly transformed the **chapel.** The remarkable **Astronomical Clock** in Clock Court, though made for him in 1540 was brought here from St James's Palace in the 19C.

150 years after Henry's death, William and Mary had plans to rebuild the palace (which had survived Cromwell, having been reserved for him), but instead Wren began alterations in 1688. He rebuilt the east and south fronts, the **State Apartments** and the smaller royal apartments. These rooms were decorated with carvings by **Grinling Gibbons** and painted ceilings by **Verrio.**

The apartments and rooms contain a superb collection of **paintings** and **furniture**, the plain **Orangery**, designed by Wren, houses the *Cartoons of the Triumph of Caesar* by Mantegna, while the **Kitchens** and the **King's Beer Cellars** and the **Wine Cellars** offer a glimpse of life in Tudor times.

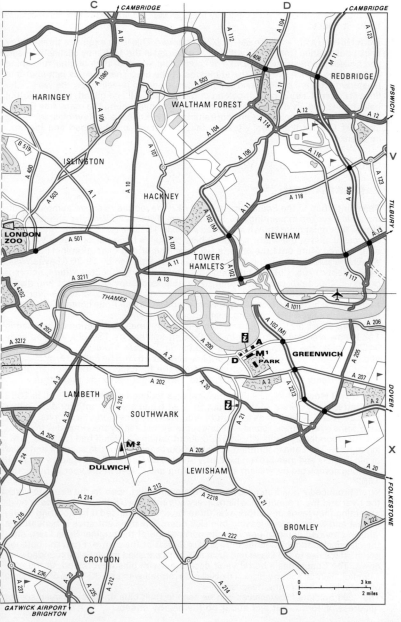

The **Gardens**★★★ as we see them today are the results of various schemes. Charles II had the mile-long canal dug and William III created the Great Fountain Garden. The famous triangular **maze** north of the palace was planted in 1690. Further north, outside the palace walls, lies Bushy Park with its **Chestnut Avenue**, particularly colourful in May. In 1768 under George III, Capability Brown planted the **Great Vine**★, now a plant of remarkable girth which produces an annual crop of 500-600 bunches of grapes *(on sale late August / early September).*

FIFTH DAY AFTERNOON

★★RICHMOND and HAM HOUSE (AX)

★★ **Richmond.** — Possessing what has been called the most beautiful urban green in England, Richmond grew to importance between the 12 and 17C as a royal seat and, after the Restoration, as the residential area of members of the Court - Windsor, Hampton Court and Kew are all easily accessible. Today private houses stand on the site of Henry VII's Royal Palace (the third on the site) which he had sumptuously rebuilt and in which he died in 1509 - as did his granddaughter, Elizabeth I in 1603. Among other fine Georgian houses in the "village" note the **Maids of Honour Row**★★ on the Green, built in 1724.

Climbing **Richmond Hill's** steep road, lined by 18C houses with balconied terraces, one has excellent views, immortalised by artists such as Turner and Reynolds. At the top **Richmond Park**★★ (ABX), which had been a royal chase for centuries, was enclosed as a 2 470 acre - 1 000ha park by Charles I in 1637. It is the largest of the Royal Parks and is known today for its wildlife, including badgers and herds of red and fallow deer. From the top of Henry VIII's Mound, near Pembroke Lodge and the Richmond Gate, on a clear day the **panorama**★★★ extends from Windsor Castle to St Paul's.

★★ **Ham House** (AX). — *One mile - 1 1/2km upriver.* This is an exquisite three-storey brick house dating from 1610 which was enlarged in the 1670s by Elizabeth Dysart and her second husband, the Duke of Lauderdale. Much of their original furnishing has survived, lavish even by the standards of the age. The house is rich in ornate plasterwork on the ceilings and splendid carved wood panelling on the walls. The **Great Staircase** of 1637, built of oak around a square well and gilded, has a beautiful balustrade of boldly carved trophies of arms. Notable among the many fine Dutch, English and Italian paintings are portraits by Lely, Kneller and Reynolds, including ladies at Charles II's Court - young, fair, delicately complexioned and far from innocent.

OTHER QUARTERS TO VISIT

★★CHELSEA (FGZ)

The completion of the Embankment in 1874 removed the riverside community atmosphere evoked in paintings by Rowlandson, Turner and Whistler and which **Sir Thomas More** must have known and loved when in 1523 he came upriver and bought a parcel of land at the water's edge, where he built a large house. Henry VIII, who often visited More until the latter's fall from favour and execution in 1535, built a riverside **palace** in 1537, the site of which is now occupied by 19-26 Cheyne Walk, dating from *c*1765. Chelsea has long attracted artists, architects, writers, actors... or rather, those prosperous enough to be able to occupy the elegant and distinguished houses on **Cheyne Walk**★ (GZ) and the streets perpendicular to the river. One such was the historian **Thomas Carlyle**, whose modest Queen Anne home at 24 Cheyne Row, **Carlyle's House** (FZ), can be visited today.

Chelsea Old Church (FZ), dating back to pre-Norman times, was seriously bombed in 1941; however, reconstructed in 1950-58, it still has its 13C chancel and early 14C chapels, the south one remodelled by Sir Thomas More in 1528. The nave and tower have been rebuilt in the original style of 1670. The **National Army Museum**★ (GZ) tells the story of the British Army from the formation of the Yeoman of the Guard by Henry VII on Bosworth Field in 1485, right up to the present day.

★★ **The Royal Hospital** (GZ). — The hospital was founded by King Charles II in 1682 as a retreat for veterans of the regular army who had become unfit for duty, either after 20 years' service or as a result of wounds. The provision of a hospital, rather than some system of pensions was undoubtedly inspired by the Hôtel des Invalides in Paris, founded by Louis XIV in 1670 about which Charles II had received glowing reports. The Latin inscription in Figure Court reads: "For the succour and relief of old soldiers and men broken by War. Founded by Charles II enlarged by James II and long completed by William and Mary, King and Queen in the year of our Lord - 1692".

Wren produced a quadrangular plan with a main court open to the south towards the river and the grounds, in which, every summer, the **Chelsea Flower Show** is held, attracting thousands of visitors over three days; he expanded it by abutting courts to east and west, always leaving one side open. The main entrance is beneath the lantern-crowned octagon porch in the north range of the original **Figure Court**, after the classical statue of Charles II by **Grinling Gibbons** at the centre. From the octagon porch, steps rise to the **Chapel** and **Great Hall**, both panelled beneath tall rounded windows. The Chapel has a barrel vault decorated with plasterwork and, at the end, a domed, painted apse by Ricci. The Hall is decorated with an 18C mural of Charles II on horseback before the hospital.

The "Old Soldiers" themselves can be seen in their blue un-dress or even scarlet full-dress uniforms, out and about on the nearby streets.

★BLOOMSBURY (JKY)

The once residential area with its many squares is dominated by two learned institutions, the British Museum *(qv)* and the ever-expanding London University. The development of Bloomsbury Square in 1661 brought a new concept in social planning; the 4th Earl of Southampton erected houses for the well-to-do around three sides of a square, a mansion for himself on the fourth, northern side and a network of service streets all around with a market nearby. A century later, in 1775, the elegant **Bedford Square★★** (JY) was developed by Gertrude, widow of the 4th Duke of Bedford. It is still complete, with its three-storey brick terrace houses with rounded doorways and first-floor balconies. Other squares, now partly incorporated into the University precinct, followed in the 19C. The most famous residents of these squares were the **Bloomsbury Group** of writers, artists and philosophers, loosely centred around the figures of Virginia Woolf, Vanessa Bell, Roger Fry and others in the 1920s.

⊘ The **Percival David Foundation of Chinese Art★** (JY) *53 Gordon Square,* displays the world-famous collection of Chinese porcelain assembled between the wars by Sir Percival David.

★HOLBORN (JKY)

The medieval manors at this former crossroads north of the City have been transformed into Lincoln's Inn and Gray's Inn - two of the four Inns of Court. The fields where beasts once grazed are less in extent but still open; on the north side of Lin-
⊘ coln's Inn Fields, at no 13, stands **Sir John Soane's Museum★** (KY) housing the highly individual collection of the architect (1753-1837) of the Bank of England - (alas replaced in the 20C). The museum was originally the home of Sir John Soane and houses a collection of Classical sculpture, architectural fragments, drawings, prints and paintings.

⊘ **Lincoln's Inn★★** (KY) as we see it today dates back to the late 15C with its buildings of brick with stone decoration, organised on the self-contained collegiate plan of inter-communicating courts. The Old Hall dates from 1490, the Old Buildings are Tudor, refaced in 1609, while the Chapel was rebuilt in 1620-23.
Gray's Inn★ (KY) dates from the 14C in its foundation, from the 16C in its buildings, many of which, however, have had to be renewed since the war. A remarkable survival from the late 16C is the row of **half-timbered houses** (1586-96), forming the
⊘ front of **Staple Inn★** (KY), as is the **Old Curiosity Shop** (KY) - *Portsmouth Street, south-west corner of Lincoln's Inn Fields,* a little half-timbered house said to be one of the oldest in London (c1500).

★MAYFAIR (GHY)

It is difficult to believe that the most exclusive quarter in London for fashion, elegant hotels and art is named after the annual cattle and general fair held in May, but which became so unruly and the neighbourhood so notorious, that it was officially closed in 1706! Today **Piccadilly★★** (GYZ), the delightful **Burlington Arcade★★** (1819) (HY), **Bond Street★** (GY) and **Savile Row** (GHY) are just some of the names synonymous with traditional high-quality tailoring. New Bond Street is also famous for its art auctioneers, **Chappell's, Phillips'** and of course, **Sotheby's.**

⊘ **Burlington House★** (HY), built by the 1st Earl of Burlington, was remodelled and refaced in 1715-16 in the Palladian style by the 3rd Earl, himself an architect, with Colen Campbell. The second of the house's 19C remodellings gave it its present neo-Italian
⊘ Renaissance appearance; it is now the home of the **Royal Academy** which holds its Summer Exhibition here every June.

★SOUTHWARK (LMZ)

The village on the south bank of the Thames, opposite the City, was in Anglo-Saxon times the *sud werk*, or south work against attacking land forces. It became famous and infamous in the 16C as a popular location for theatres - notably Shakespeare's "Globe" (LY) (1599) - and brothels. Few of the old buildings have survived, with the exception of the fine galleried **George Inn★** (LZ), rebuilt in 1676 after a fire, though
⊘ only the south range remains today, and the **Cathedral★★** *(qv).* The earliest work to be seen is the fragment of a Norman arch in the north wall. From the 13C have remained the massive piers supporting the central tower and the intimately proportioned Early English **chancel.** The **altar screen** appears in sumptuous Gothic glory; presented by Bishop Fox in 1520, it remained empty until 1905 when statues were carved to fill the niches. The nave was rebuilt in 1890-97 to harmonise with the chancel. Notable features are the **Harvard Chapel** in the north chancel aisle, the 1616 **monument** to Alderman Humble and his wives *(north of altar screen)* and the 12 **bosses** rescued from the 15C wooden roof which collapsed in 1830 *(on west wall at end of north aisle).*

ADDITIONAL MUSEUMS AND GALLERIES

★★★BRITISH MUSEUM (JY)

⊘ When Sir Hans Sloane's collection was bequeathed to the nation in 1753 Parliament was encouraged to found the British Museum. Already in the vaults in Westminster lay Sir Robert Cotton's (1570-1631) priceless collection of medieval manuscripts and the old Royal Library of 12 000 volumes assembled by monarchs since Tudor times. As more and more collections were presented a separate building became necessary. Montagu House was bought with money raised in a lottery and the Museum opened in 1759. Exhibits were displayed unlabelled, causing Cobbett to call the museum "the old curiosity shop".

To house the burgeoning collection Smirke produced plans which culminated in the replacement of Montagu House by the present building and its later additions. The early sequence of acquisitions, increased in the 19C and 20C by finds by archaeologists attached to the museum, brought the BM its reputation as one of the greatest centres of world antiquities. Notable among the Egyptian antiquities are the **mummies** and the **Rosetta Stone.** The collection of Western Asiatic antiquities is particularly wide-ranging, while the Greek and Roman antiquities include the **Elgin Marbles** (sculptures from the Parthenon) and the exquisite Roman **Portland Vase.** The Oriental collection with its fine T'ang horses is no less significant. In the Prehistoric and Romano-British and Medieval sections admire the craftsmanship of the shields, helmets and delicate golden torcs. Reminders of Roman Britain are the 4C silver set of tableware, the **Mildenhall Treasure,** then the mid-12C ivory chessmen and **Royal Gold Cup.**

British Library. — A separate institution since 1973, the library still occupies certain galleries and the round domed **Reading Room** opened in 1857 to seat 400 readers. In the Grenville and King's Library on the ground floor are found **Magna Carta,** the Gutenberg Bible as well as literary autographs, musical manuscripts, English and Continental illuminated manuscripts.

★★ WALLACE COLLECTION (GY) *Hertford House, Manchester Square*

⊘ The gathering of one of the world's finer collections of 18C French art was the life's work of the 4th Marquess of Hertford (1800-70) who lived mostly in Paris at his small château, Bagatelle, in the Bois de Boulogne. He greatly increased the family collection of Italian masters, 17C Dutch painting, 18C French furniture and Sèvres porcelain and bought extensively the 18C French painters **Watteau, Boucher** and **Fragonard.** His son Richard Wallace (1818-90), founder and benefactor of the Hertford British Hospital in Paris, having added yet more to the collection, finally brought it to England, where his widow subsequently left it to the nation in 1900.

★★ COURTAULD INSTITUTE GALLERIES (KY) *Somerset House*

⊘ Since 1990 the Courtauld Institute Galleries have been housed above the gateway in the Strand Block of Somerset House; the **Fine Rooms,** which are notable for their proportions and handsome plaster ceilings, originally housed three learned societies - the Royal Society, the Antiquaries and the Royal Academy. Somerset House, which was built from 1776-86 of Portland stone, was designed by **Sir William Chambers,** a founder member and treasurer of the Royal Society, as a square of terraced houses overlooking a central courtyard; the south front is supported on a row of massive arches which in the 18C were at the river's edge.
The galleries' collection consists of major art bequests to London University: Samuel Courtauld's private collection of **Impressionists** including canvases by Manet *(Bar at the Folies-Bergère),* Degas, Bonnard, Gauguin (Tahitian scenes), Van Gogh *(Peach Trees in Blossom, Self-Portrait with Bandaged Ear),* Cézanne *(Lake at Annecy)* and Seurat; the Princes Gate Collection, bequeathed to the nation by Count Antoine Seilern, including 30 oils by **Rubens** and six drawings by **Michelangelo** as well as works by Breugel, Leonardo, Tiepolo, Dürer, Rembrandt, Bellini, Tintoretto and Kokoschka; paintings of the Italian Primitive school and of the Renaissance to the 18C donated by Thomas Gambier-Parry and Viscount Lee of Fareham; paintings by the **Bloomsbury Group** gifted by Roger Fry (1866-1934).

★★ MUSEUM OF LONDON (LY)

⊘ In an interesting modern building the museum presents the story of London from prehistory to the present day, with exhibits as various as the sculptures from the Roman temple of Mithras, medieval pilgrim badges, the Cheapside Hoard of Jacobean jewellery, a diorama of the Great Fire, the doors from Newgate Gaol, 19C shops and interiors, the Lord Mayor's Coach, souvenirs of the women's suffrage movement... The development of domestic life and public utility services are illustrated as well as political and fashionable London.

★ IMPERIAL WAR MUSEUM (KZ) *Lambeth Road, Southwark*

⊘ The museum, founded in 1917, was transferred in 1936 to the present building, formerly the Bethlem Royal Hospital ("Bedlam"), which was designed in 1812-15 with its dome and giant portico added in 1846 by Sydney Smirke.
The museum in no sense glorifies war, but honours those who served. A wide range of weapons and equipment is on display: armoured fighting vehicles, field guns and small arms, together with models, decorations, uniforms, posters and photographs, as well as a selection from the museum's outstanding collection based on the work of two generations of Official War Artists.

ADDITIONAL SIGHTS

★★★ **The Royal Botanic Gardens, Kew** (AX). — The finest botanic gardens in the land
⊘ were begun in 1756 by **Sir William Chambers,** at the request of Augusta, Princess of Wales. The same architect designed the **Orangery★** , the three small classical temples and in 1761 the 163ft - 50m high ten-storey **Pagoda★**. As the gardens grew, more buildings were added, notably Decimus Burton's **Palm House★★** in 1848, which has recently been completely refurbished. In 1899 Burton completed the **Temperate House★** , which contains camellias, rain forest and dragon trees.
In 1987 The Princess of Wales opened the **Princess of Wales Conservatory,** a steel and glass diamond-shaped structure in which ten different tropical habitats ranging from mangrove swamp to sand desert are created and maintained by computer.

Extensive work has largely repaired the cruel losses suffered at Kew, as in Richmond Park and at the Royal Horticultural Society's Garden at Wisley, during the freak hurricane which hit southern England on 16-17 October 1987.

◉ **Kew Palace★★**, close to the river, was built for the London merchant Samuel Fortrey in 1631. The dark red brick building with distinctive Dutch attic gables was leased by George II for Queen Caroline about 1730 and purchased by George III in 1781. The interior is, therefore, that of a small country house of George III's time, with panelled rooms downstairs and intimate family portraits by Gainsborough, Zoffany and others upstairs.

★★**Syon Park** (AX). — The colonnaded east front is visible across the river from Kew ◉ Gardens. The Lord Protector, Duke of Somerset, built a Tudor mansion on the site of a former monastery, given to him by his nephew Edward VI in 1547; five years later he was charged with treason and executed. During the next hundred years many owners of the house were beheaded and when, in less troubled times, the house passed to Hugh Percy, 1st Earl of Northumberland, in 1762, he felt it needed remodelling. **Robert Adam** richly ornamented and furnished the house, while **Capability Brown** re-designed the gardens and extended them to the river. A number of notable Stuart portraits by Van Dyck, Lely and others further embellish the interior.

★★**Osterley Park** (AX). — Osterley is the place to see **Robert Adam** interior decoration ◉ at its most complete - room after room just as he designed them, in every detail from ceilings and walls to the furniture. What had started life as a late 15C Tudor brick manor house was transformed into a mansion by Sir Thomas Gresham, founder of the Royal Exchange, in 1562. In 1711 the mansion was purchased by Francis Child, a clothier's son from Wiltshire who had sought and found his fortune as a City banker. He was 69 when he bought Osterley and never lived there. It was his grandson, Francis, who commissioned Adam to transform the mansion, achieving the rich interior we admire today between 1761 and 1780.

★**Chiswick House** (BX). — A Jacobean mansion was purchased by the 1st Earl of ◉ Burlington in 1682. The 3rd Earl, Richard Boyle (1695-1753), a generous host and patron, made the first alterations and additions. On his return from his second Grand Tour (1714-19) he designed a Palladian villa (1727-29) to display his works of art and to entertain his friends. **William Kent** (1686-1748) a follower of Inigo Jones and Burlington's protegé, was responsible for much of the interior decoration and the gardens.
The lower floor - octagon hall, lobbies and library - now displays a video, engravings, sculptures and other material about the creation and restoration of the house and garden. On the principal floor the **Dome Saloon**, its eight walls punctuated by gold-highlighted doors and Classical busts, rises by way of an ochre entablature to a diamond-patterned dome.

★★**Kenwood House** (The Iveagh Bequest) (BV). — William Murray, younger son of a Scot-◉ tish peer, acquired Kenwood, a 50-year-old brick house on the north side of Hampstead Heath, in 1754, two years before becoming Lord Chief Justice and Earl of Mansfield. In 1764 he invited fellow Scot **Robert Adam** to enlarge and embellish the house. Adam transformed it, outside and in, leaving a strong imprint of his style. Particularly notable are the **Library★★** and the very fine collection of paintings.

★**Fenton House** (BV). — South of the Heath this 1693 red brick house is Hamp-◉ stead's finest, being one of its earliest and largest. Apart from the furniture, pictures and 18C porcelain, the house is particularly noted for the **Benton Fletcher collection★** of early keyboard instruments, ranging in date from 1540 to 1805.

★**Dulwich** (CX). — The houses reflect the transition from 17C manorial village to small country town where 18-19C merchants chose to reside. Commuter trains have made it into a south London suburb yet it remains rural in character. In 1613 the great actor **Edward Alleyn** (for whose acting style Shakespeare voiced his dislike in Hamlet's counsel to the player king) having married well but finding himself without an heir, established a charity for ''six poor men and six poor women and the education of twelfe poor children'' which grew to become the famous Dulwich College.
◉ **Dulwich Picture Gallery★** (CX M²), is the oldest public art gallery in England. Its origins were in the 39 pictures which Alleyn had collected, later increased by 80 likenesses of contemporary authors and players. In 1811 a legacy of 400 pictures necessitated the building of a new gallery which was designed by **Sir John Soane**. This same building houses a unique collection of Old Masters including works by Rembrandt, Poussin, Murillo, Claude, Rubens, Van Dyck and Cuyp.

★★★**London Zoo** (CV). — A very different London sight is the zoo which the London ◉ Zoological Society opened on a 5 acre - 2ha site in Regent's Park in 1828, at the instigation of Sir Stamford Raffles. Today the Zoo has spread to cover 36 acres - 144ha and has a staff of more than 100 caring for approximately 8 000 animals of 900 species. Many new and innovative buildings have been constructed to house the animals, and the emphasis is now placed on breeding endangered animals and foreign conservation projects.

The most famous of all classic flat races, the **Derby** *is in its third century. It was run for the first time in 1780 on the* **Epsom Downs** *where racing had been held for over a century and named for the 12th Earl of Derby. Limited to three-year-old colts and fillies the Derby is run over a 1 1/2 mile course designed to test the speed and stamina of the thoroughbreds. From small and elitist beginnings it has become a highly popular event attended by hundreds of thousands and watched by millions more on television.*

★★★ **LONGLEAT** Wiltshire

Michelin Map ███ N 30 or Atlas G Britain p 8

This grand Elizabethan house, in a glorious wooded lakeside setting, is built in golden stone in the Italian Renaissance style, rising through three tiers of windows to a skyline of balustrading and ornamental chimneystacks *(photograph p 31)*. The grounds consist of a park landscaped by **Capability Brown** in 1757, formal **flower gardens**, developed since Brown's day, a narrow-gauge railway, a maze and the **Safari Park**, most famous for its lions.

The house is still owned by the descendants of Sir John Thynne, who completed the building in 1580 on the site of an Augustinian priory, bought from Henry VIII in 1540. Its contents reflect the range of interests of the unbroken line of the Thynnes, from Sir John to the present Marquess of Bath - the family tree from 1215 is at the foot of the Grand Staircase. In the 19C, for example, the 4th Marquess had seven rooms along the east front Italianised after his extensive Continental travels.

⊘ **TOUR** *time: 3/4 hour*

Beneath the fine **hammerbeam roof** of the Great Hall are galleries displaying the arms of Sir John Thynne, Jacobean panelling hung with trophies and hunting scenes by the 18C painter John Wootton and a splendid pillared fireplace dating from about 1575-80. The Ante-Library, one of the rooms transformed by Crace in the 1870s, is furnished in French Empire style. The 1971 portrait of the 6th Marquess is by Graham Sutherland. The Breakfast Room, hung with yellow damask and furnished with Chippendale-style chairs set around the table, contains several family portraits. In the Lower Dining Room the table gleams with a gilt 17C **steeple cup**, silver, crystal and Sèvres china. The furniture is of Portuguese ebony and ebonised mahogany. On the panelled walls hang portraits of Sir John Thynne and the 1st Viscount. The walls of the State Dining Room are covered with Cordova leather and hung with 17C portraits. The table stands arrayed with much 18 and 19C silver. The 90ft - 27m saloon, originally the Elizabethan Long Gallery, with fine views over the park, has a massive marble **fireplace** by Crace after one in the Doge's Palace in Venice. The ceiling of the State Drawing Room is also by Crace, rich with panels after Titian and Veronese by Caldera. 17C Genoese velvet adds to the splendour, as do the various pieces of 18C French furniture.

★ **LUDLOW** Shropshire   Pop 7 496

Michelin Map ███ L 26 or Atlas G Britain p 26

Ludlow is a Norman "planned town". One-time seat of the powerful Mortimer family, the castle passed into royal ownership with the accession of Edward IV. The town prospered in the 16C and 17C because of its role as seat of the Council for Wales and the Marches. **Ludlow Festival**, held annually during the last week of June and the first week of July, has as centrepiece a Shakespeare play performed in the inner bailey of the castle.

★ **Ludlow Castle.** — Begun shortly after the Domesday survey, by Roger de Lacy,
⊘ and built in stone quarried on the fine defensive site protected by the River Teme and low limestone cliffs. After Roger Mortimer had used his power to topple Edward II in 1326, he virtually ruled the country from the castle; the most powerful and perhaps the richest man in all England. He completed the block of buildings containing the **Great Hall** and Solar, one of the leading palaces of the day. **Arthur, Prince of Wales** brought his young bride **Catherine of Aragon** to honeymoon in Ludlow in the winter of 1501 and it was here that Arthur died early the following year. The chapel with its richly ornamented west door is one of only five round chapel naves still standing in Britain. The first performance of **Milton's** masque *Comus* was given in the Great Hall in 1634.

★ **St Laurence's Church.** — The tower dominates the surrounding countryside and is mentioned in the collection of poems *A Shropshire Lad* by *AE* **Housman** (1859-1936), whose ashes are buried in the churchyard. The church was enlarged in 1199 - a reflection on the prosperity of the town - and parts of it are in a style transitional between Norman and Early English. The north transept has Decorated features and its construction must reflect the recovery of Ludlow from the Black Death, which reduced the population by a third in 1349. Nave and chancel roofs date from about 1440. The decoration of the latter, though 19C, is based on surviving fragments of the original colour. Twenty eight **misericords★** in the choir stalls date from 1447. Allegorical scenes intermingle with Yorkist and Lancastrian devices, for though the king, Henry IV, was a Lancastrian, the town's manorial lord was Richard, Duke of York; (political expediency was ever wise in troubled times !).

★ **Feathers Hotel.** — Described by Pevsner as 'the prodigy of timber-framed houses where everything of motifs that was available has been lavished on the façade'. An older house was re-fronted and enlarged in 1619. The balcony was added for electioneering purposes in the mid-1840s, and the whole was restored in 1970.

EXCURSIONS

★ **Stokesay Castle.** — *6 miles - 10km north by the A49.* Stokesay is the best
⊘ preserved example in England of a 13C fortified manor house. The hall, with a fine roof of shaped and tapered tree trunks was built by Lawrence of Ludlow, a wool merchant who bought the property from the Say family in about 1281. The solar has a notable stone fireplace and peepholes into the hall below. Fittings, including a fine Flemish overmantel, date from the 17C.

Feathers Hotel, Ludlow

Croft Castle and Berrington Hall. — *22 miles - 35km round tour. Leave Ludlow by the B4361 to the south and then take the B4362 to the right.*

⊘**Croft Castle.** — Home of the Croft family for all but 170 of the years since Domesday. The walls and towers of this Welsh Marcher castle are mainly 14-15C, while the central structure is 18C. The interior is finely decorated Georgian Gothic, with notable plasterwork ceilings. The park is famous for its ancient trees.

The **church of St Michael and All Angels** was 'enlarged or more beautifully made' in 1515, with box-pews, some Jacobean panelling and a splendid **altar tomb** of Sir Richard Croft (d 1509) and his wife, the effigies of which are probably portraits of the deceased.

Return to the B4361 and at Luston turn left in the direction of the A49.

★**Berrington Hall.** — Begun in 1778 by Thomas Harley, a contractor who supplied pay and
⊘clothing to the British Army in America. The architect was **Henry Holland**, son-in-law of Lancelot Capability Brown who laid out the gardens and lake. Thomas Harley's daughter married the son of Admiral Lord Rodney in 1781 and the original plans for a gentleman's modest country house were much altered in consequence. The interior today is a fitting setting for the remarkable collection of French and other furniture, paintings and objets d'art.

Return to Ludlow by the A49.

★ **MALMESBURY** Wiltshire   Pop 4 220
Michelin Map ▩ 403 N 29 or Atlas G Britain p 17

At the centre of this market town, a prosperous weaving centre until the 18C, is a fine 40ft - 12m stone **market cross★★** dating from 1490. On the spur of the hill stands the abbey.

★**Abbey.** — St Aldhelm (639-709), one of the first abbots of this 7C foundation, lies
⊘buried here. The great historian **William of Malmesbury** (1095-1143) was the abbey librarian; the present buildings were begun in the late 12C, and in the 14C the church extended 320ft - 98m from east to west, possessing a mighty spired crossing tower and big square west tower. The crossing tower fell about 1530, the west tower shortly after. With the Dissolution everything from the crossing eastward was allowed to disappear; the nave was saved and given to the town as the parish church in 1541.

South Porch, Malmesbury Abbey

Porch. — The masterpiece of the abbey is the south porch, an outstanding example of Norman sculpture and decoration; the eight orders around the outer doorway vibrate with geometrical patterning and Biblical figures (defaced). Inside, on the lunettes, are Apostles surmounted by a flying angel and on the inner door tympanum a Christ in glory.

Interior. — The Norman pillars with scalloped capitals support pointed arches and a **triforium** of rounded bays with zig-zag carving. On the south side note the **watching loft** from where the abbot could follow the service beyond the chancel screen.

★ Isle of MAN — Pop 65 000

Michelin Map **402** G 21 or Atlas G Britain p 42

''Whichever way you throw me, I stand'' - so says the motto beneath the three-legged symbol of this mountainous island in the Irish Sea. Manx identity is complex: settled by Celts, then by Norsemen, ruled by Scotland then by England. Its own language, Manx, akin to Gaelic, is now, alas, extinct, though the famous tailless cat survives. Not part of the United Kingdom, but a British dependency, it has its own laws, presented each year to an open-air parliament of the people; this 1 000 year-old descendant of the Norse *Thingvollr* (''assembly field'') is held at a central point on the island, Tynwald Green, a site with prehistoric associations.

The lowland pattern of unspoiled farmland, small fields bounded by stone walls or high hedgebanks, gives way as the land rises to wild open moorland, bright in late summer with gorse and heather. From the highest summit Snaefell (2 036ft - 621m), six ancient kingdoms can be seen - England, Scotland, Ireland and Wales, Man itself - and the Kingdom of Heaven. Most of the 100 miles - 160km of coastline is untouched by modern intrusions and much of it is of exceptional beauty, offering breezy clifftop walks or the delights of pretty beaches.

Manx transport. — The island still attracts multitudes of pleasure-seekers, mainly from the north of England. Its halcyon days of mass tourism were, however, the late 19C and early 20C and from this time dates an extensive network of vintage transport. Horse trams - nicknamed ''toastracks'' - ply the Douglas promenades, narrow-gauge steam railways serve the south and, most remarkable of all, double-track electric tramways lead from Douglas along the high cliffs to the northern resort of Ramsey and to the very summit of Snaefell.

Isle of Man TT Races. — Motor cyclists flock to the island each year as they have done since the first Tourist Trophy race was held here in 1907.

Douglas. — Pop 19 944. The great sweep of Victorian and Edwardian hotels facing promenades and the sandy bay give the island's capital an unmistakable identity among British resorts. Up the steep rise behind the seafront is the **Manx Museum**, ''the treasure house of the island's story'' (RH Kinvig). It has good examples of early Christian sculpture including the unique 9C **Calf of Man Crucifixion**, while the Folk-Life Galleries include a reconstructed Manx farmhouse.

EXCURSIONS FROM DOUGLAS

Laxey and **Snaefell.** — *20 miles - 32km return by the Manx Electric railway. Allow 5 hours for the return trip.*

From the eastern end of Douglas seafront the original tramcars follow a cliff-top route before turning inland to the junction at Laxey. While the main line continues through even more spectacular coastal scenery to Ramsey, the branch diverges here for Snaefell summit.

Walk about 1/2 mile - 1km up the valley.

★★**Laxey Wheel.** — This splendid monument of the industrial age, built in 1854 and now one of the emblems of the island, overlooks the Laxey valley, once the scene of intense lead and silver mining activity.

The quantity of water needed to drive the giant 72ft - 22m diameter wheel is collected by an extensive network of artificial channels. 95 vertiginous steps spiral to the top of the tower from which the water is fed to the wheel. The power is transmitted by a rod running along a viaduct to the head of the 1 640ft - 500m deep shaft which the wheel once drained at a rate of 270 gallons - 1 225 litres a minute.

Return to the station

★ **Snaefell.** — Another vintage tramcar climbs doggedly up the side of the glen, then onto the summit slopes of the mountain, terminating at the café just below the summit. Choose a clear day to enjoy stupendous **views**★★★ of the countries fringing the Irish Sea.

The South West. — *About 20 miles - 32km. Leave Douglas by either of the main roads southswestwards and subsequently follow local signs. Alternatively, all of the destinations as far as Port Erin may be reached by the Isle of Man Steam Railway.*

Castletown. — Pop 3 141. The streets and squares of the little harbour town, the island's capital until 1869, are gathered around the compact and well-preserved
⊘ **castle**. In the boat-cellar of the **Nautical Museum**, where she was constructed in 1791, is the clinker-built *Peggy.* Above her is the strange Cabin Room, built in imitation of the stern cabin of a large sailing ship of Nelson's time.

Port St Mary. — Pop 1 572. A fishing port with a south-facing sandy beach and room for many pleasure craft.

Port Erin. — Pop 2 812. The terminus of the railway, with a small Railway Museum and the aquarium of the Marine Biological Station. The site is perfect; a curving sandy beach set in the deep bay, protected by high cliffs prolonged on either side to form some of the island's finest coastal scenery.

★ **Cregneash Folk Museum.** — Crofting traditions survived longest in the remoter south-
⊘ west of the island. They are sensitively evoked in this tiny village where a number of buildings have been carefully restored.

Calf of Man. — Uninhabited, save by lighthouse keepers and bird sanctuary wardens, the island is separated from the Isle of Man proper by the turbulent waters of the Calf Sound.

★ **MANCHESTER** Greater Manchester   Pop 437 612

Michelin Map 402 N 23 or Atlas G Britain p 39

Manchester grew from a Roman settlement and played a colourful part in both Civil War and Jacobite eras. By the "Forty Five", Manchester merchants had discovered that political faction interfered with trade. They paid lip-service to the Stuart cause, but enjoyed the prosperity that Hanoverian rule had brought. Trade with the American colonies brought the city its heyday and Manchester became the centre of the rapidly expanding cotton industry. Though the smoking chimneys of the cotton mills have long gone, Manchester today still has many fine buildings erected by the Victorian successors to those hard-headed Georgian merchants. The city has developed into a major provincial centre of finance. There is much for the visitor to see and do in today's Manchester.

★ **CASTLEFIELD HERITAGE PARK** (Z) *South end of Deansgate*

Britain's first urban heritage park, Castlefield traces the development of Manchester from Roman times. The remains of the **Roman fort** became known as "the castle in the field" and the north gate and part of the west wall have been reconstructed on their original site. In the 18C Castlefield became the centre of a canal system, which had started in 1761 with the Duke of Bridgewater's canal.
Liverpool Road Station, opened as the world's first passenger station by the Liverpool and Manchester Railway in 1830, has been developed as the Museum of Science and Industry.

⊘ **Museum of Science and Industry** (Z M¹). — This comprehensive museum gives a fascinating view of Manchester's industrial heritage. The exhibits are regrouped thematically in a series of halls. Start with the **Lower Byrom Street Warehouse** with its exhibitions on printing, textiles and machine tools as well as its hands-on science centre, **Xperiment**. In the **Power Hall** the locomotives such as the H W Garratt no 2352 take pride of place. In the buildings lining Liverpool Road are exhibits on the history of the city and an underground sewer. Beyond in the Liverpool Road Station the first-class booking hall has been recreated with beyond an exhibition on the Liverpool and Manchester Railway (1830).
The **National Electricity Gallery** describes the role of electricity in the home and in the development of industry.
The final section, the **Air and Space Gallery**, occupies the former city exhibition hall beyond Lower Byrom Street and illustrates the history of flight from the exploits of the earliest flying machines to the space age. The enormous four-engined Avro Shackleton reconnaissance aeroplane was only one of the many famous aircraft manufactured by the Manchester aircraft company, Avro.

⊘ **Granada Studios Tour** (Z). — The tour takes visitors behind the scenes of television to discover for example the Sherlock Holmes and Coronation Street sets.

ADDITIONAL SIGHTS

Chetham's Hospital and Library (Y). — Founded in 1653 as the result of the will of local merchant, Humphrey Chetham, the hospital, originally a school for 40 poor boys, and library, one of the oldest in the country, are housed in the domestic buildings of the former chantry college. It is now a school for young musicians.

★ **Cathedral** (Y). — The church, refounded as a chantry college in 1421, became the cathedral of the new diocese in 1847. Six bays form the nave - the widest of any church in England - and six the choir. The **choir screen** is a unique piece of medieval wood carving. In the choir itself the **stalls and canopies**★ are beautifully carved. The **misericords** c 1500, show a strong similarity in style and their humorous depiction of medieval life to the contemporary ones in Beverley and Ripon.

Royal Exchange. (Y T). — Manchester owes its prosperity to "King Cotton". Raw cotton imported via the port of Liverpool and the canal network, a pure water supply from the Pennines, a high degree of humidity in the air and a large available working population were the factors responsible for the rapid growth of the cotton and ancillary industries. English cotton was sold throughout the world and the Manchester cotton exchange was at the very nerve centre of this trade.
Inside the exchange the prices of cotton on the day the Market last traded are still shown on the board. Today this immense hall is partly occupied by the 700-seat Royal Exchange Theatre.

⊙ **St Ann's Church** (Z). — Founded 1709, consecrated 1712 it is a good example of a Renaissance church, but returning towards simpler, sterner classical architecture. Fine Georgian mouldings border the plaster ceiling, and in the Lady Chapel is the Queen Anne style **altar table**, given by the founder, Lady Anne Bland.

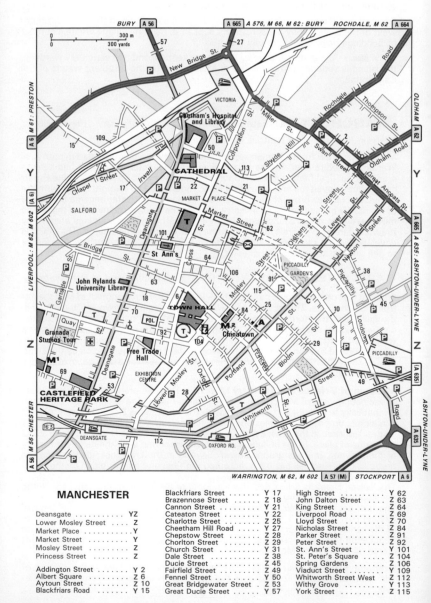

John Rylands University Library (Z). — The building was designed in late Gothic style by Basil Champneys and opened in 1900 to house the library founded in memory of a successful textile manufacturer. The library possesses many early printed books - 3 000 of which are dated before 1501 - and manuscripts from the collections of the Earls Spencer and Crawford.

Further along in Peter Street is the **Free Trade Hall** (Z), third on the site and home of the Hallé Orchestra. Sir Thomas Beecham and Sir John Barbirolli were amongst its best known conductors, and a ''triptych'' statue of Barbirolli in action is in the sculpture hall of the Town Hall *(qv)*.
Manchester can be justly proud of the strongly held principles of Free Trade which inspired the building of the Hall. The site of the hall, known as St Peter's Fields, was the scene of the **Peterloo Massacre** on 16 August 1819, when a crowd, assembled to demand Parliamentary reform and repeal of the Corn Laws, was dispersed by cavalry, with 11 dead and hundreds injured.
At the end of the streets to the right rises the imposing arched form of the G-MEX Centre. Sir John Fowler's 1876 single-span Central Station has been developed as G-MEX, an international exhibition and events centre.
The nearby refurbished hotel, typical of 19C grandeur, was where Rolls met Royce for the first time.

★ **Town Hall** (Z). — Designed in Gothic style by Alfred Waterhouse and built from 1868 to 1877, it is one of the greatest civic buildings of the Victorian era. Its tower with octagonal top stage rises 286ft - 87m above the pedestrian area of Albert Square. Two staircases lead from the low vaulted entrance hall to the **Great Hall**, with its hammerbeam roof and twelve Pre-Raphaelite style murals of Manchester events, painted by Ford Madox Brown 1876-88

★ **City Art Gallery** (Z M²). — The interior, recently restored to its 19C glory, displays an interesting Pre-Raphaelite collection with works by Millais, Hunt, Rossetti and Ford Madox Brown's *Work* (1852) illustrating the various classes of a developing industrial society. Note the works of Stubbs, Turner and Constable. The industrial landscapes of the North were captured with sensitivity by L S Lowry (1887-1976). His studio has been recreated on the ground floor.

Behind the gallery is Manchester's Chinese quarter.

Chinatown (Z). — Nearly 20 000 Chinese make the Manchester community, with Liverpool's, two of the largest outside London, and they have made the area around Faulkner Street their own with vibrant Chinese decorations, gardens and murals and the huge **Imperial Chinese Archway** (A). The Chinese Arts Centre in Charlotte Street illustrates Chinese art, crafts and customs.

ENVIRONS

Lowry Centre. — *Salford Museum and Art Gallery, Peel Park, Salford. Leave by the A6* (Y).
The centre has a large collection of works by **L S Lowry** (1887-1976), whose ''matchstick'' figure paintings provide a wry perspective on life in the industrial North. He found subject matter in the bleak surroundings of the manufacturing towns *(Industrial Landscape* and two versions of *Coming from the Mill)* and his works complement Dickens' accounts of industrial life. People also fascinated this lonely man and his portrayals are uncompromising and poignant *(The Cripples, Three Figures* and *The Funeral Party)*.

Ordsall Hall. — *Taylorson Street, Salford. Leave by the A6* (Y).
This building, with 16C timber-framed section and brick west range from 1639, sits incongruously in the middle of a modern housing development. It is a period and local history museum.

Jewish Museum. — *Cheetham Hill Road* (Y).
In the former Spanish and Portuguese synagogue (1874), a Victorian building in the Moorish style, the museum traces the history of the city's Jews, from the 18C to today's 40 000 strong community.

★★ **MELLERSTAIN** Borders

Michelin Map **401** M 17 or Atlas G Britain p 50 — 6 miles - 10km northwest of Kelso

The homely proportions of Mellerstain are the one place in Scotland to admire the detailed delicacy of Robert Adam's interiors. Surprisingly this Scottish architect worked on relatively few stately homes in his native land, with the exception of Culzean and Hopetoun House. The exterior has the added attraction of being a combined effort by father and son, with the vernacular wings by William pre-dating Robert's castellated central section by 45 years.
Although less grandiose than Culzean, Osterley or Syon, the interiors have the Adam imprint: meticulous ceilings graced by matching fireplaces, woodwork and furniture. The Library is the undoubted masterpiece. The eye moves from the centrepiece of the delicate ceiling with Zucci roundels to the unifying patterns echoed on the friezes, bookcases, doors and fireplaces.

*The **Maps**, **Red Guides** and **Green Guides** are complementary publications. Use them together.*

★★ MONTACUTE House Somerset

Michelin Map 403 L 31 or Atlas G Britain p 8

Ham Hill, two miles away, provided the warm tawny-ochre and grey-brown stone for Montacute House, the village (pop 734) and the Perpendicular parish church. The three-storeyed Elizabethan mansion was built in 1597-1601 by Sir Edward Phelips, a lawyer, Speaker of the House of Commons (1604) and Master of the Rolls (1611). In 1786 a later Edward Phelips reversed the house, making the main entrance the west front, which he altered by incorporating the porch, pillars and ornamental stone from the demolished Clifton House. The original east front, giving onto the wide terrace and gardens, is flanked by twin pavilions with ogee roofs. The Phelips family fortunes fluctuated and Montacute was let from 1911 - Lord Curzon living there from 1915-25. He entrusted the re-decoration to the novelist Elinor Glyn. In 1931 the house, in a sad state of repair, was purchased by the National Trust.

⊙ **TOUR** *time: 1 1/4 hours*

Ground Floor. — Through the original pre-18C east doorway the visitor enters the screens passage. The **Dining Room** was created by Lord Curzon out of the old buttery from which dishes were carried through the Great Hall and up the stairs to the formal dining room. The Elizabethan chimney-piece bears the **Phelips arms** of 1599. The tapestry of a **knight** against a *millefleurs* background is Flemish. Among the portraits are Mary Queen of Scots, James I and Robert Dudley, Earl of Leicester. The **Great Hall**, the communal living room until after the Restoration, retains its 16C **panelling**, the **stone screen** with archways and pillars with ramshead and leaf capitals and the **heraldic glass** in the window which includes Queen Elizabeth and Sir Edward Phelips' arms. The charming plaster relief or **Skimmington frieze**, at the far end of the hall, showing the ordeals of a henpecked husband, is an early 17C spontaneous expression of local humour.

The **Parlour**, with its original Ham stone fireplace, Elizabethan **panelling** and a **frieze** of nursery animals, contains some fine 18C furniture, amongst which is the beautiful centre table (*c*1800) by Thomas Chippendale the Younger.

In the **Drawing Room** is **Joshua Reynolds'** memorable *Portrait of a Lady.* The **stone staircase** rises by shallow flights around a solid stone pier. The tapestries are 15-16C.

First Floor. — **Lord Curzon's Room** contains a 17C **overmantel** of *King David at Prayer,* an 18C bed, a Dutch oak drop-leaf table and an 18C japanned skeleton mirror. The **Library**, formerly the dining room, is remarkable for its brilliant **heraldic glass** displaying the Phelips arms, those of the sovereign and even those of Phelips' Somerset neighbours and friends at Court. Other features of this former state room are the Portland **stone mantelpiece**, the **plaster frieze** and the Jacobean **inner porch**.

The **Crimson Bedroom**, so-called since the 19C when red flock wallpaper replaced tapestries below the plaster frieze, has a sumptuous oak **four-poster** with the arms of James I.

Top Floor. — The Long Gallery occupies the whole top floor, providing a perfect setting, through 90 portraits (on loan from the National Portrait Gallery), for a panoply of Tudor England and the early Jacobean age.

The formal garden with its exquisite pair of pavilions complements the house perfectly.

★ Isle of MULL Strathclyde   Pop 2 065

Michelin Map 401 B, C 14 or Atlas G Britain p 59
Access: see the current Michelin Red Guide Great Britain and Ireland

Though nowhere more than 26 miles - 42km across, Mull has a deeply-indented coastline some 300 miles - 480km long ranging from rocky cliffs to sandy beaches; while inland, pastoral crofting landscapes contrast with desolate moorlands.

SIGHTS

The roads are twisting and narrow; petrol stations are scarce.

Tobermory. — Pop 843. The main town and ferry port fringes Tobermory Bay, the sea grave of a Venetian treasure galleon that sailed with the Spanish Armada (1588).

⊙ **Torosay Castle.** — *1 1/2 miles - 2.5km south of the ferry port of Craignure.* Torosay (1856) is an example of David Bryce's fluency in Scottish baronial style, perfected by Robert Lorimer's delightful **gardens★**.

⊙ **Duart Castle.** — *3 miles - 5km from Craignure.* Duart, home of the Chief of the **Clan MacLean**, is perched on a rocky crag guarding the Sound of Mull, with magnificent views. In the 18C the original 13C **castle** had been destroyed by the English and fallen into disrepair. Sir Fitzroy MacLean, the 26th Chief, restored the stronghold to its present appearance in 1912. Displays include clan and family mementoes as well as dungeons and a history of the restoration of the castle.

⊙ **Staffa.** — The basaltic island on the western seaboard owes its fame to Mendelssohn's overture *Fingal's Cave*, composed following his visit in 1829.

★ **Isle of Iona.** — *Description p 138. Access from Fionnphort on the Ross of Mull.*

Michelin Map 402 P 19 or Atlas G Britain p 51

Its dramatic site, rich history and the distinctive dialect spoken by its population of hearty and humorous ''Geordies'' give this undisputed capital of England's North East an exceptionally strong identity.

The easily defended bridging point where the Tyne enters its gorge was exploited by the Roman founders of Pons Aelius, one post among many along Hadrian's Wall *(qv),* then by the Normans, whose ''New Castle'' dates from 1080. Later abundant mineral resources, particularly of coal, stimulated trade, manufacturing and engineering; **George Stephenson** (1781-1848) was born nearby as was his son **Robert**, and in the 19C Tyneside became one of the great centres of industrial Britain, dominated by figures like **William Armstrong**, later Lord Armstrong (1810-1900), whose engineering and armament works at Elswick helped equip the world's navies. The region's more recent decline is partly offset by Newcastle's great vigour as a commercial, educational and cultural centre and by public investment in projects like the ultra-modern Metro.

★★ **Site.** — The approach from the south reveals an astonishing **urban panorama**. The separate borough of **Gateshead** is linked to north bank Newcastle by six bridges. Of these, the oldest is **Robert Stephenson's** unusual **High Level Bridge** (Z), of 1848, railway

NEWCASTLE UPON-TYNE					
		Bridge Street	Z 10	Mosley Street	Z 50
		Broad Chare	Z 12	Neville Street	Z 52
		Collingwood Street	Z 25	Northumberland Street	Y 56
Blackett Street	Y	Forth Street	Z 30	Railway Street	Z 60
Eldon Square		George Street	Z 32	Rutherford Street	Z 63
Shopping Centre	YZ	Great North Road	Y 33	St. Mary's Place	Y 65
Grey Street	Z	Jesmond Road	Y 40	St. Nicholas Street	Z 66
Newgate Street	Z	John Dobson Street	Y 41	Scotswood Road	Z 70
Pilgrim Street	Z 57	Leazes Park Road	Y 43	Thornton Street	Z 80
		Low Friar Street	Z 46	Towell Street	Z 81
		Market Street	Z 47	Wellington Street	Y 84

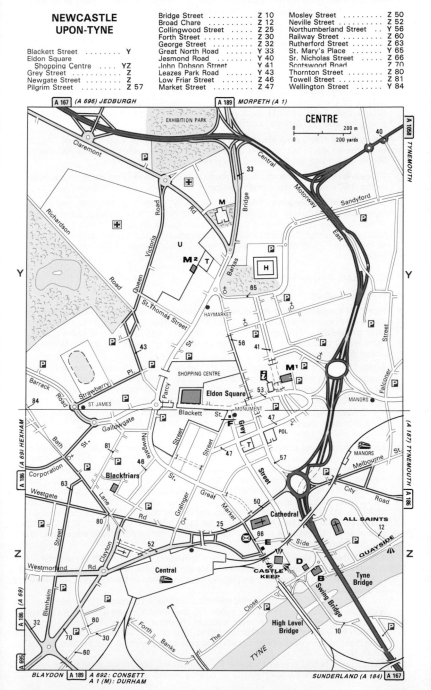

tracks above and roadway below, though the **Swing Bridge** (Z) (1876) designed by Lord Armstrong, brightly painted and nautical-looking, follows the alignment of the original crossing. Buildings of all periods and materials crowd the steep south-facing slopes, culminating in the Castle Keep and the Cathedral's lantern tower (Z).

★**Quayside** (Z). — From this ancient bridgehead the city has slowly spread via steeply-sloping streets and precipitous stairways on to the flatter land to the north. The drama of the townscape is added to by the great presence of the **Tyne Bridge** (Z) of 1928, whose monumental stone piers carry traffic high above tightly-packed Victorian commercial buildings, among which are much older survivors, like the 17C **Guildhall** (B) and the remarkable timber-framed **Bessie Surtees' House** (D). From the quayside the six bridges seen in succession upstream make an outstanding **composition★**. From the top of the slope rise the delicately-proportioned portico and tower of the 18C classical **All Saints Church★** with an unusual elliptical **interior★**.

★**Castle Keep** (Z). — The city took its name from the 'new castle' built by William ⊘ the Conqueror's son, Robert Curthose in 1080. The present keep is all that remains of its 12C successor and is a particularly good example of a Norman keep. From the roof of this massive stone edifice there is an all-embracing panorama of city, river and distant countryside. The complex railway tracks serving the many-arched **Central Station** were driven ruthlessly through the castle precinct in 1848, severing the keep from the picturesque **Black Gate** (E) to the north.

Just over a mile to the east rises the strange outline of the multi-storey flats of the colourful **Byker Wall**, outcome of successful collaboration between architects and the re-housed inhabitants of the old working-class district of Byker.

★**City Centre** (YZ). — Enlightened planning gave 19C Newcastle a new centre of classical dignity, comprising fine civic buildings, great covered markets and shopping arcades and spacious streets, of which the most splendid is **Grey Street★** (Z), curving elegantly downhill from the high column of **Grey's Monument** (F), past the great portico of the Theatre Royal. Into this heritage of **"Tyneside Classical"** have been inserted new developments such as **Eldon Square** (Y), one of Europe's largest indoor shopping and recreational centres.

★**Laing Art Gallery and Museum** (Y M¹). — The gallery's collection of English art ⊘ emphasises the 19C, notably with the apocalyptic works of the visionary **John Martin.** There are good displays of **Tyneside glass** and **silverware.**

Blackfriars (Z). — The much-restored buildings of the Dominican friary, founded in the 13C, now house a craft centre.

★**Museum of Antiquities** (Y M²). — *University.* Models of the wall, vallum, forts, milecastles and turrets, as well as a wealth of on-site finds (altars, tombstones and armour), make an interesting visit for those going on to Hadrian's Wall *(qv).* The reconstruction of the mithraeum at Carrawburgh boasts the original sculptured stones. Also on display is a set of legionary body armour *(lorica)* alongside two variants.

EXCURSIONS

★★**Hadrian's Wall.** — *Description p 131.*

★★**North of England Open-Air Museum, Beamish.** — *10 miles - 16km. Leave Newcastle to the south by any of the river bridges, then follow signs towards Consett onto the A692. At Sunniside turn left onto the A6076. After 2 miles - 3km turn right into a picnic area. A path leads via an old waggonway to the Causey Arch about 600yds - 550m away.*

Causey Arch. — One of the deep wooded "denes" characteristic of the area is boldly bridged by this pioneering stone arch of 1726, once part of a regional network of wooden waggonways linking collieries to riverside. Information displays recall this fascinating transport system which long preceded the steam railway.

Continue southwards on the A6076, turning left on entering Stanley and left again onto the A693 towards Chester-le-Street. After 2/3 mile - 1km turn left and follow signs to Beamish Museum.

★★**Beamish, North of England Open-Air Museum.** — This important and popular open-air museum ⊘ vividly recreates life in the North of England around the turn of the century.

Preserved tramcars take visitors through the extensive site to the **town**, whose shops, houses, working pub and printer's workshop, stocked and furnished authentically, recreate the urban scene of the 1920s. The **railway station** with its goods yard and signal box, has live steam, including a fine replica of Stephenson's *Locomotion* of 1825, and the transport collection boasts old road vehicles of every kind. The animals on the **home farm** are of traditional local breeds. Near the mine is the colliery village with pit cottages and gardens, and visitors can penetrate underground into the old workings of a real "drift" mine.

★**Seaton Delaval Hall.** — *11 miles - 18km northeast, via the A189* (Y) *and the A190.* ⊘ Built for Admiral George Delaval in 1718-29, this powerful Northern version of a Palladian villa is a masterpiece by the architect of Blenheim Palace and Castle Howard, **Sir John Vanbrugh.**

The north front looks across windswept countryside towards the industrial port of Blyth, the bleakness of the scene echoed in the great masses of sombre stonework. The eastern of the two symmetrical flanking wings houses sumptuous **stables.** The interior of the central portion, gutted by fire in 1822 and twice partially restored since, is of Piranesian grandeur and gloom. A fine portico adorns the south front.

The Delaval family were notorious for wild revels, but found time in the mid-18C to build extensive harbour works at nearby **Seaton Sluice.**

★ **Wallington House.** — *20 miles - 32km northwest. Take the A696 (Y) for 18 miles -*
⊘ *29km then right on minor road and follow the signs.*
The original property was bought in 1688 by Sir William Blackett from the bankrupt
Sir John Fenwick, most of the £ 2 000 price being paid as an annuity as long as
Sir John should live. When Sir John became involved in a plan to assassinate King
William III, Sir Walter voted energetically in Parliament for a Bill of Attainder, which
eventually took Sir John to the scaffold in 1697 and terminated the annuity ! But
Sir John had his posthumous revenge. King William had confiscated Sir John's horse
White Sorrel and this was the mount which stumbled on a molehill, throwing the
King and causing his death - the origin of the Jacobite toast to ''the little gentle
man in the black velvet coat''.
The house rebuilt by Sir William and refurbished by his heir Sir Walter is renowned
for its 18C plasterwork by an Italian, Francini. The original courtyard, now the hall,
is decorated with a series of painted scenes from Northumbrian history by William
Bell Scott, a reminder of the Pre-Raphaelite connections with Wallington. The large
collection of porcelain includes many 18C Chinese and Japanese items as well as
Bow and Chelsea pieces. The important collection of dolls' houses is another fascinating feature of Wallington.
The **walled garden**, as well as James Paine's **bridge** and the whole village of Cambo,
are fine examples of Sir Walter's imaginative vision. Though born just two miles
away, Capability Brown had little to do with the layout of the parkland, Sir Walter
again being the designer. Battle Hill beyond is the site of Chevy Chase where Hotspur and Douglas fought, a familiar subject in the Border ballads of this marchland
area.

⊘ **Washington Old Hall.** — *7 miles - 11km to the south in the new town of Washington, District 4.*
The hall was the seat of the forebears of **George Washington** (1732-99), the first president of the United States. A small English manor-house stands on the site of
earlier buildings. The ground floor is furnished with items typical of the 17-18C.

★★ **NEW FOREST** Hampshire

Michelin Map 📠 O, P 31 or Atlas G Britain p 9

William I made the area near his castle in Winchester a royal forest for hunting;
severe penalties were imposed on poachers or anyone who harmed the deer or trees.
The Crown ceded jurisdiction of the forest to the Forestry Commission in 1924.
Ponies, donkeys, deer, cattle and occasionally pigs still roam freely in the 144 square
miles - 373km² of unspoilt woodland, heath and marshland and not infrequently
by the roadside. Motorists should drive slowly and always with extreme care !

★★ **Bolderwood Ornamental Drive.** — This is a lovely drive through several enclosures
created in the 19C and now containing many fine, mature trees especially oak and
beech. The **Bolderwood Walks**, at the beginning of the drive, enable visitors to see some
of the forest deer at close quarters from observation platforms. Further along some
of the oak and beech pollards are at least 300 years old. At the end of the drive
just before the A35 is the venerable **Knightwood Oak** reputedly 375 years old.

Brockenhurst. — Pop 2 939. The busy small town with its ford in the main street,
is a good centre from which to explore the Forest. It is the goal or starting point
of the Rhinefield Drive.

Lyndhurst. — Pop 2 828. Capital of the New Forest, this bustling and attractive
town was where the forest verderers held court in the 17C **Queen's House.** The bold
red-brick Victorian church is notable for its Burne-Jones windows and an 1864 fresco
by Lord Leighton. In the churchyard is the grave of Alice Hargreaves, née Liddell,
who inspired Lewis Carroll to write *Alice in Wonderland.*

Minstead. — Pop 721. This attractive and largely unspoilt village, just south of
the A31, has a red-brick **All Saints Church** (13C), notable for its two-tiered gallery,
17C three-decker pulpit and two manorial pews. North of the village are the
⊘ informal **Furzey Gardens** with a 16C thatched cottage showing how New Forest
workers lived 400 years ago.

⊘ **New Forest Butterfly Farm.** — Ashurst. An enormous greenhouse full of tropical
vegetation is home to hundreds of butterflies, from Britain and abroad.

★★ **Rhinefield Ornamental Drive.** — This is a magnificent drive along an avenue of
trees planted in 1859 which are today Britain's finest collection of mature conifers.
Some of the Douglas Firs and Redwoods stand 150ft - 46m high.

Rufus Stone. — In a quiet glen, a memorial tablet marks the spot where William II,
known as Rufus, was killed by an arrow while hunting in 1100. Historians have
never ascertained whether it was an accident or murder.

*Join us in our never ending task
of keeping up to date.*

*Send us your comments
and suggestions, please.*

*Michelin Tyre PLC
Tourism Department
Davy House, Lyon Road - HARROW - Middlesex HA1 2DQ.*

Michelin Map **404** R 27 or Atlas G Britain p 28
Town plan in the current Michelin Red Guide Great Britain and Ireland

An important town in the Middle Ages (and still expanding), though nothing of the *c*1100 castle where Thomas Becket stood trial in 1164 remains. Indeed little of pre-1675 Northampton remains. That year the medieval town was destroyed by fire. Defoe called the late 17C town that replaced it the "handsomest and best town in this part of England". With the coming of the railway in 1845, finally obliterating the castle, a new town grew up. Three buildings epitomise these three ages.

Church of the Holy Sepulchre. — *Sheep Street.* One of five Norman round churches in England, founded by Simon de Senlis, veteran of the First Crusade, with a **round nave** and circular **ambulatory.**

All Saints Church. — *The Drapery.* Rebuilt after the 1675 fire (the portico is of 1701), domed and classical, with a beautiful plastered ceiling, Betjeman called it a "homely provincial version" of Wren's St Mary at Hill, in the City of London.

⊘ **Guildhall.** — *St Giles Square.* Victorian Gothic at its most confident by Edward Godwin in *c*1860, when he was only 28. The **exterior** is ennobled with kings, queens and other neo-Gothic props; the **interior** is invested with local municipal worthies, almost lost amid the imitation Early English foliage on the cast-iron columns.

EXCURSIONS

Anglo-Saxon Church Architecture. — Two marvels of pre-Conquest church building survive in the Northamptonshire countryside.

★ **All Saints, Brixworth.** — *8 miles - 13km north on the A508.*
⊘ The largest Saxon church to survive almost in its entirety, it was established by monks from Lindisfarne *(qv)* in the 7C and rebuilt after being sacked by Danes in the 9C, which accounts for its defensive tower, a useful retreat during Viking raids. Note the Roman tiles and Saxon arches in the nave and chancel.

⊘ **All Saints, Earls Barton.** — *8 miles - 13km east on the A45.*
The fortress **tower** is Saxon, built in the reign of Edgar the Peaceful (959-995), the golden age of Saxon architecture. The patterning is clearly derived from older timber-framed buildings. The tower door and west door are Norman.

★★ **Boughton House.** — *17 miles - 27km northeast on the A43, turn right at Geddington.*
⊘ Originally a monastic house owned by the Abbey of Edmundsbury *(qv)* it was bought by Edward Montagu in 1528, who made the first extensions. More were made by the first Duke of Montagu, ambassador to Louis XIV, who built the north front, commissioned Chéron's baroque ceilings, introduced the "parquet de Versailles" floors and embellished the house with furniture, porcelain and paintings. Though more was added by the fourth Duke (mid-18C), the house with its 7 courtyards, 12 entrances and 365 windows (for the days of the week, months and days in the year), has hardly changed since *c*1700.
Amongst the finest **paintings** are El Greco's *Adoration of the Shepherds,* and Murillo's *John the Baptist* in the Low Pavilion Ante Room; Teniers the Younger's *Harvest Scene* in the Little Hall; the *Earl of Southampton* by Gainsborough in the Great Hall and numerous Van Dycks, Lelys and Knellers.

Milton Keynes. — Pop 136 000. *17 miles - 27km south on the M1.*
This prosperous planned city, midway between London and Birmingham, is the last and most ambitious of Britain's postwar New Towns. Its lavishly landscaped 22 000 acre - 8 900ha site takes in three established towns (Stony Stratford, Wolverton and Bletchley) and several ancient villages, trim new residential areas, community facilities and high-tech industries, all set in parkland and linked by a web of expressways; drawing shoppers from a vast catchment area is the gleaming **City Centre** with 140 stores under its roof and parking for 10 000 cars.

⊘ **Sulgrave Manor.** — *18 miles - 29km southwest on the A45, B4525 and minor road.*
Home of the Washington family from 1539 to their departure to Virginia in 1656 and now a museum of Washingtonia, jointly owned by the American and British peoples. In the Great Hall are the Washington coat of arms (note the resemblance to the Stars and Stripes) and in the Deed Room and Porch Room, George Washington's saddle bags, velvet coat, medals and several of his letters. The manor is a good example of a Tudor home at the time of Shakespeare.

★ NORTH YORK MOORS North Yorkshire
Michelin Map **402** Q, R, S 20 and 21 or Atlas G Britain pp 46 and 47

The beauty of this expanse of open moorland lies in its unforgettable wildness, heather-covered high ground stretching eastwards towards the rugged cliffs of the Yorkshire coastline. Located within their geographical limits is one of the country's National Parks.

★ **North York Moors National Park.** — From Pickering and Rievaulx in the south, northwards to the industrialisation of Middlesbrough, stretch 553 square miles - 1 432km² of National Park. Show-place villages, like **Hutton-le-Hole** *(8 miles - 13km west of Pickering by A170 then north on minor road),* grass verges nibbled close by sheep, attract the tourist and photographer alike. The **Ryedale Folk Museum** in the village has a large collection of rural memorabilia. **Rosedale Abbey** *(4 miles - 6km north of Hutton-le-Hole on the same minor road),* with fragments of a ruined 12C Abbey, is approached down a 1 in 3 slope which gives a magnificent panoramic **view**★ across the moors.

Pickering. — Pop 5 316. A pleasant market town poised on a limestone bluff on the southern edge of the park, Pickering is noted for its **castle**. Guarding the cross-roads which gave importance to the site of Pickering, the castle is built of the rock on which it stands. The high, steep motte carries a 13C keep, but this probably replaced an earlier structure. The **Parish Church of SS Peter and Paul**, mostly Norman built on a Saxon site, houses wall paintings on the north and south walls. Depicting the lives and deeds of the saints, they were discovered in 1851 and have been restored.

From Pickering Station steam locomotives still haul trains to Grosmont, along the 18 miles - 29km of track laid in 1836, when Stephenson opened the Pickering-Whitby Railway. The line is now the property of the **North Yorkshire Moors Railway.**

Helmsley Castle. — *13 miles - 21km west of Pickering on the A170.*
Standing high above the village with its spacious square, the castle sits within two massive rings of banks and ditches, its originally D-shaped keep, 'slighted' after the Civil War, still dominating the scene. The west range and tower, on 12C foundations, survive as 16C domestic buildings, roofed and glazed, with oak panelling and plaster ceiling.

★★**Rievaulx Abbey.** — *3 miles - 5km northwest of Helmsley on the B1257.*
The first major monastery built by the Cistercians, Rievaulx was founded *c*1132 and the monastic buildings must have been completed by the last quarter of the 12C. The austere **nave** dates from about 1135-40. The walls of the Early English, 13C **presbytery** still rise to three tiers, showing little of the severity of design of the nave. The shrine of the first Abbot, William, is set in the west wall of the **chapter house**. A complex of monastic buildings, infirmary, chapel, kitchens and a warming house, give an idea of the activities and work of the community.

★★ NORWICH Norfolk Pop 169 814

Michelin Map **404** Y 26 or Atlas G Britain p 31

Astride the River Wensum and decorated with the spires and towers of thirty-two medieval churches, Norwich has been the leading city of East Anglia since Saxon times.

★★CATHEDRAL (Y) *time: 2 hours*

The Norman cathedral was begun in 1096; its choir clerestory was rebuilt in Early English style in the 14C and Perpendicular vaults added in the 15C and early 16C. Faced with Caen stone, the rich Norman **tower** and 15C **spire** act as a perfect foil to the long low nave and graceful flying buttresses at the east end.

Interior. — Above the steadfast Norman nave and transepts the four hundred bosses on the vaults portray ''a strip cartoon of the whole story of God's involvement with man from creation to last judgement'' (Dean Alan Webster). Note the **misericords** of the choir stalls, the ambulatory, St Luke's Chapel (displaying the famous Despenser Reredos) and Jesus Chapel (displaying Martin Schwarz's *Adoration of the Magi).*

Cloisters and close. — The **Prior's Door**, leading from the nave to the cloisters, with its sculptured figures of Christ flanked by a bishop, a monk and angels, is one of the most beautiful doors of the early Decorated style. The cloisters, uniquely two-storeyed, were rebuilt *c*1297-1430 in a consistent style; their tracery is superb, and there are almost four hundred **bosses** on their vaulted ceiling, illustrating good, evil, the lives of Christ, Mary and the Saints. The predominantly Georgian close, entered through **Erpingham Gate** (1420) (**A**) or **St Ethelbert's Gate** (*c*1300) (**B**) leads to Pull's Ferry, the old watergate.

ADDITIONAL SIGHTS

Castle (Z). — Built 1160, externally decorated with blind arcading (imitating Castle Rising *qv*), the motifs faithfully reproduced in the Bath stone refacing by Salvin (1833-9). Later used as a prison it now houses the **Museum and Art Gallery★**. The upper floor, where the interior of the **keep** can best be viewed, displays arms and armour. The lower floor contains the **art gallery★**; this is the best place to see the work of the landscape painters of the Norwich School, particularly John Crome (''Old Crome'' 1768-1821), and the highly individual John Sell Cotman (1782-1842) whose ability to distil the essence of landscape into bold, almost abstract patterns of watercolour still seems strikingly modern.

Walls (Z). — The stone walls (1294-1320) surrounding the city centre are 2 1/4 miles - about 4km long, the same as the City of London's: best **viewed** from Carrow Bridge and Carrow Hill.

★**Market Place** (Z). — 900 years old and the largest market in East Anglia. To the north is the chequered flint **Guildhall** (**D**), begun in 1407; to the west, **City Hall** (**H**), ''probably the foremost English public building of between the wars'' (Pevsner); to the south, Norwich's grandest parish church, **St Peter Mancroft** (**E**), Perpendicular par excellence, with a fine hammerbeam roof, a great east window with medieval glass, and a 15C font; to the east, the Art Nouveau **Royal Arcade** (**F**).

Elm Hill (Y). — A thoroughfare since 1200, once the centre of the weaving industry, Elm Hill starts at the late Perpendicular **St Simon and St Jude**. This cobbled street first passes on the left the medieval buildings of the **Blackfriars** then starts curving at the 15C **Britons Arms** on the right before ending at **St Peter Hungate** (rebuilt 1460). The latter is now a museum of ecclesiastical art containing icons, illuminated manuscripts, stained glass and a brass-rubbing centre.

Elm Hill .... **Y**
Gentleman's Walk ...... **Z** 17
London Street .... **YZ** 26
St. Andrew's Street .... **Y** 36
St. Stephen's Street .... **Z**

Bank Plain .... **Y** 2

Bethel Street .... **Z** 4
Castle Meadow .... **Z** 6
Cattle Market Street .... **Z** 7
Chapel Field North ..... **Z** 9
Charing Cross .... **Y** 10
Colegate .... **Y** 14
Exchange Street ...... **YZ** 15
Grapes Hill .... **Y** 19
Market Avenue .... **Z** 28
Rampant Horse Street ... **Z** 32

Red Lion Street .... **Z** 33
St. George's Street ..... **Z** 38
St. Giles Street .... **Y** 40
Thorn Lane .... **Z** 42
Timber Hill .... **Z** 43
Tombland .... **Y** 45
Upper King Street ..... **Y** 46
Wensum Street .... **Y** 49
Westlegate .... **Z** 50
Whitefriars .... **Y** 51

★**Sainsbury Centre for Visual Arts** (**Z**). — *University of East Anglia.* One of the most exciting buildings of the 1970s, the Sainsbury Centre was designed by Norman Foster and constructed out of thirty-seven prismatic steel trusses forming a 400ft - 122m by 100ft - 31m tube of interchangeable glass, solid and grilled panels, to create a non-museum environment to look ''at works of art from a sensual, not only an intellectual point of view'' (Sir Robert Sainsbury).
The 19 and 20C European works by Degas, Seurat, Picasso, Epstein, Bacon, Modigliani, Moore and Giacometti are delightfully juxtaposed with African, Pacific, Oriental and American Indian art in a deliberate breaking down of barriers.

EXCURSIONS

★★**Blickling Hall.** — *15 miles - 24km north on the A140* (**Y**). This splendid turreted and gabled brick mansion was built 1619-25 by Robert Lyminge, the architect of Hatfield House *(qv)*; of great Jacobean houses it is one of the most intact; the extensive late 18C alterations carried out by Thomas Ivory of Norwich, were tactfully ''in keeping''. There is a staircase of barbaric profusion; a 120ft - 37m plastered ceiling portraying the *Five Senses* and *Learning* in the Long Gallery; a splendid tapestry of Peter the Great defeating the Swedes at Poltava, presented by Catherine the Great to Blickling's owner the Earl of Buckinghamshire, in the Peter the Great Room; and paintings by Reynolds, Gainsborough and Canaletto.
The present parterre and gardens date from the late 19C, the original layout of the grounds having been landscaped away in the late 18C, probably by Humphry Repton. Far away in the park is an extraordinary 40ft - 12m high pyramidal mausoleum.

★**The Broads.** — *Leave Norwich to the north by the A1151* (**Y**). The 200 miles - over 300km of navigable waterways and the fourteen Broads (formed out of medieval peat diggings) are best explored by boat. One of Britain's premier wildlife habitats, the Broads are the home of Chinese water deer, kingfishers, herons and great crested grebes; while the Broads' villages are famous for their hammerbeamed and thatched roof churches.

Wroxham. — Pop 2 954. A boating centre on the River Bure. Boats can be hired by the hour, day or week.

Leave to the south by a local road, turn left at Salhouse before heading east to Ranworth passing through on the way Woodbastwick.

Ranworth. — The Perpendicular tower and Decorated south porch of **St Helen's Church** give no hint of the splendour inside: the finest rood screen (15C) in East Anglia, a brightly-painted (recently restored) array of saints, apostles and martyrs.

Continue via South Walsham to Acle then head north (A1064) to cross the Bure. Fork left onto the B1152.

Potter Heigham. — Pop 307. On the River Thurne, Potter Heigham, with its part Norman Church of **St Nicholas** (Norman tower, hammerbeams and thatched roof) is the capital of the northern Broads.

Knapton. — Pop 307. *18 miles - 29km north by the A1151 (Y) and B1150 to North Walsham and then the B1145.*
The glories of the **Church of SS Peter and Paul** are the 1504 double hammerbeam roof bearing 138 carved angels, each one different, and its font cover.

NOTTINGHAM Nottinghamshire
Pop 273 300

Michelin Map 404 Q 25 or Atlas G Britain p 36
Town plan in the current Michelin Red Guide Great Britain and Ireland

Famous for lace, D H Lawrence and a medieval sheriff, Nottingham was originally Snotingeham, a settlement peopled by followers of the Dane Snot. Guarding the River Trent, gateway to the North, it grew in importance, becoming one of the five Danish burghs, together with Derby *(qv)*, Leicester *(qv)*, Lincoln *(qv)*, and Stamford *(qv)*. William the Conqueror built the first fort here in 1068. At the fort rebuilt in stone, supporters of Prince John surrendered to Richard the Lionheart in 1194. Mortimer and Queen Isabella (assassins of Edward II) were captured by Edward III. Richard III marched out to defeat and death at Bosworth Field in 1485 and Charles I unfurled his standard at the beginning of the Civil War in 1642.

One of the earliest towns to industrialise (the Spinning Jenny came in 1768), it was shaken by Luddite riots (1811-16), inspiring Byron's maiden speech in the House of Lords in their defence, and shaken by riots again in 1831 when the baroque castle, home of the anti-Reform Bill Duke of Newcastle, was burnt down.

100 years after Byron's protest Nottingham spawned another writer and protester against industrial society, **David Herbert Lawrence** (d 1930) the novelist, born in nearby Eastwood in 1885.

The regional centre of the East Midlands, Nottingham still has a broad industrial base including several well-known firms, Boots pharmaceuticals, Raleigh cycles and John Player cigarettes.

Nottingham alabasters. — From 1350 to 1530 the city was the home of a school of alabaster carvers specialising in delicately-detailed scenes illustrating the life of Christ, the Virgin and the saints. The early free-standing figures and panels were superseded by altarpieces combining both panels and figures arranged in a wooden framework. The few works which survived the systematic destruction of the Reformation were often sold to the Continent.

Alabaster Altarpiece (15C)

★ Castle Museum. — Nothing of the original Norman castle survives, save the subterranean passage, **Mortimer's Hole,** from the castle to the **Brewhouse Yard,** and **Ye Olde Trip to Jerusalem** (allegedly the oldest inn in England) below. What was left after 1831 was turned into a museum and art gallery housing Bronze Age, Roman and Greek antiquities, medieval Nottingham **alabasters★** , 3 000 ceramic pieces, jewellery, glass and 16C Italian, 17C Dutch, 17C French and 18-20C English paintings. New displays tell the history of Nottingham from prehistory to 1990.

Castle Gate. — Three of the street's elegant Georgian houses have been suitably converted into a **Museum of Costume and Textiles.** Attractive period rooms are the setting for the displays of Nottingham's famous lace, together with costume (1760-1960), fans, lingerie, dolls and embroidery through the fads of centuries. The 1632 map tapestries of Nottinghamshire reward a closer inspection.

Lace Hall. — *High Pavement.* Displays illustrate Nottingham's leading role in the history of British lacemaking. Both hand and machine lace-making methods are described.

EXCURSIONS

★ **Wollaton Hall.** — *2 1/2 miles - 4km west of the city centre, by Ilkeston Road, the* ⊘ *A609.* An exuberant display of Elizabethan grandeur, built by Robert Smythson *(qv)*, his second major commission after Longleat *(qv)*. Like Longleat it is outward looking but here Smythson replaces the inner courtyard with a central hall so high it overtops the roof line and is lit through a clerestory. It's brazen and it's supposed to be, being built not for a courtier but for a coal magnate, Sir Francis Willoughby. Wollaton houses a natural history museum.

★ **Newstead Abbey.** — *11 miles - 18km north of Nottingham off the A60.* ⊘ An abbey in name only, the medieval priory was converted into a home in the 16C and it is best known as the ancestral home of **Lord Byron** (1788-1824). The ruined façade of the priory church, with its gabled niche holding a seated Virgin Mary, adjoins the main range. The 19C rooms include the apartments of Byron and a selection of Byron manuscripts, memorabilia and portraits. Lakes, gardens and parkland make for an attractive setting.

Sherwood Forest. — *The Visitor Centre is 19 miles - 30km north of Nottingham off the A614 and close by the A6075.*
Once one of the sixty-five Royal Forests which covered much of England, thick with oak, birch and bracken, it was protected from agriculture and development by royal hunting forest laws: in this perfect environment for poaching, the outlaw bands recorded by the chroniclers of Godber, Coterel, Folville and **Robyn Hode** all became legends and by the 15C Robyn Hode had become a composite folk-tale character embracing all their exploits.
Some of the woodland was subsequently cleared - ''if there was such a man as Robin Hood, he would hardly find shelter for a week'' (Daniel Defoe). Some is now heathland and much has been replanted with conifers. There are however attractive remnants. A mile north of Edwinstone, where the supposed marriage of ⊘ Robin Hood and Maid Marion took place, is the **Sherwood Forest Visitor Centre**, close by Sherwood's most famous sight, the **Major Oak**, 500 years old and 33ft - 10m in diameter.

OBAN Strathclyde	Pop 7 476

Michelin Map **401** D 14 or Atlas G Britain p 60

A busy tourist centre and service town for the hinterland and islands - a far cry from 1773 when Dr Johnson had to content himself with ''a tolerable inn'' - Oban owes its development to the railways and steamboats; hence the dominating Victorian aspect to the town.
There is a traditional piping competition on the opening day of the **Argyllshire Highland Gathering**, as well as putting the shot, throwing the hammer and tossing the caber (as straight, rather than as far, as possible).
The outstanding landmark is **McCaig's Tower** (1897), a replica of the Colosseum, built by an Oban banker to relieve unemployment and never finished.

EXCURSIONS

★★ **Loch Awe.** — *Follow the A85 to the east.*
The road follows the narrow defile of the **Pass of Brander** overlooked to the north by the lower slopes of **Ben Cruachan** (3 689ft - 1 126m).
Loch Awe, Scotland's longest, is over 25 miles - 40km long, and lies in the heart of Campbell country. **Kilchurn Castle** juts out on the northern shore. A 15C stronghold, built by Sir Colin Campbell, with 1693 extensions, it was abandoned in the mid-18C.
This excursion can be continued southwards to Inveraray *(qv)* and Loch Fyne.

★ **Sea Life Centre.** — *11 miles - 18km north of Oban, on the A828.*
⊘ This original aquarium presents the living creatures - from seals to octopus - from the seas around Britain.

★★ **ORKNEY Islands** Islands Area	Pop 19 040

Michelin Map **401** K, L, M 6 and 7 or Atlas G Britain p 74

Of the 67 islands that make up the Orkney archipelago only some 20 are inhabited. The first Neolithic settlers came in the 4th millennium BC. Some of their dwellings remain and their fine stone tombs can be seen throughout the islands. From the early Iron Age, around the 5C BC, there are fortified villages, about the massive stone buildings known as brochs. The Vikings came to Orkney from the late 8C AD, sweeping away the culture of the Pictish Orcadians. Orkney's culture still has Scandinavian elements, though the islands were pawned to King James III of Scotland in 1468, as part of the dowry of his Danish bride.
The cliffs are home to countless seabirds, and seals and otters are common.

★★ **KIRKWALL** Pop 4 167

A capital since Viking days, Kirkwall stands on the isthmus separating the eastern and western parts of the island.
Notable games include the Christmas and New Year's Day **Ba Games** when the Uppies play the Doonies, symbolising the old rivalry between ecclesiastical town and the secular authority represented by the now-vanished castle.

★★ St Magnus Cathedral. — Built by Earl Rognvald from 1137 to 1152 and dedicat-
ⓢ ed to his murdered uncle, Earl Magnus, the cathedral is Norman in character, contemporary with Durham *(qv)*. The red stone exterior is severe and plain, dominated
by the tower and steeple. The three west front doorways added later show confident originality in their combination of red and yellow sandstone. The interior, though
somewhat severe, is pleasingly harmonious, carefully controlled proportions creating a sense of vastness belying the building's modest dimensions. The square pillars on either side of the organ screen enshrine the relics of St Magnus (right), and
Earl Rognvald (left).

★ Earl's Palace. — The remains of this early Renaissance palace have splendid cor-
ⓢ belling on the windows, chimney breast and corbel course, and sculptured panels
above the main entrance and oriel windows. It was built *c*1600-7 by **Earl Patrick Stewart**,
whose execution for treason in 1615 was said to have been delayed to allow him
time to learn the Lord's Prayer. The vaulted chambers on the ground floor hold
exhibitions of Orkney history from the early Middle Ages to the present, while
the grand staircase leads to the Great Hall and other princely apartments.

ⓢ **Bishop's Palace.** — Built in the 12C alongside the cathedral, it was here that King
Haakon of Norway died after the Battle of Largs (1263). Most of what can be seen
dates from the rebuildings in the 16 and 17C, the latter by Earl Patrick Stewart.

★ Tankerness House Museum. — A fine 16C town house with excellent introduc-
ⓢ tory displays on the islands' prehistory.

EXCURSIONS

★★ Western Mainland. — *Leave Kirkwall by the A965.*

Rennibister Earth House. — *Behind the farmhouse, access by trapdoor and ladder.*
The oval chamber has five wall recesses and an entrance passage. Human bones
were found in it, though its original purpose remains uncertain.

> *Continue through Finstown on the A965.*

★★ Maes Howe. — This Neolithic burial cairn is a work of unique skill in stone building
ⓢ from people whose only tools were stones and flint. Pre 2 700 BC, it was covered
by a 26ft - 8m high and 115ft - 35m wide mound. The cairn was broken into in
the 12C by Norsemen, who left an important series of runic graffiti.

Ring of Brodgar. — The Stone Age circle, standing on the neck of land between the
lochs of Stenness and Harray, still has 27 of its original 60 stones standing. Two
entrance causeways interrupt the encircling ditch.

Unstan Cairn. — *Park in front of the house; the keys hang in a box by the back door.*
The Stone Age chambered tomb, from the mid-fourth millennium, compartmentalised by upright slabs, overlooks the Loch of Stenness.

★ Stromness. — Pop 1 646. Second largest town and principal port. The town grew,
from its original Norse settlement, in the 18C as a whaling station and the last port
of call for the Hudson Bay Company ships sailing to Canada.
ⓢ The **Pier Gallery** has a permanent collection of abstract art based on the work of the
St Ives artists, Ben Nicholson and Barbara Hepworth. Aspects of Orkney's natural
ⓢ and maritime history are presented in the **museum.**

> *The A965, the A967 and then the B9056 lead northwards to Skara Brae.*

★★ Skara Brae. — Long preserved in sand, Skara Brae *(photograph p 26)* is 5 000 years
ⓢ old. The seven best preserved Stone Age dwellings are rectangular with coursed
flagstone walls, a hearth in the middle and are connected by a subterranean sewer
system.

> *Continue to Birsay.*

★ Brough of Birsay. — *Access by foot across causeway at low tide.*
ⓢ The earliest remains are Pictish. In the 10C Norse farmers occupied the island and
Earl Thorfinn the Mighty (*c*1009-65) built a church after a pilgrimage to Rome. It
became a cathedral and was the initial resting place of St Magnus before the
construction of Kirkwall Cathedral. Excavations show a small oblong nave, short
narrow choir and rounded apse, surrounded by a Norse graveyard. A little to the
southwest is a collection of stone and turf-built **Norse long houses** with the living
quarters at the upper end and the byre lower down.

> *The A966 and A965 to the left lead back to Kirkwall.*

Scapa Flow. — *Take the A961 south past St Mary's. About 10 miles - 16km.*
From the **Churchill Barriers**, built in the Second World War by Italian prisoners of war
to link the four islands with the mainland, there is a good view of the naval base
where the German Grand Fleet scuttled itself in 1919. Beyond the first barrier is
the **Italian Chapel★**, built by the same prisoners inside two Nissen huts: a unique and
moving testament to faith in adversity.

The **Michelin Red Guide Great Britain and Ireland**
revises annually its 100 town plans showing:
— throughroutes and by-passes,
  new roads, car parks and one-way systems
— the exact location of hotels, restaurants and public buildings.

With the help of all this updated information
take the harassment out of town driving

England's oldest University, Oxford, "city of dreaming spires", developed in Saxon times around the 8C nunnery of St Frideswide (now Christ Church Cathedral) and still maintains its original street plan and walls. Religious foundations grew up and the university (essentially a federation of monastic halls and still a federation of autonomous colleges) emerged about 1200. Secularised at the Reformation, Oxford provided martyrs for both sides (Latimer, Ridley, Cranmer and Campion: Martyrs' Memorial in St Giles Street). It was the headquarters of the Royalists during the Civil War (Charles I staying at Christ Church, Henrietta-Maria at Merton College) and has been Matthew Arnold's "home of lost causes and... impossible loyalties" ever since. The 18C saw new buildings but few new ideas: reform came in the 19C, first with the Anglo-Catholic Oxford Movement, which sought to bring new life to the Anglican Church, then with the growth of scientific research and finally with the admission of women. Traumatic as the reforms appeared at the time, the essence of Oxford remains unchanged - "a city where too many bells are always ringing in the rain" (Elmer Davis).

THE CENTRAL COLLEGES *visit: allow a day*

Note that many colleges are open only in the afternoons. Start in Radcliffe Square.

Radcliffe Square (Z 35). — The heart of the University, in the centre stands James Gibbs' baroque rotunda the **Radcliffe Camera★** (Z A), with St Mary's Church to the south, Brasenose College to the west, All Souls College to the east and the "federal" university buildings around the Bodleian and Sheldonian to the north.

St Mary the Virgin (Z B). — Late 15C Perpendicular with a Decorated 13C tower (offering a **view** of the city's domes, spires, quadrangles and the surrounding hills) and a delightfully incongruous baroque porch (1637) by Nicholas Stone. St Mary's is the University Church and adjoins the earliest rooms used by the University: the early 14C **Congregation House** where the governing body convened, with above the first Library. Inside is the Vice-Chancellor's Throne.

⊘ **Brasenose College** (Z D). — Founded 1509, the Gatehouse, Front Quad and Hall are early 16C, the Library and Chapel mid-17C and the old kitchen a 14C relic of Brasenose Hall (the name refers to a doorknocker from the hall).

⊘ **All Souls College** (Z E). — Entrance in High Street. Founded in 1438 as a memorial to those killed in the Hundred Years' War, the Front Quadrangle is mid-15C and the larger North Quad 18C by Nicholas Hawksmoor. Between them is the 1442 Perpendicular **Chapel★**, with its 15C glass in the antechapel, and magnificent medieval reredos.

★★ **Bodleian Library** (Z F). — One of the world's great libraries, established in the 14C, rebuilt in the 17C, the Bodleian contains almost 5 million books, manuscripts and maps. The entrance leads to **Old Schools Quadrangle**, built in 1439 in the Jacobean-Gothic

Radcliffe Camera

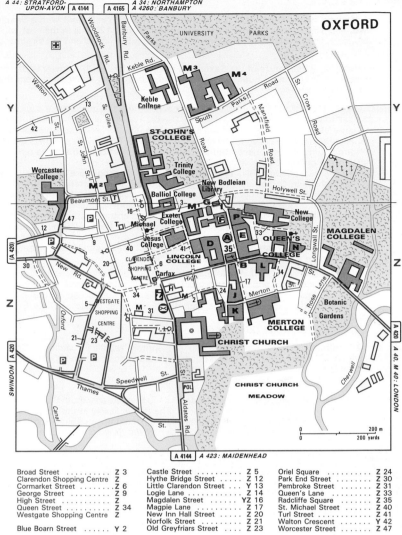

A 40: CHELTENHAM
A 44: STRATFORD-UPON-AVON **A 4144** **A 4165** A 34: NORTHAMPTON
A 4260: BANBURY

OXFORD

A 4144 A 423: MAIDENHEAD

style so characteristic of Oxford. On the right is the **Tower of the Five Orders**, richly decorated with the five classical orders of architecture. Opposite is the 15C **Divinity School**, famous for the bosses and pendants of its **lierne vaulting★**. Above is Duke Humphrey's Library (1610-12) with its gaily decorated **ceiling★★**.

★ Sheldonian Theatre (Z G). — Built 1664-9, Oxford's first classical building and Wren's first work of architecture was designed to accommodate formal University ceremonies. Alongside is Hawksmoor's 1713 Palladian **Clarendon Building** (YZ 1) built to house the University Press and now also part of the Bodleian Library. On the other side, facing onto Broad Street, is the Old Ashmolean, now a museum of the History of Science (M¹).

Exeter College (Z). — Founded 1314, combining Jacobean profuseness and Victorian values, its oldest part is **Palmer's Tower** (1432); in Gilbert Scott's 1857 chapel (modelled on the Sainte Chapelle in Paris) is a tapestry by Morris and Burne-Jones, both of whom were undergraduates at Exeter.

Trinity College (Y). — Founded 1555, Trinity was the successor to Durham College suppressed at the Dissolution. Standing well back from Broad Street behind gardens in the Front Quad, is the **Chapel★**, with Grinling Gibbons' exquisite cherub and wood carvings, in the Durham Quad the 17C Library and in the Garden Quad, facing **Trinity Gardens★**, a north range by Wren.

Balliol College (Y Z). — Founded 1282, all is Victorian except around the 15C front quad.

Jesus College (Z). — Founded 1571, its east front is very late Perpendicular, the Front Quad, Hall and Chapel Jacobean-Gothic and the Inner Quad 17-18C classicism.

★ Lincoln College (Z). — Founded 1427, the Front Quad and Hall were built in 1436 and provide a rare glimpse of what medieval Oxford must have looked like. The 1610-31 Chapel in the Back Quad contains original 17C Flemish stained glass and between the two quads are the oak panelled rooms of **John Wesley**, the founder of Methodism.

Return to Broad Street. Turn left down Cornmarket Street.

St Michael at the Northgate (Z). — The oldest building in Oxford with a Saxon tower, and 13C interior. Oxford's earliest stained glass (c1290) is in the east window, depicting St Nicholas, St Edmund of Abingdon, St Michael and the Virgin and Child.

Carfax (Z). — The centre of the Saxon and medieval city, the 14C tower is all that remains of St Martin's Church. There are impressive views of the High from the top of the tower.

Continue south down St Aldate's.

★★**Christ Church** (Z). — Founded in 1525 by Cardinal Wolsey and refounded in 1532 ⊘ by Henry VIII after Wolsey's fall from grace, "The House" is Oxford's biggest and grandest Renaissance college. The chapel, originally St Frideswide's (p 192) rebuilt in Norman times, was consecrated as England's smallest cathedral while remaining also the college chapel in the 16C.
Oxford's largest quadrangle is **Tom Quad★**. The southern ranges are by Wolsey, the northern ranges by Dr Samuel Fell (late 17C), and the fountain statue in the middle a copy of Giovanni da Bologna's *Mercury*. Above Wolsey's gatehouse is Wren's synthesis of baroque and Gothic, **Tom Tower★**, a fine domed gateway; to the south is the Tudor **Hall★★**, with its magnificent fan-vaulted entrance stairway by James Wyatt, hammerbeam roof and portraits by Kneller, Romney, Gainsborough, Lawrence, Millais; to the northeast are the 18C Peckwater Quad and **Picture Gallery** (Italian Renaissance Masters). South of the college Christ Church Meadow stretches from St Aldate's to the River Thames.

Christ Church Cathedral★. — Late Norman with a 16C roof, originally the church of St Frideswide's Priory and now the smallest cathedral in England, its glory is its 15C stellar vaulted **choir roof★**. Note the c1330 stained glass depicting Becket's martyrdom in the Lucy Chapel, the early Gothic chapter house and late Gothic cloisters.

Leave by Peckwater Quad for Oriel Square.

Oriel College (Z J). — Founded 1326 but entirely rebuilt in Jacobean-Gothic between 1619 and 1642, a second quadrangle was added in the 18C, the library by James Wyatt.

Cross Merton Street.

⊘**Corpus Christi College** (Z K). — Founded 1517, the gateway (note the fan vaulted ceiling) and Front Quad are early Tudor. The **Pelican Sundial** in the centre of the quad was designed in 1581, the 16C **Hall** has a splendid hammerbeam roof and in the 16C **Chapel** is an altarpiece of the *Adoration of the Shepherds* attributed to the studio of Rubens.

★★**Merton College** (Z). — Founded in 1264, boasting of the oldest and most pic-⊘ turesque college buildings in Oxford, her oldest quad is **Mob Quad**, a complete 14C quadrangle with the 1371-78 **Library** (the first medieval library to put books on shelves) on two sides. Adjacent is the 1294-97 Decorated **Chapel**, a naveless chancel with the 14C transepts forming the antechapel, its windows ablaze with original glass.

Turn left up Logic Lane to High Street ("the High").

University College (Z L). — Founded 1249, with a Jacobean-Gothic curved front, the western of its two vaulted gateways leads to the large mid-17C quad with the hall and chapel (note the 17C painted glass by Van Linge), and the eastern gateway to the smaller early 18C quad. Under a domed chamber in the northeast corner of the main quad is Onslow Ford's neo-classical nude statue of the drowned poet Shelley.

★**The Queen's College** (Z). — Founded 1340 in honour of Queen Philippa, it was rebuilt 1671-1760 and is the only college in Oxford unified in one style. The entrance, crowned by its cupola leads into the **Front Quadrangle**, cloistered on three sides with the hall and chapel in the building opposite. The 60ft - 18m barrel-vaulted **Hall** shows the influence of Wren; the 100ft - 30m classical **Chapel** has a ceiling painting by Sir James Thornhill who also decorated the dome of St Paul's, painted glass of 1635 by Van Linge and a finely carved organ screen as well as a good brass eagle lectern of 1662. Beyond in **North Quad** is Hawksmoor's noble **Library** with a carved pediment representing Wisdom crowned by an eagle.

Walk up Queen's Lane and New College Lane.

⊘**St Edmund Hall** (Z N). — Founded c1220, the last remaining medieval hall; though the oldest parts are only mid-17C, it still maintains its postage stamp dimensions and English horticultural charm. The adjoining church of St Peter in the East is now the college library, though the c1150 crypt is open.

⊘**New College** (Z). — Founded by William of Wykeham in 1379 three years before his other foundation, Winchester College (qv). The college still maintains some of its original buildings, the Great Quad is quintessential English Perpendicular, the hall the oldest in Oxford. The 15C **Chapel★** is vast, naveless like Merton, with 14C glass in the antechapel transepts and Epstein's **Lazarus** rising under Reynolds' 1777 west window. The cloister is a place of calm, offering a view of the 1400 Bell Tower. In the gardens is Oxford's finest section of city walls, including five bastions.

⊘**Hertford College** (Z P). — Founded as Hart Hall in 1282 and refounded as Hertford College in the 19C, its bridge over New College Lane was built in 1913 to link the two quads.

ADDITIONAL SIGHTS

★★ Ashmolean Museum (Y M²). — Built by C R Cockerell in free Grecian form (1845), the Ashmolean has grown from "Tradescant's Ark", an array of curiosities assembled by John Tradescant, gardener of Hatfield House *(qv)*, and his son, into the University's museum of archaeology. The collections are rich and varied, though their display is sometimes dauntingly old-fashioned.

Ground Floor. — The Greek and Roman sculptures of the Arundel Collection include fragments of a frieze from an Athenian temple and a torso of *c*480 BC. Among the Egyptian antiquities is an Eighteenth Dynasty fresco of a princess, showing for the first time in the history of art a rounded body on a flat surface. The decorative and fine arts of China, Japan, Tibet, India and Persia are well represented. The outstanding object in the Medieval Room is the exquisite late 9C Alfred Jewel, assumed to have been made for Alfred the Great. There is a good collection of Worcester porcelain.

First Floor. — Part of Tradescant's original "twelve cartloads", including Guy Fawkes' lantern, is in the Tradescant Room. There are archaeological treasures from Crete, Greece and Etruria but the principal interest is in paintings. The Italian 14C and 15C are well represented, particularly by Uccello's wonderful *Hunt in the Forest* and Piero di Cosimo's dream-like *Forest Fire.* Among Italian Renaissance works are pictures by Bellini, Veronese, Tintoretto and Giorgione. There are numerous minor 17 and 18C works of the Flemish, Dutch, English and French schools, some of them on the second floor, but quite outstanding is one of Claude Lorrain's luminous landscapes, *Ascanius shooting the Stag of Sylvia.*

Second Floor. — Another high point in the collection is reached in the **Pre-Raphaelite** paintings, including Hunt's *A converted British family sheltering a Christian missionary from the persecution of the Druids*, and Charles Collins' *Convent Thoughts.* A good selection of French Impressionists is complemented by a number of 20C British works, mainly of the Camden Town School.

The museum's collection of prints and drawings is vast, with numerous works by the pastoral visionary Samuel Palmer (1805-81).

★ University Museum (Y M³). — "The building will shortly sink into insignificance when compared to the contents it will display and the minds it will mould", enthused its founder Sir Henry Acland in 1860. He was wrong. The museum's natural history contents (including the Oxford Dodo) tell us more about our ancestors who were Victorian than about our ancestors who were monkeys, and sink into insignificance beside the extraordinary building: a cast-iron neo-Gothic cathedral designed like a railway station, with 19C decorated stone carvings of animals and plants by the Irish sculptor-mason family, the O'Sheas. A doorway at the end leads to the **Pitt Rivers Museum★** (Y M⁴), Oxford's bizarre anthropological collection of masks, musical instruments, jewellery, skulls, totem poles and armour, arranged by categories rather than countries and showing traditions common to different cultures.

★★ Magdalen College (Z). — Founded 1458 - pronounced "maudlen" - and originally the Hospital of St John the Baptist, the wall running along the High Street is 13C. The chapel, bell tower and cloisters are sumptuous late Perpendicular. The nave-less chapel, though Victorianised inside, is magnificently adorned with gargoyles and pinnacled buttresses. The 150ft - 46m **bell tower** is still "the most absolute building in Oxford" (James I). The unforgettable gargoyles on the cloister buttresses are a familiar feature of the Great Quadrangle. Beyond the cloister amid the meadows is New Building (1733) between Magdalen's deer park and the River Cherwell.

★ St John's College (Y). — Founded 1555 and stretching out beyond the original 16C front, the gardens are by Capability Brown; the front quad contains the remains of the medieval St Bernard's College (founded 1437), while Canterbury Quadrangle's colonnades (1631-36) give a delightful touch of Italian classicism to Oxford's predominant Jacobean-Gothic.

Worcester College (YZ). — Founded 1714, from the medieval foundation of Gloucester College, a relic of the foundation exists in the five monastic houses on the south side of the main quadrangle. The rest of the buildings are 18C classical, though the interior of the chapel was melodramatised in the 19C by William Burges. The **gardens** are graced by a lake and are among the most serene in Oxford.

Keble College (Y). — Founded 1870 and built of brick by William Butterfield in strident Victorian Gothic, Keble is a monument to the Oxford Movement and the Gothic Revival, reaching its highest expression in the ecclesiastical engineering of the **chapel**, where Holman Hunt's *The Light of the World* hangs in the Liddon Memorial Chapel.

Botanic Gardens (Z). — Established in 1621, the oldest in England, with a view of both the college towers and spires and the River Cherwell, crowded with punts in the summer; the *c*1630 gateways were built by Nicholas Stone, borrowing ideas from Italy.

EXCURSIONS

★★★ Blenheim Palace. — *Description p 61.*

Waddesdon Manor. — *25 miles - 40km, take the A34* (Y) *and the A41 to Bicester and then Aylesbury.*
Built in 1874-89 for Baron Ferdinand de Rothschild in French Renaissance style, the house contains the superb Rothschild collection of Dutch, French and English paintings, 18C French furniture, porcelain, carpets and many other works of art.

★★ **Collection.** — Twenty rooms are furnished with French 18C royal furniture, Sèvres porcelain, Savonnerie carpets and other works of art. On the walls hang portraits by Gainsborough, Reynolds and Romney. There are also pictures by Rubens *(Pink Boy)*, Cuyp, Van der Heyden, Ter Borch and other Dutch and Flemish masters. In the rooms on the first floor are collections of buttons, lace and fans, besides pastimes and mementoes of the Rothschild family. In the Blue Sèvres Room is a Sèvres dessert service of over one hundred pieces.

The house is set in 150 acres of grounds laid out by the French landscape gardener, Elie Lainé.

★ **Claydon House.** — *20 miles - 32km on the A34* (Y) *and the A41. Once past ⊘Bicester then follow signs.*

Extravagant Rococo by Hugh Lightfoot ("such work the world never saw"); its most beautiful eccentricities are its parquetry staircase (thin veneers of ebony, ivory, box and mahogany) and the "gothic chinoiserie" woodwork of the Chinese Room. More conventional but equally beautiful are the Mytens and Van Dyck oils.

★★ PEAK DISTRICT S. Yorkshire, Derbyshire, Staffordshire

Michelin Map 402 O, P 23 and 24 or Atlas G Britain p 35

The teeming industrial areas of Sheffield, Manchester, the Potteries and West Yorkshire have the unspoiled landscape of the **Peak District National Park** on their doorstep. The National Park covers 542 square miles - about 1 400 km², from Holmfirth in the north to Ashbourne in the south and from Sheffield in the east to Macclesfield in the west. The underlying rock is limestone of two very different kinds: to the north gritstone, which gives rise to the sombre moorlands and precipitous outcrops of the **Dark Peak**, culminating in **Kinder Scout** (2 088ft - 636m); to the south, the lighter stone of the more pastoral **White Peak**, a plateau divided up by drystone walls and by spectacular steep-sided dales.

It was on Kinder Scout, on 24 April 1932, that a mass trespass by ramblers was organised. They were anxious to establish a right of access to these wild spots. The 'trespass' resulted in the imprisonment of five of their number. In the end, however, it helped lead to the establishment of National Parks. Today, disused railway lines have been turned into footpaths; there are rock faces to be climbed and pot-holes to be explored, particularly around Castleton, where the caves can be visited by the not-so-energetic as well.

Well Dressing. — The annual Well Dressing *(photograph p 39)* is a unique Peak District tradition. Pagan thanksgivings to local water spirits have been transformed into Christian ceremonies, in some twenty Peak District villages. Eyam, Youlgreave, Wirksworth and Monyash are just some of the villages where the dressing takes place from early May to August each year. A large board is covered in clay, a design pricked out on it and then flowers, seeds, bark, lichens and grasses are used to fill out the design in colours. The board is then placed by the well or spring and blessed at a special open-air church service.

LANDMARKS, TOWNS and VILLAGES

The sights are listed in alphabetical order

Arbor Low. — Just off the High Peak Trail, one of the disused railway tracks, is Arbor Low, the best known of the Peak's prehistoric monuments. A 'clock-face' circle of stones lies within a surrounding bank and ditch.

Buxton. — Pop 19 502. The Romans discovered the warm springs and built baths here in about 79 AD. It was to **Old Hall**, now the Old Hall Hotel, in the Crescent, that Mary Queen of Scots was occasionally permitted to come, during her long captivity at Sheffield Manor, to 'take the waters' for her rheumatism; but it was not until the fifth Duke of Devonshire commissioned John Carr of York to build **The Crescent**, in 1780, that the town began to take on the aspect of a spa town such as Bath and Cheltenham. The Crescent, with the **Opera House** nearby is still the centre of the town, which grew in the 1860s with the advent of locomotives capable of coping with the steep gradients.

Castleton and its caves. — Pop 881. William Peveril, built a stone castle here soon after the Conquest. After centuries of neglect, the present ruined keep, mostly 12C, still dominates the village of Castleton. The village is an ideal centre from which to visit the local caves which are either natural cavities, lead-mining workings or ⊘ a mixture of both. The nearest is **Peak Cavern**, with its impressive entrance, at the foot of the hill on which the castle stands. Here for three hundred years, until 1974, there was a settlement of ropemakers, whose houses were built inside the entrance to the cave. Soot from the chimneys still blackens the roof of the cave.

⊘ West of the village on the B6061 is **Speedwell Cavern** where access is by boat via an underground canal.

Further west **Winnats Pass**, a steep ravine with high limestone cliffs, is probably a collapsed cave system.

⊘ Just off the A625 is the **Blue John Cavern★**, source of a purplish-blue form of fluorspar called Blue John. There are several distinct veins, each with its own colouring and patterns, buff, purple and black predominating. The semi-precious mineral has been worked into jewellery and larger pieces for many years; vases were found in the ruins of Pompeii. During the visit to this important range of caverns the visitor can admire lofty chambers with attractive mineral colourings and a variety of limestone formations, rippling draperies, stalactites, stalagmites and columns.

The summit of **Mam Tor** directly opposite was the site of an Iron Age fort and there are doubtless dozens of caverns as yet undiscovered in the fissured limestone below.

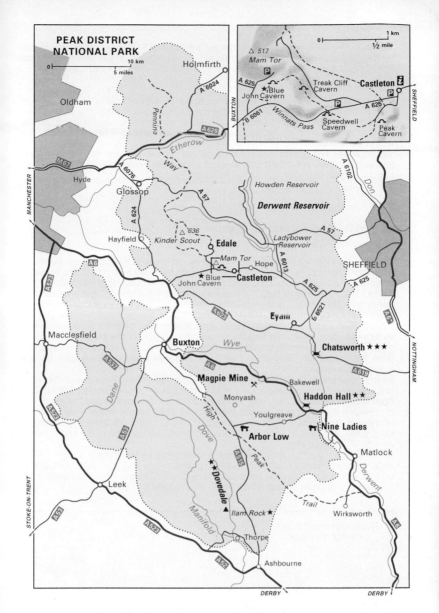

PEAK DISTRICT NATIONAL PARK

⊘ Further east is **Treak Cliff Cavern**, where, in 1926, the skeletons of Bronze Age miners were found, with their flint implements alongside them.

★★★**Chatsworth House.** — *Description p 86.*

Derwent Reservoir. — Created to supply water to the nearby cities, **Derwent, Howden** and **Ladybower Reservoirs** are today a 'Lake District' to be enjoyed by yachtsmen, cyclists and walkers alike. It was here that 617 Squadron, the "Dambusters", trained with the 'bouncing bomb', for the 1943 raid on the Ruhr dams.

★★**Dovedale.** — A dramatic two-mile gorge in the Derbyshire hills where the River Dove has washed away the soft limestone, exposing cliffs, caves and crags. Ruskin called it "an alluring first lesson in all that is admirable and beautiful".
From its entrance between Thorpe Cloud (942ft - 287m) and Bunster Hill (1 000ft - 305m), it meanders below the rocky outcrops of Lovers' Leap, The Twelve Apostles and **Ilam Rock★**. Upstream of Dovedale it continues to Beresford Dale, forever associated with Izaak Walton and John Cotton, authors of *The Compleat Angler.* The 1674 Fishing Temple built by Cotton still stands as a celebration of their friendship.

Edale. — Pop 338. Starting point of the Pennine Way, the first long-distance footpath in Britain, established on 24 April, 1965, the anniversary of the Kinder Scout trespass. It runs for 250 miles - 402km along the Pennines, backbone of northern England, from Edale, across Hadrian's Wall to Kirk Yetholm in the Cheviots. Its course is mostly through rugged upland country, unforgiving to the ill-prepared walker. It crosses motorways and skirts industrial areas, but takes the walker through outstanding natural landscapes; many villages, buildings of note and archaeological sites are scattered along its route or can be reached by short detours. Walk eastwards to the Packhorse Bridge which is one of the best of the Peak District bridges, with their narrow and low parapets to avoid the swinging panniers.

Eyam. — Pop 923. It was here, in the autumn of 1665, that the villagers, stricken by the plague, cut themselves off from the world outside, in self-imposed quarantine. Only a quarter of the inhabitants survived the twelve-month epidemic.

★★**Haddon Hall.** — *Description p 87.*

Magpie Mine. — The deep, steep-sided dales gave easy access to veins of lead, the rivers provided the power to drain the mine tunnels and the metal has been mined in the Peak since Roman times. Magpie Mine was continuously worked for two hundred years from the 1740s. Today engine houses and spoil heaps are reminders of this past activity.
Old workings and shafts can still be a danger for the unwary, so do not wander into spots where you might put yourself - and your rescuers - into danger.

Nine Ladies. — A stone circle surrounded by many barrows indicates the importance of the area to Neolithic man.

★★ PEMBROKESHIRE Coast Dyfed

Michelin Map 403 E, F 27, 28 and 29 or Atlas G Britain p 14

Uniquely amongst the National Parks of Wales and England this park comprises mostly coastal scenery, its wonderful variety of beaches backed by a cliffline revealing a complex and sometimes spectacular geology and harbouring a rich bird-life. Part of the old Kingdom of Dyfed, ''land of magic and enchantment'', the area abounds not only in the dolmens and megaliths of prehistory but also in the splendid stone crosses of Celtic Christianity. From the late 11C the native Welsh were largely displaced from south Pembrokeshire by Anglo-Normans, bent on colonisation and settlement; even today the linguistic boundary known as the **Landsker** follows the old military frontier separating the northern ''Welshry'' of distinct Celtic character from the southern ''Englishry'' with its anglicised place-names and square-towered churches.

From Amroth near Tenby in the south, to Poppit Sands near Cardigan in the north, the coastline's myriad delights are linked together by the 180 mile - 290km long **Pembrokeshire Coast Path**, offering an opportunity to the backpacker, or many less challenging but rewarding circular walks to the more casual visitor. Enquire at any of the numerous National Park information centres *(see map below)* for details of local walks and bear in mind that the coast near Castlemartin in the south serves as a NATO firing range.

Surfers, water skiers, yachtsmen, power-boat enthusiasts and sea anglers have a wide variety of sandy or pebble beaches, coves, inlets and creeks to choose from on this varied coastline. For some, access is more difficult, while for others there are parking facilities within a few yards of the beach.

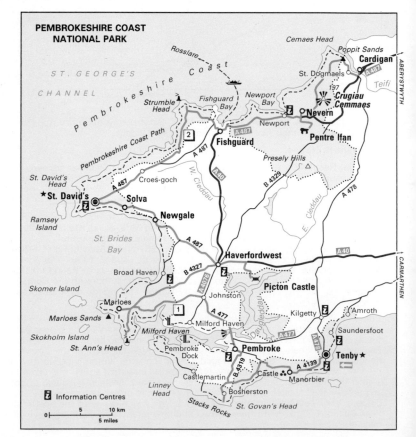

FROM TENBY TO ST DAVID'S
85 miles - 135km - local map opposite

Beginning at the delightful resort of Tenby and ending in the far mysterious west at St David's, this section of the tour introduces some of the important sights of the park while leaving much for exploration.

★ **Tenby** (Dinbych-y-pysgod). — *Description p 231.*

Go west on the A4139 and after 4 miles - 6km turn left onto the B4585.

Manorbier (Maenorbyr) — Pop 1 136. "The most delectable spot in Wales" according to Giraldus Cambrensis, traveller and historian, born here c1146. When seen from the bay, the mighty walls of his family's **castle** recall the great Crusader strongholds of the Levant.

Take a succession of local roads round the coast to Bosherston and if possible continue on down to the coast near St Govan's Head.

The stretch of coastline between St Govan's Head and Linney Head to the west has some spectacular limestone features: high cliffs, arches, stacks, sea caves and blow holes. On this indented coastline are two impressive pillars, **Stacks Rocks** (Elegug Stacks) and slightly beyond a natural arch known as the **Green Bridge of Wales**. *(NB: this area is part of the Castlemartin artillery range and beyond this point the path leaves the coast. Before visiting the last two features check locally to see if they are accessible on that day.)*

Return inland to Pembroke.

Pembroke (Penfro). — Pop 15 284. The town is strategically set on a long thin promontory with its impressive castle guarding both town and safe anchorage. The **castle**★★ has dominated the life of the town and, in its turn, Pembroke seems to have led in the rivalry between itself and the other ports of Haverfordwest and Tenby. Pembroke is built along a ridge, and the castle, originally a palisaded enclosure at the end of the ridge - now the inner ward - was completed by 1093. But the great keep, seventy feet high, with massive walls 19ft - 6m thick at the base, is the crowning glory of the castle today. The visitor enters the outer ward through the great gatehouse, and, turning left, comes immediately to the Henry VII Tower, one of the five projecting round towers that protect the curtain wall. Margaret Beaufort, young wife of Edmund Tudor, was sent for safety during the Wars of the Roses to her brother-in-law Jasper at Pembroke. It was most probably in this tower, in 1457, that the young Margaret, a widow at nineteen, gave birth to Harri Tudur, later King Henry VII. The Wogan Cavern, below the Norman Hall, is unparalleled in British castles. It is a natural vaulted cavern, some 60ft - 18m by 80ft - 24m and was probably used as a store and boathouse.

Head north by the A4139 to join the A477.

From the modern tollbridge there is a good **view** of the magnificent anchorage of **Milford Haven** described by Nelson as one of the best in the world. Sir William Hamilton set about building a town, a naval dockyard and navigation school here in 1790, an ambitious plan encouraged by Lord Nelson. By 1814, the Admiralty had founded their own dockyard at Pembroke Dock. Despite a more recent oil terminal development, commercial activity in the Haven has dwindled although various installations are visible on both banks of Milford Haven with its deep water channel. The port ceded its supremacy to Sullom Voe in the Shetlands with the development of North Sea Oil in the 1970s. The whole waterway, together with the Daugleddau estuaries, has been developed as a centre for sailing, windsurfing and waterskiing.

Continue to Johnston then turn left onto local roads in the direction of Marloes and the Dale Peninsula. Shortly before coming to Marloes take the B4327 to the left.

The lighthouse and coastguard station on the red sandstone cliffs of **St Ann's Head** survey the entrance to the waterway. The rugged western shores where Atlantic rollers crash onto the sands contrast with the sheltered bays and anchorages of the eastern shores. It was in the small cove of Mill Bay that Henry Tudor (Harri Tudur) landed on 7 August 1485 on his way to victory at Bosworth Field *(qv)* and the crown of England.

Go northwards to the village of Marloes then westwards to the car park at Marloes Mere.

The wide expanse of sand known as **Marloes Sands** separates the Dale and Marloes Peninsulas. On the beach note the **Three Chimneys**, Silurian rocks up-ended by powerful earth movements. The names of the offshore islands, Skokholm and Skomer, are the heritage of the Norse incursions. Visits can be made to the nearby bird sanctuary islands of Skomer, Skokholm and Grassholm, with their colonies of terns, guillemots, gannets and other sea birds, including the comical puffin, the emblem of this national park.

Return inland to Haverfordwest by the B4327.

Haverfordwest (Hwlffordd). — Pop 13 572. The hilltop former county town is of ancient origin and is still the urban centre for a wide area. The ruined castle houses a local museum.

The A40 and a local road to the south lead to Picton Castle.

Picton Castle - The Graham Sutherland Gallery. — The painter **Graham Sutherland** (1903-80) returned again and again to Pembrokeshire and his obsession with its landscapes is seen in this collection of his work, the largest in the country.

Return via Haverfordwest and the A487 to the coast.

Newgale. — One of several holiday villages on this coast, its splendid two-mile stretch of sand, backed by a storm ridge of shingle, makes this a favourite family holiday spot. Newgale marks the western end of the Landsker *(p 198)*.

Follow the A487 to Solva.

Solva (Solvach). — The pretty harbour at Lower Solva was built to be out of sight of sea-raiders. Today it shelters pleasure boats as well as fishing craft.

★ **St David's** (Ty Ddewi). — *Description p 213.*

FROM ST DAVID'S TO CARDIGAN

55 miles - 85km - local map p 198. The coastal road leads round to Strumble Head.

★ **St David's** (Ty Ddewi). — *Description p 213.*

Leave St David's by the A487 and 2 miles - 3km beyond Croes-goch turn left towards the coast.

Beyond is **Strumble Head** and its light, the nearest point to Ireland.

Fishguard (Abergwaun). — Pop 2 903. The lower town offers a pretty haven for pleasure craft. Brunel planned to make Fishguard a transatlantic port to rival Liverpool. For a brief period great liners like the *Mauretania* did berth here, but today it is only the ferries that sail from the eastern side of the bay towards Rosslare.

The A487 turns eastwards to skirt Fishguard and Newport Bays.

Eastwards of Fishguard the coastal landscapes are wilder and the cliffs more precipitous.

Follow the A487, and at the turn-off for Nevern, branch to the right. Minor roads lead inland to an imposing megalithic monument.

Pentre Ifan. — This massive cromlech is sited within a curve of standing stones, its capstone finely balanced on the tips of three uprights. It overlooks Newport Bay, probably an important landing place in the days of the megalith builders and traders.

Return to Nevern.

Nevern. — Pop 606. Near St Brynach's Church stands a splendid 11C Celtic wheelhead **cross**, 13ft - 4m high, richly carved in interlacing patterns.

Leave by the B4582.

Crugiau Cemmaes (646ft - 197m). — This National Trust **viewpoint** at the roadside gives a good idea of the character of this upland part of the National Park. To the south rise the rounded, heather-clad **Presely Hills** (Mynydd Preseli), from whose eastern crests came the bluestones of Stonehenge.

Go back to the crossroads then turn right.

On the coast again the long distance path ends at Poppit Sands, an extensive beach at the mouth of the Teifi estuary.

Cardigan (Aberteifi). — *Description p 83.*

★ **PENZANCE** Cornwall   Pop 19 579

Michelin Map ▣ D 33 or Atlas G Britain p 2 — Local map p 96
Town plan in the current Michelin Red Guide Great Britain and Ireland

Penzance was burned by the Spaniards in 1595 and the present town is predominantly post-1800; its wonderful **outlook★★★** on Mount's Bay and St Michael's Mount has made it a popular holiday resort for 150 years, while also being a busy market town. The town divides into three distinct quarters.

Harbour. — From the colourful **harbour** the MV *Scillonian* sails to the Scilly Isles *(see below)*; alternatively BIH helicopters fly to the Isles from the heliport. At the end of the quay stands a mid-18C granite ''cellar'' known as the Barbican, now a lively craft centre. Behind the quay a maze of alleys extends to the main streets.

Western Promenade. — The wide, half-mile promenade and the Queen's Hotel, built in 1861, reflect Penzance's early importance as a holiday resort. Inland **Regent Square, Regent Terrace** and **Voundervour Lane** are lined by 18-19C houses.

Market Jew Street and **Chapel Street.** — The 1837 **Market House** in Market Jew Street is a dignified building with a distinctive bright-green copper dome. To its west is Penlee House, the local museum. **Chapel Street★** contains remarkable Georgian and Regency houses, notably the amazingly decorated **Egyptian House** of *c*1835 and the Union Hotel, re-fronted in 1810. The 17C **No 44** and **Abbey House** may have been associated with St Michael's Mount when it was a priory. The **Admiral Benbow** is named after the 18C band of smugglers known as the Benbow Brandy Men. No 19 is the ⊘ **Maritime Museum★** displaying weapons and instruments as well as treasure found on the seabed.

★ **ISLES OF SCILLY**

Access: see Penzance in the current Michelin Red Guide Great Britain and Ireland

This wind-battered archipelago shows evidence of Bronze Age culture in the 50 or so **megalithic passage graves** dating from *c*2000-1000 BC. They have been associated with a culture from Brittany which left other traces in West Cornwall and County Waterford, Eire. From 400-1000 AD there were Christian hermits on the isles and monks on Tresco. In 930 AD Athelstan dispatched the Danes from the isles and in 1114 Henry I granted Tresco to Tavistock Abbey to establish a Benedictine priory.

In the 1830s Squire Augustus Smith became Lord Proprietor; the islands knew 40 years of prosperity during which houses, churches and schools were built, five ship-building yards were established on St Mary's and the **flower industry** was begun.

St Mary's. — Pop 1 650. 3 miles - 5km across at its widest, with a coastline of 9 miles - 15km, St Mary's is the largest and principal island on which all but a few hundred Scillonians live. The main town, **Hugh Town**, runs the length of the sand bar between the main part of the island and the hill to the west, the **Garrison**. The **Guard Gate**, built in the mid-18C gives access to the eight-pointed **Star Castle**, built in 1594 at the time of Elizabeth I's feud with Spain. The walk inside the rampart walls circles the headland and affords excellent **views**★★ of the islands. Fifteen minutes walk from the **Telegraph Tower** on the island's highest point (158ft - 48m) is a 3C BC stone burial chamber, **Bants Carn**. The large inlet, **Porth Hellick**, has a 4 000-year-old passage grave.

Tresco. — Pop 285. In the magnificent sub-tropical **Abbey Gardens**★ stands Tresco Abbey, built chiefly in 1841 to the design of the Lord Proprietor Augustus Smith. On the edge of the gardens is **Valhalla**, an extraordinary collection of figureheads and other carved ornaments from the thousand ships wrecked off the islands in the past two centuries.

Other islands to visit include **Bryher**, **St Agnes**, **St Martin's** and **Samson** - a deserted island with many megalithic remains and the ruins of 19C cottages.

★ PERTH Tayside   Pop 41 916

Michelin Map **401** J 14 or Atlas G Britain p 62
Town plan in the current Michelin Red Guide Great Britain and Ireland

Perth has always been an important centre, where road and river traffic meet, and this one-time Royal Burgh has succeeded in retaining its atmosphere as a country town. The River Tay, long noted for its magnificent salmon fishing, also has fresh-water mussels which produce some excellent pearls. Some of the finest specimens are incorporated in the Honours of Scotland, the Scottish Crown Jewels, on display in Edinburgh Castle.

Pleasantly situated on the Tay between the vast green expanses of North Inch and South Inch, the 'Fair City' has played a prominent role in Scottish history and might well have become the capital had not James I been assassinated here in 1457. Other stirring events included the murderous Clan Combat of 1396 and the destruction of the town's monasteries following John Knox' inflammatory Sermon of 1559. Perth is the setting for many recreational events and its location makes it an ideal touring centre.

★Black Watch Museum. — Balhousie Castle is the home of this collection of silver, battle honours, medals and Colours, tracing the history of the Regiment. When General Wade was given the task in the early 18C of bringing peace to the Highlands, he enlisted and armed groups of Highlanders to keep the peace. These companies became known as **The Black Watch**, for the "Watch" they kept on the Highlands and for their dark tartan, a sharp contrast to the red of Government troops. The Black Watch became a Regiment by the amalgamation, at Aberfeldy in 1739, of six independent Companies of these Highlanders. 250 years later the Black Watch remains in the service of the Crown.

★Museum and Art Gallery. — In addition to the natural history section there are interesting displays of the local glass, silver and clock-making industries. **John Millais** (1829-96) owed his Perthshire connections to his wife, and, an enthusiastic fisher and shooter himself, has captured the chill of autumn on the Tay in many of his paintings, particularly in *Chill October*.

Georgian Perth. — On completion of the elegant Perth Bridge in 1772, the town broke out of its medieval limits and north of the centre are good examples of Georgian housing in Charlotte Street, Atholl Crescent, Rose Terrace and Barossa Place.

EXCURSIONS

★★Scone Palace. — *2 miles - 3km to the northeast by the A93.*
One of Scotland's most hallowed historic sites, Scone was the centre of Kenneth MacAlpine's Scoto-Pictish kingdom from the mid-9C and, from 1120, the first Augustinian priory in Scotland. **Moot Hill** was where Scottish kings were enthroned on the **Stone of Destiny** (Stone of Scone) until it was carried off to Westminster Abbey by Edward I in 1296 to form part of the Coronation Chair. Wrecked in the wave of destruction of 1559, the abbey eventually became the seat of the Earls of Mansfield. The present neo-Gothic palace dates from 1808. Its richly furnished apartments contain a splendid array of porcelain and ivories, unusual timepieces, busts and portraits, and a unique collection of *papier-mâché* objets d'art. Moot Hill, now occupied by a 19C chapel, faces the palace. Beyond the Old Gateway was the village of Scone, moved during the 19C alterations to the palace. In the 50-acre pinetum are examples of the Douglas fir, named after the botanist David Douglas, born here in 1799.

★Dunkeld. — *14 miles - 23km to the north by the A9.*
The site of a monastic establishment from 700 AD, briefly the ecclesiastical equivalent of Scone *(see above),* then a majestic Gothic cathedral, today's Dunkeld consists of the tiny cathedral 'city' and the partly ruined cathedral in its attractive riverside precinct.

⊘ The **Cathedral's** nave of the 15C is roofless, but the 14C choir was restored in 16
to serve as the parish church and the chapter house contains the Atholl ma
soleum and a small museum. **Cathedral Street★** and **The Cross** were rebuilt afte
Dunkeld was sacked following the Battle of Killiecrankie in 1689. Today's attrac
tive townscape owes much to expert restoration by the National Trust of many
of the 17-18C houses.

★ **Drummond Castle Gardens.** — *20 miles - 32km west. On the A85 to Crieff, then*
⊘ *south on the A822.* The Gardens of Drummond Castle were originally laid out about
1630 by John Drummond, 2nd Earl of Perth. In about 1830, the parterre was
Italianised and embellished with fine figures and statues from Italy. One of the most
interesting pieces of statuary is the Sundial, designed and built by John Mylne, Master
Mason to King Charles I.

PETERBOROUGH Cambridgeshire   Pop 113 404

Michelin Map 404 T 26 or Atlas G Britain p 29
Town plan in the current Michelin Red Guide Great Britain and Ireland

A village around a monastery, a town around a cathedral, a city around brickworks,
Peterborough is now undergoing its fourth expansion as a high-tech city, doubling
its population in twenty years. Modern and Post-Modern office blocks act as foils
to the Perpendicular church of St John the Baptist in Cowgate, to the cathedral
and to the 17C guildhall.

★★ **Cathedral.** — Peterborough and Ely *(qv)* were the two great monasteries of the
⊘ Fens. The (pre-Conquest) Saxon monastery, founded *c*655, was sacked by the Danes
in 870 and then some damage and pillaging occurred after an attack by Hereward
the Wake *(qv)* in 1070. The abbey was subsequently burned down in 1116. It was
rebuilt between 1118 and 1238. The interior is a superb example of Norman
architecture.
The Early English **west front** is most memorable and fascinating with its three giant
arches and its rich incongruous early Perpendicular (14C) porch. The nave, transepts and choir with their **Norman elevations** are a robust uncomplicated expression
of structure and faith. Above, the 13C **nave ceiling** is a wonderful painted example
of medieval art, while that of the choir (presbytery) is 15C. The fan vaulting of the
retrochoir is 16C Perpendicular. In the north choir aisle Catherine of Aragon is
buried, and in the south choir aisle Mary Queen of Scots was temporarily laid to
rest (1587-1612).

★ PITLOCHRY Tayside   Pop 2 194

Michelin Map 401 I 13 or Atlas G Britain p 61

Set in the Tummel Valley and on one of General Wade's roads built throughout the
Highlands in the 1720s, Pitlochry makes a fine touring centre. Concerts and plays
are staged, from May to October, at the Pitlochry Festival Theatre.

⊘ **Pitlochry Power Station.** — A dam 54ft - 16m high and 475ft - 140m long has
created Loch Faskally. A **salmon ladder** - with an observation window from which the
visitor can see the fish at close quarters - enables salmon to move upstream to their
spawning grounds.

EXCURSIONS

★★ **Queen's View.** — *5 miles - 8km west of Killiecrankie, along the B8019.*
This beauty spot was named after Queen Victoria's visit in 1866, and commands
a wonderful view up Loch Tummel, with the cone shape of Schiehallion (3 547ft -
1 083m) to the left.

Return to the B8079 and continue north.

Killiecrankie. — It was on high land to the north of the narrow defile, the pass
of Killiecrankie, that the **Battle of Killiecrankie** (27 July 1689) was fought. John Graham (Viscount Dundee) and his Highlanders soundly defeated the government troops
of William and Mary. "Bonnie" Dundee was mortally wounded in the battle and
the leaderless Highlanders were wiped out a month later at Dunkeld to the south.
The end of the Jacobite saga, however, did not come until Culloden in 1746. From
the visitor centre a path leads to the **Soldier's Leap** where a fleeing government
soldier is said to have jumped to safety.

★★ **Blair Castle.** — *7 miles - 12km north of Pitlochry by the A9.*
⊘ Blair Castle is the home of the Duke of Atholl and was the centre of the ancient
kingdom of Atholl. A large part of the tower built here in 1269 still remains, and
the castle with its turrets, crenellations and parapets continues to command a strategic route into the Central Highlands. The Duke of Atholl retains the only private
army left in the British Isles, the Atholl Highlanders, sole survivor of the clan system, when the king relied on chieftains to raise their men to serve in his army. The
Atholl Highlanders' annual parade is on the last weekend in May.

Interior. — The closely interwoven histories of the family and castle are highlighted
by family portraits (Lely, Jacob de Wet, Honthorst, Hoppner, Zoffany, Landseer)
cross-referenced to genealogical tables, interesting collections (armour and porcelain),
Jacobite and other historic relics (one of the original copies of the National Covenant).
The 18C interiors are of particular interest, especially those with sumptuous stucco ceilings (Picture Staircase, Dining and Drawing Rooms) by Thomas Clayton.

Michelin Map 403 H 32 or Atlas G Britain p 3 — Local map p 97

Plymouth developed from the amalgamation of three towns, **Sutton, Devonport** and **Stonehouse**. Sutton, at the mouth of the River Plym, began as a small fishing port. The Plantagenet period brought trade with France and by the Elizabethan period trade had spread worldwide, so that for a time it was the fourth largest town in England after London, Bristol and York. From the 13C Plymouth also played a prime role as a naval and military port, from which warriors and explorers such as Drake, Raleigh, Hawkins and Grenville (all Devonians), Cook and the Pilgrim Fathers set sail. The Royal Naval Dockyard was founded by William III in 1691 on Bunkers Hill, Devonport, its initial five acres being much increased to the north. In World War II the city suffered serious bombing damage.

NAVAL AND MILITARY PLYMOUTH

The Hoe (Z). — On ''that loftie place at Plimmouth call'd the Hoe'' (Drayton), Sir Francis Drake (1540-96) is said to have seen the invincible Spanish Armada arriving one day in 1588 and decided to finish his game of bowls (or wait for the tide to turn?) before going to battle. It remains an ideal point from which to **view** the maritime traffic on the **Sound**, the natural harbour at the mouth of the Rivers Tamar and Plym. **Smeaton's Tower**, a red and white painted lighthouse, was erected on the Hoe in 1884 after 123 storm-battered years on Eddystone Rocks about 14 miles - 23km southwest of Plymouth. The present **Eddystone Lighthouse**, built in 1878-82, can be seen from the Hoe and oven better from the top of Smeaton's Tower. Other monuments testifying to Plymouth's role in history include Boehm's 1884 **Drake Statue** (**A**), the **Armada Memorial** (**B**) and the **Naval War Memorial** (**D**) bearing the names of 22 443 men.

The southern limit of the Sound is marked by the mile-long **Breakwater** constructed by **John Rennie** between 1812 and 1841 to counter heavy sea swell coming from the southwest.

★**Royal Citadel** (Z). — From the early 15C the land to the east of the Hoe served
⊘ as the site for a stronghold. In 1590-91 Drake began a fort intended to protect the Sound against marauding Spaniards and it was in this place that Charles II had the

PLYMOUTH

Armada Way	YZ 2
Cornwall Street	Y
Drake Circus Centre	Y
New George Street	Y 24
Old Town Street	Y 25
Royal Parade	Z
Beaumont Road	Y 3

Buckwell Street	Z 4	Lambhay Hill	Z 20
Charles Cross	Y 6	Mayflower Street	Y 22
Charles Street	Y 7	Millbay Road	Z 23
Derry's Cross	Z 9	Princess Street	Z 27
Drake Circus	Y 10	Quay Road	Z 28
Eastlake Street	Z 12	St. Andrew's Cross	Z 31
Elliot Street	Z 13	St. Andrew's Street	Z 32
Gasking Street	Y 14	San Sebastian Square	Z 33
Great Western Road	Z 16	Southside Street	Z 34
Hoe Road	Z 17	Vauxhall Street	Z 35
Kinterbury Street	Z 18	Woolster Street	Z 36

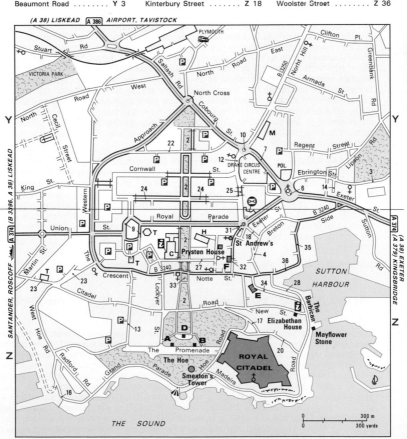

present castle built in 1666-71. The 3/4 mile **ramparts** command **views**★★ of the Sound, the Barbican and the mouth of the Tamar. The 1670 **Main Gate** originally contained a bust of Charles II with the royal arms and inscription, but this was tactfully replaced by four cannon balls when the citadel was surrendered personally to William III in 1688! The 17C Guard House, Governor's House and Storeroom have all been rebuilt and the small **chapel**, built in 1688, was enlarged in the 19C. In the courtyard the lead **statue** of George II as a warrior dates from 1728.

BARBICAN AND CITY CENTRE

Barbican (**Z**). — Old Plymouth survives in the Barbican, an area extending 1/4 mile inland from Sutton Harbour, combining modern amenities with medieval houses, Jacobean doorways, cobbled alleys and the **Mayflower Stone** on the pier commemorating the voyage of the Pilgrim Fathers, who set sail in 1620 in their 90ft - 27m ship, *The Mayflower.* Many other famous voyages are commemorated in the numerous stones and plaques on the pier.

The **Elizabethan House,** *32 New Street* and its neighbour were built in the late 16C as part of a development for merchants and sea-captains prosperous from trade and booty. The timber-framed and limestone houses are distinguished by their windows, exposed beams, large fireplaces and stout 16-17C carved oak furniture.

Coates Plymouth Gin Distillery (**Z E**). — *At the top of Southside Street.* The distillery is housed in what was once a Dominican Friary founded in 1425. Today it is possible to take a guided tour to see how gin is made.

St Andrew's (**Z**). — The church, founded in 1050 and rebuilt in the 15C, was firebombed in 1941; this left only the walls, fluted granite piers, chancel arches and the 136ft - 41m tower standing. The rebuilt church, re-consecrated in 1957, has six distinctive **windows** by John Piper, their vivid colours offset by a patinaed Delabole slate floor. Among the memorials are a 12-13C Purbeck marble effigy, tablets to Frobisher and Drake and the royal arms of Charles I, George III and George IV.

Just south of the church stands Yogge's House known locally as **Prysten House**, built soon after 1498 by Thomas Yogge, a wine merchant. It is a three-storeyed building around an inner courtyard with open timber galleries. The hall has a fine timber roof, bay window and granite fireplace.

Merchant's House (**Z F**). — *33 St Andrew's Street.* This mid-16C timbered house, its upper floors supported on stone corbels and with windows the full width and height of the front, owes its present style to William Parker, Mayor of Plymouth in 1601-02, a merchant and successful buccaneering sea-captain.

EXCURSIONS

★★**Saltram House.** — *3 1/2 miles - 5 1/2km east by the A374* (**Z**) *then south on the A38.*
In 1712 the Parker family of Boringdon bought the Tudor mansion at Saltram and in 1750 John Parker's wife, Lady Catherine, set about improving it. When she died in 1758 her son John Parker II, an MP, inherited the house; through his lifelong friend Joshua Reynolds, born locally at Plympton in 1732, he met the architect **Robert Adam**, who was then working with **Thomas Chippendale.** Following a fire, Adam, Chippendale and Reynolds all worked at Saltram, with the result that the house contains some of the finest 18C rooms in the country. In spite of alterations made in 1818 when the local architect John Foulston added a music room to the library, designed a balustraded porch with Doric columns at the front and enlarged the windows above it, the house remains much as it was in the 18C: a happy blend of Adam's architecture, Chippendale's furniture, Reynolds' portraits and an outstanding collection of porcelain.

★★**Buckland Abbey.** — *9 miles - 15km north by the A386* (**Y**) *then on by-roads.*
Originally a Cistercian abbey founded in 1278, the manor was granted to Sir Richard Grenville in 1541 after the Dissolution. His grandson, the famous naval commander Sir Richard Grenville (1541-91), converted it into an Elizabethan mansion before his rival Drake, newly knighted and already very rich, bought the estate from him in 1581. With its three domestic rooms, kitchen and museum galleries (one floor devoted to Drake), the abbey is remarkable for the way in which it accommodates the original church - its central crossing, tower, nave and chancel - within a domestic context.

★**Antony House.** — *Torpoint Ferry from Plymouth. Description p 97.*

★ **PORTSMOUTH** Hampshire   Pop 174 218

Michelin Map **404** Q 31 or Atlas G Britain p 10

Britain's premier naval base is set on **Portsea Island** between two almost landlocked harbours, Portsmouth and Langstone. There was no significant settlement on the island until the 12C but the early 15C saw the development of the naval base and in 1495 the first dry dock in the world was built. After the great expansion in Charles I's reign, during the Commonwealth and under Samuel Pepys in 1660-89, Portsmouth had become the principal naval base in the country by the end of the 17C. In the 18C when France was Britain's major enemy, the fortifications were strengthened, making the port the ideal base from which the Fleet set sail for such victories as Trafalgar. After heavy bombing in World War II the city was rebuilt and expanded all over Portsea Island and onto the mainland between Portchester and Farlington.

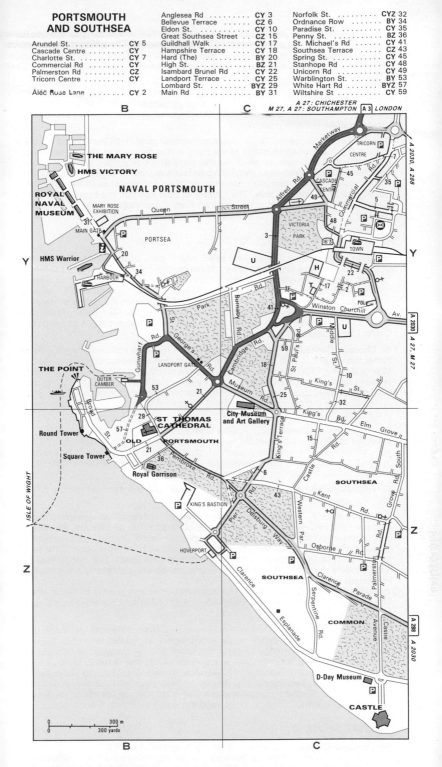

NAVAL PORTSMOUTH (BY) *time: 3 hours*

★★★ **HMS Victory.** — On 21 October 1805, Admiral Horatio Nelson's splendid 3-masted
   ⊙ flagship (laid down at Chatham in 1759) led the victorious attack on a combined
   French and Spanish fleet off Cape Trafalgar, in Spain - at the cost of her admiral's
   life. In the 1920s the *Victory* was brought into dry dock after 150 years at sea and
   she continues to serve as the flagship of the Commander in Chief, Naval Home Command and is still manned by serving Royal Naval and Royal Marines personnel. Preservation work is continuous as she is restored to the configuration she held at the
   battle of Trafalgar.

★★ **The Mary Rose.** — On 19 July 1545, the 4-masted *Mary Rose* (built 1509), vice
   ⊙ flagship of the English fleet, heeled over and sank while preparing to meet a French
   attack. Henry VIII and his army on Southsea Common could hear the cries of the
   drowning men. In the 1960s the wreck was found, preserved in the Solent silt;

205

in 1982 the hull was raised and it is now a unique Tudor time-capsule remarkably preserved after 437 years on the seabed. The **exhibition** of the many objects — treasures and possessions of her crew — recovered gives insight into Tudor nautical life. An audio-visual presentation describes the dramatic salvage operation.

⊘ **HMS Warrior.** — This sleek, black battleship was once the pride of Queen Victoria's Navy. Britain's first iron-clad battleship was commissioned in the 1860s and after 100 years of use for various purposes she has been superbly restored. HMS *Warrior* is now a living exhibition where every aspect of life in the Victorian Navy is vividly portrayed.

★★ **Royal Naval Museum.** — The museum stands alongside HMS *Victory* and the *Mary* ⊘ *Rose* in the heart of the historic naval base and is devoted to the overall history of the Royal Navy. From its windows the ships of today's Navy can be seen, still going about their business of defending Britain's shores. The galleries are packed with mementos of those who have served their country at sea through a thousand years of peace and war. The ghosts of past seamen are brought vividly to life in a series of exciting modern displays. Note in the Victory Gallery a panoramic painting by W L Wyllie and a model evoking the Battle of Trafalgar.

★ **OLD PORTSMOUTH** (BYZ) *time: 1 1/2 hours*

Harbour ramparts. — The original town which grew up around the **Camber** south of the dockyard was once entirely enclosed by ramparts; today only those on the harbour side are complete, forming a pleasant promenade with **views** of Gosport and Spithead. At the end of Broad Street the **Point** (BY) affords fine **views★★** of ships entering and leaving the port. The **Round Tower** (BZ), built on the orders of Henry V, was modified in Henry VIII's reign and again in the 19C. The **Square Tower** (BZ), built in 1494 and also much modified, contains, in a small recess, a gilded bust of **Charles I** by Le Sueur.

★ **St Thomas Cathedral** (BZ). — It was built *c*1180 as a chapel to honour **Thomas Becket**, martyred in 1170. Only the Early English **choir** and **transepts** survived the Civil War; in around 1690 the nave and tower were rebuilt and the attractive octagonal wooden **cupola** - a landmark from the sea - was added in 1703. In the south chancel aisle is a **monument** to the notorious Duke of Buckingham, murdered in 11 High Street in 1628. After the church was elevated to cathedral status in 1927, extensions were made in 1938-39.

Royal Garrison Church (BZ). — This was part of a hospital founded *c*1212, the buildings of which were used for military purposes after the Dissolution. All was demolished in 1827 except the church which still served the garrison; it was bombed in 1941 and today only the beautiful Early English chancel with leafy bosses and capitals retains its roof.

⊘ **City Museum and Art Gallery** (CY). — The displays are devoted to local history and arts from the 17C to the 20C.

Southsea (CZ). — The strip of land at the south of Portsea Island was rough marshland until the 19C when an elegant suburb of Portsmouth and a coastal resort began to grow and the Common became a pleasure area. At the southernmost tip ⊘ of the island stands the **Castle★** , built by Henry VIII in 1544-45 as part of the chain of forts protecting the ports along the south and east coast. The central **keep** surrounded by a dry moat, is still mainly Tudor; inside are displays of the growth of Portsmouth's fortifications.

⊘ The **D-Day Museum** (CZ) near the castle illustrates the major events of World War II. The centrepiece is the *Overlord Embroidery* with thirty-four panels recounting the story of the D-Day operation.

★ **Royal Marines Museum.** — Eastney. *Leave by Clarence Parade, the A288* (CZ). ⊘ Set in the original 19C officers' mess, this imaginative display describes the creation, history and modern-day work of the Royal Marine Corps. First brought into existence by Charles II as soldiers to serve on ships, the corps is famous for its capture and defence of Gibraltar in 1704. Also of note are the audio-visual presentations on the Marines' part in the Battles of Zeebrugge and Jutland, their role in World War II, in Northern Ireland and the Falklands. On the first floor are a medal collection, uniforms, portraits, silver, and a display on Royal Marine bands.

EXCURSION

★ **Portchester Castle.** — *5 miles - 8km north by the A3* (CY). ⊘ At the north end of Portsmouth harbour stands a castle all but surrounded by the sea. The first phase of its construction was in the late 3C when the Romans built defence walls 10ft - 3m wide and 20ft - 6m high enclosing 9 acres - 3 1/2ha of land; the walls still stand although the fort was used by the Saxons in the 5-6C and became a medieval castle in the early 12C in the reign of Henry I. An inner bailey with a moat was built and a strong, austere **keep** which was heightened in the mid-12C. Richard II built a palace in the inner bailey in the late 14C, though it is now in ruins. In 1133 Henry I founded an Augustinian priory within the walls and although the priory moved to Southwick 20 years later the church of St Mary has remained - Norman with a fine **west front** and ornate **doorway** and, inside, a 12C **font**.

Great Britain and Ireland are covered entirely at a scale of 16 miles to 1 inch by our map "Main Roads" 986.

PRESTON Lancashire   Pop 166 675

Michelin Map 402 L 22 or Atlas G Britain p 38

This busy town, the administrative centre of Lancashire, was the birthplace of **Sir Richard Arkwright** (1732-92). His spinning frame was one of the inventions which made cotton spinning a factory industry and transformed Preston from fashionable Georgian town into a centre of the cotton industry. Arkwright's story is told in the **Harris Museum and Art Gallery** which also has interesting collections of ceramics, glass and costume.

EXCURSIONS

Samlesbury Hall. — *3 miles - 5km east of Preston by the A59.* Well-restored example of a timber-framed manor house, begun in 1325, but mainly 15C and 16C, saved from dereliction in 1875 and again in 1924.

Hoghton Tower. — *5 miles - 8km southeast of Preston by the A675.* Fortified mansion, 16C with 17C additions, with a walled garden, built by Sir Thomas Hoghton in 1565. Spectacular approach to the 550ft - 170m hilltop site, up a long straight driveway. Here, in 1617, King James I and VI is said to have "knighted" the loin of beef, making it Sirloin for all Englishmen since.

RICHMOND North Yorkshire   Pop 7 596

Michelin Map 402 O 20 or Atlas G Britain p 45

At the foot of Swaledale and on the very edge of the **Yorkshire Dales National Park**, Richmond is an attractive country town, meeting place and market for the area. It was the home of Frances l'Anson, the "Sweet Lass" who married the writer of the 18C song, *Sweet Lass of Richmond Hill* in 1787.

★ **Castle.** — The castle was built by Alan the Red, starting in 1071, and the masonry of the curtain walls probably dates from then. The castle was strongly placed, on a cliff edge overlooking the river. It has played a remarkably small part in the history of England, both the Wars of the Roses and the Civil War passing it by. Entry is by the **keep**, 100ft - 30m of grey Norman masonry, great enough to stand beside Rochester and London's White Tower. It incorporates an 11C arch opening into the courtyard. From the roof of the keep there is a splendid **view** across the cobbled market place and over the moorland beyond. Within the courtyard, the most interesting building is **Scolland's Hall**. Built 1080, it is, with the exception of the hall-keep at Chepstow *(qv)* the oldest such building in England.

★ **Georgian Theatre Royal and Museum.** — *Through Friar's Wynd, from Market Place.* Opened 2 September 1787, it was used for many years from the 1840s as an auction room. It was restored in 1963 and is the only Georgian theatre in the country with its original form and features.

Green Howards Regimental Museum. — Housed in the 12C Holy Trinity Church in the centre of the Market Place, the museum was opened in 1973 by the Colonel in Chief, the late King Olaf V of Norway and displays include uniforms, medals, campaign relics, weapons, badges and pictures from 1688 to the present day.

EXCURSION

Bolton Castle. — *12 miles - 19km southwest, by the A6108 then right onto minor road.* Richard Scrope started building his castle in 1379. It is basically a comfortable house of the period, built round a courtyard. For defence the castle has massive corner towers, turrets and portcullises and the whole southeast corner could be sealed off as a self-contained keep. Bolton served as prison for Mary Queen of Scots in 1568-9. It is still well preserved, despite being "slighted" after the Civil War and parts are still roofed.

★ RIPON North Yorkshire   Pop 13 036

Michelin Map 402 P 21 or Atlas G Britain p 40

At 9pm every night of the year, a horn is blown in the Market Square of this small cathedral city, to "set the Watch". The custom commemorates the responsibility, in the Middle Ages, of the **Wakeman** for the safety of the citizens at night. A toll of two pence per house door was paid to him annually, and he made good from this 'insurance premium' any losses suffered.

Market Square. — Covering two acres - almost a hectare, it is one of the largest in the north of the country. The **Obelisk**, at the four corners of which the horn is blown, dates from 1781 and commemorates the sixty-year term as Member of Parliament of William Aislabie, of nearby Studley Royal *(qv)*. The **Town Hall**, built by Wyatt in 1801 has an Ionic portico and carries along its frieze the motto "Except ye Lord Keep ye Cittie ye Wakeman Waketh in Vain". The four Town Horns, including the **Charter Horn**, many centuries old and symbolising the granting of the first Charter to Ripon in 886 AD, can be seen in the Mayor's Parlour. The latest horn was presented in 1886, marking the 1000th anniversary of that Charter and came from the Chillingham herd of wild cattle *(qv)*.

Almost next door is the **Wakeman's House**, a 14C two-storeyed, timber-framed house, home of the last holder of the office, Hugh Ripley, who in 1604, under the Charter granted by James I, became first Mayor of Ripon.

★ **Cathedral.** — Built above the Saxon crypt of St Wilfrid's church, dating from 672 AD, the cathedral, started in 1154, presents first its imposing Early English west front - "the finest in England" (Pevsner). Inside the west door, immediately to your right, is the medieval font and above it, in the westernmost window of the south aisle, are roundels of 14C glass, all that remains of the great east window, shot out in 1643 by Parliamentary troops, who also destroyed the 'idolatrous images' on the **choir screen**. These were replaced, by one carver, during the 1939-45 war. To the south of the nave altar are the steps down into the **Saxon crypt★★**, under the tower, 11ft × 8ft - 3 1/2m × 2 1/2m - and only 9ft - less than 3m high. It was built by St Wilfrid on his return from Rome. Part of the central tower collapsed in 1450; its reconstruction resulted in a contrast between the Transitional style of the north and west sides, which had survived, and the Perpendicular of the rebuilt south and east sides.

Misericords and exquisite **choir stalls** were carved over five years by William Bromflete and a handful of craftsmen, the 'Ripon school', who worked here and at Beverley at the end of the 15C. On one is an "Elephant and Castle", often said to be the English misinterpretation of "Infanta of Castile" - Eleanor, Queen of Edward I - which has since been widely used as a name for public houses across the country. The **Chapel of the Holy Spirit** has a striking modern metal screen, symbolising the Pentecostal 'tongues of flame'.

EXCURSIONS

★★★ **Fountains Abbey** and **Studely Royal.** — *Description p 121.*

Newby Hall. — *4 miles - 6km southeast, by the B6265 and minor road.*
Originally a 17C mellow brick mansion extended and remodelled during the 18C by John Carr and Robert Adam. Renowned for its Adam interiors, including the Gobelins **Tapestry Room** with the *Loves of the Gods* **tapestries★** on an unusual dove-grey background and the **Gallery** designed for a rare collection of Classical sculpture brought from Italy by William Weddell in 1765. Additional features of interest include the Chippendale furniture and a collection of chamber pots (16C-19C). From the south front of the house beautiful gardens sweep down to the River Ure.

ROCHESTER Kent   Pop 23 840

Michelin Map 404 V 29 or Atlas G Britain p 12

The Romans built Durobrivae to dominate the point where Watling Street crossed the River Medway. The 12C castle still does, and dominates, too, the cathedral - the Normans were practical - and the town, a walled town cut in two by "the silent High Street, full of gables with old beams and timbers" (Charles Dickens).

★ **Castle.** — The early **curtain walls** were built by Gundulf, Bishop of Rochester and architect of Rochester Cathedral and the Tower of London *(qv).* The present massive **keep** was built by William de Corbeil, Archbishop of Canterbury, in 1127 and its ruins are an outstanding example of Norman military architecture. Note the dogtooth decoration on the arches, the great hall and the 13C bastions on the curtain wall.

★ **Cathedral.** — Bishop Gundulf (1024-1108) followed Lanfranc to England and held England's second episcopal see (f 604) from 1077 to his death in 1108. The cathedral was subsequently extended on two main occasions and is mostly 12 and 13C. Of particular interest is the Norman west front, rich in blind arcading and its centrepiece, the exuberantly sculptured **west doorway** (1160) showing a strong French influence. Beyond the six Norman nave bays the cathedral is essentially Early English. The painting on the choir wall is the *Wheel of Fortune* and dates from the 13C when the whole of the cathedral walls were similarly painted. Note the carvings on the chapter room doorway (*c*1350) and the west end of the crypt which is part of Gundulf's original work.

On the north side between the two transepts is Gundulf's *c*1100 **tower** and to the south, the ruins of the 12C cloisters.

Guildhall. — Erected in 1687, this fine Renaissance building now contains the city's civic regalia, local history museum and archives.

Chatham Historic Dockyard. — *2 miles - 3km northeast of the Cathedral.*
Established in the reign of Henry VIII, this cradle of British sea power built nearly 500 ships, including Nelson's *Victory*; its last vessel, HMCS *Okanagan,* was completed in 1966 and the Royal Navy finally moved out in 1984. The splendid complex of docks and maritime buildings now welcomes the public with interpretive displays in the visitor centre, while the making of flags and sails is demonstrated in the Sail and Colour Loft. The many historic structures include the imposing Main Gate, bearing the arms of George III, the Commissioner's House, the church and the 1 140ft - 347m long ropery, once again in production.

EXCURSION

★ **Leeds Castle.** — *11 miles - 18km southeast. Take the A229 and the M20, follow signs.*
Originally Norman, built on two islands in a lake, it was described by Lord Conway as "the loveliest castle in the world". The interior is fully furnished with treasures from the 14-19C. The castle is still used for important meetings: its fortifications protected Egyptian and Israeli negotiators during the 1970s Middle East peace talks. The park and gardens include a duckery, aviary, secret grotto and maze.

Michelin Map 404 U 30 or Atlas G Britain p 12
Town plan in current Michelin Red Guide Great Britain and Ireland

A graceful combination of Georgiana and Victoriana amid parks, vistas and with a vast semi-wild common, Tunbridge Wells owes its good fortune to the accidental discovery of its mineral springs in 1606 by Lord North and it soon became a magnet for the fashionable. Queen Henrietta-Maria spent six weeks there, in a tent, after the birth of her son, Charles II. Queen Anne provided the tiled paving after which the **Pantiles** are named and Queen Victoria spent holidays there: "Dear Tunbridge Wells, I am so fond of it".

★ **The Pantiles.** — The perfect pedestrian precinct. On two levels, an Upper Walk and a Lower Walk; the **Bath House** (1804) still shows off its chalybeate spring; the **Corn Exchange** (1802), once a theatre, displays Doric columns and Ceres, Goddess of the Harvest, on the roof; and the **Music Gallery** remains a reminder of the town's past elegance. **Union House** (1969, by Michael Levell) at one end of the Pantiles is an object lesson on how old and new can stand together in dignity. The **Church of King Charles the Martyr** at the other end is a lesson in modesty and adaptability. The 1678 church was squared in 1696, the interior turned round and given a ceiling by Wren's plasterer, Henry Doogood.

★ **Calverley Park.** — Not so much a park as a neo-classical new town by Decimus Burton. Inspired by Bath *(qv)* it is always homogenous but never repetitive, lavish in space but spare in idiom; best seen around Calverley Park Crescent.

EXCURSIONS

Knole and Ightham Mote. — *19 miles - 31km by the A26, A21 and A225 north to Sevenoaks, then follow signs to Knole.*

★★ **Knole.** — Begun in 1456 by Thomas Bourchier, Archbishop of Canterbury, this great house in its vast sweep of parkland passed to the Sackville family who extended it in c1603 and it was the childhood home of Vita Sackville-West. With seven courts (the days of the week), 52 staircases (weeks of the year) and 365 rooms (days of the year) she likened it to a "medieval village". Horace Walpole, looking through different eyes, spoke of its "beautiful, decent simplicity".
Most impressive of the rooms is the **Great Hall**, with its sumptuous Jacobean screen. In the grisailled Stair Hall is a life-size nude of the beauty Gianetta Baccelli, mistress of the house in all senses and whose portrait by Gainsborough is in the Tate Gallery *(qv)*. The **Spangle Dressing Room** displays portraits by Lely and the second oldest harpsichord case, made in England in 1622. The **Reynolds Gallery** speaks for itself. The **Ballroom** is characterised by its Jacobean chimney-piece, panelling and frieze and the **Cartoon Gallery** by Mytens' copies of Raphael's New Testament cartoons. Climax of the house is the **King's Room**, all gaudy grisailles, ostrich feathers, expensive embroidery and silver ornamentation - "the only vulgar room in the house" (Vita Sackville-West).

Go north through Sevenoaks town centre, then take the A25 towards Maidstone. Ightham Mote is signposted to the right after about 3 miles - 5km.

★ **Ightham Mote.** — Built of stone and timber in 1340, Ightham (pronounced "item") is the most perfect surviving moated manor house in England. The **Gatehouse**, Courtyard and Great Hall (note the grotesques holding up the timber beams and the stone vaulting) are Decorated. The Chapel with its painted barrel vault roof is early Tudor.

Scotney Castle Garden and Sissinghurst Castle. — *18 miles - 29km. Leave Tunbridge Wells on the A267 to the south, then take the B2169 to Lamberhurst and follow signs.*

Scotney Castle Garden. — From a bastion near the Victorian stone mansion the eye is led sharply downwards into an enchanting scene - the steep valley sides, the moated ruin of Roger Ashburnham's 14C castle and the 17C house built into it, luxuriant trees and shrubs, all drawn together in the early 19C by Edward Hussey to form the most picturesque of landscaped compositions.

Take the A21 and the B2162 north, then the A262 east.

Goudhurst. — The pretty village street rises steeply to the parish church on the hilltop. All around are the orchards and hopfields of the "Garden of England".

Continue on the A262 to Sissinghurst.

★ **Sissinghurst Castle.** — A great Tudor mansion was discovered by **Vita Sackville-West** and her husband **Harold Nicholson** in 1930. "I fell in love; love at first sight. I saw what could be made of it... a castle running away into sordidness and squalor, a garden crying out for rescue." The **Tower** became her study (note the Hogarth Press which printed the first edition of T S Eliot's *Waste Land*) and the **garden** their monument. It combines "the strictest formality of design with the maximum informality in planting"; axial walks with gardens opening off (each with a separate colour scheme), culminating in arches and statues.

Penshurst, Chiddingstone and Chartwell. — *23 miles - 37km. Leave to the west by the A264 then turn right onto the B2188.*

Penshurst Place. — Home of the Elizabethan poet **Sir Philip Sidney** (1554-86), it is set in a pretty neo-Tudor village, clustering around the 13C church of St John the Baptist, with its Sidney Chapel. The original 1346 Hall has been added on with early Tudor, Jacobean and neo-Gothic wings. Inside the Hall, the chestnut timber roof is held up by carvings of life-size peasants, while the living rooms are packed with Rococo and Palladian furniture, some by William Kent. In the outbuildings is an enchanting **Toy Museum**, containing 19C dolls, rocking horses, puppets and a Queen Anne flatbacked doll.

Continue north on the B2176 to join the B2027, which you take to the left.

Chiddingstone village is 15 and 16C, timber-framed, tile-hung, pargetted and gabled, clustered around St Mary's Church, a rare combination of 14C Gothic and Jacobean neo-Gothic. "In its way, Chiddingstone is perfect" (Pevsner).

Chiddingstone Castle. — This mansion in the castle style, was remodelled *c*1805 from an older house, by William Atkinson the architect of Scone Palace. The works of art were amassed by Denys Eyre Bower, perhaps the most remarkable English eccentric since William Beckford - unlike Beckford he was not a millionaire but a bank clerk with an extraordinary eye.

The collection includes Lely's nude portrait of Nell Gwyn, Samuel Cooper's miniature of Charles II, Japanese armour and swords, a fine selection of Japanese lacquer, as well as Royal Stuart mementoes from Mary Queen of Scots to Bonnie Prince Charlie.

Continue along the B2027 and follow signs to Hever Castle.

★ **Hever Castle.** — *Description p 136.*

Return to the B2027 then turn right onto the B2028.

★ **Chartwell.** — Home of **Sir Winston Churchill** (1874-1965). The restored Tudor house is packed with Churchilliana including many of his paintings and reflects the comfortable domestic life of the great man. The walls in the garden were partly built by Churchill himself and there is a splendid southward prospect over rolling countryside.

Westerham. — Pop 5 000. A trim former market town on a hill, birthplace of General Wolfe, conqueror of New France in 1759. His residence, **Quebec House** has interesting mementoes and his statue, sword aloft, shares the sloping green with a seated figure of Churchill.

The Weald. — This densely wooded tract of sandy hills and clay vales runs for nearly 100 miles - 160km between the bold escarpments of the North and South Downs. The even more extensive and sparsely populated forest (Weald is cognate with German **Wald**) of former times provided seemingly limitless quantities of timber for shipbuilding and wood for charcoal production associated with the exploitation of local ironstone. The area's iron industry reached its peak in the 16 and 17C; the dozens of "hammer ponds" which once supplied water-power for the many forges are its most visible trace today, though many of its products are assembled in the Anne of Cleves Museum at Lewes *(qv)*.

Proximity to London has long combined with the leafy intimacy of the Wealden landscape to make it an attractive area for residence, as much for the contemporary commuter as for the great landed proprietors of the past. A range of materials, stone, timber, brick and tile, have been used to create some of the most romantically appealing of country houses as well as the more modest hamlet, village and isolated yeoman's cottage.

Leave Tunbridge Wells by the A264 to the west, then turn left onto the B2110.

The villages of **Groombridge** and **Hartfield** both have pretty weather-boarded and tile-hung houses.

2 miles - 3km beyond Hartfield turn left following signs to Wych Cross.

Ashdown Forest. — The core of the Weald is formed by the heaths and pine and birch woodlands of this spacious sandy upland. A number of parking spots and picnic areas invite visitors to enjoy the fine views and discover the countryside on foot. Shortly before Wych Cross three rebuilt thatched barns house the small Ashdown Forest Centre, which explains the area's natural history.

★★ **RYE** East Sussex   Pop 4 127

Michelin Map **404** W 31 or Atlas G Britain p 12

A multitude of red-roofed houses building up to a massive squat-towered church, this exquisite small hill town is visible far off across the vast expanse of eastward-stretching levels. Its early history was one of struggle both on and with the sea. Associated from 1191 with the **Cinque Ports**, the maritime league of Kent and Sussex towns established by Edward the Confessor to supply ships and men for defence of the realm, Rye suffered repeated sackings by the French. Though battered by storms which violently changed the course of the River Rother in the 13C and later destroyed many of its buildings, the town is still a minor port, though the sea's retreat has left it two miles inland.

Tranquil centuries of decline and its former remoteness preserved Rye's charming townscape, though much of its medieval fabric wears a Georgian exterior. Artists and writers, among them Henry James, have lived here, drawn by its antique air or by the lonely landscapes and strange light of the surrounding marsh.

The "Sixth Continent" - Romney Marsh. — Eastwards from Rye stretch the seemingly infinite levels of Walland, Denge and Romney Marshes. This once isolated land was won bit by bit from the sea over a thousand years, yielding rich pasture for its famous sheep. The little resorts of its east coast, linked by the 15 mile - 24km miniature mainline **Romney, Hythe and Dymchurch Railway** are busy enough in the summer; a giant nuclear power station now stands on the shingle spit at Dungeness but inland are tiny villages lost in a web of meandering lanes and watercourses. Along the foot of the old cliff from Rye to Hythe runs the **Royal Military Canal**, dug to facilitate the transport of troops and heavy munitions between the Martello towers and coastal batteries.

★★ OLD TOWN

With its steep and intricate streets, a wealth of different building materials and sudden glimpses of the countryside, the whole of Rye between ruined walls and former cliff-line repays careful exploration on foot.

From the riverside warehouses of Strand Quay, where the **son et lumière** accompanying the meticulously-crafted **Rye Town Model** effectively evokes the past, the cobbled **Mermaid Street★** rises sharply. Its varied buildings include the 15C **Mermaid Inn**, reputed haunt of ruthless smuggler gangs. Looking towards Church Square is the handsome Georgian façade of Lamb House, home of Henry James from 1897 and later of the satirical novelist E F Benson.

St Mary's Church. — Begun in the 12C, this large and impressive building has a famous 16C clock, its 18ft - 5 1/2m pendulum swinging inside, its elaborate face on the outside of the north transept, flanked by jolly painted quarter boys who strike the quarters but not the hours. From the tower there is an incomparable **view★** of Rye's red-tiled roofs and all the country around.

Ypres Tower. — This sturdy little 13C citadel on its clifftop perch, long used as a prison, is now a local **museum**.

High Street. — Among the many delights of the long and gently winding street is the Dutch gabled **Old Grammar School** of 1636. The round towers of the Landgate mark the point at which an isthmus connected the island port with the mainland.

EXCURSIONS

★★ **Bodiam Castle.** — *13 miles - 21km. Leave to the northwest via the A268. After 11 miles - 18km turn left at Sandhurst and follow minor roads to Bodiam.*
In a pretty landscaped setting among low hills, overlooking the levels of the River Rother, this archetypal medieval castle sits four-square within its protecting moat. Built in 1385-88 to block movement inland by marauding Frenchmen up the then navigable river, it retains its great gatehouse, massive curtain walls and 60ft - 18m high drum towers at each corner. A brick and concrete blockhouse, a "pillbox" of the Second World War, confirms the site's strategic importance.

★ **Winchelsea.** — Pop 34 127. *2 1/2 miles - 4km. Leave via the A259 to the west.*
Planted in the late 12C by **Edward I** on a sandstone bluff, to replace its storm-wracked namesake three miles away, Winchelsea never prospered in its role as a port for the Gascon wine trade. Repeatedly attacked by the French and abandoned by a receding sea, some of its chequer-board plan remained unbuilt, though three gateways remain, the Pipewell Gate, the New Gate lost in the countryside to the south and the **Strand Gate**, looking forlornly from the old clifftop to the distant sea. Some of the 18C and 19C houses in the quiet grass-verged streets have vaulted medieval cellars, a reminder of the early wine trade. All that remains of the grand town church of **St Thomas** is an impressive chancel, its side chapels containing fine 14C **effigies★**.

★ ST ALBANS Hertfordshire   Pop 76 709

Michelin Map 404 T 28 or Atlas G Britain p 19

First there was the River Ver. On one bank was built **Verulamium**, the Roman city. Its bricks were used to build the abbey on the other bank. A town grew up which, at the Dissolution, took over the abbey as its parish church; in 1877 it became a cathedral, the town a city.

★ VERULAMIUM

The third largest city in Roman Britain, Verulanium was established in 49 AD and rebuilt at least twice: once after being sacked by Boadicea in 61 AD and again *c* 155 AD after a major fire. Rome declined and Verulamium fell. By 940 its ruins "were hiding places for robbers, body snatchers and evil women", according to the Saxon abbot. By 1591 Edmund Spencer could write "Of which there now remains no memorie, Nor anie little moniment to see". Since the excavations of Sir Mortimer Wheeler in the 1930s and Professor Sheppard Frere in the 1950s, the city has been rediscovered. The site is now a public park, Verulamium Park.

Verulamium Museum. — *St Michael's Street.*
The on-site museum displays some of the most impressive Roman works to be unearthed in Britain, providing a fascinating glimpse of Roman life: ironwork, jewellery, coins, glass, pottery and the exceptional Sea God and Lion **mosaics.**

Roman Theatre. — *Northwest of the museum, on the other side of Bluehouse Hill.*
Almost round like a modern theatre, its first use was probably for public and religious festivals. Then the stage was enlarged and behind it a row of columns was erected in imitation of a conventional Roman theatre. In *c* 300 AD it was enlarged again. Behind the theatre ran Watling Street *(qv),* in front of it was the temple, and again in St Michael's churchyard nearby was the basilica and forum.

Hypocaust. — *Verulamium Park, southwest of the museum.*
The bath suite of a large house preserved *in situ*, it reveals the central heating system: hot air from a fire passing through flues and channels under the floor.

Walls. — *Verulamium Park, south of the museum.*
The 6ft - nearly 2m thick walls of flint and brick stood more than 16ft - 5m high and were strengthened by bastions, of which two remain, together with the foundations of the London Gate.

★**CATHEDRAL** *time: 1 hour — by Verulam Road, George Street*

The original abbey was Saxon, a shrine to St Alban, England's first Christian martyr. The present cathedral, dominated by its Norman central tower, was started in 1077 by the Norman Paul of Caen. Paul was possibly the illegitimate son of Lanfranc, Archbishop of Canterbury. When Lanfranc built a five-apse abbey, Paul built a seven-apse one.

100 years later the impressive Norman nave was lengthened still further in Early English style. When five piers collapsed on the south side they were replaced by Decorated ones. The cathedral was given a new and very Victorian west front in 1879 and a ''Post-Modern'' chapter house in 1982.

Interior. — ''There is nothing to attract, though much to respect and much to investigate'', wrote Pevsner. The beauty lies not in the structure but in the smaller things, the 1350 nave screen, the 1484 reredos, the 1320 Lady Chapel, the **shrine** to St Alban and the exquisite medieval wall paintings and ceiling panels.

EXCURSIONS

★★**Hatfield House.** — *Description p 135.*

★**Luton Hoo.** — *10 miles - 16km on the A1081 and B653.*
⊘ Originally designed by Robert Adam and landscaped by Capability Brown, it was rebuilt in 1848 and sold to the South African diamond merchant and art collector Sir Julius Wernher in 1903. He commissioned Charles Mewès, architect of the Ritz Hotels in London and Paris, to redesign the interior in Beaux Arts grandeur. It is now the showcase of the **Wernher Collection**★★ of English and Dutch paintings, French tapestries, ecclesiastical art, Byzantine art and Renaissance jewellery; the English porcelain collection of his wife; and the Russian Collection of Imperial Royal Family portraits and Fabergé jewellery, belonging to his daughter-in-law, Anastasia, daughter of Grand Duke Michael of Russia.

★**Knebworth House.** — *5 miles - 8km by the A1, own access off Junction 7.*
⊘ The house is late 15C, the great hall with its richly carved screen and minstrels' gallery hardly changed since the house was built. It was **Bulwer-Lytton**, the writer of historical fantasies, who turned it into a domed Gothick fantasy, best seen in the turreted fireplace, painted panels and stained-glass windows of the **State Drawing Room**. His favourite room was his study. Edward Fitzgerald recalls visiting Lytton there, in the company of Charles Dickens. ''We saw an Eastern potentate sitting on luxurious cushions, with dreamy eyes and reposeful manner, smoking a chibouk.''

★★ ST ANDREWS Fife   Pop 11 630
Michelin Map 401 L 14 or Atlas G Britain p 56

This Fife coast resort, with its cathedral, castle and long-established university, is also famous as the ''home'' of golf.

HISTORICAL NOTES

There was an early religious settlement of St Mary, associated with relics of St Andrew. In the 12C a priory, and later a cathedral were established, leading to the foundation of the University. By 1472 St Andrews was the ecclesiastical capital of Scotland. Its importance declined in the 17C, owing to the switch in trade from the Baltic to the American colonies, and after the Act of Union in 1707. The 19C, however, saw St Andrews return to prominence as a tourist and golfing centre, an importance it has kept to this day.

Golf. — It was in 1457 that James II had his Parliament ban ''the games of futeball and the golfe'', for people were wasting their time playing these games instead of practising their archery at the butts and attending kirk! Founded in 1754, the Society of St Andrews Golfers had the title Royal and Ancient conferred on it in 1834 and today it is recognised as the sport's ruling body.

New courses have been laid out on the springy turf of the links to supplement the **Old Course**, established many centuries ago.

SIGHTS

★**Cathedral.** — The imposing **St Regulus Church** may have been built originally to house ⊘ the relics of St Andrew. Robert of Scone built the church, with its lofty tower, between 1127 and 1144. The tower today *(151 steps),* affords a magnificent **panorama**★★ across St Andrews and its main monuments. St Regulus's was replaced from 1160 by the later cathedral, the largest church ever built in Scotland. After the Reformation this once-noble building was used as a stone quarry, and reduced to the ruin we see today. The **museum** has a good collection of early Christian sculpture stones.

The ruined 13C **castle** overlooking the foreshore was once a part of the palace of the archbishop.

⊘ **St Andrews University.** — Founded in 1410 and granted a Papal Bull in 1413, it was the first in Scotland, and third only after Oxford and Cambridge. It became in the 16C a centre for reformist doctrines and thus involved in struggles with both the established Church and the Crown. This had some bearing on the plan to move the University to Perth in the 17C. The present student population (4 250) is largely residential. **St Salvator's College**, founded in 1450 by Bishop James Kennedy, remains the nucleus of the Faculty of Arts.

EXCURSIONS

★★ **East Neuk.** — *Leave St Andrews by the A917.*

The East Neuk, or East Corner, is a stretch of coastline dotted with picturesque fishing villages, each clustered around its harbour and with a wealth of vernacular architecture. These were the ports to which once came the wealth and prosperity of the fisheries and the Baltic and Dutch trade. With Dunfermline as the political capital and St Andrews as the ecclesiastical, they made of Fife the "beggars mantle with a fringe of gold", as James VI described it.

⊘ **Crail** is the most attractive village; in **Anstruther** is the **Scottish Fisheries Museum**★★, and in **Pittenweem** Kellie Lodge, the corbelled, pantiled and crow-stepped town house of the Earls of Kellie Castle *(see below).*

★ **Kellie Castle.** — *10 miles - 16km south by the B9131 and the B9171.*

⊘ Just inland behind this "fringe of gold" is Kellie Castle. It is, in fact a laird's house, an example of unspoilt 16 and 17C traditional Scottish architecture. A period of neglect from 1830 was, happily, followed by the castle being leased by **Sir Robert Lorimer**, the architect who designed the Thistle Chapel in St Giles' Cathedral, Edinburgh. With the help of his brother, an artist, and in the next generation, Hew Lorimer, the sculptor, Kellie Castle was restored to its former glory. The 17C **plasterwork ceilings** are notable, in particular that of the Vine Room.

Leuchars. — Pop 2 203. *6 miles - 10km northwest by the A91 and the A919.*

The village is known for its Junction, the railway station for St Andrews, and for ⊘ the RAF base nearby. The **church** which dominates the village from its elevated position, has a 12C chancel and apse, exceptionally fine examples of **Norman work**, ⊘ with grotesque heads over arcading on the outside walls. Nearby, **Earlshall Castle** has an exceptional painted ceiling and a fine topiary garden.

★ **ST DAVID'S** (TYDDEWI) Dyfed   Pop 1 428

Michelin Map **403** E 28 or Atlas G Britain p 14 — Local map p 198

The cathedral, not unnaturally, is the centrepiece of this tiny city. Since the decree of Pope Callixtus II in the 12C, two pilgrimages to St David's are the equivalent of one to Rome - a privilege shared only with Santiago de Compostella in Spain. There has been a Christian community and daily worship on this site, for more than fourteen centuries. St David's today is a thriving tourist-oriented community, set at the westernmost point of the **Pembrokeshire Coast Path** *(qv).*

★★ **Cathedral.** — Wales' greatest church, built in lichen-encrusted purple stone, sits in a secluded hollow, revealing itself with dramatic suddenness to the visitor passing through the gatehouse into the precinct containing both Cathedral and Bishop's Palace.

The original church, built here on the banks of the Alun by St David (*c* 462-520 AD), was burnt down in 645 and again, by the Danes, in 1078. The present building was started in 1180 by Peter de Leia (1176-98), Florentine monk and third Norman bishop. Up to the wall behind the high altar, what we see today is substantially his cathedral, though the tower fell in 1220 and an earthquake in 1248 left the westernmost pillars of the nave leaning alarmingly outwards. The whole building slopes upwards some 14ft - 3 1/2m from west to east and presents a unique and striking impression to a visitor entering the south porch, at the western end of the nave. The late 15C **nave roof** is a magnificent piece of work, in Irish oak, incorporating the dragon of Wales on the pendants. In the south choir aisle is the tomb of the historian **Giraldus Cambrensis** (1146-1223). Before the high altar is the table tomb of **Edmund Tudor**, grandfather of Henry VIII, who ordered it to be moved here from Grey Friars at Carmarthen after the Dissolution. The remains of St David's shrine, built 1275, are on the north side of the Presbytery, but the **Saint's relics**, together with those of his confessor, Justinian, rest in an oak and iron reliquary, at the back of the Holy Trinity Chapel, near where they were hidden at the Reformation and only re-discovered during restoration work in 1886.

★ **Bishop's Palace.** — The close wall surrounding cathedral and palace probably dates ⊘ from *c*1300. The Palace we see today was built mainly by Bishop Gower (1328-47), who also added the south porch and the Decorated windows to the cathedral. His palace consists of three long buildings, surrounding a courtyard, which is completed by a wall pierced by a buttressed gateway. The **Bishop's Hall** and **Solar**, with kitchen and chapel, appear to have been the main residence, the **Great Hall** to the south, with its elaborate porch and stairs from the courtyard, being reserved for the entertainment of important guests. After the Reformation the decay of palace and cathedral began. Bishop Barlow (1536-48), wished to remove the See to Carmarthen and stripped the palace roof of its lead - ostensibly for re-use on his new palace, though it was said in St David's that the sale of the lead provided generous dowries for his five daughters, each of whom married a bishop!

St Non's Chapel. — Immediately south of the city are the cliffs and coves of the Pembroke coast. Here can be found a number of sites associated with the saint: the ruined chapel dedicated to his mother, St Non, where he is held to have been born; St Non's Well and, to the west, the tiny harbour inlet at Porth-Clais, where, by tradition, he was baptised.

Except where otherwise stated,
all recommended itineraries in town, are designed as walks.

Michelin Map 403 O 30 or Atlas G Britain p 9
Town plan in the current Michelin Red Guide Great Britain and Ireland

The new town of Salisbury came into existence with the new cathedral, was granted a charter in 1227 and was controlled by the bishops until 1611. The earlier city of **Old Sarum**, a 28 acre - 11ha Iron Age hillfort two miles to the north, had been modified by the Romans and Saxons and finally became a Norman strongpoint where two successive cathedrals were built. From 1078-99 **St Osmund** was bishop of the first cathedral which was destroyed by lightning and then rebuilt and enlarged by **Bishop Roger**, who also converted the castle into an episcopal palace. His fall from power in 1139 marked the beginning of prolonged friction between the clergy and the king's men over possession of the castle-palace.

By the beginning of the 13C the inadequate water supply and the fact that they no longer needed a hilltop fort decided the citizens and clergy of Old Sarum to build their third cathedral on the banks of the River Avon. The buildings on the hilltop fell into ruin and today only the castle ruins and the ground plan of the cathedral can be seen within the earthworks, with a fine view over Salisbury Plain and New Sarum, now Salisbury.

★★★ CATHEDRAL *time: 1 hour*

Salisbury is the most stylistically unified of all the British cathedrals, built in its entirety between 1220 and 1265, except for the spire, its most famous feature, which was built from 1285-1320. This epitome of Early English style is built of silver-grey limestone from Chilmark, 12 miles - 19km away, with Purbeck marble shafts. The **west front** is impressively ornate though confused, perhaps because it suffered too much 19C restoration; the **north porch** is, however, particularly fine. Curiously, the most spectacular feature of this Early English edifice was added almost a century later and yet the **tower** and **spire**, the highest in the land, rising to 404ft - 123m, is such inspired work that it goes perfectly with the rest of the church *(photograph p 32)*.

Interior. — Perfect unity and consistent beauty of line give great poise and a certain coolness.

Nave. — The grey quatrefoil piers of Purbeck marble, surrounded by polished shafts, are caught by slim moulded capitals; the clusters of foiled columnettes in the galleries and the tall lancets of the clerestory are of the same distinctive black stone. Between the arcade pillars on the south side are the tomb chests of **Bishops Roger** (d 1139) and **Joscelin** (d 1184), the shrine of **St Osmund** (d 1099) and the chain-mailed effigy of **William Longespée** (d 1226), 3rd Earl of Salisbury, whose wife founded Lacock Abbey.

Crossing. — Marking the crossing are **giant piers** of clustered black marble columns, intended to support the original low tower but since the 14C required to bear the extra 6 500 tons of the heightened tower and spire. The piers have in fact buckled a mere 3 1/2'' - 9cm despite reinforcing internal and external buttresses, massive 15C tie-beam arches across the transepts and a decorated stone vault over the crossing.

At the centre of the crossing an **octagon** marks the outline of the spire 45ft - 14m below its apex. In 1668 **Sir Christopher Wren**, surveying the cathedral, dropped his plumbline from the spire point and a brass plate marks the spot 29 1/2 inches - 75.5cm off-centre to the southwest, where it reached the floor.

Tower ascent. — A number of spiral staircases (360 steps) lead the enterprising visitor to the base of the spire (224ft - 68m) with views of the Close and Old Sarum.

Transepts. — This symmetrical church has its main transepts exactly midway between the east and west ends and a further pair of sub-transepts with 14C scissor arches.

Trinity Chapel. — The **blue window**, *Prisoners of Conscience*, glazed in 1980 by Gabriel Loire from Chartres, contrasts with the great **west window** which contains six medieval shields and 15-16C figures. The chapel contains the slimmest of all the black Purbeck **marble shafts** in the cathedral, rising to the groined vaulting.

CLOISTERS AND CHAPTER HOUSE

Work began on the chapter house and cloisters in 1263, in Decorated style. The rib-vaulted interior of the walks has many varied bosses, including biting dragons, mermaids and human figures.

Chapter House. — This octagonal chamber, 58ft - 18m across, whose vaulted roof rises from a slender central column, is surrounded by eight ringed Purbeck marble shafts which ascend from the foliated capitals as ribs to ceiling bosses before dropping to clusters of slim columns framing the eight giant windows. Below these a frieze of Old Testament stories (restored in the 19C) fills the spandrels between the niches framing the canons' seats.

★ CLOSE

The Close, spacious and mellow with the ancient stone and terracotta bricks of its 16-18C houses, was enclosed in the 1330s against the ''riotous citizenry''. The walls are of stone from the abandoned cathedral and castle of Old Sarum. In the northwest corner is a secondary close, known as the **Choristers' Close**. There are four entries to the Close.

North or **High Street Gate.** — The gate, with a statue of **Edward VII**, opens from Choristers' Close into the town by way of an alleyway of old houses and the **Matrons' College** built in 1682 as almshouses for canons' widows.

Harnham or **South Gate.** — The distant south gate leads to the dissolved De Vaux College and St Nicholas Hospital, the latter the source of Trollope's *The Warden*.

St Ann's and **Bishop Gates.** — The gates in the east wall abut the 18C Malmesbury House and the old Bishop's Palace, an island building *c* 1220, now the Cathedral School.

★ **Mompesson House.** — Through a fine 18C wrought-iron gateway and the front ⊘ door, above which stands the stone-carved coat of arms of Charles Mompesson, who built the house in 1701, is a well-furnished interior set against ornate **baroque plasterwork**. The oak **staircase**, inserted in the 1740s at the back of the hall, is the principal architectural feature, rising by shallow flights with three crisply turned banisters to each tread. Also of note is the collection of **English drinking glasses** dating from 1700, with 370 different types of glass displayed in period cabinets in the Dining and Little Drawing Rooms.

★ **Salisbury and South Wiltshire Museum.** — *West side of the Close.*
⊘ This medieval flint and brick **King's House**, named after the visits of James I, contains a **Stonehenge** collection, a model of and relics from Old Sarum as well as sections on porcelain and pottery.

ADDITIONAL SIGHTS

Medieval Streets. — Between the cathedral and the 19C **Market Square** to the north extends a network of medieval streets, lined by gabled half-timbered houses dating from the 14-17C. The alley names indicate the trades which once flourished there - Fish Row, Butcher Row, Silver Street. At the centre in a small square stands the 15C hexagonal **Poultry Cross**.

★ **Sarum St Thomas Church.** — A Perpendicular church dating from 1220 with a low square tower of 1390, has a *Doom Painting* (*c* 1475) above the chancel arch, featuring Christ in Majesty and the New Jerusalem - perhaps a representation of 15C Salisbury. The **Lady Chapel** decorated with very small 15C frescoes, has splendid wrought-iron **railings** and finely carved **woodwork**, both dating from 1725. Admire also the roof (1470) with angel musicians on the beams.

SCARBOROUGH North Yorkshire   Pop 36 665

Michelin Map ▣ S 21 or Atlas G Britain p 47
Town plan in the current Michelin Red Guide Great Britain and Ireland

Scarborough's development as a resort can be traced back to the discovery of a medicinal spring in 1626; by 1676 the waters were claimed to cure any number of ailments, including ''The Hypochondriac Melancholy''.
The arrival of the railway in 1845 led to a prolonged building boom to accommodate the growing number of visitors and residents.
The town's two beaches are separated by the headland with its 12C castle built around a Roman signal station; to the south is the medieval town, the old fishing harbour and popular beaches; to the north, extensive stretches of sand.

⊘ **St Mary's Church.** — A Cistercian foundation, the present building dates from around 1180. **Anne Brontë**, d 1849, is buried in the churchyard.

Theatre in the Round. — It is one of Scarborough's five theatres, and owes much of its popularity to the resident playwright Alan Ayckbourn, many of whose plays have been premiered here before moving to London.

EXCURSIONS

★ **Flamborough Head.** — *21 miles - 34km south. Leave Scarborough by the A165 then turn left.*

Filey. — Pop 5 460. Filey is sheltered from the North Sea by its headland, **Filey Brigg**, and a sandy beach stretches from the charming Victorian town, right round to Flam-
⊘ borough Head. The **Filey Museum** in Queen Street is housed in two cottages dating from 1696.

Return to the A165 then turn left onto the B1229 and follow the B1255 beyond Flamborough.

★ **Flamborough Head.** — From this 215ft - 66m headland with its lighthouse, a coastal path gives access to some of the most outstanding chalk cliff scenery in the country, particularly near Bempton where the clifftops rise up to 427ft - 130m.

★ **Sledmere House.** — *21 miles - 34km south on the A64, B1249 and then right*
⊘ *onto the B1253.* Sledmere was begun in 1751, but today's exterior is the work of **Sir Christopher Sykes**, who died in 1801. Drawings exist showing that he was his own architect and draughtsman. Capability Brown laid out the park, Joseph Rose, used by both Adam and Wyatt in houses they designed, did the plasterwork. After a fire in 1911, a programme of rebuilding has left the house much as it must have looked in the early 1800s. A magnificent **Staircase Hall** and **Grand Staircase** lead up to the **Library**. All have recently been re-decorated, in colours which harmonise ideally with the architectural style. Chippendale and Sheraton furniture, French furnishings and paintings, and exquisite porcelain and antique statuary are displayed in the many fine rooms of this ''lived-in'' house.

2 1/2 miles - 4km southeast on the Great Driffield road at Garton Hill.

Built in 1865, the 120ft - 37m high **Sir Tatton Sykes Memorial** is in Gothic style, but stranger than any genuine Gothic tower.

SELBY North Yorkshire Pop 10 643

Michelin Map 402 Q 22 or Atlas G Britain p 40

The Abbey Church managed to survive the Dissolution and has remained the glory of this small Yorkshire town.

★ **Abbey Church.** — Probably founded as a Benedictine house, in 1069, thus predating both Durham and St Mary's, York. The present church was begun by Abbot Hugh de Lacey, around 1100. The **west front** is a summary of the three main styles of the building - from strength and simplicity to later elegance. The Norman doorway of *c*1170 is magnificent. Above, the work is Early English with a Perpendicular window inserted and small Early English lancets in the side bays. The **nave**, mid-Norman with its gigantic circular piers, owes a debt to Durham. The easternmost arches have distorted spectacularly, owing to a high water table. The **Jesse Window** at the east end, though much restored, is a memorable piece of work of about 1330. The **Norman font** in the west end of the north aisle has a magnificent 15C wooden cover, one of the few pieces saved from the disastrous fire of 1906. High up above the south side of the choir is a **14C window** with the arms of the Washington family - the "Stars and Stripes" motif of the American flag.

EXCURSIONS

Carlton Towers. — *6 miles - 10km south by the A1041.*
This is the Yorkshire home of the Duke of Norfolk. Henry, 9th Lord Beaumont, had the original house, built in 1614, completely re-faced in cement in 1873, to look like stone. Gargoyles, towers, turrets and battlements were added. The **Venetian Drawing Room** is one of the most complete "Victorian" interiors in the country. The **chimneypiece**, with the Stapleton "Talbot" supporters and the armorial quarterings, is the most prominent feature. There is much 19C china - Berlin, Meissen, Sèvres and Vienna - on display. The **Dining Room** occupies what was the Jacobean Hall of the original house and the table is set with silver and china from the family collection.

Lotherton Hall. — *16 miles - 26km northwest on the A63, A1 and B1217.*
The Hall was given to Leeds City Council in 1968 by the Gascoigne family, who have lived in the area since the 14C. It now, with the City Art Gallery and Temple Newsam *(qv)* houses the City's art collections. There is furniture, sculpture and fine silver from the Gascoigne family treasures, much of it collected during "Grand Tours" between 1720 and 1780. Historical costume from the 18C onwards is well represented and there is a large collection of ceramic and pottery work from the 1700s to the 1920s. In the grounds is a tiny but well preserved **Norman chapel** and a **Bird Garden** containing over 200 species from all the continents.

SHEFFIELD South Yorkshire Pop 470 685

Michelin Map 402 P 23 or Atlas G Britain p 35 — Local map p 197
Town plan in the current Michelin Red Guide Great Britain and Ireland

The hills on which medieval Sheffield grew were rich in iron ore and their thick woods provided charcoal. The five rivers running by provided water power and the local stone the grindstones - all the ingredients which, by the 14C, had made Sheffield England's chief producer of fine cutlery. Sheffield plating, the coating of copper items with silver by fusion, was a process invented in 1742 by Thomas Bolsover. Though some of its traditional industry has declined, Sheffield remains an important manufacturing centre and the commercial and cultural focus of a wide region. Its air is clean, its river valleys greener than before and part of the Peak District National Park *(qv)* lies within the boundaries of what is England's fourth largest provincial city.

★ **Cutlers' Hall.** — *Church Street.* Of dignified Grecian design, built in 1832, it is the third Cutlers' Hall on this site. It houses the Company's silver and is the setting for their annual banquet.

Cathedral Church of SS Peter and Paul. — *Church Street.*
Elevated to cathedral status in 1914, the originally cruciform building probably dates back to the 12C. Most of what is visible today is in the Perpendicular style, much altered in the restoration of 1880, with extensions in the 1930s and 1960s. The **Shrewsbury Chapel** now forms the sanctuary of the Lady Chapel, in the southeast corner and was added by the fourth Earl of Shrewsbury (d 1538). His **tomb★** shows him in armour and wearing the robes of the Order of the Garter. **St George's Chapel**, now the Chapel of the York and Lancaster Regiment, has an unusual screen of Sheffield-made swords and bayonets - the swords point uppermost denote service still being offered; bayonets, point down, signify weapons of war laid aside.

Graves Art Gallery. — *Top floor of library, Surrey Street.* This attractive suite of galleries is known for its holding of Old Masters as well as 19 and 20C French and British art, and a particularly good selection of British watercolours.

Mappin Art Gallery. — *Weston Park.* A collection of Victorian paintings and 18 and 19C English art, including Constable and Turner.

City Museum. — *Weston Park.* Here is the world's largest collection of old Sheffield Plate and of cutlery representing European and Asian craftsmanship from the Bronze Age to the present day. There are also fine collections of silver, clocks, ceramics and glass. Local archaeology exhibits include outstanding material from the Peak District and the unique Anglo-Saxon boar-crested Benty Grange Helmet.

⊘ **Sheffield Manor.** — *Manor Lane.* Originally the southern annexe of Sheffield Castle, where **Mary Queen of Scots** spent nearly fourteen of the nineteen years of her captivity, in the custody of the sixth Earl of Shrewsbury and his Countess, **Bess of Hardwick**, before being tried and executed in 1587. The **Turret House**, built 1574, still has fine plaster ceilings and houses a small museum of exhibits connected with the manor and the captive Queen.

⊘ **Bishops' House.** — *Meersbrook Park.* Timber-framed yeoman's house, *c*1500, now substantially as it was after the last alterations in 1753. It houses a small museum of Sheffield life in Tudor and Stuart times.

⊘ **Abbeydale Industrial Hamlet.** — *4 miles - 6km southwest by the A621.* By 1714, and possibly earlier, scythes were being forged here, under water-powered tilt hammers. The steel furnace was installed early in the 19C and the clay crucibles were made on site. The Abbeydale Works ceased production in 1933 and became a museum in 1970, with its manager's house and workmen's cottages open to visitors, as well as forge, grinding hull, water wheels and riveting shop.

★ **SHERBORNE** Dorset   Pop 7 405
Michelin Map 🔢 M 31 or Atlas G Britain p 8

Although the busy centre of the district's dairy-farming industry, Sherborne, with its imposing abbey church, public schools and fine buildings, some in or enriched by warm **Ham Hill stone**, has the charm of a small cathedral city.

★★ **Abbey.** — The abbey church, rebuilt during the 15C, contains elements which date
⊘ back to Saxon times when Sherborne was made the see of the Bishop of Wessex in 705. The Norman church extended as far west as the Saxon church, as the late Norman **south porch** proves. The 15C **crossing tower**, on Saxon-Norman piers and walls, has paired bell openings and twelve pinnacles; the two-tiered Perpendicular windows along the south front are divided midway by the eight-light transept window.

Interior. — The **choir** shafts rise directly from the floor to the vaulting - the earliest large-scale **fan vault** in the country - and the effect is breathtaking. Despite flying buttresses the almost flat vault had dropped 7 inches - 17.5cm after 400 years and both had to be exactly rebuilt in 1856.

Nave. — Even more impressive is the late 15C nave **vault** which, being slightly arched, did not present the same problems as the choir vault. The nave piers are not placed at equal distances and perhaps the narrower spacings towards the west end are those of the Norman piers. The string-course below the clerestory is emphasised by fleurons and corbels of angels holding shields.

Chancel arch. — A splendid, unadorned Norman tower arch divides the nave from the choir.

North aisle. — One of the **Saxon doorways** of the original church can be seen at the end of the north aisle.

★ **Sherborne Castle.** — The Old Castle, now a ruin, was built in 1107-35. In 1592
⊘ it was acquired by Sir Walter Raleigh, who then decided to build a new house, known as Sherborne Lodge, which forms the nucleus of the present house, commonly known as Sherborne Castle, on the far bank of the River Yeo. Sir John Digby enlarged the castle in 1620-30, keeping faithfully to Raleigh's style and it has remained in the family ever since.
The house, set in parkland created by **Capability Brown** in 1776-79, contains fine collections of paintings, furniture and porcelain. Particularly noteworthy is the famous painting of Queen Elizabeth I in procession and the early 17C **chimney-piece** and plaster ceiling in the Red Drawing Room. The Oak Room has 1620 **panelling** and a remarkable pair of **Jacobean inner porches**.

EXCURSIONS

Yeovil. — Pop 36 114. *5 miles - 8km west on the A30.* This busy market town with its twice-weekly livestock market has been a glove and leather centre since the 14C, the skins coming from the Polden and Quantock Hills. The majority of the buildings are 19-20C, as the town grew considerably after the opening of the Taunton-Yeovil railway in 1853. There are however a few Georgian houses and inns, most notably in **Princess Street**, **Silver Street** and the **High Street**.
⊘ The early Perpendicular church of **St John the Baptist★** (1380-1400) is characterised by five-light **windows** and original **roof bosses** depicting strange human faces and animal masks. An ogee-arched doorway leads from the chancel to the **crypt** with rib vaulting on a central **octagonal pier**. In the church, note also the 15C **font** and **lectern**.

Cadbury Castle. — *7 miles - 11km north by the B3148 and a minor road to the right.* Recent excavations give evidence of occupation in prehistoric times and of the construction of an Iron Age hillfort *c*600 BC. There are signs that the Romans occupied the castle after the 43 AD invasion and that the Saxons re-fortified it late in the 5C. The site, with its commanding **views★★**, is also reputed to be that of King Arthur's castle, **Camelot**.

Great Britain and Ireland are now covered by an Atlas at a scale of 1 inch to 4.75 miles.
Three easy to use versions: paperback, spiralbound, hardback.

Michelin Map **401** P, Q, R 1 to 4 or Atlas G Britain p 75
Access: see the current Michelin Red Guide Great Britain and Ireland

Of the 100 Shetland Islands, lying some sixty miles north of Orkney, less than twenty are inhabited. The capital, Lerwick, is on the east coast of Mainland which is 50 miles - 81km long north to south, and 20 miles - 32km across at its widest.
In contrast to Orkney, Shetland has few tracts of flat land. With its many inlets of the sea, called *voes,* the economy until recently was dominated by fishing and crofting. The oil boom of the 1970s disrupted this well-balanced economy, but even today, with **Sullom Voe** as Europe's largest oil port, the oil industry still takes second place to fishing in importance, and the area directly affected by it is limited. Elsewhere the visitor will still find the attractions of wild beauty and the empty spaces.

★★ **Up Helly Aa.** — A great torch-lit procession, reminder of the Viking heritage, takes place on the last Tuesday in January. It harks back to the placating of the Norse gods and looks forward to the return of the fire of the sun in spring. The culmination of the festival is the burning of the Viking longship - though the celebrations continue throughout the night.

Lerwick. — Pop 6 127. The natural harbour of the port capital of Shetland is sheltered by the Island of Bressay. Oil-related companies now diversify port activities traditionally dominated by fishing.

EXCURSIONS FROM LERWICK

★★ **Jarlshof.** — *Mainland. 25 miles - 40km south of Lerwick.*
The site of Jarlshof has been occupied from the middle of the 2nd millennium BC until the 17C. There are six Bronze Age houses, and a late Iron Age broch with other dwellings clustered around it. Numerous Viking longhouses tell of several centuries of occupation and there was a farmstead here in the 13C. In the 16C **New Hall** was built for Earl Robert Stewart.

★★★ **Mousa Broch.** — *Mousa Island. 12 miles - 19km south of Lerwick.*
Small fortified farms, brochs, were peculiar to Scotland, the culmination of a tradition stretching back to 500 BC. Most have crumbled, but Mousa, probably dating from the first or second century AD, still stands. Within the imposing kiln-shaped tower, more than 40ft - 15m across at the base, the courtyard was surrounded by lean-to structures, while staircase, chambers and galleries were built into the thickness of the walls.

Sullom Voe. — *Mainland. 35 miles - 56km north of Lerwick.*
Europe's largest oil terminal was established in a deep sheltered inlet, connected by two pipelines to the oilfields of the East Shetland Basin. Tankers of over 400 000 tons can be handled here and fourteen off-shore fields, 100 miles - 160km away to the northeast, pump Brent Blend oil to the terminal, which can handle 1 million barrels a day. Sullom Voe has no refining facilities, though the gases propane and butane are separated and stored for shipment.

SHREWSBURY Shropshire   Pop 57 731

Michelin Map **403** L 25 or Atlas G Britain p 26
Town plan in the current Michelin Red Guide Great Britain and Ireland

Once the capital of the Welsh dominions of Powys, medieval Shrewsbury grew up around its Norman castle, built by Roger de Montgomery in 1083 to guard the loop in the Severn. The town today has elegant Queen Anne and Georgian buildings, a wealth of 'black and white' houses and fascinating 'shuts' - medieval short cuts and alleyways. The two main bridges over the Severn are still, after centuries of border unrest, known as English Bridge and Welsh Bridge. **Charles Darwin** (1809-82), the naturalist, was born here, and a statue to him stands outside his old school, now the Library. Another famous townsman, **Clive of India** (1725-74), is commemorated with a statue in The Square.

★ **Abbey.** — Founded 1083, the Benedictine Abbey stands just outside the town, across the English Bridge. The 14C tower carries a statue of Edward III, in whose reign it was built, and there are Norman pillars in the nave dating from the 11C.

Castle. — Restored in the 14C, the castle was turned into a home for Sir William Poultney, MP for Shrewsbury (1776-1805), by Thomas Telford, in 1787. Only the mayor's parlour remains from this alteration, as the building was turned into Council Chambers in 1926. Today the Castle houses the **Shropshire Regimental Museum.**

Rowley's House. — This fine example of a three-storey Tudor merchant's timber-framed house, built in the late 16C, is now used as a local and social history museum. There is a collection of Roman artefacts from the city of Viroconium.

EXCURSIONS

★★ **Ironbridge Gorge Museum.** — *Description p 139.*

★★ **Weston Park.** — *17 miles - 27km east through Telford on the A5.*
The red brick house of 1671 is unusual in having been built by a woman, Lady Elizabeth Wilbraham; evidence of her architectural enthusiasm can be seen in her annotations to Palladio's *First Book of Architecture* in the library.
The splendidly furnished interior is remarkable for the quality of its portraits, most of the masters of this art being represented from Holbein onwards; Lely's likeness

of Lady Wilbraham is in the Drawing Room and there is that rarity, a portrait (of the Hon and Rev George Bridgeman) by Constable. Deer and rare breeds of sheep graze in the Capability Brown park, where there are also many family attractions, a miniature railway, pets corner, picnic area...

★★ **Powis Castle.** — *20 miles - 32km west to Welshpool by the A458.*
The town of Welshpool (Y Trallwng) lies at the northern end of the ridge on which is built Powis Castle. The barony of the la Pole was granted to Gruffyd ap Gwenwynwyn in 1277 on condition that his son renounce all Welsh princely titles. The massive twin towers of the gateway date from the decades prior to 1300. In 1587 the castle was bought by Sir Edward Herbert who quickly adapted it to Elizabethan standards of comfort. The Long Gallery, with its mid-17C *trompe-l'œil* panelling is dated 1592-3 while the Dining Room and Oak Drawing Room were remodelled in the early 20C. The castle houses the collections of the first **Lord Clive** (1725-74), victor of Plassey and founder of British India, and many fine paintings.
The **gardens**, their Italianate terraces enhancing the castle's craggy site, were created towards the end of the 17C. They were not later subjected to the fashionable attentions of Capability Brown and are one of the rare remaining masterpieces of the period. They make Powis appear more like a papal villa outside Rome than a medieval castle guarding the Marches.

Montgomery (Trefaldwyn). — Pop 1 035. *15 miles - 24km southwest of Shrewsbury by the B4386.*
A medieval "new town" granted a Charter by Henry III in 1227, Montgomery grew up beneath the **castle★** on the ridge above. The town has expanded little and the original rectangular layout is intact, though it now has the character of a Georgian market town. In the parish church of **St Nicholas** is the **canopied tomb** of Richard Herbert, his wife Magdalen, and their eight children, one of whom was the poet George Herbert (1593-1633).

Much Wenlock. — Pop 2 500. *12 miles - 19km southeast of Shrewsbury by the A458.*
A pleasant country town with many half-timbered houses including the 16C **Guildhall.** It grew around the Cluniac **Priory★** founded *c* 690 AD, pillaged by the Danes and later refounded. Built in the 1220s by Prior Humbert, its 350ft - 106m nave made it one of the longest monastic churches in England. The chapter house, however, with delicate interlaced arcading is Norman, as is the magnificent **lavatorium** at which the monks washed before meals; dating from around 1180, it has elaborately carved panels in "Wenlock marble" depicting Christ with St Peter and two Apostles.
The Prior's Lodging is one of England's finest medieval buildings, 12C, much extended in the 1490s, it has been a private dwelling since passing into private ownership at the Dissolution.

From nearby **Wenlock Edge★** a massive limestone escarpment celebrated by the poet A E Housman, magnificent views can be obtained across Shropshire.

Offa's Dyke Path. — *177 mile - 285km long distance footpath.*
Offa was King of Mercia from 757-796, introduced the penny into English currency and, having added East Anglia to his domains, was powerful enough to be in diplomatic contact with both the Papacy and Charlemagne. His Dyke marks a consolidation of the western (Welsh) border of his Mercian kingdom, though it is unlikely that it was ever "manned", as Hadrian's Wall had been on the Scottish border. In some places it is now barely visible; elsewhere its earthen bank rises to a height of 12ft - 4m, with a correspondingly deep ditch.
Officially opened in Knighton - Tref-y-Clawdd, "the town on the Dyke" - on 10 July 1971, **Offa's Dyke Path** runs from Prestatyn in the north to the Severn estuary near Chepstow in the south. Though the Path does not slavishly follow the Dyke itself all the way, it does however, offer the walker real moorland country, pastoral landscapes and thickly wooded valleys and some points on it are easily accessible by car, for those who want to stretch their legs for a few miles.

SKIPTON North Yorkshire   Pop 13 009

Michelin Map 402 N 22 or Atlas G Britain p 39

Today a base from which to explore the **Yorkshire Dales National Park**, Skipton is still dominated by its castle; this remarkably well-preserved medieval stronghold stands at the top of the High Street, along which, four times a week, there is a traditional market. Skipton also has a marina on the Leeds-Liverpool canal across the Pennines.

SIGHTS

★ **Skipton Castle.** — The castle was substantially strengthened by Robert de Clifford in the early years of the 14C before his death at Bannockburn in 1314. The beautiful **Conduit Court** was built by the 10th Earl, but the castle today owes much to the restorations made by Lady Anne Clifford (1589-1676), after the ravages of the Civil War. It was she who, in 1657-8, added the parapet with the Clifford motto *Desormais* over the main gate, and recorded the work of restoration on a tablet over the Tudor entrance to the castle itself.

Holy Trinity Church. — The church was enlarged in the 15C; its fine roof dates from 1488, and there is a **rood screen** of 1533. After the Dissolution, the Clifford family were buried here in the parish church, rather than as before in Bolton Priory. Three of their tombs stand within the Communion rails.

EXCURSIONS

★ **Haworth Parsonage and the Brontës.** — *12 miles - 19km south by the A629.*
Haworth is a typical Yorkshire hill village, and in the 1840s had more than 1 200
hand-looms operating. The **Keighley and Worth Valley Railway** operates a steam train
service from Haworth. But the village will always be best known as the home
of the **Brontë Sisters**, Charlotte (*Jane Eyre*, 1847), Emily (*Wuthering Heights,* 1847)
and Anne, who, having published *Agnes Grey,* also in 1847, is the only one of the
sisters not buried in Haworth. She lies in St Mary's churchyard, Scarborough.
The **Parsonage Museum** where they lived with their father, the Rev Patrick Brontë and
their brother Branwell, gives an intimate picture of the genteel hardship of their
lives.

★ **Bolton Priory.** — *5 miles - 8km east by the A59.*
Bolton Priory was founded by the Augustinians *c*1154, in a setting of great beauty
on a bend of the River Wharfe. At the Dissolution, the lead was stripped from all
the roofs save that of the nave of the church and the gatehouse; the nave survives
intact today, entered by an outstanding Early English west front.

> *Well-signposted footpaths on either side of the river lead from the ruins to the*
> *Wharfe's most famous spot, the Strid then on to Barden Bridge.*

At the **Strid** the river courses through a very narrow channel. Notices warn against
the foolhardiness of trying to jump across, - some have tried and perished, including it is said, the son of the founder of Bolton Priory, Alicia de Rumilly.

★ **Yorkshire Dales National Park.** — *12 miles - 19km northwest by the A65, then*
the minor road to Malham.
Malham has an information centre of the National Park. The park itself extends over
680 square miles - 1 760km²; it combines many of the dramatic features of limestone scenery, crags, caves, "limestone pavements", disappearing streams, with,
in the broad dales such as Airedale, Wensleydale and Wharfedale, stone-built villages set harmoniously in an ancient pattern of stone-walled fields. The lime-rich
waters of **Malham Tarn** support a unique collection of plants and animals, and nearby
is the awesome natural amphitheatre of **Malham Cove**.

> *Take minor road towards Settle, then the B6479/B6255 north to Hawes.*

Pen-y-ghent (2 273ft - 693m) lies to the east of Horton-in-Ribblesdale, and at Hawes
is **Hardrow Force**, England's highest single drop waterfall, over which Blondin once
walked a tightrope, cooking an omelette on the way!
Malham, Horton-in-Ribblesdale, Pen-y-ghent with its sinkholes and cave systems,
Hawes and Hardrow are all on the Pennine Way *(qv)*.

★★ Isle of SKYE Highland   Pop 8 139

Michelin Map ▉▉ A, B 11 and 12 or Atlas G Britain p 65
Access: see the current Michelin Red Guide Great Britain and Ireland

All the mystery and enchantment of a Hebridean isle is to be found on Skye,
the largest of the Inner Hebrides group. In Norse and Gaelic tales, Skye is the
Island of Cloud or the Winged Isle. And indeed the rapid changes of mood and weather
do form part of the isle's enchantment. Although treeless and bare the scenery is
spectacular and beguiling - how better to admire the majestic forms of the Cuillins
than when rain-laden clouds roll away to reveal a landscape streaming with sunshine.
Crofting, tourism and forestry are the principal occupations of the islanders. The
island is a stronghold of Gaelic with over 85% of the population still Gaelic speakers.

★★★ **The Cuillins.** — The scenic splendour of the Cuillins makes these peaks the isle's
most famous feature. The **Black Cuillins**, a six-mile arc of sharp peaks, encircle Loch
Coruisk; many of these peaks are over 3 000ft - 914m in height, with Sgurr Alas-
dair (3 309ft - 993m) the highest. On the other side of Glen Sligachan the softly-
rounded forms of the pink granite **Red Cuillins** contrast with their neighbours.

★ **Portree.** — Pop 1 374. Skye's pleasant little capital, arranged around a sheltered
bay, is a popular yachting centre.

Kilmuir. — On the north coast of Trotternish Peninsula, the small churchyard of
this township has a monument to Flora MacDonald (1722-90), known for her part
in the escape of Bonnie Prince Charlie after the collapse of the Jacobite cause at
Culloden. She brought the Prince, disguised as her maid, from Benbecula in the Outer
Hebrides to Portree. From here he left for France and lifelong exile.

★ **Skye Croft Museum.** — A typical crofter's house, a weaver's house, a smithy
and a ceilidh house give some idea of crofting life in the 19C.

Dunvegan Castle. — Until 1748 the only entrance to this Hebridean fortress, the
seat of the MacLeods, was by a sea gate. The castle is set on a rocky platform
overlooking Loch Dunvegan. Most notable of the treasures kept here is the fragment of silk, known as the Fairy Flag. Legend has it that the flag was given to the
4th Chief by his fairy wife, with whom he had lived for twenty years. The flag is
credited with the power to ward off disaster to the Clan, and has been twice
invoked. Other relics include the broadsword of the 7th Chief, the Dunvegan
Cup and the Horn of Rory Mor, the 15th Chief.

Clan Donald Centre. — Part of Armadale Castle houses a museum-cum-exhibition
featuring the 'Sea Kingdom', the story of the Lords of the Isles and the Gaelic culture. The stable block serves as a visitor arrival point.

★★★ SNOWDONIA Gwynedd

Michelin Map 403 I 24 and 25 or Atlas G Britain p 32

840 square miles - 2 180km² of wild beauty *(photograph p 12)* amongst the scenic mountains of Gwynedd, the National Park was designated in 1951; second largest of eleven in England and Wales. Yr Wyddfa Fawr, The Great Tumulus, or Snowdon, as it is called in English, at 3 560ft - 1 085m dominates the northern sector, Cadair Idris (2 930ft - 893m) the south. There are ninety-six peaks of over 1 970ft - 600m in the park.

Places to visit in and around the national park

Beddgelert. — Pop 646. Three valleys meet here and the village looks south to the Pass of Aberglaslyn. The dramatic scenery is enough to attract the tourist, but in the 18C the local innkeeper, anxious to encourage trade, embroidered an old legend, and made ''Gelert's Grave''. The tale has it that Llywelyn the Great had a hound called Gelert. He left Gelert guarding his baby son and returned to find the child missing and the dog covered in blood. Llywelyn, believing Gelert had killed his son, slew the poor beast before he discovered that he had in fact saved the boy from a wolf, whose body was discovered nearby.

★ Betws-y-Coed. — Pop 654. Beautifully set amid tree-clad slopes at the junction of the Rivers Conwy and Llugwy, Betws-y-Coed (Chapel in the Woods) has been the gateway to Snowdonia since Telford's great London-Holyhead road (now the A5) was driven through North Wales in the early 19C. The huge stables of the hotel are today the National Park Visitor Centre. A graceful stone arch, Pont y Pair spans the Llugwy, near where it cascades through a wooded ravine in the **Swallow Falls★** . Telford's ornate cast-iron bridge over the Conwy proclaims that it was ''Constructed in the same year the Battle of Waterloo was fought''.

Blaenau Ffestiniog. — Pop 5 000. Slate is still quarried here, but on a lesser scale than in the past. In the **Llechwedd Slate Caverns**, the story of Welsh slate is told on film, and another train takes the visitor through caverns, where tableaux depict the working conditions in the last century. At **Gloddfa Ganol Slate Mine**, the world's most extensive mine still in operation, there are walks through some of the mine's 42 miles - 68km of tunnels. From Porthmadog on the coast, the 13 mile - 21km **Ffestiniog Railway**, built in 1836 to haul slate from quarry to port, now takes tourists through magnificent scenery, past lakes and waterfalls, to Blaenau Ffestiniog.

Cadair Idris. — One of the more challenging mountains in Britain, the great ''Chair of the Giant Idris'' (2 927ft - 893m) looms above the beautiful valley of the Mawddach in the south of the park. No one should venture lightly onto its boulder-strewn upper slopes. This, in fact, applies to any walkers in the whole National Park. From dunes at sea level it is all too easy to be drawn upwards, through woodland to the higher pastures and then onto moorland. Remember that ''mountains make their own weather''. Walkers and climbers should always obtain detailed and up-to-date weather forecasts for the National Park and let someone know of their planned route and time of return, before setting out to explore.

★★ Harlech Castle. — *Description p 133.*

★★★ Snowdon. — It is from the quarrying town of Llanberis, overlooking Llyn Padarn, that the easiest ascent to the summit of Snowdon can be made, by the steam trains of the **Snowdon Mountain Railway**, opened in 1896. For the more energetic, five main footpath routes are fully described in the leaflets and maps published by the Park Authority; the most straightforward follows the ridge used by the railway, while the most scenic begins at the Pen-y-Pass car park on Llanberis Pass. For experienced walkers, the scramble along the knife edge of Crib Goch offers a certain challenge. Given fine weather, the **panorama★★★** from Snowdon summit takes in the whole of Anglesey, the Isle of Man, and the Wicklow Mountains in Ireland.

SOUTHAMPTON Hampshire   Pop 211 321

Michelin Map 404 P 31 or Atlas G Britain p 9

This great port, naturally favoured with a double tide, began as a Roman coastal garrison, Clausentum, on the east bank of the Itchen. By the 8C the Saxon port of Hamwic was already serving the royal city of Winchester and it has continued to grow, becoming one of Britain's major container ports. After severe bombing in World War II, the town began a successful recovery in the fifties and alongside medieval remains a modern city has grown up, with a lively university and renewed industry.

Old Southampton (YZ). — Happily a good deal of the medieval defences and town buildings can still be seen today. The impressive northern gate to the town, the **Bargate★ (Y)**, built *c*1180, was given its large towers *c*1285 and its forbidding north face in the 15C. The **west wall** of the early defences rises spectacularly above the **Western Esplanade (YZ)**, where Southampton Bay once lapped the shore. Note the 15C **Catchcold Tower (Y)** and the **Arcade (Z)** running from the site of **Biddlesgate** to the **Blue Anchor Postern (Z)**. At the top of Blue Anchor Lane the large early 16C **Tudor House★ (Z)** incorporating an earlier banqueting hall serves as one of the city **museums**; outside, a 16C **garden** of flowers and herbs and a ''knot garden'' have been re-created.
At the far end steps lead down to the shell of the **Norman House (Z A)**, a fine example of a 12C merchant's house which was incorporated into the town wall defences in the 14C.

SOUTHAMPTON

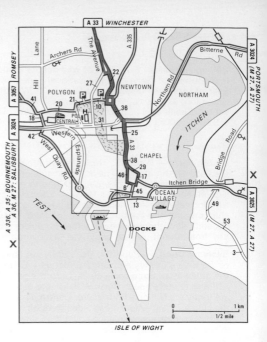

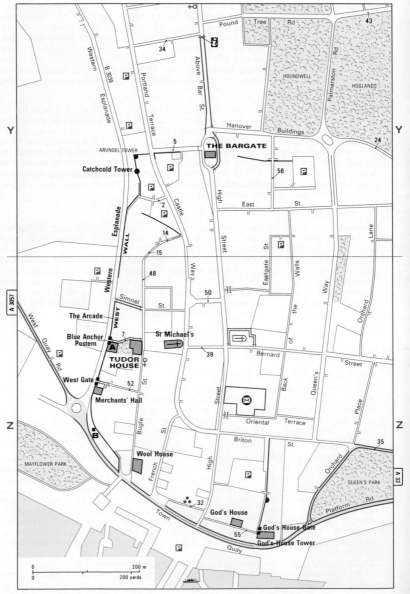

⊘ **St Michael's Church** (Z). — This is the oldest building in the medieval town, built soon after the Norman conquest and enlarged throughout the Middle Ages and in the 19C. A distinctive feature is the elegant 18C **stone spire** rising from the squat 11C **tower**. The furnishings of excellent quality include a black **Tournai marble font** of c1170, two 15C brass **lecterns** and the 1567 **tomb** of Sir Richard Lyster, who occupied Tudor House.

Back on the Western Esplanade, just beyond the 14C **West Gate** (Z) and the 1428 **Merchants' Hall** (Z) stands the **Mayflower Memorial** (Z B), erected in 1913 to commemorate the sailing of the Pilgrim Fathers in 1620. In the **Wool House** (Z), a beautlfully restored
⊘ 14C stone warehouse, now the **Maritime Museum**, displays models of ships and exhibits from the history of this great port. **God's House** (Z) was founded c1185 as an almshouse and hostel for travellers. To its east stand the early 14C **God's House Gate**
⊘ (Z) and the early 15C **God's House Tower** (Z), containing the city's archaeological museum.

⊘ **Harbour Boat Trip.** — *From Ocean Village* (X). The tour gives an impression of the immensity of the port, though its interest depends on which vessels are in dock.

EXCURSIONS

★★ **New Forest.** — *Description p 185.*

★ **Broadlands.** — *8 miles - 13km northwest by the A3057* (X), *or 1 mile - 2km short*
⊘ *of Romsey.* In 1736 the 1st Viscount Palmerston bought the small Tudor manor a mile south of Romsey and set about transforming its grounds. His son the 2nd Viscount, commissioned **Capability Brown** to continue this work and rebuilt the house in the Palladian style. He added the pedimented three-bay portico to produce a noble **west front**, overlooking his landscaped grounds and the beautiful River Test. Brown's son-in-law, **Henry Holland**, then created the east entrance front and the elegant dining room - the setting for three splendid **Van Dyck** paintings. The house is notable for the **Wedgwood Room**, with white friezes and mouldings on a blue background, a fine collection of 18C Wedgwood pieces and four portraits by Sir Peter Lely of ladies at Charles II's court. Do not miss the exquisite white and gold plasterwork of the **Saloon** and the painted medallions in the drawing room ceiling. After the death of the Prime Minister, Lord Palmerston in 1865, the house eventually passed to Lord Mount Temple, whose daughter Edwina married Louis Mountbatten in 1922 and inherited the house in 1938. The present occupant, their grandson, Lord Romsey, has had an exhibition and audio-visual presentation created in memory of Lord Mountbatten in the stable block.

★ **Romsey Abbey.** — *9 miles - 15km northwest by the A3057* (X). The town of Romsey grew up around a nunnery founded by Edward the Elder, son of Alfred the Great,
⊘ in 907 and largely rebuilt from c1120-1230. At the Dissolution the convent was suppressed and the buildings destroyed but the abbey church survived to serve as the parish church. The purity and simplicity of the **interior**★★ make this an excellent example of late Norman architecture. Note especially the elevation of the south choir aisle. In the east chapel of the south choir aisle is a **Saxon crucifix** of c1100, depicting Christ crucified, with two angels, the Virgin and St John. A second Saxon sculpture, the 11C **rood**, is outside on the south side, next to the finely decorated Abbess's Doorway.

SOUTHPORT Merseyside   Pop 88 596

Michelin Map 402 K, L 23 or Atlas G Britain p 38

The dignified resort of Southport with its tree-shaded streets, attractive flowerbeds and famous gardens is in sharp contrast to its more lively neighbour Blackpool. Elegant, spacious and tree-lined, **Lord Street** with its characteristic wrought-iron canopies and glass-roofed arcades is the epitome of a Victorian promenade. Six miles of sands and the amusement parks keep the children happy. With six first-class golf courses Southport is an important British golfing centre known for its championship course at **Royal Birkdale** to the south.

EXCURSIONS

★ **Rufford Old Hall.** — *12 miles - 19km to the east by the A565 then the A59 to*
⊘ *the right.* Built by Sir Thomas Hesketh, who held the manor between 1416 and 1458, this is one of the finest 15C houses in Lancashire. The **Great Hall**★ has a magnificent **hammerbeam roof** and ornate carved screen. The Carolean wing was reconstructed in brick in 1662. There is much original furniture, arms and armour, and a folk museum.

Several miles further on to the south.

⊘ **Martin Mere Wildfowl Trust.** — *350 acres - 140ha* of protected habitat for wildfowl. The mere is home to flamingos, black swans, geese and a winter haven to thousands of pink-footed geese, Icelandic Whooper swans as well as Bewick swans from Russia. There are hides and nature trails for the birdwatcher.

The Michelin Green Guide France

aims to make touring more enjoyable by outlining
a variety of touring programmes, easily adapted to personal taste.

Michelin Map 404 R 24 or Atlas G Britain p 36

The glory of this ''well-built clean town'' (John Byng) is its three-towered Norman Minster, the glory of the Minster the famed foliage carving of its late 13C master masons.

★★ SOUTHWELL MINSTER *time: 1 hour*

⊘Built *c*1108 on Norman lines it is the only cathedral in England to boast a complete set of three Norman towers. There was previously a Saxon church on the site; even earlier there had been a Roman villa nearby, and fragments of its mosaic flooring can be seen in the south transept.

Beautifully situated, surrounded by lawns and well-spaced graves, its **west front**, pierced by a Perpendicular seven-light window above the west door, and the rare barrel-vaulted Norman north porch are its most obvious charms.

Interior. — Intimate in spite of its Norman severity, the mood suddenly changes with the mid-14C **screen**, showing 286 images of men, gods and devils. Even more glorious is the Early English **choir** and **chapter house** (1288), the first single-span stone vaulted chapter house in Christendom, boasting some of the finest late 13C naturalism carved out of medieval stone.

EXCURSION

Newark-on-Trent. — Pop 33 143. *7 miles - 11km east on the A612 and the A617.* Though mostly a Georgian town (John Wesley called it ''one of the most elegant in England''), its two dominating features are its castle and Market Place.
⊘Raised by Alexander, Bishop of Lincoln *(qv)*, the **castle** is where King John died (1216) and King Charles gave up his struggle. Nothing of the keep overlooking the Trent survives. What is left after three sieges in the Civil War are the ghosts of a late 12C gateway, 13C west wall and the northwest and central towers.

Market Place with its endearing hybrid mixture of styles is overshadowed by the 252ft - 77m spire of **St Mary Magdalene★**. Inside note the vast transept windows (''Nothing like it was tried again until the time of the Crystal Palace'': Pevsner), the **brass** to Alan Fleming (d 1361) and the *c*1520 Dance of Death **wall painting** in the south chantry chapel.

★★ STAMFORD Lincolnshire   Pop 16 127

Michelin Map 404 S 26 or Atlas G Britain p 29

''As fine a built town all of stone as may be seen'', according to the late 17C traveller and writer Celia Fiennes. Stamford was one of the five Danelaw towns (with Derby, Leicester, Lincoln and Nottingham), so picturesque it became the first town in England to be designated a Conservation Area.

★ St Martin's Church. — *High Street St Martin's.*
Having been rebuilt *c*1480 St Martin's is entirely Perpendicular. The north chapel is dominated by the imposing alabaster monument to **William Cecil, Lord Burghley** (1520-98). In the nearby churchyard is the grave of Daniel Lambert (1770-1809), reputed to be the fattest man in England and who in spite of his size, was a keen horseman and ''very partial to the female sex''. He weighed 52 stones 11bs when he died.

★ Lord Burghley's Hospital. — *Corner of Station Road and High Street St Martin's.*
The charming late Elizabethan almshouses were built on the site of the medieval hospital of St John the Baptist and St Thomas the Martyr in 1597.

Brazenose Gate. — *St Paul's Street.*
Rebuilt here *c*1688, it was the original 14C gate of the now-vanished Brazenose College, set up in 1333 by seceding students from Brasenose College, Oxford *(qv)*.

★ Browne's Hospital. — *Broad Street.*
⊘One of the best-preserved medieval hospitals in England, it was built *c*1475, providing cubicles for ''ten poor men'' in what is now the Board Room. Both the chapel and the audit room are lit by unforgettable *c*1480 stained glass.

EXCURSIONS

★★Burghley House. — *Immediately to the southeast of Stamford.*
⊘One of the finest Elizabethan mansions, built by one of the great Elizabethans, **William Cecil, Lord Burghley**, ''the greatest, gravest and most esteemed Councillor that ever Your Majesty had'' (Essex). Extensively redecorated in the late 17C, it is distinguished for its baroque ceilings painted by **Laguerre** and **Verrio** (at their most exuberant in the **Heaven** and **Hell Rooms**) and its collection of paintings.

Paintings. — These include works by Paolo Veronese, Jean Tassel and Francesco Bassano in the **Chapel**; Gainsborough, Kneller and Lawrence in the **Billiard Room**; and Brueghel the Younger in the **Marquetry Room**. Most fascinating of all is the Pagoda Room; here are Henry VIII (by Van Cleve), William Cecil (by Gheeraerts the Elder), Elizabeth I (by Gheeraerts the Younger) and Oliver Cromwell (by Robert Walker); Capability Brown (by Nathaniel Dance) looks out over the grounds he created.

⊘**Deene Park.** — *11 miles - 18km southwest on the A43, turn right and follow the signs.* Ancestral home of the Brudenell family, whose most famous son is remembered for having led the Charge of the Light Brigade, 1854. The house is 16 and 17C, ranged around a central courtyard, with 18-19C additions.

Interior. — The most important part is the Great Hall of 1571 with its splendid Renaissance decoration and miraculously well-preserved alternate single and double hammerbeam roof. More intimate is the miniature **Oak Parlour** with 1630 panelling and portrait of Louise de Kerouaille *(qv)* and the **Drawing Room** with twelve charming Jacobean portraits of women and children.

⊘ **Kirby Hall.** — *13 miles - 21km. Take the route to Deene Park, continue 2 miles - 3km.*

Kirby Hall is a fine example of a large stone-built, Elizabethan mansion, begun in 1570 with 17C alterations. Bought and completed in 1757 by Sir Christopher Hatton, a favourite of Elizabeth I, it was further extended into one of the most magnificent mansions of the Elizabethan era. Now mostly ruins, a few rooms still survive, such as the great hall with its canted ceiling. The great garden, laid out in the late 17C, is currently being restored to its former glory.

Burghley House

★★ STIRLING Central   Pop 36 640

Michelin Map 401 I 15 or Atlas G Britain p 55
Town plan in the current Michelin Red Guide Great Britain and Ireland

Strategically important from time immemorial, the long history of Stirling has been essentially that of the castle and one-time royal residence perched on its well-nigh impregnable crag. Today it is an ideal touring centre, with a wealth of possible day trips, into the Trossachs, Rob Roy country, Fife or the Ochils, to name but a few.

HISTORICAL NOTES

From its magnificent site, controlling a crossing of the Forth at its tidal limit, Stirling has seen many battles (Stirling Bridge 1297; Bannockburn 1314). Royal association began with David I, who in 1126 granted the burgh royal status. Stirling became a permanent royal residence with the accession of the **Stewarts**, and its Golden Age came under James IV, a true Renaissance prince. After his death at Flodden (1513), his Queen Margaret brought her son to Stirling, where he was crowned as James V. His daughter **Mary Queen of Scots** was crowned in the Chapel Royal, and her infant son, the future **James VI** of Scotland and I of England, was baptised here in 1566. It was with his departure to Whitehall that Stirling's role as a royal residence ended.

★★ **Stirling Castle.** — The approach to the castle is up through the old town *(see over)*. A statue of Robert the Bruce still stands guard - on the esplanade. There is an audio-visual presentation in the **Visitor Centre**, illustrating the castle's history through seven centuries.

Palace. — Begun by James IV in 1496 it was completed by his son in 1540. A masterpiece of Renaissance ornamentation, it had little effect on Scottish architecture in general. Its outstanding feature is the elaborate design of the external elevations, which are best admired from the Upper Square. Here can be seen the façade of the Great Hall (1460-88), which can be compared with the Palace itself (1496-1540) and the Chapel (1594); these show clearly how styles changed over a period of 150 years. In the King's Old Building is the **Regimental Museum★** of the Argyll and Sutherland Highlanders, with silver, medals, colours and documents telling the story of 200 years of regimental history, from the Thin Red Line at Balaclava through two World Wars to the present day.

Old Town. — The medieval town, with its narrow wynds and steep streets spills downhill from the castle. It is best explored on foot. The splendid mansion, **Argyll's Lodging★** was built in 1632 by Sir William Alexander, founder of Nova Scotia. Everywhere are examples of fine Scottish Renaissance decoration. Only a ruined façade remains of **Mar's Wark**, the palace started in 1570 for John Erskine, Regent and Hereditary Keeper of the castle, and guardian of the young Prince James.

⊘ In the **Church of the Holy Rude★**, the infant James VI was crowned, in 1567, with John Knox preaching the sermon. At the bottom of Broad Street, one-time centre of burgh life, with its mercat cross and tolbooth, is **Darnley's House**, where the already estranged father - Darnley - stayed while his son, the future James VI, was being baptised.

EXCURSIONS

★ Dunblane. — Pop 6 783. *6 miles - 10km north of Stirling by the A9.*
⊘ A mainly residential town of some 6 000 inhabitants, Dunblane is grouped round its beautiful 13C Gothic **cathedral★★**. An ecclesiastical centre since Celtic times, the cathedral dates from David I's creation of the bishopric in 1150. It was neglected, but not pillaged, following the Reformation, and so remains today a fine example of 13C Gothic architecture. Note particularly the vigorous carving of the canopied 15C **Chisholm stalls** and their misericords. Adjoining the south side of the nave is a 12C tower, and the magnificent **west front★★**, overlooking the Allan Water, is a masterpiece. The Dean's House contains a museum of both cathedral and town.

★ Doune. — Pop 1 020. *8 miles - 13km from Stirling by the A84.*
⊘ The late 14C **castle★**, with its four-storey, 95ft - 29m high **keep-gatehouse**, stands apart from the village. With elaborate accommodation on a semi-royal scale, it is an example of a truly self-contained, secure residence of its period. In the 17C and 18C the village was famous for the manufacture of fine pistols, made entirely of metal. They are highly decorated and were used mainly by Highland cattle drovers.

⊘ The **Doune Motor Museum★** is one mile to the northwest off the A84. An interesting private collection of 40 cars, from the period 1905-66, and all roadworthy. The **Doune Hill Climbs** take place each year, in June, on a course laid out on the estate.

⊘ **Bannockburn Heritage Centre.** — *2 miles - 3km south of Stirling by the A9.*
An equestrian statue of Robert the Bruce marks the King's command post on the eve of the battle. By 1313 Bruce had retaken most of the kingdom lost to Edward I, who had died in 1307. On 24 June 1314, he routed a numerically superior English army, ineptly led by Edward II. After Bannockburn, independence for Scotland was assured, though not formalised until the Declaration of Arbroath (1320) and the Treaty of Northampton in 1328.

⊘ **Wallace Monument.** — *1 mile - 1.5km northeast. Leave Stirling by the A9 and at the Causewayhead roundabout, take the B998.*
Sir William Wallace (1270-1305) rallied Scottish forces against English rule. He recaptured the castle from Edward I's forces after his victory at Stirling Bridge in 1297. Following the Scots' submission in 1304, Wallace was captured and died a traitor's death in London in 1305. An audio-visual presentation depicts Wallace and his place in Scottish history. From the viewing platform (242 steps) atop Abbey Craig (362ft - 110m) there is a **panorama★★** of Stirling and all the country around.

STOKE-ON-TRENT Staffordshire   Pop 272 446

Michelin Map ▓▓▓ N 24 or Atlas G Britain p 35
Town plan in the current Michelin Red Guide Great Britain and Ireland

Arnold Bennett's *Five Towns* (in fact there are six: Stoke, Tunstall, Burslem, Hanley, Fenton and Longton) remain, in spite of 50 years of unification, separate entities, each maintaining an identity of its own. Stoke's potteries existed long before the time of England's most distinguished potter, **Josiah Wedgwood** (1730-95). Kilns dating *c*1300 have been found at Sneyd Green and there were Adams and Wedgwood potters in the 1600s; but it was the opening of Josiah Wedgwood's Etruria factory (1769), the exploitation of Staffordshire's coalfields and the digging of the Trent-Mersey Canal that turned a local industry into a national one and an industry into an art. Most of the great brick kilns (bottle, conical, squat, swollen, slender) have now disappeared. A few remain, particularly in Longton, standing out on the horizon, as monumental as Stonehenge.

MUSEUMS

★ Gladstone Pottery Museum. — *Uttoxeter Road, Longton.*
⊘ This unique surviving pottery factory or 'potbank' retains its original workshops, cobbled yard and distinctive bottle ovens. Dating from 1850 Gladstone Works employed 41 adults and 25 children in its early years, producing bone china until the 1960s when it was converted into a museum of British pottery. Displays illustrate the growth of the Staffordshire pottery industry, the various products, the art of colouring and decorating them and the potter at home. The potters' traditional skills are demonstrated in the workshops.

★ Museum and Art Gallery. — *Bethesda Street, Hanley.*
⊘ The city museum houses one of the finest ceramics collections (in the Potteries), starting with English pottery *c*1350, through the beginning of earthenware as an English art (**Thomas Toft's** Charles II plate), to the glorious years of the 18C and the prosperous years of the 19C (Spode and Copeland's **View of Naples** and **Minton's** bone china vases), finishing with the Art Deco follies of Clarice Cliff, the modern studio movement and examples of current industrial production.

EXCURSIONS

★★ **Little Moreton Hall.** — *10 miles - 16km north of Stoke-on-Trent centre on the ⊘ A500 and the A34.*
A beautiful moated half-timbered manor house characterised by rich and intrinsic patterns on square panels, elaborate joinery and window tracery and 16C glass. Begun in the 1440s with the building of the Great Hall, it was completed some 140 years later with the addition of John Moreton's Long Gallery. Note the tracery in the bay window of this Great Hall, the painted panelling frieze in the Parlour which tells the story of Susanna and the Elders, the arch-braced roof trusses and plaster figures of Destiny and Fortune in the Long Gallery.

★ **Wedgwood Visitor's Centre.** — *7 miles - 11km south of Stoke-on-Trent centre ⊘ on the A500 and the A34, then left for Barlaston.*
At the 1938 Wedgwood Factory (set in parkland and a model in its day) are full displays of the pottery-making process, an excellent collection of Wedgwood ware (Neo-Classical, Victorian, Art Nouveau, Art Deco and modern), and Wedgwood portraits by Stubbs, Reynolds, Lawrence and Wright of Derby.

⊘ **Chatterley Whitfield Mining Museum.** — *4 miles - 6km north of Stoke-on-Trent, off the A527 between Tunstall and Biddulph.*
Opened in 1979 as Britain's first underground mining museum on the site of the million ton per annum Chatterley Whitfield Colliery. Now the home of British Coal's National Mining Collection, this unique working museum offers guided underground tours by ex-miners, with pit-ponies, underground railway rides, and examples of mining technology from the 19C to the present day.

⊘ **Alton Towers.** — *12 miles - 19km east of Stoke-on-Trent via the A50, A521 and the B5032.*
The Towers themselves, a 19C folly, are now picturesque ruins, but the beautiful gardens and grounds are large enough to provide tranquillity and escape from the vast pleasure park that attracts 2 1/2 million visitors each year.

★★★ STONEHENGE Wiltshire

Michelin Map **403** O 30 or Atlas G Britain p 9

⊘ Stonehenge, Britain's most celebrated prehistoric monument, is 4 000 years old, dating from *c*2800-1550 BC. For centuries it has sent writers, painters and every sort of visitor into flights of fancy, for its purpose remains an enigma. Although many of the stones have fallen or disappeared it is still possible, from the centre of the circle, to see the sun rise over the Heel Stone (at the entrance) on midsummer's day; there are suggestions that it was constructed as an astronomical observatory or a sanctuary for a sun-worshipping cult, or even a combination of the two. The main axis has always been aligned with the midsummer sunrise and Stonehenge must have been a ceremonial centre celebrating the sun and marking the seasons. Certainly it was not "built by the Druids", the priesthood of the Celtic peoples who reached Britain in the 3C BC, long after the completion of the final phase of the building.

The Period. — When work began the area was inhabited by nomadic hunters and early farming settlers who had crossed the Channel and North Sea in skin boats. In 1900 BC the Beaker Folk spread into Wessex along the chalk upland tracks, growing into a community of 12-15 000, ruled by the cattle-barons of Salisbury Plain, who also controlled the metal industry. There was a growing priesthood who, at peak periods in the construction of Stonehenge, could call on the population to provide the 600 men needed to haul a sarsen stone up the Vale of Pewsey, or 200 to erect it on site.

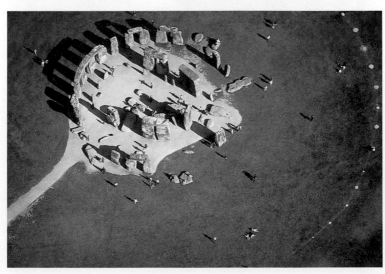

Aeriel view of Stonehenge

The building design. — Like many a medieval cathedral Stonehenge was much remodelled after its foundation. In the **first phase**, *c*2800 BC, a ditch with an inner bank of chalk rubble 6ft - nearly 2m high, was dug. This, with a ring of 56 holes, known as the Aubrey Holes, after the 17C pioneer of field archaeology John Aubrey (1626-97), encloses an area 300ft - 91m in diameter. To the northeast the bank and ditch were cut to make an entrance marked inside by two upright stones and outside by the **Heel Stone** *(near the road)*. Inside the enclosure four **Station Sarsens** were set up at the cardinal points of the compass.

In the **second phase**, *c*1900 BC, a double ring of undressed **bluestones** was set up toward the centre; these stones, weighing up to 4 tons each, were transported 240 miles - 386km from the Presely Hills in southwest Wales, mainly by water and finally along the wide **Avenue** which was built from the River Avon to the entrance of the henge. In the **third phase**, *c*1650 BC, the structure was transformed. The bluestone rings were replaced by a circle of tall trilithons. These standing stones were tapered at one end and tenoned at the top to secure the curving mortised lintels, which were linked to each other by tongues and grooves, having been levered gradually into position on ever-rising log platforms. Inside the circle five separate giant trilithons rose in a horseshoe, opening towards the Heel Stone. The entrance was marked by new uprights, one of which, the Slaughter Stone, now fallen, remains. In the **final phase**, *c*1550 BC, the dressed bluestones were re-introduced in their present horseshoe formation, within the sarsen horseshoe.

★★★ STOURHEAD Wiltshire

Michelin Map 403 N 30 or Atlas G Britain p 8

⊘The garden is one of the supreme examples of English landscape style. Its creator was the banker Henry Hoare II (1705-85), whose father had built a classical house here in 1721, designed by the architect Colen Campbell.

Henry Hoare was influenced in his garden design by the landscapes he saw on his travels and even more by the paintings of Claude and Nicholas Poussin, in which nature is presented in luminous shades and focal points are provided by classical

Stourhead

buildings. He first formed the great triangular lake, then, as he began his plantings of deciduous trees and conifers, ''ranged in large masses as the shades in a painting'', he started, with his architect, Henry Flitcroft, to build those gems of garden architecture which, if you circle the lake in an anti-clockwise direction, you may pinpoint from across the water as the Temple of Flora, the Watch Cottage, the Grotto, the Pantheon, and, high among the trees, the Temple of Apollo.

In 1765, Hoare was given the 1373 Bristol Cross, enabling him to create a vista which is entirely English, of lake, turf bridge, cross, and, in the background, Stourton church and village. His planting, now wonderfully mature, has been added to by his successors to give a wealth of exotic specimens and of ever-changing seasonal effects.

House. — In 1790-1804 wings were added to Campbell's original house, and, in about 1840, the present portico. The centre of the house was gutted by fire in 1902, but was faithfully restored. The hall, a perfect cube, contains portraits of the Hoare family. The long barrel-vaulted library contains fine pieces of **Chippendale** furniture and **Canaletto** pen and wash drawings of Venice. Further treasures are to be found in the Picture Gallery: **Claude** and **Poussin landscapes** which inspired Henry Hoare II's design for the gardens.

EXCURSION

Shaftesbury. — Pop 4 831. The excellent **views★** from the town on the crest of its 700ft - over 200m spur account for King Alfred's choice of the site as a strongpoint in his struggle against the Danes. The **abbey** founded in 888 by Alfred for his daughter became the wealthiest nunnery in England. Canute died here in 1035 and Marie de France, the 12C Anglo-Norman lyric poet, half-sister to Henry II, was among the abbesses. It was said in the 15-16C that if the Abbess of Shaston (Shaftesbury) were to marry the Abbot of Glaston (Glastonbury) their heirs would own more land than the king! In 1539 Henry VIII dissolved both abbeys and today only the ground plan remains visible.

★ STRATFORD-UPON-AVON Warwickshire   Pop 20 941

Michelin Map 403 P 27 or Atlas G Britain p 27

Stratford is Arden country, its timber frames hewn from the surrounding Forest of Arden, its favourite son's mother called Mary Arden. **William Shakespeare** (1564-1616) *(photograph p 36)* forsook his home town and his wife, Anne Hathaway, for London, where success came to him as a jobbing playwright, but one able to distil sex and violence, farce and philosophy into the most potent lines in the language. He returned to Stratford in 1611, rich and famous enough to acquire a coat of arms and lived at New Place until his death.

★**Shakespeare's Birthplace** (A). — The half-timbered house where the dramatist was born is part museum (including a First Folio), part shrine. Note the graffiti on the upstairs windows (Scott, Carlyle, Ellen Terry and Henry Irving). In the adjoining **Shakespeare Centre** (M¹) is an exhibition of costumes from the BBC Shakespeare series and in the **garden** are many of the flowers mentioned in the plays.

Harvard House. — Half-timbered, dating from 1596, it was the home of Katherine Rogers, mother of **John Harvard** (b 1607), founder of Harvard University.

New Place. — Of Shakespeare's retirement home, built in 1483, only the foundations remain, but next door in **Nash's House**, home of Shakespeare's granddaughter, behind the much-restored frontage, is an exhibition about the history of Stratford.

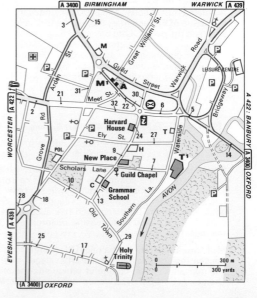

STRATFORD-UPON-AVON

Bridge St. 6
Henley St. 22
High St. 24
Sheep St. 27
Wood St. 32

Alcester Rd 2
Birmingham Rd 3
Bridge Foot 5
Chapel Lane 7
Chapel St. 9
Chestnut Walk 10
Church St. 13
Clopton Bridge 14
Clopton Rd 15
College Lane 17
Evesham Place 18
Evesham Rd 20
Greenhill St. 21
Sanctus St. 25
Shottery Rd 28
Trinity St. 29
Union St. 30
Windsor St. 31

Town plans:

the names of main shopping streets are indicated in red at the beginning of the list of streets.

⊘ **Guild Chapel.** — The Chapel of the Guild of the Holy Cross (founded 1269), Stratford's ruling body before the Reformation, is predominantly Perpendicular, with wall-paintings of Christ, Mary, St John, St Peter and the Last Judgement in the **chancel**.

Grammar School. — *Exterior only.* Built *c*1417 as the Holy Cross Hall and turned into a school after the Reformation; amongst its pupils was William Shakespeare.

⊘ **Holy Trinity Church.** — With an Early English tower and transepts and early Perpendicular nave and aisle, Holy Trinity would be notable even without **Shakespeare's grave**, on the north side of the chancel. "Blessed be the man who spares these stones / And cursed be he that moves my bones." No one has touched them.

⊘ **Royal Shakespeare Theatre** (T¹). — Opened in 1932 as the Shakespeare Memorial Theatre and now the headquarters of the **Royal Shakespeare Company**. Adjoining it, created in the shell of the original theatre all but destroyed by fire in 1926, is the **Swan Theatre**, built in 1986 with a Jacobean-style apron stage and galleried seating. The Royal Shakespeare Company Collection includes paintings, sculpture and historical theatre material and organises backstage tours.

EXCURSIONS

★★★ **Cotswolds.** — *Description p 100.*

★ **Mary Arden's House.** — *4 miles - 6km north, off the A3400 in Wilmcote.*
⊘ Home of Shakespeare's mother, Mary Arden, displaying herring-bone timber framing and mercifully unrestored. Between the house and neighbouring **Glebe Farm** (preserved as a *c*1900 farmhouse) are dovecots, cowsheds, barns and outbuildings.

⊘ **Anne Hathaway's Cottage.** — *1 mile - 2km west of Stratford via Shottery Road* (28). More a farmhouse than a cottage, its back was rebuilt after a fire in 1969. Upstairs are some dramatic tie-beams. The interior contains the Hathaway bed and the exterior is charmed by a herb-scented garden, orchard and Shakespeare tree garden.

★ **Ragley Hall.** — *10 miles - 16km west off the A46, 2 miles - 3km beyond Alcester.*
⊘ Noble rather than stately Ragley was designed and built by Robert Hooke in Palladian style for the Marquess of Hertford, between 1679 and 1683. James Gibbs added some of the most perfect plasterwork **ceilings** he ever conceived around 1750, and thirty years later Wyatt built the gigantic portico. The walls are hung with paintings by Wootton, Van Loo, Reynolds, Hoppner, Lely and Cornelius Schut. The surprise is the **South Staircase Hall** decorated by Graham Rust between 1969 and 1983, with its ceiling of *The Temptation* and murals portraying classical gods, monkeys, birds and contemporary members of the Seymour family, all in a post-Realist baroque style.

★ **Upton House.** — *14 miles - 22km southeast on the A422.*
⊘ A late 17C house, bought by Viscount Bearsted, son of the founder of the Shell company and exhibiting his spectacular collection of porcelain and paintings. In the **Hall** is a view of Venice by Canaletto and a landscape by Wootton. In the **Long Gallery** are Dutch paintings - note Jan Steen's *Four Senses* as well as the Chelsea and Bow porcelain. The **Boudoir** is reserved exclusively for French 18 and 19C works, including Boucher's *Venus and Vulcan*, while the **Porcelain Lobby** is packed with Sèvres, Chinese, Chelsea and Derby china and porcelain. In the Games Room are Hogarth's *Morning* and *Night* and in the **Billiard Room** Hondecoeter's *Turkey Cock.* The pride of the collection is in the **Picture Gallery**, where among works by Holbein, Hogarth, Guardi, Rembrandt - an attribution, Tintoretto, Breughel the Elder and Bosch hangs El Greco's *Christ taken in Captivity,* believed to be the model for his altarpiece in Toledo Cathedral.

⊘ **Broughton Castle.** — *22 miles - 35km southeast on the A422 to Banbury then southwest on the B4035.*
A moated manor house of *c*1300, extended in 1554 and 1599, Broughton became the centre of Parliamentary opposition to Charles I, the leaders Hampden, Pym, Warwick and the owner, Lord Saye and Sele meeting in the Council Chamber. The Great Hall, dining room and chapel show the 1300 interior at its best, while the King's Chamber chimneypiece and the Great Parlour ceiling show the best of the Elizabethan extension work. The 18C Gothick Gallery, with busts of Inigo Jones and Ben Jonson, by Rysbrack, fits admirably with the 1300s through its simplicity and restraint.

SWANSEA (ABERTAWE) West Glamorgan — Pop 172 433

Michelin Map ■403■ I 29 or Atlas G Britain p 15
Town plan in the current Michelin Red Guide Great Britain and Ireland

Swansea is the lively urban centre for southwest Wales, after Cardiff the country's second city, and a commercial and pleasure port with a ferry service to Cork. Three centuries of industrial activity in the **Lower Swansea Valley** created one of Britain's most spectacularly derelict landscapes. Since the late 1960s a thoroughgoing programme of reclamation has succeeded in greening most of this former wilderness of ruined factories and polluted land, though much remains to interest the industrial archaeologist.

★ **Maritime Quarter.** — The mid-19C South Dock has been renovated as a marina, the centrepiece of a new "inner-city village" of spruce apartments, public squares and quayside walks, on one of which sits the statue of Swansea-born poet **Dylan**
⊘ Thomas (1914-53). The varied exhibits of the **Maritime and Industrial Museum**★ are

housed in a brightly-converted former warehouse and include a complete, re-erected woollen mill; several retired vessels, among them a lightship, are moored at the quayside, and historic vehicles of the Mumbles Tramway can be seen in the tramshed. Nearby is the **Swansea City Museum**, a resolutely old-fashioned general museum worth visiting for its own sake and also for its display on the restoration of the Lower Swansea Valley.

EXCURSIONS

★**Gower Peninsula.** — A chain of superb beaches and magnificent cliffs extends along the south coast of the 14 mile - 22km peninsula, Britain's first designated Area of Outstanding Natural Beauty.

4 miles - 7km west on the A4067.

The Mumbles. — Swansea's own seaside resort, overlooked by Oystermouth Castle, was the terminus of the famous Mumbles Railway. Opened for horse-drawn traffic in 1804, this was the world's first scheduled passenger railway. It closed in 1960.

11 miles - 17km west on the A4118, B4271 and minor road towards Reynoldston.

In clear conditions the **panorama**★★ from this moorland ridge of **Cefn Bryn** extends far across the Bristol Channel to Hartland Point on the Devon coast (43 miles - 69km), to the Brecon Beacons (37 miles - 59km to the north) and westward to the Presely Hills (36 miles - 58km).

Rejoin the A4118 and continue west, turning right onto the B4247 after 2 miles.

Rhossili. — Pop 415. The approach to this tiny village in the far southwestern corner of the peninsula does not prepare the visitor for the breathtaking **views**★★★ which open up from the coastguard cottages housing the National Trust visitor centre. The cliffs falls dramatically away to the great 3 mile - 5km arc of Rhossili Bay with the surf crashing on its wonderful sandy beach. High above is Rhossili Down (633ft - 193m), and to the south, a mile-long sea-serpent in rock, Worms Head, accessible only at low tide.

Aberdulais Falls. — *11 miles - 17km northeast on the A483, A48 and A465.* In a pretty wooded gorge, the waters of the River Dulais crash down through huge boulders and past the remains of the works of the Aberdulais Tinplate Co, founded 1830. The site's industrial history goes back to 1584, when copper smelting began; in the late 18C-early 19C it was frequented by artists (including Turner) who found it an appropriately picturesque subject.

Kidwelly (Cydweli). — *21 miles - 34km to the northwest by the A483, A4070 and the A484.* Bishop Roger of Salisbury's first ringwork was certainly complete by the foundation of the priory about 1130, though the present **castle** dates from the 1280s. The walls enclosed the Norman town to form a 'bastide' such as are found in North Wales at Conwy and Caernarfon. St Mary's Church, built *c*1320, in Decorated style, originally served a Benedictine monastery.

★ **TAUNTON** Somerset   Pop 47 793

Michelin Map 404 K 30 or Atlas G Britain p 7

The country town of Taunton is an agricultural and commercial centre at the heart of the fertile Vale of Taunton Dean, cider apple country.

Castle. — Dating from the 11-12C the castle is especially known for its ownership by successive bishops of Winchester. The Civil War put Taunton and the castle in particular, under siege three times. It was rescued in the 19C and is now in part a museum.
After his unsuccessful rebellion against Henry VII in 1497 **Perkin Warbeck** was brought to trial in the great hall. Following defeat at Sedgemoor in 1685 Charles II's natural son, the **Duke of Monmouth**, and some of his followers were tried by **Judge Jeffreys** in the great hall; 144 of them were condemned to death in the notorious **Bloody Assizes.** Monmouth himself was executed on Tower Hill a month later.

★**St Mary Magdalene.** — The lovely red and tawny-gold stone of the soaring **tower** (1488-1514) of St Mary Magdalene is Taunton's outstanding landmark. In the true Somerset tradition it is a triumphant culmination to this splendid medieval church. Inside, the roof carvings (bosses and angels) are typical examples of Somerset craftsmanship.

★ **TENBY** (DINBYCH-Y-PYSGOD) Dyfed   Pop 5 226

Michelin Map 403 F 28 or Atlas G Britain p 14 — Local map p 198

This little medieval town on its rocky promontory combines all the ingredients of a seaside resort in a compact and pleasing pattern.
Dinbych-y-Pysgod - little fort of the fishes - originated in a tiny Welsh fortress on Castle Hill. Later it became a satellite of the main Norman stronghold at Pembroke, was sacked by the Welsh and on its rebuilding surrounded by sturdy ramparts. Its popularity as a watering-place dates from the Napoleonic wars.

★★ **Harbour and seafront.** — A perfect composition of jetty, massive retaining walls, Fishermen's Chapel and rugged warehouses, backed by Georgian and Regency houses crowded prettily together and rising to crown the low cliff. Superb sandy beaches extend north and south. Castle Hill has a local museum with paintings by

Augustus and Gwen John and other Tenby artists, and is topped by a statue of Prince Albert waiting patiently for a Victoria who in fact never came here. Cut off at high tide is St Catherine's Island with its Palmerstonian fort of 1869.

Town. — Landward is a good stretch of the **town walls**, enclosing a characteristically intricate web of medieval streets, widening out at **St Mary's**, one of Wales' most substantial parish churches, with a 152ft - 46m spire. The **Tudor Merchant's House** is a late 15C town dwelling, virtually unchanged externally and well preserved inside, with Flemish chimneys and period furniture.

EXCURSIONS

★ **Caldey Island.** — *Authorised boats leave Tenby harbour every 1/2 hour. The crossing takes twenty minutes. Allow 1 hour.*
In 1136 Caldey was given to the Benedictine order and a monastery established, replacing the original 6C settlement. Today a self-sufficient Cistercian community with a score or so of helpers runs a dairy and perfumery on the island.

Carew Castle. — *5 miles - 8km west of Tenby just off the main A477.*
Much of the castle standing today dates from the late 13C-early 14C. The most striking feature, however, is the North Range. Started about 1558 by Sir John Perrot, reputedly the son of Henry VIII and Mary Berkeley, wife of Sir Thomas Perrot, it was unfinished at his death. The magnificent Elizabethan architecture, with rows of tall mullioned windows, reflected in the mill pool, recaptures some of the elegance of the period.
The nearby **tidal mill**, the only one of its kind remaining in Wales, is a restored late 18C building and has an audio-visual presentation to explain its workings to visitors. The **Celtic Cross** near the entrance to the castle is one of the earliest Christian monuments in Wales. Heavily ornamented with Celtic and Scandinavian designs, it was erected as a memorial to Maredudd ap Edwin, joint ruler of Deheubarth, killed in battle in 1035.

Laugharne. — *17 miles - 27km east by the A478, A477 and the B4314 to Pendine.*
Down on the coast is Amroth, a former mining village and starting point of the Pembrokeshire Coast Path *(qv).*
A little further round the coast, the seven-mile stretch of **Pendine Sands** offers excellent bathing and angling. In 1924-26 Sir Malcolm Campbell and Parry Thomas established world land-speed records here, Parry Thomas being killed in his 1927 attempt to beat the existing record of 174.8mph - 281.3km/h.

Continue east on the A4066.

Laugharne (Talacharn). — Pop 1 003. The controversial poet **Dylan Thomas** (1914-53) lived in this small town on the Taf estuary from 1938, latterly in **The Boathouse**, now a museum of his life and work. He is buried in St Martin's churchyard. The character - and characters - of Laugharne are reflected in his "play for voices" *Under Milk Wood.*

★ TEWKESBURY Gloucestershire Pop 9 454

Michelin Map **403** N 28 or Atlas G Britain p 27

The little town, founded in Saxon times, is dominated by the imposing presence of the great Norman abbey church, its tower visible over much of the flat country between the Malverns and the Cotswold Hills. Bypassed by the railway and hemmed in by the floodlands around the confluence of the navigable rivers Severn and Avon, Tewkesbury grew little in the 19C and has conserved its historic character almost intact. In 1471 it was the scene of bloody slaughter, both during and after the **Battle of Tewkesbury**, which marked the decisive defeat of the Lancastrian cause in the Wars of the Roses.

★★ **ABBEY** time: 1 hour

The church combines a noble simplicity of structure with great richness of detail and recalls the wealth and importance of the former Benedictine abbey. Many of the latter's noble benefactors are buried here and the church has been called "the Westminster Abbey of the feudal baronage". At the Dissolution it was saved from demolition by the townsfolk, who bought it for £453.

Exterior. — The complex eastern end of the church, with its cluster of chapels contrasts with the grandeur of the **west front**, with its 65ft - 20m high recessed arch. But it is the huge 12C **tower** which impresses most, its solidity relieved by the elaborate patterning of its upper stages.
There are two survivals from monastic days, the **Abbey House** and, just outside the precinct, the handsome **Gatehouse.**

Interior. — With its eight bays defined by massive cylindrical columns, the Norman **nave**★★ is one of the most inspiring sights in English church architecture. The beautiful 14C vault replaced an earlier timber roof.
The church's many monuments are grouped around the choir. Hugh and Elizabeth Despenser lie solemnly side by side, an intricate canopy of delicately carved limestone - an early example of fan vaulting - suspended above them. The extraordinary figure of Edward Despenser kneels in prayer on the roof of his chantry chapel, while Bishop Wakeman is grotesquely commemorated by a **memento mori**, a decomposing cadaver crawling with vermin.
The 14C **stained glass windows** of the choir depict local notables as well as Biblical scenes, while its **vault**★ is a gloriously intricate web of ribs and bosses. A ring of suns, the Yorkist emblem, was added to mark the victory of 1471.

EXCURSION

Deerhurst. — Pop 100. *4 miles - 6km southwest on the A38, B4213 and a minor road.*

The village of Deerhurst is remarkable in possessing two important **Anglo-Saxon buildings**, a former priory and a chapel. The earliest parts of **St Mary's★**, an extraordinary building, once the church of a flourishing monastery, may date from as early as the 8C. Though much rebuilt and added to, its character is strongly Saxon; the roughly-built walls contain masonry laid in a herringbone pattern; a curious triangular-headed window opens into the tall nave from the tower; carvings include a Madonna and Child, the heads of beasts and, high up outside, an angel. The fine **font** is Saxon, too. Much later is the 15C **brass**, commemorating not only Sir John Cassey and his wife, but also her pet dog Terri.

Standing on a low knoll rising from the floodplain of the nearby Severn, **Odda's Chapel** was dedicated by Earl Odda, in 1056. Still attached to the farmhouse it once served as a kitchen, it was "rediscovered" only in the 19C. It consists of a nave and chancel, both of touching simplicity.

★★ THAMES Valley

Michelin Map **404** Q, R 28 and 29 or Atlas G Britain p 18
For a description of the lower Thames, see under London

"Sweet Thames! run softly, till I end my song" - this much-quoted refrain from Edmund Spenser's *Prothalamion* (1596) still captures the nature of England's most famous river, whose gently winding course westward from Kew, back to its source in the Cotswolds, offers many varied pleasures as it passes through typically English countryside of low hills, woods, meadows, country houses, pretty villages and small towns. Reading is the only industrial centre.

For long sections no road follows its course but there is usually a towpath. The result is that while the motorist may admire the river in towns along its route, the Thames' quiet beauty can only be fully appreciated from a boat or on foot. In the summer months many Thames-side towns and villages offer boat trips or the chance to hire a boat - and such an experience need not be as full of mishaps as the journey described in Jerome K Jerome's amusing idyll *Three Men in a Boat* - essential reading for any traveller on the Thames.

Swan-Upping. — Every July a colourful procession mounts the river, from Sunbury-on-Thames to Whitchurch Lock. Her Majesty's Swan Keeper and representatives of two City Livery Companies, the Worshipful Company of Dyers and the Worshipful Company of Vintners, take "up" out of the water the new cygnets and nick their bills to denote ownership. Swans with no nicks belong to the Crown, those with one nick to the Dyers' Company and those with two nicks to the Vintners' Company. The ceremony dates back to the 12C. Swans have always been indigenous to England and claimed as the property of the Crown and a very few nobles. Today only the two Livery Companies share the privilege with the Crown, but the tradition of "Swan Upping" continues.

LOWER THAMES

For a description of the Lower Thames' main sights (**Kew Gardens★★★**, **Richmond★★** and **Hampton Court★★★**), look under London. Local map pp 170-171.

FROM WINDSOR TO OXFORD

71 miles - 114km - allow at least a day - local map p 234.

★★★ **Windsor Castle.** — *Description p 246.*

★★ **Eton College.** — Perhaps the best known of all British schools, Eton College was founded in 1440 by the young Henry VI. It comprised a church, almshouses and a community of secular priests giving free education to 70 poor Scholars and choristers. The following year Henry founded King's College, Cambridge, where the boys could continue their education, a system modelled on that introduced by William of Wykeham *(qv)* at Winchester 50 years earlier. The school provided education for boys in addition to the Scholars and, as it became fashionable for the nobility to send their sons to Eton, their number increased greatly.

The paved **School Yard**, centre of college life, is dominated by the 16C red brick **Lupton's Tower** on the east side. To the north is **Lower School**, the 15C brick building originally constructed by Henry VI to house his Scholars. **Upper School** on the west side was built in the 17C to accommodate the increasing number of boys. In the centre of the yard stands a 1719 bronze statue of the founder.

The **College Chapel★★**, built from 1449-82 is one of the best examples of Perpendicular architecture in England, even though the fan vaulting was completely reconstructed in 1957. The **wall paintings★** representing the miracles of the Virgin (north side) and the adventures of a mythical Empress (south side) were executed from 1479-88; uncovered in 1923, restored from 1961-75, they can now be appreciated as the finest 15C wall paintings in England. The stained glass is by Evie Holme (east window) and John Piper. Note also the tapestry reredos and panelling produced by William Morris from designs by Burne-Jones.

The brick **Cloister Court** dates back to Henry VI's time, although the second floor on the north and east sides and the College Library on the south are 18C. Below this is the 15C College Hall, where the collegers eat. In the undercroft to college hall is the Museum of Eton Life.

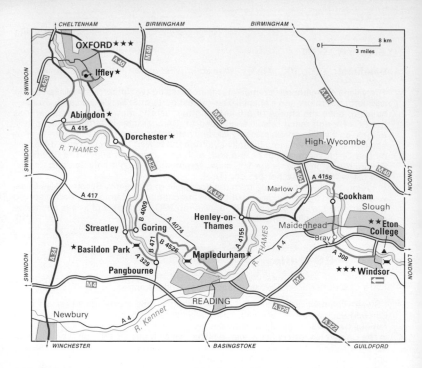

Cookham. — Pop 5 865. This charming village has been immortalised by the artist **Sir Stanley Spencer** (1891-1959). The former Wesleyan Chapel which Spencer attended as a boy is now the **Stanley Spencer Gallery★**. Cookham features in many of his paintings, notably *Christ preaching at Cookham Regatta* and *The Betrayal.*

Henley-on-Thames. — Pop 10 910. In the first week of July oarsmen come from all over the world to this charming town for the **Henley Royal Regatta,** England's premier amateur regatta. The elegant 5-arched **bridge,** designed in 1786, bears carved heads of Father Thames and the goddess Isis. It is overlooked by the 1550 tower of the 13C **St Mary's Church,** enlarged *c*1400. Note, inside, early 17C monument to Lady Periam and, in the churchyard, almshouses and the timber-framed Chantry House. The town has a good number of Georgian and earlier timber-framed inns and houses.

★ Mapledurham. — An Elizabethan manor house beside a 14C church and a fully operational watermill dating back to the 15C form an almost perfect riverside picture. The house was completed *c*1612 by Sir Richard Blount. Though many changes were made over the centuries there is still much to admire, notably the great oak staircase, fine Jacobean plasterwork, many portraits and the chapel, an imaginative piece of Strawberry Hill Gothick.

Pangbourne. — Pop 3 445. The River Pang joins the Thames at this village where **Kenneth Grahame** lived from 1922-32 and wrote his children's book *The Wind in the Willows.* At the Swan Inn, built in 1642, rain finally caused Jerome K Jerome's *Three Men* to abandon their boat and return to London.

★ Basildon Park. — The splendid Palladian villa of mellow Bath stone, overlooking a lush part of the Thames valley, was built by John Carr in 1776. In the early 20C it was planned to have it moved to the United States, but fortunately only some of the fittings were sold and are now in New York's Waldorf Astoria Hotel. The house was saved from demolition in 1952 by Lord and Lady Iliffe, who restored it and recently donated it to the National Trust.
The **west front** is dominated by a giant recessed portico of four Ionic columns rising from the first floor to the pediment at roof level. The house is entered through low ground-floor arches and narrow twin staircases which climb to the portico and the entrance to the hall. The beautifully restored house is rich in exquisite **plasterwork** on ceiling and walls, notably in the blue and gold dining room, green drawing room and the pink, lilac, green and grey hall. The almost over-sumptuous Octagon Room, overlooking the Thames, was decorated *c*1840. In addition to a fine collection of 18C paintings, note the Graham Sutherland portrait of Lord Iliffe in the Library.

Streatley and **Goring.** — The villages, with the weir and Goring Lock, are set in what is acknowledged as one of the most beautiful parts of the Thames, offering enjoyable riverside walks.

★ Dorchester. — Pop 1 045. This historic village on the Thame, a tributary of the Thames, dates back to the Bronze Age. The Romans built their own town Dorocina on the site. In 635 AD St Birinus baptised King Cynegils of Wessex in the river; a Saxon church was built, on the site of which the Norman **abbey church** now stands. Most of the church is in fact Decorated, its crowning glory being the enormous six-light **east window** of 1340. The north wall has an equally spectacular **Jesse Window,** depicting in its tracery Christ's lineage back to Jesse. Opposite are the flamboyantly pinnacled sedilia and piscina. In the village several great coaching inns have survived as well as many fine houses and thatched cottages.

★ **Abingdon.** — Pop 29 130. The town grew up around an abbey founded in the 7C, though the only remaining abbey buildings are the 13C **Chequer** with its tall chimney, the *c*1500 **Long Gallery** with an oak beamed roof and the 15C **gateway** beside the medieval church of St Nicholas. A notable feature is the 17C **County Hall★** by Christopher Kempster, who assisted Wren in the construction of the dome of St Paul's Cathedral. Abingdon's skyline is characterised by the 15C spire of the wide 5-aisled **St Helen's Church**, mostly rebuilt in the 15C; note the 14C paintings on the roof of the inner north aisle. Delightful 15C **almshouses★** border the churchyard.

★ **Iffley Church.** — Iffley, now one of Oxford's suburbs, has one of the best preserved ⊘ Norman village churches in England, with a central tower and a profusion of zigzag moulding, typical of the late 12C.

★★★ **Oxford.** — *Description p 192.*

TINTAGEL Cornwall — Pop 1 566

Michelin Map **403** F 32 or Atlas G Britain p 3 — Local map p 97

Tintagel especially and the West Country in general have always been associated with Arthurian legend dating back to the 8C. There is probably some historical basis for the figure of **Arthur** as a 5-6C chieftain, but what is certain is that Arthur's court and the quest for the Holy Grail fired the imagination of some of the greatest writers of the Middle Ages throughout Europe - William of Malmesbury, Geoffrey of Monmouth, Wace, Chrétien de Troyes, Wolfram von Eschenbach, Gottfried von Strassburg, Sir Thomas Malory - and more recent authors including Tennyson, Swinburne, T H White...

Arthurian Legend in Cornwall. — In the innumerable written and unwritten versions of Arthurian legend Tintagel often figures as the castle where Arthur lived with his Queen Guinevere and the **Knights of the Round Table**, among whom were Parsifal, Gawain, and Tristan, nephew of King Mark who is also said to have lived at Tintagel. The magician **Merlin** lived in a cave below the castle and on a rock off Mousehole *(qv)*; the sword **Excalibur**, forged in Avalon and withdrawn by Arthur from the stone, was finally thrown into Dozmary Pool on Bodmin Moor; Camelot is believed to be Cadbury Castle *(qv)*. The battle of Mount Bladon in *c*520, when Arthur defeated the pagan Saxons, was possibly fought at Badbury Rings in Dorset or near Swindon, and the **Battle of Camlan**, where he was slain by his stepson Mordred, on the banks of the River Camel on Bodmin Moor. Mortally wounded, Arthur sailed into the sunset to the Isles of Scilly or the Isle of Avalon, held to be near Glastonbury where his and Guinevere's tomb was ''discovered'' in the 12C.

⊘ **Tintagel Castle.** — *Access by a steep road from the main street.*
The castle ruin lies on an impressive **site★★★** overlooking the sea from precipitous rocks. As well as the ruined walls from the 1145 chapel and great hall, the area is strewn with the remains of the 6C Celtic monastery. Recent archaeological excavations have revealed possible signs of a Dark Age chieftain's hall.

★★★ TROSSACHS Central

Michelin Map **401** G 15 or Atlas G Britain p 55

The Trossachs is one of Scotland's most famous scenic areas, with rugged mountains and wooded slopes reflected in the waters of many lochs. From Callander and Loch Venacher in the east, to Loch Katrine and even to the shores of Loch Lomond *(qv)* in the west, this whole area of great scenic beauty is easily accessible. So start your visit early, if you can, to avoid the crowds and the tourist coaches; make the most of this fascinating and unspoilt area.

Rob Roy MacGregor (1671-1734). — Much of this area is MacGregor country, home territory of that outlawed leader of the clan and hero of Sir Walter Scott's novel, *Rob Roy* (1818). Rob, his wife and two of their sons lie in the churchyard of Balquhidder, on Loch Voil to the north.

Queen Elizabeth Forest Park. — Planned forestry was practised in the Loch Ard area as early as 1794, supplying building materials, fuel and an associated tanning industry. The Forestry Commission purchased land in 1928; and some 42 000 acres - 17 000ha were designated the Queen Elizabeth Forest Park in 1953. Details of leisure opportunities (forest drives, walking, cycling, picnics and fishing) within the ⊘ forest park boundaries are available from the visitor centre at **David Marshall Lodge** north of Aberfoyle.

Places to visit in and around the Trossachs

★ **Callander.** — Pop 2 286. This busy summer tourist centre became known to millions as the Tannochbrae of television's *Dr Finlay's Casebook*. Callander has been popular with visitors for over a century and is the main eastern gateway to the Trossachs. The visitor centre offers an introduction to the area and the famous Highland rogue, Rob Roy MacGregor.

Loch Venacher. — The Trossachs road, the A821, skirts the lower slopes of **Ben Ledi** (2 882ft - 879m) overlooking the banks of Loch Venacher, before reaching the scattered settlement of **Brig o'Turk** at the mouth of Glen Finglas. The village has associations with the Ruskins and Millais, whose double tie in 1853 was followed by an annulment of the Ruskins' marriage and Effie's remarriage to Millais. This spot later became a favourite haunt of the Glasgow Boys *(qv)*.

★★ **Loch Katrine.** — *1 mile - 1.5km from the A821 to the pier, visitor centre and car park. There is no access round the loch for vehicles.*
For those who do not relish hill walking, the only, but very rewarding, way to see this lovely loch, source of Glasgow's water supply since 1859, is to take a **boat trip** on the SS *Sir Walter Scott.* Two of the loch's isles - Ellen's and Factor's Isles - figure respectively in works by Sir Walter Scott, the poem *The Lady of the Lake* and the novel *Rob Roy.* Scott's romantic poem did much to popularise the Trossachs and the Wordsworths and Coleridge followed in his footsteps in 1830. The boat turns at Stronachlachar, from where a road leads west to Loch Lomond. Glen Gyle at the head of the loch, was the birthplace of Rob Roy.

To the south of Loch Katrine looms the twin-peaked form of **Ben Venue** (2 393ft - 727m). Beyond, a hilltop viewpoint affords a magnificent **panorama★★★** across the Trossachs, with Ben Venue, Loch Katrine with its ring of mountains, Ben An, Finglas Reservoir, Ben Ledi with Brig o'Turk at its feet and Loch Venacher.

Aberfoyle. — Pop 546. The village, busy now with tourists every summer, was made famous as the place from where Rob Roy abducted Baillie Nicol Jarvie, factor to the Duke of Montrose. Jarvie had evicted Rob's family, and in reprisal, was held captive on what is today known as Factor's Isle in Loch Katrine.

A road leads west through the forest park to Loch Lomond.

★★ **Loch Lomond.** — The blue waters of this 653ft - 200m deep loch are flanked by rugged mountains in the north and pastoral woodlands in the south. Rising on the far side of the loch from the pier at Inversnaid are the rugged forms of the Cobbler, Bens Vorlich, Vane and Ime. The West Highland Way, starting from Milngavie, north of Glasgow follows the east shore northwards to Fort William passing on the way the lower slopes of **Ben Lomond** (3 192ft - 974m). This shapely peak is the most southerly of the Highland Munros (mountains over 3 000ft - 912m). The *Countess Fiona* operates out of Balloch in the south and calls at the highly attractive village of **Luss★** with its mellow stone cottages, Tarbet, Inversnaid and Rowardennan.

Lake of Menteith. — This stretch of water is one of the venues for the Grand Match between north and south, organised by the Royal Caledonian Curling Club and is also popular with fishermen. The remains of **Inchmahome Priory** on one of the tiny islands include the mid-13C ruins of the church and chapter house. The infant Mary Queen of Scots was brought here for safety for a while in 1547, before embarking for France and her marriage to the Dauphin.

★★ TWEED Valley Borders

Michelin Map ⁴⁰¹ K, L and M 17 or Atlas G Britain p 50

On its long and beautiful course the Tweed flows past a wealth of famous landmarks - castles, abbeys, great houses - making the exploration of its banks a delight for the tourist.

HISTORICAL AND GEOGRAPHICAL NOTES

River and landscapes. — The Tweed, third longest river in Scotland after the Tay and the Clyde, rises in the Tweedsmuir Hills and reaches the sea at Berwick-upon-Tweed; for the last part of its journey it serves as the border between England and Scotland. It is ringed by hills in its upper reaches - the Cheviots to the south and the Lammermuir Hills to the north - and its valley is constricted and irregular. In its middle reaches it is broad with majestic curves, overlooked by ruined abbeys and prosperous Border towns.

The Tweed Valley has long been a favoured area of settlement. Iron Age and Roman forts, and monastic houses are found all over the region. It was much fought over and the troubled times are remembered in many a Border ballad and poem.

Today, the valley is primarily agricultural, though the traditional woollen and knitwear industries are the mainstay of the towns.

The River Tweed is one of the foremost salmon rivers in Scotland, though many other species of fish attract the angler too.

FROM MOFFAT TO THE SEA
130 miles - 210km - allow 1 day - local map below

Moffat. — A small town at the head of Annan Valley, Moffat makes a good base from which to explore the Tweedsmuir Hills, source of the Tweed.

Take the A708 Selkirk road.

★★**Grey Mare's Tail.** — At the head of Moffat Water Valley is the Grey Mare's Tail, a spectacular 200ft - 60m waterfall. The road leads on up the now narrow V-shaped valley to cross the pass and then to descend the valley of the Little Yarrow Water. Here, by St Mary's Loch, is Tibbie Shiel's Inn, meeting place of **James Hogg** (1770-1835), ''the Ettrick Shepherd'' and his friends. On the northern side of the Tweedsmuir Hills is the source of the River Tweed.

Take the road to the left, signposted Tweedsmuir following Megget Water, turn right onto the A701.

Broughton. — Pop 220. In this trim roadside village is the **John Buchan Centre** (Old Church), a tribute to the author and statesman **John Buchan**, Lord Tweedsmuir (1875-1940).

The B7016 to the right joins the B712, running parallel to the Tweed. At the junction with the A72, turn right.

One mile short of Peebles, on a rocky outcrop overlooking the river is **Neidpath Castle**, a 14C L-plan tower house. It is typical of the fortified dwellings needed for safety in the days of border and clan warfare.

Peebles. — Pop 6 404. A good centre from which to explore the Tweeddale countryside, or to fish for salmon. The author **Robert Louis Stevenson** lived here, as did the explorer **Mungo Park** whose journeys opened up much of Africa. **William Chambers**, publisher of the famous Dictionary, was born here and donated the Chambers Institute, a library and a museum to the town.

6 miles - 10km down river, by the A72. Cross the Tweed at Innerleithen.

★★**Traquair House.** — There was a royal hunting lodge here as early as 1107, which was transformed into a Border 'peel', or fortified tower house, during the Wars of Independence. This typical tower house has a wealth of relics, treasures and traditions and many associations and personal belongings of Mary Queen of Scots.

Return to the A72 and continue eastwards by the B7060 then the A7 to the left towards Abbotsford.

★★**Abbotsford.** — A fantasy in stone, typical of **Sir Walter Scott** (1771-1832), the man who did so much to romanticise and popularise all things Scottish. Scott was born the youngest of thirteen children of an Edinburgh solicitor. When in 1799 he became sheriff of Selkirkshire, he bought a house at Achiestiel, and later, in 1812, the farmhouse which he re-named and transformed into Abbotsford. In the study is preserved his massive writing desk; following a financial crisis in 1826 Scott wrote a staggering three novels a year whilst he re-paid his creditors; he died here at Abbotsford, overlooking his beloved River Tweed, on 21 September 1832. There is in the house a collection of some 9 000 rare books and some of the many items relating to Scotland and its history collected by Sir Walter throughout his life.

By the A7 return to the A72 then turn right.

★**Melrose.** — Pop 2 143. Grouped around the abbey ruins, Melrose is overshadowed by the **Eildon Hills.** Their strange triple peak - of volcanic origin - was once believed to have been the work of Michael Scott, a 13C wizard, who is buried in the abbey.

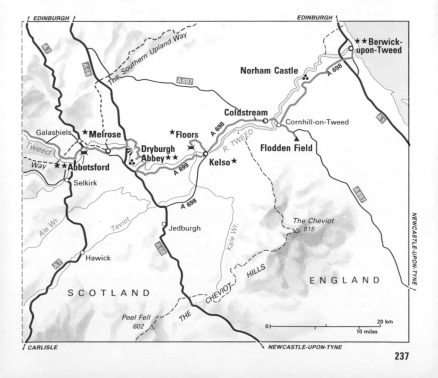

Melrose Abbey

Melrose and other towns in the Borders, like Galashiels and Hawick, have a long and proud tradition of producing outstanding Rugby League and seven-a-side teams.
David I founded **Melrose Abbey★★** in 1136. The original buildings were damaged in the 14C, notably in 1322 by Edward II's retreating army. Robert the Bruce, whose heart is buried here, ensured their rebuilding. The ruins date from the late 14C to the early 16C and, uncharacteristically for a Cistercian foundation, are distinguished by a profusion of decorative sculpture. The remains of what was perhaps the richest abbey in Scotland were restored in the 1820s on the initiative of Sir Walter Scott.

Leave Melrose by the B6361 running along the Tweed. Past the viaduct, turn left onto the A68, then, once over the river, right on a minor road to Leaderfoot, then up Bemersyde Hill and turn right onto the B6356.

★★ Scott's View. — The AA viewpoint (593ft - 181m) faces west across the winding Tweed to the three conical peaks of the Eildons. In the near foreground is Bemersyde House, the home presented in 1921 by the nation to **Earl Haig**, who is buried in Dryburgh Abbey.

Continue by the local road to Dryburgh Abbey.

★★ Dryburgh Abbey. — One of the group of Border abbeys founded by David I, Dryburgh was begun in 1150. It was repeatedly attacked by the English in the 1300s and was badly damaged when the town of Dryburgh was razed in 1544. A sheltered meander of the Tweed provides a splendid setting for the ruins of the abbey. The conventual buildings are one of the best preserved groups.

Return to the B6356 then take the B6004 towards St Boswells where you turn left onto the A699 alongside the Tweed.

★ Kelso. — Pop 5 547. Standing at the confluence of the Tweed and its main tributary, the Teviot, Kelso grew from a fording place into a thriving market town. Here again are the ruins of a fine abbey, founded in 1128, but many times destroyed, the latest being in 1545, despite a desperate resistance put up by the monks to the "Rough Wooing". The town has some remarkable Georgian architecture and the cobbled town square features the elegant Town House of 1816. The bridge was built in 1803 by John Rennie, and served as a model for Waterloo Bridge.

★ Floors Castle. — *On the outskirts of Kelso.* The distinctive pinnacled silhouette stands on a terraced site overlooking the Tweed. The main block, built to the designs of William Adam, was extended when Playfair added the wings. Many of the rooms were refurbished early this century by the American wife of the 8th Duke of Roxburghe, to accommodate her outstanding collection of tapestries and furniture.

Continue down river on the A698.

Coldstream. — A busy market town grew up at this crossing place of the Tweed. Here General Monck raised his regiment of Northumbrian troops, having been given the task by Cromwell of policing Scotland's east coast. On 1 January 1660 the General and his regiment set out for London on the march which eventually led to the Restoration of Charles II. The small local museum has an excellent section on the **Coldstream Guards**, the regiment's name after 1670.

Follow the A697 across the Tweed to Cornhill-on-Tweed then Branxton.

Flodden Field. — A monument inscribed "To the brave of both nations" marks Pipers Hill, the centre of the English positions. In two hours, on 9 September 1513, the smaller English army slaughtered the flower of Scotland's chivalry and their King, James IV, who had led them into battle in support of his recently renewed 'Auld Alliance' with the French.

Return to the A698 then take a local road to Norham Castle in its riverside site.

⊘ **Norham Castle.** — Hugh Puiset, Bishop of Durham, completed the massive stone keep of his castle about 1174. From the 12C to 16C, Norham guarded one of the main crossings of the Tweed. It was in Norham Church on 20 November 1292 that John Balliol swore fealty to Edward I, after being chosen as King of Scotland three days previously, at Berwick.

Continue along the A698 to Berwick-upon-Tweed.

★★ **Berwick-upon-Tweed.** — *Description p 54.*

★ **WARWICK** Warwickshire   Pop 21 701

Michelin Map 403 P 27 or Atlas G Britain p 27
Town plan in the current Michelin Red Guide Great Britain and Ireland

''This perfect county town'' (Pevsner), its castle ''the most perfect piece of castellated antiquity in the kingdom'' (Lord Torrington). The town is Queen Anne style, the castle 14C. Both have a unity and neither encroaches on the other.

★★ **Warwick Castle.** — On the site of a Norman motte and bailey stronghold - which
⊘ may even have been a Saxon strongpoint - Thomas De Beauchamp 11th Earl of Warwick (1329-69) rebuilt his castle. It was home also to Richard (1382-1439) the 13th Earl, executioner of Joan of Arc, and to Richard Neville, Earl of Warwick (1428-71), the ''king-maker''.
Overlooking the River Avon in a landscape by Capability Brown, the curtain walls and gatehouse are 14C, the Bear Tower and Clarence Tower 15C.

Interior. — Collections of paintings, furniture and arms and armour are housed in the State Rooms, Great Hall and Armoury. The Great Hall was neo-Gothicised by Salvin; the Red and Cedar Drawing Rooms are packed with Lelys, Van Dycks, Dahls and Boulle furniture; and in the Blue Boudoir is a fruit carving by Grinling Gibbons and portrait of Henry VIII after Holbein. Also in the former Private Apartments is a Madame Tussaud's exhibition entitled *A Royal Weekend Party 1898.* Other attractions include the dungeons, torture chamber, rampart walk and ghost tower.

Leycester Hospital, Warwick

★ **Leycester Hospital.** — *High Street.*
⊘ Founded in 1571 by Lord Leicester (Queen Elizabeth's favourite) and built with timber frames around a charming partly-cloistered courtyard, the oldest parts are the 1383 chapel and 1450 guildhall, built by Warwick the ''king-maker''.

★ **Collegiate Church of St Mary.** — *Church Street.*
⊘ Dating back to 1123 the church was rebuilt after a fire in 1694. Its glory is the 15C **Beauchamp Chapel** with the **tomb**★ and superb gilded bronze effigy of Richard De Beauchamp, Earl of Warwick, as well as the tomb of Robert Dudley, Earl of Leicester.

EXCURSION

★ **Kenilworth Castle.** — *5 miles - 8km, take the A46 and the A429 north.*
⊘ Immense and awe-inspiring, its sandstone ruins were once the home of Simon de Montfort, while in the **Great Hall** Edward II stood a prisoner in a black dress before being taken to his death at Berkeley Castle *(qv).* Strengthened by John of Gaunt, and the seat of the Earl of Leicester, it was wrecked after the Civil War and overgrown with ivy became the backcloth to Sir Walter Scott's *Kenilworth* (1862).

Michelin Map 403 M 30 or Atlas G Britain p 16

The calm of the cathedral within its precinct contrasts majestically with the bustle of the Market Square in England's smallest cathedral city.

★★★CATHEDRAL

Wells was the first cathedral church in the Early English style; it took more than three centuries to plan and build, from c1175 to 1508.

West Front. — Despite weathering and much destruction by the Puritans, the west front is one of England's richest displays of 13C sculpture. The screen front is nearly 150ft - 46m across, twice as wide as it is tall, extending round the bases of the west towers — strange constructions which continue the gabled lines of the screen in slim and soaring pinnacled buttresses and tall paired lancets, only to stop abruptly. The 300 statues, half of them life-size, rise to a climax in the centre gable with a frieze of the Apostles and Our Lord flanked by two six-winged cherubim.

Nave. — Viewed from the west to the east end the most striking feature is the scissor arch, constructed together with similar arches at the north and south sides of the crossing in 1338-48, when the west piers of the crossing tower began to subside. The nave itself was completed in 1239. Note the stiff leaf **capitals** at the top of the piers and the stone pulpit, dating from c1547 at the east end of the nave.

Chancel. — Immediately striking is the Jesse or **Golden Window** of medieval glass and the embroidered stall backs.

South Transept. — The capitals portray men's heads, animal masks hidden among leaves and everyday scenes such as a man with toothache and even two men caught in the act of stealing apples from an orchard. The **corbels** also portray figures, including an angel. The circular font, with Jacobean cover, is the only relic of an earlier cathedral on an adjacent site.

Retro-Choir. — The **piers** produce a forest of ribs to support intricate tierceron **vaulting**. Note the 13C cope chest and medieval **misericords** showing a man killing a wyvern or Alexander the Great being lifted to heaven by two griffins.

Lady Chapel. — At the centre of the unequal octagon a finely painted boss forms the climax to the **star vault**. Note original figurework of c1315 glass.

North Transept. — In the transept is an **astronomical clock** of 1390, with the sun and a star revolving round the 24-hour dial and, above, a **knights' tournament** in which one knight is struck down at every quarter hour.

Chapter House. — A wide curving flight of **steps** leads to the splendid octagonal chapter house, the building of which was completed by 1306. From its slender clustered centre pier 32 ribs fan out to meet those rising from each angle in an en-circling octagonal rib.

Cathedral Precinct. — Three 15C **gates** lead from the city streets to the calm of the **Green** and the spectacular view of the cathedral exterior. The 1459 **Chain Gate** at the north east of the Green gives access to **Vicars' Close**, a 150yd - 137m long street of identical cottages built in c1348 for members of the cathedral in minor orders. On the south side of the cathedral stands the 700 year old **Bishop's Palace★**, stoutly walled and encircled by a moat. Inside are walled gardens and the welling springs from which the city gets its name - 3 400 000 gallons a day, or 40 gallons a second (c15 million litres a day, 180 litres a second). There are also the ruins of the old banqueting hall, the present palace and a beautiful **view★★** can be ob-tained of the east end of the cathedral.

EXCURSIONS

★**Caves at Wookey Hole.** — *2 miles - 3km northwest of Wells on a minor road.* The approach is through wooded pastureland at the foot of the Mendip plateau. The hole is in a 200ft - 61m cliffside from which the River Axe emerges.

The **caves★** contain six chambers through which the river flows, always present, in echoing cascades and deep blue-green pools. **Stalactites, stalagmites,** "frozen" water-falls and translucent pools fill the caverns through which one walks for some 429yds - 392m. There is no evidence of Stone Age occupation, but the caves were inhabited by Iron Age man in 150 BC and later by Romano-British and Celtic peoples.

★★**Cheddar Gorge.** — *9 miles - 14km northwest by the A371.* The Gorge is two miles - 3km long with a 1:6 gradient, twisting and turning in its descent from the Mendips. The cliffs are of limestone, gaunt and grey where the fissured walls and pinnacles rise vertically 350-400ft - 107-122m. From near the foot of the gorge **Jacob's Ladder**, a staircase of 322 steps, leads up to a panoramic **view★** of the Men-dips, the Somerset Levels and the Quantocks.

Caves. — The caves are near the gorge bottom on the east side *(right, going up)*. **Cox's Cave** was discovered in 1837 and **Gough's Cave** in 1890. The series of chambers follows the course of underground streams through the porous limestone. The stalag-mites and stalactites, petrified falls, lace curtains and pillars are coloured accord-ing to the minerals in the limestone - rust red (iron), green (manganese) and grey (lead). These dramatic formations increase by 1 cubic inch - 16cc every 400 years. In the **museum** the weapons, utensils in flint, bone and antler horn, iron and bronze, pottery and the skull of Cheddar Man indicate that the caves were inhabited inter-mittently from the Palaeolithic to the Iron Age and even in Roman times.

Michelin Map 401 D, E 10, 11 and 12 or Atlas G Britain p 66

The Atlantic seaboard of Wester Ross is wild and dramatic, with magnificent mountains and placid lochs. The main touring centres are Kyle of Lochalsh, Gairloch and Ullapool, and from these the visitor may drive, walk, climb, fish or sail, to enjoy to the full this glorious area.

★★★① FROM KYLE OF LOCHALSH TO GAIRLOCH

120 miles - 192km it visiting Ellean Donan Castle - allow a day

The route covers some of the finest scenery in the Wester Ross region - Loch Maree studded with islands, the Torridon area and the Applecross peninsula. Some of the roads will be busy in the height of the tourist season, but many stretches will allow the luxury of enjoying the scenery in solitude. Remember to keep the petrol tank well topped up.

Kyle of Lochalsh. — Pop 803. This is the ferry port for Skye *(qv)* and a busy place in summer.

★ **Eilean Donan Castle.** — *9 miles - 15km east of Kyle of Lochalsh by the A87.*

The castle enjoys an idyllic setting *(photograph p 41)* on its island in the loch, with the mountains behind. It is now linked to the shore by a bridge and the rooms open to the public have a variety of MacRae mementoes. The MacRaes were the guardians of the castle and hereditary bodyguards to the MacKenzies. Following an abortive Jacobite landing, with Spanish troops in support, in 1719, the castle was abandoned for two hundred years. A complete reconstruction was undertaken in the 20C.

Return to Kyle and leave by the road running along the coast to the north, with its views across to Skye and the Cuillins.

★ **Plockton.** — Pop 425. Once a "refugee" settlement at the time of the Highland clearances, Plockton, with its palm-lined main street is a centre for yachtsmen and windsurfers.

At Achmore, take the A890 to the left, and at the junction with the A896, go left again, towards Lochcarron. At Tornapress, the visitor can elect to continue on the A896 to Shieldaig, but the minor road across the peninsula, via Bealach-na Bo well repays the effort. It has hairpin bends and 1:4 gradients, and is not recommended for caravans - or learner drivers.

Bealach-na Bo. — 2 053ft - 626m. On the way up to the pass the hanging valley frames spectacular vistas of lochs and mountains, while from the summit car park the **panorama**★★★ westward of Skye and its fringing islands is superb.

Applecross. — Pop 235. Site of the monastery founded in the 7C by St Maelrubha, now a holiday centre with a red sandy beach.

Either continue north along the coast, via Fearnmore, to Torridon, or retrace your tracks to Tornapress and then to Torridon by the A896.

Torridon. — There is a countryside centre here with an audio-visual introduction to the area. Information is available on walking and climbing routes.

Glen Torridon. — A flat-bottomed glacial valley, overlooked by the seven summits of "The Grey One" **Liathach** (3 456ft - 1 054m) on the left, with **Beinn Eighe** (3 309ft - 1 010m) to its northeast.

At Kinlochewe, take the A832 to the left.

Aultroy Visitor Centre. — The centre explains the fascinating ecology of the 11 757 acre - 4 758ha **Beinn Eighe National Nature Reserve**, Britain's first, with its splendid remnants of the native Scots pine forest.

★★★ **Loch Maree.** — Loch Maree epitomises the scenic beauty and grandeur of the west coast. Between a shoulder of Beinn Eighe and the towering **Slioch** (3 217ft - 980m) to the north, the loch is studded with islands, on one of which, Isle Maree, St Maelrubha set up his cell in the 7C.

★ **Victoria Falls.** — A platform and the riverside path give good views of these falls, named after Queen Victoria's visit in 1877.

Gairloch. — Pop 125. The ideal centre for touring the Torridon area, exploring the hills and enjoying the sandy beaches of this part of the west coast, with splendid views of the Hebridean Islands. The pier at the head of the loch still has all the bustle of a fishing port. The **Gairloch Heritage Museum** illustrates life in the past, including a croft house room, shop, schoolroom, the ironworks of the 17C and illicit whisky distilling.

★★② FROM GAIRLOCH TO ULLAPOOL

56 miles - 90km - about 4 hours

This run will take you along the coastline with its bays, beaches and headlands all backed, inland, by breathtaking mountain scenery.

Take the A832 across the neck of the Rubha Reidh peninsula.

Stop, before descending to the River Ewe, and look back from the roadside **viewpoint**★★★, at the superb view of Loch Maree with its forested islands.

★★★ **Inverewe Gardens.** — These outstanding gardens, in a magnificent coastal setting, are made possible so far north by the influence of the Gulf Stream. Here, on the same latitude as Leningrad, in 64 acres - 26ha of carefully tended gardens, many kinds of plants are shown to their best advantage. The property was bought for Osgood MacKenzie in 1862. The peninsula was barren, exposed to the Atlantic gales and with an acid peat soil. A rabbit-proof fence was erected. Scots and Corsican pine were planted as windbreaks, and soil was brought in. A lifetime of planning and planting, carried on after his death by his daughter, has created this memorial to him. The gardens were given to the National Trust for Scotland in 1952. Colour is found at most seasons, with azaleas and rhododendrons in May, the rock garden in June, herbaceous borders in mid-summer and heathers and maples in the autumn.

Continue along the A832, following the shoreline of Loch Ewe and across the neck of the Rubha Beag peninsula.

The island in Gruinard Bay was the scene of an anthrax experiment during the war. *(The public is strictly forbidden to land on the island.)*

Continue on the A832, turning left at its junction with the A835.

★★ **Falls of Measach.** — The waters of the River Droma make a spectacular sight as they drop over 150ft - 45m in the wooded cleft of the Corrieshalloch Gorge.

Continue northwest on the A835.

The road follows the north shore of **Loch Broom**★★, with its scattered houses and traces of former field patterns, lying in a particularly attractive setting.

★ **Ullapool.** — Pop 1 006. The village was laid out in the 18C by the British Fisheries Society and flourished as a fishing port during the herring boom. Fishing still plays an important part in the local economy and factory ships can usually be seen, in season, anchored at the mouth of the loch. Ullapool is the car ferry terminal for Stornoway, a haven for yachtsmen and an unrivalled centre for sea angling. Various boats sail to the **Summer Isles** where seals and sea birds are the principal attraction. For details apply to the tourist information office in the car ferry terminal.

WHITBY North Yorkshire   Pop 12 982

Michelin Map 402 S 20 or Atlas G Britain p 47

Port and holiday resort, Whitby, at the mouth of the River Esk, is divided into an east side, steeped in history, with the abbey on its headland, and a relatively modern west side. It was in Whitby that the explorer **Captain Cook** (1728-79), served his seafaring apprenticeship. The beaches from Robin Hood's Bay to the south, past **Staithes** to **Saltburn** to the north, are popular for bathing and wind-surfing.

Whitby Abbey. — Founded 657 AD by St Hilda, Abbess of Hartlepool, on the probable site of a Roman signal station, on land given to her by Oswy, King of Northumbria. It was the setting for the **Synod of Whitby** in 664 AD, at which the Roman, rather than the Celtic rite was chosen. Here the poet **Caedmon**, who worked on the abbey lands, "sang the Creation of the world" as Bede tells us. That abbey was possibly destroyed by the Danes in 867, and we see today the remains of the new abbey re-founded in 1078, rebuilt in its present form between 1220 and 1320. The high quality of the Early English style is typical of other abbeys in the north, particularly at Rievaulx, which is contemporary with Whitby.

St Mary's Church. — 199 steps lead up from the town to this basically Norman church, which shares the clifftop with the abbey. It was modified in Stuart and Georgian times, leaving a charming mixture of white-painted galleries, 'barley sugar' columns and box pews.

EXCURSION

★ **Captain Cook Birthplace Museum.** — *28 miles - 45km west in Stewart Park, Marton, near Middlesbrough. Take the A171 to Ormesby, turn left on the B1380 and follow signs, or take the coast road the A174.*
An excellently appointed museum, near the site of the cottage where Captain Cook was born, traces his early life, his naval career and survey voyages to Canada and Australia, as well as his three Pacific voyages of discovery 1768-89.

WICK Highland   Pop 7 770

Michelin Map 401 K 8 or Atlas G Britain p 74

Wick stands near the mouth of the river of the same name - after the Norse term *Vik,* meaning a bay. It is a thriving market town and was once the country's premier herring port with two good harbours - one designed by Thomas Telford and later improved by Stephenson. The **Wick Heritage Centre** presents the town's history by means of an attractive series of tableaux.

EXCURSIONS

★ **Duncansby Head.** — *19 miles - 31km to the north by the A9.*

John o'Groats. — 876 miles - 1410km from Land's End. This settlement takes its name from a Dutchman, Jan de Groot, who started a ferry service to the Orkneys in the 16C. The eight-sided tower of the hotel recalls the tale of this ferryman who, to settle disputes amongst his seven descendants, built an octagonal house, with eight doors and an octagonal table.

Take the local road eastwards.

The northeastern headland of mainland Scotland, **Duncansby Head**★, overlooks the treacherous waters of the Pentland Firth, a seven-mile-wide channel. Standing just offshore, the **Stacks of Duncansby**★★, pointed sea stacks, rise a spectacular 210ft - 64m up from the water.

Two Caithness Prehistoric Monuments. — *18 miles - 29km south of Wick by the A9.*

★ **Hill o'Many Stanes.** — This fan-shaped arrangement of 22 lines of stones was laid out in the Bronze Age, perhaps for some astronomical purpose. Similar settings exist elsewhere in northern Scotland.

Continue on the A9 and turn right at West Clyth onto a local road.

★ **Grey Cairns of Camster.** — Dating from the Neolithic period (4 000 - 1 800 BC), the **Long Cairn★★**, 195ft - 60m long by 33ft - 10m wide, incorporates two earlier bee-hive cairns. Both the **Long** and smaller **Round Cairn** can be viewed from the outside but access to the inner chambers is for the agile only, as the entrance passage-ways must be negotiated on hands and knees.

★★ Isle of WIGHT   Pop 118 594

Michelin Map **404** P, Q 31 and 32 or Atlas G Britain p 9
Access: see the current Michelin Red Guide Great Britain and Ireland

The 147 square mile - 380km² island has been a holiday destination since Queen Victoria chose Osborne for her country retreat. Visitors attracted by the mild sunny climate and varied scenery can choose the popular sandy beaches of the eastern coastal resorts, notably **Sandown**, the more elegant **Shanklin**, and **Ventnor** with its **botanic gardens** on the sunny ledge of the Undercliff; or the rolling hills of the ridge of chalk downs running east from Culver Cliff through the quieter western part to The Needles. A 65 mile - 105km **coastal path** around the island connects with cross-country trails offering spectacular views of downs, cliffs and sea. The following is a brief selection of sights.

Alum Bay. — The westernmost bay of the island, where alum was mined, is a remarkable geographical phenomenon, with its sandstone **cliffs** richly coloured with more than 20 mineral hues. In the afternoon sun a boat trip to the **Needles**, sea stacks 100ft - 30m offshore, gives fine views of the colourful cliffs framed by chalk cliffs.

Tennyson Down was one of Alfred, Lord Tennyson's (1809-92) favourite walks during the years he lived at Farringford; a 38ft - 12m high granite cross commemorates the great poet.

⊘ **Arreton.** — The handsome stone **manor house** bears the date 1639 on the front porch; among the period furnishings note the fine panelling in the hall and dining parlour. The upper floors now house a **museum of childhood**, a collection of toys and dolls from the past. **St George's Church** contains elements of Early Norman and Early English work and a radio museum.

★ **Brading.** — Pop 2 040. The remains of the 3C **Roman Villa★** southwest of the vil-
⊘ lage comprise the ground plan of the west wing - with good 4C **mosaics** of figures from Classical mythology - and a display of artefacts. **St Mary's Church★**, built *c*1200, has a late 13C west tower with a recessed spire; in the Oglander Chapel are impressive family tombs, notably that of the diarist Sir John Oglander (d 1655), represented as a recumbent medieval knight. The timber-framed house (*c*1500)
⊘ beside the church contains a **wax museum**. In 1607 Sir John Oglander took over **Nun-**
⊘ **well House★** *(1 mile - 2km west)* which stayed in the family until recently. Charles I's last night of freedom was probably spent here.

★★ **Carisbrooke Castle.** — In 1100 Richard de Redvers built the keep and curtain walls
⊘ on the site of a Roman stronghold. In the 14C the fortifications were strengthened and withstood a French attack in 1377, and in the late 16C bastions and further defence lines were added to enclose the entire site. Until 1944 the castle was the residence of the Crown-appointed Governors of the island, one of whom, Colonel Robert Hammond, was host, then jailer to the fleeing King Charles I in 1647-48. After passing through an Elizabethan gateway dated 1598 the visitor crosses a bridge to the massive 14C **gatehouse** with twin drum towers. The Norman curtain wall encloses the high motte and 12C shell **keep** (with **views★** for miles around), the 13C chapel rebuilt in 1904, and the late 12C **Great Hall** which has a 1390 chimney-piece and houses a **museum** of Isle of Wight history. In the 16C well-house a donkey still turns the 1587 treadmill to draw water from the Norman well.

⊘ **Godshill.** — Above this much-visited village stands the 14-15C church of **All Saints**, notable for its unique mid-15C **Lily Cross mural** on the east wall of the south transept, showing Christ crucified on a triple-branched lily, under a wagon roof. Other features are the fine early 16C monument to Sir John Leigh and a double nave plan. West of the church stands a group of attractive thatched cottages, which form with the church tower behind a quintessentially English rural scene.

★★ **Osborne House.** — This remarkable Italianate villa overlooking the Solent was built
⊘ for Queen Victoria and Prince Albert by the famous London builder Thomas Cubitt. Work began on what Queen Victoria described as "a place of one's own, quiet and retired" in 1845 and it was completed in 1851. The Prince Consort's choice of style, with Tuscan columns and campanile and an eleven-bay Palladian front to the household wing, was inspired by the fact that the site with its view of the sea reminded him of the Bay of Naples. The Royal Family regularly took vacations at Osborne and after Albert's death in 1861 Queen Victoria spent much of her 40 years of widowhood there, insisting that everything be kept exactly as it had been during Albert's life.

After the Queen's death, Edward VII gave most of the estate to the nation, opening it to the public. The richly decorated and furnished private apartments give a remarkable picture of the private life of the Royal Family in the 19C, a touching example being the **twin desks** in the **Queen's Sitting Room** where the Queen and her Prince worked side by side. The only significant alteration made after Albert's death was the addition of the **Durbar Wing** to the L-shaped building in 1890: the work of Bhai Ram Singh and John Lockwood Kipling, the father of Rudyard, it reflects Queen Victoria's pride in her Indian possessions and her title Empress of India.

In the **grounds** a real **Swiss Cottage**, imported from Switzerland, was erected in 1853, with a delightful tiled kitchen where the royal children apparently learned to cook. A second Swiss Cottage, built in 1862 contains a **museum** of miscellaneous objects collected by the royal family.

Shorwell. — Pop 612. This peaceful village nestling below the downs is notable for **St Peter's Church★**; it is mainly Perpendicular except for the early 13C south doorway and late 12C north chapel containing **monuments** to members of the Leigh family of Northcourt, just north of the church. Over the door is a large *c*1440 **wall painting★** of St Christopher wading through the water. Other treasures are a 1541 Cranmer Bible, a 1579 "Breeches" Bible, a Jacobean font cover and a pulpit canopy with hour glass and a Dutch wooden panel.

Quarr Abbey. — In 1907 French Benedictine monks from Solesmes in the Loire Valley bought the Victorian Quarr House; one of the community, Dom Paul Bellot, a graduate of the Ecole des Beaux Arts in Paris, designed the abbey church which was built in 1911-12. This masterpiece of construction in brick is the most impressive modern building on the island and it is tempting to imagine the career of this genius, had he not become a monk.

⊘At the east end of the **Abbey Church** stands a solid square tower; the high cylindrical south tower rises from an enormous plain wall. The entrance at the west end through a huge brick arch topped by steep gables, leads into the low, short nave which opens out to a long high choir without aisles or transepts. The church is bathed in yellow light from the tall east windows, by the superb soaring arches inside the east tower.

★★ WILTON House Wiltshire

Michelin Map **403** O 30 or Atlas G Britain p 9

The first Earl of Pembroke, William Herbert, received the property of the dissolved Benedictine convent at Wilton from Henry VIII in 1544 and built a house on the site. When a fire destroyed all but the east front in 1647 the 4th Earl commissioned Inigo Jones to design the house anew, incorporating a state room for his collection of portraits by **Van Dyck**. Successive generations have each left their mark; the 8th Earl, founder of the **Royal Wilton Carpet Factory** *(in King Street)* appointed agents to find new pictures and marbles, and the 9th Earl built the 1737 **Palladian Bridge** and redesigned the **garden**. In 1801 the 11th Earl called in James Wyatt, who greatly altered the house. He rebuilt the west and north fronts and built the two-tier Gothic cloister in the original inner court, providing galleries for statuary and historic mementoes such as Napoleon's despatch box and hand-written verses by **Sir Philip Sidney**, who composed his poem *Arcadia* here while staying with his sister.

⊘**State Apartments.** — The suite of six apartments by Inigo Jones are characterised by their stunning decoration, classical in style but opulent, with Italian ceiling paintings, large marble chimneypieces, superbly carved cornices, overmantels, and columns - all decorated in gold leaf. The **Cube Room** (30 × 30 × 30ft) and the **Double Cube Room** (60 × 30 × 30ft), reflecting Jones' preference for simple geometrical relations, are both decorated in gold and white, the latter being a setting for the Van Dyck portraits. Among other notable paintings is a **Rembrandt** portrait (*c*1629) in the Great Ante-Room.

Smoking Rooms. — Besides the moulded detail in cornices, doorways and chimneypieces, typical of Inigo Jones' style, note the **equestrian portraits** and 55 **Spanish Riding School gouaches** commissioned by the 10th Earl, and the outstanding **furniture**, including a late 17C walnut table and Chippendale Spanish mahogany bookcases.

★★ WINCHESTER Hampshire   Pop 34 127

Michelin Map **404** P, Q 30 or Atlas G Britain p 9
Town plan in the current Michelin Red Guide Great Britain and Ireland

This ancient cathedral city was the capital of **Wessex** and of England, from the early 9C to about 100 years after the Norman conquest. There are signs of early habitation in the area (notably the Iron Age hillfort on St Catherine's Hill) but it was only after the Roman invasion of 43 AD that the city known as **Venta Bulgarum** was founded. After the Romans withdrew, the city declined until the Saxon king, Cenwall of Wessex, built a church there in 648 and created a bishopric in 662. After 878 **Alfred the Great** consolidated his defence of Wessex against Danish attacks by setting up a series of fortified **burhs**, of which Winchester was the largest.

At the time of the Norman conquest the city was already of such importance that **William I** was crowned there as well as in London. He built a castle in the southwest angle of the city walls and established a new cathedral in 1070. After the 12C Winchester yielded to London as the preferred royal residence. During the Civil War the Norman castle was largely destroyed, the cathedral damaged and the city looted by Parliamentary troops. After the Restoration the city recovered and in 1682 Charles II commissioned Wren to design a great palace, though work stopped on the monarch's death in 1685.

★★★ **CATHEDRAL** *time: 2 hours*

⊙ The cathedral stands surrounded by lawns on the same site as the 7C Saxon minster, the foundations of which were located in the 1960s. An early bishop of Winchester, **St Swithun**, was buried outside the west end of the minster in 862. There was torrential rain on the day in 1093 when his grave was transferred inside the new church, though he had expressly asked to be buried in the open air; this gave rise to the legend that if it rains on St Swithun's Day (July 15) it will rain for forty days.

William Walkelyn, appointed bishop by William I, began building the new cathedral in 1079. In 1202 the east end was reconstructed, in the early 14C the Norman choir was rebuilt in the Perpendicular style and the nave and west front were rebuilt between 1346 and 1404. After further remodellings of the nave, Lady Chapel and chancel from 1486-1528, the longest Gothic church in Europe (556ft - 169m) was complete.

When, in 1652, Parliament ordered the cathedral (ransacked in the Civil War) to be destroyed, it was saved only by a petition of the citizens. Early in the 20C the east end, built on marshland and supported on a 13C beech tree raft, began to sink, causing the walls to crack and the roof to fall; the cathedral was saved by a diver, William Walker, who worked alone from 1906-12 replacing the rotting rafts with cement.

Exterior. — Built largely of stone from the Isle of Wight, the cathedral's exterior with its squat Norman tower is impressive, though less exciting than the interior.

Nave. — The twelve-bay nave is the cathedral's most striking feature. Under **Bishop William of Wykeham** (1324-1404), the Norman pillars were reconstructed to support graceful Perpendicular arches surmounted by a line of balconies with high clerestory windows above, reaching up to the **stone lierne vault**, with bosses. In the south aisle, Bishop Edington's Chantry (d 1366) is in simple contrast with that of William of Wykeham.

The fine 12C **font** (north aisle) is of black Tournai marble. Nearby is the simple **tomb** of the novelist **Jane Austen**, with no mention of her literary achievements and a 1900 window and brass to her memory. The **west window** (glorious in the afternoon sun) is made up of glass broken by Cromwell's soldiery.

Transepts. — The arcades of rounded arches, surmounted by twin-arched galleries below irregular clerestory arches, form the only unaltered part of the Norman church. In the **Holy Sepulchre Chapel** in the north transept are exquisite 13C wall paintings.

Chancel. — The canopied **choir stalls**, dating from 1308 have a remarkable set of **misericords** with more than five hundred smiling faces. In 1100 the interment of the ''ungodly'' King William Rufus in the chancel gave rise to controversy. Above the high altar stands the early 16C **stone reredos** with three tiers of statues (restored in the 19C) of Christ crucified, saints, English kings, bishops of Winchester... The early Tudor wooden **vault** has outstanding **bosses.**

Retro-choir and Lady Chapel. — The early 13C retro-choir, replacing the Norman apse, is a beautiful piece of Early English design. The chapels and chantries are dedicated to 15C and 16C bishops of Winchester. The Lady Chapel, also early 13C, was extended under Henry VII with the addition of huge seven-light windows, Tudor woodwork and **wall paintings** of the miracles of the Virgin, inspired by those at Eton College.

Library. — *Access from south transept.* A rich collection of manuscripts and books is housed in a room added to the cathedral in the 12C. The jewel of the library is the beautifully illustrated **Winchester Bible**, produced by the monks of the priory in the 12C.

Cathedral Close. — Of the few remaining monastic buildings south of the cathedral, note the **Deanery**, formerly the Prior's Lodging, with a three-arched porch and a 15C
⊙ hall. The 14C **Pilgrims' Hall**, now part of the choir school, has possibly the oldest **hammerbeam roof** in existence. Beside the sturdy **St Swithin's Gate** stands the 15C timber-framed **Cheyney Court** and early 16C stables, also timber-framed and now part of the Pilgrims' School.

ADDITIONAL SIGHTS

★ **Winchester College.** — The college was founded in 1382 by **Bishop William of Wyke-**
⊙ **ham** to provide an education for 70 poor scholars, 16 choristers and 10 ''commoners'' (now 500) from wealthy families, to be continued at New College, Oxford *(qv)*, which Wykeham had already founded in 1379. Pupils are still known as ''Wykehamists''.

The school is entered by the 14C **Outer Gate** in College Street. Through the Middle Gate is **Chamber Court**, the centre of college life, surrounded by Wykeham's original late 14C buildings. **Hall** on its south side (1st floor) has fine 16C wooden panelling on which hang portraits of former pupils and a 16C portrait of the founder. The **Chapel**, with its prominent 15C pinnacled tower was heavily restored in the 19C, but retains its medieval **wooden vault**, one of the first attempts at fan-vaulting in England and the original 14C **choir stalls** with fine misericords. In the centre of Wykeham's 14C cloister stands the early 15C **Fromond's Chantry**, the only example in England of a chapel so placed. The red brick and stone **School** (west of cloister), was built in 1683-87 for the increasing number of ''commoners''. Sir Herbert Baker's simple peaceful **War Cloister**, built in 1924, commemorates Wykehamists who fell in two World Wars.

★ Castle Great Hall. — The Hall is the only surviving part of the castle, built in Norman times and slighted by order of Parliament in the Civil War. The 110 × 55 × 55ft room (34 × 17 × 17m), dating from 1222-36 is a splendid example of a medieval hall, with its timber roof supported on columns of Purbeck marble. On the west wall hangs the 18ft - 5m diameter oak **Round Table** mentioned in 14C records; it is decorated with paintings of the Tudor Rose in its centre, King Arthur and a list of his knights around the edge.

High Street. — At the east end *(The Broadway)* stands a bronze statue to Alfred the Great, erected in 1901. Among the buildings in the pedestrian street are the former **Guildhall** (now a bank), built in 1713, opposite the timber-framed **God Begot House**★ dating from 1558. Note also the 15C stone carved **Butter Cross**, around which markets were held.

★★ St Cross Hospital. — *1 mile - 2km south - a beautiful walk across the meadow.* The oldest charitable institution in England was founded by Bishop Henry de Blois in 1136. In 1445 Cardinal Beaufort added his Almshouses of Noble Poverty. The cruciform **Chapel**, built from around 1160 to the late 13C, is a fine example of transitional Norman architecture and is rich in zig-zag stone carving on the arches and chancel vaulting. In the **Lady Chapel** is a **Flemish triptych** of *c*1530. The **Brethren's Hall** has a minstrels' gallery and an impressive open-timbered late 15C roof. A range of two-storey **15C cottages** forms the west side of the close.

★★★ WINDSOR Castle Berkshire

Michelin Map 404 S 29 or Atlas G Britain p 20 — Local map p 234
Town plan in the current Michelin Red Guide Great Britain and Ireland

England's largest castle is also the largest inhabited stronghold in the world and has been a favourite royal residence, frequently extended and rebuilt, since William the Conqueror first built a motte and bailey on the site in 1070. By 1110 it had become a royal lodge where Henry I held his first court. Henry II erected the first stone buildings between 1165 and 1179, constructing one range of royal apartments in the Upper Ward (to the east of the Round Tower) and one in the Lower Ward. Faced with rebellion by his sons he modernised the defences, rebuilding the earthen walls and wooden Round Tower in stone. Under Henry III (1216-72) this work was virtually completed. Edward III (1327-77) reconstructed the royal apartments for his newly-founded Order of the Garter. Under Charles II that part of the castle comprising the State Apartments was rebuilt, but the principal changes were made in the early 19C when George IV commissioned Sir Jeffry Wyatville as his architect; he built the machicolated walls and several towers, raised the massive Round Tower, giving the castle its famous outline, and remodelled the State Apartments, adding the Waterloo Chamber.

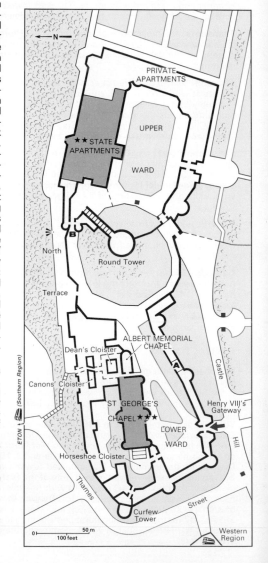

Access to the castle is through **Henry VIII's Gateway**, built in 1511 and bearing the king's arms, the Tudor rose and the Spanish pomegranate of Catherine of Aragon.

Ahead is **St George's Chapel**★★★ *(see over)* and through an archway to the left is the *c*1480 **Horseshoe Cloister** of brick and half-timbered houses built by Edward IV for the minor clergy, which, though heavily restored in the 19C, retains great charm.

St George's Chapel, Windsor

The **Curfew Tower** beyond was built by Henry III, its conical roof being added in the 19C. To the right of Henry VIII's Gateway are the **Military Knights' Lodgings (A)** for retired army officers who, in scarlet uniforms dating from William IV, play a prominent part in the Garter ceremonial and attend Chapel on Sundays. The impressive **Round Tower**, raised to its present height by Wyatville in the 19C, stands on the site of William I's original fortress. An opening in the outer wall left of the tower leads to the **North Terrace**, built *c*1570, which affords **views★★** of Eton College and to the east, London. Between the outer wall and the tower mound, the **Norman Gateway (B)**, with its twin towers and portcullis still in position, was built by Edward III in 1359.

★★★ST GEORGE'S CHAPEL *time: 3/4 hour*

This great Perpendicular chapel was begun by Edward IV to replace Henry III's chapel to the east which Edward III had enlarged and dedicated to his **Most Noble Order of the Garter.** It took over half a century to build and was thus completed after the Royal Chapels of Eton and King's College, Cambridge. The **Royal Beasts** above the flying buttresses of the west end trace the royal descent from Edward III, the Lancastrians on the south side, the Yorkists on the north.

Nave. — Although the nave is wide for its height, the slender clustered piers lead the eye uninterruptedly to the crowning glory of the chapel, the almost flat **lierne vault**, rich with coloured bosses - completed in 1528. The blank panelling between the tall arcades and the clerestory windows is topped with crowned and smiling angels. The aisles are notable for their **fan vaulting**. The impressive Perpendicular **west window** depicts 75 figures mainly in early 16C glass, the remainder being 19C.

Chancel. — Beyond the beautifully fan vaulted **crossing**, the chancel is overlooked by two **oriels**, one, in stone, belonging to Edward IV's chantry chapel and reached by a small staircase in the wall, the other a wooden Renaissance structure built by Henry VIII as a gallery for Catherine of Aragon. The **iron grille** below it was made in 1482 by John Tresilian. The ornate three-tier **stalls★★★**, abounding in misericords and other carvings, were built in 1478-85; the top tier, surmounted by a richly carved canopy, is for the Knights of the Garter. The banners, crests, helmets, mantling and swords of the living Knights mark their places. The stall plates are of the living and deceased since the foundation of the Order in 1348 (about 900 Knights in all). The middle tier is for the Military Knights, minor canons and choirmen; and the lowest tier is for the choirboys. The reredos was rebuilt in 1863 as a memorial to Prince Albert, as was the former **Lady Chapel** which Queen Victoria had remodelled and decorated with sumptuous marbles and wall paintings, all highlighted in gold. Note also Edward III's 6ft 8in long **battle sword** in the south chancel aisle.

★★STATE APARTMENTS *time: 1 1/2 hours*

⊙ Only the north range can be visited, the east and south being the present royal apartments. From the North Terrace the tour begins at the **Grand Staircase**, built for Queen Victoria in 1866, with its display of arms and armour including that of Henry VIII, below Sir Francis Chantrey's statue of George IV. It leads to the **Grand Vestibule** where Sir James Wyatt's lively fan vaulting and lantern contrast with the heaviness of the staircase. The marble statue of Queen Victoria, seated, was made in 1871.

Public Rooms. — These rooms provide examples of the work done for George IV by Wyatville (Wyatt's nephew) from 1820-30. In the **Waterloo Chamber** hangs a series of portraits by Sir Thomas Lawrence, of the monarchs and leaders, both military and political, involved in Napoleon's final defeat. The **Garter Throne Room**, created on older foundations, is the room in which the Knights Companion assemble and the monarch invests new knights before the annual service in St George's Chapel. Both rooms boast panels and carvings by **Grinling Gibbons (1648-1721)**. The **Grand Reception Room** is Wyatville at his most exuberant - ornate French rococo hung with Gobelins tapestries and decorated with gilt plasterwork, massive chandeliers and bronze busts. The same artist created the long, sober **St George's Hall** out of the hall built by Edward III for the Knights of the Garter and the baroque chapel which Hugh May had built for Charles II. The Garter Knights' escutcheons are set in the panelling of the plaster ceiling, made to look like wood. Note portraits of James I to George IV by Lely, Kneller and Van Dyck.

The Queen's Rooms. — The 19C **Queen's Guard Chamber**, containing busts of Sir Winston Churchill and the Dukes of Marlborough and Wellington, leads into the panelled Queen's Presence Chamber which, with the adjoining **Queen's Audience Room**, is essentially unchanged since the time of Charles II; Hugh May planned them with ceilings painted by Verrio and superb carvings by Gibbons; the Gobelins tapestries are late 18C additions. The white marble Adam fireplace in the Presence Chamber was brought from Buckingham Palace by William IV. Wyatt and his nephew share responsibility for the blue silk **Queen's Ball Room**; the elder architect remodelled the room and Wyatville designed the ceiling as well as that of the red **Queen's Drawing Room**. Eight Van Dyck portraits hang in the Ball Room while the Drawing Room contains a variety of paintings including Holbeins.

The King's Rooms. — Wyatville created a suite for royal visitors out of the **King's Closet** and **Dressing Room**, in which Charles II preferred to sleep, and the **King's State Bedchamber**. The bed, made in France in the reign of Louis XVI, was given hangings with the cipher of Napoleon III and Empress Eugénie for their state visit in 1855. The paintings in the Dressing Room include portraits by Andrea del Sarto, Holbein, Dürer, Memling, Rubens, Van Dyck and two Rembrandts.
Although the **King's Drawing Room**, containing five Rubens paintings and one by Janssens, has retained little from Charles II's time, the **King's Dining Room** has survived intact. The room in which the King dined in public, in accordance with age-old custom, is a feast of wood carving by Henry Phillips and Grinling Gibbons and has a painted ceiling by Verrio depicting a Banquet of the Gods.

Queen Mary's Dolls' House. — The Dolls' House, designed by **Sir Edwin Lutyens**, was presented to Queen Mary in 1923. The fascination of this piece is that everything is exactly on a 1:12 scale - not only the furniture, but even the printed leatherbound books in the library, paintings, the garden designed by Gertrude Jekyll and the vintage cars in the garage.

★WINDSOR PARK

In the mid-18C George II charged his son, William Duke of Cumberland, with the task of organising the vast Windsor Forest. 4 500 acres - 1 821ha of overgrown woodland were cleared, streams were diverted to drain the marshes into newly dug ponds which eventually flowed into the especially created 130 acres - 53ha of **Virginia Water**. George III continued this land reclamation work and established two farms.
⊙ Today the park is divided into **Home Park**, which is private and **Great Park**, most of which is public. A significant feature of the park is the **Long Walk**, a 3 mile - 5km avenue running south as far as the **equestrian statue** of George III which is in Great Park. Under Charles II the avenue was planted with elm trees, in 1685, the year in which he died, but in 1945 the diseased trees had to be replaced by chestnuts and planes.
The **Royal Mausoleum**, Frogmore Garden, in Home Park was begun in 1862, the year after Prince Albert's death, specifically so that Queen Victoria and Albert could be buried side by side. The Romanesque style exterior is topped with a dome, while the rich interior reflects the Consort's passion for the Italian Renaissance.

★WINDSOR TOWN Pop 30 832

The old town, extending round two sides of the castle walls, comprises one main street, Thames Street, which is intersected by the road leading down from the castle gate and then continues as High Street and Sheet Street. The network of old cobbled streets bordered by High Street, Castle Hill, Church Lane and Street and Albans Street contains a number of 16-18C timber-framed houses with oversailing upper floors rising to pointed gables.
The short High Street is distinguished by St John's parish church, re-built in 1822 and the **Guildhall**, begun by Sir Thomas Fitch c1637 and completed by Sir Christopher Wren in 1690. In the niches of the pilastered upper floor are statues of Queen Anne and Prince George of Denmark.

★★ WOBURN Abbey Bedfordshire

Michelin Map 404 S 28 or Atlas G Britain p 28

A Cistercian abbey for 400 years, Woburn Abbey was refurbished in 1630 but not given its magnificence until **Henry Flitcroft** (1697-1769) rebuilt the west range in 1747 and **Henry Holland** the south range in 1787. The east range also by Holland was pulled down in 1950 leaving only the north range in the 17C style.

⊘ APARTMENTS

4th Duke's Bedroom. — The **Mortlake tapestries** (1660s) are based on Raphael's *Acts of the Apostles*. The white mid-18C ceiling depicts the Four Seasons and the sculpture of Hermaphroditus and Salmacis is by Delvaux.

State Rooms. — With the state rooms we enter Flitcroft's range: **Queen Victoria's Bedroom**, with etchings by Victoria and Albert displayed; **Queen Victoria's Dressing Room**, the walls covered with superb 17C Dutch and Flemish paintings including Aelbert Cuyp's *Nijmegen on the Vaal* and *Fishermen on Ice*, and Van Dyck's *Jan Snellinck;* **Blue Drawing Room** with its 1756 ceiling and its fireplace by Duval and Rysbrack; **State Saloon**, with its ornamental ceiling and Rysbrack chimneypiece; and **State Dining Room** graced by a Meissen dinner set and a portrait by Van Dyck. At the end of the range the **Reynolds Room** houses 10 of his portraits and the **Canaletto Room** twenty-one of his Venetian views.

Library. — The finest room of Holland's range divided into three parts by fluted Corinthian columns; on the walls hang **Rembrandt's** *Self-Portrait* and *Old Rabbi*.

Long Gallery. — Also divided by columns (this time by Flitcroft) the gallery is packed with 16C paintings including the *Armada Portrait* of Elizabeth I.

The Armada Portrait by George Gower

GROUNDS

The two stable courtyards behind are by Flitcroft, the pretty Chinese Dairy by Holland, the 3 000 acre - more than 1 200ha park landscaped by Humphry Repton. The 1 000 head of deer range through nine species including Milu, originally the Imperial herd of China and preserved at Woburn.

⊘ **Wild Animal Kingdom.** — *Separate entrance 1 mile - 1.5km from the house.* There is nothing new in elephants, tigers, lions, zebras, bison, rhinos and wildebeest grazing in the park. Already in 1894 it was said there was no better animal collection outside London Zoo.

★ WORCESTER Hereford and Worcester   Pop 75 466

Michelin Map 403 N 27 or Atlas G Britain p 27
Town plan in the current Michelin Red Guide Great Britain and Ireland

Its great red sandstone cathedral rising above the bend in the River Severn, its wealth of timber-framed buildings and Georgian mansions, its porcelain and its sauce make Worcester one of the most English of English cities.
The cathedral choirs of Hereford, Gloucester and Worcester combine to present a programme of concerts known as the **Three Choirs Festival.**

CITY CENTRE *time: 3 hours*

Guildhall. — *High Street.* Completed in 1724 (red brick and stone dressings) with statues of Charles I, Charles II and Queen Anne in niches, Labour, Peace, Justice, ⊘ Plenty and Chastisement on the parapet. Inside is a splendid **Assembly Room**, its Italianate ceiling contrasting beautifully with the simple classicism beneath.

Walk along Pump Street, turn right into Friar Street.

Friar Street. — Lined with timber-frames, its most impressive is Greyfriars (c1480) with an enchanting garden, the interior hung with tapestries and crewel work.

Turn right into College Street, enter the cathedral through the north porch.

★★ **Cathedral.** — An early church was rebuilt in the late 11C by Wulstan (the Saxon Bishop of Worcester who thrived under his new Norman masters and was later canonised). His superb **crypt** survives, though the greater part of the cathedral, including the tower, was reconstructed in the 14C. The **choir** is an outstanding example of Early English. There are many monuments: note **King John's tomb** in the choir, the 14C **Beauchamp tomb** in the nave, the c1470 alabaster effigy of Virgin and Child in the southeast transept; **Prince Arthur's Chantry**, with its delicate tracery, is late Perpendicular work.

Leave the cathedral by the Prior's Door in the south aisle.

Cloisters. — Rebuilt in 1374, with wonderful medieval bosses. The east walk leads to the c1150 **chapter house**, a very early example of central shaft vaulting.

Edgar Tower. — Sensibly fortified against anticlerical rioters, the tower was the main entrance to the medieval monastery, now the serene cathedral precincts.

Turn right up Severn Street.

★ **Royal Worcester Porcelain Works.** — Founded in 1751, its success lay in its use of Cornwall soaprock to simulate Chinese porcelain, and ability to adapt to changing fashions (Chinoiserie, Classicism, Romanticism). The **Dyson Perrins Museum★** displays some of Royal Worcester's finest products: Humphrey Chamberlain's vase of Wellington and Blucher, James Hadley's veiled Lady and Chicago Exhibition Vase, George Owen's honeycombed masterpieces and Dorothy Doughtey's bird series.

Turn right into King Street and cross Sidbury.

The Commandery. — Originally St Wulstan's Hospital (11C) but mostly early 16C, the Commandery was the headquarters of Charles II at the Battle of Worcester (1651). Parts of the hospital can still be seen in the Painted Chamber and Dying Room, while the 15C hall has a superb **hammerbeam roof**, minstrels' gallery and stained glass.

EXCURSIONS

★ **The Elgar Trail.** — *Signposted with "violin" signs.*
Much of the music of **Sir Edward Elgar** (1857-1934), most "English" of composers, evokes this countryside of broad, tranquil vale and soaring hills. The circular route of about 40 miles - 65km links the **Elgar Birthplace Museum** at Lower Broadheath near Worcester with his grave in the Roman Catholic churchyard in Little Malvern at the foot of the hills that so inspired him.

Great Malvern. — Pop 30 153. *8 miles - 13km, take the A449 south.*
A settlement around a priory, its medicinal waters were popularised in the late 18C, its Greek Revival **Pump Room** and **Baths** built in 1819-23. The **Priory Church** contains some of the finest 15C stained glass in the country. From **Worcestershire Beacon** (1 395ft - 426m), highest of the Malvern Hills which rise steeply above the town, there is a **view** of 15 counties and three cathedrals (Worcester, Gloucester and Hereford).

★ WYE Valley Gwent, Hereford and Worcester, Gloucestershire

Michelin Map 403 L, M 28 and 29 or Atlas G Britain p 16

The Wye twists and turns through changing landscapes on its 135 mile - 220km run from Plynlimon to the Bristol Channel; the final section of its valley, between Ross and Chepstow, is deep and narrow; limestone crags emerge in places from the magnificent woodlands of oak, beech, yew and lime which clothe the steep slopes. One of the resorts of the 18C and early 19C connoisseurs of Romantic scenery, it has remained popular ever since. From Monmouth to Chepstow the **Offa's Dyke Long Distance Footpath** *(qv)* high up on the east bank gives ever-changing views through the trees of the river winding far below; the river bank itself is followed by the less strenuous **Wye Valley Walk.** This waymarked walk follows the River Wye between Chepstow and Hereford.

Forest of Dean. — Eastward from the lower part of the Wye Valley extends this tract of wooded hills, "Queen of Forests All" according to Drayton. A royal hunting preserve since Canute's day, it has supplied timber for the navy as well as being worked for coal and iron. In 1938 it became England and Wales' first Forest Park; a tendency to replace immemorial oakwoods with conifers has been checked and the Forestry Commission welcomes visitors to its domain with many a picnic site, camping ground and well-signed footpaths.

At Soudley, between Blakeney and Cinderford, on the B4227, is the **Dean Heritage Centre**, whose exhibits include a reconstruction of the type of coal mine still being worked by the Forest's "Free Miners".

Severn Bore. — East of the Forest are the splendid tidal waters of the River Severn. The Severn Bore occurs at every tide; imperceptible on most days, around the time of the equinoxes it manifests itself as a roaring wall of water up to 6ft - 2m high, best seen near the village of Minsterworth on the A48.

FROM ROSS-ON-WYE TO CHEPSTOW
32 miles - 52km — allow a day

Ross-on-Wye. — Pop 8 281. The **Market House★** built in sandstone in the 1670s carries a medallion of Charles II placed by John Kyrle, "Man of Ross", benefactor of many of the buildings in the town. **St Mary's Church**, mainly 13C, has a 208ft - 63m spire, the top of which was rebuilt in 1721, thanks to his generosity. A cross in the churchyard is a memorial to the 315 plague victims "buried nearby, by night, without coffins" during 1637. Tudor almshouses in Church Street were restored in 1575 by the Rudhall family, some of whose tombs are in the church.

Go south on the B4228 for 3 miles - 5km, turn right at the Wye bridge and follow signs to Goodrich Castle.

★ Goodrich Castle. — The picturesque sandstone ruin on its high spur commands an ancient crossing of the Wye. The keep, with its original entrance (now a window) on the first floor, is Norman; the majority of the castle dates from around 1300. During the Civil War, the Royalist garrison was forced into surrender by the use of a large mortar, "Roaring Meg", which was specially cast by the besiegers nearby, and can today be seen in Churchill Park, Hereford.

From Goodrich village follow signs to Symonds Yat, then to Yat Rock. The road becomes narrow and steep. Park in the Forestry Commission car park.

★ Symonds Yat. — From the Yat Rock, 473ft - 144m, there is a famous and vertiginous **view★** of the extraordinary loop in the Wye, as well as a fine prospect of the rich Herefordshire farmlands to the north.

Go south on the B4432 and B4228, then west on the A4136.

Monmouth. — Pop 7 379. The town has retained much of its medieval street plan intact, though little remains of the castle in which **Henry V** (1387-1422) was born. His statue is set in a recess in the handsome Georgian **Shire Hall**, which in 1724 replaced an Elizabethan Market Hall. Below him stands another local notable, the Hon C S Rolls, co-founder of Rolls-Royce and a pioneer of flying, while the visits paid by Nelson to the town are remembered in the museum nearby. **Great Castle House**, headquarters of the Royal Monmouthshire Royal Engineers, is a splendid stone building of 1673. Wide Monnow Street leads down to the town's emblem, the 13C fortified bridge-gate.

Go 8 miles - 13km west by the A40.

On the right is the striking silhouette of **Raglan Castle★**. Its Great Tower, the "Yellow Tower of Gwent", begun in 1435, is a fortress within a fortress and reflects the insecurity of an age when a lord had to be able to isolate himself from even his own liveried men, in case they should decide to change their allegiance.

From Monmouth southwards the A466 follows the sinuous course of the river.

★★ Tintern Abbey. — The steep wooded slopes of the winding valley provide the picturesque setting for this most romantic of ruins. In the latter part of the 18C the Abbey became a favoured destination of sentimental tourists, among them William Wordsworth, who here...

> "... felt
> A presence that disturbs me with the joy
> Of elevated thoughts".

A Cistercian house was founded in 1131 by Walter de Clare, Anglo-Norman lord of Chepstow. The Cistercians, unlike the Benedictines, settled in simple houses devoid of ornament and followed a rule of silence "far from the habitations of men". The modest original church was replaced in the late 13C under the patronage of Roger Bigod by a much more lavish structure. Abbot Richard Wyche surrendered his abbey to the King's commissioners in 1536.

Much of the 13C abbey church still stands. The nave, originally for the lay brothers, was separated from the choir, presbytery and high altar by a stone screen, the remains of which were removed in the 19C, providing a view, never seen by the original worshippers, along the whole 236ft - 72m of the church. Beyond, set in the turf, are the foundations of the chapter house, infirmary, cloisters, kitchens and dining hall as well as the abbot's lodging and guest house.

Continue on the A466. After about 2 1/2 miles - 4km turn into the signposted picnic area and viewpoint.

Wyndcliff. — 365 steep steps climb the limestone cliff nearly 800ft - 240m above the river. From the **Eagle's Nest viewpoint★** at the top, the eye is led over the final reaches of the Wye to the mighty span of the Severn Bridge and far into the countryside beyond. *(The viewpoint can also be reached by a more level footpath from a car park signposted 1/2 mile - 3/4km further along the A466.)*

Continue into Chepstow.

Chepstow. — Pop 9 039. The still partly walled town slopes sharply down from the great Town Gate to the ancient crossing of the Wye, bridged by John Rennie's elegant cast-iron structure of 1816. From here is the best view of **Chepstow Castle★**. This splendid stronghold was begun in 1067 by William FitzOsbern, one of the Conqueror's closest associates, then engaged in securing the western boundary of his domain.

He chose a site with excellent natural defences: a long narrow spur with cliffs dropping sheer into the river to the north and a deep dell to the south. The various parts of the castle are strung out along the ridge; in the east is the 13C Lower Bailey, guarded by the Outer Gatehouse and Marten's Tower. Beyond the Middle Ward rises the heart of the original castle, FitzOsbern's Great Tower, a hall-keep which is probably the earliest secular stone building in Britain. The Upper Ward leads to the castle's western extremity and highest point, the outer defence works of the Barbican.

In 71 AD, the Roman Ninth Legion built a fortress, **Eboracum**, later capital of the northern province. Here in 306 AD Constantine the Great was proclaimed Emperor. After the departure of the Roman legions the Anglo-Saxons made **Eoforwic** the capital of their kingdom of Northumbria. In 627 AD King Edwin was baptised by Paulinus here. In 866 AD the Vikings took the city, which became **Jorvik**, one of their chief trading bases in northern Europe. Viking rule lasted until 954 AD, but Scandinavian influence and custom, as well as street names, continued long after the Norman conquest of Britain.

Medieval York, its prosperity based on wool, was a city of 10 000 people and forty churches, the richest city in the country after London. With the decline of the wool trade after the Wars of the Roses (1453-87) and following the Dissolution the city's prosperity waned. The many elegant Georgian buildings in York reflect more the desire of well-to-do northerners to have a town house in what had become an important centre of social and cultural life, rather than the city's return to its former economic importance.

★★★ YORK MINSTER (BY) *time: 1 1/2 hours*

The dedication of the Cathedral Church to St Peter emphasises the close links with Rome after the union of the Celtic and Roman traditions at Whitby in 664 AD *(qv)*. The Minster is the largest Gothic church north of the Alps. It is 534ft - 160m long and 249ft - 76m wide across the transepts. The vault is 90ft - 27m above the floor and the towers rise to 198ft - 60m. The west front, completed by the addition of the towers in 1430-70, presents an almost 13C ''French'' outline. It is curious that such a design caught on so late in England, which has its own glorious ''screen'' façades of Lincoln and Wells.

Interior. — The nave, built between 1291 and 1350, is in Decorated style; the transepts of the mid-13C are the oldest visible parts of the present building. The **Chapter House★★**, octagonal with a magnificent wooden vaulted ceiling, can be dated to just before 1300. The **Choir Screen★★** is by William Hyndeley, late 15C. Its central doorway is flanked by statues of English kings from William the Conqueror. The finest monument in the Minster is the **tomb (1)** of the man whose initiative began the present building, **Archbishop Walter de Gray**, Archbishop from 1215 until his death in 1255 *(east side of south transept)*. His crozier, paten, chalice and ring, are displayed in the Treasury.

★★★ **Stained Glass.** — The Minster contains the largest single collection of medieval stained glass to have survived in England. The **West Window (2)** with its curvilinear heart-shaped tracery was painted in 1339 by Master Robert for Archbishop William de Melton. It was the largest in the Minster at the time, but was surpassed by the **East Window (3)** in the Lady Chapel, painted by John Thornton of

YORK MINSTER

0 ⌐————————¬ 30 m
    50 feet

■ 1220-1260 Early English

▨ 1280-1350 Decorated

□ 1361-1472 Perpendicular

Coventry between 1405 and 1408. It is the largest expanse of medieval glass in the country, and revitalised the already well-established York school of glass painting. The **Five Sisters Window (4)**, lancets of grisaille glass from *c*1250, is the oldest window still in its original place in the Minster.

The **Pilgrimage Window (5)**, *c*1312, shows grotesques, a monkey's funeral and scenes of hunting, reminiscent of some of the misericord carvings of the time. Next to it is the **Bellfounders Window (6)**, given by Richard Tunnoc, who was buried in the Minster in 1330. He is depicted presenting his window to the Archbishop, amongst scenes of casting and tuning a bell. The **Jesse Window (7)**, depicting Jesus' family tree, dates from 1310.

Foundation Museum. — In 1966-7 the foundations of the east wall, west towers and the 16 000 ton Central Tower were found to be yielding. A programme of reinforcement was begun which lasted five years. Thousands of tons of soil and rubble were removed, exposing walls both of the Roman headquarters building and the early Norman cathedral (c1080-1110), with its remarkable oak reinforced foundations. New concrete foundations, tied to the old by stainless steel rods, were poured into place and today's visitor can see the clearly indicated lines of the Roman and Norman buildings. The **Treasury** (access by Foundation Museum) displays a collection of York domestic silver, from 1485 to 1858, and church plate belonging to the Minster and on loan from churches all over the north of England.

★★★NATIONAL RAILWAY MUSEUM (AY)

⊙ Opened in 1975, the museum presents in an exemplary way the history of railways in the country of their invention. The Main Exhibition Hall, in an old steam engine shed covering nearly two acres, almost a hectare, displays over fifty locomotives. Probably the most famous is *Mallard*, which on 3 July 1938 reached 126mph - 203km/h, a world speed record for steam. Also displayed is *Evening Star*, built at Swindon in 1960, the last steam locomotive to be built for British Railways, together with a working replica of Stephenson's *Rocket*. Amongst the collection of rolling stock are several Royal and private coaches, a travelling Post Office coach, dining cars and sleepers. Because there are more engines than available space, the selection is frequently changed. A balcony gives a magnificent overall view and houses railwayana, an audio-visual theatre and a display covering the history of railways in Britain.

THE TOWN

★★ **The Walls** (ABCYZ). — A walk of about three miles - 5km will take the visitor right around medieval York. The **Multangular Tower (BY)**, western corner of the Roman fort, still stands in the Yorkshire Museum Gardens, near the ruins of St Mary's Abbey *(see opposite)*. The 13C walls follow the course of the Roman wall to the north of the Minster, and are built atop the earthen bank raised by the Anglo-Danish kings. The Normans built fortified gateways - today's **'Bars'** - through this earthen bank, where roads led into the city. **Bootham Bar (BY)** is on the site of the Roman gateway. The walls lead around the Deanery Garden to **Monk Bar (BY)** and on to Aldgate. Here a swampy area and the River Foss constituted the defences, and brick-built walls, c1490, run from **Red Tower (CY)**, pass **Walmgate (CZ)** and continue around the south of York Castle, to **Fishergate Postern (CZ)**, built in 1505 on what was then the riverbank. Here York Castle took up the defences. Beyond Skeldergate Bridge, and **Baile Hill (BZ)**, the walls resume, running to **Micklegate Bar (AZ)**, traditional point of entry of the monarch into York, and where the severed heads of traitors were exposed after execution. From here the walls turn northeast and lead to the **North Street Postern (BY)**, where the ferry crossed the Ouse, before the building of Lendal Bridge.

★ **York Castle Museum** (BZ). — In what was the **Debtors Prison** and the **Female Prison**, ⊙ two striking buildings from 1705 and 1777 respectively, there is now a museum of everyday life. "Kirkgate" is an authentic reproduction of a Victorian street, with a **Hansom cab**, a design perfected by a York architect, **Joseph Hansom** (1803-82). The **Coppergate Helmet**, a Saxon helmet found in 1982 during the Jorvik Centre excavations, is displayed here. Iron with brass fittings, c 750 AD it probably belonged to a Northumbrian noble. There are costumes, period rooms, pubs and shops as well as the actual cell in which Dick Turpin was held before his execution, on 7 April 1739. The famous "Ride to York" which Ainsworth attributed to Turpin in his novel *Rookwood* was not, in fact, made by Turpin but by John Nevinson, a highwayman who was hanged in York in 1685.

Clifford's Tower (BZ). — Built 1250-75 by Henry III, to replace the Conqueror's timber fort, burnt down by a mob attacking besieged Jews there in 1190. The name commemorates Roger de Clifford who was captured during a battle at Boroughbridge and hanged in chains from this tower on 16 March 1322.

★ **Fairfax House** (BZ). — Built by Viscount Fairfax for his daughter Anne, in 1755, ⊙ this Georgian house was saved from destruction in 1983-4, having been used for fifty years as a dance hall and cinema. It houses a collection of Georgian furniture, paintings, clocks and porcelain. Ceilings by Cortese and carved wooden mouldings have been painstakingly restored or replaced.

⊙ **Merchant Adventurers' Hall** (BZ). — A brick undercroft, with a Chapel first consecrated in 1411, is crowned by a timber-framed Great Hall, built c1357.

★ **Jorvik Viking Centre** (BZ). — During building operations between 1976 and 1981, ⊙ archaeologists uncovered four rows of buildings from the Viking town, with remarkably well preserved items, even to boots and shoes, pins, plants and insects. Two rows now illustrate an archaeological 'dig' and two have been accurately reconstructed. "Time Cars" take the visitor on a journey back into Jorvik, with sights sounds and smells as they would have been on an October day in 948 AD. In February each year the York Archaeological Trust stages the **Jorvik Viking Festival**, with longship races, feasting and fireworks.

★ **Shambles** (BY). — The most visited amongst the many picturesque streets of the city, with overhanging timber-framed houses. Nearby **Pavement (BY 45)**, with the Guild church of All Saints, is so called because it was the first street in medieval York to be paved.

Great Britain and Ireland
are now covered
by an Atlas
at a scale of
1 inch to 4.75 miles
Three easy to use versions:
Paperback, Spiralbound, Hardback.

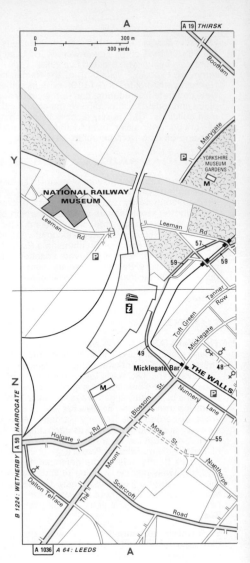

⊘ **Assembly Rooms** (BY). — Designed by Richard Boyle, 3rd Earl of Burlington, and built in 1731, these have a finely proportioned **Egyptian Hall** with Corinthian columns and clerestory lighting. The Rooms were needed for dancing and for gaming following the growing social life of York, which by this time had three stage-coach services a week to and from London.

St Mary's Abbey (BY). — St Mary's was founded 1088 by William Rufus. The ruins of this Benedictine abbey, mostly late 13C, are the setting, in June-July every four years, for the **York Cycle of Mystery Plays**, the life of Christ told in a series of plays dating from around 1340.

⊘ **York City Art Gallery** (BY). — An extensive collection of paintings, from 1350 to the present day, including many portraits and nude studies by the York painter **William Etty** (1787-1849), who is buried in St Olave's churchyard, Marygate.

⊘ **Treasurer's House** (BY). — Rebuilt in the 17C and 18C, this was the house of the Treasurers of York Minster and has a magnificent series of rooms with furniture and pictures from many periods. The **Great Hall** has had its false ceiling removed, and has an unusual staircase c1700. The early 18C ceiling in the **Dining Room** has decorated beams and panels. The fascinating collection of 18C drinking vessels illustrates the skill and ingenuity of the glassmaker. Stems, bowls and feet were variously fashioned: twisted, fluted, folded, engraved, cut and faceted.

EXCURSIONS

⊘ **Sutton Park.** — *8 miles - 13km north by the B1363* (BY).
A house by Thomas Atkinson, c1750, it contains beautiful 18C panelling and furniture, as well as a fine collection of Meissen and Imari porcelain. The gardens contain many unusual and interesting plants.

⊘ **Samuel Smith Old Brewery, Tadcaster.** — *7 miles - 11km southwest by the A64* (AZ).
Established 1758, the brewery still preserves the old-fashioned methods of brewing, makes its own casks and uses shire horses for local deliveries.

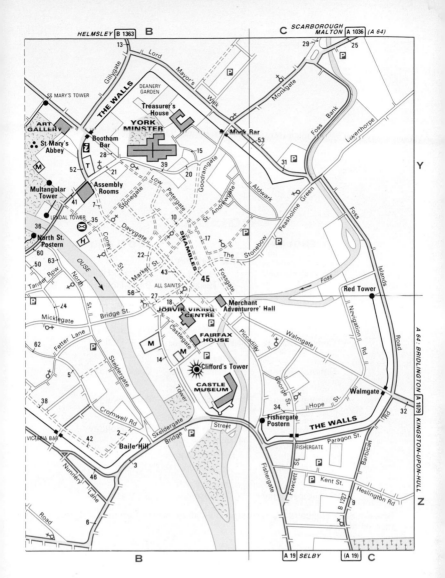

MYSTERY PLAYS

*Mystery Plays, originally known as **miracles,** have enthralled ever since they were first performed during the Middle Ages. Originally moral lessons involving much singing and music they were generally based on events from the New Testament or the story of Christ and were told through a cycle of plays. As the medieval drama moved out of the hands of the clergy into those of the craftsmen's guilds so, the dramatisations moved out of the church onto the steps and parvis in front of it.*

*Two of these cycles have survived and are performed in outdoor settings at **Coventry** (every three years 1993, 1996...) and **York** (every four years 1992, 1996...).*

Michelin Guides

*The **Red Guides** (hotels and restaurants)*
Benelux - Deutschland - España Portugal - main cities EUROPE - France - Great Britain and Ireland - Italia

*The **Green Guides** (works of art, historic buildings and beautiful scenery)*
Austria - Canada - England: The West Country - France - Germany - Greece - Italy - London - Mexico - Netherlands - New England - New York City - Portugal - Rome - Scotland - Spain - Switzerland

and 10 guides on France

HOLIDAYS

ENGLAND		SCOTLAND
	New Year's Day:	
General Holiday	**1 January**	General Holiday
	2 January	Bank Holiday
	Good Friday:	
General Holiday	**Friday before Easter**	Bank Holiday
	Easter Monday:	
General Holiday	**Monday after Easter**	Bank Holiday
	May Day:	
General Holiday	**First Monday in May**	Bank Holiday
	Spring Bank Holiday:	
General Holiday	**Last Monday in May**	Bank Holiday
	August Bank Holidays:	
	First Monday in August	Bank Holiday
General Holiday	**Last Monday in August**	
	Christmas Day:	
General Holiday	**25 December**	General Holiday
	Boxing Day:	
General Holiday	**26 December**	Bank Holiday

Scotland: Bank Holidays are for banks only although they do apply to certain commercial offices.

Practical
information

TRAVELLING TO BRITAIN

Passport. — Visitors coming to Britain must be in possesion of a valid national passport of other proof of identity and nationality.

Visa. — Citizens of the Commonwealth (including Australia, Canada and New Zealand), the Republic of South Africa or the USA as well as the member states of the European Community do not require a visa.

Customs. — Tax free allowances for various commodities are decided by the EC but remember that the Channel Islands and Isle of Man have different regulations. Details of these allowances and restrictions are available at most ports of entry to Britain. For further information apply to HM Customs and Excise, Dorset House, Stamford Street, London SE1 9PS, ☎ 01 928 0533. It is forbidden to bring domestic animals (dogs, cats...) into Britain.

By air. — The various national and other independent airlines operate services to London (Heathrow, Gatwick and London City) and to the major provincial airports (Aberdeen, Birmingham, Cardiff, Edinburgh, Glasgow, Liverpool, Manchester, Newcastle, Prestwick). Information, brochures and time-tables are available from the airlines and from travel agents.

By sea. — There are numerous cross-Channel (passenger and car ferries, hovercraft) and other ferry or shipping services from the continent. For details apply to travel agencies.

TRAVELLING IN BRITAIN

Documents. — Nationals of EC countries require a valid **national driving licence**; nationals of non-EC countries require an **international driving licence**.
For the vehicle it is necessary to have the **registration papers** (log-book) and a **nationality plate** of the approved size.

Insurance. — Insurance cover is compulsory and although an **International Insurance Certificate** (Green Card) is no longer a legal requirement in Britain it is the most effective proof of insurance cover and is internationally recognised by the police and other authorities. Certain UK motoring organisations (AA, RAC) run accident insurance and breakdown service schemes for members. Europ-Assistance has special schemes for members.

Highway Code. — The minimum driving age is 17 years old. Remember to **keep to the left** and overtake on the right. In Britain the compulsory wearing of **seat belts** includes rear seat passengers and all children under 14 when rear belts are fitted. Important **traffic signs** are given at the end of the Michelin Red Guide Great Britain and Ireland. In many service stations dual-pumps are the rule with **unleaded pumps** being identified by green pump handles or a green stripe. Leaded two-star petrol is no longer available in Britain; unleaded two-star has been substituted.

Speed limits. — The maximum permitted speed on motorways or dual carriageways is 70mph - 112km/h, on other roads 60mph - 96km/h and in towns and cities 30mph - 48km/h.

Route planning. — The **Michelin map series** at a scale of 1: 400 000 covers the whole of Britain (see the layout diagram on page three) as does the **Michelin Road Atlas** of Great Britain and Ireland at a scale of 1: 300 000. In addition to a wealth of road information they indicate tourist features such as beaches or bathing areas, swimming pools, golf courses, race courses, scenic routes, sights, country parks... These publications are an essential complement to the annual Red Guide and the Green Guide and they are all carefully cross-referenced.

Car Rental. — There are car rental agencies at airports, air terminals, railway stations and in all large towns throughout Britain. European cars usually have manual transmission but automatic cars are available on demand. An international driving licence is required for non-EC nationals. Most companies will not rent to those aged under 21 or 25, check in advance.

Motoring Organisation. — The major motoring organisations in Great Britain are the Automobile Association and the Royal Automobile Club. Each provides services in varying degrees for non-resident members of affiliated clubs.
Automobile Association, Fanum House, Basingstoke, Hants, RG21 2EA, ☎ (0256) 20123.
Royal Automobile Club, RAC House, Lansdowne Road, Croydon, Surrey CR9 2JA, ☎ (081) 686 2525.

By train. — Those visiting by train should consider buying a **Britrail Pass** which gives unlimited travelling on the entire British Rail network. There are several versions of this pass which must be purchased in your home country. For further information on this and other regional rail passes consult the British Rail International office or sales agent:
United States, Britrail Travel Inc, 1500 Broadway, 10th Floor, New York, NY 10036-4015, ☎ (212) 382 3737.
Canada, 409 Granville Street, Vancouver BC, V6C 1T2, ☎ 604 683 6896.
94 Cumberland Street, Toronto, M5R 1A3 Canada, ☎ 416 929 3333.
Australia, Thomas Cook Pty Ltd, 44 Market Street, Sydney NSW 2000.
New Zealand, Atlantic and Pacific Travel Intl, Parnell Place, 164 Parnell Road, PO Box 3839, Parnell, Auckland 1.
France, British Rail International, 55, rue St-Roch, 75001 Paris.
Belgium, British Rail International, 306 Avenue Louise, 1050 Brussels.
Switzerland, British Rail International, Centralbahnplatz 9, CH-4002 Basle.

ACCOMMODATION

Places to stay. — The **Michelin Red Guide** of hotels and restaurants is an annual publication which presents a selection of hotels and restaurants. The range is wide, from the modest inn to the most luxurious grand hotel, from the centrally situated modern establishment catering to the needs of today's business man to the secluded away from it all retreat. Places listed in the Red Guide are underlined in red on the Michelin map series at a scale of 1: 400 000. In addition the Guide contains a wealth of general information: tourist information centres, early closing days, main shopping streets, pedestrian precincts, agents for different makes of car, car parks and one-way streets...

Booking a room. — The local Tourist Information Centre will give you, free of charge, an information booklet listing all hotels, bed and breakfast and other accommodation. Many will book accommodation for you for a small fee. Remember that room prices, even for a double room, can be quoted per person.

Bed and breakfast (B&B). — Many private individuals take in a limited number of guests. Prices include bed and cooked breakfast. Some offer full board or an evening meal but meal times tend to be rigid and the menu is usually a set one. Again the local Tourist Information Centre may provide a list of the bed and breakfast establishments in the area and book if necessary for a fee. Look out for the B&B signs.

Rural accommodation. — A stay on one of Britain's many different types of working farms - arable, livestock, hill or mixed - set in the heart of glorious countryside is an ideal way to spend a holiday. For further information apply to the British Tourist Authority for their booklet *Stay on a Farm*. The Farm Holiday Bureau based at the National Agricultural Centre, Stoneleigh, Warwickshire CV8 2LZ also produces a guide, *Farm Holiday Bureau UK.*

University accommodation. — During student vacations many universities and colleges offer low-cost accommodation in their halls of residence. Apply to the British Universities' Accommodation Consortium Ltd, Box C 85, University Park, Nottingham NG7 2RD.

Youth Hostels. — Britain's 260 youth hostels are open to members of the Youth Hostel Association (Trevelyan House, St Albans, Herts AL1 2DY, ☎ 0727 55215) or to those with an international membership card.

Camping and caravanning. — The British Tourist Authority publishes *Camping and Caravanning in Britain* and local Tourist Information Centres supply lists of camping and caravan sites. The following clubs also publish guides for members: The Camping and Caravanning Club of Great Britain and Ireland, 11 Lower Grosvenor Place, London SW1W OEY; The Caravan Club, East Grinstead House, London Road, East Grinstead, West Sussex.

Tourism for the Disabled. — The Red Guide indicates hotels with rooms accessible to the disabled; as suitable rooms may be limited it is advisable to book in advance. The Royal Association for Disability and Rehabiliation (RADAR), publishes an annual guide with detailed information on hotels and holiday centres as well as sections on transport, accommodation for children and activity holidays. Apply to RADAR, 25 Mortimer Street, London W1N 8AB, ☎ 071 637 5400. Other organisations such as the British Tourist Authority, National Trust and the Department of Transport publish booklets for the disabled.

GENERAL INFORMATION

Medical treatment. — If a traveller becomes ill in Britain he is entitled to treatment at one of the National Health Service Accident and Emergency departments of hospitals. For an overnight or longer stay in hospital you will probably be required to pay. It is therefore advisable to take out adequate insurance cover before leaving on holiday. In case of an emergency, dial the free nationwide emergency number (999) and ask for either Fire, Police or Ambulance.

Currency. — The decimal system (100 pence = £ 1) is used throughout Britain, although the Channel Islands and Isle of Man have different notes and coins, and Scotland has different notes.

Banks. — Banks are generally open from Monday to Friday, 9.30am-3.30pm. Some banks offer a limited service on Saturday mornings; all banks are closed on Sundays and holidays *(see below)*. Most large hotels have exchange facilities, and Heathrow and Gatwick Airports have 24-hour banking facilities.

Credit Cards. — The main credit cards (American Express; Access/Eurocard/Mastercard; Diners Club; Visa/Barclaycard) are widely accepted in shops, hotels and restaurants and petrol stations. Most banks have cash dispensers which accept international credit cards.

Post. — Post Offices are generally open Monday to Friday, 9.30am-5.30pm and Saturday mornings, 9.30am-12.30pm. Stamps are also available from many newsagents and tobacconists.

Telephone. — Over 170 countries can be dialled direct; the dialling codes are found at the front of telephone directories and in codebooks. Enquiries about directory numbers and codes outside the United Kingdom will be answered by the International Operator (☎ 155); these calls are now charged for.
Prepaid **British Telecom** and **Mercury** phonecards, in varying values, are available from post offices and many newsagents, and can be used in booths with phonecard facilities for national and international calls.

Shopping. — The big stores and larger shops are open Mondays to Saturdays from 9am-5.30/6pm. Smaller individual shops may close during the lunch hour. Most towns have an early closing day (ECD) when shops close at midday (see the Michelin Red Guide Great Britain and Ireland).

Standard Time. — In winter standard time throughout the British Isles is Greenwich Mean Time (GMT). In summer British clocks are advanced by an hour to give British Summer Time (BST). The actual dates are announced annually but always occur over weekends in March and October.

Electricity. — 240 volts (AC) is the usual voltage and an adaptor or multiple point plug is required for non-British appliances.

Embassies and Consulates

Australia: Embassy, Australia House, The Strand, London WC2B 4LA; ☎ 071 379 4334.

Canada: Embassy, Macdonald House, 1 Grosvenor Square, London WIX OAB; ☎ 071 629 9492.
       Consultate: 151 St Vincent St, Glasgow G2 5NJ; ☎ 041 221 4415.

New Zealand: Embassy, New Zealand House, The Haymarket, London SW1Y 4TQ; ☎ 071 930 8422.

USA: Embassy, 24-31 Grosvenor Square, London W1A 1AI; ☎071 499 9000.

TOURIST INFORMATION

British Tourist Authority Overseas Offices. — For information, brochures, maps and assistance in planning your trip apply to the official tourist office in your country.

United States:
Chicago - 625 North Michigan Avenue, Suite 1510, Chicago, Illinois 60611, ☎ (312) 787 0490.
Dallas - Cedar Maple Plaza, Suite 210, 2305 Cedar Springs Road, Dallas, TX 75201 1814, ☎ (214) 720 4040.
New York - 40 West 57th Street, New York, NY 10019, ☎ (212) 581 4700.
Los Angeles - World Trade Center, 350 South Figueroa Street, Suite 450, Los Angeles, CA 90071, ☎ (213) 628 3525.

Canada. — Toronto - Suite 600, 94 Cumberland Street, Toronto, Ontario, M5R 3N3, ☎ (010 1 416 961 8124/925 6326).

France. — 63, rue Pierre-Charron, 75008 Paris, ☎ 42 89 11 11.

Australia. — Associated Midland House, 171 Clarence Street, Sydney, NSW 2000, ☎ (02) 29 8627.

New Zealand. — Suite 305, Dilworth Building, Cnr Customs and Queens Streets, Auckland, ☎ (09) 31 446.

There are BTA offices in Germany, Belgium, Brasil, Denmark, Spain, Hong Kong, Ireland, Italy, Japan, Norway, Netherlands, Sweden and Switzerland.

The British Tourist Authority (BTA) works in close cooperation with the three National Tourist Boards (England, Scotland and Wales), the Regional Tourist boards and other tourist organisations. The Michelin Red Guide gives the addresses and telephone numbers of local Tourist Information Centres **ℹ**.

Historic Properties. — The following are organisations which own or maintain historic buildings, monuments, gardens or ruins and which give free admission to members:

Cadw (Welsh Historic Monuments). — Over 120 properties: Cadw, Brunel House, 2 Fitzalan Road, Cardiff CF2 1UY, Wales; ☎ (0222) 465511.

English Heritage. — Over 350 properties: Fortress House, 23 Saville Row, London W1X 1AB; ☎ (071) 973 30000.

Historic Scotland. — Over 300 properties: 20 Brandon Street, Edinburgh EH3 5RA, Scotland; ☎ (031) 224 3101.

There are reciprocal arrangements between the above organisations and membership of one organisation entitles you to half-price admission at others.

National Trust:
England: 36 Queen Anne's Gate, London SW1 9AS; ☎ 071 222 9251.
Wales: Trinity Square, Llandudno, Gwynedd LL30 2DE; ☎ (0492) 860123.
Scotland: 5 Charlotte Square, Edinburgh EH2 4DU; ☎ (031) 226 5922.
Northern Ireland: Rowallane House, Saintfield, Ballynahinch, Co Down BT24 7LH; ☎ (0238) 510721.

The Royal Oak Foundation. — American public charity affiliated with the National Trust to promote the preservation of the Anglo-American heritage. Royal Oak members automatically receive the rights and privileges of full Trust members.

There are reciprocal arrangements between the English and Scottish National Trusts and with similar overseas national trusts.

'Open to View'. — This is a ticket which gives access to a large number of stately homes, castles and gardens (over 600) throughout Britain, and is available in a fifteen-day or one-month version. Contact the local British Tourist Authority office or Tourist Information Centre for details.

*The **Michelin Map Series** (1: 400 000 or 1 cm: 6.30 miles)*
*covers the whole of **Great Britain.***

When choosing your lunchtime or overnight stop
use the above maps as all towns listed in the
***Red Guide** are underlined in red.*

When driving into or through a town
use the map as it also indicates all places
*with a town plan in the **Red Guide.***

LEISURE ACTIVITIES

National Parks. — *See p 12.*

Association of Railway Preservation Societies. — Publishes an annual free guide to Steam Railways and Museums, available through Tourist Information Centres or by sending a stamped addressed envelope to Mr R Williams, 16 Woodbrook, Charing, Ashford Kent TN27 0DN ☎ (023 371) 2130.

Wildfowl and Wetlands Trust. — Eight centres around Britain concentrate on protecting the wildlife and environment of specific areas, and provide facilities for birdwatching. Addresses of regional centres from the headquarters in Slimbridge, Gloucestershire GL2 7BT ☎ (0453) 890333.

National Gardens Scheme. — Publishes an annual guide to private gardens of interest that open for a limited time to the public, in aid of charity; available through bookshops at £ 1.50 or by post at £ 2.25 inc p&p from Hatchlands Park, East Clandon, Guildford, Surrey GU4 7RT ☎ (0483) 211535.

British Waterways Board. — As managers and promoters of the canals and waterways they have information on all related activities. Information can be obtained through local Tourist Information Centres, or ring Watford ☎ (0923) 226 422 for details of regional offices.

SPORTS

Coarse Fishing. — For information and local addresses throughout Britain, contact Mr Watkins, National Federation of Anglers, Halliday House, 2 Wilson Street, Derby DE11 1PG, ☎ (0332) 362000.

Game Fishing. — For information on membership application contact Mr J H Ferguson, Salmon and Trout Association, Fishmongers' Hall, London Bridge, London EC4R 9EL, ☎ (071) 283 5838.

Sea Angling. — For information on sea angling in England contact Mr D Rowe, National Federation of Sea Anglers, 14 Bank Street, Newton Abbot, Devon, ☎ (0626) 331330.

Canoeing. — For information on membership application contact British Canoe Union, Mapperley Hall, Kucknow Avenue, Nottingham NG3 5FA, ☎ (0602) 821100.

Boating. — For information and leaflets on all boating, barging and cruising contact Association of Pleasure Craft Operators, 35a High Street, Newport, Shropshire TF10 8JW, ☎ (0952) 813572.

Water-Skiing. — For information on where to water-ski in Britain, where to learn or on membership application contact British Water Ski Federation, 390 City Road, London EC1V 2QA, ☎ (071) 833 2855.

Cycling. — For leaflets and membership application information contact Cyclists Touring Club, Cotterell House, 69 Meadrow, Godalming, Surrey GU7 3HS, ☎ (0483) 41 7217.

CALENDAR OF EVENTS

25 January
Throughout the UK . . . .   Burns Suppers.

Last Tuesday in January
Lerwick, Shetland . . . . .   Up Helly Aa: great torchlit procession, burning of Viking longship, nightlong celebrations.

April
River Thames . . . .   Oxford-Cambridge Boat Race: from Putney to Mortlake.

Early May
Spalding . . . .   Flower Parade and Festival: street procession of floats decorated with tulip heads.

8 May or previous Saturday if 8th falls on Sunday or Monday
Helston . . . .   Flora Day Furry Dance: five processional dances are performed at 7am, 8.30am, 10am, noon and 5pm. Most spectacular are at 10am and noon.

Last weekend in May
Blair Castle . . . .   Atholl Highlanders Annual Parade.

May-August
Glyndebourne . . . .   Festival Opera Season.

Early May-August
Peak District . . . .   Well Dressing: in such Peak villages as Eyam, Monyash, Warksworth and Youlgreave.

May
London . . . .   Chelsea Flower Show: The Royal Hospital.

May-August
Glyndebourne . . . . Festival of Music or Opera.

May-October
Pitlochry . . . . Pitlochry Festival Theatre Season.

Late May-early June
Isle of Man . . . . TT Races : motor cycles races.

June
Doune . . . . Doune Hill Climbs.

2nd or 3rd Saturday in June
London . . . . Trooping of the Colour: the Queen's official birthday parade on Horse Guards Parade.

June
Wimbledon . . . . Lawn Tennis Championships.

Early July
The Thames . . . . Swan-Upping.

July
Llangollen . . . . International Eisteddfod.

July-September
London . . . . Henry Wood Promenade Concerts : Royal Albert Hall.

First week in July
The Thames . . . . Henley-Royal-Regatta: England's premier amateur regatta.

July
King's Lynn . . . . Festival of Music and the Arts.

Third weekend in July - end October
Fountains Abbey . . . . . . Floodlit evenings: Fridays and Saturdays only, dusk to 10.30pm with background Gregorian chant.

August
Jersey . . . . Battle of Flowers.

August
Aboyne . . . . Highland Games.

3 weeks in August
Edinburgh . . . . Edinburgh International Festival: arts festival including the Military Tattoo and the Fringe.

August
Gloucester, Hereford and Worcester . . . . Every third year each cathedral is the setting for The Three Choirs Festival.
Snape Maltings . . . . Aldeburgh Festival: the late Benjamin Britten's Festival.

First Saturday in September
Braemar . . . . Highland Gathering

September
Oban . . . . Argyllshire Highland Gathering

September and October
Blackpool . . . . Blackpool Illuminations.

1st Sunday in November
London-Brighton . . . . . . Veteran and vintage car rally.

5 November
Throughout Britain . . . . . Torchlight processions, tarbarrel rolling, fireworks and giant bonfires commemorate Guy Fawkes and the Gunpowder Plot.

November
London . . . . State Opening of Parliament.

2nd Saturday in November
London . . . . Lord Mayor's Procession and Show.
Ludlow . . . . Festival: performances of Shakespeare in castle's inner bailey.

ADMISSION TIMES AND CHARGES

As admission times and charges are liable to alteration, without prior notice, the information is given for guidance only. The times are those of opening and closure unless otherwise indicated; most places do not admit visitors during the last hour or half hour.

The prices quoted apply to individual adults; where a property belongs to the National Trust (NT), English Heritage (EH), Cadw, the National Trust for Scotland (NTS) or Scottish Heritage (SH) the abbreviations, given in brackets, appear after the charge. Many places offer reduced rates for children and OAP's and some a discount family ticket.

Groups should apply in advance in writing or by telephone; some places have special days for groups and many offer special rates for group bookings. Some buildings are small and have limited space and facilities.

Every sight for which there are times and charges is indicated by the symbol ⊙ in the margin in the main part of the Guide. The entries below are given in the same order as in the alphabetical section of the Guide.

A

ABERDEEN

King's College Chapel. — Open Mondays to Saturdays, 9am-5pm; except during weddings and services.

St Machar's Cathedral. — Open daily 9am-5pm; closed 1 and 2 January.

Maritime Museum. — Open Mondays to Saturdays, 10am-5pm; Sundays in July and August 2-5pm; closed Christmas and New Year holidays; ☎ (0224) 585788.

Provost Skene's House. — Open Mondays to Saturdays, 10am-5pm; closed 25 December and 1 January; ☎ (0224) 646333.

Art Gallery. — Open Mondays to Saturdays, 10am-5pm (8pm Thursdays); Sundays 2-5pm; closed Christmas and New Year holidays; ☎ (0224) 646333.

Excursions

Drum Castle. — Open May-September daily 2-6pm; October weekends 2-5pm (last tour 45mins before closing time); grounds all year daily 9.30am-sunset; £2.80 NTS.

Balmoral Castle. — Grounds open May, June and July when the royal family is not in residence.

Pitmedden Garden. — Open May-September 10am-6pm (last admission 5.15pm); ☎ (06513) 2352; £2.20 NTS.

ABERYSTWYTH

National Library of Wales. — Open Mondays-Fridays 9.30am-6pm, Saturdays 9.30am-5pm; closed public holidays; ☎ (0970) 623816 ext 201.

Vale of Rheidol Light Railway. — Aberystwyth to Devil's Bridge time: 3 hours including 1 hour stop at Devil's Bridge. July and August 4 trains on weekdays; daily in April-June and September and weekends in July and August 2 trains; single: £6.80, return: £9; ☎ (0685) 4854.

Excursions

Elan Valley Visitor Centre. — Open Easter-late October, daily 10am-6pm.

Strata Florida. — Open late March-late October Mondays-Saturdays 9.30am-6.30pm, Sundays 2-6.30pm; late October-late March Mondays-Saturdays 9.30am-4pm, Sundays 2-4pm; £1.25 Cadw.

Llanbadarn Fawr. — Open 9am-dusk.

ALNWICK

Castle. — Open late April-early October, daily 1-5pm (last admission 4.30pm); closed Saturdays in May and September; ☎ (0665) 510777; £2.50.

Excursions

Dunstanburgh Castle. — Open April-September daily 10am-6pm; October-March Tuesday-Sundays 10am-4pm; closed 24-26 December and 1 January; 95p EH and NT.

Warkworth Castle and Hermitage. — **Castle:** open April-September daily 10am-6pm; October-March Tuesday-Sundays 10am-4pm; closed 24-26 December and 1 January; **Hermitage:** weekends summer only; 95p EH.

Cragside House. — Open April-October Tuesdays-Sundays 1-5.30pm; closed Mondays but open bank holiday Mondays; house: £1.50, house and country park: £3.50 NT.

Northumberland National Park. — Three National Park Visitor Centres are open from Good Friday for the summer season: Ingram ☎ (066 578) 248; Rothbury ☎ (0669) 20887; Once Brewed ☎ (049 84) 396.

Chillingham Wild Cattle. — They are to be seen in the Park at Chillingham: open April-October, weekdays 10am-12noon, 2-5pm; Sundays 2-5pm; closed Tuesdays; park warden ☎ (06685) 250.

ANGLESEY

Plas Newydd. — Open late March-late September, Sundays to Fridays, 12noon-5pm; closed Saturdays; October Fridays and Sundays only 2-5pm; ☎ (0248) 714795; £3 NT.

Beaumaris Castle. — Open late March-late October Mondays-Saturdays 9.30am-6.30pm, Sundays 2-6.30pm; late October-late March Mondays-Saturdays 9.30am-4pm, Sundays 2-4pm; ☎ (0248) 810361; £1.50 Cadw.

Court House and Gaol. — Court house: late May-September daily 11.30am-5.30pm, except when court is in session; 90p; Gaol: guided tours late May-September daily 11am-6pm; £1.50.

ARRAN

Brodick Castle. — Open Easter-mid October, daily 1-5pm (last admission 4.30pm); April and October Mondays, Wednesdays and Saturdays only 1-5pm (last tour 4.40pm); ☎ (0770) 2202; castle and gardens: £2.80 NTS.

AVEBURY (EH)

Alexander Keiller Museum. — Open May-October daily 10am-6pm; October-May 10am-4pm, closed Mondays in winter; ☎ (067 23) 250; 80p.

AYR

Burns Cottage and Museum. — Alloway. Open June-August, 9am-7pm; Sundays 10am-7pm; April, May, September, October 10am-5pm; Sundays 2-5pm; November-March 10am-4pm and closed Sundays; closed Christmas and New Year holidays; ☎ (0292) 41215; £1.50 including Burns Monument and Gardens.

Land o'Burns Visitor Centre. — Open June-late September, daily 10am-6pm; October-May, daily 10am-5pm; closed Christmas and New Year holidays; ☎ (0292) 43700; 40p.

Culzean Castle. — Castle: late March-late October daily 10.30am-5.30pm (last admission 5pm); £2.80. Country Park: open all year, facilities as for castle; £4.50 per car NTS.

B

BARNARD CASTLE

Castle. — Open April-September daily 10am-6pm; October-March Tuesdays-Sundays 10am-4pm; closed 24-26 December, 1 January; 85p EH.

Bowes Museum. — Open May-September, Mondays-Saturdays 10am-5.30pm (5pm March, April, September; 4pm November-February); Sundays 2-5pm (4pm in winter); closed over the Christmas and New Year period; ☎ (0833) 690606; £1.60.

Excursions

Raby Castle. —Open May-June Wednesdays and Sundays only 1-5pm (last admission 4.30pm); July-September daily except Saturdays 1-5pm; grounds 11am-5.30pm; ☎ (0833) 60202 ; £2.50.

BARNSTAPLE

Parish-Church. — Open Mondays-Saturdays in summer; may be closed Saturdays in winter and closed Sundays throughout the year.

BATH

Roman Baths. — Open July and August daily 9am-7pm; March and October daily 9am-6pm; November-February daily 9am-5pm; closed 25-26 December; ☎ (0225) 461111 ext 2782; £3.50.

Bath Abbey. — Open Easter Monday-late October Mondays to Saturdays, 9am-6pm; November-Easter Eve 9am-4.30pm; Sundays 1-2.30pm and 4.30-5.30pm; donation 80p.

Pump Room. — Open March-October daily 9am-6pm (7pm July and August); November-February daily 9am (10am Sundays)-5pm; closed 25 and 26 December; ☎ (0225) 461111 ext 2782.

No 1 Royal Crescent. — Open March-October 11am-5pm; November-mid December 11am-4pm; closed Mondays; ☎ (0225) 428126; £2.50.

Assembly Rooms. — Open March-October weekdays 9.30am-6pm, Sundays 10am-6pm; November-February weekdays 10am-5pm, Sundays 11am-5pm; closed 25-26 December; ☎ (0225) 461111 ext 2782 NT.

Museum of Costume. — Same opening times as the Assembly Rooms above; £2.20.

Excursions

Tithe Barn. — Open Easter-September, daily, 10am-6pm; closed 1 January, 24-26 December; ☎ (02216) 4783; £1.10 EH.

Corsham Court. — Open Good Friday-September daily except Mondays 2-6pm (last admission 5.30pm); closes the rest of the year at 4.30pm (last admission 4pm) and on Mondays and Fridays as well as during December; ☎ (0249) 712214; £3.

St Cyriac's. — Lacock. Open Easter-October, daily, 2-5pm; Sundays only the rest of the year 2-5pm.

Fox-Talbot Museum. — Open March-early November daily 11am-5pm; closed Good Friday; £2 NT.

Lacock Abbey. — Open April-late October, Wednesdays-Mondays, 1-5.30pm; closed Tuesdays; £3.50 NT.

Dyrham Park. — Open April-early November daily except Thursdays and Fridays 12noon-5.30pm (last admission 5pm); park open all the year daily 12noon-dusk; ☎ (027582) 2501; house, ground and park £4, park only £1.20 NT.

American Museum. — Claverton Manor. Open late March-early November, daily, 2-5pm; gardens 1-6pm; closed Mondays; ☎ (0225) 460503; £3.50.

BATTLE

Abbey and battlefield. — Open Good Friday-September daily 10am-6pm; 4pm the rest of the year; closed 24-26 December and 1 January; £1.70 EH.

BEAULIEU

National Motor Museum. — Open, daily, May-September 10am-6pm (5pm October-April); closed 25 December; ☎ (0590) 612345; £6.50, children £4.50: all inclusive ticket for the museum, abbey ruins and the Palace House.

Excursions

Buckler's Hard Maritime Museum. — Open Spring bank holiday-early September, daily, 10am-9pm; 6pm Easter-Spring bank holiday; 4.30pm in winter; closed Christmas Day; £2.20.

BERKELEY CASTLE

Castle. — Open May-September, Tuesdays-Saturdays 11am-5pm, Sundays 2-5pm; April Tuesdays-Sundays 2-5pm; October Sundays only 2-4.30pm; bank holiday Mondays 11am-5pm; closed Mondays except bank holiday Mondays; ☎ (0453) 810332; £2.90.

Excursion

Wildfowl and Wetlands Trust, Slimbridge. — Open daily 9.30am-5pm (4pm in winter); ☎ (0453) 890065; £3.50.

BERWICK-UPON-TWEED

Berwick Barracks: Kings Own Scottish Borderers Museum (EH) **and Burrell at Berwick Collection.** — Open Easter-September, Mondays-Saturdays, 10am-12.30pm and 1.30-6pm, Sundays 11am-12.30pm and 2-6pm; October-Easter, Tuesdays-Saturdays, 10am-12.30pm and 1.30-4pm; ☎ (0289) 304493; £1.40.

Excursions

Holy Island. — The island can only be reached by a causeway at low tide; time tables are posted at either end of the causeway.

Lindisfarne Priory, Holy Island. — Open daily 10am-6pm (4pm in winter); ☎ (0289) 89200; £1.40 EH.

Lindisfarne Castle. — Open April-September daily except Fridays 1-5.30pm; October Wednesdays and weekends 1-5.30pm; ☎ (0289) 89244; £2.20 NT.

Bamburgh Castle. — Open April-October, daily, 1-5pm; ☎ (06684) 208; £1.80.

Farne Islands. — Open April and August-September daily 10am-6pm; restricted access during breeding season (May-July); landing fee: £2.80 NT. Boats leave from Seahouses harbour, some operators have landing permits, others sail around the islands; boat trip fee: £3.50.

BEVERLEY

Guildhall. — Open Easter-September Tuesdays and bank holidays 10am-4.30pm; ☎ (0482) 867430.

Beverley Minster. — Open May-September 9am-8pm (5pm the rest of the year); Sundays in summer 12noon-5pm, in winter 2.30-5pm; donation.

St Mary's Church. — Open June-September, weekdays, 9.30am-7pm, Saturdays 10.30am-7pm, Sundays 1.30-5pm; October-May, weekdays 9.30am-4.45pm, Saturday mornings only; ☎ (0482) 864506.

Excursions

Burton Constable. — Open late July and August, Sundays to Thursdays, 1-5pm; June and early July Sundays only 1-5pm; ☎ (0964) 562400; £2.75.

Burton Agnes Hall. — Open April-late October, daily, 11am-5pm; ☎ (0262) 89324; £2.25.

William Wilberforce Museum. — Kingston upon Hull. Open Mondays-Saturdays 10am-5pm, Sundays 1.30-4.30pm; closed 1 January, Good Friday, Christmas and Boxing Days; ☎ (0482) 222737.

BIRMINGHAM

Museum and Art Gallery. — Open Mondays-Saturdays 9.30am-5pm, Sundays 2-5pm; ☎ (021) 235 2834.

Barber Institute of Fine Arts. — Open Mondays-Fridays, 10am-5pm; Saturdays 10am-1pm; closed Sundays, bank holidays and statutory university holidays; ☎ (021) 472 0962.

Museum of Science and Industry. — Open Mondays-Saturdays 9.30am-5pm; Sundays 2-5pm; closed Christmas and New Year holidays.

Aston Hall. — Open April-late October, daily, 2-5pm; ☎ (021) 327 0062.

Excursion

Black Country Museum. — Open April-October 10am-5pm; November-March 10am-dusk; closed Christmas Day; ☎ (021) 557 9643; £4.50.

BLACKPOOL

Illuminations. — Early September-first Sunday in November; for exact dates ☎ (0253) 21623.

Blackpool Tower. — For details of opening times ☎ (0253) 22242.

Excursion

Windmill. — Lytham St Anne's. Open Easter-September daily except Mondays and Fridays 10am-4.30pm.

BLENHEIM PALACE

Palace. — Open mid March-October, daily, 10.30am-4.45pm; closed in winter; **Park:** all the year round 9am-5pm; ☎ (0993) 811325; palace and park £5.50.

BOSTON

St Botolph's Church. — Open Easter-September Mondays-Saturdays 9am-4.30pm, Sundays 11am-4pm; the rest of the year Mondays-Saturdays 9am-4pm, closed Sundays.

Boston Guildhall Museum. — Open Mondays-Saturdays 10am-5pm; Sundays April to September only 1.30-5pm; closed Christmas and New Year holidays; ☎ (0205) 365954; 70p.

Fydell House. — Open during university term times, weekdays, 10am-12.30pm and 2-4pm; ☎ (0205) 368588.

Excursions

Tattershall Castle. — Open April-October, daily, 10.30am-6pm; November-March daily 12noon-4.30pm; last admission half an hour before closing; closed 25 and 26 December; ☎ (0526) 42543; £1.80 NT.

Ayscoughfee Hall. — Spalding. Open Mondays-Thursdays 10am-5pm, Fridays 10am-4.30pm, Saturdays March-October only 10am-5pm.

Springfields. — Spalding. Open April-September daily 10am-6pm; ☎ (0775) 724843; £2.

BOURNEMOUTH

Russel-Cotes Art Gallery and Museum. — Open Mondays-Saturdays 10am-5pm; closed Sundays, Good Friday and Christmas Day; ☎ (0202) 551009; £1.

Shelley Rooms. — Open Mondays-Saturdays 2-5pm; closed Sundays, bank holidays, Good Friday and Christmas Day; ☎ (0202) 551009.

Excursions

Waterfront Museum. — Poole. Open Mondays-Saturdays 10am-5pm, Sundays 2-5pm; ☎ (0202) 683138; £2.

Compton Acres. — Open April-October daily.

Corfe Castle. — Open March-October daily 10am-4.30pm; November-February weekends only 12noon-3.30pm; ☎ (0929) 480921; £2 NT.

BRADFORD

National Museum of Photography, Film and Television. — Open Tuesdays-Sundays 10.30am-6pm; closed Mondays, 1 January, May Day and 25, 26 and 27 December; ☎ (0274) 727488.

Wool Exchange. — Open by arrangement ☎ (0274) 725001.

BRECON BEACONS

Brecknock Museum. — Brecon. Open Mondays-Saturdays 10am-5pm; closed Good Friday, 24 December-1 January.

Brecon Beacons Mountain Centre. — Southwest of Brecon. Open daily 9.30am-6pm, 5pm March-June and September-October, 4.30pm the rest of the year; 50p parking fee.

Dan-yr-Ogof Caves. — Open Easter-October 10am-4.30pm; £4.

BRIGHTON

Royal Pavilion. — Open June-September 10am-6pm; October-May 10am-5pm; closed Christmas and Boxing Days; ☎ (0273) 603005; £2.80.

St Bartholomew's. — Open daily 9am-2pm, Sundays and bank holidays services only.

Art Gallery and Museum. — Open Tuesdays-Saturdays 10am-5.45pm, Sundays 2-5pm; closed Mondays (except bank holidays), Good Friday, Christmas, Boxing and New Year's Days; ☎ (0273) 603005.

BRISTOL

Industrial Museum. — Open Saturdays-Wednesdays 10am-1pm and 2-5pm; closed Thursdays and Fridays, 25-27 December, 1 January, Good Friday; ☎ (0272) 251470.

Maritime Heritage Centre. — Open Mondays-Saturdays 10am-6pm (5pm in winter).

SS Great Britain. — Open daily 10am-6pm (5pm in winter); closed 24 and 25 December; ☎ (0272) 260680; £2.50.

St Mary Redcliffe. — Open June-August daily 8am-8pm (6pm on Sundays and the rest of the year).

Bristol Cathedral. — Open daily 8am-6pm; closed afternoon of Christmas Day; suggested donation: £1.

Georgian House. — Open Mondays-Saturdays 10am-1pm and 2-5pm; closed 1 January, Good Friday and 24-26 December; ☎ (0272) 211362.

Red Lodge. — Open Mondays-Saturdays 10am-5pm.

St Nicholas Church Museum. — Open Mondays-Saturdays 10am-5pm.

Quakers Friars. — Closed temporarily.

John Welsey's New Room. Open Mondays-Saturdays 10am-1pm and 2-4pm; closed Sundays all the year and Wednesdays in winter; ☎ (0272) 264740; suggested donation: 50p.

Temple Meads: Brunel's Station Building. — Open Mondays-Thursdays 10am-3.30pm, Fridays 10am-12noon; closed 21 December-3 January and bank holidays; ☎ (0272) 292 688.

Cathedral of SS Peter and Paul. — Clifton. Open daily 7am-9pm (8pm in winter).

Bristol Zoological Gardens. — Clifton. Open daily 9am-6pm (5pm in winter); closed Christmas Day; ☎ (0272) 738951; £4.

Excursion

Clevedon Court. — Open April-September Wednesdays, Thursdays and Sundays 2.30-5.30pm (last admission 5pm), also open bank holiday Mondays; ☎ (0272) 872257; £2.50 NT.

BURY ST EDMUNDS

St Edmundsbury Abbey. — Open March-October 7.30am-half hour before dusk; November-February 7.30am-4.15pm; Sundays open at 9am; ☎ (0284) 764667; E H.

Cathedral of St James. — Open summer 9am-8pm, Sundays 8am-6pm; winter 9am-5.30pm, Sundays 8am-5pm.

St Mary's Church. — Open Easter-October subject to staff availability weekdays 11am-3.30pm (2pm in winter), Sundays 2-4pm.

Excursions

Ickworth House. — Open May-September Tuesdays, Wednesdays, Fridays and weekends 1.30-5.30pm (last admission 5pm), April and October weekends only 1.30-5.30pm; park open daily dawn-dusk; ☎ (0284) 735270; House, garden and park: £3.50 NT.

National Horse Racing Museum. — Newmarket. Open March-December Tuesdays-Saturdays 10am-5pm, Sundays July and August noon-5pm, the rest of the year 2-5pm; ☎ (0638) 667333; £2.

Guildhall Museum. — Lavenham. Open April-early November daily 11am-5pm; closed Good Friday and Christmas Day; ☎ (0787) 247646; £1.80 NT.

Times and charges

C

CAERNARFON

Caernarfon Castle. — Open late March-late October daily 9.30am-6.30pm; late October-late March Mondays-Saturdays 9.30am-4pm, Sundays 2-4pm; ☎ (0286) 77617; £3 Cadw.

Segontium Roman Fort. — Open May-September Mondays-Saturdays 9.30am-6pm, Sundays 2-6pm; 5.30pm March, April and October, 5pm Sundays; 4pm the rest of the year; closed Good Friday, 24-26 December, 1 January; ☎ (0286) 5625; voluntary charge Cadw.

Llanbeblig Church. — Open weekdays 10am-4pm, Sundays 11am-2pm; church is locked, written application is advised to ensure being able to visit.

CAIRNGORMS

Cairn Gorm Chairlift. — The chair lift operates Easter-early November 9am-5pm; February and March 8.30am-5pm; November-February 8.30am-4.30pm; two stages: adult Rtn £3.50, party and family tickets available.

Strathspey Railway. — Steam train service June-September daily; April-May. Oct weekends only; for timetable ☎ (047 983) 692; single journey: 20min.

Highland Folk Museum. — Kingussie. Open April-October Mondays-Saturdays 10am-6pm, Sundays 2-6pm; November-March Mondays-Fridays only 10am-3pm; closed fortnight over Christmas and New Year; ☎ (0540) 307; £1.70.

Highland Wildlife Park. — Open June-September, daily, 10am-5pm, 4pm April, May, October; ☎ (05404) 270; admission charge per vehicle: £8.

Glenlivet. — Open Easter-October Mondays-Fridays 10am-4pm.

Glenfiddich Distillery. — Guided tours (time: 1/4 hours), all year except Christmas and New Year holidays, weekdays 9.30am-4.30pm; Easter-mid October Saturdays 9.30am-4.30pm, Sundays 12noon-4.30pm; ☎ (0340) 20373.

Baxters. — Open Mondays-Fridays 9.30am-4.30pm; weekends also May-September.

Tugnet Ice House. — Open June-September daily 10am-4pm.

CAMBRIDGE

St John's College. — Open July-mid April weekdays 11.30am-5.30pm, Sundays 12.30-5pm; closed mid April-June; £1.

Trinity College. — Open daily 9am-6pm except during examination period May-June; Wren Library open 12noon-2pm in term time.

Gonville and Caius College. — Open afternoons only, late March-5 May and 10 June-end September; closed 6 May-9 June and all day at weekends and bank holidays.

Trinity Hall. — Open daily during daylight hours; closed mid April-late June and 24 December-2 January.

Clare College. — Open July-late April 9am-5pm, gardens only open Mondays-Fridays 2-4pm.

Old Schools, Squire Law Library and Senate House. — Not open to visitors; view from outside only.

Great St Mary. — Open 9am-5pm; access to tower: 50p.

King's College. — Daily until 6pm, limited access mid April-September. **King's College Chapel:** term weekdays 9.30am-3.45pm, summer vacation 9.30am-5.45pm.

Corpus Christi College. — Open during daylight hours; restrictions during examination period May-early June; closed late December-early January.

St Catherine's College. — Open all the year 11am-5pm; closed mid May-late June, 29 June, 1 July and 21-31 December.

Queen's College. — Open last week in late June-September daily 10.15am-12.45pm and 1.45-4.30pm; October-third week in May 1.45-4.30pm; closed for exams third week in May-last week in June; 50p.

Fitzwilliam Museum. — Open Mondays-Saturdays 10am-5pm, Sundays 2.15-5pm; closed Mondays except bank holidays, Good Friday, 24 December-1 January; ☎ (0223) 332900.

Kettle's Yard. — House open Tuesdays-Sundays 2-4pm; gallery Tuesdays-Saturdays 12.30-5.30pm, Sundays 2-5.30pm.

Magdalene College. — College and chapel daily 9-6.30pm; Hall daily 9.30am-12.30pm; Garden daily 1-6.30pm; all closed during exams; Pepys' Library late April-August weekdays 11.30am-12.30pm, 2.30-3.30pm, mid January-mid March and early October-early December weekdays 2.30-3.30pm.

Jesus College. — Courts, gardens and chapel open daily 10am-6pm; closed during Christmas period and Easter term (April-June).

Emmanuel College. — Gardens open 9am-5pm.

Pembroke College Chapel. — Open all the year 9am-5pm; closed May and June and some public holidays; guided tour (15min) 2-5pm.

Excursion

Audley End. — Open April-September daily except Mondays 1-5pm ; park 12 noon-6pm; ☎ (0799) 22 399; £4.

CANTERBURY

Canterbury Cathedral. — Open Easter-September Monday-Saturday 8.45am-7pm; October-Easter 8.45am-5pm; Sundays throughout the year 12.30-2.30pm; crypt throughout the year 10am-4.30pm; ☎ (0227) 762862.

St Dunstan's Church. — Open summer weekdays 9am-6pm, Sundays 8am-7.15pm; winter weekdays 9am-3pm, Sundays 9am-4pm

West Gate. — Open Mondays-Saturdays; 50p.

Hospital of St Thomas the Martyr, Eastbridge. — Open Mondays-Saturdays 10am-5pm; Sundays 11am-5pm.

Franciscan Gardens and Greyfriars Monastery. — Open mid-May-October Mondays-Saturdays 2-4pm; closed Sundays; voluntary donation.

Poor Priests Hospital. — Open Mondays-Saturdays 10.30am-5pm; June-October Sunday afternoons 12.30-5pm ; closed Good Friday, 25 and 26 December; ☎ (0227) 452747; £1.20.

St Augustine's Abbey. — Open Good Friday-September daily 10am-6pm; October-Maundy Thursday, Tuesdays-Sundays 10am-4pm; closed 1 January and 24-26 December; ☎ (0227) 767345; 95p EH.

St Martin's Church. — Open daily 9am-6pm, Sundays after morning service-6pm.

The King's School. — Open daily; some buildings closed during the school holidays; ☎ (0227) 768764/475500.

Excursions

Richborough Castle. — Open Good Friday-September daily 10am-6pm; October-Maundy Thursday, Tuesdays-Sundays 10am-4pm; closed 1 January and 24-26 December; ☎ (0304) 612013; £1.30 EH.

Eurotunnel Exhibition Centre. — Folkestone. Open late May-late-September 10am-6pm; winter 10am-5pm; closed Mondays except for bank holidays; ☎ (0303) 270111; £2.70.

St Leonard's Church. — Hythe. Open 8am-5pm; crypt May-September 10.30am-12noon and 2.30-4pm; crypt 20p.

Port Lympne Zoo Park. — Open summer 10am-7pm (last admission 5pm); winter 10am-5pm (last admission 3.30pm) ☎ (0303) 264646; £5.

CARDIFF

Cardiff Castle. — Open May-September daily 10am-6pm; 5pm March, April and October; 4.30pm November-February; guided tours of castle: May-September daily at 20 minute intervals 10am-12.40pm and 2-5pm; March, April and October daily at 30 minute intervals 10am-12.30pm and 2-4pm; November-February daily 10.30am, 11.45am, 2pm and 3.15pm; ☎ (0222) 8222083; guided tour of castle and admission to both Military Museums, Roman wall and Norman Keep; £3.

National Museum of Wales. — Open Tuesdays-Saturdays 10am-5pm, Sundays 2.30-5pm; closed Mondays, 1 January, Good Friday, 25 and 26 December; ☎ (0222) 555105; £1.

Llandaff Cathedral. — Open daily 7am-7pm (6.30pm Wednesdays); suggested donation: 40p.

Welsh Industrial and Maritime Museum. — Open Tuesdays-Sundays 10am-5pm, Sundays 2.30-5pm; closed Mondays, 1 January, Good Friday, 24-26 December; ☎ (0222) 481919; £1.

Excursions

Welsh Folk Museum, St Fagans. — Open daily 10am-5pm; closed Sundays November-Easter, 1 January, Good Friday, 24-26 December; ☎ (0222) 555105; £3.

Castell Coch. — Open late March-late October daily 9.30am-6.30pm; late October-late March Mondays-Saturdays 9.30am-4pm, Sundays 2-4pm; ☎ (0222) 810101; £1.75 Cadw.

Caerphilly Castle. — Open late March-late October daily 9.30am-6.30pm; late October-late March Mondays-Saturdays 9.30am-4pm, Sundays 2-4pm; ☎ (0222) 883143; £1.50 Cadw.

Caerlon. — **Roman Monuments.** - Open late March-late October daily 9.30am-6.30pm; late October-late March Mondays-Saturdays 9.30am-4pm, Sundays 2-4pm; ☎ (0633) 422518; £1.25 Cadw.

Roman Legionary Museum. — Open mid-March-mid-October Mondays-Saturdays 10am-6pm, Sundays 2-6pm (4.30pm the rest of the year); closed 1 January, Good Friday, 24-26 December; ☎ (0633) 423134; £1 (combined ticket available for museum and Roman monuments).

Valley Inheritance Centre. — Pontypool. Open February-December weekdays 10am-5pm, Sundays 2-5pm; ☎ (0495) 752036; 90p.

Big Pit, Blaenavon. — Open March-December daily 10am-5pm; underground tours (1 hour) last tour 3.30pm; ☎ (495) 790311; £4.

CARDIGAN

Excursions

Cilgerran Castle. — Open late March-late October daily 9.30am-6.30pm; late October-late March Mondays-Saturdays 9.30am-4pm, Sundays 2-4pm; ☎ (0239) 615136; £1.25 Cadw.

Museum of the Welsh Woollen Industry. — Dre-fach Felindre. April-September Mondays-Saturdays 10am-5pm; October-March Mondays-Fridays 10am-5pm; closed 1 January, Good Friday, 24-26 December; £1.

CARLISLE

Tullie House. — Open Easter-September 10am-7pm, October-Easter weekdays 10am-5pm; ☎ (0228) 34781; £2.80.

Castle. — Open April-September daily 10am-6pm; October-March daily 10am-4pm; closed 1 January and 24-26 December; £1.60 EH.

Church of St Cuthbert with St Mary. — Open daily 10am-12.30pm, Sundays 10am-12noon. **Tithe Barn:** viewed from the exterior only.

Excursion

Lanercost Priory. — Open March-September daily 10am-6pm; 65p EH.

CASTLE HOWARD

House and Costume Galleries. — Open late March-early November daily 11am-4.30pm: ☎ (065) 384444; £5.

CHANNEL ISLANDS

Jersey

Elizabeth Castle. — St Helier. Open Easter-October daily 9.30am-5pm; ☎ (0534) 23871; £1.20.

Jersey Museum. — Open Mondays-Saturdays 10am-5pm; closed 1 January, Good Friday, 25-26 December; ☎ (0534) 30511; £1.20.

Fort Regent. — Open daily 9am-11pm; closed 25-26 December; ☎ (0534) 73000; £2.

Mont Orgeuil Castle. — Gorey. Open Easter-October daily 9.30am-5pm; ☎ (0534) 53292; £1.20.

Jersey Pottery Workshops. — Gorey. Open Mondays-Fridays 9am-5.30pm; closed weekends and bank holidays; ☎ (0534) 51119.

St Matthew's Church. — Milbrook. Open Mondays-Fridays 9am-6pm, Saturdays 9am-1pm.

Samarès Manor House. — Guided tour of the house: April-October Mondays-Saturdays, 10.30am, 11.15am, 12noon; £1.50; Gardens: April-October daily 10am-5pm; £2; ☎ (0534) 70551.

Jersey Zoo. — Open daily 10am-6pm (dusk in winter); closed 25 December; ☎ (0534) 64666; £3.50.

Guernsey

Castle Cornet. — Royal Guernsey Militia Museum and Guernsey Maritime History Museum: open April-October 10.30am-5.30pm; ☎ (0481) 26518; £2.

Hauteville House. — Guided tours (3/4 hour) April-September Mondays-Saturdays 10-11.30am and 2-4.30pm; closed Sundays and local holidays; £1.50.

Sausmarez Manor. — Guided tours late May-late September Wednesdays-Fridays and bank holiday Mondays 10.30-11.45am and 2.30-4.30pm; ☎ (0481) 35571; £1.50.

Sausmarez Park. — Open all the year round. **Guernsey Folk Museum:** open April-September 10am-5.30pm; £1.60.

CHATSWORTH

House and Garden. — Open Easter-October daily house 11am-5.30pm (last admission 4.30pm); garden 11am-6pm (last admission 5pm); ☎ (0246) 582204; £4.25.

Excursions

Hardwick Hall. — Open April-October: Hall Wednesdays, Thursdays, Saturdays, Sundays 12.30-5pm; Gardens daily 12noon-5pm; ☎ (0246) 850430; Hall and Gardens £4.50, Gardens only £1.80 NT.

Haddon Hall. — Open April-October Tuesdays-Sundays 11am-6pm; closed Mondays; ☎ (0629) 812855; £3.

Bolsover Castle. — Open Good Friday-September daily 10am-6pm; October-Maundy Thursday Tuesdays-Sundays 10am-4pm; closed Mondays in winter, 1 January, 24-26 December; ☎ (0246) 823349; £1.50 EH.

CHELTENHAM

Museum and Art Gallery. — Open Mondays-Saturdays 10am-5.20pm, Sundays May-September only 2-5.20pm; ☎ (0242) 237431.

Pittville Pump Room. — Open Tuesdays-Saturdays 10.30am-5pm (last admission 4.40pm), Sundays April-October only 10.30am-5pm; closed Good Friday and winter bank holidays; ☎ (0242) 512740; 55p.

Gustav Holst Birthplace Museum. — Clarence Road. Open Tuesdays-Fridays 12noon-5.20pm, Saturdays 11am-5.20pm; ☎ (0242) 524846.

Excursion

Sudeley Castle. — Open late March-October daily 11am-5pm; ☎ (0242) 604357; £4.20.

CHESTER

Town Hall. — Council Chamber and Assembly Rooms open Mondays-Fridays 9am-5pm; ☎ (0244) 324324.

Grosvenor Museum. — Open Mondays-Saturdays 10.30am-5pm, Sundays 2-5pm; closed Good Friday, 24-25 December.

Excursion

Chester Zoo. — Open daily 10am-dusk; closed 25 December; ☎ (0244) 380280; £4.60.

CHICHESTER

Cathedral. — Open daily 7.40am-7pm (5pm in winter).

St Mary's Hospital. — Guided tours (1 hour) Tuesdays-Saturdays 11am-12noon and 2-5pm (4pm in winter); ☎ (0243) 783377.

Pallant House. Open Tuesdays-Saturdays 10am-5.30pm; closed Sundays and Mondays; ☎ (0234) 774557; £1.80.

Excursions

Petworth House. — Open April-October Tuesdays-Thursdays and weekends 1-5.30pm (last admission 5pm); grounds 12.30-5.30pm; ☎ (0798) 42207; £3.30 NT.

Arundel Castle. — Open June-August Sundays-Fridays 12noon-5pm (last admission 4pm); April, May, September, October Sundays-Fridays 1-5pm; closed Saturdays; ☎ (0903) 882173; £3.50.

Weald and Downland Open Air Museum. — Open March-October daily 11am-5pm; November-February Wednesdays, Sundays and bank holidays only 11am-4pm; ☎ (024363) 348; £3.

Goodwood House. — Open early May-September Sundays and Mondays 2-5pm, plus Tuesdays, Wednesdays and Thursdays in August; ☎ (0243) 774107; £3.

Fishbourne Roman Palace. —Open May-September daily 10am-6pm; March, April, October, November 10am-5pm; December-February Sundays only 10am-4pm; ☎ (0243) 785859; £2.50 family ticket available.

Bignor Roman Villa. — Open June-September Tuesdays-Sundays 10am-6pm; March-May and October 10am-5pm; ☎ (07987) 259; £1.85.

CHIPPING CAMPDEN

St James' Church. — Open 9am-6pm (4pm in winter).

Excursions

Hidcote Manor Garden. — Open April-October daily except Tuesdays and Fridays 11am-7pm; ☎ (0386) 438333; £3.80 NT.

Chastleton House. — Closed to the public.

Times and charges

CIRENCESTER

Church of St John the Baptist. — Open weekdays 9.30am-5pm, Sundays 12noon-6.30, October-March 2.15-6pm.

Corinium Museum. — Open April-October weekdays 10am-5.30pm, Sundays 2-5.30pm; the rest of the year closed 5pm, Mondays and Christmas; ☎ (0285) 655611; 80p.

Excursions

Westonbirt Arboretum. — Open daily 10am-8pm or sunset whichever is the earlier; admission charge.

Chedworth Roman Villa. — Open March-October Tuesdays-Sundays 10am-5.30pm (last admission 5pm); November-early December Wednesdays-Sundays 11am-4pm; ☎ (024 289) 256; £2.20 NT.

COLCHESTER

Castle and Museum. — Open Mondays-Saturdays 10am-5pm, Sundays April-October only 2-5pm; ☎ (0206) 712931; £1. Guided tours of castle vaults and prisons; daily July and August, weekends only April-October.

St Botolph's Priory. — Open any reasonable time EH.

Excursions

Flatford Mill. — Not open to the public.

Gainsborough House. — Sudbury. Open Easter-October Tuesdays-Saturdays 10am-5pm, Sundays 2-5pm; closes 4pm the rest of the year; closed Mondays, Good Friday and 25 December-1 January; ☎ (0787) 72958; £1.50.

Melford Hall. — Long Melford. Open May-October Wednesdays, Thursdays and weekends 2-5.30pm; April and October weekends 2-5.30pm; ☎ (0787) 880286; £2.40 NT.

CONWY

Conwy Castle. — Open late March-late October daily 9.30am-6.30pm; late October-late March Mondays-Saturdays 9.30am-4pm, Sundays 2-4pm; ☎ (0492) 592398; £2 Cadw.

Plas Mawr. — Open April-September daily 10am-6pm (4pm in October); February, March and November Wednesdays-Sundays 10am-4pm; £1.

Aberconwy. — Open Easter-early November daily except Tuesdays 11am-5.30pm (last admission 5pm); £1 NT.

Excursions

Bodnant Garden. — Open mid-March-October daily 10am-5pm; ☎ (0492) 650460; £2.50 NT.

CORNWALL COAST

South Coast

Antony House. — Open June-August Tuesdays, Wednesdays, Thursdays and Sundays; 2-5.25pm; April, May, September, October Tuesdays, Wednesdays and Thursdays 2-5.25pm; ☎ (0752) 812191; £3 NT.

St Mawes Castle. — Open Easter-September daily 10am-6pm; October-Easter Tuesdays-Sundays 10am-4pm; closed 1 January, 24-26 December; ☎ (0326) 270526; 80p.

Trelissick Garden. — Open Easter-September weekdays 11am-6pm, Sundays 1-6pm; March-Easter and October 11am-5pm, Sundays 1-5pm; November-late December weekdays 11am-4pm, Sundays 12noon-4pm; ☎ (0872) 862090; £2.50 NT.

Pendennis Castle. — Open Good Friday-September daily 10am-6pm; October-Maundy Thursday daily 10am-4pm; closed 1 January and 24-26 December; £1.40 EH.

Glendurgan Garden. — Open March-October Tuesdays-Saturdays 10.30am-5.30pm (last admission 4.30pm); ☎ (0326) 250906; £2 NT.

Gweek Seal Sanctuary. — Open March-October 9.30am-6pm; November-February 9.30am-4.30pm; ☎ (0326) 22361; £3.75.

St Michael's Mount. — Open April-October daily 10.30am-4.45pm; the rest of the year by guided tours Mondays, Wednesdays and Fridays 11am, 12noon, 2pm and 3pm; ☎ (0736) 710507; £2.80 plus 60p ferry fare NT.

North Coast

Geevor Tin Mine. — Open Easter-October Sundays-Fridays 10am-5pm; closed Saturdays except during school holidays; admission charge.

Chysauster. — Open Good Friday-September daily 10am-6pm; October-Maundy Thursday daily 10am-4pm; closed 1 January and 24-26 December; 85p EH.

Wayside Museum. — Zennor. Open April-October daily 10am-6pm; ☎ (0736) 796945; £1.50.

Barbara Hepworth Museum. — St Ives. Open July-August Mondays-Saturdays 10am-6.30pm, Sundays 2-6pm; April, June and September weekdays only 10am-5.30pm; October-March weekdays only 10am-4.30pm; ☎ (0736) 796226; 50p.

Trerice. — Open April-October daily except Tuesdays 11am-6pm (5pm in October); ☎ (0637) 875404; £3.20 NT.

COTSWOLDS

Arlington Mill Museum. Bibury. Open mid-March-November daily 10.30am-7pm, the rest of the year weekends only 10.30am-dusk; £1.80.

Cotswold Countryside Collection. — Northleach. Open Easter-early November weekdays 10am-5.30pm, Sundays 2-5.30pm; ☎ (0451) 60715; 80p.

Snowshill Manor. — Open May-September Wednesdays-Sundays 11am-1pm and 2-6pm; April and October weekends only 11am-1pm and 2-5pm; ☎ (0386)852410; £3.50 NT.

Broadway Tower. — Broadway Country Park. Open during daylight hours.

COVENTRY

New St Michael's. — Open Easter-September weekdays 9.30am-7pm, Sundays 12noon-7pm; October-Easter weekdays 9.30am-5.30pm, Sundays 12noon-5.30pm; cathedral: £1 donation; visitors centre: £1.25.

Guildhall of St Mary. — Open April-October weekdays 10am-1pm and 2-5pm (4pm Sundays and bank holidays); ☎ (0203) 833041.

Whitefriars. — Open Thursdays-Saturdays 10am-5pm; ☎ (0203) 832433.

Museum of British Road Transport. — Open April-December daily 10am-5pm; January-March Fridays-Sundays only 10am-5pm; ☎ (0203) 832425; £2.

CULROSS

Town House. — Open Easter then May-September daily 11am-1pm and 2-5pm; ☎ (0383) 880359; 80p NTS.

The Study. — Open Easter then April-October weekends only 2-4pm; ☎ (0383) 880359; 50p NTS.

Palace. — Open April-September 9.30am-7pm (4pm in October), Sundays 2-7pm (4pm in October); closed November-March; £1.20 HS/NTS.

D

DARTMOOR

Buckfast Steam Railway. — Open June-September daily; May Wednesdays and weekends; April and October Wednesdays and Sundays; ☎ (03644) 2338.

Castle Drogo. — Open April-September Saturdays-Thursdays 11am-5.30pm; October Saturdays-Thursdays 11am-4.30pm; ☎ (0647) 433306; £3.80 NT.

Lydford Gorge. — Open April-October daily 10.30am-6pm; November-March 10.30am-4pm; ☎ (082 282) 441; £2.80 NT. The walk is arduous and not suitable for the very young or elderly.

DARTMOUTH

Dartmouth Castle. — Open Good Friday-September daily 10am-6pm; October-Maundy Thursday Tuesdays-Sundays 10am-4pm; closed 1 January, 24-26 December; £1.15 EH.

Excursions

Elizabethan Museum. — Totnes. Open mid March-October Mondays-Fridays 10.30am-1pm and 2-5 pm; ☎ (0803) 863821; 60p.

Guildhall. — Totnes. Open Easter-September weekdays 10am-1pm and 2-5pm; ☎ (0803) 863411; 30p.

Totnes Castle. — Open Good Friday-September daily 10am-1pm and 2-6pm; October-Maundy Thursday Tuesdays-Sundays 10am-1pm and 2-4pm; closed 1 January, 24-26 December; 85p EH.

River Dart boat service. — Late March-October daily; circular cruise 1 hour £2.50; 1 1/2 hour cruise £3. Dartmouth-Totnes single £3, Rtn £4.60.

Kents Cavern. — Torquay. Open July-August daily 10am-9pm (6pm Saturdays); April-June and September-October 10am-6pm; November-March 10am-5pm; closed 25 December; ☎ (0803) 294059; £2.60.

Torre Abbey. — Torquay. Open April-October daily 10am-6pm; ☎ (0803) 293593; £1.50.

DENBIGH

Castle. — Open late March-late October daily 9.30am-6.30pm; late October-late March Mondays-Saturdays 9.30am-4.30pm, Sundays 2-4pm; ☎ (074571) 3979; £1.25 Cadw.

Excursion

Cathedral. — St Asaph. Open May-September daily 7.30am-8pm; October-April 7.30am-6.30pm.

DERBY

Cathedral. — Open daily from 9am; donation £1.

Museum and Art Gallery. — Open Mondays 11am-5pm; Tuesdays-Saturdays 10am-5pm; Sundays and bank holiday Mondays 2-5pm; ☎ (0332) 255586.

Royal Crown Derby Museum. — Open Mondays-Fridays 10am-4pm; closed Saturdays and bank holidays; ☎ (0332) 47051; factory tours (1 1/2 hours) at 10.30am and 1.45pm; £2.

Excursions

Kedleston Hall. — Open April-October Saturdays-Wednesdays 1-5.30pm (last admission 5pm); closed Thursdays and Fridays; ☎ (0332) 842191; £3.50 NT.

Sudbury Hall. — Open April-October Wednesdays-Sundays 12.30-4.30pm; ☎ (028378) 305; £2.80 NT.

DEVIZES

Devizes Museum. — Open Mondays-Saturdays 10am-5pm; closed Sundays; closed public holidays; ☎ (0380) 727369; £1.50.

Excursion

Bowood House. — Open March-October daily 11am-6pm; ☎ (0249) 812102; £4.

DORCHESTER

Dorset County Museum. — Open Mondays-Saturdays 10am-5pm; closed Good Friday, 25 and 26 December; ☎ (0305) 262735; £1.50.

Excursions

Maiden Castle. — Open any reasonable time; EH.

Swannery. — Abbotsbury. Open April-October daily 9.30am-5pm; ☎ (0305) 871684; £2.30.

Sub-Tropical Gardens. — Open March-October daily 10am-5pm; November-February Tuesdays-Sundays 10am-dusk; closed 1 January and 25 December; ☎ (0305) 871387; £2.50.

House. — Milton Abbas. Open Easter and summer school holidays 10am-6.30pm.

DORNOCH

Excursion

Dunrobin Castle. — Open June-September Mondays-Saturdays 10.30am-5.30pm, Sundays 1-5.30pm; May Mondays-Thursdays 10.30am-12.30pm; ☎ (04083) 3177; £2.80.

DOVER

Castle. — Open Good Friday-September daily 10am-6pm; October-Maundy Thursday daily 10am-4pm (last admission 45 mins before closing time); closed 1 January and 24-26 December; ☎ (0304) 201628; £3 EH.

DUMFRIES

Robert Burns Centre. — Open April-September Mondays-Saturdays 10am-8pm, Sundays 2-5pm; October-March Tuesdays-Saturdays 10am-1pm and 2-5pm; admission free, audio-visual presentation 50p.

Burns House. — Open Easter-October Mondays-Saturdays 10am-1pm and 2-5pm, Sundays 2-5pm; October-March 10am-1pm and 2-5pm closed Sundays and Mondays; ☎ (0387) 55297; 70p.

Excursions

Drumlanrig Castle. — Open late April-late August weekdays except Thursdays 11am-5pm, Sundays 1-5pm; ☎ (0848) 31682; £3.

Sweetheart Abbey. — Open April-September weekdays 9.30am-6pm; Sundays 2-6pm; October-March weekdays 9.30am-4pm; Sundays 2-4pm. 80p HS.

Shambellie House. — Open mid-May to mid-September Thursdays-Mondays 10am-5.30pm, Sundays 12noon-5.30pm; closed Tuesdays and Wednesdays; ☎ (038) 785375.

Caerlaverock Castle. — Open April-September weekdays 9.30am-6pm, Sundays 2-6pm; October-March weekdays 9.30am-4pm, Sundays 2.4pm; £1 HS.

Ruthwell Cross. — Keykeeper.

DUNDEE

The Frigate Unicorn. — Open April-October daily 10am-5pm (4pm on Saturdays); October-March daily 10am-4pm; ☎ (0382) 200900; £1.25.

RRS Discovery. — Open June-September daily 10am-5pm; late March-May and first fortnight in October weekdays 1-5pm, Sundays 11am-5pm; ☎ (0382) 201175; £2.

Excursion

Claypotts Castle. — Broughty Ferry. Open April September weekdays 9.30am-6pm, Sundays 2-6pm; closed in winter; £1 HS.

DUNFERMLINE

Dunfermline Abbey Church. — Open April-September, Mondays-Saturdays 9.30am-6pm, Sundays 2-6pm; October-March, Mondays-Saturdays 9.30am-4pm, Sundays 2-4pm; closed Thursday pm and Fridays in winter; £1 HS.

Dunfermline District Museum. — Open Mondays-Saturdays 11am-5pm; closed Sundays and public holidays; ☎ (0383) 721814.

Andrew Carnegie Birthplace. — Open April-October weekdays 11am-5pm, Sundays 2-5pm; November-March daily 2-4pm; ☎ (0383) 724302.

Excursion

Loch Leven Castle. — Open April-September Mondays-Saturdays 9.30am-6pm; Sundays 2-6pm; closed in winter; £1.20 includes ferry HS.

DUNSTER

Castle. — Open late March-September Saturdays-Wednesdays 11am-5pm; October-early November Saturdays-Wednesdays 12noon-4pm; closed Good Friday; ☎ (0643) 821314; £4 NT.

Dunster Water Mill. — Open July and August daily 11am-5pm; April-June and September-October Sundays-Fridays 11am-5pm; ☎ (0643) 821759; £1.30 NT.

DURHAM

Cathedral. — Open daily 7.15am-8pm (5.45pm in winter).

Castle. —Guided tours July-September weekdays 10am-12noon and 2-4.30pm, Sundays 2-4.30pm; the rest of the year Mondays, Wednesdays and Saturdays 2-4.30pm; ☎ (091) 374 3800; £1.30.

Excursion

Oriental Museum. — Durham University. Open Mondays-Saturdays 9am-1pm and 2-5pm, Sundays 2-5pm; ☎ (091) 374 2911; 50p.

E

EASTBOURNE

Eastbourne Heritage Centre. — Open Tuesdays-Fridays 2-5pm also open bank holidays and Sundays 2-5pm; ☎ (0323) 411189; 50p.

EDINBURGH

Castle. — Open April-September 9.30am-5.05pm (last admission), Sundays 11am-5.05pm; October-March 9.30am-4.20pm (last admission), Sundays 12.30pm-3.35pm; closed Christmas and New Year's holidays; ☎ 031 225 9846; £2.80 HS. Opening hours may be altered during the Tattoo, state and military events.

Royal Scots Regimental Museum. — Open May-September 9.30am-4.30pm, Sundays 11am-4.30pm; October-April 9.30am-4pm; closed weekends and the week between Christmas and New Year; ☎ 031 336 1761 ext 4267.

Scotch Whisky Heritage Centre. — Open daily 9am-6.30pm; winter 10am-5pm; closed Christmas and New Year's Holidays; ☎ 031 220 0441; £2.75.

Gladstone's Land. — Open April-October weekdays 10am-5pm (last tour 4.30pm), Sundays 2-5pm; ☎ 031 226 5856; £2 NTS.

Lady Stair's House. — Open June-September Mondays-Saturdays 10am-6pm; 5pm the rest of the year; ☎ 031 225 2424.

St Giles' Cathedral. — Open April-September 9am-7pm; October-March 9am-5pm.

Parliament Hall. — Open Mondays-Fridays 10am-5pm; closed at weekends and on public holidays.

John Knox House. — Open Mondays-Saturdays 10am-4.30pm; closed 25 and 26 December and 1 and 2 January; ☎ 031 556 9579; £1.20.

Museum of Childhood. — Open June-September weekdays 10am-6pm; October-May 10am-5pm; ☎ 031 225 2424 ext 6645.

Times and charges

Cannongate Tolbooth. — The People's Story Museum open Mondays-Saturdays 10am-6pm; October-May 10am-5pm; closed 25 December and New Year's Day; ☎ 031 225 2424 ext 6638.

Huntly House. — Open June-September Mondays-Saturdays 10am-6pm; 5pm the rest of the year; ☎ 031 225 2424 ext 6678.

Palace of Holyroodhouse. — Guided tours (time: 1 hour); ticket office open late March-late October weekdays 9.30am-5.15pm, Sundays 10.30am-4.30pm; November-March weekdays 9.30am-3.45pm, closed on Sundays; ☎ 031 556 1096; £2.30. Closed during Royal and State visits, especially in May and early June, check in advance.

Abbey of Holyroodhouse. — Same opening times as the palace. Visitors are free to visit on their own at the end of the guided tours.

Georgian House. — Open April-October weekdays 10am-5pm (last tour 4.30pm), Sundays 2-5pm; £2.20 NTS.

National Portrait Gallery. — Open Mondays-Saturdays 10am-5pm, Sundays 2-5pm; closed 25, 26 December, 1, 2, 3 January; ☎ (031) 556 8921.

Royal Museum of Scotland: Antiquities. — Queen Street. Open weekdays 10am-5pm, Sundays 2-5pm; closed 25-26 December and 1-2 January; ☎ 031 225 7534 ext 219; same times for the Chambers Street Museum.

Scott Monument. — Closed for repairs.

National Gallery of Scotland. — Open Mondays-Saturdays 10am-5pm, Sundays 2-5pm; closed 25, 26, 31 December, 1, 2 January, 1 May; ☎ (031) 556 8921.

Excursions

Dalmeny Parish Church. — Key can be obtained at hall or gate cottage.

Dalmeny House. — Guided tours May-September 2-5.30pm; closed Fridays and Saturdays; ☎ 031 331 1888; £2.80.

Hopetoun House. — Open Easter then late April-September daily 10am-5.30pm (last admission 4.45pm); ☎ 031 331 2451; £3.

The Binns. — Guided tours May-September daily, except Fridays, 2-5pm (last tour 4.30pm); ☎ (050 683) 4255; £2.50 NTS.

Linlithgow Palace. — Open April-September weekdays 9.30am-6pm, Sundays 2-6pm; October-March weekdays 9.30am-4pm, Sundays 2-4pm; £1.20 HS.

Cairnpapple. — Open April-September weekdays 9.30am-6pm, Sundays 2-6pm; closed in winter; 80p HS.

Rosslyn Chapel. — Open April-October Mondays-Saturdays 10am-5pm, Sundays 12noon-4.45pm; £1.50.

ELGIN

Cathedral. — Open April-September weekdays 9.30am-6pm, Sundays 2-6pm; October-March weekdays 10am-4pm; Sundays 2-4pm; closed Thursday pm and Fridays in winter; 80p HS.

ELY

Cathedral. — Open daily 7am-7pm (in winter 6.15pm and 5pm on Sundays); ☎ (0353) 667735; £2.40. In summer the Stained Glass Museum is open and there are guided tours of the cathedral.

EXETER

Maritime Museum. — Open daily 10am-6pm (5pm in winter); closed 25 and 26 December; ☎ (0392) 58075; £3.

Guildhall. — Open Tuesdays-Saturdays 10am-5pm; closed Sundays.

St Nicholas Priory. — Open daily except Mondays 10am-1pm and 2-5pm; closed 25, 26 December and bank holidays; 70p.

Excursions

Bicton Gardens. — Open April-September daily 10am-6pm; March and October daily 10am-4pm; ☎ (0395) 68889; £3.75.

F

FALKLAND

Palace of Falkland. — Open Easter-October weekdays 10am-6pm (last admission 5pm), Sundays 2-6pm; ☎ (0337) 57397; £2.80 NTS.

FOUNTAINS ABBEY

Fountains Hall. — Open April-October daily 10am-6pm (4pm the rest of the year); ☎ (0765) 86333; NT.

Abbey and Studley Royal. — Open July and August daily 10am-8pm; April-June daily 10am-7pm; October 10am-6pm; November-March 10am-5pm; ☎ (0765) 86333; summer: £2.70, winter: £2.40 NT.

G

GLAMIS CASTLE

Castle. — Guided tours Easter then late April-mid October daily 12noon-5.30pm (opens 11am in July and August); ☎ (030784) 242; £3.30.

Excursions

Angus Folk Museum. — Glamis. Open Easter, late April-late September daily 11am-5pm (last tour 4.30pm); £1.40 NTS.

Aberlemno Stones. — The stones are boarded up between November and April.

Meigle Museum. — Open April-September weekdays 9.30am-6pm, Sundays 2-6pm; closed in winter; 80p HS.

Arbroath Abbey. — Open April-September weekdays 9.30am-6pm, Sundays 2-6pm; October-March weekdays 9.30am-4pm, Sundays 2-4pm; 80p HS.

Edzell Castle. — Open April-September weekdays 9.30am-6pm, Sundays 2-6pm; October-March 9.30am-4pm, Sundays 2-4pm; closed Thursday am and Fridays in winter; £1.20 HS.

GLASGOW

Burrell Collection — Open Mondays-Saturdays 10am-5pm (closes 10pm Wednesdays), Sundays 12noon-6pm; closed 25 December and 1 January; ☎ 041 649 7151.

Pollok House. — Open Mondays-Saturdays 10am-5pm (closes 10pm Wednesdays), Sundays 12noon-6pm; closed 25 December and 1 January; ☎ 041 632 0274.

Cathedral. — Open April-September Mondays-Saturdays 9.30am-1pm and 2-7pm (5pm the rest of the year); Sundays 2-5pm (4pm in winter).

People's Palace. — Open weekdays 10am-5pm, Sundays 12noon-6pm; closed 25 December and 1 January; ☎ 041 554 0223.

Hunterian Museum. — Open Mondays-Fridays 9.30am-5pm, Saturdays 9.30am-1pm; closed certain public holidays; ☎ 041 330 4221.

Hunterian Art Gallery. — Open Mondays-Fridays 9.30am-5pm, Saturdays 9.30am-1pm; closed local public holidays.

Art Gallery and Museum Kelvingrove. — Open Mondays-Saturdays 10am-5pm, Sundays 12noon-6pm; closed 25 December and 1 January; ☎ 041 357 3929.

Museum of Transport. — Open Mondays-Saturdays 10am-5pm, Sundays 12noon-6pm; closed 1 January and 25 December; ☎ 041 357 3929.

City Chambers. — Guided tours (45mins) weekdays 10.30-11.15am and 2.30-3.15pm; ☎ 041 227 4017.

Hutchesons' Hall. — Open Mondays-Fridays 9am-5pm; Saturdays 10am-4pm; NTS.

Royal Exchange. — Open Mondays-Saturdays, except Wednesdays, 9.30am-8pm.

Glasgow School of Art. — Open Mondays-Thursdays 9.30am-8pm, Fridays 9.30am-5pm, Saturdays 10am-12noon; holiday Mondays 9.30am-4.30pm; ☎ 041 332 9797; £1.

Tenement House. — Open Easter-October daily 2-5pm last tour 30mins before closing; the rest of the year weekends only 2-4pm; ☎ 041 333 0183; £1.40 NTS.

Excursions

Hill House. — Helensburgh. Open late March-22 December daily 1-5pm (last admission 4.30pm); closed 23 December-27 March; ☎ (0436) 73900; £2.20 NTS.

Bothwell Castle. — Open April-September weekdays 9.30am-6pm, Sundays 2-6pm; October-March weekdays 9.30am-4pm, Sundays 2-4pm; closed Thursday pm and Fridays in winter; 80p HS.

David Livingstone Museum. — Blantyre. Open Mondays-Saturdays 10am-6pm, Sundays 2-6pm; closed 25 December and 1 January; ☎ (0698) 823140; £1.50.

GLASTONBURY ABBEY

Abbey. — Open June-August 9am-6pm; the rest of the year 9.30am-6pm or dusk if earlier; ☎ (0458) 32267; £1.50.

GLEN COE

Glen Coe Centre. — Open late May-early September 9.30am-6.30pm; April-late May and early September-late October 10am-5.30pm; 30p NTS.

Glencoe Folk Museum. — Open mid-May-September Mondays-Saturdays 10am-5.30pm; 60p.

GLOUCESTER

National Waterways Museum. — Open daily 10am-6pm (5pm in winter); closed 25 December; ☎ (0452) 307009; admission charge.

Bishop Hooper's Lodging: Gloucester Folk Museum. — Open Mondays-Saturdays 10am-5pm; July-September also on Sundays 10am-4pm; closed 1 January, Good Friday, 25-26 December; ☎ (0452) 26467.

Excursion

Crickley Hill Country Park. — Open during daylight hours; ☎ (0452) 863170.

GRAMPIAN'S CASTLE COUNTRY

Haddo House. — Open June-August daily 11am-6pm (last tour 5.15pm); April-May and September-October daily 2-6pm; ☎ (065 15) 440; £2.80 NTS.

Fyvie Castle. — Open June-August 11am-6pm (last tour 45 mins before closing); April-May and September 2-6pm; October weekends 2-5pm; ☎ (065 16) 266; £2.80 NTS.

Crathes Castle. — Open late March-October daily 11am-6pm (last tour 5.15pm); castle, gardens, grounds £3.30 NTS.

Craigievar Castle. — Open May-September daily 2-6pm (last tour 5.15pm); £2.80 NTS.

Castle Fraser. — Open July-August daily 11am-6pm (last tour 45 mins before closing); May-June and September 2-6pm; October weekends only 2-5pm; ☎ (03303) 463; £2.80 NTS.

Kildrummy Castle. — Open April-September weekdays 9.30am-6pm; Sundays 2-6pm; weekends only in winter; 80p HS.

Dunnottar Castle. — Open April-October weekdays 9am-6pm, Sundays 2-6pm; November-March Mondays-Fridays 9am-dusk, Sundays 2pm-dusk; ☎ (0569) 62173; £1.

GRANTHAM

Excursions

Belvoir Castle. — Open April-September Tuesdays, Wednesdays, Thursdays and Saturdays 12noon-5.30pm, Sundays 11am-6pm; ☎ (0476) 870262; £3.

Belton House. — Open April-October Wednesdays-Sundays 1-5.30pm (last admission 5pm); gardens 11am-5.30pm; £3.50 NT.

GREAT GLEN

Urquhart Castle. — Open April-September weekdays 9.30am-6pm; Sundays 9.30am-6pm; October-March 9.30am-4pm, Sundays 2-4pm; £1.20 HS.

Official Loch Ness Monster Exhibition. — Drumnadrochit. Open July-September 9am-9.30pm; June, September-October 9.30am-8pm; November-Easter 10am-4pm; Easter-May 9.30am-5.30pm; £2.85.

H

HADDINGTON

St Mary's Church. — Open Easter-September weekdays 10am-4pm, Sundays 1-4pm; brass rubbing centre: July-September Thursdays, Fridays, Saturdays, Mondays 1-4pm, April-July Saturdays 1-4pm.

Excursions

Tantallon Castle. — Open April-September weekdays 9.30am-6pm, Sundays 2-6pm; October-March weekdays 9.30am-4pm, Sundays 2-4pm; closed Thursday pm and Fridays in winter; £1.20 HS.

Lennoxlove. — Guided tours May-September Wednesdays and weekends 2-5pm; ☎ (062 082) 3720; £2.

HADRIAN'S WALL

Corstopitum (Corbridge Roman Site). — Open April-September daily 10am-6pm; October-March Tuesdays-Sundays 10am-4pm; closed 24-26 December, 1 January; £1.40 EH.

Chesters. — Open April-September daily 10am-6pm; October-March 10am-4pm; ☎ (0434) 681379; £1.60 EH.

Housesteads. — Open Easter-September daily 10am-6pm; October-Easter 10am-4pm; closed 24-26 December, 1 January; ☎ (0434) 344363; £1.60.

Vindolanda. — Open July-August 10am-6.30pm; May-June 10am-6pm; April, September, 10am-5.30pm; March and October 10am-5pm; November and February 10am-4pm; ☎ (06977) 47485; £2.50.

Roman Army Museum. — Open July-August 10am-6.30pm; May-June 10am-6pm; April, September 10am-5.30pm; March and October 10am-5pm; November and February 10am-4pm; ☎ (06977) 47485; £2.

Birdoswald. — Open Easter-October daily 9.30am-5.30pm; during the rest of the year phone ☎ (06977) 47602; £1.50, concessionary rate for EH members.

HARLECH CASTLE

Castle. Open late March-late October daily 9.30am-6.30pm; late October-late March Mondays-Saturdays 9.30am-4pm, Sundays 2-4pm; ☎ (0766) 780552; £2 Cadw.

Excursions

Portmeirion. — Open March-October daily 9.30am-5.30pm; October-mid January 10am-5pm; ☎ (0766) 770228; £2.40.

Criccieth Castle. — Open late March-late October daily 9.30am-6.30pm; late October-late March Mondays-Saturdays 9.30am-4pm, Sundays 2-4pm; closed 24-26 December; ☎ (0766) 522227; £1.75. Cadw.

Llanystumdwy. — **Lloyd George Museum and Highgate:** open Easter-September daily 10am-5pm; ☎ (0286) 679098; £2.

HARROGATE

Royal Pump Room and Royal Baths Assembly Rooms. — Open weekdays 10am-5pm, Sundays in summer only 2-5pm; closed 25-26 December and 1 January; ☎ (0423) 503340; £1.10.

Excursions

Harewood House. — Open late March-October daily 10am-5.30pm; November, February and early March Bird Gardens and grounds only 10am-3pm; ☎ (0532) 886225; from £2-£5.

Castle Keep. — Knaresborough. Open Easter weekend then May-September 10am-5pm; closed the rest of the year; 50p.

Harlow Carr Botanical Gardens. — Open daily 9am-dusk; ☎ (0423) 565418; £2.50.

HATFIELD HOUSE

House. — Open late March-mid October weekdays (guided tours only: 1 hour) 12noon-4.15pm, Sundays 1.30-5pm; bank holiday Mondays 11am-5pm; closed Mondays and Good Friday; ☎ (0707) 262823; £3.90; gardens late March-mid October daily 11am-6pm; £2.15.

HEREFORD

Bulmer Railway Centre. — Open Easter-September weekends and bank holidays only 2-5pm; 50p (£1.50 if engine(s) in steam).

Cider Museum. — Open April-October daily 10am-5.30pm; November-March Mondays-Saturdays 1-5pm; closed 25 December and 1 January; ☎ (0432) 354207; £1.50.

HEVER CASTLE

Castle. — Open mid March- early November daily 12noon-6pm (last admission 5pm); gardens 11am-6pm; ☎ (0732) 865224; £4.40.

HEXHAM

Abbey. — Open May-September 9am-7pm; October-May 9am-5pm; donations welcome.

I

INVERARAY CASTLE

Castle. — Open July-August weekdays 10am-6pm, Sundays 1-6pm; early April, June, September-mid October weekdays except Fridays 10am-1pm and 2-6pm, Sundays 1-6pm; last admissions 12.30pm and 5.30pm; ☎ (0499) 2203; £2.50.

Excursion

Auchindrain. — Open June-August daily 10am-5pm; April, May, September daily except Saturdays 10am-5pm; ☎ (0499) 5235; £2.

INVERNESS

Museum and Art Gallery. — Open Mondays-Saturdays 9am-5pm, Sundays in July and August 2-5pm; ☎ (0463) 237114.

St Andrew's Cathedral. — Open weekdays 7.45am-9.30pm; October-April 7.45am-6.30pm.

Excursions

Cawdor Castle. — Open May-early October daily 10am-5.30pm (last admission 5pm); ☎ (06677) 615; £3.20.

Fort George. — Open April-September 9.30am-6pm, Sundays 2-6pm; October-March weekdays 9.30am-4pm, Sundays 2-4pm; £1.75 HS. The regimental Museum: April-September 10am-6pm, Sundays 2-6pm; October-March weekdays only 10am-4pm.

Culloden Visitor Centre. — Open late May-mid September daily 9am-6.30pm; April-late May, mid September-October 9.30am-5.30pm; November, December, February-March 10am-4pm; ☎ (0463) 790607; £1.50 NTS.

IONA

Infirmary Museum. — Open all the year 9am-5pm; ☎ (06817) 404; donation welcome.

IPSWICH

Christchurch Mansion. — Open weekdays 10am-5pm, Sundays 2.30-4.30pm; closed 24-26 December; ☎ (0473) 213761.

Ancient House. — Bookshop open normal trading hours: Mondays-Saturdays 9am-5pm.

IRONBRIDGE GORGE MUSEUM

Museum sites. — Open daily in summer 10am-5pm; some sites close from November-mid February; for further details contact ☎ (0952) 433522 or 432166; passport ticket giving admittance to all museum sites: £6.95. During the peak summer months there is a park and ride bus service which operates between the various museum sites, with the exception of the Jackfield Tile Museum.

J

JEDBURGH

Jedburgh Abbey. — Open April-September weekdays 9.30am-6pm, Sundays 2-6pm; October-March weekdays 9.30am-4pm, Sundays 2-4pm; £1.50 HS.

Mary Queen of Scots House. — Open Easter-mid November daily 10am-5pm; ☎ (0835) 63331; £1.

Castle and Jail. — Open Easter-September weekdays 10am-5pm, Sundays 1-5pm; ☎ (0835) 63254; 60p.

Excursions

Bowhill. — Open July daily 1-4.30pm; ☎ (0750) 20732; admission charge.

Hermitage Castle. — Open April-September weekdays 10am-6pm, Sundays 2-6pm; October-March Saturdays 9.30am-4pm, Sundays 2-4pm; 80p HS.

K

KING'S LYNN

Excursions

Houghton Hall. — Open Easter Sunday-last Sunday in September Thursdays, Sundays and bank holidays 1-5pm; ☎ (048522) 569; £3.

Oxburgh Hall. — Open March-September daily 1.30-5.30pm; October weekends only 1.30-5.30pm; ☎ (036 621) 258; £3.30 NT.

Holkham Hall. — Open late May-September Sundays-Thursdays 1.30-5pm, Sundays and bank holiday Mondays 11.30am-5pm; ☎ (0328) 710227; £2.

Sandringham House. — Open late April-September Mondays-Thursdays 11am-4.45pm, Sundays 12noon-4.45pm; house, grounds and museum: £2.20; the house is closed when a member of the royal family is in residence; ☎ (0553) 772675.

Castle Rising. — Open April-September daily 10am-6pm; October-March Tuesdays-Sundays 10am-4pm; 85p EH.

Castle Acre Castle. — Open any reasonable time. **Castle Acre Priory:** open April-September daily 10am-6pm; October-March Tuesdays-Sundays 10am-4pm; closed 24-26 December and 1 January; £1.15 EH.

St Clement's Church. — Terrington. Key available at all reasonable times, for keykeeper see church noticeboard.

St Peter's Church. — Walpole St Peter. Open daily 9.30am-4pm; voluntary donation.

St Mary's Church. — West Walton. Keykeepers indicated on noticeboard outside the church.

All Saint's Church. — Walsoken. Key from the rectory.

L

LAKE DISTRICT

Boat trips on Lake Windermere. — Three boats sail continuously calling in at Lakeside pier, Bowness pier and Ambleside pier; full lake cruise: 3 hours; March-November 16 sailings daily out of Bowness and 8 daily from the other two piers; ☎ (05395) 31188; full lake cruise: £6.75, single journey: £2.35.

Ferry across Lake Windermere. — Time: 5 minutes; sailings every 20 minutes; car: £1 single fare, cyclist: 20p, foot passengers: 10p.

Hill Top. — Hawkshead. Open late March-early November Mondays-Wednesdays and weekends 11am-5pm (last admission 4.30pm); closed Thursdays and Fridays; £2.90 NT. The cottage is so small that numbers of visitors may have to be limited at peak times. The Beatrix Potter Gallery in the main street of Hawkshead has an exhibition on her work as an author, artist and farmer in the area with a selection of her watercolours.

Brantwood. — Open mid March-mid November daily 11am-5.30pm; mid November-mid March 11am-4pm; ☎ (05394) 41396; £2.40, grounds only 50p, family ticket available.

Ruskin Museum. — Coniston. Open Easter-October daily 10am-5.30pm; 50p.

Dove Cottage and Museum. — Open daily 9.30am-5.30pm (last admission 5pm); closed mid January-mid February; ☎ (09665) 544; £3.50, museum only £1.90, family ticket available.

Rydal Mount. — Open March-November daily 9.30am-5pm; November-March 10am-4pm; closed Tuesdays; ☎ (05394) 33002; £2.

Brockhole National Park Visitor Centre. — Open late March-early November daily 10am-5pm (10pm July and August); closed the rest of the year; ☎ (09662) 6601; £1.90.

Pencil Museum. — Keswick. Open daily 9.30am-4pm; closed 25-26 December, 1 January; ☎ (07687) 73626; £1.

Museum of Lakeland Life. — Kendal. Open late May mid-November daily 10.30am-5pm, Sundays 2-5pm; winter Mondays-Fridays 11am-4pm, weekends 2-5pm; closed 25-26 December, 1 January; ☎ (0539) 722464; £1.50.

Levens Hall. — Open Easter-September daily 11am-5pm, last admission 4.30pm; ☎ (05395) 60321; £3.25.

Cartmel Priory Gatehouse. — Open summer daily 9am-5.30pm; winter 9am-3.30pm; donation welcome NT.

Furness Abbey. — Open April-September daily 10am-6pm; October-March Tuesdays-Sundays 10am-4pm; closed 24-26 December, 1 January; £1.40 EH.

LANCASTER

Castle. — Open Easter-September daily 10.30am-4pm; subject to court requirements check in advance ☎ (0524) 64998; 80p.

Priory Church. — Open weekdays 9.30am-6pm (5.30pm in winter), Sundays 12noon-6pm.

Maritime Museum. — Open Easter-October daily 11am-5pm; November-Easter 2-5pm; ☎ (0524) 64637; 75p.

LEEDS

City Art Gallery. — Open Mondays-Saturdays 10am-6pm (closes Wednesdays 9pm; Saturdays 4pm), Sundays 2-5pm; closed 25-26 December and 1 January; ☎ (0532) 462495. **Henry Moore Centre for the Study of Sculpture** open Mondays-Fridays 10am-4.30pm; ☎ (0532) 462451.

St John's Church. — Open Mondays, Tuesdays, Thursdays, Fridays and Saturdays 11am-12noon.

Kirkstall Abbey. — Open April-September Mondays-Saturdays 10am-6pm, Sundays 2-6pm (closes 5pm in winter); closed 25-26 December and 1 January; 90p.

Excursions

Temple Newsam. — Open Tuesdays-Sundays 10.30am-4.15pm (dusk in winter); ☎ (0532) 647321; 90p.

Nostell Priory. — Open July and August weekdays except Fridays 12noon-5pm, Sundays 11am-5pm; April-June, September and October Saturdays 12noon-5pm, Sundays 11am-5pm; closed public holidays; ☎ (0924) 863892; £3 NT.

LEICESTER

Jewry Wall and Archaelogy Museum. — Open weekdays 10am-5.30pm, Sundays 2-5.30pm; closed Good Friday, 25-26 December; ☎ (0533) 541333.

Guildhall. — Open weekdays 10am-5.30pm, Sundays 2-5.30pm; closed Good Friday, 25-26 December; ☎ (0533) 532569.

St Mary de Castro Church. — Open Easter-October Saturdays and bank holidays 2-5pm.

Trinity Hospital. — Chapel view by appointment only.

Newarke Houses Museum. — Open Mondays-Saturdays 10am-5.30pm, Sundays 2-5.30pm; closed Good Friday, 25-26 December; ☎ (0533) 554100.

Museum and Art Gallery. — Open Mondays-Saturdays 10am-5pm, Sundays 2-5.30pm; closed 25-26 December, Good Friday; ☎ (0533) 554100.

LEWES

Castle. — Open weekdays 10am-5.30pm, Sundays 11am-5.30pm; ☎ (0273) 474379; £2.50.

Lewes Living History Model. — Open April-mid September weekdays 10am-5pm, Sundays 11am-5pm; ☎ (0273) 474379; £2.50.

Anne of Cleves House. — Open April-October Mondays-Fridays 10am-5.30pm, Sundays 2-5.30pm; ☎ (0273) 474610; £1.50.

Excursions

Sheffield Park Garden. — Open April-mid November Tuesdays-Saturdays 11am-6pm, Sundays and bank holiday Mondays 2-6pm (last admission 1 hour before closing); closed Good Friday and Tuesdays after bank holiday Mondays; ☎ (0825) 790655; £3.60-£3.10 according to the season NT.

Bluebell Railway. — Trains operate June-September daily 10am-6pm; March-May and October-December weekends only 10am-6pm; January-February Sundays only 11am-5pm; closed Christmas Day; times may vary, confirm in advance ☎ (082 572) 2370; train fare £3.50 admission to premises £1.

LEWIS and HARRIS

Arnol Black House. — Open April-September Mondays-Saturdays 9am-6pm; October-March 9am-4pm; closed Sundays; 80p.

LICHFIELD

Dr Johnson's Birthplace. — Open daily 10am-5pm; closed Christmas and 1 January; 75p.

Cathedral. — Open daily 7.45am-6.30pm (4.30pm Sundays in winter); suggested donation £1.

LINCOLN

Cathedral. — Open 7.15am-8pm (6pm in winter); donation requested.

Castle. — Open weekdays 9.30am-5.30pm, Sundays 11am-5.30pm (closes 4pm in winter) last admission 1/2 hour before closing; ☎ (0522) 511068; 50p.

Usher Gallery. — Open weekdays 10am-5.30pm, Sundays 2.30-5pm; closed 25 December and 1 January; ☎ (0522) 527980; 30p.

Greyfriars (City Museum). — Open weekdays 10am-5.30pm, Sundays 2.30-5pm; 50p.

Excursions

Doddington Hall. — Open May-September Wednesdays and Sundays daily 2-6pm; ☎ (0522) 694308; £3.

Gainsborough Old Hall. — Open Mondays-Saturdays 10am-5pm, Sundays 2-5pm in summer only; closed 1 January, Good Friday, 25-26 December; ☎ (0427) 612669; £1.

LIVERPOOL

Merseyside Maritime Museum. — Open daily 10.30am-5.30pm; closed 1 January, Good Friday, 24-26 December; the maritime park and piermaster's house are closed from April-November; ☎ (051) 207 0001; £1.50.

Tate Gallery Liverpool. — Open April-September Tuesdays-Sundays 11am-7pm; October-March Tuesdays-Fridays 11am-5pm, Sundays 11am-6pm; closed 1 January, Good Friday, May Day, 24-26 December; ☎ (051) 709 3223.

The Beatles Story. — Open daily 10am-6pm; closed Christmas Day; ☎ 051 709 1963; £3.

Walker Art Gallery. — Open weekdays 10am-5pm, Sundays 2-5pm; closed 1 January, Good Friday, 24-26 December; ☎ (051) 207 0001.

Bluecoat Chambers. — Open Mondays-Saturdays, gallery Tuesdays-Saturdays; ☎ (051) 709 5297.

Excursions

Speke Hall. — Open April-October daily except Mondays 1-5.30pm; November-mid December weekends only 1-4.30pm; closed Good Friday, 24-26 December; ☎ (051) 427 7231; £2.50 NT.

Lady Lever Art Gallery. — Port Sunlight. Open weekdays 10am-5pm, Sundays 2-5pm; closed 1 January, Good Friday, 24-26 December; ☎ (051) 645 3623; voluntary donation.

Boat Museum. — Ellesmere Port. Open April-October weekdays 10am-5pm; November-March 11am-4pm; closed 24-26 December; ☎ (051) 355 5017; £3.60.

Ness Gardens. — Open March-October daily 9.30am-dusk; November-February 9.30am-4pm; closed 25 December; ☎ (051) 336 2135; £2.50.

Pilkington Glass Museum. — St Helens. Open Mondays-Saturdays 10am-5pm, Saturdays 2-4.30pm; closed Christmas to New Year; ☎ (0744) 692014.

Knowsley Safari Park. — Open March-October daily 10am-4pm; closed the rest of the year; ☎ (051) 430 9009; £7 per car including all passengers.

Wigan Pier. — Open daily 10am-5pm; closed 25-26 December; ☎ (0942) 323666; £5.

LLANDUDNO

Excursion

Rhuddlan Castle. — Closed temporarily. Cadw.

LLANGOLLEN

Plas Newydd. — Open May-September 10am-7pm, October 10am-5pm; ☎ (0978) 861514; £1.

Excursions

Valle Crucis Abbey. — Open late March-late October daily 9.30am-6.30pm; late October-late March Mondays-Fridays 9.30am-4pm, Sundays 2-4pm; ☎ (0978) 860326; £1.25 Cadw.

St Giles Church. — Wrexham. Open April-September Mondays-Fridays 10am-4pm.

Erddig. — Open April-mid October Saturdays-Wednesdays 12am-5pm (last admission 4pm); grounds 11am-6pm; closed Thursdays and Fridays; ☎ (0978) 355314; £4 NT.

Chirk Castle. — Open late March-September daily except Mondays and Saturdays 12noon-5pm; October-early November weekends only 12noon-5pm; ☎ (0691) 777701; £3 NT.

LONDON

Tower of London. — Open March-October weekdays 9.30am-6pm, Sundays 2-6pm; November-February weekdays only 9.30am-5pm (last admission 1 hour before closing); closed 1 January, Good Friday, 24-26 December; ☎ (071 709) 0765 ext 235; £5.50.

Tower Bridge. — Open April-October daily 10am-6.30pm; November-March 10am-4.45pm (last admission 45mins before closing time); closed 1 January, Good Friday, 24-26 December; ☎ (071 407) 0922; £2.50.

St Paul's Cathedral. — Open daily 7.30am-6pm; entrance restricted during special services; access to ambulatory, crypt and galleries £1; guided tours available ☎ (071 248) 2705.

St-Martin-in-the-Fields. — Open daily 8am-8pm; Mondays, Tuesdays and Fridays lunchtime concerts.

National Gallery. — Open weekdays 10am-6pm, Sundays 2-6pm; closed 1 January, Good Friday, May Day, 24-26 December; ☎ (071 839) 3526.

Banqueting House. — Open Mondays-Saturdays 10am-5pm; closed English bank holidays also subject to closure at short notice for Government functions; ☎ (071 839) 3787; £2 Historic Royal Palaces.

Palace of Westminster. — Access restricted; tours on application to a Member of Parliament only.

Westminster Abbey. — Open daily 8am-6pm; choir, transepts and royal chapels Mondays-Fridays 9am-4.45pm, Saturdays 9am-2.45pm and 3.45-5.45pm (last admissions 3/4 hour before closing time); royal chapels £2.60; for guided tours ☎ (071 222) 5152.

Buckingham Palace. — Not open to the public.

Queen's Gallery. — Open Tuesdays-Saturdays 10.30am-5pm, Sundays 2-5pm; closed Easter and Christmas; ☎ (071 799) 2331; £2.

Victoria and Albert Museum. — Open weekdays 10am-5pm, Sundays 2.30-5.50pm; closed August bank holiday and Christmas; ☎ (071 938) 8500; suggested donation £3.

Science Museum. — Open Mondays-Saturdays 10am-6pm; Sundays 11am-6pm; closed 1 January, 24-26 December; ☎ (071 938) 8000; £2.50.

Natural History Museum. — Open weekdays 10am-6pm, Sundays 1-6pm; ☎ (071 938) 9123; £3.

Kensington Palace. — Open weekdays 9am-5pm, Sundays 1-5pm (last admission 4.15pm); closed 1 January, Good Friday, 24-26 December; £3.50 Historic Royal Palaces.

Tate Gallery. — Open weekdays 10am-5.50pm, Sundays 2-5.50pm; closed 1 January, Good Friday, May Day bank holiday, 24-26 December; ☎ (071 821) 1313.

Boat trips. — There are regular services all the year round from Westminster down river to the Tower (20mins), Greenwich (45mins) and the Thames Barrier (1 1/4 hours) and from April-October up river to Kew (1 1/2 hours), Richmond (2 1/2 hours) and Hampton Court (3 hours 45 mins); ☎ (071 730) 4812.

Royal Naval College, Greenwich. — Open daily 2.30-5pm (last admission 4.30pm); closed Thursdays.

National Maritime Museum. — Open April-September Mondays-Saturdays 10am-6pm, Sundays 2-6pm; closes 5pm October-March; closed 1 January, Good Friday, 23-25 December; ☎ (081 858) 4422; £2.90 passport ticket £4.90.

Queen's House and Old Royal Observatory. — Same times and charges as for the National Maritime Museum above.

Cutty Sark. — Open Easter-October weekdays 10am-6pm, Sundays 12noon-6pm; November-Easter closes at 5pm; closed 24-26 December; ☎ (081 858) 3445; £2.50.

Hampton Court. — Open mid March-mid October daily 9.30am-6pm; mid October-mid March 9.30am-4.30pm; closed 1 January, 23-26 December; ☎ (081 977) 8441; £4.50, family ticket £13.50.

Ham House. — Open April-September daily except Mondays 11am-5pm; ☎ (081 940) 1950; £2 NT.

Carlyle's House, Chelsea. — Open April-October Wednesdays-Sundays 11am-5pm (last admission 4.30pm); ☎ (071 352) 7087; £2.20 NT.

Chelsea Old Church. — Open May-September 9.30am-1pm and 2-5pm; closes the rest of the year 4.30pm.

National Army Museum. — Open Mondays-Saturdays 10am-5.30pm, Sundays 2-5.30pm; closed 24-26 December, 1 January, Good Friday; ☎ (071) 730 0717.

The Royal Hospital. — Open weekdays 10am-12noon and 2-6pm, Sundays 2-4pm.

Percival David Foundation of Chinese Art. — Bloomsbury. Open weekdays 10.30am-5pm; closed Easter, Christmas-New Year inclusive and bank holidays; ☎ (071 387) 3909; voluntary donation.

Sir John Soane's Museum. — Open Tuesdays-Saturdays 10am-5pm; closed bank holidays.

Lincoln's Inn. — Open March-September Mondays-Fridays 9.30-11.30am; £2.

Old Curiosity Shop. — Open April-October 9am-5.30pm, Sundays 9.30am-5pm; the rest of the year closes 5pm on weekdays and 4pm on Sundays; closed Good Friday and 25 December; ☎ (071 405) 9891.

Burlington House. — Open daily 10am-6pm; closed Good Friday and 24-26 December; ☎ (071 439) 4996/4997; admission charge varies according to exhibition.

Royal Academy. — Burlington House. Open daily 10am-6pm; ☎ (071 439) 4996; £1-£5 according to the exhibition.

Southwark Cathedral. — Open Mondays, Wednesdays and Fridays; 12.30-4pm; £1.

British Museum. — Open weekdays 10am-5pm, Sundays 2.30-6pm; closed 1 January, Good Friday, first Monday in May, 24-26 December; ☎ (071 580) 1788.

Wallace Collection. — Open Mondays-Saturdays 10am-5pm, Sundays 2-5pm; closed 1 January, May Day, 24-26 December; ☎ (071 935) 0687.

Courtauld Institute Galleries. — Open Mondays-Saturdays 10am-6pm (late opening 8pm Tuesdays), Sundays 2-6pm; closed 1 January, Easter weekend, 25-26 December, Monday bank holidays; ☎ (071 873) 2526; £2.50.

Museum of London. — Open Tuesdays-Saturdays 10am-6pm, Sundays 2-6pm; closed Mondays except bank holiday Mondays, 1 January, 24-26 December.

Imperial War Museum. — Open daily 10am-6pm; closed 1 January, 24-26 December; ☎ (071 820) 1683; £3, free on Fridays.

Royal Botanic Gardens, Kew. — Open daily from 9.30am; closed 25 December; ☎ (081 940) 1171; £3.

Kew Palace. — Open April-September daily 11am-5.30pm; ☎ (081 940) 3321; £1.

Syon Park. — Open April-October daily 9.30am-5.30pm; closed 25-26 December; ☎ (081 560) 0881; house and gardens £3.75; house only £2.50; gardens only £1.50.

Osterley Park. — Open Wednesdays-Fridays 1-5pm, weekends 11am-5pm; March weekends 11am-5pm; closed Good Friday, May Day, 24-25 December; ☎ (081 560) 3918; £2.50 NT.

Chiswick House. — Open Good Friday-September daily 10am-6pm; October-Maundy Thursday daily 10am-4pm; closed 24-25 December; ☎ (081 995) 0508.

Kenwood House. — Open April-September weekdays 10am-6pm; October-March 10am-4pm; closed 24-26 December; ☎ (081) 348 1286.

Fenton House. — Open April-October Saturdays-Wednesdays 11am-6pm (last admission 5pm); March weekends only 2-6pm; ☎ (071 435) 3471; £2.80 NT.

Dulwich Picture Gallery. — Open Tuesdays-Fridays 10am-1pm and 2-5pm, Saturdays 11am-5pm, Sundays 2-5pm; closed Mondays and bank holidays; ☎ (081 693) 8000; £1.50.

London Zoo. — Open March-October weekdays 9am-6pm, Sundays 9am-7pm; November-February daily 10am-dusk; ☎ (071 723) 3333; adults £5.20 children £3.20.

LONGLEAT

House. — Open Easter-September daily 10am-6pm; October-Easter 10am-4pm; closed 25 December; ☎ (09853) 551; £3.50. **Narrow Gauge Railway:** early March-early November daily 11am-6pm; £1. **Safari Park:** early March-October 10am-6pm; ☎ (09853) 328; £4.50.

LUDLOW

Castle. — Open May-September daily 10.30am-5pm; October-November and February-April daily 10.30am-4pm; £1.50.

Excursions

Stokesay Castle. — Open April-September daily 10am-6pm; March and October 10am-5pm; November weekends only 10am-dusk; closed Tuesdays and December-February; ☎ (0588) 672544; £1.50 EH.

Croft Castle. — Open May-September daily 2-6pm; April and October 2-5pm; ☎ (056 885) 246; £2.40 NT.

Berrington Hall. — Open May-September Wednesdays-Sundays 1.30-5.30pm; April 12.30-5.30pm; October 12.30-4.30pm; closed the rest of the year; ☎ (0568) 615721; £2.70 NT.

M

MALMESBURY

Abbey. — Open daily April-September 10am-6pm; October 10am-5pm; November-March 10am-4pm.

MAN, ISLE OF

Manx Museum. — Open weekdays 10am-5pm; closed 25-26 December, 1 January; ☎ (0624) 675522.

Castletown Castle. — Open Easter-September weekdays 10am-5pm, Sundays 2-5pm; ☎ (0624) 675522; £1.

Nautical Museum. — Castletown. Open Easter-September weekdays 10am-5pm, Sundays 2-5pm; ☎ (0624) 675522; £1.

Cregneash Folk Museum. — Open Easter-September Mondays-Saturdays 10am-5pm, Sundays 2-5pm; ☎ (0624) 675522; £1.50.

MANCHESTER

Museum of Science and Industry. — Open daily 10am-5pm (last admission 4.30pm); closed 23-25 December; ☎ (061 832) 2244; £2.50.

Granada Studios Tour. — Open late March-late September Tuesdays-Sundays grounds: 9.45am-7pm (11.30pm Wednesdays), first tour 10am, last tour 4pm (9pm Wednesdays); late September-late March Wednesdays-Sundays grounds: 9.45am-5.30pm (6.30pm weekends), first tour 10am, last tour 3pm (4pm weekends); ☎ (061 832) 9090; £7.95.

St Ann's Church. — Open daily 9am-5pm; closed bank holidays and Sunday afternoons.

City Art Gallery. — Open Mondays-Saturdays 10am-5.45pm, Sundays 2-5.45pm; closed 1 January, May Day, 24-26 December; ☎ (061 236) 5244.

Lowry Centre. — Salford Museum. Open Mondays-Fridays 10am-4.45pm, Sundays 2-5pm; closed Saturdays, 1 January, Good Friday, 25-26 December; ☎ (061 736) 2649.

Ordsall Hall. — Open Mondays-Fridays 10am-12.30pm and 1.30-5pm, Sundays 2-5pm; closed 1 January, Good Friday, 25-26 December; ☎ (061 872) 0251.

Jewish Museum. — Open Mondays-Thursdays 10.30am-4pm, Sundays 10.30am-5pm; closed Fridays, Saturdays and Jewish holidays; ☎ (061 834) 9879; £1.50.

MELLERSTAIN

House. — Open May-September daily except Saturdays 12.30-5pm (last admission 4.30pm); ☎ (057 381) 225; £3.

MONTACUTE HOUSE

House. — Open April-October Wednesdays-Mondays daily 12noon-5.30pm (last admission 5pm); closed Tuesdays, Good Friday; ☎ (0935) 823289; £4 NT.

MULL, ISLE OF

Torosay Castle. — Open May-mid October daily 10.30am-5pm; mid October-April gardens only during daylight hours; ☎ (06802) 421; £3.

Duart Castle. — Open May-September daily 10.30am-6pm; ☎ (068 02) 309; £2.

Access to Staffa. — Open all the year; landing fee NTS.

Access to Isle of Mull. — Ferry service from Oban.

N

NEWCASTLE UPON TYNE

Castle Keep. — Open April-September Tuesdays-Sundays 9.30am-5pm; October-March Tuesdays-Sundays 9.30am-4pm; closed Mondays except bank holiday Mondays; £1.

Laing Art Gallery and Museum. — Open Tuesdays-Fridays 10.30am-5.30pm, Saturdays 10.30am-4.30pm, Sundays 2.30-5.30pm; closed Mondays and some public holidays; ☎ (091) 232 7734; £1.

Excursions

Beamish, North of England Open-Air Museum. — Open April-October daily 10am-6pm (last admission 4pm); November-March daily except Mondays 10am-5pm (last admission 4pm); closed for one week prior to 25 December and 30 December-1 January; ☎ (0207) 231811; mid July-August: £6; rest of summer £5, November-March: £3.

Seaton Delaval Hall. — Open May-September Wednesdays and Sundays 2-6pm; ☎ (091) 237 3040; £1.

Wallington House. — Open April-October Wednesdays-Mondays 1-5.30pm (last admission 5pm); closed Tuesdays; ☎ (0670) 74283; £3 NT.

Washington Old Hall. — Open April-October 11am-5pm (last admission 4.30pm); closed Fridays; ☎ (091) 416 6879; £1.50 NT.

NEW FOREST

Furzey Gardens. — Minstead. Open daily 10am-5pm (4pm in winter); closed 25-26 December; £1.95.

New Forest Butterfly Farm. — Open late March-late October daily 10am-5pm; ☎ (0703) 293367; £3.

NORTHAMPTON

Guildhall. — Closed during building work.

Excursions

All Saints, Brixworth. — Open summer 10am-6pm; winter 11am-4pm; donation welcome.

All Saints, Earls Barton. — Open daily 9am-5pm.

Boughton House. — Open late July-August daily 2-5pm; ☎ (0536) 515731; £3.

Sulgrave Manor. — Guided tours (1 1/2 hours) April-September daily 10.30am-5.30pm; March, October-December daily 10.30am-4pm; February open by appointment only; closed 25-26 December; ☎ (0295) 76 205; £2.50.

NORTH YORK MOORS

Ryedale Folk Museum. — Open late March-late October daily 10.30am-5.30pm (last admission 4.45pm); ☎ (07515) 367; £2.

Pickering Castle. — Open April-September daily 10am-6pm; October-March Tuesdays-Sundays 10am-4pm; closed 24-26 December and 2 January; 85p EH.

North Yorkshire Moors Railway. — Open Easter-October daily 10am-6pm; ☎ (0751) 73535; Rtn £4.80.

Helmsley Castle. — Open April-September daily 10am-6pm; October-March Tuesdays-Sundays 10am-4pm; closed 24-26 December and 2 January; £1.15 EH.

Rievaulx Abbey. — Open April-September daily 10am-6pm; October-March Tuesdays-Sundays 10am-4pm; closed 24-26 December and 2 January; £1.40 EH.

NORWICH

Castle: Museum and Art Gallery. — Open Mondays-Saturdays 10am-5pm, Sundays 2-5pm; closed Good Friday; ☎ (0603) 223624; summer £1, winter 50p.

Sainsbury Centre for Visual Arts. — Open Tuesdays-Sundays; ☎ (0603) 592470; 50p.

Excursion

Blickling Hall. — Open April-October Tuesdays, Wednesdays, Fridays-Sundays 1-5pm; gardens 12noon-5pm; closed Good Friday; ☎ (0263) 733084; £4.50 NT.

NOTTINGHAM

Castle Museum. — Open April-September daily 10am-5.45pm (4.45pm the rest of the year); ☎ (0602) 483504; free weekdays, Sundays and bank holidays; 40p.

Museum of Costume and Textiles. — Open daily 10am-5pm; closed 25 December; ☎ (0602) 483504.

Lace Hall. — Open daily 10am-5.30pm (5pm in winter) last admission 1 hour before closing; closed 25-26 December; ☎ (0602) 484221; exhibitions £1.50.

Excursions

Wollaton Hall. — Open April-September weekdays 10am-7pm, Sundays 2-5pm; October-March weekdays 10am-dusk, Sundays 1.30-4.30pm; closed 25 December; free weekdays 40p, Sundays and holidays.

Newstead Abbey. — Open Good Friday-September 11.30am-6pm (last admission 5pm); grounds open all year round dawn-dusk; ☎ (0623) 793557; house £2, grounds £1.20.

Sherwood Forest Visitor Centre. — Open April-October daily 10.30am-5pm; October-March 10.30am-4.30pm; ☎ (0623) 823202. Country Park open during daylight hours.

O

OBAN

Excursions

Kilchurn Castle. — Open site HS.

Sea Life Centre. — Open July-August daily 9am-7pm; mid February-June and September-late November daily 9am-6pm; ☎ (0631) 72386; £3.50.

ORKNEY ISLANDS

Kirkwall

St Magnus Cathedral. — Open 9am-1pm and 2-5pm; closed Sundays and holidays.

Earl's Palace and Bishop's Palace. — Open May-September weekdays 9.30am-6pm, Sundays 2-6pm; closed in winter; 80p HS combined ticket with Bishop's Palace.

Tankerness House Museum. — Open April-September weekdays 10.30am-12.30pm and 1.30-5pm, Sundays May-September only 2-5pm; £1.

Excursions

Maes Howe. — Open April-September weekdays 9.30am-6pm, Sundays 9.30am-6pm; October-March weekdays 9.30am-4pm, Sundays 2-4pm; £1.20 HS.

Pier Gallery. — Stromness. Open summer weekdays 10.30am-5pm, Sundays 2-5pm; winter weekdays only 10.30am-5pm; ☎ (0856) 850209.

Museum. — Stromness. Open May-September weekdays 10.30am-5pm; October-April weekdays 10.30am-12.30pm and 1.30-5pm; 40p.

Skara Brae. — Open April-September weekdays 9.30am-6pm, Sundays 9.30am-6pm; October-March weekdays 9.30am-4pm, Sundays 2-4pm; £1.50 HS.

Brough of Birsay. — Open site HS.

OXFORD

Colleges. — Many of the colleges are only open in the afternoon; the exact visiting times are often displayed at the porter's lodge.

Brasenose College. — Open 10am-5pm in summer (4.30pm in winter); closed 25-26 December.

All Souls College. — Not open at present.

Bodleian Library. — Guided tours (1/2 hour) for the Divinity School and Duke Humphrey's Library mid March-October weekdays 10.30am, 11.30am, 2pm and 3pm, Saturdays 10.30am and 11am; the rest of the year Wednesdays and Saturdays only; closed Easter, last week in August, 24 December-1 January; £2.

Sheldonian Theatre. — Open mid February-mid November 10am-12.45pm and 2-4.45pm (3.45pm in winter); closed Sundays and for rehearsals, concerts and university events; 50p.

Exeter College. — Open 2-5pm; closed Easter and Christmas.

Trinity College. — Open daily 2-5pm; closed 27 March-8 April and 9 August-3 September.

Balliol College. — Open daily 10am-6pm; closed 10 days at Christmas and Easter and last two weeks in August and first week in September; ☎ (0865) 277777.

Jesus College. — Open daily 2-4.30pm; closed for one week at Easter and Christmas.

Lincoln College. — Open weekdays 2-5pm, Sundays 11am-5pm; closed 5 days at Christmas and 1 January.

Christ Church. — Chapter house and hall open April-September weekdays 9.30am-6pm, Sundays 12.45-5.30pm; October-March weekdays 9am-5pm, Sundays 1-5pm; hall closed daily from 12noon to 2pm; cathedral weekdays 9am-5pm, Sundays 1-5pm; picture gallery April-September weekdays 10.30am-1pm and 2-5.30pm, Sundays 2-5.30pm (4.30pm the rest of the year); chapter house, cathedral and hall: £1.50; picture gallery: 50p.

Corpus Christi College. — Open all year 2-5pm except Christmas and Easter.

Merton College. — Open Mondays-Saturdays 2-4.30pm (4pm in winter); 30p.

St Edmund Hall. — Open during daylight hours; closed Christmas.

New College. — Open mid March-mid April and July-September 11am-5pm; winter 2-5pm; £1 Easter and Summer.

Hertford College. — Open 2-5pm.

Additional Sights

Ashmolean Museum. — Open Tuesdays-Saturdays 10am-4pm, Sundays 2-4pm; closed certain holidays for confirmation ☎ (0865) 278000.

University Museum. — Open Mondays-Saturdays 12noon-5pm.

Keble College. — Open 10am-5pm (sunset in winter).

Botanic Gardens. — Open 9am-5pm (4.30pm in winter); closed 25 December and Good Friday; ☎ (0865) 276920; £1 July and August, free the rest of the year.

Excursions

Waddesdon Manor. — House closed for refurbishment; grounds and aviary only open late March-late December Wednesdays-Sundays 12noon-5pm; ☎ (0296) 651211; NT.

Claydon House. — Open April-October Saturdays-Wednesdays 1-5pm (last admission 4.30pm); closed all public holidays within the above dates with the exception of Good Friday; ☎ (0296) 730349; £2.80 NT.

P

PEAK DISTRICT

Peak Cavern. — Castleton. Guided tours (40mins) Easter-October 10am-5pm; ☎ (0433) 20285; £2.

Speedwell Cavern. — Guided tours (1 hour) Easter-September 9.30am-5.30pm; October-Easter 9.30am-5pm; ☎ (0433) 20512; £3.75. 105 steps down to boat, not suitable for the disabled.

Blue John Cavern. — Guided tours (45mins-1 hour) February-December daily 9.45am-6pm (dusk in winter); closed 1 January, 25-26 December; ☎ (0433) 20642; £3.60.

Treak Cliff Cavern. — Open daily summer 9.30am-6pm (4pm in winter); closed 25 December; ☎ (50433) 20571; £2.95.

PEMBROKESHIRE COAST

Manorbier Castle. — Open Easter then May-September 10.30am-5.30pm; £1.20.

Pembroke Castle. — Open April-September daily 9.30am-6pm; October-March 10am-4pm; closed Sundays November-February; ☎ (0646) 681510; £1.50.

Picton Castle: The Graham Sutherland Gallery. — Open April-October Tuesdays-Sundays 10.30am-5pm; winter by appointment; ☎ (0437) 751296; £1.

PENZANCE

Maritime Museum. — Open Easter-October Mondays-Saturdays 10am-5pm; ☎ (0736) 62476; £1.50.

Isles of Scilly

Star Castle: St Mary's Museum. — Open April-October Mondays-Saturdays 10am-12noon and 1.50-4.30pm (in addition mid June-September 7.30-9pm); November-March Wednesdays only 2-4pm; 50p.

Tresco Abbey Gardens. — Open daily 10am-4pm; closed 25 December; ☎ (0720) 22849; £2.50.

PERTH

Black Watch Museum. — Open Easter-October Mondays-Fridays 10am-4.30pm; Sundays 2-4.30pm; October-Easter 10am-3.30pm, closed Sundays; ☎ (0738) 71781 ext 8530.

Museum and Art Gallery. — Open daily 10am-5pm.

Excursions

Scone Palace. — Open April-mid October Mondays-Saturdays 9.30am-5pm, Sundays 1.30-5pm (Sundays in July and August 10am-5pm); October-March by appointment only; ☎ (0738) 52300; £3.30.

Dunkeld Cathedral. — Open April-September daily 9.30am-7pm; October-March weekdays 9.30am-4pm, Sundays after Armistice Day 2-4pm; ☎ 03502 249.

Drummond Castle Gardens. — Open May-August daily 2-6pm (last admission 5pm); September Wednesdays and Sundays only 2-6pm; £1.20.

PETERBOROUGH

Cathedral. — Open May-September daily 7am-8pm; October-April daily 7am-6.15pm; Sundays 7.30am-5.30pm; suggested donation £1.

PITLOCHRY

Pitlochry Power Station. — Open April-October daily 9.40am-5.30pm; closed November-March; ☎ (0796) 3152; 50p.

Excursion

Blair Castle. — Open June-September daily 10am-5pm; April-May and October weekdays 10am-5pm, Sundays 2-5pm; ☎ (079 681) 207; £3.30.

PLYMOUTH

Royal Citadel. — Currently under major refurbishment; not open until 1992.

Elizabethan House. — Open April-October weekdays 10am-5.30pm, Sundays 2-5pm; November-March 10am-4.30pm; in January and December it closes between 1-2pm; closed Mondays; ☎ (0752) 264878; 65p.

Coates Plymouth Gin Distillery. — Open Easter-September weekdays 10.30am-4pm; ☎ (0752) 667062; £1.25.

St Andrew's. — Open April-October weekdays 10am-4pm;

Prysten House. — Open April-October Mondays-Saturdays 10am-4pm; 50p.

Merchant's House. — Open April-October Tuesdays-Saturdays 10am-5.30pm, Sundays 2-5pm; November-March weekdays only 10am-5.30pm; ☎ (0752) 264878; 65p.

Excursions

Saltram House. — Open March-September daily except Fridays and Saturdays 12.30pm-6pm; October 12.30pm-5pm; closed Good Friday; ☎ (0752) 336546; £4.40 NT.

Buckland Abbey. — Open late March-September 10.30am-5.30pm, October 10.30am-5.30pm; November-late March weekends only 2-5pm; last admission 45mins before closing time; ☎ (0822) 853607; £3.60 NT.

PORTSMOUTH

HMS Victory. — Open March-October Mondays-Saturdays 10.30am-5.30pm, Sundays 1-5.30pm; November-February weekdays 10.30am-5pm, Sundays 1-5pm; £3.50.

The Mary Rose. — Guided tours (1 1/2 hours) March-October 10am-5.30pm (last admission 1 hour before closing time); November-February 10.30am-5pm; closed 25 December; ☎ (0705) 812931; £3.50.

HMS Warrior. — Open April-October weekdays 10.30am-5.30pm, Sundays 10am-5.30pm; November-April daily 10.30am-5pm; £3.50.

Royal Naval Museum. — Open daily 10.30am-5.30pm (last admission 4.30pm); closed 25 December, 1 January; £1.50, family ticket £4.10.

City Museum and Art Gallery. — Open daily 10.30am-5.30pm; ☎ (0705) 827261; 80p.

Southsea Castle. — Open daily 10.30am-5.30pm; ☎ (0705) 827261; £1.

D-Day Museum. — Open daily 10.30am-5.30pm (last admission 4.30pm); closed 24-26 December; £3 summer, £2.25 October-March.

Royal Marines Museum. — Open Easter-August daily 10am-5.30pm; September-Easter 10am-4.30pm; closed 3 days at Christmas; ☎ (0705) 819385; £2.

Excursion

Portchester Castle. — Open April-September daily 10am-6pm; October-March Tuesdays-Sundays 10am-4pm; closed 24-26 December and 1 January; £1.15 EH.

Times and charges

PRESTON

Harris Museum and Art Gallery. — Open Mondays-Saturdays 10am-5pm; closed Sundays and bank holidays; ☎ (0772) 58248.

Excursions

Samlesbury Hall. — Open mid-January mid-December daily 11.30am-5pm (4pm in winter); £2.

Hoghton Tower. — Guided tours (1 1/2 hours) Easter-October Sundays 2-5pm; Saturdays also in July and August 2-5pm; ☎ (025 85) 2986; £2.50.

R

RICHMOND

Castle. — Open mid March-September weekdays 10am-6pm; October-mid March 10am-1pm and 2-4pm, Sundays 2-4pm; closed Mondays, 24-26 December; ☎ (0748) 2493; £1.30.

Green Howards Regimental Museum. — Open April-October weekdays 9.30am-4.30pm, Sundays 2-4.30pm; March and November 10am-4.30pm; February weekdays only 10am-4.30pm; closed weekends; ☎ (0748) 2133; £1.

Excursion

Bolton Castle. — Open March-November daily 10am-5pm; ☎ (0969) 23981; £2 EH.

RIPON

Cathedral. — Open daily 8am-8pm (6.30pm in winter); suggested donation £1.30.

Excursion

Newby Hall. — Open Easter-September Tuesdays-Sundays 12noon-5pm; gardens 11am-5.30pm; closed Mondays unless a bank holiday; ☎ (0423) 322583; house and gardens: £4.50, gardens only: £2.50.

ROCHESTER

Castle. — Open April-September daily 10am-6pm; October-March except Mondays 10am-4pm; closed 24-26 December and 1 January; ☎ (0634) 402276; £1.30 EH.

Cathedral. — Open daily 7am-6pm ; suggested donation £1.

Guildhall. — Open daily 10am-5.30pm; closed 24-25 December; ☎ (0634) 848717.

Chatham Historic Dockyard. — Open April-October Wednesdays-Sundays 10am-6pm November-March Wednesdays and weekends only 10am-4.30pm; closed 25 December; ☎ (0634) 812551; £4.50, family ticket £10.

Excursion

Leeds Castle. — Open April-October daily 11am-5pm; November-March 11am-4pm; closed 25 December-1 January; ☎ (0622) 765400; £5.50.

ROYAL TUNBRIDGE WELLS

Excursions

Knole. — Open late March-October Wednesdays-Saturdays 11am-5pm (last admission 4pm), Sundays 2-5pm; ☎ (0732) 450608; £3 NT, car park £5.50 includes one admission to the house.

Ightham Mote. — Open April-October Mondays, Wednesdays, Thursdays, Fridays 12noon-5pm; Sundays 11am-5pm; ☎ (0732) 810378; weekdays £3, Sundays £3.50 NT.

Scotney Castle Garden. — Open April-mid November Wednesdays-Fridays 11am-6pm, weekends 2-6pm; closed Good Friday; ☎ (0892) 890651; £2 NT.

Sissinghurst Castle. — Open March-October Tuesdays-Fridays 1-6.30pm, weekends 10am-6.30pm; closed Mondays; ☎ (0580) 712850; weekdays £4, Sundays £4.50 NT.

Penshurst Place. — Open late March-September Tuesdays-Sundays 1-5pm; ☎ (0892) 870307; £3.50.

Chiddingstone Castle. — Open May-September Wednesdays-Sundays 2-5.30pm (Tuesdays mid June-mid September), Sundays 11.30am-5.30pm; Easter-April and October public holidays and weekends only; £3.

Chartwell. — Open April-October Tuesdays, Wednesdays, Thursdays and weekends 12noon-5pm; March and November 11am-5pm; ☎ (0732) 866368; £3.70 NT.

Quebec House. — Westerham. Open April-October daily except Thursdays and Saturdays 2-6pm; ☎ (0959) 62206; £1.70.

RYE

Romney, Hythe and Dymchurch Railway. — Open Easter-September daily; also weekends in March and October; ☎ (0679) 62353.

Rye Town Model. — Open April-October daily 10.30am-5.30pm; ☎ (0797) 226696; £1.50.

Ypres Tower: Rye Museum. — Open Easter-mid October daily 10.30am-5.30pm (last admission 5pm); ☎ (0797) 223254; £1.50.

Excursion

Bodiam Castle. —Open April-October daily 10am-5.30pm; November-March weekdays 10am-5.30pm or sunset, closed Sundays; ☎ (0580) 830436; £1.70 NT.

S

ST ALBANS

Verulamium Museum. — Open March-October weekdays 10am-5.30pm, Sundays 2-5.30pm; November-February 10am-4pm, Sundays 2-4pm; ☎ (0727) 866100 ext 2912; £1.20.

Roman Theatre. — Open April-October daily 10am-5pm; November-March 10am-4pm; £1.

Excursions

Luton Hoo. — Open late March-mid October Tuesdays-Sundays 1.30pm-5.45pm; gardens 12noon-6pm; ☎ (0582) 22955; £3.70.

Knebworth House. — Open late March-September daily 12noon-5pm; closed Mondays except bank holidays, park 11am-5.30pm; ☎ (0438) 812661; £3.50, park and playground only £2.

ST ANDREWS

Cathedral. — Open April-September weekdays 9.30am-6pm, Sundays 9.30am-6pm; October-March weekdays 9.30am-4pm, Sundays 2-4pm; £1 HS.

St Andrews University — Guided tours (1 hour) mid June-early September Mondays-Saturdays 10.30am and 2.30pm; ☎ (0334) 76161; £1.

Excursions

Scottish Fisheries Museum. — Anstruther. Open late March-late October Mondays-Saturdays 10am-5.30pm, Sundays 11am-5pm; late October-late March Mondays-Saturdays 10am-4.30pm, Sundays 2-4.30pm; closed 25-26 December, 1-2 January; ☎ (0333) 310628; £1.60.

Kellie Castle. — Open May-October daily 2-6pm (last tour 5.30pm); weekends only in April 2-6pm; ☎ (033 38) 271; £2.50 NTS.

Leuchars Church. — Open March-October daily 9.30am-6pm (5pm in winter).

Earlshall Castle. — Open May-September daily 2-6pm; also Good Friday-Easter Monday 2-6pm; ☎ (0334) 839205: £2.50.

ST DAVID'S

Bishop's Palace. — Open late March-late October daily 9.30am-6.30pm; late October-late March Mondays-Saturdays 9.30am-4pm, Sundays 2-4pm; ☎ (0437) 720517; £1.50 Cadw.

SALISBURY

Cathedral. — Open 7.30am-8.30pm (6.30pm in winter) ; ☎ (0722) 328726; £1.

Mompesson House. — Open late March-early November Saturdays-Wednesdays 12noon-5.30pm; closed Thursdays and Fridays; ☎ (0722) 335659; £2.30 NT.

Salisbury and South Wiltshire Museum. — Open Mondays-Saturdays 10am-5pm, Sundays in July and August 2-5pm; closed Christmas; ☎ (0722) 332151; £1.80.

SCARBOROUGH

St Mary's Church. — Open June-September 10am-12noon and 2-4.30pm.

Excursions

Filey Museum. — Open June-15 September daily 2-5pm; ☎ (0723) 513640; 30p.

Sledmere House. — Open early May-September daily except Mondays and Fridays 1.30-5.30pm; also open Easter weekend and Sundays in April; ☎ (0377) 86637; house, park and gardens £2.50, park and gardens only £1.

SELBY

Abbey Church. — Open June-August 9am-7pm, Saturdays March and October 5pm; November-March 9am-4pm.

Excursions

Carlton Towers. — Open May-September Sundays only 1-5pm; ☎ (0405) 861662; £2.

Lotherton Hall. — Open daily except Mondays (unless bank holidays) 10.30am-6.15pm; in winter 10.30am-12noon and 1pm-dusk; closed 25-26 December; ☎ (0532) 813259; £1.

SHEFFIELD

Cutlers' Hall. — Open by appointment; ☎ (0742) 728456.

Cathedral of SS Peter and Paul. — Open 7.30am-6pm, 10am-4pm on public holidays.

Graves Art Gallery. — Open weekdays 10am-6pm; closed Sundays; ☎ (0742) 734788.

Mappin Art Gallery. — Open Tuesdays-Saturdays 10am-5pm, Sundays 2-5pm; closed Mondays.

City Museum. — Open Tuesdays-Saturdays 10am-5pm, Sundays 11am-5pm; ☎ (0742) 768588.

Sheffield Manor. — Open July-August; phone to confirm; ☎ (0742) 768588.

Bishops' House. — Open Wednesdays-Sundays 10am-4.30pm; ☎ (0742) 557701; 60p.

Abbeydale Industrial Hamlet. —Open Wednesdays-Saturdays 10am-5pm, Sundays 11am-5pm; closed 24-26 December; ☎ (0742) 367731; £1.80.

SHERBORNE

Abbey. — Open daily 9am-6pm (4pm in winter); ☎ (0935) 812452.

Sherborne Castle. — Open Easter Saturday-September Thursdays, Saturdays and Sundays 2-5.30pm; ☎ (0935) 813182; £3.

Excursion

St John the Baptist Church. — Yeovil. Open April-October weekdays 9am-4pm, Sundays 8am-1pm; November-March 9am-1pm, Sundays 8am-1pm.

SHETLAND ISLANDS

Jarlshof. — Open April-September weekdays 9.30am-6pm, Sundays 2-6pm; closed in winter; £1.20 HS.

Mousa Broch. — Via motor boat from Sandwick by arrangement with the proprietor Tom Jamieson, Leebitton ☎ (09505) 367; charge; 15min boat trip from Sandwick jetty.

SHREWSBURY

Abbey. — Open Easter-November daily 9.30am-5.30pm; winter 11am-2pm.

Castle: The Shropshire Regimental Museum. — Open daily 10am-5pm (last admission 4pm); closed Sundays October-Easter and Christmas holiday period; ☎ (0743) 58516; 70p.

Rowley's House. — Open Mondays-Saturdays 10am-5pm, Sundays Easter-October only 12noon-5pm ; ☎ (0743) 61196; 60p.

Excursions

Weston Park. — Open Easter-September 1-5pm, park 11am-5pm; ☎ (095 276) 207; house £1, park £2.75.

Powis Castle. — Open July-August Tuesdays-Sundays 12noon-5pm; April-June and September-early November Wednesdays-Sundays 12noon-5pm; Clive Museum and gardens 11am-6pm; early November-March only Clive Museum and Gardens open Sundays 2-4.30pm; ☎ (0938 554) 336; castle, garden and museum £5, garden and museum £3 NT.

Montgomery Castle. — Open daily.

Much Wenlock Priory. — Open 1 April-September daily 10am-6pm ; October-March 10am-4pm; closed Mondays; ☎ (0952) 727466; 85p EH.

SKIPTON

Castle. — Open weekdays 10am-6pm, Sundays 2-6pm (October-February 4pm); ☎ (0756) 792442; £2.20.

Excursions

Haworth Parsonage. — Open April-September daily 10am-5pm; October-March 11am-4.30pm; closed 24-26 December and three weeks late January and early February; ☎ (0535) 42323; £2.50.

Keighley and Worth Valley Railway. — Keighley to Oxenhope 5-mile line: 30min single journey; trains operate late-June-late September Mondays-Fridays and March-late October weekends 10am-dusk; for details of timetable ☎ (0535) 643629; Rtn £3.50, all day rover £4.50.

Bolton Priory Church. — Open weekdays 9am-7.30pm (Fridays 4pm), Sundays 8am-7.30pm; £2 car parking fee, unless attending service.

SKYE

Skye Croft Museum. — Open Easter-October Mondays-Saturdays 9am-5.30pm; closed Sundays; £1.

Dunvegan Castle. — Open late March-October weekdays 10am-5.30pm, Sundays 1-5.30pm; ☎ (047 022) 206; £3.30.

Clan Donald Centre. — Armadale Castle. Open Easter-October daily 9.30am-5.30pm (last admission 5pm); ☎ (047 14) 305; £2.50.

SNOWDONIA

Llechwedd Slate Caverns. — Blaenau Ffestiniog. Open March-September daily 10am-6pm (last tour 5.15pm); October-February 10am-5pm; weekends only in December 10.30am-5pm; ☎ (0766 830) 306; admission charge.

Gloddfa Ganol Slate Mine. — Open Easter to last Thursday in November Mondays-Fridays 10am-5.30pm; ☎ (0766) 830664; £2.75.

Ffestiniog Railway. — Porthmadog to Blaenau Ffestiniog: 2 1/2 hours Rtn; trains operate late March-early November daily, also certain days in winter; ☎ (0766) 512340; Rtn £9.80, family ticket available.

Snowdon Mountain Railway. — Llanberis to summit: return journey 2 1/2 hours. Open mid April-mid September Sundays-Fridays 9am-5pm, Saturdays 9am-3.30pm; mid March-mid April and mid September-October daily 9.30am-3.30pm; ☎ (0286) 870223.

SOUTHAMPTON

Tudor House Museum. — Open Tuesdays-Fridays 10am-12noon and 1-5pm; Saturdays 10am-12noon and 1-4pm. Sundays 2-5pm; ☎ (0703) 632493.

St Michael's Church. — Open April-October weekdays 10.30am-4.30pm, Sundays 2-4.30pm.

Wool House: Maritime Museum. — Open Mondays-Fridays 10am-1pm and 2-5pm (4pm Saturdays), Sundays 2-5pm.

God's House Tower. — Archaeological Collection. Open Tuesdays - Saturdays 10am-12noon and 1-5pm (4pm Saturdays), Sundays 2-5pm; ☎ (0703) 632493.

Harbour Boat Trip. — Cruise down Southampton Water: 2 hours, daily at 2.30pm and as season demands 11.30am; ☎ (0703) 223278; £5.

Excursions

Broadlands. — Open August-September daily 10am-5.30pm (last admission 4pm); Easter-July Saturdays-Thursdays 10am-5.30pm, closed Fridays; ☎ (0794) 516878; £4.50.

Romsey Abbey. — Open daily 8.30am-6pm.

SOUTHPORT

Excursions

Rufford Old Hall. — Open April-October Mondays-Thursdays and weekends 1-5pm (last admission 4.30pm); closed Fridays; ☎ (0704) 821254; £2.30 NT.

Martin Mere Wildfowl Trust. — Open daily 9.30am-5pm, 4pm in winter; closed 24-25 December; ☎ (0704) 895181; £3.

SOUTHWELL

Southwell Minster. — Open Easter-mid October 8am-7pm (4pm the rest of the year); suggested donation £1.

Excursion

Newark-on-Trent: Castle. — Open April-October daily except Mondays and Thursdays 1-5pm; ☎ (0636) 79403.

STAMFORD

Browne's Hospital. — Open May-September daily; October-April by appointment; ☎ (0780) 63746; £1.20.

Excursions

Burghley House. — Open Easter-early October daily 11am-5pm; ☎ (0780) 52451; £3.80.

Deene Park. — Open Easter, May, Spring and Summer bank holiday Sundays and Mondays, also every Sunday June-August 2-5pm; ☎ (078 085) 278; £3.

Kirby Hall. — Open Good Friday-September daily 10am-6pm; October-Maundy Thursday daily 10am-6pm, closed Mondays; closed 24-26 December, 1 January; ☎ (0536) 203230; 85p.

STIRLING

Stirling Castle. — Open April-September Mondays-Saturdays 9.30am-5.15pm, Sundays 10.30am-4.45pm; October-March 9.30am-4.20pm, Sundays 12.30-3.35pm; ☎ (0786) 62517; £2 HS.

Visitor Centre. — Open late March-September weekdays 9.30am-5.15pm, Sundays 10.30am-4.45pm; October-late March weekdays 9.30am-4.20pm, Sundays 12.30pm-3.35pm; closed 25-26 December, 1-3 January; ☎ (0786) 50000; £1.75 NTS.

Argyll and Sutherland Highlanders Regimental Museum. — Open April-September weekdays 10am-6pm, Sundays 11.30am-5.30pm; October weekdays only 10am-4.30pm; ☎ (0786) 75165.

Church of the Holy Rude. — Open May-September 10am-5pm.

Excursions

Dunblane Cathedral. — Open April-September weekdays 9.30am-7pm, Sundays 9.30am-5pm; October-March daily 9.30am-4pm.

Doune Castle. — Open April-September weekdays 9.30am-6pm, Sundays 2-6pm; October-March weekdays 9.30am-6pm, Sundays 2-6pm; closed Thursday pm and Fridays in winter; £1 HS.

Doune Motor Museum. — Open April-October daily 10am-4.30pm; ☎ (0786) 841203; £2.

Bannockburn Heritage Centre. — Open Good Friday-October daily 10am-6pm (last audio-visual show 5.30pm); ☎ (0786) 812664; £1.20 NTS.

Wallace Monument. — Open June-August daily 10am-7pm; April, May, September 10am-6pm; February, March and October 10am-5pm, closed Wednesdays and Thursdays; last admission 1 hour before closing time; ☎ (0786) 79000; £1.20.

STOKE-ON-TRENT

Gladstone Pottery Museum. — Open March-October weekdays 10am-5pm, Sundays 2-5pm; November-February Tuesdays-Saturdays 10am-5pm; ☎ (0782) 319232; £2.50.

Museum and Art Gallery. — Open Mondays-Saturdays 10am-5pm, Sundays 2-5pm; ☎ (0782) 202173.

Excursions

Little Moreton Hall. — Open April-September daily except Tuesdays 1.30-5.30pm (last admission 5pm); March and October weekends only 1.30-5.30pm; ☎ (0260) 272018; £2.30, weekdays: £2.90 weekends NT.

Wedgwood Visitor's Centre. — Open Easter-October Mondays-Fridays 9am-5pm, weekends 10am-4pm; November-Easter weekdays 9am-5pm, Saturdays 10am-4pm, closed Sundays; ☎ (0782) 204218; £2.

Chatterley Whitfield Mining Museum. — Open daily 10am-5pm; last underground tour 4pm; ☎ (0782) 813337; £3.75.

Alton Towers. — Park open late March-early November daily 9am-6pm, 7pm or 8pm according to the season; rides and attractions 10am-5pm, 6pm or 7pm according to the season; November-March grounds and gardens only 10am-dusk; ☎ (0538) 702200; peak season prices: adults £10.50, children aged 4-13 £7.99.

STONEHENGE

Site. — Open Easter-September daily 10am-6pm (4pm in winter): closed 1 January, 24-26 December; ☎ (0272) 734472; £1.60.

STOURHEAD

Gardens. — Open daily 8am-7pm or dusk if earlier; ☎ (0747) 840348; summer £3.50, winter (November-February) £2.30 NT.

House. — Open April-early November Saturdays-Wednesdays 12noon-5.30pm or dusk if earlier (last admission 5pm); closed Thursdays and Fridays; ☎ (0747) 840348; £3.50 NT.

Excursion

Shaftesbury Abbey. — Open April-October daily 10.30am-5.30pm; closed the rest of the year; ☎ (0747) 52910; 75p.

STRATFORD-UPON-AVON

Shakespeare's Birthplace. — Open March-October weekdays 9am-5.30pm, Sundays 10am-5.30pm; January-February and November-December weekdays 9.30am-4pm, Sundays 10.30am-4pm; closed mornings of Good Friday and 1 January, all day 24-26 December; £2.20.

Harvard House. — For opening times; ☎ (0789) 204016 Shakespeare Birthplace Trust; £1.

New Place. — Open March-October, Mondays-Saturdays 9.30am-5pm, Sundays 10.30am-5pm; November-February Mondays-Saturdays 10am-4pm, Sundays 1.30-4pm; £1.50.

Guild Chapel. — Open Mondays-Saturdays 10am-4pm.

Holy Trinity Church. — Open April-October weekdays 8.30am-6pm, Sundays 2-5pm; November-March weekdays 8.30am-4pm, Sundays 2-5pm; 40p.

Royal Shakespeare Theatre. — Theatre tours vary according to rehearsal schedules; they usually include the Royal Shakespeare and Swan Theatres as well as the RSC Collection; ☎ (0789) 296655; £3.50.

Royal Shakespeare Company Collection. — Open weekdays 9.15am-8pm, Sundays 12noon-5pm (11am-4pm November-March); £1.50.

Excursions

Mary Arden's House. — Open March-October Mondays-Saturdays 9.30am-5pm, Sundays 10.30am-5pm; December-November Mondays-Saturdays 10am-4pm, Sundays 1.30pm-4pm; closed Good Friday, 24-26 December and 1 January; ☎ (0789) 293455; £2.50.

Anne Hathaway's Cottage. — Open March-October weekdays 9am-5.30pm, Sundays 10am-5.30pm; January-February and November-December weekdays 9.30am-4pm; Sundays 10.30am-4pm; closed mornings of Good Friday and 1 January, all day 24-26 December; £1.80.

Ragley Hall. — Open Easter-September Tuesdays-Thursdays and weekends, house 12noon-5pm, park and garden 10am-6pm; garden and park open daily in July and August; house, garden and park £4, garden and park £3.

Upton House. — Open May-September Saturdays-Wednesdays 2-6pm; April and October weekends and bank holiday Mondays 2-6pm; ☎ (0295) 87 266. £3.10 NT.

Broughton Castle. — Open July-August Wednesdays, Thursdays and Sundays 2-5pm; mid May, June and first fortnight in September Wednesdays and Sundays only 2-5pm; ☎ (0295) 812027; £2.60.

SWANSEA

Maritime and Industrial Museum. — Open daily 10.30am-5.15pm; closed 25-26 December; ☎ (0792) 650351.

Swansea City Museum. — Open Tuesdays-Saturdays 10.30am-5.15pm; closed 25-26 December; ☎ (0792) 653763; 30p.

Excursion

Aberdulais Falls. — Open April-early November Mondays-Fridays 10am-5pm, weekends and public holidays 11am-6pm; early November-24 December daily 11am-4pm; £1.25 NT.

Kidwelly Castle. — Open late March-late October daily 9.30am-6.30pm; late October-late March weekdays 9.30am-4pm, Sundays 2-4pm; closed 25-26 December, 1 January; ☎ (0554) 890104; £1.50 Cadw.

T

TAUNTON

Castle. — Somerset County Museum. Open Mondays-Saturdays 10am-5pm; closed Good Friday, 25-26 December; £1.

TENBY

Tudor Merchant's House. — Open Easter Sundays-November Mondays-Fridays 11am-6pm, Sundays 2-6pm; closed the rest of the year; ☎ (0558) 822800; £1.25 NT.

Times and charges

Excursions

Boat service to Caldey Island. — Boats operate late April-mid October Mondays-Saturdays 10am-6pm; closed Sundays; ☎ (0834) 2801; £3.50.

Carew Castle. — Open Easter-October daily 9.30am-5pm; ☎ (0646) 651782; £1.15.

The Boathouse: Laugharne. — Open Easter-October daily 10am-5.30pm; October-March weekends only 11am-3.30pm; ☎ (0994) 427420; £1.35.

TEWKESBURY

Abbey. — Open daily 7.30am-5.30pm; donation requested.

Excursions

Deerhurst: St Mary's Church. — Open April-October daily 9am-8pm; November-March 9am-4pm; ☎ (0684) 293235.

Deerhurst: Odda's Chapel. — Open 10am-5pm (4pm in winter); closed 25-26 December, 1 January; EH.

THAMES VALLEY

Eton College. — School Yard, College Chapel, Cloister Court and the Museum of Eton Life are open April-early October 10.30am-4.30pm but during term time (mid April-June and early September-early October it is only open between 2-4.30pm); a guided tour (1 hour) takes place on above days at 2.15pm and 3.15pm; £2.20 ordinary admission, £2.80 guided tour; Chapel and College may be closed without prior notice.

Cookham: Stanley Spencer Gallery. — Open Easter-October daily 10.30am-5.30pm; November-Easter weekends only 11am-5pm; ☎ (06285) 20890; 50p.

Mapledurham. — Open Easter Sunday-September weekends and bank holidays 2.30-5pm, park 12.30-7pm; the rest of the year only the watermill and park are open Sundays 2-4pm; ☎ (0734) 723350; £4 combined ticket.

Basildon Park. — Open April-October Wednesdays-Saturdays 2-6pm (last admission 5.30pm), Sundays and bank holiday Mondays 12noon-6pm; closed Mondays and Tuesdays; ☎ (0734) 843040; £2.80 NT.

Dorchester: Abbey Church. — Open daily 7.30am-8pm (6pm in winter).

Iffley Church. — Open summer Tuesdays-Sundays 10am-5pm; winter 10am-4pm; closed Mondays.

TINTAGEL

Tintagel Castle. — Open April-September daily 10am-6pm; October-March Tuesdays-Sundays 10am-4pm; closed 24-26 December, 1 January; ☎ (0326) 270526; £1.40 EH.

TROSSACHS

David Marshall Lodge. — Open Easter-September daily 10am-6pm; car park 35p.

Loch Katrine: Boat Trips. — No access round the loch for vehicles SS *Sir Walter Scott* leaves from Trossachs Pier, early May-September; three trips daily Sundays-Fridays at 11am, 1.45pm and 3.15pm; two cruises on Saturdays at 2pm and 3.30pm; ☎ (041) 336 5333; round trip £2.80.

Inchmahome Priory. — Open April-September daily 9.30am-6pm; closed in winter; £1.50 inclusive of ferry HS. To attract the ferryman's attention when he is on the island, turn the white board on the jetty.

TWEED VALLEY

Broughton: John Buchan Centre. — Open May-September Mondays-Saturdays 2-5pm; closed Sundays; ☎ (0899) 21050; 50p.

Neidpath Castle. — Open early April-mid October weekdays 10am-1pm and 2-5pm; Sundays 1-5pm; £1.

Traquair House. — Open July-August daily 10.30am-5.30pm; Easter holidays then late May-June and September 1.30-5.30pm; ☎ (0896) 830323. £2.75.

Abbotsford. — Open mid March-October Mondays-Saturdays 10am-5pm, Sundays 2-5pm; ☎ (0896) 2043; £2.

Melrose Abbey. — Open April-September Mondays-Saturdays 9.30am-6pm, Sundays 9.30am-6pm; October-March weekdays 9.30am-4pm, Sundays 2-4pm; ☎ (089682) 2562; £1.50 HS.

Dryburgh Abbey. — Open April-September Mondays-Saturdays 9.30am-6pm, Sundays 2-6pm; October-March weekdays 9.30am-4pm, Sundays 2-4pm; £1.50 HS.

Floors Castle. — Open July-August daily 10.30am-5.30pm; May, June and September Sundays-Thursdays 10.30am-5.30pm; October Sundays and Wednesdays 10.30am-4pm; £2.70.

Coldstream: Coldstream Guards Museum. — Open Easter-October Mondays-Saturdays 10am-1pm and 2-5pm, Sundays 2-5pm; 50p.

Norham Castle. — Open 10am-6pm (4pm in winter); closed 2 days in the week telephone in advance ☎ (02289) 82379; 85p EH.

W

WARWICK

Castle. — Open March-October daily 10am-5.30pm; November-February 10am-4.30pm; closed 25 December; ☎ (0926) 495421; £5.75.

Leycester Hospital. — Open April-October Mondays-Saturdays 10am-5.30pm; November-March 10am-4pm; closed Sundays, Good Friday, 25 December; ☎ (0926) 492797; £1.50.

Collegiate Church of St Mary. — Open April-October daily 9am-6pm (4pm in winter).

Excursion

Kenilworth Castle. — Open Easter-September daily 10am-6pm; October-Easter daily except Mondays 10am-4pm; closed 24-26 December, 1 January; ☎ (0926) 52078; £1.30 EH.

WELLS

Cathedral. — Open daily 7.15am-8.30pm, 6.30pm in winter; suggested donation £1.50.

Caves at Wookey Hole. — Open March-October daily 9.30am-5.30pm; November-February 10.30am-4.30pm; closed the week before Christmas; ☎ (0749) 72243; £4.50.

Cheddar Gorge Caves and Museum. — Open Easter-September daily 10am-5.30pm; October-Easter daily 10.30am-4.30pm; closed 24-25 December; ☎ (0934) 742343; Jacob's Ladder 75p; Gough's Cave £2.50; Cox's Cave £2.50; Museum 75p.

WESTER ROSS

Eilean Donan Castle. — Open Good Friday-September daily 10am-5.30pm; ☎ (059 985) 202; £1.

Torridon Countryside Centre. — May-September Mondays-Saturdays 10am-6pm, Sundays 2-6pm; ☎ (044 587) 221.

Aultroy Visitor Centre. — Open early May-early September daily 10am-1pm and 2-5pm; ☎ (044 584) 254.

Gairloch Heritage Museum. — Open Easter-September daily 10am-5pm; ☎ (0445) 83 243; 50p.

Inverewe Gardens. — Open all the year 9.30am-sunset; ☎ (044 586) 229; £2.50 NTS.

Boat trips to the Summer Isles. — For further details apply to the tourist information office in the car ferry terminal or to the various huts on the waterfront.

WHITBY

Abbey. — Open April-September daily 10am-6pm; October-March 10am-4pm; ☎ (0947) 603568; 95p EH.

Excursion

Captain Cook Birthplace Museum. — Marton. Open Easter-October daily 10am-6pm; October-Easter daily 9am-dusk; closed 25-26 December, 1 January; ☎ (0642) 311211; 60p.

WICK

Wick Heritage Centre. — Open June-September Mondays-Saturdays 10am-5pm; ☎ (0955) 3268; £1.

ISLE OF WIGHT

Arreton Manor House. — Open April-October Mondays-Fridays 10am-6pm, Sundays 12noon-6pm; closed Saturdays and bank holidays; £2.50.

Roman Villa. — Brading. Open April-September daily 10am-5.30pm (Sundays 10.30am); ☎ (0983) 406223; £1.50.

Wax Museum. — Brading. Open May-September daily 10am-10pm; September-April 10am-5pm; ☎ (0983) 407286; £3.

Nunwell House. — Near Brading. Open last Sunday in June-last Thursday in September daily 10am-5pm; ☎ (0983) 407240; £2.30.

Carisbrooke Castle. — Open April-September daily 10am-6pm; October-April daily 10am-4pm; closed 24-26 December, 1 January; ☎ (0983) 522107; £2.60 EH.

All Saints Church. — Godshill. Open April-December weekdays 8am (10am Sundays)-6pm the rest of the year except January 8am-dusk.

Osborne House. — Open June-October daily 10am-5pm; Easter-early June grounds and Swiss cottage only; closed the rest of the year; ☎ (0983) 200022; £4.30 EH.

Quarr Abbey Church. — Open daily 5.30am-8.30pm; limited access to church only.

WILTON HOUSE

House. — Open April-mid October Tuesdays-Sundays 11am-6pm; ☎ (0722) 743115; £4.20.

WINCHESTER

Cathedral. — Open daily 7.15am-6.30pm; ☎ (0962) 853137; suggested donation £1.50.

Pilgrims' Hall. — Telephone in advance ☎ (0962) 854189.

Winchester College. — Open April-September tours at 11am, 2pm and 3.15pm; closed October-March; £2.

Castle Great Hall. — Open weekdays 10am-5pm (4pm Saturdays November-February); closed Good Friday, 25-26 December; ☎ (0962) 846476.

St Cross Hospital. — Open April-October weekdays 9.30am-12.30pm 2-5pm (3.30pm the rest of the year); closed Sundays, Good Friday, 25 December; ☎ (0962) 851375; £1.

WINDSOR CASTLE

St George's Chapel. — Open weekdays 10.45am-4pm, Sundays 2-4pm (closes 3.45pm on weekdays in winter); closed most of January; ☎ (0753) 865538; £2. The chapel is subject to closure at short notice.

State Apartments. — Open May-September weekdays 10.30am-5pm, Sundays 12.30-5pm; March and October weekdays 10.30am-4pm, Sundays 12.30-4pm; November-February weekdays only 10.30am-3pm; ☎ (0753) 831118; State Apartments £2.90; Doll's House £1.40.

Great Park. — Open 10am-6pm or sunset when earlier; £2.20.

WOBURN ABBEY

Apartments. — Open late March-early November weekdays 11am-4.45pm, Sundays 11am-5pm; January-late March 11am-4pm; ☎ (0525) 290666; £5.

Wild Animal Kingdom. — Open early March-early November daily 10am-5pm; ☎ (0525) 290666; £6.

WORCESTER

Guildhall: Assembly Room. — Open March-December weekdays 9am-5pm; closed Christmas; ☎ (0905) 723471 ext 2010.

Greyfriars. — Open April-October Wednesdays, Thursdays and bank holiday Mondays 2-5.30pm; £1.30 NT.

Royal Worcester Porcelain Works: Dyson Perrins Museum. — Open Mondays-Fridays 9.30am-5pm, Saturdays and bank holidays 10am-5pm; closed 25-26 December; ☎ (0905) 23221. Tours of Royal Porcelain Factory also available.

The Commandery. — Open weekdays 10.30am-5pm, Sundays 2-5pm; closed 25-26 December; ☎ (0905) 355071; £1.70.

Excursion

Elgar Birthplace Museum. — Lower Broadheath. Open May-September daily 10.30am-6pm; October-April 1.30-4.30pm; closed Wednesdays and from mid January-mid February; ☎ (0905 66) 224; £2.

WYE VALLEY

Forest of Dean Heritage Centre. — Open April-October daily 10am-6pm; November-March 10am-5pm; closed 25-26 December; ☎ (0594) 822170; £2.25.

Goodrich Castle. — Open April-September daily 10am-6pm; October-March 10am-4pm, closed on Mondays; closed 24-26, December, 1 January; ☎ (0600) 890538; £1.15 EH.

Raglan Castle. — Open late March-late October daily 9.30am-6.30pm; late October-late March Mondays-Saturdays 9.30am-4pm, Sundays 2-4pm; £1.75 Cadw.

Tintern Abbey. — Open late March-late October daily 9.30am-6.30pm; late October-late March Mondays-Saturdays 9.30am-4pm, Sundays 2-4pm; ☎ (02918) 251; £1.75 Cadw.

Chepstow Castle. — Open late March-late October daily 9.30am-6.30pm; late October-late March Mondays-Saturdays 9.30am-4pm, Sundays 2-4pm; ☎ (02912) 4065; £2 Cadw.

Y

YORK

York Minster. — Open 7am-8.30pm (6pm in winter).

National Railway Museum. — Open Mondays-Saturdays 10am-6pm, Sundays 11am-6pm; closed 24-26 December, 1 January; ☎ (0904) 621 261; £3.20.

York Castle Museum. — Open Mondays-Saturdays 9.30am-4pm, Sundays 10am-4pm; closed 25-26 December, 1 January; ☎ (904) 653611; £3.

Fairfax House. — Open March-December Mondays-Thursdays and Saturdays 11am-5pm, Sundays 1.30-5pm (last admission 4.30pm); closed January and February; ☎ (0904) 655543; £2.25.

Merchant Adventurers' Hall. — Open mid March-early October daily 8.30am-5pm; early November-mid March 8.30am-3.30pm, closed Sundays; closed 25 December, 1 January; ☎ (0904) 654818; £1.50.

Jorvik Viking Centre. — Open April-October daily 9am-7pm; November-March 9am-5.30pm; closed 25 December; ☎ (0904) 643211; £3.20.

Assembly Rooms. — Closed.

York City Art Gallery. — Open Mondays-Saturdays 10am-5pm, Sundays 2.30-5pm; closed 1 January, Good Friday, 25 26 December; ☎ (0904) 623839.

Treasurer's House. — Open April-October daily 10.30am-5pm (last admission 4.30pm); ☎ (0904) 624247; £2.30 NT.

Excursions

Sutton Park. — Open May-September Wednesdays and bank holiday Mondays 1.30-5.30pm; house and gardens £2.50.

Samuel Smith Old Brewery. — Tadcaster. Guided tours early January-mid December Mondays-Thursdays 11am, 2pm, 7pm; £1.50.

Punch and Judy Sign

INDEX

County Abbreviations

Bedfordshire : Beds
Berkshire : Berks
Buckinghamshire : Bucks
Cambridgeshire : Cambs
Derbyshire : Derbs
East Sussex : E Sussex
Gloucestershire : Glos
Hampshire : Hants
Hereford and Worcester :
   Heref and Worc
Hertfordshire : Herts
Lancashire : Lancs
Leicestershire : Leics
Lincolnshire : Lincs

Mid Glamorgan : Mid Glam
Northamptonshire : Northants
North Glamorgan : N Glam
Northumberland : Northumb
North Yorkshire : N Yorks
Nottinghamshire : Notts
Oxfordshire : Oxon
South Glamorgan : S Glam
South Yorkshire : S Yorks
Staffordshire : Staffs
Warwickshire : Warw
West Sussex : W Sussex
West Yorkshire : W Yorks
Wiltshire : Wilts

ACKNOWLEDGEMENTS OF PHOTOGRAPHS AND DRAWINGS

p	12	A. William, Guildford
p	15	A. William, Guildford
p	22	R. Thrift/The National Trust, London
p	26	B. Gerard/EXPLORER, Paris
p	30	A. F. Kersting, London
p	31	M. Stevens, Trowbridge
p	32	A. F. Kersting, London
p	36	Musées Nationaux, Paris
p	39	VISIONBANK, London
p	41	D. Faure/SCOPE, Paris
p	51	After photo by J. Ch. Pratt, D. Pries/DIAF
p	53	After photo from the National Motor Museum, Beaulieu
p	54	The Bridgeman Art Library, London
p	55	J. Allan Cash Ltd/PIX, Paris
p	58	Birmingham Museum and Art Gallery, Birmingham
p	64	A. F. Kersting, London
p	70	A. Williams, Guildford
p	72	A. F. Kersting/ARTEPHOT, Paris
p	77	A. F. Kersting, London
p	86	A. F. Kersting, London
p	90	J. Whitaker/National Trust, London
p	91	J. Allan Cash Ltd/PIX, Paris
p	94	GIRAUDON/Paris *(above)*
p	94	T. Adina/EXPLORER, Paris *(below)*
p	97	A. Williams, Guildford
p	100	N. Meers/The National Trust, London
p	101	After photo by A. F. Kersting, London
p	106	Derby Museums and Art Gallery, Derby
p	127	A. F. Kersting, London
p	132	H. Phillips/The National Trust, London
p	136	A. F. Kersting, London
p	140	The Ironbridge Gorge Museum Trust, Ironbridge
p	142	A. F. Kersting, London
p	158	Ph. Roy/EXPLORER, Paris
p	164	Ed. Pritchard/FOTOGRAM-STONE, Paris
p	168	British Tourist Authority, London
p	177	A. Williams, Guildford
p	178	M. Stevens, Trowbridge
p	189	Nottingham Castle Museum and Art Gallery, Nottingham
p	192	A. Williams, Guildford
p	225	A. Williams, Guildford
p	227	A. Howarth/EXPLORER, Paris
p	228	A. Williams, Guildford
p	238	J. Allan Cash Ltd/PIX, Paris
p	239	A. F. Kersting, London
p	247	A. F. Kersting, London
p	249	By kind permission of the Marquess of Tavistock
p	257	VISIONBANK, London
p	299	J. Bottin, Paris

MANUFACTURE FRANÇAISE DES PNEUMATIQUES MICHELIN

Société en commandite par actions au capital de 2 000 000 000 de francs
Place des Carmes-Déchaux - 63 Clermont-Ferrand (France)
R.C.S. Clermont-Fd B 855 200 507

© Michelin et Cie, Propriétaires-Éditeurs 1991
Dépôt légal 4ᵉ trim. 1991 - ISBN 2.06.701.541-9 - ISSN 0763-1383

Printed in France 08-91-30
Impression : MAME Imprimeurs, Tours n° 13804

Do you know

the series
of

Michelin
Green Guides

in English

CANADA
 MEXICO
  NEW ENGLAND
  NEW YORK CITY
  WASHINGTON DC

EUROPE

AUSTRIA
 FRANCE
  GERMANY
   GREAT BRITAIN
   GREECE
   ITALY
    LONDON
     NETHERLAND
     PORTUGAL
     ROME
      SCOTLAND
      SPAIN
       SWITZERLAND
       THE WEST COUNTRY (G.B.)

FRANCE

BRITTANY
 BURGUNDY
  CHATEAUX OF THE LOIRE
   DORDOGNE
   FRENCH RIVIERA
    ILE DE FRANCE
     NORMANDY COTENTIN
      NORMANDY SEINE VALLEY
      PARIS
       PROVENCE

To get the most out of your vacation
Michelin Guides and Maps

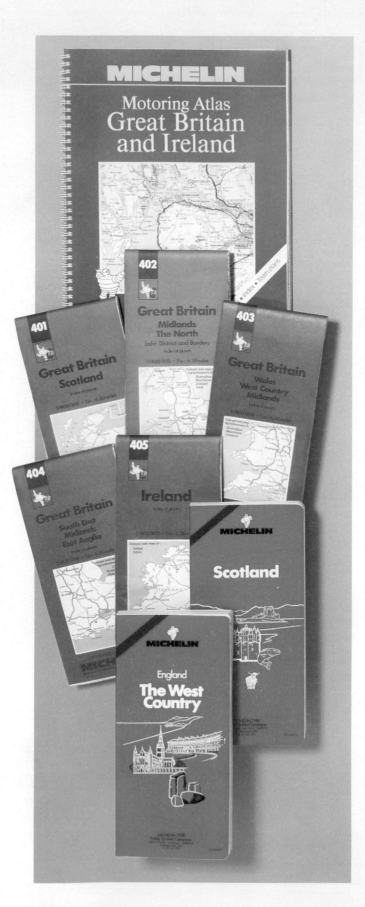